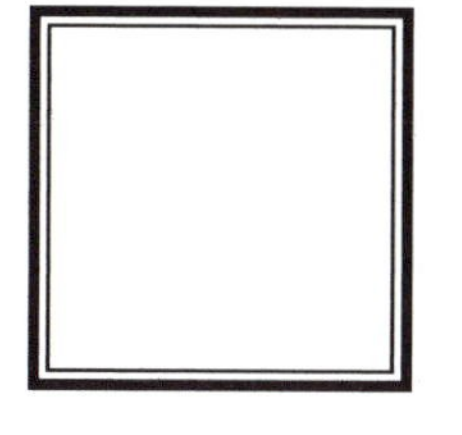

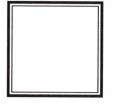

The Modern Middle East

From Imperialism to Freedom, 1800–1958

EMORY C. BOGLE
University of Richmond

Prentice Hall
Upper Saddle River, NJ 07458

Library of Congress Cataloging-in-Publication Data

Bogle, Emory C., (1937–)
The modern Middle East: from imperialism to freedom, 1800–1958 /
Emory C. Bogle.
p. cm.
Includes bibliographical references (p.) and index.
ISBN 0-13-206509-6 (pbk.)
1. Middle East—History—1517– I. Title.
DS62.7.B64 1996
956—dc2095-15863
CIP

To

My Parents:

FRED BOGLE and RUTH BOGLE

and

Mr. and Mrs. IBRAHIM ABU RISH
for treating me like their son

Editorial Director: Charlyce Jones Owen
Acquisition Editor: Sally Constable
Editorial/production supervision, interior design,
and electronic page makeup: Mary Araneo
Editorial assistant: Tamara Mann
Buyer: Nick Sklitsis
Cover designer: Bruce Kenselaar

Printed in the United States of America

10 9 8 7 6 5 4 3 2 1

ISBN 0-13-206509-6

PRENTICE-HALL INTERNATIONAL (UK) LIMITED, *London*
PRENTICE-HALL OF AUSTRALIA PTY. LIMITED, *Sydney*
PRENTICE-HALL CANADA INC., *Toronto*
PRENTICE-HALL HISPANOAMERICANA, S.A., *Mexico*
PRENTICE-HALL OF INDIA PRIVATE LIMITED, *New Delhi*
PRENTICE-HALL OF JAPAN, INC., *Tokyo*
SIMON & SCHUSTER ASIA PTE. LTD., *Singapore*
EDITORA PRENTICE-HALL DO BRASIL, LTDA., *Rio de Janeiro*

Contents

Acknowledgments

The University of Richmond contributed to this project through two sabbaticals, a favorable teaching schedule, acquiring sufficient resources, relieving me of other duties, and encouraging the faculty to publish.

Colleagues in the field of Middle East studies offered invaluable assistance. Abdul Karem Rafeq of the College of William and Mary was the kindest, most knowledgable, most thorough reader an author could ever imagine. It is an understatement to say that his observations and encouragement were invaluable. Peter Sluglett of Durham University in England gave me an unexpected boost when he used his valuable time to respond so kindly to my manuscript. Moawiyah Ibrahim of Yarmouk University in Jordan offered insights, encouragements, and opened important doors which will eternally indebt me to him. Amin Allimard of Virginia Commonwealth University, who knows modern Iran so well, was helpful beyond words with his endorsement of that portion of the text. Bob Olson of the University of Kentucky offered prompt and important comments as well as encouragement. Mohammad Ghanoonparvar of the University of Texas took initiatives with the manuscript that moved the manuscript from my desk to publication. Hafez Farmayan of the University of Texas kindly encouraged and guided me at crucial stages. A stamp of approval from Terry Dolan of the Old and Middle English Department of University College, Dublin, Ireland, provided inspiration and hope.

I wish to thank the following colleagues in the University of Richmond Department of History: John Rilling, John Treadway, Barry Westin, Martin Ryle, and Allen Golden for reading the manuscript and offering critical comments and to John Gordon, Harry Ward, Ernie Bolt, Harrison Daniel, Dan Roberts, and Bob Remini for their encouragement. Houman Sadri of the political science department offered helpful comments on Iran.

The departmental secretaries Nancy Jordan, Gladys Llewellyan, Mary Anne

Wilbourne, Debbie Govoruhk, and Eleanor Neal were helpful and patient with me at all stages of the project.

My graduate assistants, Michael Mortlock, Joe Rowley, and Royce Grubic helped find important information, made helpful suggestions and performed arduous tasks. Michael Bell mady my computer work and led it to otherwise unreachable uses.

Friends, who took special interest in the project, deserve mention for their interest and confidence in me: Khalil Abu Rish, Ender Agirnasli, Murat Agirnasli, Renee Stephano, Joanne McCracken, Mattisin Abu Jaber, W.D. Taylor, Nadim Abou Said, Akram Hatoum, Susan Gordon, Fathi Abu Rish, Ron and Delores Smith, Sabah and Jameel Abed, Hanna Bazuzzi, Linda Howlette, Nellie Texler, Pierre Harrek, Suheil Rayes, Julie Daffron, George W. McCall III, Kamal Mahmoud, and Foaud Abouhana. Jack Bowling was more helpful than he could ever realize.

Finally my sons, Rhett and Andrew, frequently assured me that my efforts were worthwhile and meaningful. Andrew was also an astute and helpful reader.

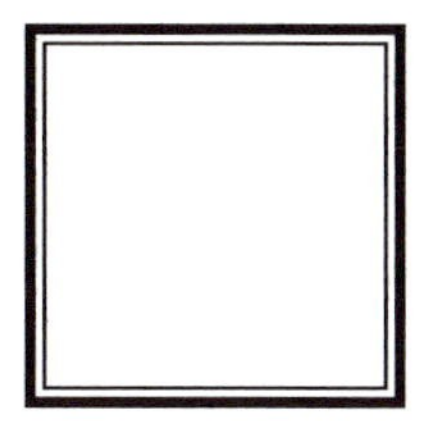

Introduction

No area of the world has a longer, more tumultuous history than the region presently known as the Middle East. It is, therefore, understandable that teacher and student alike find it difficult to comprehend. The region's apparently passive role in history over recent centuries, when Europe and the New World attracted most scholarly attention, created a void in Western memory. It recently regained the attention and concern it customarily received throughout previous millennia. The centuries of Western scholarly and popular amnesia of the Middle East, however, provided the perfect atmosphere for fanciful reverie to run rampant.

Most Western impressions were built around sand, camels, tents, flowing robes, luxury, poverty, intrigue, dervishes, turbans, waterpipes, and decadence spun into romantic tales of a predictable moral message. The same tales were told in the West for any time and place all the way from Morocco to Afghanistan in the same monotonous desert landscape filled with Muslim infidels who marveled at the Western heroes and their Western magic.

These misconceptions contrasted starkly with the West's knowledge of the ancient Middle East from the Garden of Eden through the time of the New Testament. In those times God had ruled the region and brought forth prophets and rulers who created the values upon which all God-fearing, God-abiding people and nations based their religion, government, society, and relationships with their fellow human beings. The lineages of entire ancient families were better known than that of their own immediate families. Westerners knew the location and significance of ancient Middle Eastern cities, towns, villages, rivers, streams, wells, mountains, rocks, and burial spots better than they knew similar geographical features within fifty miles of their homes. It was as if, regardless of later heritage, the ancient Middle East were the Mother Country of most people west of Constantinople.

Westerners virtually blocked out interest in Middle East developments after the rise of Islamic dominance in the seventh century. This attitude was certainly more widespread after the failure of the crusades. By that time Westerners seemed to believe that infidels had profaned God's land. God seemed to have abandoned the area, and no longer bothered to send prophets to express His will. From a Western perspective, the infidels continued to demonstrate their unworthiness as they failed to comprehend and adopt the modern science and technology of the enlightened West.

The people of the Middle East reciprocated Western ignorance with their own ignorance of the West. Middle Easterners had no way of knowing, before it was too late, that they were at the mercy of the Western nation-states' modern science, technology, industry, tax systems, military capacity, and will to expand their influence. The entire region fell under Western domination before it could wrest a modicum of control over its own destiny. The ease of the Western conquest of the Middle East reenforced the Western belief that Islamic domination had been a perverse aberration all those lost centuries. Close inspection of the region confirmed to Western observers that conditions in the Middle East conformed to popular Western portrayals. Once Western influence entered the modern Middle East, the Westerners attempted to transform the Middle East in its own image.

Since speed characterizes the twentieth century, the gradual, almost imperceptible changes that occurred over centuries in the West, altered the Middle East in about five decades at an accelerated pace. Middle Eastern nations, groups, and individuals choose their ideas and values from the entirety of human experience, instead of only from local and regional traditions.

The scope and pace of these dramatic changes have challenged every person, group, and institution in the Middle East beyond comprehension. Consensus and custom, which guided previous attitudes and values, could not prevail in the new tumult. The present could hardly be defined, while there was an urgency to determine what the future should be.

The forces of change all seem modern, and one might assume that the present direction would be limited to a choice among some combination of modern ideas and institutions. But that could not be in so ancient a land, where, from the modern perspective, centuries of apparent continuity mask the reality of five thousand years of ferment and change. There is a strong sense of history in each person and group, which is almost always incorrect and self-serving. This condition is important since modern attitudes dictate that national boundaries conform to developments in the entire known past. In a land so ancient, which is saturated with tales and legends, and God's direct interference, controversy over the past invites confusion and conflict in the present. National and personal pride and identity are involved at both the micro and macro level in all these deliberations.

Changes in earlier ages were usually violent and brutal with the victor in command of telling the story. Might unabashedly prevailed on the battlefield and in historical memory. Few of the vanquished either retained their separate identity or gained a forum to express the injustices that were invariably the result of weakness. The weak vanished or became absorbed before a message for help could reach a possible ally.

In modern times, the opportunity to tell one's story or call for help about past and present injustices is only a microphone or telephone away. Knowledge and imagination are the only limits on one's story. Imagination has never been a scarce commodity in the Middle East. Neither has conspiracy. Modern scholarship has actually exacerbated the Middle East penchant for belief in intrigue and conspiracy, because it has verified many ancient and modern conspiracies. For the first time, modern communications provide a worldwide forum to rectify old wrongs. Pride dictates not only an explanation of past failures but demands compensation. The permanence of modern boundaries under international law and mutual defense treaties compels groups and nations to establish their ancient and just claims before they consent to the ineradicable lines of modern maps and international law books.

It is little wonder there is such a constant sense of urgency in the Middle East, which remains one of the most geopolitically important areas of the world and possesses resources vital to the continuation of the modern standard of living.

AN OVERVIEW

No dramatic event or development occurred in 1800 to justify it as the beginning of a work of this length. That year is primarily notable for the fact that it began a new century that would propel the Middle East into world affairs on a scale much greater than had been the case for several previous centuries. The weakness of both the Ottoman and Persian empires in comparison with the individual and collective strength of the modern European nations invited Western intervention into the region during the nineteenth century. Intervene they did. The two regional empires faced overwhelming European military forces, which only the mutual jealousies of the Europeans nullified. The Europeans, in fact, countered each other with diplomatic and military pressures to prevent the aggrandizement of any of their number at the expense of the two enfeebled Middle Eastern empires. By mutual consent, however, the European states culturally penetrated the archaic empires and established their economic dominion over them. At the end of the century, it was clear that Europeans would determine the future of both the Ottoman and Persian empires.

The vast Ottoman Empire exercised jurisdiction over the predominantly Slavic-Christian Balkan region, the predominantly Turkish Anatolian peninsula, the Arabic-speaking portion of southwest Asia, and most of the Islamic- and Arabic-speaking portion of northern Africa. The outdated administrative and military methods of the empire were inadequate to retain this immense region in face of the many internal and external forces of modern times. The discontented among the Balkan Greeks and Slavs, who became infected with modern nationalism concepts, found willing supporters in the Christian nations to the west and to the north. The Christian states capitalized on this discontent to justify their efforts to "liberate" their fellow believers from Ottoman control. The Balkans rejected Ottoman efforts to pacify them with offers of increased participation in the governing process and chose to pursue the more enticing goal of full independence with European assistance. By the end of the century other non-Turkish elements of the empire also demonstrated an inclination for independence, while most of North Africa fell under British and French imperial control.

The Ottoman government struggled to survive and to maintain its holdings. The constitutionally governed British and French were willing to assist the Ottomans against Russian aggression, but found it awkward to support a traditional monarchy. The Ottomans, therefore, accepted the necessity of granting greater liberties to their subjects in return for Western assistance. The ensuing *Tanzimat*, or modernization period, produced mixed results. Government-sponsored education, both at home and abroad, educated a segment of the population that could administer a "modern" society, but it also spawned an element that demanded even greater changes. The Ottoman government, the Porte, also soon determined that modernization had the advantage of extending much greater central authority over Ottoman subjects. Despite accusations to the contrary, the so-called "Sick Man" of Europe became efficient enough that many of the newly educated subjects began to resist an increased authoritarianism. The Sultan and the Porte faced resistance to modernization from such disparate groups as traditionalists, nationalistic minorities, and advocates of a secular, constitutional government. Internal and external enemies challenged the government, which frequently attempted accommodation with its critics, while it gradually moved toward adopting a strong preference for Turks and Turkish-oriented policies.

War, and the constant threat of war, retarded Ottoman attempts to modernize and survive. A reduction in agricultural production caused by farmers having to spend so much time as soldiers consumed precious revenues and decreased the capacity to generate revenues. An appetite for borrowing from foreigners resulted in heavy indebtedness at exorbitant rates and fostered a gradual intrusion of foreign control over the Ottoman economy. The empire lost its financial independence, control over its trade, and its already meager manufacturing capacity.

New approaches failed to stave off disaster. A closer affiliation with Germany seemed to offer relief in the late nineteenth century. In response to continued internal upheaval, the government reinstated a constitution in 1908. The Balkan provinces, however, soon obtained their independence, Austria annexed Bosnia and Herzogovina, and Italy annexed Libya. These reverses inspired an even stronger Turkish orientation of the government, which increased Arab dissatisfaction and led to a subsequent movement toward separation from the empire.

The Turkish-dominated Ottoman government allied with the Central Powers early in World War I in an effort to break the hold of other European powers over their nation. The Entente powers quickly decided to divide the Ottoman Empire among themselves if they should triumph. Great Britain made domination over the Middle East a major goal during the war and established military control over the Arabic-speaking portion of the empire. Arab nationalists, under the leadership of Sharif Hussein of the Hijaz, embraced the British war effort in return for a British promise of independence after the war. After the Entente victory, the British allowed their French ally control over a small portion of the Ottoman Empire during the peace settlement, but retained control over most of the Arabic-speaking portion. The two victors acquired League of Nations approval of their acquisitions with the justification that the former Ottoman subjects required assistance to prepare them for their eventual independence.

The League of Nations mandate for Palestine made no pretense of preparing that region for independence because the British mandatory authority had the responsibility of creating a "national home" for the Jews in Palestine. A well organized Jewish nationalist movement called Zionism obtained this unusual commitment in recognition of their years of suffering persecution in all of the European countries. The League of Nations experiment proved to be one of the most contentious experiments of all time as it rallied the otherwise divided Arabs against the entire peace settlement and fostered disagreement among the victors.

Under the leadership of Mustapha Kemal, the Turks refused to accept Entente plans to divide the Turkish homeland among them. Their military resistance, which was anchored on Turkish pride and diplomatic support from the new Soviet Union, succeeded in dismantling the peace settlement with Turkey. Kemal, who became better known as Ataturk, used his success to impose a secular republic in Turkey that virtually destroyed all vestiges of the Ottoman past. His success also inspired Arabs and Persians to assert themselves against the new imperial forces.

Arab attempts to defy the designs of their new mentors did not enjoy similar success. The British and French ignored the validity of the two Arab kingdoms that a duly elected Arab congress created in 1920. Great Britain and France employed a combination of force and manipulation to establish control over both the Levant and the Fertile Crescent regions of Arabic southwest Asia. They arbitrarily established borders and governments in a number of new Arab states that met the needs of the mandatory powers to the utter dismay of the inhabitants of the region. The superior force of the European states prevailed to impose boundaries within the Arabic region that not only ignored Arab aspirations for unity, but created untenable conditions for some of the states after the boundaries became permanent.

While some Arabs benefited from the new configuration of their lands, most chafed at the gerrymandered result. The individual new Arab states lacked economic viability, defendable borders, and adequate access to the seas. Cultural unity, family and tribal affiliations, economic integrity, and the capacity to utilize the human and natural resources among the Arabs suffered to accomplish the goals of the mandatory authorities, who had the blessing of the greater community of nations.

The resulting endemic Arab unrest aroused a passion for Arab unity that transcended all other considerations. Arab nationalism grew, however, parallel to the growth of the entrenched interests of the individuals and groups who exercised power in the spurious individual Arab states, which remained under foreign domination. The general agreement for unity, therefore, collided with the conflicting visions for unity among the ambitions of different individuals and groups. Ironically, disagreements over different possible plans for unity became a new, dominant source of divisiveness among the Arabs. The occupying forces alertly used internecine Arab conflicts to their advantage.

Only widespread resistance and the threat of the Axis powers in the late 1930s moved the mandatory powers to accommodate Arab desires for freedom. The outbreak of World War II, however, brought even greater restrictions on the Arab populations and governments from the mandatory authorities. Arab support for their oppressor's enemies dictated that the entire Middle East region become unable to succor the Axis powers in any way. Great Britain, as in World War I, enjoyed the military power to shape the Middle East, while Germany prevented French participation. The British changed five Middle Eastern governments during the war and prevented the Arabs and Iranians from gaining their freedom.

Perfunctory declarations of war against the Axis in the last days of the war from compliant Arab governments qualified them for independence and membership in the United Nations. In many respects their independence was still illusory as the British and French maintained many residual rights and a military presence. The Arab states had no substantial experience in self-government and no military ability worthy of modern nations. This was a decided handicap for many reasons, but especially in view of the increased Zionist threat.

After World War II, Zionism was imbued with an urgency far greater than it had possessed in earlier years. Worldwide support for Zionism was also stronger following a realization of the horrors the Nazis had inflicted upon European Jewry during the war. Zionist attacks upon the British from 1945 to 1947 convinced the British to leave Palestine. The United Nations partitioned Palestine into Jewish and Arab sectors with the understanding that the entity would remain under United Nations guidance. A full-scale war ensued between the Arabs and Jews of Palestine. The British withdrew on May 15, 1948 and Israel declared its independence with United Nations approval. Weak Arab armies from all the neighboring states were no match for the well-organized, and determined, new nation of Israel. When the conflict ended in a truce in 1949, all of the Arab nations refused to recognize the legitimacy of the new Jewish state.

Israel was not only the new Arab enemy, it was a monument to Arab weakness. Failure in the war against Israel exacerbated the many existing problems between the Arabs and the Western states, among the Arab states, and within each Arab state. There was a widespread belief that the defeat of Israel, which the Arabs viewed as an outpost of Western imperialism, was impossible without Arab unity. Most Arabs could also agree that the existing Arab governments were both incompetent and illegitimate.

A dramatic seizure of power in Egypt by young, unknown junior military officers on July 23, 1952 began a new phase in Middle Eastern affairs. Gamal Abdel Nasser soon emerged, not only as the leader of Egypt, but as the leader of the entire Arab-speaking world. His transformation of Egypt through radical social changes indicated to the Arab masses that he could lead them into the mainstream of the modern world. His willingness to obtain assistance from the Eastern Bloc eliminated the restraints the West had been able to maintain upon Arab technological and military advancement. His nationalization of the Suez Canal extended his appeal beyond Egypt to the surrounding, underdeveloped, Arab-speaking nations.

While most of the Arab masses jubilantly embraced Nasser's every word and action, most of the Arab governments loathed him, but they usually feared outward expressions of their feelings. His appeal and stature made him unassailable. As the leader of the largest and most powerful Arab nation, the Arab masses viewed him as the natural leader who could rectify previous Arab humiliations.

There were other important Arab agendas, however, that prevented fulfillment of Arab unity under Nasser. The Hashemites in Iraq and Jordan openly resisted the threat to their governments and their long-standing claims to Arab leadership. The Ba'ath party, which was centered in Syria, resented Nasser's appeal since it eclipsed their concept for an Arab world united under their control. Strong communist movements in Syria and Iraq feared Nasser because of his treatment of Egyptian communists and because his nationalist orientation conflicted with their own world view. Some minorities, especially the Maronites of Lebanon, feared for their fate in a unified Arab state composed of Muslims, many of whom seemed to lack any religious convictions in pursuit of secular answers to Arab problems. Entrenched elements in each Arab state feared Nasser and all other movements that threatened their privileged positions.

Nasser's detractors appeared hopeless in 1958 as in rapid succession his supporters seemed to prevail throughout the Levant and the Fertile Crescent. In February 1958, Syria's regime willingly merged their country with Egypt in order to avoid civil war or a communist takeover. General Arab elation with this major step in Arab national unification shook all existing Arab regimes. In the spring, a civil war erupted in Lebanon between supporters and opponents of Nasser. A popularly supported military coup on behalf of Nasser seemed imminent in Jordan, where King Hussein had only recently escaped losing his throne to Nasser's supporters. On July 14, an especially bloody coup annihilated the Iraqi royal family. This coup, in apparent support of Nasser, seemed the *coup de grace* to Arab disunity and weakness. Almost everyone believed that the weak governments of the Arabian peninsula, which also lacked any military capacity, would also fall to the forces of Arab unity.

Most Arabs believed that the dramatic developments of 1958 were both just and inevitable. They could not imagine that anything could or should thwart their reemergence into the power equation of the modern world. They envisioned themselves as a proud people who had been submerged under Turkish and European imperial domination for centuries, after having been major contributors to the intellectual and spiritual benefit of mankind. Justice, history, their strategic location, and their vital human and natural resources demanded Arab freedom. Even United States military presence to save the regime in Lebanon and British military protection of King Hussein in Jordan could not dampen their ardor. From an Arab point of view, those two tiny states were both artificial and inconsequential. The days of foreign control over Arab affairs were ended. There were only some loose ends to tidy up under the leadership of Nasser, the greatest Arab since the Prophet Muhammad.

The Persians had their own bitter experience with imperialism in the nineteenth and twentieth centuries. The Persian Empire, in fact, was more moribund than the Ottoman Empire at the beginning of the nineteenth century and was also unprepared to face the challenges of modern times. The modest central institutions of the Qajar dynasty were inadequate to subdue the restive tribes that composed much of its population. Its minimal resources and paucity of modern knowledge were equally damning. Dependence upon trade with Russia added to its problems. Russia, as with the Ottoman Empire, was a major threat to the continuation of Persia as an independent empire. Great Britain's willingness to help Persia resist Russian aggression only introduced another force that divided Persian loyalties and deprived it of control over its own affairs.

While Anglo-Russian rivalry in Persia helped preserve its territorial integrity in the nineteenth century, it was helpless to prevent almost constant interference by the two rivals over the Persian economy. Persia's inability to manage its financial, commercial, and administrative affairs forced the Persians to become dependent upon Russian, British, and other Western experts. Resentment of foreign interference unified Persians to express collective resistance, frequently under the leadership of religious officials, when nothing else could. Cooperation between religious leaders and merchants provided some successes in deterring the almost complete foreign domination of Persia's economy and public utilities.

The helplessness of the Qajar rulers against their internal and external enemies forced them to experiment with constitutionalism in 1906. The coalition of merchants, religious leaders, and a small number of intellectuals that forced the Shah to accept constitutionalism had too many differences to make the constitution work. The traditionalist forces of the clergy and the merchants had no desire to allow the secular agenda of the intellectual revolutionaries to succeed. Consequently, the secularists faced a combination of forces that prevented implementation of their new constitution. Russia also exerted pressure to prevent the success of constitutionalism. The frenzy that accompanied the constitutional movement had, in fact, given the opportunity for radical ideas that had been spawned in Russia to spread widely in the dissatisfied elements of northern Persia, which contained the empire's greatest population centers and proven economic resources. Near anarchy reigned in Persia as the tribes revolted in the absence of central authority. Persians were in no position to prevent Russia and Great Britain from establishing their mutually recognized spheres of influence in Persia in 1907. Both used neutral Persia for their own interests during World War I.

Great Britain dominated Persian affairs after the Russian revolution in 1917. The Russian revolutionary forces, like everything else Russian, spilled over into Persia. Separatist movements that were affiliated with Russian revolutionary groups developed in northern Persia. British attempts to dominate Persia were untenable, since Persia was economically dependent upon commercial relations with Russia, regardless of the nature of its regime.

Reza Khan, a military leader of the Russian-trained Cossack Brigade, seized power and slowly asserted his military control over northern Persia by 1921. He made peace with the new Soviet regime and served as Prime Minister until 1926 when he crowned himself as the new Shah. By then he had subdued the tribes and had come close to establishing his will over Persia in the same way Ataturk, whom he admired, had done in Turkey.

Reza Shah charted an independent course in foreign affairs and eliminated the hold foreigners had formerly exercised in Persian affairs. His extraction of higher revenues from the Anglo-Iranian Oil Company in 1933 gave him more income and helped assuage Persian national pride. He ruthlessly eliminated internal threats and forced through legislation that had an interestingly similar anti-religious character to that of Ataturk. Once he eliminated their economic base and domination over education, the clergy no longer had a foundation for opposition, as they had in the past.

A close affiliation with Germany by the mid-1930s signaled the independence of Iran (renamed in 1935) from Russian and British influence. Iran, in fact, became the Middle Eastern center of pro-German activities in 1941 after the British suppressed the pro-German government of Iraq. The Soviet Union and Great Britain could not countenance such independence of action in Iran. They overthrew Reza in 1941 but allowed his son, Muhammad, to assume the crown. The United States also joined in the occupation of Iran once it became involved in the European theater of World War II.

The three foreign occupiers withdrew from Iran by 1946, but the USSR had laid the foundation for a powerful influence in northern Iran with its support of the Tudeh party. Separatist elements, which were at least as strong as those that followed World War I, threatened to place parts, or all, of Iran under direct or indirect Soviet control. Nationalists in close association with the Shah suppressed the Tudeh movement by 1947.

Having rid themselves of the Soviets, the Iranian nationalists turned their attention to Britain's continued influence through its ownership and control of Iran's petroleum industry. Muhammad Mossadegh used his forum in the legislature to make nationalization of Iran's petroleum industry the central issue in Iran. Public support for his proposal was so strong that the Shah and other hesitant elements were forced to adopt his nationalist policy. A revived Tudeh party played a prominent role in Mossadegh's success. The entire Middle Eastern region and much of the underdeveloped world erupted in jubilation when Iran nationalized the British owned petroleum company in 1951. It was the largest blow any nation in the region had delivered to Western imperialism.

Mossadegh proceeded to acquire more power than even most of his staunchest supporters could abide. An international boycott of Iranian petroleum, which it was as yet unable to administer by itself, added to the hardship of Mossadegh and the country. When he and his supporters forced the Shah to flee in 1953, most assumed that both royal and foreign domination had ended. The Shah's return in six days, with United States assistance, dispelled that belief. Elements loyal to the Shah overthrew Mossadegh and proceeded to suppress the Tudeh party in 1953.

Iran achieved much greater control over its petroleum industry in a new, multinational structure of the National Iranian Oil Company in 1954. Great Britain's direct influence over Iranian affairs was gone just as Russia's had subsided with the demise of the power of the Tudeh party. By 1958, Iran seemed in control of its affairs under a benevolent Shah, who had a new source of advice, protection, and technology from the United States. Few feared this new state's participation in Iranian affairs, since it enjoyed a good reputation for supporting freedom and had no history of pursuing imperialistic goals in the region. By 1958 Iranians had every reason to believe that, after a century and a half of foreign domination, they, like the Arabs, were free to determine their own fate.

The future did not bear out the optimistic hopes of Arabs and Iranians in 1958. It is, however, worthwhile to attempt to look more closely at the challenges they had faced before that date to understand why there was so much hope for a better future, with freedom from imperialism, in 1958.

1

Confrontation with Modernity

HISTORICAL TIMELINE

- **1536** ⇛ Sublime Porte was allied with France.
- **1683** ⇛ Successful defense of Vienna against Ottomans.
- **1699** ⇛ Christian reconquest of Hungary.
- **1774** ⇛ Treaty of Kuchuk Kainarji took place on July 21.
- **1787** ⇛ Austro-Russian agreement to partition Ottoman Empire.
- **1792** ⇛ Sultan made peace with Austria and Russia with Treaty of Jassy on January 9.
- **1798** ⇛ Napoleon attacked Egypt on July 1.
- **1799** ⇛ Napoleon left Egypt on August 24 and returned to France.
- **1801** ⇛ Joint Ottoman and British effort drove French back to France.
- **1807** ⇛ Selim III deposed on May 29; replaced by Mustafa IV.
- **1807** ⇛ Franco-Russian detente at Tilsit.
- **1808** ⇛ Selim was murdered, Mustafa was deposed on July 28; he was replaced by Mahmoud II.
- **1809** ⇛ Treaty of the Dardanelles on January 5 gave Britain favorable trade relations with the Ottoman Empire and closed the Straits to all foreign warships in peacetime.
- **1812** ⇛ Treaty of Bucharest was signed on May 28.
- **1821** ⇛ Greek Revolution began.

1824 ⇛ Sultan Mahmoud II allied with Muhammad Ali of Egypt.

1826 ⇛ Mahmoud II announced the creation of the new model army on May 28.
⇛ Revolt of the Janissaries against Mahmoud's reforms.

1827 ⇛ Treaty of London on June 6, in which the European powers threatened to use force against the Ottomans on behalf of the Greeks.
⇛ The British fleet crushed the Ottomans and the Egyptians at Navarino on October 20.

1828 ⇛ Russian forces had Istanbul at their mercy by August.

1829 ⇛ Treaty of Adrianople [Edirne] on September 14 ended the War of Greek Independence.

1832 ⇛ Establishment of first Turkish newspaper ,*Takuim-i Vekayi.*
⇛ Egypt conquered Levant as compensation for military efforts to end the Greek revolution.

1833 ⇛ Russians came to Ottoman defense in February to thwart threat from Muhammad Ali.
⇛ Treaty of Kutahya on July 8 gave Muhammad Ali concessions from the Ottoman Empire.
⇛ Treaty of Hunkiar Iskelski in August gave Russia a preferred status with the Ottoman Empire.

1834–1848 ⇛ Reign of Muhammad in Persia.

1837 ⇛ Persian conflict with Britain over Persian attempt to annex Herat region of Afghanistan.
⇛ Mustafa Rashid entered ministry of Sultan Mahmoud II.

1838 ⇛ Muhammad Ali announced Egyptian independence from Ottoman suzerainty.
⇛ Death of Sultan Mahmoud II on July 1, succeeded by Abdul Mejid I.
⇛ Treaty of Balta Limani gave British trade concessions in the Ottoman Empire.

1839 ⇛ Muhammad Ali claimed complete independence from Sultan.
⇛ Egyptians defeated Ottoman army at the battle of Nezib in Syria on June 24 and moved into central Anatolia to threaten Istanbul.
⇛ *Hatt-i-Sharif* (Illustrious Rescript of Gulhaneh) November 3 decreed by Sultan Abdul Mejid I gave Ottoman subjects greater freedom and rights.

1840s–1860s ⇛ Shayhk Nasif al-Yaziji modernized Arabic through extensive poetry in the contemporary idiom. He also wrote on grammar, rhetoric, and logic.

1840 ⇛ Western powers forced Egypt out of Syria but Sultan acknowledged Muhammad Ali's right to pass title to his progeny.
⇛ Egypt forced to accept capitulations that prevailed in the other parts of the Ottoman Empire.

⇛ Ottoman Council of Judicial Ordinances assumed role as central institution of Ottoman government.

1841 ⇛ Muhammad Ali withdrew Egyptian troops from Crete.
⇛ Straits Convention on July 13 closed the Straits to foreign war ships during peace.

1842 ⇛ Orthodox Church claimed the right to rebuild the dome of the Church of the Holy Sepulchre resisted by Rome.

1843 ⇛ Beginning of *qamaqamate* in Lebanon.

1845 ⇛ New phase of *Tanzimat* initiated by Sultan Abdul Mejid I.
⇛ Charter of the University of Istanbul.

1847 ⇛ Christmas brawl between Latin and Orthodox monks at the Church of the Nativity in Bethlehem.
⇛ Creation of the Ottoman Ministry of Education.

1848–1896 ⇛ Reign of Shah Nasir al-Din of Persia.

1848 ⇛ Persia and Ottoman Empire agreed on borders.
⇛ Revolutions swept the Hapsburg Empire.
⇛ Wallachian revolutionaries declared union with Moldavia in the independednt state of Rumania free of Ottoman control.

1849–1854 ⇛ Russo-Persian War.

1850s–1870s ⇛ Butrus al-Bustani helped modernize the Arabic language through his dictionary, his encyclopedia, and other extensive writings on the need for Arabs to learn modern science and other knowledge. He strongly emphasized national identity.

1850 ⇛ Promulgation of a commercial code for the Ottoman Empire.

1852 ⇛ Napoleon III gained concessions for Roman Catholic Church within the Ottoman Empire.

1853 ⇛ Russians invaded Danubian principalities on July 2.
⇛ Vienna Note of July 28 attempted to resolve the problems between France and Russia over religious matters within the Ottoman Empire.
⇛ Russians destroyed an Ottoman fleet at Sinop on November 30.

1854 ⇛ Ottoman High Council of the *Tanzimat* assumed legislative duties from the Council of Judicial Ordinances, maintained its judicial function.
⇛ Great Britain and France declared war on Russia on March 28.
⇛ Austria and Prussia agreed to a mutual defense treaty on April 20.
⇛ Porte and Austria reach agreement on the defense of the Danubian principalities on June 14.
⇛ Russia withdrew from Danubian principalities on August 8.
⇛ Ottomans made the first loan in the West to finance the Crimean War.
⇛ Anglo-French seige of Sevastopol began September 14.

1855 ⇛ Fall of Sevastopol on September 9.

1856 ⇛ Peace of Paris on March 30 ended the Crimean War.

Middle Eastern affairs were inextricably intertwined with Europe by the nineteenth century. The intermittent relationship between the two regions from the early part of the century developed into an association that the Europeans gradually dominated. Ironically, most of the Middle East fell under European control as a result of a desperate attempt by the Middle East empires to survive the challenge of European political, economic, and military superiority. Europe, which was the source of the challenge, also seemed to be the source of the solution for the Ottoman and Persian empires, which encompassed most of the entire Middle Eastern region. Adding to the incongruity, both empires were initially under the greatest threat from Russia, which was, itself, decidedly the least developed major European nation. The perceived Russian threat, however, stimulated the other European nations to become heavily involved in Middle Eastern affairs in an effort to prevent Russian aggrandizement and to maintain its virtual landlocked condition. During the process, Russia's European opponents became firmly ensconced in the Middle East long after Russia ceased to be a direct threat to the region. The prolonged and intense struggle transformed the Middle East and threatened to deny its people the opportunity to control their own affairs and fate.

European penetration, which led to its domination of the Middle East, centered on financial, military, and technological assistance. In addition, the Europeans justified much of their activity upon a moral and humanitarian effort to protect the rights of non-Muslims. The supposed humanitarian motivations were, in fact, crucial in the modern era when public opinion became increasingly decisive in the formulation of national policies. In time, the Europeans espoused a motivation that was more inclusive as they expressed the desire to provide the Middle East with modern European-style constitutional government. A significant portion of the Middle Eastern population, many of whom had received European educations, became partners in this quest, even though they resented European influence in other areas of the region's development. In general, traditionalists were unable to counter the appeal of foreign and indigenous Western influence that portended to provide a modern standard of living and participatory government to the region's population.

The decentralized Ottoman and Persian empires were incapable of withstanding the many challenges the West presented. Policies and practices that had been sufficient in the past became anachronistic and deficient to sustain the two ancient empires against both external and internal forces. The valiant efforts each of them made often seemed to exacerbate their decline into subservience to the West.

THE OTTOMAN EMPIRE

The Ottoman Empire was not a nation, but a federation of different peoples and regions, which were spread over an immense area under differing degrees of control by the Sultan and his government, the Porte. Consequently, there was no sense of Ottoman nationalism in the modern sense of the term. While all subjects of the empire were Ottomans, their sense of identity was usually much more local, except for an affiliation with their particular religion.

Despite being pushed out of Hungary at the end of the seventeenth century, the empire still stretched south of Russia from the entire Balkan peninsula, all the way to the Arabian Gulf. It was composed of Turks, a plethora of different Christian Slavs, Arabs, Greeks, Armenians, Kurds, Jews, Druze, and others. In addition, most of north Africa was part of the Ottoman Empire, but its historical marginal authority there was even weaker by the nineteenth century. A majority of the subjects were Muslim, and Islam was the official religion of the empire. Turkish was the official language. Non-Muslim subjects had the time-honored status of *dhimmis*, which gave them freedom to practice their religion, and allowed exemption from military service in return for a special tax.

Most individuals and groups had accommodated themselves to the empire over the centuries and had never seriously attempted to acquire their independence. The empire had never been very efficient, and for long periods, regions of this far-flung entity existed with little interference from Istanbul, unless outright rebellion occurred. Individuals and localities sought, and often achieved, a kind of anonymity within the empire. An Ottoman in the provinces could often proudly say, "the Sultan does not know my name." Such anonymity could bring freedom from taxation and from conscription into the Sultan's military service. In this respect, the rule of the Ottomans was bearable and preferable to a smaller, regional state whose authority would be more immediate.

One could make a strong case that only an amorphous entity such as the pre-reformed Ottoman Empire could have ruled so vast an area prior to the development of rapid communication and transportation. Its minimal authority was like some law of nature, which allowed ebb and flow, shifting and crumbling, mutation and transformation, while the general appearance and pattern of life remained the same.

While Muslims thought of Islamic law, the *Sharia,* as a universal law, it was not applicable to unbelievers, who did not accept or understand its premises. Therefore, one system of law could not prevail in an empire that contained many non-Muslim subjects. This led to the unavoidable conclusion that, in many areas of public and private life, a different arrangement was necessary for non-Muslim subjects, since there was no secular law. Quite naturally, the Porte turned to the leaders of the different religious groups within its empire to provide justice and perform other functions to their respective communities. The necessity of providing justice according to religious affiliation enhanced the subjects' religious identity and increased the role of religious leaders in Ottoman society at every level. Confessional identification was so strongly ingrained that, like many other Ottoman practices, it endured long after the Ottoman Empire ceased to exist.

The entire empire was organized around *millets,* or religious communities, and the Porte communicated with each *millet* through its recognized leader or executive council. Each *millet* was responsible for collecting taxes, distributing government services, and administering justice for its members. In some respects all Muslims had preferential treatment in the largest *millet.* Traditionally, however, only the Greek and Armenian Orthodox Christians and the Jews held special *millet* status. Other non-Muslim Ottomans were under the protection of the ambassadors of foreign nations whose religion was the same or similar to theirs. The most important such arrangement was with France, which had enjoyed the status of protector of the Roman Catholics since the sixteenth century.

The number of *millets* grew in the later part of the nineteenth century with the increased interest of foreign countries in the empire, until by the outbreak of World

War I they numbered seventeen. At that time, every major European nation, and even the United States, protected the *millets* associated with them. These religious *millets* became convenient vehicles for foreign governments to influence the empire's internal affairs.

FOREIGN CAPITULATION AGREEMENTS

Religious *millets*, combined with capitulary commercial treaties, created a heavy financial burden for the Porte and understandably aroused resentment in Ottoman society. The capitulations, in fact, had laid the foundation for the *millets*. The capitulation treaties began in the fifteenth century when foreign merchants made arrangements with the Porte to provide them special legal protection due to the inapplicability of Muslim law to their behavior. The Porte, thus, capitulated its jurisdiction over some activities within its realm, first to foreign merchants and later to foreign states. It, therefore, became customary for commercial treaties to include special tariff duties as well as extraterritorial legal privileges. Under the capitulations, foreign nationals paid few or no tariffs and taxes, and they were only subject to Ottoman law by the permission of their government. Distinctions between the capitulation treaties of the various nations were virtually nonexistent in the nineteenth century, as each enjoyed most-favored-nation status. As long as one nation, such as Great Britain, insisted on continued protected status for its nationals, all the others retained them as well.

The capitulations were an abuse of Ottoman sovereignty by nature, but they became worse in the nineteenth century as non-Muslim Ottomans became citizens of foreign nations and obtained protection under the capitulations. Without the inconvenience of leaving the empire, Ottomans could become citizens of foreign governments by obtaining a document called a *barat*. The attending privileges were sufficiently favorable to entice many Ottoman subjects to exercise this option. Muslims by law and choice did not change their religion or nationality. Only Christians and Jews, therefore, enjoyed the benefits of the *barats* in commerce and trade, which they already dominated. The protracted intercourse of these indigenous "foreigners" with the West not only brought them prosperity, but knowledge and skills in languages for them and their offspring, which widened an existing breech between them and Ottoman Muslims. It was little wonder that many Muslims not only resented the *barat* holders' unwarranted success but often regarded them as Fifth-Column elements within the empire.

PERSIA

For millennia Persia was a land of cultural, literary, and military accomplishments on a mythic and epic scale to its own inhabitants and to the entire world. Persia defined splendor, military might, cultural refinement, and erudition in the arts and literature. Peoples within hundreds of miles of its several different capitals were subject to falling under its direct or indirect rule, which could occur as a result of brutal conquest or the cleverest of diplomacy. The Persian shahs (emperors) could and did establish both security and devastation, oppression and emancipation, pros-

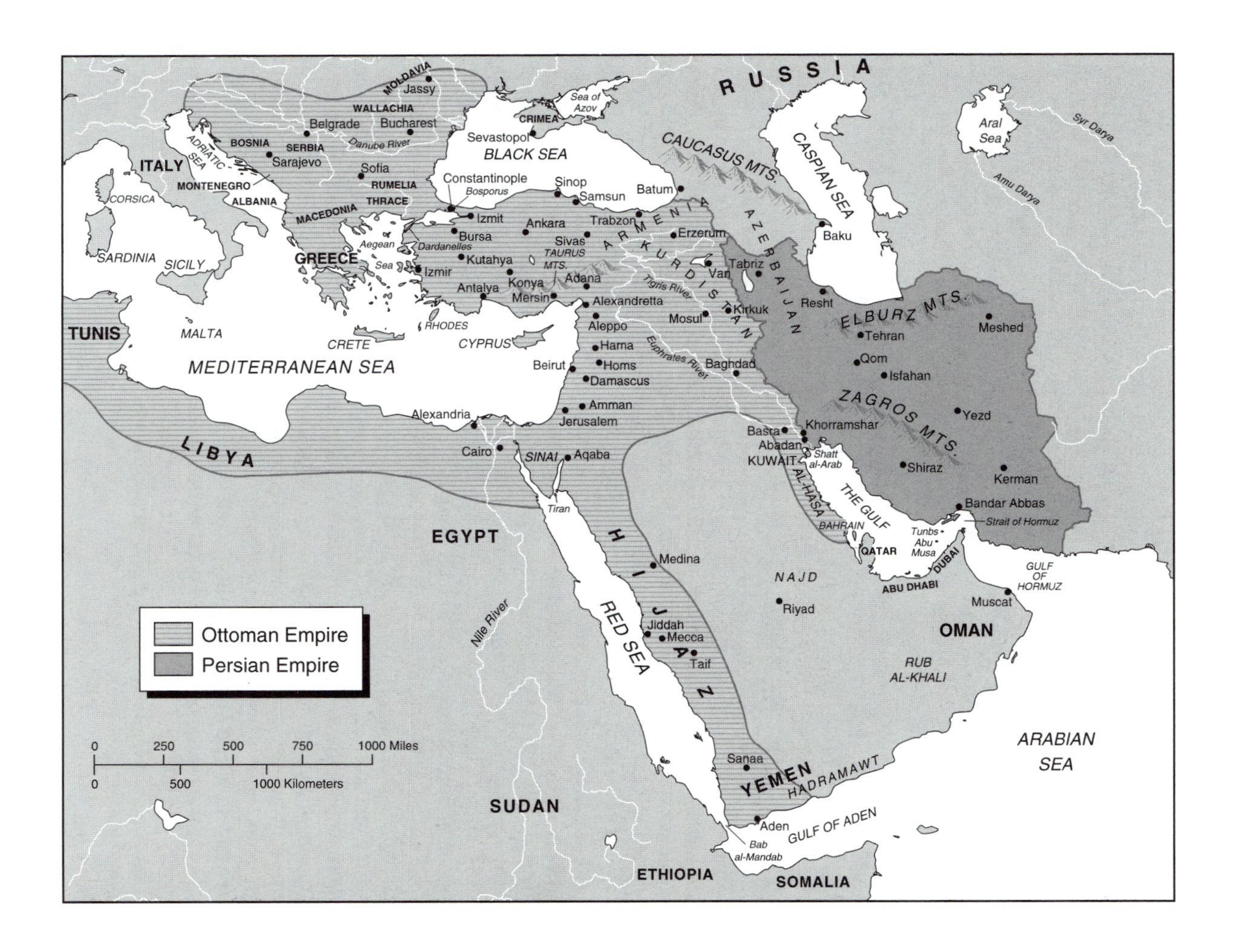

RUSSIA
MOLDAVIA
Jassy
WALLACHIA
Belgrade
Bucharest
Danube River
BOSNIA
SERBIA
Sarajevo
Sofia
RUMELIA
THRACE
MACEDONIA
MONTENEGRO
ALBANIA
ADRIATIC SEA
ITALY
CORSICA
SARDINIA
SICILY
GREECE
Aegean Sea
Dardanelles
Bosporus
Constantinople
Izmit
Bursa
Kutahya
Izmir
Antalya
Konya
Mersin
Adana
TAURUS MTS.
Ankara
Sivas
Sinop
Samsun
Trabzon
Batum
Erzerum
ARMENIA
KURDISTAN
AZERBAIJAN
Van
Tabriz
Resht
Baku
CAUCASUS MTS.
CASPIAN SEA
Sea of Azov
CRIMEA
Sevastopol
BLACK SEA
Aral Sea
Syr Darya
Amu Darya
ELBURZ MTS.
Tehran
Meshed
Qom
Isfahan
ZAGROS MTS.
Yezd
Shiraz
Kerman
Bandar Abbas
Strait of Hormuz
Tigris River
Euphrates River
Kirkuk
Mosul
Baghdad
Basra
Abadan
Khorramshar
KUWAIT
Shatt al-Arab
AL-HASA
THE GULF
BAHRAIN
QATAR
Tunbs
Abu Musa
DUBAI
ABU DHABI
GULF OF HORMUZ
Muscat
OMAN
RUB AL-KHALI
NAJD
Riyad
ARABIAN SEA
TUNIS
MALTA
CRETE
RHODES
CYPRUS
MEDITERRANEAN SEA
Alexandretta
Aleppo
Hama
Homs
Beirut
Damascus
Amman
Jerusalem
Alexandria
Cairo
SINAI
Aqaba
Tiran
LIBYA
EGYPT
Nile River
HIJAZ
Medina
Jiddah
Mecca
Taif
RED SEA
Sanaa
YEMEN
HADRAMAWT
Aden
GULF OF ADEN
Bab al-Mandab
SUDAN
ETHIOPIA
SOMALIA
Ottoman Empire
Persian Empire
0
250
500
750
1000 Miles
0
500
1000 Kilometers

perity and ruin. Persia accurately became associated with the vilest vices and the grandest luxuries.

By the nineteenth century, Persia had experienced three centuries of decline, which often threatened its extinction from a combination of foreign annexation and the unencumbered power of local chieftains. Persia's decline and disarray resulted largely from the frequent rule of indulgent shahs, who usually attempted to live in splendor but failed to provide the strong leadership the empire required. Even the heartland of Persia needed firm leadership to prosper, because it was not intrinsically wealthy and was composed of many ethnic and linguistic groups, whose local loyalties were greater than their sense of identity to the central government. Down through the centuries the almost constant infusion of tribute from conquered areas and the continuity of strong monarchical leadership had overcome the intrinsic weaknesses of the empire.

The emergence of strong neighbors on the periphery of Persia gradually confined it to the limited territories that presently constitute the modern state of Iran. Russia to the north, the Ottoman Empire to the west, and a strong British presence to the south and east ended Persia's capacity to expand and extract tribute. Persia's inability to modernize militarily, administratively, and economically made it an easy prey for foreign control. Russia and Great Britain took full advantage of Persia's weakness in the nineteenth century and gradually established control over most of the once proud empire. Weak as the Ottoman Empire was, it could also thwart Persian expansion into Mesopotamia and deny its predominantly Shiah Muslim population full access to their most sacred shrines south of Baghdad.

The central government lost prestige and the capacity either to enforce its will or collect revenue from the outlying regions of the empire. Local tribal leaders openly defied central authority in the countryside, while the cities and towns increasingly fell under the influence of merchants and religious leaders. During the nineteenth century, the shahs attempted to remedy their plight through concessions to foreigners and the use of foreign expert advisers at the expense of the independence of both themselves and their country.

Most Persians detested the growth of foreign influence over their country in the nineteenth century, but those who were in a position to establish a government to prevent such encroachment balked at strengthening the shah's authority. They were also unable to establish an effective alternative to monarchical rule. The infiltration of foreign influence became so widespread that almost all elements of the upper echelons of Persia's population fell under suspicion of being foreign agents. In many cases the suspicions were well founded. Mistrust among the leaders exacerbated an already tragic inability to maintain Persian sovereignty.

Persia was too old and had been too grand for its population to accept passively the fate that resulted from their own flaws. Their common plight under foreign control periodically brought united efforts to expel foreign control and to punish their fellow countrymen who had bartered away the country's patrimony. Personal ambitions and fundamental differences among the Persians failed to coalesce into a concerted effort to determine their own destiny.

Any unity that resulted from this trauma was the widespread fear and hatred of foreigners and foreign influence. Persia's unique status as the largest Shiah nation in the world prevented it from even obtaining succor from the larger Islamic world that generally regarded it as schismatic. The fact that it was the only nation to use the Persian language isolated it further.

THE LAND AND PEOPLE

A large percentage of Iran's population lives near its borders because much of the interior is virtually uninhabitable desert. Close to ninety percent of the land can sustain little or no population as a result of the lack of water, unfertile soil, and severe weather conditions. Mountains define most of Iran's perimeter, even on the Caspian Sea to the north and on the Gulf in the southwest, where the mountains reach almost to the water's edge. Vast portions of the mountains also lack water or have weather conditions that defy human habitation. Most of the population resides across the northwest part of the country, which usually receives adequate rainfall and enjoys the benefit of the narrow, rich agricultural area on the southern shore of the Caspian Sea. This also helps explain why Tehran replaced Isfahan as the capital of the country, although much of its glory is associated with the former capital. Tabriz, which is located in Azerbaijan province in the northwest part of the country, has also served as the capital even though it is subject to invasion from both Turkey and Russia.

Iran's modern borders only became solidified well into the twentieth century in large part because similar kinds of people live on both sides of its borders with Turkey, the Soviet Union, Afghanistan, Pakistan, and Iraq. Even the Gulf does not serve as a good line of delineation, since Persians comprise much of the population along the entire shoreline of the Gulf and on its islands. This is especially troublesome on the island of Bahrain, which has an Arab minority ruling over a largely Persian population. The southwest boundary with Iraq along the Shatt al-Arab is the most contentious because the province of Khuzistan, which the Arabs call Arabistan, has a predominantly Arab population. The fact that it is the center of Iran's oil extraction and production adds to the problem. All of these problems revolve around Abadan, which historically has been the center for refining and shipping Iran's crucial oil resources. Only under duress has Iraq agreed for Iran to use the Shatt al-Arab to transport its petroleum to the markets of the world.

Historically, Iran has been a nation of farmers and herdsmen who were dependent upon a landed aristocracy and tribal leaders for their economic welfare and security. A small number of families owned almost all of the land and exercised nearly total control over the lives of Iran's inhabitants. The central government of the shahs sometimes could extend its authority to the general population, but even then it usually did so through the land-owning elite. This is not the least reason representative government did not work after the implementation of a constitution in 1906, because even the broadest franchise reflected the desires of the landed class, which instructed the peasants how to vote. The results from those elections could not please the unruly urban constitutionalists who were under the influence of merchants and clerics.

Several distinct peoples comprise the Iranian population, but the fact that most speak some form of the Persian language gave the country a foundation for unity. The fact that even most who spoke other languages were Shiah Muslims provided additional hope for a national identity. For instance, while the Bakhtiari, Lurs, and Kurds are identifiably different from the mainstream Persian communities, they all speak Persian dialects. The Kurds are, however, predominantly Sunni Muslims as are the Pushtu-speaking Baluchi tribesmen in the southeast corner of the country. The Turkish speaking Azarbaijani in the economically important northwestern part of Iran share belief in Shiah Islam with most other Iranians. The same is true of the Turkish-speaking Qashqai in the west-central part of the country. These and smaller tribally organized ethnic groups had adequate reasons to feel kinship with Iran's dominant Persian population. The Arabs in Khuzistan are a notable exception because of their language and because most are Sunni Muslims. They have, however, benefited from the oil industry in their province, which is Iran's most important economic asset. Some Iranians and Arabs alike regard these Khuzistan Arabs as a potential Fifth Column, which identifies with Arab, rather than Iranian, interests. In this respect, they share an onus similar to Shiah Arabs in southern Iraq whom many Iraqis believe owe their first allegiance to the Shiah nation of Iran. There were sound reasons, other than tradition, however, to make the various distinctive tribes hesitant to accept loyalty to the state, unless the central government could either offer them overriding reasons to willingly submit or could force them to do so. The virtual independence of the tribal leaders, who exercised great authority over their people, was the most obvious reason to spurn efforts to bring them under central authority.

THE EGYPTIAN EXCEPTION

Unlike other areas of the Arab Middle East, the continuity of Egypt's history from earliest times dwarfed its heritage as an Arabic and Islamic society. The pyramids symbolically attested to a proud and continuous tradition of leadership in world civilization from 5000 B.C. Arabs came in the seventh century and Arabic soon became the dominant language. Islam, which came with the Arabs, also became the religion of most except for the ten percent who remained Coptic Christians. Still, the descendants of the pharonic past evinced an aura of historical depth that relegated the Islamic era to a mere patina. The Arabs, like various other invaders over the centuries, were never able to detach the Egyptians from their early identity. Many Egyptians agreed with the early twentieth-century Arab nationalist, Neguib Azouri, that "Egyptians do not belong to the Arab race."

However, as the largest, most modern Arab community, and the country with the most experience with quasi-independence, Egypt consistently obtained the mantle of leadership of the Arab world in modern times. Egyptians could offer skills, knowledge, and understanding that were essential to the more ardent nationalists with better "Arab" credentials from elsewhere in the Arab world. Some Arab nationalists felt uneasy with Egypt's leadership, however, since they realized that Egypt, more than any other Arab state, could at any time shed its Arab identity and withdraw to pursue an independent course.

Egypt is 385,000 square miles of virtually rainless desert. It receives its life from the Nile River, which flows from Upper Egypt in the south to Lower Egypt and the Mediterranean in the north. Almost all of Egypt's arable land lies within a few miles of the river until it splits into a broad delta just north of Cairo, which is located about one hundred miles inland from the Mediterranean Sea. These physical features dictate that Egypt's ever burgeoning population lives on five percent of its land along the Nile, whose annual flooding brings water and rich new soil from the interior of Africa. The warm climate allows year-round farming when water is available. It is little wonder that down through the ages rulers and subjects alike have dreamed of retaining the Nile's precious waters instead of allowing it to rush to the sea.

While Egypt's population is hardly homogeneous, the minorities have usually presented no significant challenge to central authority. However, during the nineteenth century, the close affiliation of some Christians and Jews with certain Western nations aroused resentment. Non-Egyptians residing in Cairo, and especially in Alexandria, offered special skills and talents that enriched Egyptian society, particularly in manufacturing, foreign trade, and banking. These Greek, Armenian, and Levantine Christian Arabs, along with Jews, generally prospered regardless of the vagaries in the greater Egyptian society by remaining aloof from politics. By the twentieth century, however, some among these groups were the initial adherents of leftist, secular ideologies that traditional Muslims and Copts found offensive.

Ninety percent of Egypt's population embraced Sunni Islam with the same ease with which they approached most aspects of their lives. Fanaticism was not unknown but it was rare. There was a strong commitment to Islam as a way of life and many Egyptians pursued academic careers in Islamic sciences. Those who did had the benefit of Al-Azhar, which, since it was founded in 970 A.D., was the oldest institution of higher learning in the world. Interpretations from its *ulama*, or faculty, were often considered definitive throughout the Islamic world. The moderate but persuasive call for Islamic reform and rejuvenation from Jamal al-Din al-Afghani, Muhammad Abduh, and Rashid Rida was much more in keeping with the general tenor of Egyptian Islam than was the more militant approach of Hasan al-Banna. The expansion of their teachings far beyond Egypt's borders epitomized Egyptian leadership in almost every important feature of Arab life.

EMERGENCE OF MUHAMMAD ALI

Because of both the nature of Egypt and the Ottoman Empire, Egypt was seldom under the close control of Istanbul. However, the Ottoman Pasha, or governor, usually paid annual tributes to the Sultan, contributed troops for the Ottoman military needs, and enforced laws that applied to the entire empire. By all accounts, however, Egypt was in particularly poor condition at the end of the eighteenth century because of Mamluk-inspired ruthlessness and greed. The unprincipled tyranny of the remnants of this caste of slave-administrators provided Napoleon his ostensible reason for invading Egypt in 1798 to liberate the Egyptians. Sultan Selim III rejected Napoleon's claim that the invasion by the Ottoman's oldest European ally was also to his benefit. He sent an Ottoman army to repel the French intrusion.

This episode changed Egypt and the Middle East in many ways, but the most obvious change occurred because it gave Muhammad Ali, an Albanian, the opportunity to lead an Albanian army to Egypt. After he expelled the French, the Albanian attacked the Mamluks and gained widespread support in Egypt, especially in Cairo. Selim initially resented the unauthorized actions of Muhammad Ali but finally recognized him as the Pasha of Egypt in 1805. By 1812 Muhammad Ali had subdued the Mamluks, killed hundreds of their leaders, and confiscated their properties.

Muhammad Ali's acquisition of the Mamluk estates initiated an approach that ended with his accumulation of more land, wealth, and power than any individual had enjoyed since the pharaohs. He confiscated lands from those who failed to endorse his authority, those who could not demonstrate clear title to their land, and those whose land taxes were in arrears. Much religious *waqf* land failed to meet his standards and also became his personal property. This, of course, gave him unprecedented wealth and direct influence over the lives of the tenants on his vast lands. His administrators dictated the crops Egyptian farmers would grow and provided a state-controlled marketing monopoly for domestic and international sales. Egypt once again became the bread basket of the Mediterranean as it had been in antiquity. The *fellahin*, farmers, were able to keep little more of their production than they kept during the Mamluk period, but they were more secure if they maintained the Pasha's demanding production expectations.

Under Muhammad Ali's direction, Egypt became closely affiliated with Europe a full century before any other part of the Middle East. Predictably, his first concern was for military modernization, for which he turned to independent French advisers. Soon, however, he also enticed Europeans, mostly Frenchmen, to establish schools and medical facilities in order to provide an educated and healthy Egyptian population. He knew this would be necessary if Egypt were to become a worthy partner with the European states he wished to emulate. Young Egyptians, thus, became familiar with European ideas, technology, and institutions far sooner than their surrounding Arab brethren. Cholera, which had amounted to a virtual plague in the delta region, diminished. This resulted in subsequent population growth, which would in time become nearly as dire a problem as the disease had been. Significant improvements of irrigation, especially the construction of a barrage in the southern delta, improved the food supply and increased Egypt's agricultural exports.

The Pasha resented that his profits from grain exports returned to the European economy to purchase manufactured goods. He decided to establish his own industries based upon the new techniques of Europe's industrial revolution. Again, under European supervision, he established textile, sugar, and glass factories, as well as foundries and shipyards. These efforts, which attest to Muhammad Ali's foresight, inclination to innovation, and desire to obtain self-sufficiency, had marginal success. Egypt lacked the raw materials for modern industrialization based on coal and iron. Its work force was unaccustomed to the regimentation in confined quarters associated with nineteenth-century industrialization. Lack of familiarity with the care and upkeep of modern machinery led to the premature deterioration of machines before they had repaid their investments. No small part of Egypt's failure at industrialization, however, resulted from successful European efforts to prevent the emergence of another competitor for the world's markets.

This was particularly true in textile manufacture, which has traditionally been the avenue to industrialization for many kinds of societies. The Pasha's textile manufacturing efforts suffered from the same maladies as his other attempts at industrialization. Under ordinary circumstances, Egypt should have been able to overcome the difficulties related to cotton manufacture, since it had an abundance of the world's best cotton. Egypt, for instance, began growing the coveted, long-staple cotton in 1820, which would become the basis of Egypt's economy for the future.

OTTOMAN CONFLICTS WITH THE WEST

Western public opinion, and to some degree western governments, were unaware that non-Muslims enjoyed any rights at all within the Ottoman Empire. The new consciousness of representative government and individual rights in the West by the nineteenth century impelled westerners to intercede to acquire the same kind of "natural rights" in behalf of their Judeo-Christian compatriots in the Islamic Ottoman Empire. The precedents and vehicles for interference toward this end, combined with the weakness of the empire, created pressure for westernization throughout the nineteenth century.

Ottoman weakness vis-a-vis the West in the early modern period was a dramatic change that required time for both camps to understand and make adjustments. For centuries, the Ottoman Empire struck terror into the hearts of Christians to its west and north, as it expanded and thrived on almost constant warfare and conquest. Eastern Europe, in particular, had lived in perpetual fear that it would follow Hungary under the yoke of the Sultan of Istanbul. The Mediterranean and its adjacent waterways were usually navigable for the Christian West only by the sufferance of the Ottomans. The Ottomans were confident that their success was the will of God, while Christians were sure that the Sultan-Caliph and his armed hoards were instruments of the devil.

Though less than efficient, the Ottomans enjoyed centuries of superiority because their administrative and tax systems easily provided the capacity to wage war on the weak, decentralized Christian nations. The sheer size of the Ottoman Empire generated more revenues for the Sultan's central coffers than western rulers could imagine.

The successful Christian defense of Vienna in 1683, and the subsequent reconquest of Hungary in 1699, signaled the end of Ottoman expansion. The previous Christian fear of extinction or absorption gave way to an uneasy tension with its Islamic neighbor.

By the beginning of the eighteenth century, the Christian states, including Russia, had adopted modern administrative and military practices, which their improved economies could sustain. Several individual Christian states, thus, became more than a military and economic match for the Ottoman Empire. While they had no collective will to use their new strength against the "terrible Turks," the Ottoman Empire became a favorite target for economic and cultural expansion for France and Great Britain, and for territorial expansion for Russia and the Austrian Empire.

In fact, throughout the eighteenth century, the Ottomans were almost constantly at war with the latter two over border disputes and Austro-Russian interference in Poland. France, which had been closely associated with the Sublime Porte (the Ottoman government) since 1536, urged the Ottomans to resist Austro-Russian aggression. France, which was occupied with its global wars with Great Britain during this period, benefitted from the Ottomans' distraction of its great European land rivals.

The mutual distrust of Austria and Russia prevented their cooperation and allowed the Ottomans to acquit themselves well enough in these conflicts. By 1774, however, Russia was able to defeat the Ottomans in the Aegean Sea and on land in Wallachia, Moldavia, and the Crimea. Russia's victories led to the momentous Treaty of Kuchuk Kainarji on July 21, 1774. While Russia actually returned some conquered territory, it made more important inroads into Ottoman sovereignty, as the Ottomans consented to Russian commercial navigation on both the Danube River and the Black Sea. The treaty guaranteed Russian pilgrims the right to visit the Holy Land, and allowed Russia to construct a Russian Orthodox church in Istanbul. Although it seemed innocuous at the time, the greatest Russian gain was tacit Ottoman consent to the tsar's right to protect Orthodox Christians in the Ottoman Empire. The treaty further implied that Russia had protective rights over the Ottoman provinces of Bessarabia, Wallachia, and Moldavia.

The Ottoman situation seemed even worse when, in 1787, Austria and Russia agreed on a plan to partition the Sultan's lands. The Ottomans escaped the consequences of the scheme, however, in large part because their tormentors, along with Prussia, became involved in the partition of Poland during the French revolutionary wars.

These distractions of the Europeans gave respite to the Ottomans until Napoleon's unexpected attack on Egypt in July 1798. Although Egypt had not been under effective Ottoman control for some years, the Porte could not ignore such an overt attack on one of its territories. The attack was also upsetting because the Porte had not allowed the revolution in France to alter the traditionally positive Franco-Ottoman relations. By the time Lord Nelson's British fleet destroyed Napoleon's ships at Aboukir Bay, the French army had already subdued Egypt and attacked Syria. Following Napoleon's return to France in 1799, a joint Ottoman-British effort drove the French forces back to France in 1801. This dramatic, but apparently trivial, episode in the French revolutionary wars, left a lasting impression on the Middle East, because many Ottomans got their first prolonged look at the riches, knowledge, and technology of the west.

Throughout the Napoleonic wars, the Ottoman Empire remained under pressure from all sides. While the Porte reestablished good relations with France after 1801, the Franco-Russian detente at Tilsit in 1807 caused a new strain. Ottoman compliance with the French Continental Blockade of British goods brought it into conflict with Great Britain, which only ended with the Treaty of the Dardanelles in 1809. The Ottomans ceased their embargo on British goods, and Great Britain reiterated its recognition of Ottoman control over traffic through the straits. Russia's resentment of Ottoman concessions to British interference, however, led to a Russian invasion of Wallachia, Moldavia, and Bessarabia. At the May 28, 1812 Treaty of Bucharest, Russia annexed Bessarabia and received Ottoman consent to virtual autonomy for Serbia, which had been in revolt against the Porte.

Following Napoleon's demise, the European powers were preoccupied with domestic matters and a fear of the loss of their own thrones, which led to unprecedented cooperation among them on strictly European matters. There was little inclination to foreign adventure among the European monarchs as they sought to maintain stability against nationalist and liberal movements after the Congress of Vienna in 1815. Circumstances in Europe, therefore, provided the Ottomans with a reprieve from European interference.

MUHAMMAD ALI'S MILITARY ADVENTURES AND THE GREEK REVOLT

Muhammad Ali's wealth and control over the lives of his subjects enabled him to develop a formidable military strength that threatened Ottoman authority. His vibrant economy, which generated surplus capital, provided him with funds other rulers envied. Foreign advisers assured him access to the proficient use of modern military techniques and weapons. The large population, which he governed with virtually no restriction on his authority provided him with large numbers of soldiers;

their absence from the fields neither seriously affected adequate food production nor reduced revenues. His shipyard in Alexandria could rapidly produce worthy naval vessels.

Understandably, this man who had obtained control of Egypt through military conquest soon turned much of his attention to war and further conquest. Although Muhammad Ali's military capacity was a threat to his suzerain in Istanbul, the Sultan found it necessary to call upon him for help. At his request, Egyptian troops under the leadership of the Pasha's son, Ibrahim, suppressed the troublesome Islamic fundamentalist *wahhabi* movement from the Hijaz to the Gulf coast in 1818 and obtained the governorship of the Hijaz, with Islam's holiest shrines, as a reward. Muhammad Ali's Egypt threatened to become the dominant force on the Arabian peninsula from the Red Sea to the Gulf. Another of his sons, Ismail, brought much of the Sudan under Egyptian control by 1826.

Ottoman relations with Europe took a new turn when a major Greek revolution against Ottoman control began in 1821. Western affinity for everything Greek prompted both the French and British governments to favor Greek independence. Russia's concept of its right to protect Orthodox Christianity, and its constant conflicts with the Ottomans, also moved Russia to support the Greek cause. While the Greeks enjoyed some early successes, the conflict proceeded with great bloodshed and brutality on both sides. Since no European ally was available, in 1824 Sultan Mahmoud II enticed Muhammad Ali of Egypt to assist him against the Greeks in return for Egyptian control over the island of Crete and the right of the Egyptian pasha's son, Ibrahim, to become governor of the Greek peninsula.

By the end of 1825, the Ottoman-Egyptian forces had substantially defeated the Greek rebels. However, on July 6, 1827, Great Britain, France, and Russia agreed in the Treaty of London to interfere in the war unless the Ottomans accepted a truce. When the Porte ignored the threat, an Anglo-French fleet proceeded to Navarino and crushed the Ottoman-Egyptian fleet on October 20. Meanwhile, Russia launched a successful land attack and, by August 1828, had the Ottoman capital at its mercy, much to the distress of Britain and France.

Anglo-French interference prevented a greater Russian victory by negotiating a settlement that led to the Treaty of Adrianople (Edirne) on September 14, 1829. The treaty recognized the independence of a small Greek state, as well as autonomy for Serbia, Wallachia, and Moldavia. Russia received Georgia, Nakhivan, and Erivan in the east and a capitulation commercial treaty similar to those the Porte had with the Western states. This war indicated that unless the Ottoman Empire became stronger, it was no longer capable of defending itself against Russia.

In 1831, however, problems with Muhammad Ali of Egypt disproved the assumptions that Russia was the Sultan's greatest threat. The emerging conflict with the Egyptian pasha also dispelled the Ottoman belief that the British and French would interfere to maintain the status quo. The test of these assumptions occurred when Muhammad Ali claimed Syria in compensation for his aid to the Sultan against the Greeks and the subsequent failure of Egypt to obtain Crete because of the Ottoman-Egyptian defeat. When the Porte rejected his claim, Muhammad Ali's son, Ibrahim, attacked Syria from the south at Acre and quickly conquered Damascus, Homs, and Aleppo, after which he turned west and secured Alexandretta by capturing Adana. The Egyptian army marched northwest into the heartland of Turkish Anatolia, where it defeated the main Ottoman army at Konya in December 1832. Ibrahim's relentless thrust took him to Kutahya, which was only two hundred miles south of Istanbul, and possible control of the Ottoman Empire.

Mahmoud's initial pleas to France and Great Britain for assistance fell on deaf ears. Louis Philippe's France was closely allied to Muhammad Ali and Britain was preoccupied with developments in Belgium and its own Great Reform Bill. Ironically, it was Russia, in an effort to protect its beneficial post-Adrianople relationship with its old enemy, that came to the Sultan's aid. A Russian fleet arrived in the Bosphorus in February 1833, and a Russian army soon encamped near the Ottoman capital. Just as had been the case at the end of the Greek revolution, the presence of a Russian army near Istanbul alarmed Ottomans and the French and British, alike. Even so, Russia's on-site strength was inadequate to deter a determined Egyptian attack. The British and French threatened to use force unless the Sultan removed the Russians and negotiated with Ibrahim. Under these pressures Mahmoud II had no choice but to agree to Muhammad Ali's demands for Crete, along with governorships for Ibrahim over Syria, Adana, and the Hijaz. The Treaty of Kutahya on July 8, 1833 granted these terms and Ibrahim withdrew his troops from the Ottoman heartland but remained in Syria.

Russian troops remained another month until the tsar had extracted the Treaty of Hunkiar Iskelesi, which was named after the place of the Russian encampment. With this treaty, Nicholas I established a special relationship with the Ottoman Empire, which would reduce both British and French influence with the Porte. It reaffirmed the earlier Treaty of Adrianople and bound the two signatories to an eight-year mutual defense pact. Understandably, the British, French, and Prussians objected to Russia's increased influence over the Ottomans. They were especially upset with the Porte's agreement to close the straits to all warships in time of war. In their eyes, the treaty gave Russia the right to interfere in, if not control, both the internal and foreign affairs of the Ottoman Empire. Time would determine whether their fears were accurate. Recent developments had proven, however, that the Ottoman Empire's condition only allowed it to react to others, rather than to initiate events.

OTTOMAN REFORM UNDER SELIM III AND MAHMOUD II

From fairly early in the eighteenth century, some Ottomans realized that the empire must adopt some Western military and administrative practices or perish. But for other elements in Ottoman society, such alternatives were anathema because of their Western and Christian origin. The *ulama* and the janissaries were foremost in resisting all innovations of foreign origin. The *ulama*, who were the leading religious authorities under the leadership of the Shaykh-al-Islam, justified their objections to change for religious reasons. The janissaries, as the traditional elite military corps, claimed to resist on behalf of both religion and the customary superiority of Ottoman methods over everything Western. It became apparent that innovations, even if they meant survival, would be impossible without the reduction or elimination of these centers of tradition.

Selim III (1789–1807), who was better educated than most of his predecessors, decided to institute major reforms after the Treaty of Jassy in 1792 relieved him of the war with Austria and Russia. Military reform was foremost in his plans. Like his contemporary, Muhammad Ali in Egypt, Selim used French instructors to create the *Nizam-i Cedid*, or New Order, and introduce Western discipline and equipment into the Ottoman army. French became the language of instruction in his new army and naval colleges for training new officers in the art of Western warfare. Selim III also established permanent embassies in London, Paris, Vienna, and Berlin to enhance the acquisition of knowledge from the West. His attempts at large-scale reforms in taxes, coinage, and prices, however, proved both impossible to implement and unpopular. His innovations, and the fact that he had never produced a son, were more than the traditionalists could abide. On May 29, 1807, therefore, the Shaykh-al-Islam and the janissaries deposed Selim and placed his cousin, Mustafa IV, on the throne.

In July 1808, however, the Grand Vizir (the Sultan's chief minister) and advocates for modernization in the army marched from Edirne to Istanbul and gained control of the government. Since the traditionalists had murdered Selim III, the reformists deposed Mustafa IV and replaced him with his brother, Mahmoud II.

Mahmoud was committed to reform, but he had to contend with the traditionalists, war with Russia, and the Greek revolution before he could attempt anything substantial. The janissaries violently resisted his early reforms and killed Bayrakdar Mustafa, the military commander who had put Mahmoud on the throne. But on May 28, 1826, when he seemed to have crushed the Greek revolt, he announced the creation of a new, model army similar to Selim's *Nazim-i Cedid*. Mahmoud had anticipated a janissary uprising even though some of their top officers and the *ulama* had agreed to accept the new style of army. He was, therefore, ready with 14,000 artillerymen when the janissaries revolted on June 15. Most of the janissaries were either buried beneath the rubble of their barracks or taken into custody. His decrees, which abolished the janissary corps and their close religious allies, the Bektashi dervish brotherhood, removed major obstacles for even greater change.

Most of Mahmoud's reforms were designed to improve Ottoman military capacity. This required both military instruction and a system of education that would prepare Ottoman officers to learn methods of modern warfare both abroad through the importation of foreign specialists. As they engaged in their efforts to modernize the Ottoman army, Selim, Mahmoud, and their successors had no way of anticipating the additional changes which would occur as a result of increased Ottoman exposure to Western influence.

INFLUX OF WESTERN IDEAS AND PRACTICES

Since few Ottoman Muslims learned Western languages, culture, and knowledge, Ottoman Christians and Jews had a virtual monopoly on these arcane subjects within the empire. This was particularly true of Armenians and Greeks, who had traditionally served as translators of documents and correspondence, and, in general, as the interpreters of Western thought and culture. But the Ottoman effort to understand and incorporate Western military science, beginning in the reign of Selim III, introduced more Ottoman Muslims to Western knowledge. Cadets at the new schools and Ottomans who went abroad to study, or to serve in the newly established embassies, used their new linguistic skills to read Western literature, and political and social commentaries, along with their military sciences.

French was the Western language that most of the Ottomans learned in their schools and their foreign travel. Intensified contact with the West corresponded with the occurrence of the French revolution and the decades of revolutionary fervor throughout Europe that followed it. The French revolutionary governments actively proselytized their cause through their citizens and embassy personnel in Istanbul, as well as through personal contacts with Ottomans in France. As a result of this contact with Europe, Christian Ottomans learned to resent the restrictions that the Muslim superstructure of the Ottoman Empire placed upon them. Young Muslims began to question the validity of their society, in which religious authority and privileged classes dominated much as they had in prerevolutionary France. This infusion of the European Enlightenment and revolutionary concepts into the Ottoman Empire was an unexpected by-product of Ottoman modernization. It was not coincidental that most of the reforming officials and lay leaders of reform had studied in the new schools and had travelled in Europe.

The increased level of education in the Ottoman Empire also created a new reading public. The introduction of European printing presses in Istanbul, Cairo, and other cities within the empire provided books, newspapers, and pamphlets in Turkish, Arabic, and French to satisfy the new appetite for reading. The first Turkish newspaper, *Takvim-i Vekayi* (Calendar of Events), was established in 1832. This new medium not only spread Western ideas, it also created a means of communicating other information throughout the empire, which prevented occurrences from being of merely local knowledge and significance.

OTTOMAN PROBLEMS WITH EGYPT

New developments did not make old problems go away. In 1838, Muhammad Ali announced his intention to declare total independence from his Istanbul suzerain, and make his holdings hereditary in his family. Mahmoud had continued to resent the Treaty of Kutayha and had sent an army into Syria to deal with Ibrahim as a first step toward curbing Muhammad Ali and confining him to Egypt. Ibrahim's annihilation of the Ottoman army near Aleppo at the battle of Nezib on June 24, 1839 provided a bitter end to Mahmoud's reign.

His successor, Abdul Mejid I, not only faced the shock of the Aleppo defeat, but also the horror of having his naval commander turn his fleet over to Muhammad Ali, because he rejected the prospect of the Ottoman fleet participating in a joint Ottoman-Russian campaign against the Egyptians. Under these circumstances the Sultan nearly conceded to all of Muhammad Ali's demands, but most of the Great Powers interfered to prevent drastic Ottoman concessions. France alone, because of its close alliance with Muhammad Ali, was inclined to accept Egyptian hereditary rights to Syria and Cilicia.

The possible extension of French influence through the success of Muhammad Ali helped drive Great Britain and Russia together in this particular crisis. Russia sought British assistance in guaranteeing the exclusion of foreign warships from the straits. Nicholas I also hoped to reduce Anglo-French cooperation through improving Russia's relations with Britain. The Anglo-Russian concern did not threaten to cause a major war because, while France endorsed Muhammad Ali's demands, it refused to offer him military support. Great Britain, Russia, Austria, and Prussia, therefore, agreed in July 1840 to force Muhammad Ali to limit his claims of hereditary rights to Egypt alone, or risk losing everything.

After his failure to comply, British, Austrian, and Ottoman troops landed in

Beirut and drove Ibrahim out of Syria. A British naval blockade of Alexandria forced Muhammad Ali to give up claims to everything but Egypt, which would become hereditary in his family but remain under the suzerainty of the sultan. The Great Powers forced Egypt to withdraw from the Arabian peninsula, as well, just at the time that a renewed Egyptian military effort threatened to establish Egypt as the dominant force in the Gulf region. Of perhaps even greater importance to Egypt, the defeat in Syria in 1840 resulted in Muhammad Ali having to accept the capitulation agreements the Western nations had imposed upon the entire Ottoman Empire. As Marx pointed out, Europe's cheap commodities battered down Egypt's ability to compete and it became an open market for foreign products. Egypt suffered not only the destruction of its nascent textile industry but, like the rest of the empire, a decline of its cottage handcraft manufactures. Egypt, in fact, became dependent on the exportation of raw cotton. The wealth generated by cotton compelled an inordinate proportion of Egypt's farming to embrace the cultivation of the vital fiber at the expense of food production. This adversely affected the Egyptian diet and determined that Egypt's solvency depended upon the international demand for cotton and the price it could command.

After curtailing the expansion of Muhammad Ali, the Great Powers concluded the Straits Convention of July 13, 1841, in which they endorsed the earlier Russo-Turkish bilateral agreement to exclude all foreign warships from the straits.This interference of the Great Powers on behalf of the Porte was motivated by their own self-interests, rather than out of specific concern for the Ottoman Empire. Their joint efforts against Muhammad Ali had the effect, however, of eliminating Russia's special relationship with the Porte, which dated back to the treaty of Hunkiar Iskelesi in 1833.

BRITISH INFLUENCE

Russia was, in fact, too close, too powerful and too covetous of Ottoman assets for the Porte to feel comfortable in relying mainly on its old, traditional enemy for protection. Great Britain was, by contrast, far away and powerful, but had vital interests in preventing Russian intrusion into the Balkans, the straits, and beyond. Despite their differences, Russia also preferred working with the British, rather than with the French, on Ottoman affairs. Also, the close French affiliation with Muhammad Ali's domestic policies and foreign adventures had reduced its traditional influence with the Porte.

All of these factors were important in a new orientation of Ottoman affairs by the late 1830s. Great Britain, in fact, began to emerge as the dominant foreign influence over Ottoman affairs, largely through the close relationship between its ambassador, Lord Stratford de Redcliffe, and Mustafa Reshid, who dominated the policies at the Porte from 1837 until his death in 1858. Indicative of the new relationship, Mustafa Reshid granted the British greater trade concessions at the treaty of Balta Liman in 1838 in an early attempt to obtain British aid against Muhammad Ali.

British Prime Minister Palmerston's close cooperation with the unreformed Ottoman and Russian governments, however, caused some dissatisfaction at home. This had forced him to seek the wider scope of the Straits Convention, rather than the bilateral agreement that the Russians desired. Concern for domestic sensitivity had also moved him to urge European-style reforms in the Ottoman Empire.

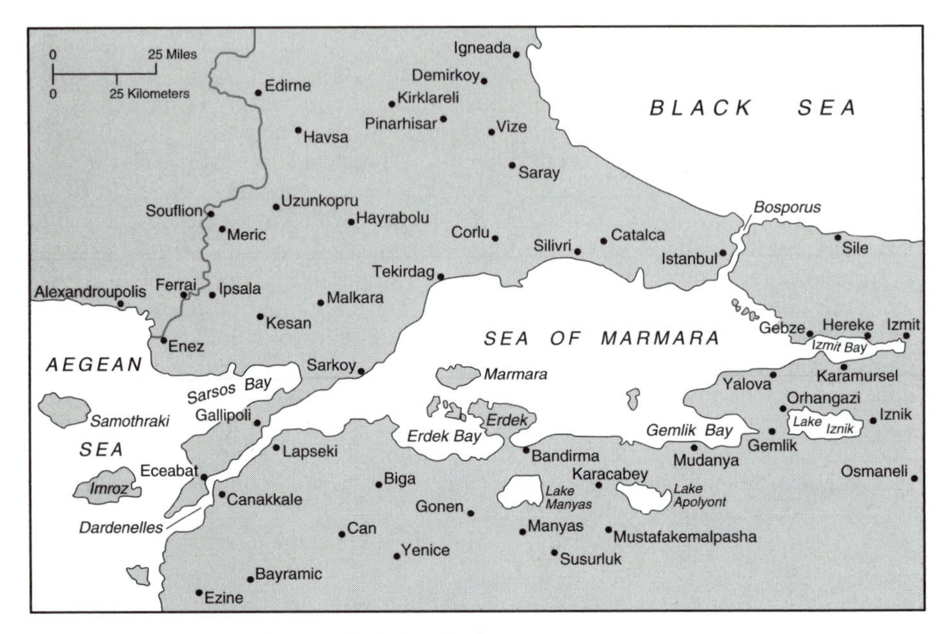

Sea of Marmara and the Turkish Straits

Mustafa Reshid, who had become enamored with European society, was a willing instrument for Palmerston's proposals for reform. The timing of the declaration of the *Hatt-i-Sharif* of Gulhaneh on November 3, 1839, which signalled the beginning of the Tanzimat reform, was the result of British pressure and was also an indication of Britain's new influence over the Ottoman Empire. (See below.)

Anglo-Russian-Ottoman cooperation was difficult to maintain once the circumstances that spawned it subsided. It began to disintegrate in 1848 when revolutionaries in Wallachia seized control and declared their union with Moldavia in the independent state of Rumania. The Rumanians' close contact with Western Europe had instilled in them the revolutionary fervor that all the Great Powers wanted to suppress. Rumanian independence threatened the Russian, Austrian, and Ottoman Empires alike because of its possible inspiration to their many minorities. The same Russian army, therefore, that crushed the Hungarian revolution of 1849 also swept through Rumania. The Great Powers and the Porte approved Russia's action, but they resisted Nicholas I's insistence that the Ottomans should extradite Rumanian, Polish, and Hungarian rebels (including the likes of Lajos Kossuth), who had fled to the Ottoman Empire for safety. Only the deployment of British and French fleets to Besika Bay prevented a Russian invasion of the Ottoman Empire to punish the rebels.

RUSSIAN AND BRITISH INFLUENCE IN PERSIA

Persia, which had a long history of conflict with neighboring Russia, attracted Great Britain as an ally in that struggle early in the nineteenth century. The British became heavily involved in Persian affairs primarily out of concern for the possible interference of Russia in Britain's predominance in India. The British concluded that a strong Persia could deter Russia's advance southward in its constant quest for access to the world's maritime shipping lanes. Napoleon's attempts to involve Persia against both Russia and Britain also helped shape the new relationship between Britain and Persia. In addition, the British needed to work closely with Persia in all matters related to Afghanistan, since it was also a major bulwark against Russia's drive to the south. The convergence of Russian and British interference into Persian affairs relegated the long-standing conflict between Persia and the Ottoman Empire to a minor concern.

Anglo-Russian preoccupation with Napoleon in 1813–1814 worked to Persia's benefit as its war with Russia, which had begun in 1804, ground to a halt. Britain interceded in Persia's behalf to get the best border arrangement possible, even though Persia had to agree to Russia's claim to most of the Caucasus and had to pledge to construct no naval presence on the Caspian Sea. Britain extracted some concessions from Persia but offered a substantial subsidy and assistance in training the Persian army in return. Perhaps just as important to Shah Fath Ali, the British and Russians agreed to support the continuation of the Qajar dynasty in Persia. Both of the Great Powers had a vested interest at that time in maintaining stability in Persia under a monarchy with which they had established a working relationship. A new war broke out between Persia and Russia in 1825 that solidified Russian supremacy in the Caucasus and resulted in Russia making a significant intrusion into Persian affairs. It ended with the Treaty of Turkumanchai in 1828, through which Russia obtained a major indemnity for returning Tabriz. It also resulted in a capitulary agreement, which provided Russia a favorable trade relationship and extralegal authority over Russians who encountered legal problems with Persia.

The Russians and British kept their promise to assure the Qajar succession first with the ascension of Muhammad (1834–1848) and then with Nasir al-Din (1848–1896). Persia had serious differences with both that resulted in armed conflict. The Russo-Persian war, which occurred along their border from 1849 to 1854, proved indecisive. Persia's efforts to annex the Herat region in western Afghanistan in 1837 and again in 1856 required British military responses. The British prevailed in both conflicts after holding considerable Persian territory in the Gulf region until the Persian government ceased its attempts to gain dominion over territory it believed belonged to Persia. Nasir al-Din recognized the independence of Afghanistan in 1857 at the Treaty of Paris. The British also obtained special economic concessions and a capitulation agreement similar to the one Russia had enjoyed since 1828. Persia also continued to have border conflicts with the Ottomans until 1847, which resulted in the establishment of the basic modern border between Iran and Iraq.

Persia's internal situation should have ruled out any foreign adventures. Serious efforts to modernize Persia met steady opposition from the vested interests of the clergy, the landed elite, and the tribal leaders. The merchants often had mixed feelings, since modernization generally increased trade and merchant profits. Many merchants shared with the other elements a fear of the concomitant growth of power that modernization gave to the central government. They also feared and resented the fact that modernization brought in an influx of foreign entrepreneurs, who invariably surpassed their Persian counterparts in capital assets and modern business practices. The clergy were in the forefront of opposition because they could cite Islamic laws and traditions that modernization violated. The dismissal and assassination of former Prime Minister Mirza Taqi, Nasir al-Din's particularly gifted reformer, demonstrated the fate that others of like mind could expect. Consequently, Persia remained far less centrally administered and educated than the Ottoman Empire, which faced many of the same challenges. The shahs' influence usually did not reach much beyond Tehran, while resentment simmered throughout the country at all attempts, and suspected attempts, they made to modernize and extend their authority.

The inability to collect revenue for modernization foiled royal attempts to construct a better infrastructure, improve education, or build a better army. All of these, of course, were necessities for constructing a modern nation. This helps explain why Persia turned to granting concessions to foreigners and increasingly turned to them for expert advice.

OTTOMAN REFORM

Ottoman attempts to modernize for self-preservation in the early nineteenth century accelerated dramatically from the end of the fourth decade under pressure from its European protectors. In part, the Europeans imposed their will upon the Ottomans in an effort to establish a more Western-like society, which they could justify protecting from Russian expansion. The increasingly important public opinion in the West understood the wisdom of confining the Russian bear behind the Turkish straits. Also, a posture of protection for Christians within the Islamic realm had widespread appeal. The supposed altruistic Western interference in Ottoman affairs gained further momentum by allowing European economic and cultural expansion.

In time, both the Sultans and the Porte not only found the adoption of European practices less onerous but, in fact, very helpful. For, while the changes required major concessions to Ottoman minorities, they provided both an excuse and a method for extending Istanbul's authority into all phases of life in every area of the empire. The Ottoman government essentially wagered that the benefits of modernization outweighed the risks of extensive foreign influence.

Familiarity with Western ideas and institutions increased during the reigns of Selim III and Mahmoud II, mostly as a by-product of military modernization. (See above.) A significant shift in the nature of, and motivation for, the adoption of Western practices began to occur toward the end of Mahmoud's reign after Mustafa Reshid entered his ministry in 1837. Reshid Pasha's commitment to transforming Ottoman government and society made him the father of Ottoman reform. His frequent role as either Foreign Minister or Grand Vizir from 1837 to 1858 afforded him the opportunity to make many changes, while he trained and inspired many others to follow his lead. Unlike most of the other reform leaders, he arrived at his convictions for reform from a traditional educational background, rather than from the new French language schools. His inspiration seems to have resulted from an acquaintance with the Muhammad Ali's Egypt early in his diplomatic career. He only learned French and English while serving as ambassador to France and England from 1834 to 1837, when he became convinced that many Western practices were necessary in Ottoman government and society.

THE TANZIMAT

Reshid Pasha led a receptive Mahmoud II to make changes in Ottoman internal policies from the time he became the Sultan's foreign minister in 1837. It was, therefore, less than traumatic for Reshid to draft the *Hatt-i-Sharif* of Gulhaneh, which Mahmoud's successor, Abdul Mejid I, decreed on November 3, 1839. British demands for such changes in return for help against Muhammad Ali no doubt influenced the timing of the announcement.

The *Hatt-i-Sharif* (Illustrious Rescript) was the first major step in the entire *Tanzimat* (Reorganization) movement which lasted until 1876. Promulgation of the *Hatt-i-Shari*f and subsequent reforms of the Tanzimat served as an open admission that customary practice was unjust. The Tanzimat, however, raised internal and external expectations that the Ottoman Empire would soon mirror European values and policies.

The expectations for the entire Tanzimat era were well founded on the overall theme of the *Hatt-i-Sharif,* which recognized the obligation of the Ottoman state to serve all of its subjects. It promised equal treatment of all subjects, regardless of their religion, on matters of life, honor, and property. It provided for the creation of an equitable, centralized tax system, and the elimination of the cumbersome and decentralized system of tax farming. Capital punishment could only occur after a fair and open trial. Conscriptions for the army would be equitably assessed and special attention would be given to agricultural labor needs. It created a Council of Judicial Ordinances to legislate all laws and submit them to the Council of Ministers and the Sultan for approval.

The Council of Judicial Ordinances moved into its new building at the Porte in 1840 and became the new center for government. The Sultan approved the vast majority of its legislation, which increased dramatically over the next few years, as suggestions for new laws and regulations poured from the provincial and local councils. It also served as the highest court of the realm, with authority to try high officials and hear appeals from lower courts. The combined legislative and judicial duties of the council, however, proved to be a larger burden than the ten-man institution could fulfill.

The huge empire was difficult to alter in face of entrenched tradition, religious and ethnic complexity, and a paucity of professional administrative methods and personnel. The immediate lack of change following the Illustrious Rescript disappointed reformers. But in 1845 Abdul Mejid initiated a new phase of the Tanzimat when he acknowledged the failure of reform, which he attributed to his officials' misconception of the Rescript and the ignorance of the general population. He proposed an emphasis on education as the necessary remedy. The University of Istanbul appeared on paper, but many years passed before it opened on a regular basis. He was much more successful in opening additional secular secondary schools that were few in number but prepared a nucleus of students for higher education. He created a Ministry of Education in 1847 to supervise the growth of education. When an assembly of two representatives from each province seemed hesitant to speak openly with him, he sent out commissioners to accumulate information on problems in the realm.

His, and his successors', surprisingly assiduous attention to reform becomes more comprehensible when one realizes that they came to regard "reform" as a method of extending central authority throughout the empire and as a way of generating additional revenues for their constantly empty coffers. Their activities were not unlike those of seventeenth- and eighteenth-century European monarchs who had employed similar tactics to create centralized absolutist monarchies.

The Tanzimat, therefore, incensed liberals and conservatives alike, but for different reasons. Centralization under the guise of reform brought criticism from reformers, while certain elements resisted any change by whatever name. The oft-maligned ineffectiveness of the Tanzimat was effective enough, however, to lead logically to the later "despotism" of Abdul Hamid II.

Abdul Mejid I's investigatory commissions led him to realize the need for better commercial law in his lands. He, therefore, resurrected an earlier controversial proposal of Mustafa Reshid and promulgated a new commercial code in 1850. It was significant because it was the first secular law code of the empire. The *ulama* correctly perceived it as a harbinger of further attacks on the inviolability of the *Sharia*.

By 1854 it became obvious that the work load of the Council of Judicial Ordinances exceeded its capacity. A new High Council of the Tanzimat assumed the legislative responsibilities while the Council of Judicial Ordinances retained its judiciary functions. The Tanzimat Council was more powerful than its parent council as only the Sultan surpassed its authority. Unlike its predecessor, it had the right to initiate legislation, allowing it to enact laws that could originate from any source in the empire. All laws, however, required its approval. An abundance of information and suggested laws and regulations poured into the Tanzimat Council from the new administrative system, which reached down to the *mukhtars* (local Ottoman officials) at the village level. The new council, however, soon became as overworked as the old one had been.

THE CRIMEAN WAR

French participation in thwarting Nicholas I's efforts to subdue all Eastern European rebels exacerbated the problem of protection of Christians within the Ottoman Empire, which had been brewing for a decade. Napoleon III, who liked to pose as the champion of Catholicism, began to reassert the French right to protect Ottoman Christians, which it had enjoyed since the sixteenth century. But Russia's right to intervene in behalf of Orthodox Christianity had been in the ascendant in the Ottoman Empire since the Treaty of Kuchuk Kainarji in 1774. Since that time, Russian and Greek Orthodox priests had gained control over most of the Holy Land's shrines, and Orthodox pilgrims substantially outnumbered Latin pilgrims to the shrines.

In 1843, the tsar ordered the Orthodox Patriarch of Jerusalem to reside in the City of Peace, rather than in the more comfortable circumstances of Istanbul. The resulting increase of Orthodox presence throughout the Holy Land prompted the pope in 1847 to move the Latin Archbishop of Jerusalem and his staff from Istanbul to Jerusalem for the first time in the long history of that office. These developments indicated the new importance of the Holy Land to the Roman and Orthodox branches of Christianity and to their respective political protectors. Interestingly, these developments also made Muslims uncomfortable about the fate of Jerusalem,which is their third most holy city, for the first time in centuries. The issue of the disposition of Jerusalem, therefore, became much more prominent among Muslims as a result of the Christian conflicts over the city cherished by Muslims, Christians, and Jews. The French government and Latin church authorities resisted Orthodox claims to the right to rebuild the dome of the Church of the Holy Sepulchre in 1842, because the Russian style would symbolize Orthodox supremacy. The brawl between Orthodox and Latin monks at the Church of the Nativity in Bethlehem at Christmas in 1847 could not have even been pleasant even for the Muslims.

Matters worsened in 1852 when Napoleon III, whom Nicholas regarded as a usurper, gained new concessions for the Latin church. While the concessions fulfilled Napoleon's objectives, they were an affront to Nicholas, who was determined to demonstrate his influence over Christianity in the Ottoman Empire. By way of preparation for a bold move, the tsar discussed with Great Britain the possibility of partitioning the Ottoman Empire. The suggested partition allowed for Britain to receive Egypt and Crete, while Russia would become the protector of new states in Bulgaria, Serbia, and Rumania. He apparently interpreted the noncommittal British response as consent to force the issue of the Orthodox claims with the Porte.

As a result of his military weakness, the Sultan was ready to give in to Russian demands for more concessions in the Holy Land and recognize the Russian protectorate over Ottoman Christians. In return, the tsar offered to protect the Ottoman Empire against further French aggression and demands. Under direct instructions from London, Lord Stratford de Redcliffe, the British ambassador, convinced Abdul Mejid to refuse the Russian offer. Nicholas responded with an ultimatum at the end of May 1853, in which he threatened to invade the Danubian principalities unless the Sultan met his demands.

Because of their customary resistance to Russian expansion into the Balkans, the British and French dispatched their fleets to Besika Bay to protect the Sultan. Russia refused to alter its course and invaded the Danubian principalities on July 2, 1853. Representatives of the Great Powers met in Vienna to find a peaceful solution and issued the Vienna Note on July 28, which provided for the Sultan to acknowledge the rights of Ottoman Christians and also confirmed earlier Russo-Ottoman treaties. Nicholas accepted the Note's terms, but the Porte did not, because Nicholas had received the proposal before the Ottoman government had seen it. The Porte's rejection was understandable since all the provisions of the Christian-drafted Note called for Ottoman concessions. The Porte also insisted that the authority of the Sultan, rather than pressure from Russia, guaranteed the status of Christians in the Ottoman Empire. To induce the Porte to accept a compromise acceptable to Russia, the British pulled their fleet back from its protective posture for the Sultan in the Dardanelles. However, the Porte refused to make concessions because it remained confident of Anglo-French support and enjoyed enthusiastic public support for a strong stand.

Russia's predictable refusal to the Porte's October ultimatum to withdraw its troops led to Ottoman offensives into the Danubian principalities in the west and across their border with Russia in the east. Simultaneously, an Ottoman fleet entered the Black Sea to protect against a Russian naval attack through the Bosphorus. A Russian fleet, however, caught the Ottoman ships at anchor off the Ottoman coast at Sinope and destroyed the Ottoman fleet on November 30. The

British threatened to move their fleet to the Black Sea unless Russia withdrew. Russia's answer was to break off relations with Great Britain and France, who, in turn, declared war on Russia on March 28, 1854.

Austrian and Prussian concern with the possibility of Russian aggrandizement during the conflict led them to a mutual defense treaty on April 20, in which they further agreed to prevent Russian annexation of the Danubian principalities. On June 14, Austria also concluded an agreement with the Porte, whereby an Austrian army would occupy the principalities and prevent uprisings in Bosnia, Albania, and Montenegro during the war. Russia withdrew from the principalities on August 8 on the condition that Austria also keep Ottoman, British, and French troops out of the principalities.

Austria's occupation of the principalities with the mutual consent of the Russians and the Ottomans diverted Anglo-French efforts to the Crimean peninsula. On September 14, 1854 they laid siege to the Russian port city of Sevastopol, but it did not fall until nearly a year later, on September 9. The Allies won battles at the Alma River and Balaclava during the siege of Sevastopol, but the Russians defeated the Ottomans at Kars in the east and were ready to push westward through Anatolia by the end of November 1855. During the winter lull, Austria threatened to enter the war against Russia unless St. Petersburg negotiated a peace on the principal of the Vienna Note. Nicholas I's death on March 2, 1855 along with an Ottoman declaration of new guarantees for its Christian subjects, offered opportunities to end the war just when it seemed that it might, in fact, broaden. When the Sultan issued the *Hatt-i-Hamayun* on February 18, 1856, which guaranteed equality for his Christian subjects, both Russia and its enemies could claim the reasons for the war no longer existed. On February 25, the new tsar, Alexander II, faced too many domestic problems to continue the drain of an unpopular war; he agreed to cease hostilities and attend a peace conference in Paris.

The Peace of Paris, which ended the Crimean War, was signed on March 29, 1856. It upheld the Straits Convention of 1841 and opened the entire length of the Danube River to commercial navigation for all nations. Russia's ceding of southern Bessarabia to Moldavia eliminated Russian access to the Danube, which was placed under the authority of an international commission to guarantee free navigation. The Russians and the Ottomans closed all naval bases on the Black Sea and agreed to retain only light coast guard vessels on those waters. All the Great Powers recognized and guaranteed the autonomy of Wallachia, Moldavia, and Serbia. The Ottoman Empire joined the Concert of Europe and on April 15, 1856 signed a treaty with the European Powers that guaranteed its independence and territorial integrity. Russia withdrew its claim to protection over Ottoman Christians.

Superficially, the Crimean War seemed to have little adverse effect on the Ottoman Empire. Its incorporation into the Concert of Europe and the Great Power guarantee of its independence and integrity appeared to make it more secure than it had been for nearly two centuries.

The war, in fact, had a great impact on the Ottoman Empire and drastically altered its relationship with the Western nations. The most obvious effect of the war was that it marked the beginning of Ottoman financial indebtedness to the West. The first loan to finance the war in 1854 initiated a practice that bankrupted the Ottoman treasury over the next twenty years. The war also exposed many Ottomans to the superiority of Western technology and accelerated their acquisition of

European ideas. Increased numbers of young Ottomans soon sought education and travel in the West. The unprecedented newspaper coverage of the Crimean War whetted Western interest in Eastern affairs. In short, Western Europe and the Ottoman Empire began to merge into a single financial and intellectual community that the West dominated.

2

Change without Benefit

HISTORICAL TIMELINE

1855 ⇛ Fall of Sevastopol on September 9.

1856 ⇛ *Hatt-i-Hamayun* (Imperial Rescript) on February 18 extended rights of Ottoman subjects.
⇛ Alexander II, tsar of Russia, agreed to peace conference in Paris on February 25.
⇛ Peace of Paris signed on March 29 to end the Crimean War.
⇛ Ottoman Empire signed treaty with other powers on April 15 to guarantee the independence and integrity of the empire.
⇛ Ferdinand de Lesseps obtained permission for Suez Canal Company to construct a canal.

1857 ⇛ Persian conflict with Britain over Herat region of Afghanistan ended in the Treaty of Paris on May 2, by which Persia recognized Afghanistan's independence.

1858 ⇛ Cadastral department established in the Ottoman Empire.

1859 ⇛ Establishment of the Ottoman Civil Service School.
⇛ Maronite-Druze war began in Lebanon.

1860 ⇛ Faris al-Shidyak published the first important newspaper in the Arabic language. He was an important link between Arab and European cultures.
⇛ Large-scale massacre of Christians in Damascus on July 9.
⇛ Ottoman government intervened in Lebanese and Syrian hostilities on July 17.

- ⇛ France, Britain, Austria and Prussia sent ships to Beirut in August; French landed 7,000 troops.

1861
- ⇛ *Reglement Organique* (Organic Statute) for Mount Lebanon on June 9 established the *Mutesarrifate,* which put it under the protection of the Great Powers and lasted until 1914.
- ⇛ Abdul Aziz became Sultan.
- ⇛ Tanzimat Council and Council of Judicial Ordinances merged to become the Supreme Council of Judicial Ordinances.
- ⇛ Shinasi began publication of the *Description of Ideas.*
- ⇛ *The Army Newspaper* began as a complement to the *Calendar of Events,* which was first published in 1831.

1862
- ⇛ Acquisition of telegraph system through Persia to India, linking Persia to the outside world.

1864
- ⇛ *Description of Ideas* turned over to Namik Kemal.

1865
- ⇛ Emergence of the Young Ottomans.

1866
- ⇛ Founding of Syrian Protestant College, which later became the American University of Beirut.
- ⇛ Greek uprising in Crete.

1867
- ⇛ Ottoman Empire's debt required 34 percent of the state's revenue.
- ⇛ Ziya Pasha and Namik Kemal failed in the Ottoman Empire and fled to Europe.
- ⇛ Pasha Ismail of Egypt received the enhanced title of Khedive and Egypt received increased independence.

1869
- ⇛ Midhat Pasha became Ottoman governor of Iraq.
- ⇛ Compulsory education was implemented for all Ottoman males.
- ⇛ The Suez Canal opened on November 17.

1871–1879
- ⇛ Jamal al-Din al-Afghani was in Egypt to help shape pan-Islamic views that inspired Egyptian and Arab nationalists.

1871
- ⇛ Russia reestablished naval presence in the Black Sea.

1872
- ⇛ Shah Nasir al-Din attempted to sell concession to Baron de Reuter, a British subject, for industrial and economic development of Persia. Russia objection caused withdrawal of offer.

1873
- ⇛ Publication of Kemal's play *Vatan or Silistria* (*Fatherland or Silistria*).

1875–1910s
- ⇛ Muhammad Abduh at his height in his pan-Islamic and Egyptian nationalist activities.

1875
- ⇛ Founding of University of St. Joseph in Beirut.
- ⇛ Creation of the secret society in Beirut that expressed unrest among some Arabs with Ottoman domination.
- ⇛ Ottoman Empire's debt required 44 percent of state revenue.
- ⇛ Christian insurgents rebelled in Herzegovina on July 24.
- ⇛ Khedive Ismail sold his 44 percent interest in the canal to British government.

- ⇛ Porte suspended payment on half of its debt in October.
- ⇛ The Great Powers demanded additional reforms from the Ottoman Empire in the Andrassy Note of December 30.

1876

- ⇛ Khedive Ismail of Egypt declared an inability to pay his debts.
- ⇛ International community established the Egyptian Public Debt Fund to manage Egyptian financial affairs in May.
- ⇛ Balkan Revolt spread to Bulgaria on May 2.
- ⇛ French and Prussian consuls killed by Muslims in Salonica on May 6.
- ⇛ Midhat Pasha returned to the Ottoman government on May 10.
- ⇛ Berlin Memorandum issued by *Dreikaiserbund* (Three Emperor's League) on May 13 called for more Ottoman reforms on behalf of Balkan Christians.
- ⇛ Abdul Aziz, former Ottoman Sultan, died by apparent suicide on June 6.
- ⇛ Russian and Austrian foreign ministers met at Reichstadt on June 8 to agree upon the partitioning of the Ottoman Empire.
- ⇛ Ottoman Ministers of War and Foreign Relations were murdered on June 15.
- ⇛ Porte temporarily suspended payment on all debt in July.
- ⇛ Ottoman Sultan Abdul Hamid II succeeded his brother Murat V, who was deposed on August 31.
- ⇛ Midhat's draft of a constitution for the Ottoman Empire was published in newspapers on October 10.
- ⇛ Porte withdrew the Ottoman army from Serbia on November 3 to attempt to appease Christian rebels and the Great Powers.
- ⇛ Porte agreed on November 4 to a Great Powers conference to discuss the Balkans.
- ⇛ Istanbul Conference opened on December 12 to resolve the Balkan crisis.
- ⇛ The Ottoman Empire promulgated its first constitution on December 23.

1877

- ⇛ Russia and Austria reach an agreement at Budapest on January 15, which allowed Austria to occupy Bosnia and Herzegovina in return for Austia's neutrality in Russia's impending war with the Ottoman Empire.
- ⇛ Istanbul Conference ended on January 20 without finding a resolution of the differences between Russia and the Ottoman Empire.
- ⇛ Ottoman Empire obtained new loans from British and French bankers to finance its war with Russia.
- ⇛ Midhat Pasha was dismissed from the Ottoman government and exiled on February 5.
- ⇛ Opening of first Ottoman parliament March 19.
- ⇛ Russia declared war on the Ottoman Empire on April 24.
- ⇛ Armenians openly aided the Russian invasion of the Ottoman Empire.
- ⇛ Russian troops threatened Istanbul from both east and west by November.

1878 ⇛ Armistice agreed to on January 30 to end the Balkan war.
⇛ Abdul Hamid II dismissed parliament and withdrew the constitution on February 14.
⇛ Treaty of San Stefano of March 3 ended the Russo-Turkish war.
⇛ British formal occupation of Cyprus in June.
⇛ Congress of Berlin began June 13 to prevent Russia's victory against the Ottoman Empire from resulting in a larger war.
⇛ Said Pasha began his long tenure as Grand Vizir of the Ottoman Empire.
⇛ *Translator of Events* began publication in Istanbul.
⇛ Public Debt Fund of Egypt restricted Khedive Ismail's personal spending.

1879 ⇛ Great Powers and Ottoman government reached an interim agreement on Ottoman debt.
⇛ Sultan Abdul Hamid II deposed Khedive Ismail of Egypt on June 26 in response to European pressure. Tewfik became Khedive.

1880 ⇛ Traditional date for the beginning of Arab nationalism.

1881 ⇛ Alexander III became tsar of Russia March 13 and instituted pogroms against Jews.
⇛ French occupation of Tunisia May 12.
⇛ Egyptian government under influence of Colonel Arabi by September and set Egypt on a course of conflict with Great Britain and France.
⇛ Ottoman Public Debt Administration (O.P.D.A.) was formed on November 23 to administer Ottoman debts and revenues.

A web of European influence covered the Middle East by the second half of the nineteenth century, just as the Europeans entered the newest phase of their age-old conflicts. New communication and transportation methods, new needs, and new desires of the Europeans provided a global scope to almost every policy they perceived and/or implemented. No political or cultural unit in the Middle East larger than the family, however, was prepared to resist an accelerated European intrusion into the region. The Ottoman and Persian empires and Egypt had major internal problems that required their full attention and resources. The loudest voices in the Middle East advocated the adoption of European methods to meet both internal and external challenges. Not all, of course, agreed, albeit sometimes for different and conflicting reasons. There was little dispute that European capital was necessary for military modernization, infrastructure construction, and health and educational improvement. An active new press, which often had to operate clandestinely, spread the new ideas and proposals to the widest possible audiences.

All areas of the Middle East understandably seemed compelled to make changes as rapidly as possible to meet modern demands. Unfortunately, the region's deficiencies in capital, resources, and education were too dire for the time frame in which they had to respond. By contrast, Europe's apparent rapid transformation had evolved on a foundation of considerable duration. European developments were, in short, a natural manifestation of its cultural and institutional maturation. External and internal attempts to impose European ways upon the Middle

East, therefore, produced mixed results, which only additional time could assimilate into Middle Eastern conceptionalization and performance. It is little wonder that Middle Eastern attempts to Westernize led to financial chaos, mismanagement, and bankruptcy. Efforts to impose constitutionalism into decentralized political entities only accentuated ethnic and regional distinctions, rather than providing a means for cooperation. As if these issues were not enough, the region had to deal with multifaceted nationalism in almost every form, not the least of which was Europe's imperialistic expansion.

Although European influence descended upon the Middle East in so many other ways, the physical penetration of the Suez Canal seems symbolic of the entire phenomenon. That facility, which apparently would serve the needs of all and facilitate trade, increased in value every year to become the direct or indirect reason for a significant amount of European interest in the region. Middle Easterners soon suspected that every Western activity entailed ulterior motives that were harmful to the region and its people. Consequently, few in the region, who cooperated with the West, could escape the accusation of treason, regardless of their own motives.

HATT-I-HAMAYUN

The new Ottoman approach to government yielded noticeable results in improved services and greater revenues, but indebtedness from the Crimean War terminated reforms. Pressure from the Great Powers at the end of the Crimean War, however, extracted a more specific promise from Abdul Mejid I to improve the rights of his non-Muslim subjects. His *Hatt-i-Hamayun* (Imperial Rescript) of February 18, 1856 reiterated the main features of the earlier rescript and addressed the *dhimmi* concerns in greater detail. For instance, there was to be no distinction in the rights of any imperial subjects, including the right to enter any school or branch of government. Non-Muslims were allowed to enter the army and no longer had to pay a special tax in lieu of such service. Leaders of religious communities were to have more freedom through the appointment to their positions for life. It abolished all restraints upon free religious practice and promised laws to prevent so much as a derogatory remark against anyone's religious preference. It is doubtful that any society had ever committed to such a standard of civil rights protection for its people, albeit as the result of outside coercion.

NEW TANZIMAT GENERATION

By the end of the Crimean war Mustafa Reshid's influence was on the decline and the new stage of the Tanzimat was under the influence of his protégés, Ali Pasha and Fuad Pasha, who had worked their ways up through the bureaucracy and the diplomatic corps. Ali, Fuad, Midhat Pasha, Ahmad Sevdet Pasha, and other capable administrators were determined to modernize their homeland to preserve it against foreign attack and internal disintegration. They continued the trend of wresting power from the palace in favor of the Porte. Their efforts began to give integrity to earlier changes and make major new adjustments.

For the Tanzimat to work, the central government had to impose unprecedented control over the localities in order to override the practices of local arbitrary rulers. In theory, rule from Istanbul would implement the many reforms as well as generate a more equitably collected revenue. Among the greatest obstacles was a lack of trained personnel, which the foundation of the Civil Service School (1859) began to remedy.

Tanzimat successes, in fact, depended on the work of individuals like Midhat Pasha, who devised methods that worked for their administrative regions. His governorships over Bulgaria and Mesopotamia demonstrated the positive effects a capable administrator could achieve in implementing the Tanzimat. Midhat's policies in Bulgaria became the model for the 1864 Provincial Reform Law, which governed provincial policies for the duration of the empire. The new law placed more authority in the hands of provincial governors to eliminate the delays of referring decisions to Istanbul. It provided for provincial assemblies with representatives from each locality composed of equal numbers of Muslims and non-Muslims.

NEW SECULAR INSTITUTIONS

The entire approach required more educated people than the existing school system provided. The traditional religious schools were inadequate for the new kinds of knowledge necessary for modernization and Mahmoud II's secular schools were too few in number. The army took the initiative and built secular secondary schools throughout the empire to supplement the traditional *madresseh* (largely religious) education. Education became compulsory for boys throughout the empire in 1869, although many localities neither enforced the law nor built the schools. Resistance to the new secular schools came from both Christians and Muslims, who feared foreign ideas and languages as well as the diminution of their respective values. Like other Tanzimat reforms, the secular schools altered people's lives. Almost imperceptibly, the Ottoman Empire also changed; in areas where, only a short time before, no education had been available, students were able to begin careers of distinction in the new schools.

New and fairer methods of assessing taxes and conscripting for the army were impossible without reasonably accurate information about the empire's assets. The establishment of a cadastral department in 1858 was a vital step toward providing this information. The Porte ordered regional cadastral surveys and implemented the Tanzimat as quickly as the process permitted. This innovation, however, was no more uniformly successful than any of the others, as in some places the system simply did not work. The close-to-universal resistance to an official registration of property holdings assured only hesitant compliance under duress.

The Porte vacillated between the new approach and the old tax-farming system. Revenues grew, but never at an adequate rate for rising needs and expectations. The exemption of foreigners and Ottomans with *barats* denied the Porte a major source of potential income. There was, however, no reduction in income from the *dhimmis* after the Imperial Rescript of 1856 exempted them from the head tax. Non-Muslims generally did not want to serve in the army, and chose, instead, to exercise the right, which Muslims had traditionally enjoyed, of paying a special tax.

The Porte's inability to fashion a rational system led to additional experimentation rather than resignation. The expansion of participation in government down to the local level created an unprecedented volume of information in Istanbul, which overwhelmed the Tanzimat Council and the Council of Judicial Ordinances.

The Porte merged the two into the Supreme Council of Judicial Ordinances in 1861 and subdivided their functions into: a) legislation, b) judicial cases, and c) administration and finance. When this approach also proved unsatisfactory, the councils were reorganized into two institutions, not unlike the original arrangement after the creation of the Tanzimat Council. The incorporation of many more members of the different *millets*, at the insistence of Europeans, however, made the new organization more representative of the empire. The Council of State performed legislative and regulatory functions, while the Council of Judicial Regulations was the center of the new secular courts.

THE YOUNG OTTOMANS

Criticism and resentment of the Tanzimat from traditionalists was predictable, but the same forces that inspired Tanzimat leaders also produced critics of a liberal hue, who disliked supposed reform and wished to develop what they regarded as a more efficient despotism. The leading critics, who called themselves the Young Ottomans, had in common an education in the new secular schools and service in the Tanzimat bureaucracy. All of them also came to regard Ali and Fuad as their bitter enemies, although some had risen to prominence under their patronage during their early careers.

Like Ali and Fuad, the Young Ottomans had studied Western ideas and institutions and were equipped to employ their knowledge to advocate both a different approach and different goals for Ottoman reform. Their assumption of the name "Young Ottomans" reflects much of their creed because they were Ottoman nationalists whose religious attitudes and other values were more traditional than the Tanzimat leaders. They desired to change the empire, but wanted to retain its basic character by avoiding wholesale adoption of Western ways. Foreign interference and privileges were, therefore, major targets of their criticism, which they expressed in their newspapers, pamphlets, plays, and other publications.

The Young Ottomans maintained that the Porte, armed with the Tanzimat laws and methods, was as authoritarian as the sultans had ever been. They assiduously advocated constitutionalism as the only remedy to eliminate arbitrary government and save the empire. Such an approach, they suggested, would bring the various ethnic and religious groups into the governing process, rather than pacify them with privileges, which engendered separatism. For this reason, they promoted the adoption of a constitution with a representative parliament to satisfy foreign critics and generate a sense of pride through participation among the empire's diverse populations.

As the second generation of their society to assimilate Western culture, the Young Ottomans demonstrated a level of sophistication that the Tanzimat leaders lacked. They built upon the idealism of Mustafa Reshid, rather than upon the pragmatic approach to government reorganization that obsessed Ali and Fuad. They also learned French and English language much earlier in life and were equipped to study Western literature and institutions in greater depth.

After their attitudes drove them apart from Ali and Fuad and out of the government, they did not have the day-to-day responsibility to make and implement policies. In addition, the termination of their political careers provoked their resentment and forced them back to their studies, which was a luxury the fully occupied

Tanzimat administrators could not afford. Like the European literary figures they admired, particularly Montesquieu, they turned to writing and publishing to achieve their influence. The rapid growth of publishing facilities and a more widely educated public in the empire assured their alternative approach a receptive audience.

Ibrahim Shinasi and Namik Kemal were the two most important leaders of the Young Ottoman Society, while Ziya Pasha and Ali Suavi ranked next in order of influence. Prince Mustafa Fazil, the younger brother of Khedive Ismail of Egypt, encouraged and financed the Young Ottoman leadership after pressures at home forced them to move their operations to Europe. After Ali Pasha forced Shinasi out of a promising career on the Council of Education, he turned to journalism. Even before he left public employment, financial support and encouragement from the future sultan, Murat V, and Prince Mustafa Fazil allowed Shinasi to begin his own newspaper *Description of Ideas* in 1861. This periodical became the main organ for Young Ottoman expression for the next decade. Shinasi regained government employment briefly and participated in the initiation of a second official newspaper, *The Army Newspaper* to complement the *Calendar of Events*, which had been in print since 1831. In 1864 he turned over the *Description of Ideas* to his protégé, Namik Kemal, and went to France where he remained for four years before returning home to die. In France he wrote persuasively on behalf of constitutionalism and parliamentarianism as the answers to the problems of his homeland. Other Young Ottomans soon joined him in France where they could write freely and transmit their views home through protected French channels.

Ziya Pasha, who was the same age as Shinasi, achieved early success in the Ottoman government before falling out of favor for his views in 1867, when he joined Shinasi in Europe. He shared Shinasi's strong views on constitutionalism, but was probably more committed to the need for the empire to retain its religious foundation and particular cultural identity. His most important writings urged the Porte to adopt only Western practices that would not destroy the empire's Islamic character. In this respect his views were similar to those of Jamal al-Din al-Afghani, Muhammad Abduh, and other important Pan-Islamicists later in the century.

Namik Kemal arrived at his critical views at a much younger age than the others, as he absorbed an early orientation from his mentor, Shanasi, who was fifteen years his senior. This helped him become the most prolific and most influential Young Ottoman after he assumed editorship of the *Description of Ideas* in 1864. After he fled to Europe in 1867, he continued his passion for translating European works into Turkish. He found Montesquieu's *Spirit of the Laws* particularly fascinating and applicable to the Ottoman milieu because of its emphasis on the historical and geographical uniqueness of each country. Montesquieu's views on the separation of powers also correlated better with the English system of government, which Kemal admired above all others.

Kemal's belief in constitutionalism at least matched Shinasi's, and he became a more adept and imaginative homogenizer of Western and Islamic ideas than Ziya. His more thorough knowledge of the European Enlightenment engendered a stronger ardor than that of his colleagues for individual rights and freedom. His extensive writings stressed the imperative of individual rights under constitutional guarantees, all of which he affirmed was implicit in Islam. Rather than make him suspect, his novel combination of Eastern and Western ideologies broadened his appeal to many who would have otherwise rejected the assimilation of foreign ideas. Kemal's unbridled patriotism was apparent in his 1873 play entitled *Vatan or Silistria* (*Fatherland or Silistria*), which stressed the valor of Ottoman soldiers against the Russians in 1854. The popular play resulted in his imprisonment, but did nothing to diminish the appeal of his ideas, which he published to strengthen the empire.

Ali Suavi's Pan-Turanism separated him from his more urbane colleagues in the Young Ottoman Society. Especially toward the end of his career he worked to instill a sense of pride in all people of Turkish blood, while the other Young Ottomans tried to cultivate a feeling of brotherhood among all Ottomans. He, like the others, called attention to the inadequacies of the Tanzimat as an answer to the empire's problems.

PROBLEMS IN LEBANON

Problems in Lebanon soon tested the resolve of the Great Powers to protect the status quo within the Ottoman Empire, as well as the Porte's commitment to protect its non-Muslim subjects. The withdrawal of Ibrahim's Egyptian administration in 1840 had removed effective central control in Lebanon. A conflict began in the Maronite community of Lebanon with the clergy-supported rebellion of Maronite peasants against their Maronite overlords. A blacksmith named Taniyus Shahin led the revolt, which threatened to cause upheaval among Maronite and Druze peasants alike.

Druze leaders, however, were able to capitalize upon the resentment of the new Christian freedoms and direct the frustration of Druze peasants toward the Maronites. Maronite leaders welcomed the diversion of attention from the social upheaval and the Maronite community soon became heavily armed with French assistance. Druze leaders quietly did the same with British and Ottoman assistance. A trivial incident between the drivers of two pack animals in 1859 turned what had been a conflict in the Maronite community into a sectarian blood bath between Maronites and Druze.

While the Maronites were far more numerous and better armed, the Druze were unified and convinced from Maronite statements that they were fighting for their very survival. Druze armed bands attacked Maronite villages throughout southern Lebanon and the Biqa valley, killing their inhabitants and driving others from the countryside into Beirut, Sidon, and Damascus. The most devastating Druze attacks occurred in June 1860 at Hasbayya, Rashayya, Zahleh, and Dar al-Qamar, where nearly all Maronites died or fled.

Ottoman officials and troops did not interfere in behalf of the Maronites and might, in fact, have overtly aided the Druze onslaught. The Ottoman governor arranged a peace in Beirut on July 6, but three days later Muslims killed thousands of Christians in Damascus and spread panic among the entire Christian population of Greater Syria. There was no doubt that Ahmad Pasha, the governor of Damascus, had played a major role in the Damascus massacre.

The European Great Powers could not ignore the developments in any part of Greater Syria after the Damascus massacre. The Porte realized European concern and dispatched Fuad Pasha, the foreign minister, to Beirut on July 17 to restore order and render justice to prevent foreign intervention. France, Britain, Russia, Austria, and Prussia, however, all sent ships to Beirut and a French contingent of nearly 7,000 went ashore. Fuad Pasha acted decisively and quickly brought many Ottoman officials to trial. The Ottoman commanders of Rashayya and Hasbayya were among the 111 officers and soldiers shot for their parts in the Lebanese massacres. Fuad's justice was also swift in Damascus, where Ahmad Pasha and fifty-six others were hanged. Many others received lesser punishments in both places. No Druze leaders were executed, although Said Jumblat inadvertently died in prison before his probable release.

These severe punishments did not satisfy the Great Powers, who engaged in months of discussion with Fuad Pasha before they arrived at the *Reglement Organique* for Lebanon on June 9, 1861. The Organic Statute completely altered the size and administration of Lebanon. It established an autonomous Lebanon, which consisted only of "The Mountain," where most of the Maronites and Druze populations were located. The truncated new entity was cut off from the sea, since it did not contain any of the seaport cities of Beirut, Sidon, or Tripoli. Exclusion of the Biqa valley from Lebanon denied the new creation an adequate agricultural capacity. The predominantly Druze-Maronite enclave, thus, had the opportunity to develop separately from the Ottoman Empire, although it had severe economic limitations.

Lebanon, in fact, became a protectorate of the Great Powers and the Ottoman Empire, with an Ottoman-appointed Catholic governor. Abdul Mejid appointed a talented Armenian, Daoud Pasha, who served with distinction and to the satisfaction of the Great Powers. Oddly, the only significant resistance to the new arrangement came from the Maronites, under the leadership of Yusuf Karam, who advocated that Lebanon become a Christian state in which Maronites, closely allied to France, should dominate. The small Lebanon, which also included Greek Orthodox, Sunni and Shiah Muslims, did not satisfy emerging Maronite nationalist desires. It was, however, self-governing and paid neither taxes nor tribute to Istanbul. By contrast, the Porte, which lost most jurisdiction over Lebanon, was obligated to provide additional funds if the newly independent entity was unable to generate enough for its needs.

These measures, which solved a serious problem for a time, set the precedent for Lebanon being considered distinctly different from other areas in the Middle East. Its special status attracted educational and religious missionaries. These individuals were under the protection of the European states and served to make the differences between Lebanon and its neighboring areas more pronounced.

CRETE

The withdrawal of Muhammad Ali's troops from Crete in 1841 helped precipitate unrest in Crete, just as it had in Lebanon. However, unlike in Lebanon, the Porte was able to demonstrate in Crete that it could solve problems when the Great Powers refrained from interfering. The chief problem arose over Cretan Greeks' disappointment in having been excluded from the new Greek state in 1829. The government in Athens naturally encouraged Cretans and other Greeks to agitate for union with Greece, and helped generate a major Greek uprising on Crete in 1866. The Ottoman governor attempted to rectify Greek grievances, but before he could obtain a solution, thousands of Greek volunteers invaded Crete to aid their compatriots' cause. Preoccupation of the Great Powers with the Austro-Prussian war prevented a response to unfounded Greek claims that Ottoman troops were slaughtering Cretan Greeks. In the absence of outside interference, Ottoman forces quickly restored order and Ali Pasha arrived in Crete to remedy the causes of the disturbance.

Ali proceeded to implement the best features of the fairly well-developed Tanzimat reforms, after calling an assembly of Christians and Muslims to advise in a restructuring of Crete's administration. The arrangement provided for the representation of Christians and Muslims alike on all levels of the new governing councils. Ali established mixed courts and implemented a fair tax system, which was based on the subjects' ability to pay. The Great Powers pressured an unwilling Greece to accept Ali Pasha's remarkable solution, and, in so doing, recognized the ability of a reformed Ottoman Empire to govern its minorities by the emerging modern standards most European states espoused.

THE BALKANS

The strength of Pan-Slavism and the mutual fear and ambition of Austria and Russia, as well as British, French, and Prussian concern for any significant shifts in the balance of power, prevented the Porte from solving the problems in the Balkans as it had handled the problem in Crete. Also, internally, the Ottoman Empire was less capable of solving problems by the time the problems in the Balkans began to erupt in the 1870s. By 1871, Fuad Pasha and Ali Pasha, the leaders of a cabinet-centered (Porte) reform movement (Tanzimat) were both dead. Their deaths made it easier for Abdul Aziz, who became sultan in 1861, to grasp control of the government, which had for some time been in the hands of the Porte, on behalf of the palace.

The resurgence of Russian influence over Ottoman affairs, along with the growth of traditionalist religious forces and Turkish nationalism, served to turn Ottoman domestic issues into international problems. Russia's greater influence over Ottoman policy through its ambassador, Nicholas Ignatiev, was well illustrated by an Ottoman agreement to allow Russia to reestablish its naval presence in the Black Sea in 1871. Also, after 1871, a strong reaction began to emerge under the leadership of the *ulama* and the Pan-Turanists (Turkish nationalists). They resented and resisted the Tanzimat reforms and the prominent role that Ottoman Christians and foreigners played in Ottoman affairs. The dire conditions of Ottoman finances by the 1870s also impeded the Porte's capacity to act. In addition, it fueled the resentment of those who blamed Ottoman weakness upon Christian and foreign influence.

A general Balkan conflagration began with an apparently ordinary uprising in Herzegovina on July 24, 1875. The Christian insurgents rebelled against the Porte's attempt to collect normal taxes during a time of bad harvests. This uprising was, in fact, as much a manifestation of Slavic desire to escape the yoke of Islamic Ottoman control as it was an outcry against temporary administrative injustices. Word soon spread throughout the world that the Ottomans were using the bloodiest tactics against Christians. The Porte's image suffered even more after the revolt spread into Bosnia and the Ottoman government announced that its financial strain required it to reduce interest payments on foreign-held bonds. Representatives of Austria, Prussia, and Russia met in Berlin to discuss the situation and issued the

Andrassy Note on December 30, 1875. The Porte accepted the Note's demands for reform, which were along the same lines as those adopted for Crete, but with the significant addition that foreign officials should be present to assure their implementation. The insurgents, however, did not accept the terms of the Note, which led the Porte to use force against them. The members of the Three Emperors' League met again in Berlin and issued the Berlin Memorandum on May 13, 1876, which delineated more detailed provisions for Ottoman reforms in Bosnia and Herzegovina. France and Italy also agreed to the new ultimatum and its threat of force unless the Porte relented.

By May 2, the revolt had already spread to Bulgaria and gathered a momentum that only Balkan independence could satisfy. Nationalist fervor alone can explain the uprising in Bulgaria, which had become prosperous and largely self-governed as the result of Midhat Pasha's full implementation of Tanzimat reforms in that vital province. Midhat Pasha had even consented to the Bulgars establishing their own church and approved their expulsion of the Greek patriarch and priests, whom the Bulgars found so odious.

The insurrection began with Christians killing Muslims in Bulgaria. With an insufficient number of regular Ottoman troops on hand to deal with the uprising, the Ottoman governor used untrained irregulars, who used unsanctioned brutality against the Christian rebels. The most notorious incident occurred at Batak, where most of the Christian population perished. In the early stages of the Bulgarian violence more Muslims than Christians probably lost their lives, but Europe only heard and cared about the Muslim atrocities against Christians. Western newspapers were full of stories about the "Bulgarian horrors," which gave inflated figures for massacred Christians as high as 100,000. The deaths of the French and Prussian consuls at the hands of a Muslim mob in Salonica in May 1876 added to the Western sense of outrage. Public opinion in the West was so furious against the Porte that no Western government would have dared to offer aid to the Ottomans if Russia attacked.

The Christian uprisings in the Balkans, combined with pressure from foreign governments, aroused nationalist feelings in Istanbul as well. Religious students and the *ulama* led demonstrations against the government's inability to prevent Muslim deaths and foreign intervention. The highest military officials deposed Sultan Abdul Aziz and placed Murat V on the throne in the hope of terminating internal and external criticism. Murat immediately made administrative and financial changes and guaranteed the equality of all Ottoman subjects, regardless of ethnic and religious affiliation. This sensitive, young sultan had never been at ease with the way he obtained the throne. The death of his deposed predecessor by apparent suicide, was more than his fragile constitution could bear. The bizarre murder of the ministers of war and foreign relations on June 15 added to Murat's trauma and led to claims among the conservatives that Midhat Pasha was responsible for their deaths as well as that of the former sultan. There was, however, widespread knowledge in Istanbul that Midhat Pasha had urged Murat to adopt a constitution, which provided for parliamentary government and ministerial responsibility.

Serbia and Montenegro's declaration of war delayed a solution to Murat's mental condition. The outbreak of war prompted a Russian proposal to partition the Ottoman Empire among Russia, Austria, Great Britain, and France as a means of preventing war.

Under threats from Russia, the Porte withdrew its armies from Serbia on

November 3. British threats to give Russia a free hand against the Ottomans induced the Porte to agree the next day to a Great Powers conference to discuss the Balkans crisis. The Porte anticipated that the conference would demand extensive reforms. These would include the granting of varying degrees of autonomy or independence to the Balkan provinces, as well as Western supervision of many Ottoman policies.

The Great Powers expressed surprise that the Porte adopted a constitution soon after the Istanbul conference opened on December 12. Midhat Pasha and Murat had, however, openly discussed the possibility during the latter's short reign. Midhat had also ascertained that Abdul Hamid would accept such a course before he agreed to help Hamid obtain the throne. Midhat's draft had been published in newspapers as early as October 10, and the Porte had debated details of the proposed constitution since that time.

Sultan Abdul Hamid II's proclamation of the constitution on December 23, 1876, created a dilemma for the Great Powers. They either had to accept, at face value, the equal protection it guaranteed all Ottoman subjects or deny its validity and impose their own will. Forced separation of parts of the empire denied its sovereignty, as did any kind of foreign supervision. Special courts for religious groups were also contrary to the constitution's provision for secular courts with equal protection for all subjects.

THE RUSSO-TURKISH WAR OF 1877

The Great Powers ignored the Ottoman constitution and made demands that exceeded the Porte's worst fears. Lord Salisbury, the British representative, played a central role in drafting and presenting the demands. He informed the Porte that his government would not deter Russian reprisals, unless the Porte consented to the demands. Honor forced the Porte, with widespread public support, to refuse the harsh demands. Abdul Hamid was less convinced that refusal was wise, and dismissed Midhat Pasha soon after the Istanbul Conference broke up on January 20.

Russia thought that it already had the Great Power's consent to use force after the Ottomans rejected the conference's demands. St. Petersburg strengthened its position by an agreement with Austria at Budapest on January 15. The most important provision of this agreement was Russia's consent for Austria to occupy Bosnia and Herzegovina in return for Austria's neutrality in a Russo-Ottoman war. This agreement and the earlier conference were both contrary to the provisions of the Treaty of Paris, but Russia felt free to declare war on the Ottomans on April 24, 1877.

Russia launched its usual attack into the Balkans and into eastern Anatolia. Soon, Serbia, Greece, Rumania, and Montenegro joined the attack. By November, it was evident that tsarist forces could advance upon Istanbul from both the east and the west. The magnitude of Russia's victory would enable it to dictate peace and dismember the Ottoman Empire. Russia, thus, seemed on the verge of fulfilling most Pan-Slav aspirations by freeing the Slavs from Ottoman rule. It would also gain control of the vital Dardanelles Straits, which would provide Russia the coveted outlet to the warm waters of the Mediterranean and the oceans.

The possibility of Russia being in full control of the straits and Istanbul led the British government to forget the "terrible Turks" and consider the consequences of Russians being astride its lifeline to India. British official, and public, opinion also changed and became fervently committed to keeping Russia out of Istanbul and the Dardanelles Straits. The careful plans to avoid a Great Powers war seemed to have failed, as an Anglo-Russian war would have undoubtedly involved the other Great Powers.

THE TREATY OF SAN STEFANO

Russia agreed, however, to an armistice on January 30, 1878, shortly after the British dispatched a fleet to the Dardanelles. With British interference imminent, Russia hurried to conclude a treaty with the Porte at San Stefano. The overwhelming might of Russian arms so near the capital prevented the Porte from calling on British help, because such a provocation could evoke a Russian *coup de grace*. The terms of the Treaty of San Stefano on March 3 severed most of the Balkans from the Ottoman Empire. The Porte recognized the independence of Serbia, Montenegro, and Rumania. The treaty created a huge Bulgaria, which would reach to the Aegean Sea and remain only marginally part of the Ottoman Empire. Russia's dominance there would essentially give it an outlet to the Mediterranean, even without control of the Dardenelles Straits. Bosnia and Herzegovina, which would likely be under Austrian administration, were to become autonomous. Russia annexed northeastern Anatolia with its large Armenian population. It also regained full protectorate over Ottoman Orthodox Christians. The Porte had to agree to an astronomical indemnity, which it could not hope to pay, since it was already bankrupt before the war began. The indemnity and Russian authority over Ottoman Orthodox subjects would have virtually allowed Russia to dictate all future Ottoman policies. Only rigid British opposition and Russia's financial inability to fight another war to retain its gains kept the San Stefano Treaty from being final.

Since Britain could not allow San Stefano to stand, one British fleet moved to Istanbul and on June 4 another occupied Cyprus, with the hesitant consent of the Porte. Britain's recently acquired controlling interest in the Suez Canal made the island of Cyprus essential for protecting its Mediterranean and Asian interests from further Russian intrusions. The Porte agreed to British occupation and administration of Cyprus in return for the British promise to prevent additional Russian expansion into Anatolia.

THE CONGRESS OF BERLIN

Otto von Bismarck invited the Great Powers to attend the Congress of Berlin to prevent the Treaty of San Stefano from leading to a major war. Many of the provisions of the congress had already been decided before the Great Powers met formally in Berlin on June 13, 1878. However, the refinements required another month of negotiations. As a result, Big Bulgaria disappeared, to the everlasting disappointment of Bulgarians, and was divided into three parts with differing degrees of affiliation with the Ottoman Empire. The resulting small Bulgaria was an autonomous, Christian-dominated Ottoman principality, which was essentially free of obligations to the Porte except for an annual tribute. Eastern Rumelia remained an Ottoman province with some Ottoman military presence, but under a governor of Great Power approval. The Porte regained customary authority over Macedonia and Thrace with the stipulation that it implement reforms.

The Congress upheld San Stefano and recognized the independence of Serbia, Rumania, and Montenegro. Bosnia and Herzegovina theoretically remained part of the Ottoman Empire, but, since the congress placed them under Austrian administration, they effectively became part of the Austrian Empire. After all its efforts and successes in the war, Russia gained only Batum, Kars, and Ardahan in eastern Anatolia. Britain obtained consent to continue its occupation of Cyprus. In compensation for other Great Power gains, France seems to have gained approval to occupy Tunis at some propitious time in the future.

The Congress of Berlin averted war and reasserted Great Power parity in Ottoman affairs at the expense of Russia and the Ottoman Empire. Germany enhanced its reputation as the only European state devoid of designs against Ottoman sovereignty. The Ottoman Empire unwillingly moved closer to a full extrication of its Christian Slav population. Serbia and Bulgaria chafed at what they regarded as unnatural truncations of their national borders. Italy and Greece resented their failures to receive their shares of Ottoman territory. These and other factors assured that the Balkan problem, or "Eastern Question," was not solved, but only in remission.

THE SUEZ CANAL

More than a century would pass before Egypt would regain the influence or power it had enjoyed under Muhammad Ali until 1840. Economic stagnation that resulted from the imposition of the hated capitulations was probably as much a reason as the failure of Ibrahim, Abbas, and Said to match the ability of their father and grandfather. Notably, during Said's tenure (1854–1863), the corporate structure of the Suez Canal Company emerged, although resistance from Great Britain and the Ottoman government prevented any appreciable construction. Said's French diplomatic friend, Ferdinand de Lesseps, obtained formal consent in 1856 to construct a 105-mile canal to connect the Mediterranean and Red seas. A 15-percent ownership in the canal provided Said a personal incentive beyond any hopes he had for it as an asset to his country. Gifts of shares to important French officials, probably including Emperor Napoleon III, influenced the approval of France, whose citizens bought most of the ordinary shares. Said demonstrated his faith in the project by purchasing most of the shares sold in Egypt to bring his total ownership to 44 percent.

The canal, which transformed the Middle East, was fully operational by 1869. Most of the construction occurred after Ismail became pasha in 1863 and gave the canal his constant attention from 1866. Ismail staged inimitable celebrations with influential foreign guests that he felt Egypt's modern engineering feat deserved. The canal was a remarkable achievement that cost thousands of Egyptian lives in the malaria-infested region and cost more than twice as much to construct than de Lessep's original estimate of about $42 million. Although construction was sometimes treacherous, the fact that the Mediterranean and Red seas have the same sea level eliminated the need for locks and three natural lakes along its route provided part of the waterway.

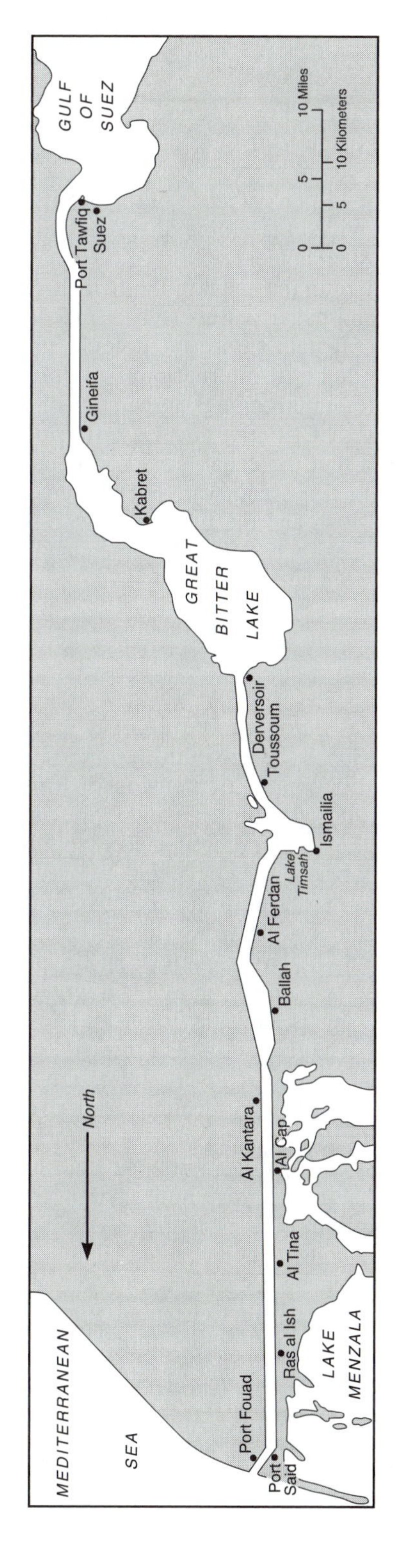

The Suez Canal

The Egyptian-registered but French-dominated Universal Company of the Maritime Canal of the Suez operated the canal with a ninety-nine year lease from Egypt. Egypt received a 15-percent share of the profits for rent and, of course, the ruling family had a claim to a 44-percent share of the profits commensurate with its ownership position. Tolls provided the source of revenue to defray the cost of construction and to provide the shareholders with profits. Ismail's dire financial situation forced him to sell his share in the canal to the British government in 1875. By that time, British merchant and naval vessels were decidedly the heaviest users of the canal and it became Great Britain's primary strategic interest in the region until 1956. As the canal's importance to international shipping and other concerns increased, there was need for international agreement on its use. All the major European Powers, along with Ottoman and Egyptian officials, agreed at the Istanbul Convention in 1888 that the canal would be open to both merchant and naval vessels of all nations in peace and war. The agreement has never stood the test of reality, as both the British and the Egyptians, who have controlled it since 1888, have denied their enemies its use for either merchant or naval shipping during wars in which they have been belligerents.

KHEDIVE ISMAIL

Ismail, the son of Ibrahim, was European in every way except by birth and lineage when he assumed power in 1863 at the age of thirty-three. He assumed in an almost naive way that Egypt could become an extension of Europe. His education in France and his familiarity with both European and Ottoman cultures provided him unique potential to succeed. Egypt's unprecedented economic growth at his accession to power gave him every reason to believe that he lived in the best of all possible worlds and that it was his destiny to improve it. His funds appeared boundless as Egyptian cotton filled the void of providing the popular fiber for European textile mills during the American Civil War. Almost all Egyptian land not needed to produce food began to grow cotton. The pasha, his predominantly Turkish and Circassian large-landowner friends, and the urban middle class enjoyed incomes beyond their fondest dreams. The *fellahin* (small farmers) prospered little from the bonanza, but work was available in the cities for those who left the land.

Ismail acquired the title of Khedive, which was derived from a Persian word for prince, in 1867. This title, which was given to him by Sultan Abd al-Aziz, enhanced his credibility just as Egypt's inordinate hold on the European cotton market ended. The new status, in fact, gave him freedom from Ottoman control in most areas except some diplomatic appointments, the appointment of officers above the rank of colonel, the construction of more advanced naval vessels, and the use of the Ottoman flag and coinage. Egypt was autonomous and close to independent, although it still owed annual tribute to Istanbul. Interestingly, cordial relations prevailed between Ismail and the Ottoman Empire. Abd al-Aziz was the first Ottoman Sultan to visit Egypt since it had become part of the Ottoman Empire early in the sixteenth century.

European governments and bankers courted the charming and urbane Khedive, whose friendship and business dealings appeared to be politically and financially rewarding. The splendor he orchestrated in connection with the opening of the Suez Canal in 1869 did nothing to diminish his appeal. The Europeans mistook his profligate propensity for giving lavish gifts and building on a grandiose scale as an indication of untold wealth, rather than as an indication of misguided optimism and weakness in spending far beyond his means. His new title, his nearly 50-percent ownership in the canal, and his apparent capacity to establish dominion over the Sudan and Ethiopia established him as a good credit risk.

Ismail accepted loans with reckless abandon and used the funds to transform Egypt. Grand public buildings and modern utilities, monuments, schools, libraries, theatres and parks rapidly materialized in Egypt in numbers and magnitude that had taken much wealthier empires centuries to acquire. The pasha was a patron of the arts, as well, and he opened the Cairo Opera House in 1869 as part of the Suez Canal opening extravaganza. Book and newspaper presses proliferated to establish Cairo as the most important communications center in the Middle East.

Although built with borrowed money he could not repay on schedule, most of Ismail's construction was of enduring value. Egyptians would have these buildings and utilities forever, regardless of whether the lenders ever received their payments. Ismail's attention to railroads, canals, telegraphs, gas, water, and schools indicated his intention of transposing more than a facade of modern European life to Egypt. He, in fact, concentrated on an infrastructure necessary for a modern society and state. Perhaps the schools he built were his greatest contribution because, by the end of his reign, few nations in the world were educating as large a proportion of their population as Egypt. Most of his actions throughout his rule indicated that, for all his European proclivities, he was, first and foremost, an Egyptian.

EGYPTIAN DEBT AND SUBSERVIENCE

In fairness to Ismail, he was hardly alone in becoming financially overextended to European capitalists in the second half of the nineteenth century. The availability of more capital than the Europeans could invest in their own economies led them to look overseas. A combination of the capitulation treaties and a desperate desire on the part of the Middle Eastern and North African countries to modernize made them willing partners in accepting the usurious rates of restless large and small European investors. An international debt commission took control of Tunisia in 1869, the Ottoman government experienced a similar fate in 1881, and Persia was well on its way toward the same end by the 1870s.

Ismail, who was inclined to do things larger than others, fell harder and sooner than some of his Middle East contemporaries. His situation was so dire by 1874 that he began to tax beyond his population's capacity to pay, although he left the larger landowners essentially untouched. He forgave part of the large landowners' future taxes in return for substantial, one-time immediate payments. In desperation he sold his share in the Suez Canal to the British government for £4 million in 1875 and borrowed £55 million at a rate of nearly 40 percent, which his creditors deducted from the loan's face value. The latter transaction demonstrates the desperation of both parties to do business when good sense dictated none should have occurred. At least 60 percent of Egypt's annual budget was already required to pay indebtedness. European bondholders and bankers knew, however, that their governments could force Egypt to pay.

Great Britain and France took the lead in collecting Egypt's indebtedness to all European nationals when Ismail informed his creditors in 1876 that he could not make any payments despite considerable austerity measures. His retirement of some army officers, and reduction of the salaries of others, followed by a moratorium on all salaries, aroused this previously politically inactive element into Egyptian politics. The international creditors forced Ismail to accept a Public Debt Fund in May 1876 with an Englishman and a Frenchman in control of the purse strings and, as such, control of Egypt's public policies. The resulting arrangement reduced debt payments to just under 50 percent of Khedival revenues, while the foreign overlords guaranteed that the integrity of the agreement would prevail. Ismail's seldom-used Assembly of Delegates failed in their attempt to play a more active role in Egypt's finances to avoid the humiliation of foreign control.

Ismail chafed at the restrictions and began to appeal to the Egyptian public to assert themselves against foreign interference. The determined Europeans responded in 1878 with restrictions upon the Khedive's personal expenditures and forced him to accept an Englishman and a Frenchman in his cabinet. This would, for the first time, constitute real governing authority on the part of the Europeans. Other Europeans obtained high-paying positions to guide Egypt's good behavior while Egyptians continued to lose pay and government employment. Additionally provocative was the Public Debt Fund's insistence that Nubar Pasha, a noted Armenian nationalist, become prime minister to preside over Ismail's cabinet. Aroused public opinion made it impossible for Egypt's cabinet to appear in public without armed protection.

In response to the popular outcry and army pressure Ismail dismissed his unwanted cabinet and chose one composed of Egyptians. He and the assembly approved a liberal constitution that gave both the cabinet and the legislature an active role in governing. Indicative that most Europeans opposed Egypt's move to independence, the German Chancellor Bismarck, arbiter of the Congress of Berlin that had peacefully settled the Balkan problem, demanded that the Sultan dismiss Ismail. Abdul Hamid reluctantly complied and deposed Ismail on July 26, 1879 in favor of his son, Tewfik. Ismail went into exile in Italy and died in Naples in 1895.

Attention to Ismail's ignominious demise and his policies that led to foreign domination should not prevent an appreciation of the positive, enduring results of his reign. Egypt became and remained the center of Arab culture and information for the entire Arab world. His educational system continued to educate people from all over the Arab world who could then lead their region to freedom from foreign domination. Their prolonged close affiliation with Europeans provided Egyptians with a better understanding of European ideas and institutions than any other Arab society possessed. Egyptians were better prepared than other Arabs to determine which Western practices and beliefs were most compatible with traditional Middle Eastern values. Ismail's frenetic attempt to make Egypt an extension of Europe accelerated Egypt's already substantial affiliation with Europe. Still, Egypt's exposure to European influence from the time of Muhammad Ali to 1956 did not destroy the essence of Egypt. The eclectic result no doubt fell short, however, of the best of both worlds Ismail had originally envisioned.

OTTOMAN PROBLEM OF INDEBTEDNESS

Debt was one of the biggest Ottoman problems from the beginning of the Crimean War, when the empire contracted its first foreign loan. The Porte's insolvency prevented it from implementing its policies and invited domestic and foreign concern and criticism. By 1867 the debt required 34 percent of the state's revenue and by 1875 the debt reached 44 percent of its income. Europeans continued to purchase Ottoman bonds because the return exceeded almost any other investment, and the Porte always found a way to pay in anticipation of further borrowing. Even before European bankers took control of Ottoman finances, their political and economic influence within the empire usually guaranteed that European bondholders received priority in Ottoman disbursements. Consequently debt grew, services declined or disappeared, and Ottoman military and administrative officials went unpaid for extended periods of time. Prolonged failure to pay the army was crucial since it created a deep-seated dissatisfaction in the one element of the empire that could alter the form of government.

Ottoman financial woes also increased for reasons other than the payment on the national debt. The scandalously low cost to Europeans of doing business with the empire turned it into an economic colony of Europe. The empire's handcrafts manufacturing could not compete with the industrialized production techniques of its western neighbors. The meager output of the past actually declined as Ottoman subjects purchased the machine-made products of the West. Conversely, the empire could only market raw goods in the West, some of which they repurchased in finished form to the benefit of Western economies.

The financial situation became so dire that the Porte suspended payment on half of their debt in October 1875 and ceased payment temporarily on all debts in the summer of 1876, during the middle of the Balkan crisis. When the Porte negotiated new loans with British and French bankers in 1877 to finance the Russo-Turkish war, it had to guarantee the exorbitant rate of 40 percent return to Western bondholders.

THE OTTOMAN PUBLIC DEBT ADMINISTRATION

Continuation of this ridiculous economic situation was impossible for all parties by 1879, and the Great Powers began to work with the Porte on a solution that would avoid a complete Ottoman default. In that year they reached an agreement to limit the amount of revenue the Ottomans had to apply to the debt, but the empire had to consign all revenues on silk, tobacco, spirits, and many licenses toward liquidating the debt. This arrangement was a major step toward a more drastic and comprehensive solution in 1881, when the Powers and the Porte established the Ottoman Public Debt Administration (O.P.D.A.). This administrative and fiscal institution proved sound for all parties. However, it had the effect of placing the empire into a friendly receivership of its foreign debtors.

The O.P.D.A. consisted of representatives from Great Britain, France, Germany, Russia, Austria, Italy, the Ottoman Empire, and a representative of the Ottoman Bank. The international community already had experience from their solution to a similar situation in Egypt. The O.P.D.A. consolidated all Ottoman debt, including the outstanding indemnity to Russia, and established a schedule for liquidating the entire indebtedness by managing many Ottoman finances. While foreigners provided the executive management of the O.P.D.A., most of the staff were Muslim Ottomans, who gained valuable experience in Western administrative techniques. The O.P.D.A. was independent of the Ottoman Ministry of Finance and received all the revenues from silk, tobacco, spirits, many licenses, and some other taxes that had not been a part of the 1879 arrangement. It also had the right to manage additional revenues from future taxes. Tributes from the Balkan states also went directly into its treasury.

Embarrassing as the O.P.D.A. was to the empire, it had the advantage of requiring only 20 percent of the empire's revenue to establish a method of defraying the debt. For the first time in at least thirty years, the Porte had financial breathing room and funding to implement new administrative procedures, develop its infrastructure, modernize, and provide services without accumulating a crippling debt.

The Porte did not, however, rely solely on the O.P.D.A. to put its house in order. The creation of a Central Auditing Council, and the regular use of financial experts, began to place Ottoman finances on a sounder basis for immediate needs and future planning. The O.P.D.A.'s restructuring also did not end the Ottoman need to borrow abroad, but the improved financial condition allowed it to borrow at lower rates. For European investors, lending to the Porte continued to be lucrative but less risky. Ottoman borrowing also became less necessary as it adopted the different tact of encouraging foreign companies to invest directly in projects such as railroads and utilities within the empire.

THE 1876 OTTOMAN CONSTITUTION

The convergence of the debt crisis and the Balkan crisis in 1876 led to the deposition of Murat V and the return of Midhat Pasha to the government. Midhat, who had adopted the Young Ottoman's views on constitutionalism, urged Murat V to embrace constitutionalism and began to draft such a document. When Murat's mental instability became so acute that his deposition seemed likely, Midhat extracted a promise of a constitution from Abdul Hamid before he agreed to support his elevation to the throne. Such a move struck a surprisingly responsive chord because the Young Ottomans, especially Nemik Kemal, had helped move many elements of Ottoman society, including traditionalists, to believe in constitutionalism.

After assuming power in September, Abdul Hamid II promulgated a constitution on December 23, 1876 in the midst of the Istanbul Conference, which was in session to prevent a general war over the Balkan crisis. While it granted representative parliamentary government, individual liberty, religious freedom, freedom of the press, and generally reiterated earlier Tanzimat reforms, the Sultan retained most of his power, including the right to appoint and dismiss ministers without reference to the bicameral parliament. It created a Chamber of Deputies with 120 elected members and a 26-member Chamber of Notables appointed by the Sultan. The Council of State was responsible for drafting proposed laws, whether they originated from the Porte or the parliament. Legislation required the approval of both the Council of Ministers and the Sultan to become law. The parliament's greatest authority rested in its right to approve all taxes and the budget. Christians and Jews enjoyed representation disproportionately high for their populations. This modern constitution appeared to be a logical culmination of the Tanzimat that alleviated the grievances of the Young Ottomans.

THE FAILURE OF PARLIAMENTARY GOVERNMENT

The parliament met on March 19, 1877 and pursued its duties with surprising vigor. However, the growing Balkan problem and the war with Russia distracted its attention from its main functions. The dismissal and exile of the constitution's architect,

Midhat Pasha, on February 5 because of his inability to avoid war with the Powers at the Istanbul Conference also helped undermine the entire constitution. After the parliament engaged in heated criticism of the Porte, and even the Sultan's, mismanagement of the war, and the situation which had led up to it, Abdul Hamid II dismissed the parliament on February 14, 1878. While he did not abolish the constitution, he withdrew it with the explanation that conditions made its continuation impossible. This brief experimentation with constitutional government thus ended, rather than fulfilled, the Tanzimat movement.

Abdul Hamid's improved financial condition after the establishment of the O.P.D.A. in 1881 strengthened his resolve to govern without the tumultuous parliament and to utilize the centralizing features of the Tanzimat for his personal rule.

AN ENDURING TRANSFORMATION UNDER THE TANZIMAT

For all the apparent failure to implement the full scope of the Tanzimat at its various stages, the reform movement had a significant effect on the Ottoman Empire. Its very promulgation, for instance, was an admission that traditional practices were inefficient and unfair. Such admissions, in fact, accompanied each stage of promulgation and, thereby, the Ottoman government openly condemned its own policies. The admissions and the consent to reforms fed both domestic and foreign appetites for further change, which only the fullest and quickest implementation of reform could satisfy.

The acknowledged inequities, however, were valid only in comparison with contemporary European institutions and practices, rather than with general historical practice in the Ottoman region. The Europeans themselves had only recently adopted the practices into their considerably more homogeneous states, which they tried to impose upon the Ottoman Empire. Foreigners, thus, attempted to impose institutions and practices upon the Ottoman Empire that arose out of European antecedents. There is little wonder that such transplantation was difficult since the Ottomans had neither a way of anticipating the developments, nor the foundation for assimilating such momentous changes.

As young Ottomans began to receive an education different from the traditional Islamic education of their forefathers, they were intellectually nurtured on the most radical literature Europe had ever produced. Also, by the time Western revolutionary ideas became widespread among the newly educated Ottomans, the ideas had lost their cosmopolitan flavor through a cross-fertilization with romantic nationalism. This helped create a formula for disaster for an empire of such ethnic diversity.

Other areas of the world experienced European economic and cultural imperialism simultaneously with the Ottoman Empire, but it was the first to feel the impact of the forceful imposition of European political, judicial, and social institutions. Under normal circumstances it could have been an exciting and fruitful experiment for the Ottoman Empire, but the empire was almost constantly at war from the beginning of the Tanzimat period. The absence of men from the fields was disastrous for agricultural production and reduced the tax base of a government, which was still experimenting with ways to institute a fair and dependable tax system.

But contrary to the observations of even well-informed foreign observers and disappointed Ottoman critics, the "Sick Man of Europe" was different as a result of the Tanzimat. Attitudes had changed among both the reform-minded and traditionalists; a new structure of government was in place and the empire was financially healthier and integrated into the European economy on a less servile basis. In addition, after considerable public debate, a constitution had developed beyond theory and existed somewhere in the government's archives, as a concrete alternative to arbitrary rule and continued domination of a Turkish minority over the empire's diverse ethnic groups.

ANGLO-RUSSIAN COMPETITION FOR INFLUENCE IN PERSIA

Persia's semi-isolated location limited attempts to influence or control it by Russia and Great Britain in the second half of the nineteenth century, when the European nations engaged in a new burst of imperial expansion. Russia was always the primary instigator as it coveted additional Persian lands and attempted to establish its economic control over Persia. Much of Great Britain's activities began with attempts to counter Russian advances, which the British believed threatened their hold on India. Persia was in need of outside assistance, but the competition between its two giant potential helpers caused considerable conflict that resulted in little benefit for Persia. Internal opposition to modernization added to the problem. As a result Persia stagnated. Its industry, agriculture, and military preparedness changed little to distinguish it from its past. Jealousies between Great Britain and Russia, for

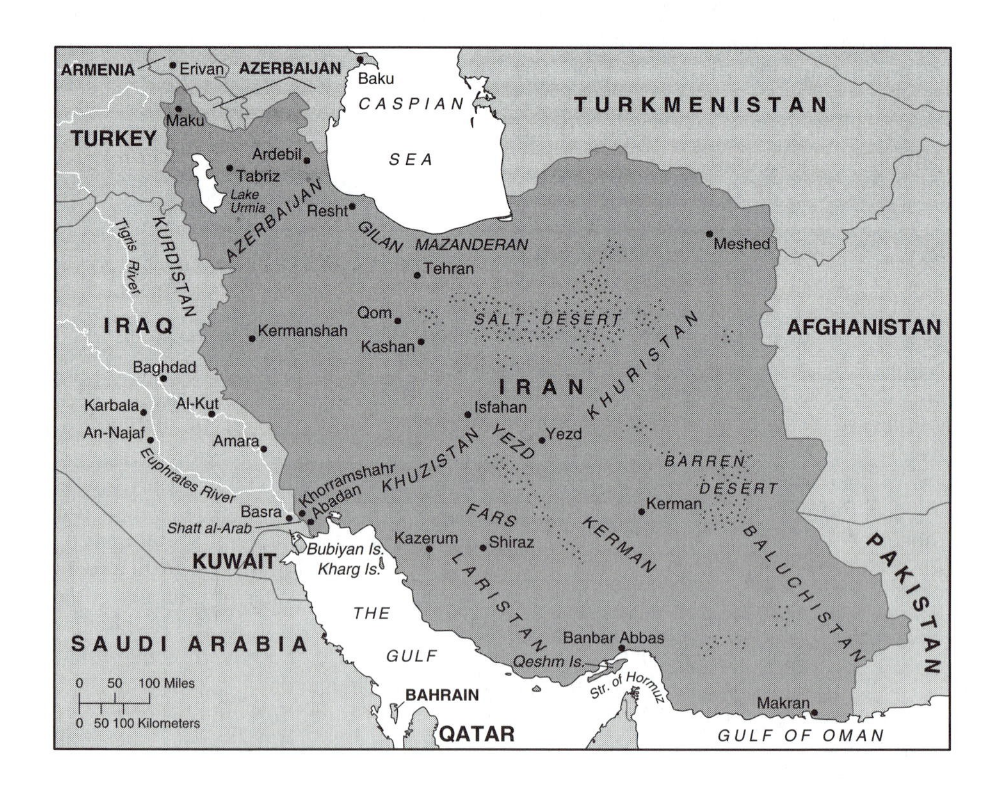

instance, prevented the construction of either adequate roads or railroads. Ironically, this proved critical to both foreign competitors during World War I, when the absence of a transportation infrastructure in Persia prevented Britain and its other allies from sending supplies that could have saved the Russian monarchy and kept it in the war.

Shah Nasir al-Din became aware of Iran's relative backwardness through his three trips to Europe and realized that Persia's very existence was in jeopardy. However, he lacked the means of either improving his revenues or developing Persia's economy. He attempted to remedy his situation through granting concessions to foreigners who possessed both the capital and expertise to modernize. His first major acquisition was a British-built telegraph system, which ran through Persia to India in 1862. This system linked Persia to the outside world, while a branch of it served Persia's internal needs. In an attempt to modernize, the shah sold Baron Julius de Reuter, a British subject, a comprehensive concession to develop Persia's industry and economy in 1872. Russia's opposition to this major intrusion into its sphere of influence, however, forced Nasir al-Din to withdraw the concession, although de Reuter was able to salvage the right to establish the Imperial Bank of Persia several years later. Russia, thus, retained its near monopoly on the Persian markets.

THE TOBACCO MONOPOLY CONTROVERSY IN PERSIA

When Major Gerald Talbot, another Englishman, received a fifty-year concession on the entire tobacco trade of Persia on March 8, 1890, he ignited a crisis that mirrored all of Persia's problems and helped create new forces that would shape its future. This concession in behalf of the Imperial Tobacco Corporation of Persia was a strictly private venture, but it renewed the Anglo-Russian conflict. It also united on an unprecedented level the merchant and clerical forces that opposed foreign interference and the expansion of royal authority.

For a modest annual fee of £15,000 and 25 percent of the profits, the Imperial Tobacco Corporation received the exclusive right to control production, sale, and manufacturing of Persian tobacco both domestically and internationally. This meant, of course, that the company's agents and influence would have permeated almost every corner of Persia, where almost half the population of 5 million people used some form of tobacco. The concession also prevented the Persian government from altering any form of taxation on tobacco for the fifty-year period of the monopoly.

More than a year passed before any indication arose that this new source of royal revenue would cause a problem. The poor choice of personnel, especially the use of so many foreigners, ignited much of the original opposition. The deportation of a Shiraz clergyman, who voiced his strong opposition to the concession, helped make the tobacco concession a *cause célèbre*. Tabriz, in the heavy tobacco-producing province of Azerbaijan, became the center of opposition by the summer of 1891. This area was all the more sensitive since Russian influence was so strong in this highly populated and volatile region. Merchants began to question whether the arrangement was economically sound, because they felt that the Ottoman Empire enjoyed a much more lucrative arrangement for a similar kind of concession.

Russian diplomats in Tabriz joined in the opposition and promised Russian assistance to protect Persian national and religious interests.

By the end of the summer 1891 the clergy, especially in Tabriz, became involved in the resistance and made continuation of the concession untenable. Leading Azerbaijani *mujtahids* (Islamic jurists) approved every type of opposition, including violence, against agents of the tobacco company and everyone who cooperated with it. Jamal al-Din al-Afghani, the well known Pan-Islamic activist, was in the forefront of the opposition and helped involve Muhammad Hasan Shirazi of Karbala in Iraq, the leading Shiah divine of the time. With this distinguished leadership the entire nation seemed to rise in opposition to protect the national and religious interests of Persia. The principal claim of the clergy was that tobacco in and from the hands of nonbelievers was unclean and unacceptable to Persians. The clergy's success was complete when even the shah's harem honored the boycott.

The shah understood that rescinding the concession represented a major political and financial defeat for him and jeopardized Persia's capacity to attract foreign capital investments. He was powerless, however, to resist the forces arraigned against him. His military capability was limited in both numbers and quality. The arrears in the army's pay and its sympathy with the opposition removed use of the army as an option. There was also the very strong indication that Russia was willing to employ military forces to assist the rebellion that broke into major violence in Tehran in December 1891. Serious doubt arose about the ability of the shah to remain in power. Fortunately for him, he was able to end the crisis before Ayatollah Shirazi's ruling on February 2, 1892 arrived in Persia. This ruling called for the "eternal abolition" of all foreign concessions in Persia without any compensation for their termination. Nasir al-Din had agreed to abolish the concession in December, before the greatest violence had occurred in Tehran, but the opposition's insistence on total victory kept the crisis alive. The delay in communications between the various centers of resistance and with Ayatollah Shirazi in Karbala also lengthened the conflict as the shah attempted to make all necessary modifications. Persians were satisfied with the shah's actions and resumed smoking on January 26, 1892.

Britain was alarmed that the tobacco issue had placed it in such an awkward position and had aroused such vehement anti-British sentiments. It was also concerned that the apparently innocent capitalist venture of a British company had presented the Russians with the opportunity for a major diplomatic and financial victory. While the British government had the responsibility to protect the business interests of its nationals, it had a greater concern in this instance to preserve the independence of the shah and prevent a further deterioration of British status in Persia. Britain, therefore, agreed that its greater interests in Persia required the termination of the tobacco concession.

New conflicts developed, however, when British officials began to assist the tobacco company in obtaining compensation for the loss of the concession. The shah's government agreed it had an obligation to compensate the tobacco company, but it lacked the funds. De Reuter's Imperial Bank offered to lend the £500,000 compensation to the Persian government in return for a lien upon Gulf-area customs duties. The Russian bank, which was a branch of the Russian government, offered Persia better terms for the necessary loan. The British government opposed this alternative, since it would have given Russia the right to interfere directly in Persia's internal affairs and international trade. Strong British pressure on the shah and on the Imperial Bank forced the shah to accept a loan on May 14, 1892 from de Reuter's bank that matched the terms Russia had offered. The bank, indeed, received a lien on the Gulf customs duties as collateral. The final resolution of this matter did not occur until March 25, 1893 when very complicated and secret negotiations led to the transfer of all Imperial Tobacco Corporation's assets to the Persian government, which in turn worked out a method of selling Persian tobacco to a French firm that had a binding obligation to sell Persian tobacco to the original British company.

Fear of a resurgence of opposition from Persian religious authorities shaped the complicated arrangement for getting Persian tobacco to the Western market and providing the shah with increased revenues. The clergy had demonstrated during the tobacco controversy that they were the strongest single force in Persian society when issues arose to provide them the opportunity to arouse popular sentiments. The long-standing symbiotic relationship between the clergy and the bazaar merchants coalesced into a firmer partnership that could for the first time marshall popular opposition to the formerly accepted right of the shah to rule with impunity. The assassination of shah Nasir al-Din in 1896 by one of Jamal al-Din al-Afghani's closest associates demonstrated the new level of clergy participation in Persian affairs.

Russia was a clear winner in the controversy because it proved, as it had in opposing de Reuter's 1872 concessions, that Persia could do little in foreign affairs that Russia opposed. It was simpler for the Persian government to accept the obvious and bow to Russian desires in order to avoid future conflicts. Accordingly, Russia increased its hold on Persian commercial affairs, primarily through the establishment of a branch of its Central Bank in Persia. The Russian bank provided a large loan in 1900. Persian customs duties, other than those that the tobacco compensation encumbered, were used as security. In this way, Russia was able to interfere in Persia's internal affairs. This was exactly the situation the British had tried to avoid. By this agreement, in fact, Persia was supposed to buy out the de Reuter lien and give Russia a lien on Persia's entire customs income.

THE OIL CONCESSION

Russia's domination over Persian commercial affairs was ephemeral, because British businessmen remained firmly entrenched in the concessions they had obtained in the second half of the nineteenth century. The twentieth century would prove to be even more fruitful for British interests in Persia. Britain's ability to supersede Russia resulted in large part from a sixty-year monopoly an Australian, William Knox D'Arcy, obtained in 1901 to find and develop petroleum and natural gas in all but the northernmost portion of Persia. This was the first oil concession granted by any Middle Eastern government. He received the concession with the payment of £20,000, stock in the company for an equal amount, and 16 percent of the annual profits. Hardship and failure marked the first six years of D'Arcy's venture and he had to obtain financial and technical assistance from the Burmah Oil Company to continue his exploration. Finally, on May 26, 1908 a massive oil strike occurred in Khuzistan at Masjid es-Suleiman in the foothills of the Zagros Mountains. Masjid es-Suleiman is about one hundred miles from the Iraqi border and one hundred and thirty miles north of the Gulf.

Persia, thus, gained unimagined new importance in world affairs and possessed a commodity that could free it from poverty. Like so much in Persia, however, foreigners owned the right to control every aspect of this precious asset and commanded new leverage over the government and economy of the nation. Within a few months of the gusher at Masjid es-Suleiman the well-capitalized Anglo-Persian Oil Company took over D'Arcy's concession and began to exploit this richest-known source of petroleum. Indicative of Persia's plight, the company, and later the British government, made the most crucial arrangements for their operations in Persia with Shaykh Khazal of Mohammarah, rather than with the Persian government. Shaykh Khazal sold them the rights for the pipeline from the wellhead to the Shatt al-Arab and the land for the refinery on Abadan island. Just as importantly, the Shaykh provided security for the entire operation in return for a retainer. When the British government bought 51 percent of the Anglo-Persian Oil Company in the summer of 1914 and gained controlling interest in the company, Persia willy-nilly found that a foreign nation was in control of its most important financial asset.

3

In Peril of Disintegration

HISTORICAN TIMELINE

1882 ⇛ British bombarded Alexandria, Egypt on July 13.
⇛ British defeated the Egyptians at Tel al-Kebir on September 13.
⇛ Dr. Leon Pinsker published *Self-Emancipation*, an important first step in the development of the Zionist movement.
⇛ Seven thousand Jews departed Russia for Palestine—First *Aliyeh*.
⇛ Ben Yehudah (Eliezer Perlmann) migrated to Palestine.

1883 ⇛ Midhat Pasha died by strangulation in Yemen.

1885 ⇛ Stefan Stambulove's coup in East Rumelia led to annexation to Bulgaria.

1887 ⇛ The Ottoman Society of Union and Progress was founded at the Medical College.

1888 ⇛ Germans obtained railroad concession in the Ottoman Empire October 6.
⇛ Istanbul Convention agreed that all naval and merchant vessels of all nations could use the Suez Canal at all times.

1890 ⇛ Major Gerald Talbot, an English citizen, received a fifty-year concession on the entire tobacco industry of Persia on March 8.
⇛ Armenian terrorists' attacks on Ottoman targets began in eastern Anatolia.

1891 ⇛ Persians boycotted the use of all tobacco. There was violent opposition in December against the tobacco concession. The Shah agreed to end the concession in December.

1892 ⇛ Khedive Tewfik of Egypt died on January 7. His son, Abbas Hilmi III, became khedive.
⇛ On February 2, Ayatollah Shirazi, the leading Shiah divine of the time demanded the "eternal abolition" of all concessions to foreigners.

1893 ⇛ Complicated and secret negotiations ended in an agreement on March 25, whereby all Imperial Tobacco Corporation assets became the property of the Persian government with stipulations to sell all tobacco to a French firm. The French firm, in turn, had a binding obligation to sell to the original British company.

1895 ⇛ Abortive coup against Sultan Abdul Hamid II by Ottoman Society of Union and Progress.

1896 ⇛ There was a Greek revolt in Crete in February.
⇛ Greece sent troops into Crete and Macedonia.
⇛ Nasir al-Din was assassinated on May 1 by Mirza Muhammad Kirmani, a disciple of Jamal al-Din al-Afghani.
⇛ Reign of Shah Muzaffar al-Din in Persia, 1896–1907.
⇛ Peak of Armenian terrorism; the capital was attacked and the Ottoman Bank seized on August 26.
⇛ Attempted assassination of Sultan Abdul Hamid II.
⇛ General Kitchener defeated the Madhi in Sudan and attached Sudan to Egypt.
⇛ Theodor Herzl published *The Jewish State*, which increased the popularity of Zionism in Western Europe.

1897 ⇛ First Zionist Congress was held in Basel, Switzerland during August.
⇛ Sultan Abdul Hamid II instituted a two-fold plan of repression and reconciliation toward the Young Turks.
⇛ Muhammad Rashid Rida travelled from Syria to Egypt to play an important role in pan-Islamic activities. He enhanced Arab nationalism by insisting on the need for an Arab caliph.

1898 ⇛ Abd al-Rahman al-Kawakibi moved from Syria to Egypt where he began to write and speak on behalf of the need for an Arab caliph.

1899 ⇛ Germans received permission to build a railway to Baghdad on November 25.
⇛ France agreed to British control of Sudan following peaceful resolution of Fashoda Incident.

1900 ⇛ Russian Central Bank made a large loan to Persia that was indicative of Russia's hold on Persia's economic and political affairs.
⇛ University of Istanbul opened.

1901 ⇛ William Knox D'Arcy, a British subject, obtained a monopoly on May 28 to find and develop petroleum and natural gas in all but the northernmost portion of Persia.
⇛ Damad Mahmud (brother-in-law of the Sultan) and his two sons, Sabah al-Din and Lutfallah, joined the Young Turks.

1901–2 ⇛ Herzl had two personal interviews with the Sultan Abdul Hamid.

1902 ⇛ Abdul Aziz Ibn Saud seized the fortress of Musmak, in the town of Riyadh, on January 15.
⇛ First Young Turk Congress in Paris on February 4.
⇛ British constructed a dam on the Nile at Aswan.

1903 ⇛ Sixth Zionist Congress. Herzl encouraged acceptance of British offer of Uganda as a temporary Jewish home.
⇛ Hijaz railway reached Amman.
⇛ Murzstag Program declared on October 2.

1904 ⇛ Theodor Herzl died at age 45.
⇛ Second *Aliyeh* began; lasted until 1914.

1905–1914 ⇛ Widespread unrest in Persia was associated with the Constitutional Movement.

1905 ⇛ Russia adopted a constitution on October 30.
⇛ Negib Azoury published his *Le Reveil de la Nation Arabe.*
⇛ Conflict with merchants and religious community in Tehran during December ignited the Constitutional Movement.

1906 ⇛ Shah Muzaffar al-Din agreed to most demands of the Persian Constitutionalists on January 13, but retained officials he had promised to dismiss.
⇛ Large-scale *basts* occurred at mosques and at the British legation over a period of several months.
⇛ Shah agreed on September 17 to hold an election for a *majlis.*
⇛ Arthur Balfour was convinced of the need for a Jewish homeland by Chaim Weizmann.
⇛ *Vatan* (Fatherland) Society was founded in the Ottoman Empire.
⇛ Misunderstanding between British officers and Egyptian villagers at Dinshawai created increased ill feelings toward the British in Egypt.
⇛ Muzaffar al-Din and Muhammad Ali of Persia, his designated successor, agreed to the constitution on December 30.

1907-1909 ⇛ Reign of Shah Muhammad Ali of Persia.

1907 ⇛ Sir Eldon Gorst became consul general of Egypt.
⇛ On August 31, Russia and Britain agreed to divide Persia into spheres of influence.
⇛ Shah agreed to supplemental fundamental laws for Persia on October 7.
⇛ Unrest existed at all levels of Persian society as every element

experienced unusual freedom. Central government was able to exercise little authority.

⇛ *Vatan* and Ahmed Riza of the Young Turks joined together and formed the Committee of Union and Progress in the Ottoman Empire.

⇛ Second Congress of Young Turks in Paris during December.

1908 ⇛ Constitutionalists attempted to force the Persian Shah to dismiss all anticonstitutionalist elements from his court.

⇛ Persian leftists attempted to assassinate Shah Muhammad Ali in February.

⇛ Massive gusher in Khuzistan province of Persia at Masjid es-Suleiman on May 26.

⇛ Shah used military force against Majlis on June 23 and dissolved the legislative body.

⇛ Tabriz became the center of constitutional activity after the shah dissolved Majlis. Revolutionaries became more radical in close affiliation with Russian revolutionaries.

⇛ Separatist states with leftist ideologies developed in Azerbaijan and Gilan. Government troops were unable to suppress the movements.

⇛ Young Turk Revolution on July 23; Abdul Hamid II restored the constitution.

⇛ Austria annexed Bosnia and Herzegovina October 6.

⇛ Greek annexation of Crete on October 7.

⇛ Sharif Hussein Al Hashemi became the Turkish governor of the Hijaz.

1909 ⇛ Society of Islamic Unity emerged in the Ottoman Empire during March.

⇛ Muslim students and soldiers stormed the Ottoman parliament and forced the cabinet to resign on April 13. (Islamic Counterrevolution to the Young Turk Revolution.)

⇛ The Anglo-Persian Oil Company took over D'Arcy's concession on April 14.

⇛ Russian troops took control of the Persian city of Tabriz on April 20.

⇛ Ottoman Army marched on Istanbul and deposed Adbul Hamid II on April 24. Mehmed V became Sultan to end the Islamic Counterrevolution.

⇛ Young Turks were fully in power after suppression of the Counterrevolution.

⇛ Persian tribal troops and constitutionalists forced Shah Muhammad Ali to abdicate on July 13.

⇛ Shah Ahmad of Persia (1909–1925) was twelve years old when he assumed the title. Abd al-Qasim was regent until Ahmad assumed full powers of his position on July 21, 1914.

⇛ Dissension among Persian constitutionalists led to many assassinations and inability to govern throughout 1909 and 1910.

⇛ Formation of the Literary Club and *Al-Qahtanyyia*, two important movements in the early development of Arab nationalism.

1910 ⇛ Albanian uprising against Ottoman rule from April to June.

1911 ⇛ The Persian constitutional government hired Morgan Shuster, an American, as treasurer-general in May. Shuster proved efficient and unwavering in his duty to Persia as a national unit.

⇛ Muhammad Ali invaded from Russia on July 11 in an attempt to regain his throne. He received little support and was defeated by October.

⇛ Lord Kitchener replaced Gorst as high commissioner of Egypt.

⇛ Italy attacked Libya on September 29 and formally annexed it on November 4.

⇛ The British and the Russians asserted themselves more strongly beginning in November. Russian pressure caused dismissal of Shuster on December 25 and extracted a promise from the Persians not to hire foreigners without Russian approval.

⇛ This Russian interference essentially ended the constitutional experiment, but support of constitutional government continued to be as strong as before the suppression.

⇛ Formation of *Al-Fatat*, a leading organization in developing Arab nationalism.

⇛ British government signed exclusive oil concession with shaykh of Bahrain.

1912 ⇛ Formation of the Ottoman Party for Administrative Decentralization in Cairo and the Reform Committee in Beirut, two important organizations that shaped Arab nationalism.

⇛ First Balkan War began on October 18.

⇛ Albania declared its independence on November 28.

⇛ Negotiations to end the Balkan War began in London on December 16.

1912–1913 ⇛ There was effectively no central authority or executive as the British and Russians ruled much of Persia. The regent fled to Europe in May 1912 and Ahmad did not begin to function as the monarch until July 21, 1914.

1913 ⇛ Enver Bey led attack on the Porte on January 23 to reassert CUP control of the Ottoman Empire.

⇛ Treaty of London on June 10 ended the First Balkan War.

⇛ Arab Congress convened in Paris on June 18 to discuss grievances with the Ottoman government.

⇛ Second Balkan War began on June 29.

⇛ Treaty of Bucharest on August 10 ended the Second Balkan War.

⇛ Major Aziz al-Misri formed *Al-Ahd*, composed primarily of Arab officers in the Ottoman army. The secret organization on behalf of Arab nationalism became the model for many later such groups throughout the Middle East.

⇛ General Liman von Sanders gained control of Ottoman Empire military planning in November.
⇛ Kitchener created a legislative assembly for Egypt, which gave new political parties the opportunity to participate in the governing process.
⇛ British government signed an exclusive oil concession with the Shaykh of Kuwait.

Indications were strong that anything approximating continued independence for the Middle Eastern empires would end with the nineteenth century. The Congress of Berlin indicated the level of interest the European nations had in Ottoman affairs and territory. European control of the Public Debt Fund in Egypt obstructed any hope its residents had of managing themselves, even though there was minimal control from Istanbul. Successful public resistance to several major Russian and British projects in Persia in no way reduced the general domination the two foreign powers exercised over Persian affairs. The region's vulnerability only left in question how the European powers would divide the territorial and extraterritorial concessions. Toward the end of the century Germany, Austria, and Italy began to contend for shares in the spoils with the traditional rivals of Russia, Great Britain, and France.

Great Britain seized the initiative and established its physical control of Egypt, which France had dominated culturally for nearly a century. With British consent, France increasingly concentrated its efforts upon northwest Africa. However, France retained a strong interest in the Levant, where it retained a strong cultural and economic presence. Russia benefitted from its linguistic and religious kinship with the Slavic Balkans and the mutual antipathy for the Ottomans it shared with the Armenians. In addition, the economic dependence of northern Persia upon Russia provided Russia with opportunities to influence Persia that no other nation could rival. Great Britain's concern regarding Russia's success in Persia provided constant tension among all the parties and the prospect of war between the two European states. While the Germans continued to manifest no interest in Middle Eastern territory, their increased involvement in Ottoman financial affairs, infrastructure development, and military preparedness alarmed the other Europeans. The Ottoman Empire, Russia, and the Balkan provinces were equally uncomfortable with Austria's unabashed efforts to expand into the Ottoman Balkan area. The prospects were good, however, that Austria would persist on that course because of its inability to expand elsewhere in an era of general European expansion. Likewise, Italy's marginal ability and strong appetite for empire made Ottoman islands and Libya its best hope for aggrandizement. Even Greece looked for the opportunity to acquire Ottoman lands, not only in the Aegean Sea, but on the mainland of western Anatolia.

Ottoman and Persian resentment of all forms of European aggression caused considerable internal turmoil, which abetted European efforts as much as it discouraged them. This reaction was not as pronounced in Egypt, where a nearly universal agreement that Great Britain was the cause of all problems deterred Egyptians from addressing issues that transcended the British presence. Intellectual support for constitutions in the Ottoman Empire and Persia succeeded in establishing constitutional governments based upon secular European principals. Widespread early elation soon led to the dictatorship of a small element within the Ottoman Empire and disarray in Persia. Europeans and dissident elements within each empire seemed to be the primary beneficiaries of the constitutional experiments. An unbridled secularism soon prevailed in the Ottoman government and Persia lapsed into anarchy.

A seemingly unrelated nationalist movement among the Jews of the Russian Empire paralleled these developments in the Middle East. Intensified persecution in Russia and apprehension about their newly obtained rights in Western Europe imbued some Jews with the desire to reestablish a Jewish state in Palestine. Like similar nationalist movements of that era, Zionist appeal spread to enough Jews throughout Europe to establish a solid organizational and financial foundation. Strong as the movement became it remained powerless to fulfill its goals unless Ottoman authorities extended them an unlikely invitation or one of the powerful European states adopted their cause and provided the Zionists a military force. Fortunately for them, the British established a physical presence in Egypt about the same time the Zionist movement began in Russia. This would prove to be the opportunity for Zionists to join the European Powers in obtaining concessions and land in the troubled Middle East.

While the ancient empires endured to the end of the nineteenth century, their plight was fatal early in the twentieth. Austria, Italy, and Greece fulfilled many of their territorial aspirations at Ottoman expense. Russian client-states emerged in the Balkans and the Armenians enjoyed Russian assistance in their quest for independence in eastern Anatolia. Great Britain continued its occupation of Egypt and Cyprus. Russia and Great Britain avoided war through an agreement to recognize each other's right to control the most viable parts of Persia. In the face of these developments Ottoman leaders forsook their amelioratory Ottoman outlook and adopted a strong Turkish identity that threatened to alienate all non-Turkish elements within their realm. The Persians fought essentially meaningless battles among themselves, since they were unable to confront their European occupiers. The Zionists waited, in case the massive reshuffle of the Middle East would result in land for them to escape centuries of European mistreatment.

BRITISH OCCUPATION OF EGYPT

The reinstatement of the hated European-dominated cabinet under Tewfik accelerated Egyptian opposition under the leadership of Muhammad Abduh, the noted advocate of Islamic revival, and Colonel Ahmad Arabi. Arabi, one of the few Egyptian officers to rise from the peasant class, became the catalyst around which other elements in Egypt expressed their pronounced nationalist aspirations. With strong support from the Assembly, and from the population in general, he influenced Tewfik to establish an Egyptian nationalist cabinet in September 1881. He assigned himself the job of war minister. In anticipation of foreign military intervention, he moved troops to the Mediterranean coast and began to construct defensive barricades.

These developments in Egypt occurred at a time of considerable international ferment. The Europeans were about to impose the Ottoman Public Debt Administration upon the bankrupt empire; Bismarck was forming both the Triple Alliance and the Three Emperor's League; France and Italy were in contention over their conflicting aspirations in Tunisia; France, which had the most to lose from the developments in Egypt, feared that the British would use the crisis to replace

French ascendancy in Egypt. Also, strong elements in both Great Britain and France opposed further imperial expansion.

Too much was at stake in Egypt, however, to allow an unsatisfactory solution for the European governments and investors. European ambassadors met in Istanbul to urge the Sultan to arbitrate or impose his own solution. His efforts failed. British and French ships patrolling off the Egyptian coast incited violent attacks against Europeans and their property. British ships responded with a bombardment of Alexandria on July 13, 1882. Concern for the property and lives of Europeans provided the excuse for a British invasion. Great Britain launched a military invasion that France refused to join because of antiimperialist sentiments in the Chamber of Deputies. British troops secured Alexandria and won a decisive battle against the Egyptian army northeast of Cairo at Tel al-Kebir on September 13. Cairo fell four days later and the British proceeded to occupy all other important population centers, especially along the Suez Canal. This supposedly temporary occupation to accomplish specific, limited goals lasted until 1956. Elimination of British control dominated Egyptian domestic and international policies and aspirations during that entire period.

Derek Hopwood's observation that "Egypt gained independence too early" alludes to its obtaining greater freedom sooner than any other Arab part of the Ottoman Empire. Despite its early development, Egypt's freedom allowed it to acquire independent indebtedness that delivered it into British domination other Arab areas were able to avoid until after World War I. In addition, Britain's unilateral hold on Egypt freed it from League of Nations guidelines and provisions for eventual independence other Arab areas, except Palestine, enjoyed.

BRITISH RULE IN EGYPT

The British expressed no intention of remaining in Egypt and they never received formal authority from either their own government or any international body to justify their occupation. Their domination of the Egyptian Public Debt Fund, which protected the interests of multinational financial and political concerns, provided any authorization they enjoyed. Otherwise, Britain's ranking diplomat, who took the titles of British Agent and Consul-General, was simply first among equals with other foreign diplomats. A succession of three British holders of these titles, in fact, became the chief executive of Egypt, although a formal Egyptian government remained in place from the Khedive down through village administrators. For the first few years the French continued to sully British hegemony, but French capacity to be a factor subsided after Egypt obtained financial solvency in 1890, the French were no longer a factor. A peaceful Anglo-French settlement in 1899 of their differences over the Sudan, followed soon thereafter by the Entente Cordiale in 1904, removed even France as a restraint on British domination.

Lord Dufferin, one of Britain's most capable diplomats and administrators, left his post as ambassador in Istanbul for seven months following the British invasion of Egypt. He intended to establish an administrative, financial, and judicial structure that would eliminate the need for continued British control. The combination of Gladstone's antiexpansion attitudes, along with constitutional sentiments in England, were too strong to endorse a blatant extension of British authority over Egypt unless it served the higher purposes of establishing participatory government, humanitarian rights, and economic development.

Dufferin's structure seemed to meet these goals. Under his influence Tewfik created provincial councils, a Legislative Council to consider all nationwide laws, and an eighty-member General Assembly, composed of the cabinet, the Legislative Council, and provincial representatives, which had the right to vote on all new direct taxes. The Assembly, however, had no legislative authority beyond this important, but limited, function. Dufferin began a process of clarifying the complicated court and legal system composed of different foreign and domestic approaches to jurisprudence. His attention to Egypt's need for greater agricultural production initiated extensive irrigation projects that helped restore national solvency within a few years. A reduction of the number of British soldiers and plans for replacing them with Egyptian soldiers under a British *Sirdar*, or commander in chief, was another important attempt to soften the humiliation of foreign occupation.

Sir Evelyn Baring, who with his French counterpart had dictated Egyptian financial policy from the inception of the Debt Fund, returned after having fled during the Arab insurrection. This first British Agent and Consul-General was hardly benign in implementing Lord Dufferin's constructive policies. A convinced imperialist, he sternly resisted Egyptian and French efforts to thwart his decisive acquisition of control over every important element of Egyptian government and policies. His obvious neglect of education in Egypt resulted from his approach that could only use Egyptians in positions where a secondary education was adequate. The existing schools could more than fulfill those needs. His authoritarian approach got results. Perhaps his permission for a free press to continue in Egypt reflected a disdain for any serious threat it could generate against continued British control. The one notable failure during his first decade as Consul General was the Mahdi's dramatic destruction of Gordon and his army in Khartoum in 1885. In Egypt order prevailed, administrative and financial integrity improved, and increased agricultural production portended a return to solvency by the late 1880s. Great Britain had, it seemed, fulfilled its original reasons for invading and occupying Egypt.

International discussions to achieve British withdrawal failed because of British insistence on maintaining a strong presence in Egypt, especially in the Suez Canal region. Gladstone was out of office in 1886 and his successors were deeply involved in competition with France over supremacy in Africa and were committed to achieving a "Cape-to-Cairo" control over that continent. Britain's agreement to allow all nations to use the canal in the Istanbul Convention of 1888 was the only concession it was willing to make to its hold on Egypt. For all practical purposes Egypt had evolved into a British colony.

THE ABBAS CHALLENGE

Tewfik's sudden death in January 1892 brought his eighteen-year-old pro-French son, Abbas Hilmi III, to power. The previous tranquility ended as the young khedive attempted to choose his own ministers and pursue a course independent of Baring, who became Lord Cromer in 1892. Abbas encouraged the nationalists, who were becoming both more numerous and more outspoken. Pan-Islamic disciples of Jamal al-Din al-Afghani, followers of the Egyptian Islamic nationalist leadership of Muhammad Abduh and Ali Yusuf, and the advocates of Mustafa Kamil's secular nationalism received inspiration and encouragement from Abbas. Egyptian speeches, articles, and meetings were little more than a nuisance without widespread popular and army support. Also, Abbas soon perceived that he had to restrain outward association with the nationalists as Cromer had the influence and power to depose him.

The frustrated nationalists witnessed the increase in British strength. General Kitchener vanquished the Mahdi in 1896 and attached Sudan to Egypt with French approval in 1899. France, in fact, seemed to become a more willing accessory to British control at that point, as they prepared to take firmer control over their own portions of Arab-speaking Africa. The British had demonstrated how decisively they could intimidate the Ottoman government when they prevented the Sultan from separating Taba, in northeastern Sinai, from Egyptian jurisdiction in 1906.

An unfortunate and unpredictable accident aroused the fairly docile Egyptian population to join the nationalist movement in May 1906. British officers accidentally killed an Egyptian woman during a heated dispute they had with villagers while hunting pigeons at Dinshawai which is near the central delta town of Tanta. An officer and another villager died before the fracas ended. The severity of the punishment a special tribunal meted out to the villagers elevated the incident to national and international notoriety. Twelve villagers received prison sentences, two of which were for life and the others from one-to-fifteen years. Eight were publicly flogged. Four were hanged. The punishments seemed to indicate the disparity between the British and their Egyptian collaborators' perception of the comparative value of British and Egyptian lives. Outrage among some in England, even in Parliament, and in other parts of Europe, nearly matched the almost universal outrage in Egypt. Many more Egyptians began to speak or endorse Mustafa Kamil's *al-Watani* (Nationalist) party's slogan of "Egypt for the Egyptians." The patient Egyptians would require considerably more provocation and vigorous leadership to translate their frustrations into overt action against their Egyptian and British masters. There is no way of knowing how many others found direction, like Anwar Sadat, for their lives in desire to revenge the Dinshawai Affair.

Sir Eldon Gorst, who had earlier served eighteen years in Egypt, replaced Cromer in 1907 and attempted to deal more gently with the Egyptians. By taking Abbas into his confidence he helped remove the khedive as a rallying point for dissension. He lost the support of some elements who did not desire the centralization of power in the palace. He never found the right combination of Egyptian partners either to forge a workable government or to satisfy the politically active opposition before he died in 1911.

Lord Kitchener, a former *Sirdar* who had defeated the Mahdi, assumed control in a manner reminiscent of Cromer. The international situation determined that his tenure could not be one of business as usual. War, and portents of war, filled the region. The Second Moroccan Crisis occurred in midyear; Italy invaded Libya immediately west of Egypt in September; civil war and a Russian invasion plagued Persia; the Balkan states were working out their final alliances in preparation for their impending war with the Ottoman Empire; Germany and Great Britain were at loggerheads over naval strength and the Berlin to Baghdad railway; and Armenian nationalism threatened the very heart of Anatolia. While maintaining a firm grip, Kitchener made some overtures to remedy economic hardship and the yearning of Egyptians to participate in government. A law, for instance, prevented foreclosure on the smallest landowners that would leave them landless and totally devoid of livestock. He created a Legislative Assembly in 1913 in which the newly developed political parties could actually function in the legislative process. Under the dynamic leadership of Saad Zaghlul of Muhammad Abduh's People's Party, this new body proved more of a force in Egyptian nationalist sentiments and political process than either Abbas or Kitchener expected. While most of the elected legislators were nationalists, as landowners they were neither radical nor revolutionary. They did, however, make constitutional government with Kitchener's hand-picked cabinets virtually impossible. Their election of Zaghlul as presiding officer assured the continuation of this impasse before their summer recess began in June 1914 and the khedive went to Istanbul for his vacation.

With the outbreak of World War I Kitchener left Egypt to serve as British War Minister. The British would not let Abbas return and replaced him with his uncle Hussein Kamil, whom they gave the new title of Sultan. These actions formally ended the affiliation between Egypt and the Ottoman Empire. Great Britain declared war on the Ottoman Empire on November 5 and declared a protectorate over Egypt on December 18. After thirty-two years of occupation, Great Britain finally had a formal framework for its control over Egypt. It ruled Egypt under martial law throughout the war, so Zaghlul and the Legislative Assembly would have to wait until after the war to determine whether there was substance to the new constitutional structure.

THE REIGN OF ABDUL HAMID II

Abdul Hamid II, the son of Abdul Mejid and the nephew of Abdul Aziz, was thirty-four years old when he succeeded his mentally ill brother, Murat V, in 1876. He was better prepared and better informed about Ottoman affairs than most of his predecessors when he assumed the throne. His previous attitude and behavior indicated that he was not particularly disposed to despotism by either nature or conviction. But the misbehavior of parliament and the rebellious posture of the non-Muslim minorities during the Russo-Turkish war convinced him to assert a strong, personal hand.

Although he did not call parliament for thirty years, he never officially abrogated the constitution and, in fact, selectively utilized some of its provisions in his years of personal rule. His use of the Tanzimat infrastructure for his autocratic rule vindicated the Young Ottomans, who had opposed it for that potential soon after its implementation. Until his later years he personally monitored even small details of imperial administration. Little, therefore, occurred without his personal approval. Power moved from the Porte to the palace, where he and his carefully chosen advisers and administrators kept strict control over formulating and executing policies. The capacity of his police and spies to keep him informed created a justifiable apprehension among both his subjects and his officials.

The fate of Midhat Pasha early in Abdul Hamid's reign served as an example to those who opposed his rule. The sultan's disapproval of the Father of the Constitution's handling of the Istanbul Conference led to his dismissal as Grand Vizir, but he remained in the sultan's employment as governor of Syria and then in Izmir. Midhat Pasha's persistent advocacy of the full restoration of constitutional government, however, led to his trial in 1881 and imprisonment in remote Taif, where he was mysteriously strangled two years later. Midhat Pasha's fate and common references to the "despotism" of Abdul Hamid evoke an unfounded image of bloodthirstiness, because the worst fate most of even his highest rebellious officials suffered was demotion to a post that was somewhat removed from their normal base of power.

Repressive as Abdul Hamid's measures were, his reign spawned an active opposition amidst substantial progress toward modernization. State supported secular schools produced thousands of graduates, who possessed the tools and abilities to both support and criticize the regime. A very active press poured out views that frequently contradicted and criticized official policy, while it also introduced Ottoman subjects to attitudes contrary to internal tranquility. Intellectuals with a full spectrum of views emerged from the educational system and published their views in every literary form. Both at home and abroad, organized groups developed in opposition to the sultan. Balkan and Armenian dissidents pursued their irredentist courses and sought to carve independent nationalist states from the empire. The regime was not repressive enough to prevent these developments, but it was vigorous enough to provide Ottoman society with many of the facilities of its more modern neighbors.

Said Pasha was Abdul Hamid's foremost administrator, serving as Grand Vizir most of the time from 1878 to 1903, and also as the first Grand Vizir after the Young Turk revolution. His stature kept him involved in important affairs through the various shifts in governments after 1908. His major importance, however, resulted from his role in formulating much of Abdul Hamid's program. Said Pasha and the sultan's other ministers were in a position to approach development realistically after the O.P.D.A. established a bearable means of liquidating the foreign debts. (See above.) The fact that many of the same foreign banking institutions had been involved in a similar process in Tunisia (1869) and in Egypt (1876) accelerated the Ottoman settlement. With finances under control Abdul Hamid began to improve his empire's infrastructure.

OTTOMAN RAILROAD DEVELOPMENT

Railroad construction received special attention because of its economic and military importance. Railroads could integrate the Ottoman economy with Europe and integrate the more developed western part of the empire with the less-developed east. They could improve the overall economy and thereby produce more revenue. Railroads could facilitate the development of eastern Anatolia to accommodate the settlement of Muslims, who were constantly being pushed out of the emerging Christian Balkan states. The empire's deep indebtedness from 1854, as well as a general lack of expertise, had prevented any significant railroad development prior to Abdul Hamid's reign.

The few hundred miles of railroad that existed when he came to power had been built largely with British assistance, and were primarily located west of Istanbul. He initiated a major extension of the empire's railroads on September 27, 1888, a month after the first train arrived in Istanbul from Europe. The concession to construct a line to Ankara went to the Anatolian Railroad Company, which was a consortium created by the Deutsche Bank. The German-dominated company's acquisition of the contract indicated Germany's penetration of Ottoman affairs following the ascension of Kaiser Wilhelm II and the decline of Bismarck's control over German foreign policy.

In Europe, the Deutsche Bank raised the capital to build the railroad and arranged for Ottoman payments through the O.P.D.A.. The Porte's guarantee of a substantial profit made this, and later Ottoman railroad construction, attractive enough to instill envy among other European bidders and to enhance the resentment of foreign governments for Germany's financial and political gains. The line to Ankara understandably prompted the greater ambition of connecting the capital with the Arabian Gulf. When the Anatolian Railroad Company also received the contract to construct the controversial Berlin-to-Baghdad Railway, the Great Powers expressed additional dismay at Germany's growing role in the Ottoman economy. Britain, in particular, was alarmed with the possibility of its new rival, Germany, being able to transport troops all the way to Mesopotamia, and conceivably to the heart of British interests in the Arabian Gulf.

The Porte's awareness of the military potential of the railroad motivated it to accelerate its construction, and to insist that it be strategically located, particularly to place it out of the range of naval bombardment. The new system reached Konya in 1896, by which time local lines had already connected the major cities in Greater Syria. Crucial connections through the mountains between Konya and Syria were not completed by 1914, but the Hijaz Railway already connected Damascus and Medina by that date. The empire's railroad network did not compare favorably with any of those in Europe by 1914; however, the approximately four thousand miles of track represented a major achievement compared to what Abdul Hamid had inherited.

OTHER MODERNIZATION

With the help of British and French technicians, Abdul Hamid was considerably more successful in providing telegraph service for most of his empire. Most of the major population centers had telegraph connections by the end of the century. The sultan quickly realized its importance in providing him rapid information for his autocratic purposes. He did not recognize its potential role as a training center and instrument for communication among conspirators throughout the empire who plotted his removal. The most profound change of Abdul Hamid's reign occurred in education, largely as a result of the priority it received in Said Pasha's overall concept for modernization. He realized both the necessity for an educated citizenry who could understand the concepts and values of a modern state, and the need for educated personnel to perform its many new and complicated functions. Toward this goal, the government created scores of new schools from the primary level to advanced specialized schools in all major professional and administrative fields. After more than a half century of existing on paper and occasionally functioning in a limited capacity, the University of Istanbul finally opened in 1900. The expanded and revitalized educational system, which was built on Tanzimat antecedents, provided the sultan's regime with the educated class he envisioned. The same system, however, produced his strongest critics, who studied European ideas and the forbidden works of the Young Ottomans. His educational system, therefore, became the incubator that nurtured both the desire to restore constitutional government, as well as the individuals who were capable of creating and maintaining such a government.

INTERNAL CRITICS

Educated people developed a thirst for additional knowledge, which the greatly expanded publishing facilities provided, as the number of presses in the capital doubled during Abdul Hamid's reign. Since censorship and suppression of publications were common, the more outspoken critics of Abdul Hamid usually fled to Egypt or Europe, where their writings could be more explicit. Other clever writers developed literary techniques that symbolically conveyed their messages, but also allowed them to remain in the empire and alter public opinion.

Ebuzziya Tevfik, Ahmad Ihsan, and Tevfik Fikret were the most influential writers to stay in the empire and produce works that undermined the regime's credibility. Ebuzziya was a prolific writer, translator, editor, and publisher, whose largely literary and historical works fed the appetite of his readers for topics beyond the empire. Ahmad Ishan began by concentrating on science in his periodical, *Treasury of Science*, but it evolved into the first highly illustrated publication of the empire, and expanded to the fields of art, biography, literature, and fiction. After Tevfik Fikret became the editor of *Treasury of Science*, it attracted the most adroit practitioners of what came to be known as the "New Literature." These writers rejected the trend toward using a simpler style and vocabulary. Instead, they perfected the art of adapting French symbolism into Turkish motifs, which eluded the censors and indirectly transmitted messages that undermined Hamidian values.

These sophisticated writers deprecated the works of Ahmed Midhat, who was one of the most important writers of the Hamidian period by virtue of the volume of his publications and the simplicity of his style. Although he was the son and protégé of Midhat Pasha, his good relationship with the court allowed him to write very openly and reach a much larger audience than the more gifted "New Literature" writers. He was the editor of the official newspaper, *Calendar of Events*, but he became more influential through his own daily, *Translator of Events*, which he founded in 1878. This widely read paper included not only the news, but also published the works of some of the most prominent literary figures of the era. His three-volume history of the world and his fourteen-volume history of European states introduced many readers to developments beyond the Ottoman and Islamic experience. He also wrote thirty-three novels and essays on almost every conceivable subject before the events of 1908 terminated his publishing and writing career.

THE GROWTH OF TURKISH IDENTITY

While much of the publication during the Hamidian period imitated European styles and introduced European subjects, there was also a significant growth in both Pan-Islamic and Pan-Turanist attitudes and literature. The sultan supported the growth of Pan-Islam to enhance his international stature and to counter the fascination with Western ways. European imperialism throughout the Islamic world from the latter part of the nineteenth century stimulated a sense of common bond among Muslims, who had an improved capacity to interact through modern communications.

Abdul Hamid, as caliph, actively sought to acquire leadership over the mutual concerns of the worldwide Muslim *umma*. He experienced French domination over both Tunisia and Algeria after 1881, while Britain dominated the Muslim world from Egypt to India after 1882. There were millions of Muslims in the Russian Empire, while Italy and Greece made covetous, imperialist overtures to acquire predominantly Muslim territory. Other millions of Muslims were trapped in the new, Christian-dominated Balkan states.

Istanbul gradually became the focus for Muslim grievances throughout the Islamic world. Prominent Muslim leaders, whose constituents were threatened, journeyed to Istanbul to consult with the sultan and his advisers. Abdul Hamid encouraged the development of Islamic studies and expanded the range of Islamic subjects taught in the secular schools. He began to replace Christians in the Ottoman administration with Muslim Arabs. By assuming this leadership role, the sultan established a sense of apprehension that harsh treatment of Muslims anywhere could cause unfavorable reaction everywhere in the Islamic world. He was, thereby, in a position to reciprocate the long-standing criticism European society had leveled against Ottoman treatment of Christians under its jurisdiction.

The growth of Pan-Turanism, however, was contrary to the concept of Ottomanism that the sultan and others who wanted to retain the empire cultivated. They had no desire to foster attitudes in any group that would accent ethnic differences and tear the empire apart. Still, a heightened awareness of a separate Turkish identity grew steadily and references to "Turks" and "Turkish" became widely used in the Ottoman press, sometimes interchangeably with Ottoman.

Turks, traditionally, had little sense of Turkish identity as they had so fully identified with the brotherhood of Islam. For Turks, all people were either Muslims or *dhimmis*. But the loss of most Christian segments of the empire, and awareness of the scholarly works of foreigners on the origins of the Turkish peoples and their language combined to create a strong sense of Turkish pride and identity in the last half of the nineteenth century.

Foreign scholars helped arouse Turkish nationalism, much as German writers had influenced the growth of Pan-Slavism some decades earlier. Native Ottoman scholars built upon the foreigners' foundation to produce their own works. Shemsettin Sami, an Albanian, utilized foreign works as inspiration for his extensive, original research into the development of the origins of the Turkish language, customs, and names, which he published in influential dictionaries and histories. His publications, as well as those of later Turkish scholars, cultivated Turkish nationalism, which instilled fraternity and a working relationship among peoples of Turkish lineage all across Asia.

PROBLEMS IN THE BALKANS

Developments within the empire encouraged the growth of Turkish nationalism as much as the scholarly Pan-Turanists. Problems with the Balkans in the west and with the Armenians in the east invited the continued interference of the Christian Powers, and led to a growing attitude among the Turks that Christian subjects would never submit to even the highest ideals of Ottomanist cooperation. While the Congress of Berlin had prevented a war among the Great Powers, the Balkan states continued to nurture grievances.

Greece and Serbia each harbored desires to annex East Rumelia. However, contrary to the Berlin agreement, Bulgaria got the impression that the Powers would allow Bulgaria to annex this area. Clearly, Bulgaria was best situated to absorb East Rumelia, and had the additional advantage of considerable support for such action within the province itself. In September 1885, a coup led by Stefan Stambulov took control and offered East Rumelia to Prince Alexander of Bulgaria. The Great Powers did not intercede with this alteration of the Berlin agreement. Bulgaria, thus, annexed East Rumelia, although later negotiations retained a facade of Ottoman suzerainty over the lost province.

Greece never tired of claiming the historical right to extend its borders to conform with those of the ancient Byzantine Empire, including Istanbul. It was, therefore, dissatisfied with its paltry acquisitions at Berlin. Greece used the situation in Crete to keep its ambitions before the court of international Great Power politics. When a revolt broke out among the Greek population of Crete in 1897, Greece landed 10,000 troops and ignited a short war with the Ottoman Empire. Greece also invaded Macedonia, where it suffered a decisive defeat against an Ottoman army. The Great Powers, however, interfered on behalf of Greece and coerced the Porte to grant Crete autonomy in a manner that essentially made it part of Greece. Greece openly annexed the island in 1908, during the confusion that followed the Young Turk revolution.

The strategically important and agriculturally rich Ottoman area of Macedonia was the yet-unclaimed portion of the Balkan peninsula, which all the Balkan states coveted. It became an even greater hotbed once radical groups within the province violently attempted to win its independence from Ottoman control and establish a separate nation. Great-Power pressure forced the Porte to implement changes to prevent further problems from either the rebels or the Balkan states. Russia and Austria seized the opportunity, however, to impose the Murzsteg program in early October 1903, whereby Russian and Austrian officials supervised their own reform system in abject violation of Ottoman sovereignty. This was only a temporary solution to the problem until the Balkan states could find an opportunity to alter it to their satisfaction.

ARMENIA IN REVOLT

Nationalism spread to the Armenians, just as it did to most other Christian groups within the empire in the late nineteenth century. Historically, Armenians had lived rather tranquilly in the empire. Many of them had risen to positions of high prominence in the government, and many more had prospered in commerce, finance, and all phases of business and the crafts. Their status generally increased after the Greek revolution engendered suspicion and resentment toward Greeks, who often competed with Armenians for the same positions.

But the Russo-Turkish war of 1877 altered their own good reputation, since some Armenians openly supported the Russian invaders. An Armenian delegation had also attended the Congress of Berlin in pursuit of a separate Armenian state. Ottoman officials never trusted Armenians after that time, although some of Abdul Hamid's most trusted confidants were Armenian. The rebellious elements did not trust their kinsmen who remained loyal to the sultan, and dismissed such allegiance as indicating a lack of principles and personal greed for gain.

Russian Armenians also played a significant role in fanning Armenian nationalism within the Ottoman Empire. In the 1880s they assisted in motivating, financing, and training their Ottoman brethren. The nationalists sought conflict with Ottoman authorities, which would initiate repression and win other Armenians to their movement, as well as call worldwide attention to their cause.

The Armenian rebels from both sides of the border aggravated the eastern Anatolian provinces with terrorist attacks beginning in 1890. Ottoman reprisals gained great attention in the western media, similar to earlier stories about Ottoman atrocities toward Greeks and Bulgarians. Their activities reached a peak in the summer of 1896, when they launched their attacks in the capital itself to gain the highest possible visibility. Armenian groups took over the Ottoman Bank, used armed force to enter the main offices of the Porte, and on another occasion attempted to assassinate Abdul Hamid.

Demands from the West were uniformly on behalf of the Armenians, but the sultan was able to delay implementing any actions, except for appointing more Christian officials in areas of high Armenian population concentration. Since most Armenians did not rally to the rebels' call for revolt, the movement died out by 1897. This violent flare-up, however, and the continued advocacy for a separate Armenian state from activists abroad, instilled a fear in many Ottoman officials that the Armenians were a dangerous Fifth Column, which would welcome any future Russian invasions into eastern Anatolia.

YOUNG TURKS

Ottoman dissidents, who wanted to preserve the empire as urgently as the Armenian rebels wanted to leave it, also caused Abdul Hamid's government trouble by the 1890s. By then the expanded educational system, the extensive and active press, as well as considerable progress toward modernization, had the undesired effect of mobilizing many disillusioned junior officers and officials, as well as other youths, into active opposition to Abdul Hamid's regime. The diverse views among them prevented consistent cooperation, but they all shared a belief in the necessity of restoring constitutional government. Most of their leaders also had in common a voluntary or involuntary exile in Europe. The dissidents abroad remained nothing more than a troublesome nuisance for Abdul Hamid, until a sufficient number of like-minded individuals stayed within the empire to enact the changes they envisioned.

While these new activists received much of their inspiration from the writings of the earlier Young Ottomans, they were more inclined than their predecessors to move beyond criticism into overt political action. They patterned their activities after the nationalist Young Italy and Young German movements and came to be known as the Young Turks. The movement evolved slowly through the entire educational system, but it crystallized among five students in the Medical College. These five individuals formed the Ottoman Society of Union and Progress in 1887. The society soon grew in membership, particularly among teachers, students, army officers, and minor officials. It also developed chapters in the heavily populated regions in the western part of the empire.

Restoration of the constitution and the deposition of Abdul Hamid were the society's foremost demands. Its suspected affiliation, therefore, with an abortive coup against the sultan in 1895 impelled many members to flee to Europe, where most joined the already established groups of either Ahmed Riza or Mehmed Murat.

Ahmed Riza, who was independently wealthy, gave up a promising career in the Ministry of Education and went to France, where he became a devotee of the Positivist movement. His bimonthly newspaper, *Meshveret* (Consultation), became the principal organ for transmitting Young Turk views on the Comtian approach to systematic change back home. Ahmed Riza and his followers did not advocate radical demarcation from the past. They staunchly supported the continuation of a centralized empire, but under constitutional governance.

Mehmed Murat, better known as Murat Bey or Mizanci, was a Russian refugee of Turkish lineage, who had held prominent positions in the government before fleeing to Egypt and then to Geneva. He gained a considerable following in both places, and his newspaper, *Mizan* (Balance), became more popular than *Meshveret*. Mehmed Murat also helped start another influential Young Turk newspaper, *Osmanli*, in Geneva.

The activities of the Young Turks moved Abdul Hamid to make a two-fold counterattack of both repression and reconciliation in 1897. A special court convicted many Young Turks, who were sent to prison in Libya. Simultaneously, Abdul Hamid sent a trusted secret police officer to Europe with an offer of amnesty and government employment to dissidents there, if they were willing to recant their antigovernment activities. Mehmed Murat accepted the sultan's offer in return for a position on the Council of State, while some others acceded to lesser inducements. These defections threw the already fragmented movement into pronounced disillusionment and disarray.

The Young Turks received an unexpected boost, however, in 1901 when the sultan's brother-in-law, Damad Mahmud, along with his two sons, Sabah al-Din and Lutfullah, defected to Paris to join Ahmed Riza. Prince Sabah al-Din soon became the leader of the most radical branch of the Young Turks in Europe and established his own society and newspaper. He advocated a decentralized empire, with each region and ethnic group having autonomy over its own affairs. He further approved both violent actions and foreign interference to overthrow Abdul Hamid and implement the society of his vision. In a search for unity, he convened a general congress of all Young Turks in Paris in February 1902, but it accentuated their differences, rather than drawing them together. Ahmed Riza and his followers could not support the decentralization Sabah al-Din advocated; the nationalist minorities had moved beyond accepting their continuation in the Ottoman Empire, even under constitutional rule.

The lack of unity persisted, as did the growth of new societies. The most important was *Vatan* (Fatherland), which developed in 1906 among young army officers in the Fifth Army in Greater Syria. A young lieutenant named Mustafa Kemal participated in its formation, and in establishing a new branch in the Third Army in Salonica, which was much closer to the center of Ottoman power. The officers and some bureaucrats who joined the Fatherland society, shared many of the Young Turks' concerns, but they had the more immediate problem of lack of pay and inadequate arms. They saw the empire disintegrating into separate nationalist enclaves and states under the leadership of an incompetent autocrat. It seemed to them that Abdul Hamid's growing concern for dissident groups and for his own personal safety rendered him ineffective. Since their views were similar to those of Ahmed Riza, they joined him to form the Committee of Union and Progress in 1907.

A second Young Turk congress met in Paris in December 1907, under the sponsorship of both Sabah al-Din and Ahmed Riza. The prominent role of the

Armenians in planning and conducting this congress guaranteed that it would be more radical than the previous congress. The demand of the European exiles indicated that their mood had become more militant. Their mutual resentment of the regime even resulted in an initial demonstration of unity. Ahmed Riza and his followers originally supported their resolutions, which called for the deposition of Abdul Hamid and a restoration of the constitution. They also endorsed the use of violence, strikes, nonpayment of taxes, and any other means of coercion, to save their fatherland from Hamidian despotism.

THE YOUNG TURK REVOLUTION

Congresses, debates, and newspapers in Europe could only strike glancing blows at best, and their participants remained safe from retaliation. Conceptional utterances and actual developments, however, had created a strong inclination toward revolution within the empire, especially in Macedonia. The unpaid officers and bureaucrats had swelled the ranks of the Committee of Union and Progress (CUP), which also found widespread support in the general population for a change in the government. Local resolutions for the restoration of the constitution poured into Istanbul, along with overt threats of forceful implementation if necessary. The sultan sent investigators to ferret out the instigators, but his factfinders met with violence or death.

Enver Bey and other officers took to the mountains in open mutiny and invited others to join them. Finally, the Third Army threatened to march on the capital, but Abdul Hamid curtailed this measure by reinstating the constitution on July 23, 1908. While there had been some bloodshed and a great deal of noise prior to the sultan's announcement, the so-called Young Turk Revolution was one of the least violent popular revolutions on record.

THE YOUNG TURKS IN POWER

Restoration of the constitution in the Ottoman Empire in 1908 seemed to be following the vogue, as Russia had adopted a constitution in 1905 and Persia had adopted one in 1906. Its restoration, however, after thirty years of arbitrary rule raised expectations beyond any government's ability to satisfy. However, most of the groups had not developed their ideology beyond restoring the constitution. Members of all ethnic and religious groups celebrated their new emancipation with each other in the streets, as if their past bitterness and conflict had only stemmed from a single malevolent individual, whose strength the constitution had vanquished. All groups expected the return of constitutional government to rectify their innately contradictory goals. It could not. The new freedoms under the constitution only allowed a fuller, more open discussion and the exacerbation of their differences. The low profile of the CUP in the immediate aftermath of the revolution also obscured the fact that the army had made the revolution, and that it alone possessed the capability to determine its future direction.

Abdul Hamid retained his throne. After all, he had originally issued the constitution and had ultimately realized the efficacy of reinstating it. Within a week, he demonstrated even more good intentions by abolishing the secret police and extending liberties that the constitution had never allowed. Soon thereafter his government expressed its intention to remedy all the major problems of the realm, including the abolition of the capitulations and an alteration of laws and judicial procedures to facilitate the elimination of the millets. A plethora of new laws, arrived at through the old legislative process, addressed the most pressing problems. Austerity measures were adopted in an effort to provide for the continuation of government services and also to pay the military personnel and government bureaucrats.

Elections for a new parliament were set for November in an atmosphere of open debate and journalistic freedom, which only apprehension regarding the true intentions of CUP dampened. The new Union Party, which was the CUP in disguise, campaigned on the broad nationalist platform of Mehmed Riza. It also stressed the need for economic development, personal liberty, and fairness. Its limited opposition came primarily from Prince Sabah al-Din's Liberal Union party, which continued his advocacy of decentralization.

Seats in the new parliament had been assigned according to the population ratios of the different millets within the empire. Only the Arabs were underrepresented, but they were neither technically a different millet nor had they yet managed to assert their separate identity as strongly as the other ethnic groups. The 147 Turkish representatives gave them a majority in the parliament, which also contained 60 Arabs, 27 Albanians, 26 Greeks, 14 Armenians, 4 Jews, 5 Bulgars, 4 Serbs, and 1 Vlach. The Greeks and the Armenians openly claimed that they were underrepresented in the parliament; politically aware Arabs felt their numbers were too few, since there were a third more Arabs than Turks in the empire.

The Union party dominated the new parliament, holding all but the single seat that the Liberal Union obtained. But neither the parliament nor the constitution prevailed. Even with the Union party in control, Ottomanism and cooperation perished as the minorities' representatives, especially the Greeks and Armenians, pressed for separation from the empire.

THE TRADITIONALIST COUNTERREVOLUTION

The threat to parliamentary government arose from conflicting visions of the empire that spanned the entire religious and political spectrum. Muslim traditionalists were the largest and most united element, and they had the additional advantage of widespread mass appeal, especially in Istanbul. Constitutional government, with its secularism and Christian participation, also threatened their lives and visions of the empire more than it challenged that of any other group. To Muslim traditionalists, the liberties of non-Muslims under constitutional government were purchased with an infringement of Muslim values.

Members of the ulama and the religious brotherhoods agitated openly and vigorously against the secularism of the constitution and the Union party. Muslim rallies attracted mass support and a crucial following within the First Army, which was stationed in the capital. By March 1909 the movement developed into the Society of Islamic Unity, which, in cooperation with the Liberal Union party, demanded the end of the secularization under the Unionists. On April 13, 1909 a mob composed mainly of soldiers and religious students stormed into the parliament, killing two members and forcing the cabinet's resignation. The sultan accepted the demands of the counterrevolutionaries and appointed a new cabinet acceptable to the Islamic traditionalists.

The violent change in government corresponded with a major Armenian uprising in southeastern Anatolia. The combination of these events moved officers of the Third Army in Salonica to form an army to march on the capital. The army reached the capital on April 24, after having met in route with members of the parliament and former cabinet members two days earlier. After brief resistance, the counterrevolutionaries folded before the army, which reconvened parliament and deposed Abdul Hamid. His brother, Mehmed V, became sultan and Abdul Hamid was quickly moved to Salonica under the custody of the Third Army.

C.U.P. DICTATORSHIP AND MINORITY UNREST

After suppression of the counterrevolution the CUP was apparently back in control from its headquarters in Salonica. It lacked unity, however, and some groups broke off to form their own parties. Other groups, which could not qualify their candidates for election, also developed. The near anarchy, which had existed much of the time since 1907, continued with only the threat of the Third Army's use of force preventing even more widespread violence. Under these circumstances the constitution was amended to establish ministerial responsibility to the parliament and to extend personal and group liberties. Other laws, however, authorized suppression of dissidents similar to those Abdul Hamid had enforced on his own authority. However, neither legislation nor physical force could curb the new manifestations of discontent that erupted all over the empire.

This competition among various factions for control over the government conformed with the classical pattern of postrevolution adjustment in societies considerably less complicated than the Ottoman Empire. The failure of the Islamic counterrevolution, however, effectively removed the traditionalists from further participation in the process. From its suppression, all changes became inextricably related to troubles with the minorities in the Balkans. The challenge of the minorities was even more difficult to abide after the Greeks had taken advantage of the distraction of the Young Turk revolution to annex Crete. In addition, Austria annexed Bosnia and Herzegovina on October 5, 1908.

An Albanian uprising early in 1910 demonstrated the fragile nature of the empire. Albanians had been in the forefront of the entire Young Turk movement, with Ibrahim Temo as one of the founders of the movement in the Medical College. The CUP's greater efficiency, however, had convinced the Albanians that their situation was worse under the new government than it had been under Abdul Hamid. The Albanian's agitation led to major concessions from CUP, rather than the use of force against them. The inability to satisfy the usually reliable Albanians within the newly structured empire convinced the members of the CUP that Ottomanism was doomed and moved them toward a narrower Turkish posture.

ITALIANS SEIZE LIBYA

An Italian attack on Libya in September 1911 set off a chain of events that effectively ended the last vestige of Ottoman control in North Africa, as well as in most of the Balkan peninsula. Italy's aggression was its means of demonstrating that it was, indeed, a Great Power, and as such had both the need and right to an overseas empire similar to that of the other Powers. Italy had carefully obtained approval for its attack on Libya from the Great Powers, who ignored their previous agreements to maintain the territorial integrity of the Ottoman Empire. Italian naval superiority prevented the Porte from sending significant forces to resist the Italian invasion. Enver Bey and Mustafa Kemal, two of CUP's most accomplished military officers, distinguished themselves in a losing effort and were able to organize a guerrilla resistance, but they were unable to prevent Italy's formal annexation of Libya on November 4, 1911.

The disaster in Libya encouraged the CUP's opponents to move against it. Rival parties, particularly the Liberal Union, and dissident army officers forced the CUP out of office and curtailed most of its activities. They closed the CUP's newspaper, *Tanin*. The apparent end of the CUP might, in fact, have worked to its advantage, because it was out of power when its successors, led by the Liberal Union, lost most of the Balkans during the next two years.

BALKAN WARS

Italy's victory, as well as the Austrian and Greek annexations, emboldened the Balkan states to reconcile their differences and seize the riches of Macedonia. Bulgaria assumed the leadership and made separate alliances with Greece, Montenegro, and Serbia to prepare for a joint effort to remove the Ottoman Empire from territories west of Istanbul.

As war in the Balkans approached in the summer and fall of 1912, the Porte was militarily weak as a result of the Italian war and Abdul Hamid's neglect of the military. The Porte made accommodations with both Albania and Italy to relieve pressure on those fronts. It granted Albanian requests to control most of its own affairs through Ottoman officials of Albanian origin. The Porte acknowledged Italy's conquest in Libya in return for continued Ottoman control over the appointment of most religious officials and supervision over religious practice.

The First Balkan War began on October 8, 1912 and soon Macedonia and Crete fell under the control of the attacking nations. Bulgarian troops threatened the Ottoman capital, to the horror of its occupants, but the southeastward thrust of the Bulgarians also prevented them from acquiring their real objectives to the west where Greece and Serbia occupied most of Macedonia. The Porte's request for a truce led to negotiations in London, which began on December 16.

CUP voiced its criticism of the conduct of the war, as did thousands of others who took to the streets in the major cities. The government concentrated on subduing the CUP. It closed most of CUP's remaining facilities and arrested some of its leaders. But the CUP made a dramatic recovery when Enver Bey led an attack on the Porte on January 23, 1913 after receiving word that the negotiators in London had agreed to abandon Edirne. His decisive action began the restoration of CUP fortunes, as CUP regained some positions in the new ministry. The war had gone so badly that little could be done except to attempt to receive the best terms in London. The Porte agreed to the Treaty of London on June 10, whereby it conceded Crete and all lands west of a line between Enos and Midye. CUP had major repre-

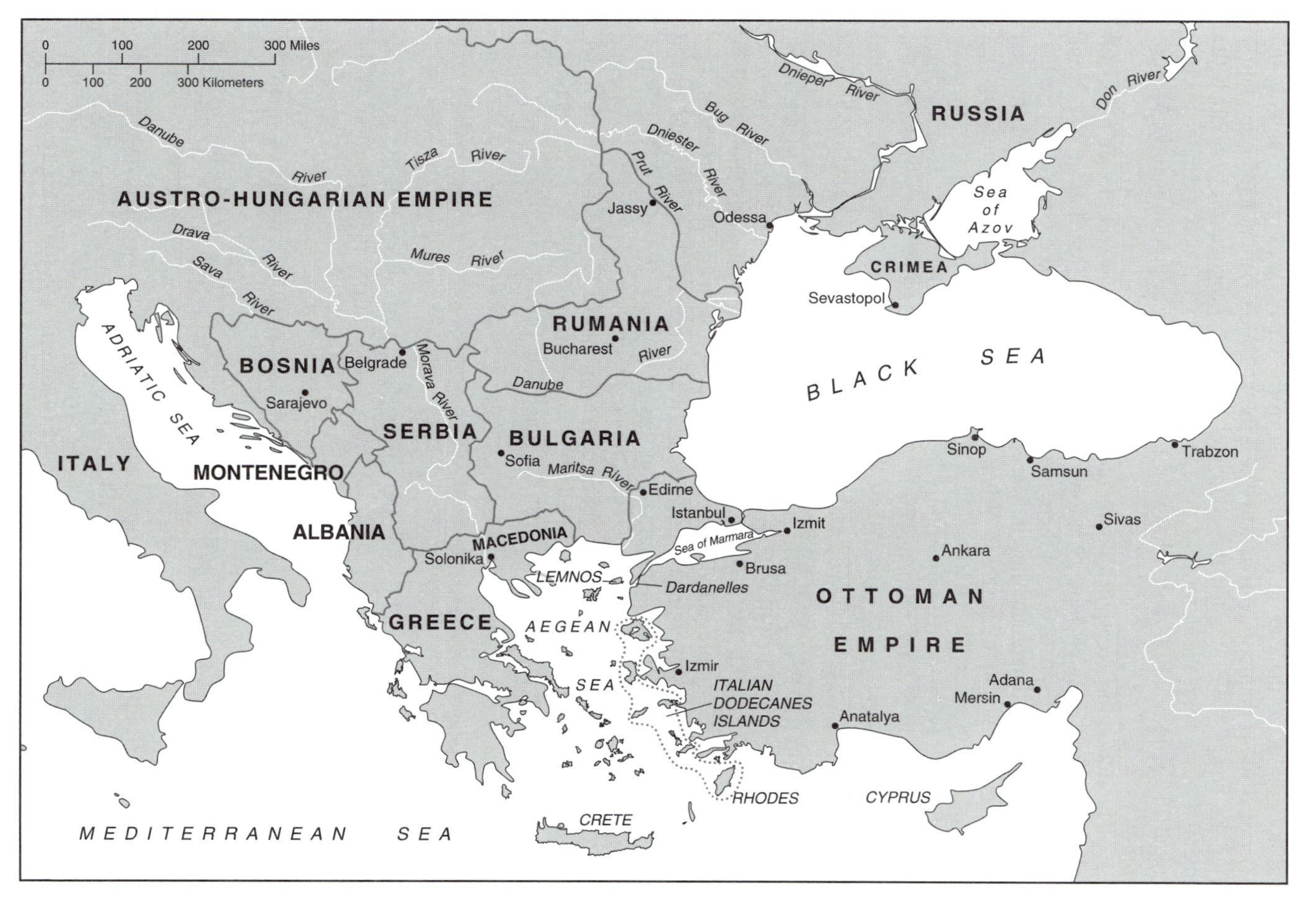

The Balkans after 1913

sentation in the government that signed the peace that lost the Balkans, although it had not conducted the war. Any diminution of the CUP's prestige for signing the peace was more than compensated by the Liberal Union's attempted coup shortly after the peace. CUP avoided the coup and used the provocation to abolish the Liberal Union. With the demise of the Liberal Union, CUP was virtually unchallenged in its domination over what was fast becoming a predominantly Muslim empire.

The ink on the Treaty of London had hardly dried, however, before a Second Balkan War broke out on June 29 among the victors of the First Balkan War. None of the victors were satisfied with their spoils. Bulgaria attacked Greece and Serbia, whom they believed had benefited in Macedonia, while the Bulgarians had engaged the Ottoman armies in the first war. When Rumania and Montenegro joined against Bulgaria, the latter was forced to withdraw its armies from Thrace to meet the challenge. Enver Bey seized the opportunity to lead an Ottoman army to regain Edirne and thereby recover some Ottoman pride. The Second Balkan War ended with the Treaty of Bucharest on August 10 to the aggrandizement of both Greece and Serbia, while Bulgaria again experienced frustration at its minimal gains in the two wars.

The Ottoman Empire, however, was obviously the loser in both of the wars. Albania had declared its full independence on November 28, 1912 during the war. Macedonia had been divided among Greece, Serbia, and Bulgaria. The loss of its European territories represented a considerable reduction in Ottoman revenues.

Constitutional government, thus, had in five short years, lost lands that the old regime had held for centuries. Ottomanism was discredited, if not dead. The empire was predominantly Islamic after the Balkan wars, with Turks and Arabs composing most of its population, except for significant numbers of Greeks and Armenians. The new alignment encouraged the CUP to move unabashedly toward creating a modern nation built around the Turkish language and Turkish institutions.

TURKIFICATION

By 1913 Talat Pasha, Jemal Pasha, and Enver Pasha had emerged as the dominant leaders of CUP. Each had demonstrated his ability during the formation of the movement, with Talat concentrating on politics, while Jemal and Enver played key roles in the army. Enver had repeatedly displayed his decisiveness in open revolt against Abdul Hamid, his conduct of the Libyan campaign, his attack upon the Porte in 1913, and his recovery of Edirne. This avid Turkish nationalist had become even more noteworthy because, as a result of his duty as military attache in Berlin, he had become convinced that the Ottoman Empire must work in close alliance with Germany.

The CUP approach to government was inordinately secular, based on the foundation of the Tanzimat, but now unencumbered with the need to pacify Balkan ethnic, religious, and nationalist desires. Its ideological leader was Ziya Gokalp, a non-Turk of Kurdish lineage, who received his education in the new Ottoman educational institutions. This innovative philosopher, who became fascinated with the study of Positivism, created a blend of traditional Islamic ethics and modern social sciences. He advocated a thorough break with the past in order to prevent outmoded ideas and institutions from impeding the creation of a modern state. Total subjugation of traditional religion, therefore, was essential to his approach to a rational, secular society, which also fostered a strong dedication to Turkish nationalism. Islam would remain the official religion of the state, but provide only spiritual and ethical guidance totally removed from both the educational and judicial fields the Islamic leaders had traditionally dominated. The state had to incorporate all institutions and individuals, including women, into its efforts to produce an organically interdependent citizenry, committed to fulfillment of the potential of the fatherland.

The Turkish Hearth, which developed out of the Turkish Homeland Society, took the ideas of Gokalp and the policies of the CUP to the masses in a widespread attempt to promote Turkish nationalism, even among the non-Turks of the empire. The Young Turks' strident nationalism helped Turks identify with their newly truncated nation, but it did not win the support of most non-Turks. Even the Arabs had begun to develop an identity separate from their Muslim Turkish brothers. The removal of many Arabs from the government as part of the CUP's Turkification did not make Arab acceptance of Turkish nationalism any more likely.

The CUP enthusiastically approached modernization and was able to streamline the bureaucracy, improve utilities and other services, and reduce the role of the ulama and religious institutions, while making some strides toward improving the economy by 1914. The military received special attention as its budget doubled and the use of foreign advisers increased. The use of German advice under General Liman von Sanders caused an international incident as both Russia and Britain resented the scope of his duties. He and his cadre of German officers, however, greatly improved the Ottoman army with the full cooperation of the Germanophile Minister of War, Enver Pasha. To reduce Great Power resentment, the CUP turned to Britain for naval modernization and to France for improvement of the gendarmerie and finances.

By 1914 the reduced Ottoman Empire was still spread out over too large an area to govern with its still inadequate communications system. Although the troublesome Balkan area was by then primarily a problem for Austria and Russia, the Ottoman Empire contained a large number of minorities that resented its authority over them. The empire was, however, a more rational entity than it had been since the time its policies fell under close Western scrutiny. There was a very definite movement toward modernization in the hands of individuals who had been educated and trained in the new educational system. There were even indications that oil discoveries in some of the Arab areas could generate a new source of revenue that would allow the empire to balance its foreign trade. The present looked better than the past, and the future held prospects of greater improvement, if the empire could break the cycle of wars, which had plagued it for more than a century.

CONSTITUTIONAL INTERLUDE IN PERSIA

Widespread unrest from 1905 to 1914 in the political and economic heart of northern Persia aided Britain's quest to establish control over Persia's oil in the southwest. The country appeared to gravitate even further under Russian influence, in part due to the weak leadership of the sickly shah, Muzaffar al-Din. Russia's grip on Persia's economy was stronger than ever and a Belgian firm under Joseph Naus was unusually relentless and efficient in collecting the Persian custom duties that were pledged to repay the Russian loans.

Suffering of merchants and workers in the cities proved a rallying point for others who were dissatisfied with a combination of foreign influence and the incompetent and despotic practices of the shah's officials. The merchants and workers, like most other Persians, turned to the clergy for guidance and redress of grievances. The clergy, of course, had serious grievances of their own. They had a strong tradition of opposition to the intrusion of non-Islamic forces in Persia's affairs. In addition, the clergy had been in almost constant conflict with the Qajar dynasty's attempts to construct secular alternatives to the clergy's traditional monopoly on education, law, and the right to serve as the principal advisers on government policies. The clergy's desire to establish, beyond question, the right of people to take sanctuary (*bast*) in religious institutions was another of their strongest reasons for joining the opposition. Dissatisfaction among a small element of the bureaucracy, middle-level clergy, and members of the professional classes stemmed from their desire for Persia to adopt some degree of Western constitutional and administrative practices. The generally uneducated population, which was also deeply imbued with traditional Islamic beliefs, was unprepared, however, to resist Qajar authority for the purpose of implementing an agenda that might originate from people under the influence of the Western liberal tradition. The paucity of newspapers and modern secular education also ensured that resistance to arbitrary imperial government would be on behalf of traditional Persian values. This also helps explain why some elements of both the landed aristocracy and tribal leadership joined the constitutional movement. In short, Persia's constitutional interlude occurred to preserve Persia's independence from foreign influence and restore the traditional role in society of Persia's different population elements.

A combination of accumulated grievances, the prospect of the authoritarian Muhammad Ali succeeding to the throne, Russia's distraction in its war with Japan, and some unpropitious behavior of various government officials incited huge protests in Tehran that spread to the other large cities. The flogging of ten merchants in December 1905 for violating the government's prices on sugar generated a large-scale *bast* in the Mosque of the Shah among other merchants, which some noted clergymen joined. The shah's principal religious official forced them out of this customary sanctuary, but they retired to the Abd al-Azim Shah shrine where more joined them. The shah agreed to their demands on January 13, 1906, but retained the officials he had agreed to dismiss and refused to implement policy changes as he had promised. The violence that followed led to arrests, the death of two religious students, and the removal of some of the religious leaders to Qumm. Participation in the *bast* in the mosques grew dramatically and thousands also sought refuge on the grounds of the British legation in Tehran. There was a very strong belief among the demonstrators that Britain's constitutional heritage made it a natural supporter of their efforts. Britain's concern, in fact, seems to have been that Persia was on the verge of anarchy. British officials counselled the ailing shah to meet the demands for a "house of justice," by which most of the demonstrators seem to have meant a means of guaranteeing responsible government through Islamic law.

Shah Muzaffar al-Din agreed on September 17, 1906 to hold an election of a *Majlis* (parliament) in October. The new situation gave individuals in Tehran who had atypical views, which reflected Western constitutional concepts, the opportunity to assert themselves. They drafted a constitution in October, before all of the elections occurred in the outlying provinces. This was, however, the constitution that the Majlis considered and approved, although many of the landed class, the clergy, and their peasant and worker followers later were uncomfortable with many of its provisions. At the insistence of the leaders of the constitutional movement, both Shah Muzaffar al-Din and his expected successor, Muhammad Ali, signed the document on December 30, 1906. Russian officials had agreed that the shah needed to make concessions to curb the uprising, but they shared with Muhammad Ali a strong distaste for this document, which restricted the autocratic power of the Persian monarchy. Both the heir to the throne and his Russian supporters realized that a more popularly based Persian policy would oppose Russia's continued domination of Persian affairs.

Constitutionalists, as opposed to those who simply wanted to restore a balance between the monarch and traditional forces, celebrated their delivery of Persia to a modern form of government. The triumph over Qajar "tyranny" allowed the liberal elements a period of prominence as they were more strongly committed than any other group to a full implementation of constitutional government. Muhammad Ali had no intention, however, of complying with the constitution when he succeeded to the throne on January 8 after his father's death. His attempt to impose upon the Majlis the conservative Amin al-Sultan as premier, indicated his attitude. A Social Democrat assassinated the proposed premier, however, and large and determined public demonstrations and strikes in almost all of the major cities forced Muhammad Ali to accept even further concessions after the Majlis met. In the Supplementary Fundamental Law, the shah accepted the principle that his power derived from the people, not from God, and consented to his ministers being answerable to the Majlis. The more radical elements obtained consent from the more moderate elements to impose these restrictions on the monarch by acknowledging Twelver Shiah Islam as the official religion of the state and supporting a provision to allow a committee of *mujtahids* to approve all legislation. All understood that Muhammad Ali accepted these restrictions under duress and that neither he nor the Russians were comfortable with the independence of the legislative branch.

The unexpected agreement between Russia and Great Britain on August 31, 1907 to divide Persia into spheres of influence alerted the constitutionalists that they would have to cope with Russian opposition to their new government without any assistance from the British. By that arrangement Britain agreed to allow Russia full influence over northern Persia in exchange for Russian approval of a British sphere of influence in the southeast portion of Persia adjacent to the Pakistan border. Britain already had a major presence along the Gulf in the southwest, where it controlled the custom duties and would soon acquire major oil fields. While neither Great Power had any formal claim to the region in the center of Persia, they had a stranglehold on that region as well. British and Russian concerns about the emergence of Germany's military and economic strength had inspired them to reconcile their century of conflict over Persia. For the moment, at least, Persians could not as overtly play the competing interests of the two Great Powers against one another. Persia, in fact, was left alone to fend with each the best it could.

The animosity between the new shah and the Majlis determined that the central government would seldom enjoy a coherent approach to Persia's many challenges. Centrifugal forces, however, were stronger than either of these central sources of authority that could not work together. Tribes asserted their autonomy with new vigor and success, localities refused to heed the government of Tehran, and conflicting groups of all persuasions tore individual localities and the nation further apart. Elements of the clergy aligned themselves with each of the contending forces that aspired to shape the nation in their image.

The constitutional experiment endured longer and enjoyed more vitality than it would have otherwise, however, because of the activities of the *anjumans* (societies), which until that time had operated quietly in secret. Like all other intellectual movements in Persia, the *anjumans* counted a large number of the clergy among their members. The various societies differed in composition and ideology as they spread to all of the larger communities of Persia, but most had in common the desire to curb authoritarian government and secure Persia's sovereignty. Their members were generally well educated by Persian standards and had knowledge, and interest, in modern, Western ideas and practices. Most discussed the need for reform in Persia and confined their efforts to defining the nature of the reform and planning means of increasing the number of people in Persia who would be receptive to their ideas. In short, most were far from revolutionary in both their outlooks and in recognition of the overwhelming forces that opposed structural change in Persian government or society.

The sudden implementation of constitutional government provided the *anjumans* with an unexpected opportunity to participate in activities they had believed would only be possible in some distant time. Consequently, some *anjumani* demonstrated more militant behavior with their new freedom than they had ever indicated before. The role of the most radical *anjumans* from Tehran and Tabriz in shaping the constitution helps explain why that document was such a departure from the past. However, the new approach that they advocated ascended upon a nation that was unprepared through education or media exposure to understand either the underlying principles or the efficacy of their ideas. Their newspapers, broadsheets, and speeches advocated changes that were radical departures from traditional Persian beliefs and practices. Persia, in fact, had never experienced such an outpouring of unfettered publications as the constitutional period allowed to exist in places where the constitutionalists were able to establish their control.

The *anjumanis* often emerged as the leaders of all aspects of the constitutional movement, from providing a conceptual foundation to organizing military operations. They never understood that most of the people who participated in the dramatic activities of the constitutional movement had agendas separate from their own. The formerly reformist *anjumanis* sometimes evolved into revolutionaries in the heat of the constitutional movement. And, as in most other revolutions, the participants had a common target they wished to destroy, rather than a common alternative they wanted to provide. The most activist *anjumanis* had a hopeless task, since they desired to establish a democratic, even a socialist, society. Had they succeeded, the clergy and landed classes would have elected a majority because of their influence over the largely illiterate nation.

The Majlis' attempt to force Muhammad Ali to purge all anticonstitutionalists from his court in 1908 resulted in failure. Thus ended any possibility of the more liberal elements being able to shape Persia's future. The shah had no intention of complying, while the parliament lacked both the military and financial capacity to enforce its command. A leftist attempt to assassinate the shah in February also added to his determination to end constitutionalism. Muhammad Ali simply unleashed his loyal, Russian-led Cossacks against the Majlis on June 23, arrested some members, executed others, and dissolved the Majlis. This frontal attack upon the center of constitutionalism demonstrated Muhammad Ali's attitude toward the constitution as he brutally reestablished his control. A noted *mujtahid*, Ayatollah Fazallah Nuri, had helped prepare widespread approval in Tehran for the shah's *coup* through effective preaching against the non-Islamic, pro-Western nature of the entire constitutional movement.

Tabriz became the center of constitutional activity after the shah's reassertion of control in Tehran. The city had been prominent in the constitutional movement from its inception under a combination of clerical and liberal *anjumani* leadership. Radical *anjumani*, under the influence of radical Russian socialist ideologies, gained ascendancy and established Tabriz as the center of Persia's leftist activity in the twentieth century. Experienced Russian-trained Iranian and Russian activists augmented the indigenous Azerbaijani elements to establish a movement that advocated policies unacceptable to most Persian constitutionalists, who were either affiliated with the Democrats or Moderates. The prominence of Armenians in both the ideological and military efforts in Azerbaijan also helped discredit the movement in much of the nation, which was strongly Muslim and opposed to political radicalism and religious equality. The Tabriz society's radicalism also helped discredit the Democrats for much of the larger Persian population. The Democrats, in general, advocated a strong, secular central government, which was free from foreign control. They supported a strong national army, a broad electoral franchise, and compulsory, secular education for all, including women, as a means of obtaining political and economic sovereignty. Support for industrialization was prominent in their program and some elements of the Democrats had strong socialist leanings from the beginning. The Moderates, who were strongly under *ulama*, landlord, tribal leader, and bazaari merchant control, supported a limited franchise, greater local autonomy, the prevalence of Islamic law, and the sanctity of private property.

Constitutionalists, working in full cooperation with various Russian-based radical groups, declared Azerbaijan a separate state and invited other parts of the nation to join its leadership, rather than accept Muhammad Ali's coup. Leftist cadres from Russia helped secure the city and enough adjacent territory to withstand a siege from the shah's limited forces. Similar developments in Gilan, under the Caucasian Armenian, Yeprom Khan, and Khuchik Khan, a conservative advocate of local autonomy, indicated the inability of the shah to govern after suppressing the constitution. For nine months Tabriz suffered great hardship in resisting the shah's troops. Russian forces entered the city in April 1909 as something of a face-saving effort for both sides, with the apparent approval of Britain, since both Great Powers were uncomfortable with Persia's instability. Indicative that Russia's use of force was not in behalf of the shah is the fact that Russia made no effort to prevent the success of a strange new supporter of the constitutionalists, Najaf Quli Khan of the Bakhtayari tribe. In league with other tribesmen and Yeprom Khan's leftist forces, Najaf Quli Khan marched on Tehran and seized control on July 13, 1909. A Grand Assembly compelled Muhammad Ali to abdicate. The shah went into exile in the Russian port of Odessa and his twelve-year-old son, Ahmad, became shah under a regency. The Najaf *ulama's* approval of the execution of Ayatollah Fazallah Nuri as punishment for his support of the shah indicated that the constitutional movement still enjoyed some strong clerical support. The Grand Assembly reduced the qualifications for voting, established four new seats to accommodate Zoroastrians, Christians, and Jews, and reduced Tehran's representation, which had been disproportionately high.

The constitutionalists had reestablished their control of Tehran, but they were more divided than before and still faced British and Russian opposition. When the Second Majlis convened in November 1909, the Moderates enjoyed an almost two-to-one majority over the Democrats, but the latter wielded more influence over the government, due to their military support from the Bakhtayari and Yeprom Khan, who became chief of police in Tehran. Each party assassinated important opponents and continued to experience considerable internal differences. The tribes became very active as a result of the confusion in the capital and asserted their authority in their regions. The unprecedented expansion of Bakhtayari control over the central government and local governorships was an additional stimulus for the other tribes, which were jealous. Most tribesmen disliked the entire constitutional development, but appreciated the fact that the constitutionalists retained the monarchy, which had no capacity to interfere in their local affairs.

This government, like those before it, had the same problem of insufficient funds to operate the government and expel foreign influence. Russia, in fact, kept a large force in northern Persia throughout this entire period. The government took the innovative step of hiring an American, W. Morgan Shuster, as Treasurer-General in May 1911. The reputation for efficient administration that he had earned in the Philippines proved well founded as he assiduously attempted to collect taxes in a nation that had a long tradition of tax evasion. The absence of any central authority for more than five years had compounded the problem even further. With the aid of Major C.B. Stokes, an Englishman he put in charge of tax collection in Azerbaijan, Shuster began to move Persia toward solvency in a very short time. As a complete outsider he regarded the entire nation as Persia and, like the government he served, refused to recognize the extraterritorial rights of either Great Britain or Russia. His single-minded pursuit of his task impressed Persians as much as it distressed the Great Powers. Some analysts suspect that fear that he would suceed in reclaiming Persia for Persians inspired the Russians to allow Muhammad Ali to cross the border on July 11, 1911 in an attempt to regain his throne. The former shah received little support in Persia, while Russia refrained from interfering and claimed to have had no prior knowledge of Muhammad Ali's plan. His effort ended in defeat by October, but he lingered in Persia until the following March, when he returned to Russia.

Muhammad Ali's defeat required direct British and Russian interference to quell the growing independence of Persia's constitutional government. British troops entered the southern provinces and additional Russian troops crossed into Persia and took control of Tabriz, Rasht, and Mashad. Russia took the lead and demanded Shuster's dismissal on November 29, as well as a promise that the Persian government would refrain from hiring foreign advisers without Russian approval. When the Majlis, with widespread public support, refused to meet the Russian demands, Russia threatened to march on Tehran. Under this pressure the cabinet dismissed the Majlis on December 24 and fired Shuster on Christmas Day. Russians encountered heroic resistance from enraged Persian citizens in almost every place they occupied. They created a lasting bitterness for their bombardment and pillaging of the Imam Reza mosque in Mashad, which also caused many Persian casualties.

Thus, the constitutional experiment ended with Persia in worse condition than when it began. The nation's weakness and internal fragmentation meant that it was destined to remain the object of foreign domination and control. Constitutionalists had not proven they could govern, although the constitution remained in place. The death or exile of most of the leftist elements, however, gave reason to believe that the constitution could fulfill the basic desires of most Persians for the elimination of royal despotism, freedom from foreign control, and preservation of Twelver Islam if a truly representative government exercised control.

THE EMERGENCE OF ZIONISM

The ancient Jews left an indelible impression on history, although their political influence and numbers were neither of great duration nor size. When Christianity and Islam spread throughout the world they gave honor and fame to Judaism, from which they had developed, as both acknowledged their debt to Jewish lineage, ethics, and law. Oddly, many in the Gentile world revered Judaism and despised the Jews.

Derision of Jews, no doubt, was related to their persistent retention of a sense of nationhood long after they had lost possession of their land in Palestine. The weakened Jews, following their split after the reign of Solomon, fell under the control of the Persians, Babylonians, and Greeks before they attained a measure of autonomy within the Roman Empire. After a Jewish revolt against Roman rule in 70 A.D., however, the emperor Vespasian subdued the Jews in Palestine and destroyed their temple in Jerusalem. Another Jewish revolt against Rome in 135 A.D. resulted in an even greater defeat and the removal of most Jews from Palestine. Their widespread dispersal, known as the *diaspora*, ended any political unity of the Jews. However, they maintained a strong attachment to the lands of Palestine, which their scriptures taught that God had promised them.

Their prayers for "next year in Jerusalem" persisted for centuries until it was little more than a formality, although it expressed a genuinely deep yearning for the land of their past glory. Most Jews lived in Christian and Muslim lands after the *diaspora*, where their status varied from time to time and place to place, with only the uncertainty of their status remaining constant. Seldom did their hosts respect their way of life and offer them full legal protection. Most Jews, however, retained their laws and customs in the face of their inferior status and periodic persecution. The massacre of Jews and confiscation of their property became a fate which most assumed would persist wherever they might move.

Despite their uncertain status, Jews became prominent in scholarly fields and in the arts. The superior education of some Jews, along with their knowledge and understanding of the world, enabled them to gain administrative positions and advisory influence over the powerful. Some Jews prospered in the *diaspora*, because for centuries Christian and Islamic laws forbade their people from charging interest for lending money. Since Jewish law contained no prohibition against collecting interest from Gentiles, Jewish bankers provided a necessary service for governments and individuals whose plans exceeded their financial means. Jews, therefore, had a high profile in banking and in the trade and manufacture of precious metals and jewels. Not uncommonly they were forced to forgive large debts and consent to new loans on pain of either incarceration or banishment.

The success of the few helped draw attention and resentment to all Jews. Most Jews, however, scratched out a living as small shopkeepers, artisans, or landless peasants. Since most retained their orthodox religious practices and dress, they were easily identifiable. Their businesses and residences, in fact, were usually confined to designated areas known as *ghettos*. Few Jews ever owned land even after the liberalization of the laws of Western Europe in the nineteenth century allowed those living there to do so.

The constitutions of most Western European states in the nineteenth century granted Jews full citizenship, but many years of ingrained persecutions and resentment prevented them and their non-Jewish fellow citizens from feeling at ease. Western European Jews were careful, therefore, to refrain from any actions that might call attention to them as a separate people. Only the Jews who migrated to the United States had a real sense of security and full citizenship. This was the first time, since their own nation had disappeared in the first century, that the Jews found acceptance. Legal restrictions and poverty prevented the truly desperate eastern European Jews from migrating to the United States.

After the tsars had absorbed most of Poland, perhaps as many as five million Jews lived in the Russian Empire. While their plight had never been good in either Poland or Russia, it became unbearable under the Russification policies of Alexander III, who became tsar in 1881. Systematic, government-inspired and -instigated *pogroms* removed any hope that Jews could maintain their religion and customs in Russia. Full assimilation, which also meant adoption of Russian Orthodox Christianity, or expulsion seemed the only choices for Russian Jews after 1881. While their Jewish brethren in Western Europe accommodated themselves to their new freedoms, Jews within the Russian Empire and elsewhere in Eastern Europe responded to leaders who sought to establish a separate Jewish state where their laws and customs would represent the norm. Since such an entity was impossible any place in Europe, Jewish nationalists looked to Palestine, Africa, and South America for possible locations for a Jewish state. No area or circumstance, however, could rival the appeal of Palestine as the homeland for Jewish national fulfillment. This desire to return to Zion nourished Jewish nationalism, which soon acquired the designation of Zionism.

While there had been earlier stirrings of Zionism in Rumania and Russia, it became a viable movement in 1882 with the publication of Dr. Leon Pinsker's *Self-Emancipation*, and the exodus of 7,000 Jews from Russia to Palestine in the first *Aliyah*, or "going up" to Zion. Individually or collectively these occurrences did not represent the heart of the Zionist movement, but they signalled the convergence of ideology and action in an environment that could support a coherent effort. Fortuitously, the same year marked Great Britain's occupation of Egypt, where it became both strategically located and motivated to serve as the Great Power midwife of Zionism.

Although the members of the first *Aliyah* were committed to working the soil, few were successful. The natural hardship of living in that land, combined with some bad seasons and inadequate financial support drove most back to the cities, or to work on the farms under the sponsorship of the French philanthropist, Baron Edmond de Rothschild. Some returned to Europe or migrated to the United States. They also lacked legal status within the Ottoman Empire and had the added disadvantage of being spread over too large an area to allow proper coordination. The few colonies that survived were spread from Jaffa to Galilee in the northwest quadrant of Palestine.

Historically, the Gentile world regarded Jews as a separate religion with accompanying peculiarities of diet, dress, and custom. To many of the leading Zionists, however, religion was incidental to their goal of establishing a Jewish state. Most prominent Zionist leaders were, in fact, secular socialists, and some were atheist Marxists. In either outlook, the emphasis was upon creating an egalitarian Jewish state, which would be based upon the common sharing of responsibilities and the results of their labor. They intended to establish a society dominated by Jewish values, customs, traditions, and the Hebrew language, as an answer to Jewish desire for a nationalist expression, and as an escape from perpetual persecution. Religion was neither essential, nor necessarily incompatible to this approach. It did, however, contradict the views of traditionalist Jews, who maintained that only God could reestablish Zion. Since the secularists dominated the Zionist movement as well as the early migrations to Palestine, their views prevailed in the formulation of Zionist institutions in Palestine.

Inspiration and direction for early Zionism came from some leaders who did not have strongly detailed economic, political, or social views on the proposed society, but helped define its general character. Dr. Leon Pinsker's *Self-Emancipation* (1882) maintained that the continued persecution of the Jews was the result of the strong sense of Jewish identity, devoid of a physical homeland. He alleged that neither Jews nor Gentiles could regard Jewish nationalism seriously until the Jews acquired land to accompany their sense of nationhood. Nationhood without an identifiable land was impossible.

Asher Ginzberg, a Ukrainian who adopted the name of Ahad Haam (One of the People), however, disliked the emphasis in early Zionism upon rapidly developing a Jewish state, as he did not believe that one could emerge to accommodate most Jews. He advocated the fuller development of an awareness among Jews of the values and attributes that set them apart. Ahad Haam led an element of Zionist intellectuals who realized the necessity of creating a true sense of Jewish culture and traditional values throughout worldwide Jewry. He visualized the development of some kind of Jewish community in Palestine that would serve as an example and inspiration for all Jews wherever they might have to live.

Eliezer Perlmann, a Lithuanian Jew who took the name of Ben Yehudah when he migrated to Palestine in 1882, performed an important role in creating a genuinely Jewish society in Palestine, rather than a transplanted eastern European society, by developing a usable, modern Hebrew language for the Jews. His rabbinical training provided him with the scholarly tools and knowledge of classical Hebrew to perform his mission. His commitment to Zionism provided him with the passion to create a modern language based on the roots of ancient Hebrew. He and his wife spoke nothing but Hebrew after they arrived in Palestine, even though much of his work in creating a modern Hebrew language still lay ahead.

Although he was not a socialist, Ahron David Gordon, a Ukrainian, held views that strongly supported the attitudes of the early socialist agrarian Zionist settlers in Palestine. Gordon was a leading advocate of the idea that Jews had to get back to the soil and other primary production in order to create a viable Zionist society. Their centuries as peddlers, merchants, and other sorts of middlemen had not only tainted the Jewish reputation, but had also warped the actual spirit of the Jews.

Gordon inspired the participants of the second *Aliyah* of between 15,000 and 20,000 pioneers, who went to Palestine from 1904 to 1914. They were committed to working the soil with their own hands rather than using Arab laborers, as many of their predecessors had done. Most were also confirmed socialists, who were determined to create a Jewish society as well as a Jewish presence in Palestine. The *kibbutz*, or small, group-owned farm, was the vehicle for fulfilling their insatiable desire for agrarian labor and a Jewish society.

Most of the previously mentioned Zionist leaders had a limited audience and a restricted forum for their ideas prior to the emergence of Theodor Herzl as the leader of united Zionism. His background and approach prevented him from understanding or appreciating the urgency, socialism, or yearning for the soil of eastern Jews. However, he quickly began to use his erudition and knowledge of Western ways and institutions to transform Zionism from a movement among impoverished Eastern European Jews into a worldwide cause, which also attracted Great Power attention.

Herzl was reared and educated in Vienna, where he received a doctor's degree in law, before he turned to the new profession of journalism. His coverage of the Dreyfus case for *The New Press* had a profound effect on attracting him to the plight of Jews who were not as fortunate as himself. He decided that only a homeland for Jews could relieve them from harassment and persecution. Men of similar or higher station to himself rejected his view, but he published *The Jewish State* in 1896. This short work defined the basic needs and functions of such a state, and was devoid of any definable ideology, which could divert other Zionists with specific social, economic, and political ideas from the main purpose of establishing a state. While many distinguished Jewish leaders disliked the whole idea, the simplicity of his brief work captured the imagination of the Jewish masses, who had neither rank nor reputation to protect.

His instant fame prompted him to convene the first Zionist Congress in Basel, Switzerland in August, 1897. The congress adopted a flag, a national anthem, and established an administrative framework for further development toward creating a Jewish homeland in Palestine. The congress also helped spawn several hundred new Zionist societies until there were nearly a thousand worldwide by 1898. The basic problem of the whole scheme at that time, however, was the reality that Palestine was part of the Ottoman Empire. Herzl pursued the possibility of obtaining permission from the sultan, Abdul Hamid II, to allow large-scale Jewish migration into Palestine. Attempts to gain the authorization through the intercession of Kaiser Wilhelm II failed, as did Herzl's personal interviews with the sultan in 1901 and 1902. This approach of using Great Power political channels as a means of acquiring a Jewish homeland became dubbed "political" Zionism. It was in contrast to the "practical" Zionists who were determined to establish a presence in Palestine by whatever means and then find a way of establishing its legitimacy.

Despite Herzl's success in coordinating Zionist efforts, his failure to find a haven for the Jewish homeland threatened his leadership of the Zionist movement. This became quite clear when he proposed in 1903 that the sixth Zionist congress accept the British offer of Uganda as a temporary home for the Jews. The proposal prompted the eastern European Jews to leave the conference, and dramatically emphasized the differences between the "political" and the "practical" Zionists. This dichotomy regarding method corresponded closely to the east-west representation within the World Zionist Organization. Herzl never solved the cleavage, as he died an apparent failure at the age of forty-five in 1904, after nine years of moving the pent-up emotions of centuries toward the expectation of a homeland. Although Zionists were split, he had helped them become accustomed to working together and had supervised the formulation of some common institutions, including the Jewish National Fund to purchase land in Palestine.

As a result of the second *Aliyah* there were about 85,000 Jews in Palestine by 1914. The majority, however, were either indigenous Jews, who lived much like their Arab neighbors, or pious Halakhah Jews, who lived on foreign charity while they meditated and waited for death in the Holy Land. Neither of these were inclined, nor able, to help in building a Jewish state.

On the eve of World War I in 1914, Zionism had made considerable progress, although it might not have appeared so just before the war greatly restricted Zionist activities and reduced their numbers. There were forty-three Jewish agrarian settlements in Palestine in which Hebrew was widely used. Tel Aviv, the first totally Jewish city for centuries was established adjacent to Jaffa. There were several international Zionist organizations to fund and foster Jewish migration to Palestine. Zionists had a flag, an anthem, and an active Jewish press. Leaders such as David Ben-Gurion, Yitzhak Ben-Zvi, and Levi Eshkol were in residence with years of experience in Palestine. The Palestinian Zionist settlers' commitment to a socialist society supplemented their Zionist nationalism to provide an ideology and a definite sense of direction. Their numbers, however, were too small to be more than of symbolic importance, and they lacked legal recognition from their host government or any other nation.

4

Arab Regions of the Ottoman Empire

HISTORICAL TIMELINE

740 ⇛ Zaid, the son of Imam Hussein and grandson of the Prophet Muhammad, inspired the creation of a new branch of Shiah Islam.

750 ⇛ The Abbassids gained control of the Islamic Empire and replaced the Umayyads, whose capital was in Damascus.

766 ⇛ The Abbassid dynasty built the city of Baghdad to serve as the capital of the Islamic Empire.

1584 ⇛ The Maronite Church established a college in Rome to train priests.

1830 ⇛ Great Britain began to implement the Trucial System whereby it arbitrated affairs among the Gulf shaykdoms.

1831 ⇛ The Ottoman government decided to use military force against the Mamluks to reestablish direct control over Iraq.

1832 ⇛ Egypt, under the control of Muhammad Ali, extended its control over the Greater Syria region until 1840.

1840 ⇛ The beginning of the *qaymaqamate* period for Mount Lebanon that lasted until 1861. This approach provided for separate governors for the Maronite Christian and Druze regions.

1858 ⇛ The Ottoman Land Law was implemented with widespread influence throughout the empire because it forced individuals to register their lands. Many feared to do so and lost ownership of their lands to those who did register the land.

1859 ⇛ Large scale war began between Druze and Maronite Christians on Mount Lebanon.

1861 ⇛ Maronite-Druze war ended and the Western Powers pressured the Ottoman Empire to establish the *Mutesarrifate,* which placed Mount Lebanon under a single neutral governor. The area had its own law called the *Reglemen Organique.*

1865 ⇛ American Presbyterian missionaries established the Syrian Protestant College in Beirut, which evolved into the American University of Beirut.

1869 ⇛ Midhat Pasha became the Ottoman governor of Iraq and held that post until 1872.

1875 ⇛ The Society of Jesus (Jesuits) established the University of St. Joseph in Beirut.

1902 ⇛ Abdul Aziz Ibn al-Saud seized control of Riyadh on January 15 and began a process that would lead to his creation of the Kingdom of Saudi Arabia.

1908 ⇛ An oil strike at Masjid es-Suleiman in western Persia was the first major oil discovery in the Gulf region.

1911 ⇛ The Ottoman government gave Yemen considerable independence in the Treaty of Daan.

1913 ⇛ Great Britain established an unofficial protectorate over Kuwait that became formal when Great Britain and the Ottoman Empire became belligerent in World War I.

1914 ⇛ The Anglo-Ottoman Convention on March 9 settled many outstanding issues between Great Britain and the Ottoman Empire regarding the Arabian peninsula.

1922 ⇛ The Uqair Conference established the boundaries between Iraq and Saudi Arabia.

The Arab-speaking regions of the Ottoman Empire in southwest Asia failed to prosper in their prolonged affiliation with the Ottoman Empire. It is probably unfair to say they declined under Ottoman jurisdiction, because forces beyond the control of anyone in the region had diminished its economic role and strategic importance before the Ottoman era. Southwest Asia had not recovered from the Mongol devastation by the time the European nations had discovered direct contact with the Far East and eliminated the traditional role of southwest Asia as a trading conduit between the East and West. The rapid rise of intense manufacturing and then industrialization in the West eradicated the need for the Levant's largely handcraft productions. Ottoman preoccupation with European and Russian threats helped focus its development in Western Anatolia to the neglect of the eastern sectors. In fact, the absence of a stronger Ottoman military presence in the Arab-speaking areas harmed both urban and rural production because marauders often controlled the roads and countryside. The lack of prosperity, however, was not a cause for unrest because the condition was so general and lasted so long that residents regarded it as normal.

Given the amorphous nature of the Ottoman Empire, most Arab-speaking Ottoman subjects identified primarily with their religion, their family, and their immediate locality. Damascus, Aleppo, Mecca, and Medina were distinct for attracting a sense of allegiance from Ottoman subjects beyond their immediate environs. Baghdad's failure to recover from the Mongol onslaught prevented it from enjoying its previous appeal, although Baghdad, Basra, and the northern Gulf region formed an identifiable economic unit. Despite its importance to three major religions, Jerusalem remained little more than a large town. It and other Palestinian towns traditionally regarded Damascus, and later Beirut to a lesser degree, as the political, cultural, and economic hub of Greater Syria.

The prospect of an Arab state or states was not even an academic subject among Arab-speakers until the very last days of the nineteenth century. Even then, the small number of Arab-speakers who began to express a stronger sense of separate Arab identity generally visualized a continued affiliation with the Ottoman Empire.(See Chapter 10 on Arab Nationalism.) In short, there was no sentiment among the Arabs in southwest Asia to support the strange configuration of separate states that later developed to accommodate the desires of European nations.

It seems advisable to look briefly at the separate regions of the Ottoman Empire that would later become states.

SYRIA

If the modern state of Syria sometimes seems to behave like a mother who, through no fault of her own, has lost her children, there is good reason. The several different kinds of governments and the multiethnic and multireligious population of Syria have generally agreed that Lebanon, Jordan, Israel, the West Bank, Gaza, the Sinai, and parts of Iraq and Turkey all belong to "natural" Syria. While originally Syria directed its venom against the parties it held responsible for this abomination, it also frequently castigates the alienated areas for continuing the estrangement.

The fact that it shares a long history of being part of many other empires over thousands of years has little to do with modern Syria's posture. It is, however, related to the fact that "Syria" has been in almost constant usage to designate much of the area of the Levant from Roman times. It has much more to do with its capital, Damascus, being the administrative center for Arabic and Islamic expansion. Mecca and Medina, after all, were too removed and too logistically inconvenient to serve that purpose. Thus, *Ash-Sham* (the North), centered on the Umayyad capital of Damascus, became associated with the Arabs emerging from obscurity to become the most culturally and intellectually advanced people in the world west of Persia. The same base guided the spread of Arabic and Islam throughout western Asia, across north Africa, and into southern Europe. Much of Persia, India, and China adopted Islam and gained some familiarity with Arabic from the Syrian foundation.

Four centuries of Ottoman rule continued the role of Syria as the locus of guidance over the region. Ottoman governors in Damascus dispatched decrees, armies, and tax collectors from *Ash-Sham*, which increasingly meant the city of Damascus. Religious, tribal, business, and scholarly leaders trekked to Damascus from all over the region to pay their respects to Ottoman authorities and to familiarize themselves with important developments. Pilgrims annually converged on Damascus to join the great caravan that moved southward through the north-south valleys on the *hajj* to the Hijaz. Aleppo, about two hundred miles north of Damascus, was a major trading center that thrust Syrian influence eastward into Mesopotamia and throughout southeastern Anatolia.

Greater Syria, roughly everything north of the Arabian peninsula and west of the Euphrates and to the Amanus Mountains to the north, was famous for trade and manufactures of all kinds. Damascus and Aleppo enjoyed especially strong reputations for their many skilled artisans and clever merchants who made and sold the finest goods for customers hundreds of miles away. The many devastations from invaders, including the Mongols, were unable to subdue the indomitable business acumen of Syrian businessmen for long. A more than adequate agricultural base enabled the region to be self-reliant as it imported goods from all over the orient and brokered them to far-flung markets. Except in times of bad harvests the region usually had ample food for exportation as well.

Syria's Religious and Ethnic Composition

The cosmopolitan nature of Syria's activities decreased the likelihood of its own ethnic and religious complexity seeming strange. Strong differences and even enmities existed, but so did a mutual interdependence that promoted a general atmosphere of live-and-let-live, except in times of intense rivalries. The rugged landscape of northern Greater Syria and the large, urban areas offered a haven to minorities that found life untenable in more accessible regions and smaller population centers. The many different overlords usually allowed the small, anomalous communities to exist, and even thrive, on the condition that they paid their taxes and tributes, employed their talents, made no special demands, and caused no troubles.

The overwhelming domination of Sunni Muslim Arabs by the thirteenth century rendered all other groups harmless. At least 75 percent of the population embraced this orthodox mainstream of Islam. The Sunni sense of security, especially after the expulsion of the Christian crusaders, allowed toleration of many forms of Christianity, Shiah Islamic sects, and quasi-Islamic sects such as the Druze and Alawis. Among the Christians the Greek Orthodox were decidedly the largest in number and demonstrated a propensity to identify with their fellow Arabs both culturally and ideologically. The Maronite Catholics, who were centered in Mount Lebanon, were the second largest group. Their strong affiliation with Rome and France aroused suspicions that both their loyalties and intentions were contrary to the best interests of the Muslim and non-Maronite Christian communities. Other Christian groups, Greek Catholics, Syrian Orthodox, Syrian Catholics, Roman Catholics, Armenian Orthodox and Catholics, Nestorians, and later, some Protestants, were too small in number to constitute either a problem or a threat.

The Alawis and the Druze were large enough groups to pose a potential problem. Both split off from Ismaili Shiah Islam and embraced beliefs and practices that are not usually associated with Muslims. Of the two, the Alawi are considerably the more numerous, with about 10 percent of the Syrian population. Until recently, however, they were of marginal importance. Traditionally, these residents of Latakia province in northwestern Syria were probably the poorest and most deprived people in the entire Middle East. Usually landless, virtually unskilled, and without education, they served as agrarian workers who found opportunities to join the army a blessing. The Druze, who were centered in the Shuf mountains south of Beirut and more numerously in Jebal Druze (Druze Mountain) in southern Syria, were fewer in numbers than the Alawis, but considerably stronger in every other respect. Their strong commitment to retain their unique identity in their mountain strongholds made them formidable foes to any government or group they perceived as enemies. The several major intrigues, conspiracies, and atrocities against them made them hesitant to accept authority outside of their own traditional leaders.

Kurds and Armenians were quite different from the other major identifiable groups because the Arabic language and Arabic culture were theirs only by adoption. The Kurds, who were predominantly Sunni Muslims, had their own lands across northcentral and northeastern Syria. From the late nineteenth century, many Syrian Kurds shared the aspiration with Kurds beyond Syrian borders of creating a Kurdish state independent from the Ottoman Empire. This became more of a problem for the modern state of Syria as nationalist activities continued among the Kurds, who were separated by the boundaries of Syria, Turkey, and Iraq. During the late nineteenth century, the Armenian Christians entered Syria in significant numbers in order to escape Turkish persecution in their native Anatolia. The Armenian population in Syria increased dramatically following their systematic expulsion from Anatolia in 1915. As refugees, they had no land and offered their labor in an urban market that was already distressed from the influx of cheap European goods. Armenians became famous for their skills as artisans and craftspeople. Their propensity to remain aloof from politics diminished their threat once the economy adjusted to their presence.

Syria's Ottoman Experience

As in other Arab-speaking regions of the Ottoman Empire, Syria experienced a general decline while a part of that empire from the early sixteenth to the early twentieth centuries. Again, as elsewhere, lack of encouragement, failure to provide protection, and the absence of a constructive economic policy led to decay in both agriculture and manufacturing. The intrusion of nomadic tribes was particularly detrimental to agriculture, which led to a subsequent decline in towns, cities, manufacturing, and trade. Population growth diminished over the years. In short, the tradition of the Levant as a vibrant center of economic and intellectual activity ended.

While factors beyond Ottoman control and responsibility contributed to the decline, the end result was the same. Foremost in the uncontrollable factors was the emergence of European ability to trade directly with the Far East by sea routes around southern Africa. Trade gradually ceased that had formerly passed through the Middle East for the employment and profit of a large percentage of the population.

Concomitant with the growth of European seamanship was the dramatic increase in western manufacturing, and eventually, industrial capacity. This, combined with European acquisition of plentiful new sources of gold and silver from the New World, spelled disaster to the Levant. Traditionally, for instance, the West bought manufactured goods from the Levant with the meager gold and silver supplies that it possessed. Precious bullion had always flowed eastward to purchase luxury goods from the mysterious Orient. By the nineteenth century, this practice ended as the sophisticated banking systems of the West, which transcended a bullion-based monetary system, financed unspeakably strong military and industrial capabilities of the large, centralized Western states.

The Ottoman Empire in general, and Syria in particular, fell victim to Europe's new ability to dominate the world industrially and militarily. The capitulation treaties the European states extracted from the embattled Ottoman government established an unfavorable trade relationship with the Middle East that mainly benefited a handful of Christians and Jews. Syria's tradition as a manufacturing and trading center made the changes more dramatic and harmful to it than to most other Middle Eastern regions. The influx of cheap European goods created a market for European-style products that the native workers could neither match in quality nor price. Massive urban unemployment reduced the demand for agricultural products and former urban workers often reverted to subsistence agriculture in an effort to feed themselves. Not surprisingly, a significant population decline was a major repercussion of the economic hardship.

The economic and population degeneration in urban areas reverberated throughout the region. As the region lost prosperity, it lost stature in Istanbul, where the government did less to protect it. Since the cause of decline was primarily insidious economic factors, military forces the region could not support were withdrawn. Unfettered nomads found it easier to assert themselves and provide an additional force to agrarian deterioration.

This, coupled with Ottoman reform attempts in the second half of the nineteenth century, adversely affected land ownership. The Ottoman effort to modernize and centralize led to an attempt to register all lands in individual names, rather than by family or tribe as had been done in the past. Most Syrians, like their compatriots throughout the region, feared that association with specific land would bring unavoidable taxes and military service. This antipathy to government caused many to seek an alternative that alienated them from land that was legally theirs. As in Iraq, large landowners, powerful shaykhs, and knowledgeable merchants registered large quantities of land in their names, which condemned most rural families to sharecropping and penury. The results reached far beyond obvious economic matters. Owners of large, even huge, tracts obtained legal title to most of the land, which became the principle criterion for voting in later years when representative government developed. Potential landowners, therefore, not only became landless, they also became disenfranchised as a result of their ignorance of modern ways.

The Ottoman government's struggle for modernization tied it economically and culturally to Europe. Capitulation treaties led to an influx of foreign investments as well as European manufactured goods. In Syria, the French gained ownership of important public facilities and broadened their influence over education, which always promoted a strong emphasis upon the French language and literature. The French and other foreigners worked closely with Christians, and created a disparity in financial and educational abilities between them and the Muslim majority. The creation of Mount Lebanon as an autonomous enclave under European protection in 1861 accelerated this process. Western-sponsored colleges and other educational institutions familiarized young Ottomans, especially Christians, with Western ideas and practices that were incompatible with prevailing ideas and institutions.

The brief Ottoman experiment with constitutional government in 1878 called attention to the difference between Arabs and other Ottomans. Arabs, who had lived fairly contentedly within the Turkish-dominated empire, began to question their status as other ethnic groups challenged the Ottoman government with demands for privileges and even independence. Increased familiarity with European ideas and contemporary nationalist movements inspired Arabs, especially Syrians, to invoke demands for natural rights and to emulate European nationalist strategies and practices. The first significant manifestation of Arab separatism occurred in Beirut in 1875 when the secret society published its demands. Beirut, Damascus, and Aleppo soon became centers of Arab nationalism and Syrians always considered themselves both the formulators of Arab national consciousness and the most capable leaders for implementing it. (See Chapter 10 on Arab Nationalism.)

While some Syrians were in the forefront of Arab nationalism, the vast majority of the population remained politically inactive and accepted continuation within the Ottoman Empire as a natural and unavoidable fate. After four hundred years of Ottoman domination, few could imagine that any diminution of Ottoman control could be anything but transitory.

LEBANON

The modern state of Lebanon is an important Middle East nation even though it is territorially tiny, lacks political integrity, contains no vital resources, is militarily weak, and often, if not usually, has been in political disarray. Much of its importance simply derives from the fact that it exists at all, and, therefore, has the right to continue to exist by the charters of both the Arab League and the United Nations. Also, its peculiar composition of different religious groups, which distrust each other and seek support from outside forces, inflates small, local incidents into international concerns.

As a result of its geographical location, its historical development, and the diversity of cultural orientation of its small population, Lebanon has been unable to agree on its identity. All of the other twenty-four nations that developed out of the Ottoman Empire have steadily enhanced their sense of nationhood since World War I, regardless of how arbitrary their borders were. For any other nation it would seem absurd for its leaders to meet to seek a solution after weeks, months, or years of internal strife and only be able to agree that Lebanon is "an Arab country," and fail to agree on anything else before resuming their conflict. Such sessions seem necessary to reassure the Lebanese and the rest of the world that there is "a Lebanon" and that for all the interference of outside forces, their troubles are, in fact, fraternal. Like a modern Janus, Lebanon looks with equal clarity to the West and to the Arab East. This is a major cause of Lebanon's continued instability. The fact that most Lebanese feel some degree of comfort from this dual orientation is probably the peculiar attribute that makes them distinctly Lebanese rather than Syrian.

Although it is sometimes difficult to remember because Lebanon has been racked with strife for so long, there is much to bind the Lebanese together. Even the most rural Lebanese citizens have had good experiences and fond memories because of the cultural diversity in their lives that results from living near people with customs different from their own. They have shared each others feasts, celebrations, weddings, and funerals. Each has benefitted from the special talents in manufacturing, farming, cooking, dancing, and making music of their different neighbors. Each can recall acts of kindness and generosity toward them from members of other groups. Occasionally, they have even shared the horror of the same oppressors and triumphed over common foes. Almost every identifiable group has been allied with, and against, every other identifiable group. Most Lebanese have had a more intimate relationship with the languages, goods, and ideas of the West than with their Arab brethren to the south and east. The Lebanese speak the language of their Arab brethren in other nations and comprehend their ideas and values, whether they embrace them or despise them. Most Lebanese have improved their standard of living because of Lebanon's full integration into the economic and intellectual systems of both the West and the Arab world. The Lebanese have fulfilled the unique role, which many of them have claimed, of being the bridge between the East and the West. No other people have done it so well, and no other people can be Lebanese. And, for all their internal differences, their common experiences have created a distinctly Lebanese personality and kinship.

Contributing to its instability is the fact that Lebanon is like a Middle East village where there are no secrets. Everyone knows who is corrupt, who is saintly, who is ruthless, and who has stolen what from whom. No one wants anyone else to obtain a position of power that threatens the honor or independence of everyone else. Like a village, it is also too weak to prevent the overwhelming force of outsiders from preying upon their differences to dominate them or escalate minor quarrels into full-scale blood baths.

Historical Heritage

The area that presently constitutes Lebanon had been successively part of the Roman, Byzantine, and Ottoman empires for centuries prior to 1920. Its name, which derives from the Aramaic word for "white" to describe its snowcapped mountains, predates all three of those empires. In recent centuries, however, "the Lebanon" usually referred to Mount Lebanon, which constitutes less than one-half of the modern state. France added territory to the north, south, and east of Mount Lebanon when it obtained control of the area following World War I. Still, Lebanon remains tiny, with a maximum distance of 125 miles from north to south and 50 miles from east to west. Lebanon's mountainous terrain makes these distances deceptive, because surface travel varies from difficult to impossible, and is seldom possible on a straight line. The ruggedness of its terrain accounts for much of Lebanon's religious complexity, as persecuted groups such as the Maronites and Druze found the mountain stronghold their only hope for survival.

The mountains also provide Lebanon with a temperature diversity that many other Middle Eastern countries lack. Temperatures vary considerably between the lower coastal areas and the higher altitudes of the interior. Lebanese love to relate accounts of snow skiers on the mountain slopes looking down on sunbathers on the beaches. The snow on the mountains and the myriad of springs also provide Lebanon with rivers and streams and an abundance of pure water, which its neighbors envy. The low coastal areas allow the cultivation of citrus fruits and bananas, but most of Lebanon's agriculture is built around the cultivation of fruits, vegetables, grapes, olives, and grains on small farms in the interior.

The Lebanese, who inherited the traditions of the ancient Phoenicians, have built their substantial wealth from the port city of Beirut, which customarily has served as the trading center for goods from all over the world destined for the Arab countries in southwest Asia. In general, Beirut's superior capacity for providing banking, warehousing, accounting, linguistic, and management services, as much as its physical location, accounts for its success as the commercial and service center of the Arab world. Continuation of this role depends on good relations with its Arab neighbors. A glance at a map quickly reveals that Lebanon's prosperity is totally dependent upon access to the roads of Syria to conduct its trade with Arab neighbors. This fact, devoid of other historical and political considerations, explains the inordinately strong role Syria plays in every aspect of Lebanese life.

For centuries, maps and travellers' accounts referred to the area presently in Lebanon as part of Syria. Emigrants who left the region prior to 1920 usually identified themselves as Syrians, even if they had lived on Mount Lebanon. The region was under the authority of the Ottoman governor of Damascus after the Ottoman Empire gained control early in the sixteenth century, but more immediate administrative functions were often in the hands of pashas in Beirut, Tripoli, Sidon, or depended upon emirs on The Mountain. Druze emirs dominated The Mountain during the Ottoman period until late in the eighteenth century when Maronite Christian numerical and financial strength afforded them political ascendancy. The predominance of Druze and Maronites on The Mountain always gave it a different character under the Ottomans. Since the population of the coastal cities was mostly Sunni Muslim, those places did not require special treatment. The heavily Shiah Muslim population of the Biqa valley and the area south of Sidon generally remained quiet and hoped the Ottoman authorities would overlook their questionable practice of the true faith and suffer them to live unperturbed in their more easily accessible areas.

Lebanon's Religious Diversity

Lebanon, like the entire eastern rim of the Mediterranean Sea, has a rich mixture of religious faiths. Most Lebanese Muslims are either Sunnis or Shiahs (Twelvers). The largest Lebanese Christian sect, the Maronites, are almost exclusively identified with Lebanon, even though they originated in the fourth century along the Orontes River in what is present-day Syria. They sought refuge in the protective mountains of Lebanon in the eighth century. The Maronites take their name from their founder, Marun, a monk who insisted on the single nature of Christ. Although still schismatic, the Maronites affiliated with Roman Catholicism in the late twelfth century and have remained under papal jurisdiction since. Maronite bishops elect their own Patriarch, who often wields great influence over all aspects of Maronite life. The establishment of a Maronite College in Rome in 1584 to train Maronite priests not only enhanced the sect's relationship with Rome, but assured the Maronites fuller knowledge of Western ideas and values. Their cultural kinship with France also developed in the sixteenth century and French remains the language of choice of many Maronites. After France became their protector against their predominantly Muslim neighbors, the Maronite community generally was willing to follow the lead of "Mother" France. Their French connection accelerated Maronite acculturation with the West and provided them with Great Power support for political and military aggression that other Christian groups in the Middle East did not dare to make.

Other significant Christian groups include the Greek Orthodox, Greek Catholics, Armenian Orthodox, Armenian Catholics, Roman Catholics, Nestorians, and various Protestants in small numbers. All have tried to accommodate their lives to remain unobtrusive in the complex Lebanese mosaic. The Greek Orthodox have been the most intellectually and politically active of these Christian groups. They have consistently identified with the mainstream of Arab politics and have often provided strong leaders for both Arab nationalism and internationalist causes.

The Druze of Lebanon have enjoyed a long history of influence, although more of their number reside in southern Syria. The sect developed out of Ismaili Shiahism in early eleventh-century Egypt, when the early believers regarded the reigning Fatimid caliph in Egypt, Abu Ali Mansur al-Hakim, as the incarnation of God. Al-Hakim's adviser, Muhammad ibn Ismail al-Darazi, actually formulated the ritual and scriptures that comprise Druze belief and practice, which are a closely guarded secret that only their holiest leaders know in full. Since it contains a great deal of Christianity, Greek philosophy, and eastern Asian teachings, it is a distinctly different religion, which is outside the body of Islam. The Druze religion spread all the way to India, but persecution ultimately confined it to its two major bastions of Mount Lebanon and Jebal Druze in southern Syria, which the Druze fiercely protect. The Druze do not accept converts, but they believe their numbers are constantly replenished through reincarnation. Druze domination in Lebanon in modern times is limited to the Shuf region of Mount Lebanon, which is located to the southeast of Beirut. While it has never matched the Franco-Maronite alliance, the Druze have retained a strong relationship with Great Britain, especially since the British cooperated in ousting Muhammad Ali's Egyptian troops from Lebanon in 1840.

Egyptian and European Interference

Egyptian rule of Syria, including Lebanon, from 1832 to 1840 altered the region in many ways. Muhammad Ali's close alliance with France assured the Maronites favorable treatment. Consequently, the Maronites prospered at the expense of the Druze, who enjoyed better relations with the Ottomans. The Egyptian tax and conscription policies wore out their welcome in Lebanon, even among the Maronites, by the late 1830s. The Druze regained some of their lands and privileges with the Ottoman return, but they and the Maronites soon resisted full reestablishment of Ottoman authority. The intercession of the European Great Powers resolved the problem of governance on Mount Lebanon by encouraging the Porte to establish a dual *qaymaqamate* (rule by regional governors). In the predominantly Christian northern part of The Mountain a Christian *qaymaqam* governed, while the southern part of The Mountain was under the jurisdiction of a Druze *qaymaqam*. Refinement of the system to accommodate members of each group who lived in their opposite's region, and Muslims and other Christians who had no identity with either, failed to bring peace or satisfaction to The Mountain. The Ottomans continued to have trouble with both groups, but restrictive measures drew the Druze closer to their traditional leaders, while the Maronite peasants rejected their own leaders as tyrannical overlords. Ottoman policies favored the Druze by the time The Mountain erupted in a wholesale Maronite-Druze war in 1859. Druze triumph in that war brought decisive Great Power interference that led to Mount Lebanon becoming a separate Ottoman district under Great Power protection. (See Chapter 1.)

Mount Lebanon was governed by the provisions of the *Reglement Organique* from 1861 to 1915, with a *mutasarrif* (rule by a single governor), or special governor of the Porte, as the head of government. The Porte was responsible to the Great Powers for its conduct of government on The Mountain during this period, which was known as the *Mutasarrifate*. The seven Christian *mutasarrifs*, who by the arrangement were obligated to be non-Maronite and non-Lebanese, varied from outstanding to quite adequate. Lebanon prospered; industry and agriculture flourished; roads, public buildings, public services, and education grew in the well-governed enclave of the Ottoman Empire, which was insulated against most of the vagaries of Great Power and Ottoman entanglements.

Some of these developments resulted from the foundation that had been laid during the period of Egyptian occupation. Western Christian missionaries also accelerated these developments as they increased their activities under the protection of the Great Powers. The missionaries concentrated on education as the best means of converting Lebanese to their particular faith or retaining the loyalty of existing members of their folds. Protestant missions and schools joined the quest for converts and raised the ante, which others tried to meet. Their efforts culminated in the establishment of the Syrian Protestant College in 1866, which evolved into the American University of Beirut. Roman Catholic missionaries, who had been active much earlier, increased all of their activities and by 1875 the Jesuit-sponsored University of St. Joseph in Beirut provided Catholic secondary students a safe atmosphere to continue their education. While they were beyond the boundaries of Lebanon at the time, many of the students came from the secondary schools that had been established earlier on The Mountain. First Lebanese and Syrian people, and then students from all over the Arab world, benefitted from these outstanding universities, which had no rivals for excellence in secular education in the Arab world for another century.

Some Druze, but very few Muslims, entered the Christian educational system, while their own confessions refused to develop schools of comparable quality. A wide disparity, therefore, arose between the educational preparation of the Christian and Muslim populations. Lebanese Christians learned Western arts, sciences, and medicine, which increased their affinity for Western culture. Their education provided them with skills and attitudes which soon spread to the entire Arab world. Lebanese intellectuals were in the forefront of the development of the modern Arab literary movement. Their understanding of Western concepts of individual rights, constitutionalism, and nationalism propelled them into the leadership of Arab dissatisfaction with Ottoman, and later with Western, domination. (See Chapter 10 on Arab Nationalism.)

Lebanese and Arab Nationalism

The Lebanese-Syrian-led Arab nationalist movement, which began about 1880, had widespread support after the Young Turks gained control of Ottoman affairs in 1909, as even Muslim Arabs experienced a diminution of their status. Lebanese were divided, however, on their vision for the future of their Arab nation. Most Maronites and Druze feared they would lose their status and significance in a larger Arab state, which would probably be affiliated with Damascus. Maronites led in suggesting an alternative of annexing the coastal cities and their surroundings, along with the Biqa valley to The Mountain, to form a separate, economically viable Lebanese state. Greek Catholics and some other Christian groups embraced this outlook as preferable to life in a predominantly Muslim state. Greek Orthodox nationalists, who had no desire to reside under Maronite domination, generally supported the concept of a larger nation that would include their co-religionists in Syria and Palestine. Muslim nationalists, for the same reasons, did not support a separate Lebanese state. Elements of the Sunni population essentially boycotted the new entity and refused to serve in elective or appointive positions, and, to their long-term detriment, avoided the opportunity to fill their share of military offices.

TRANSJORDAN

Transjordan, which evolved into Jordan in 1949, became a separate nation solely out of political expediency for Great Britain. Although its history is ancient, and even rich in some respects, it was always as part of small, transient entities, or as a relatively minor part of several large empires. Following the Muslim arrival in the seventh century, Arabic and Islam dominated the culture of this sparsely populated land that is blessed with few natural resources. Except for some architectural edifices, evidence of non-Arab habitation in premodern times requires the diligent work of archaeologists. The Jews are the one modern, non-Arab people who can associate their history with this land prior to the Islamic conquest.

Unlike other parts of the Fertile Crescent, Transjordan never seems to have had prolonged periods of prosperity to sustain a large population, although archaeologists have discovered some of the oldest evidence of civilization within its borders. Instead, it was always an outpost region with a few strategic points that merited special fortification to secure trade routes and deter invaders. In fact, only the westernmost section enjoyed the resources to support anything more complicated than nomadic animal husbandry. The Ajlun area in the northwest was in many respects a socioeconomic extension of the fertile Lower Galilee region west of the Jordan River. Similarly, the Ghor Valley, which lies immediately east of the Jordan River, has the same subtropical climate as the Jericho region on the West Bank. The fact that the lower Jordan River Valley has sustained continuous civilization longer than any other place on earth testifies to the bounty of this small, unique area that is also the lowest place on earth. A short distance east of the Ghor, however, the terrain soon gives way to rugged, semibarren highlands around Amman. East and south of Amman lie the Syrian and Arabian deserts that encompass about three-fourths of Transjordan.

Consequently, resources and climate divided Transjordan into a land of farmers along the Jordan River, while traditional bedouin culture prevailed elsewhere. Even the agricultural area was under the domination of bedouin shaykhs who usually owned the land, protected the farmers, extracted tribute, meted out justice, and settled disputes. The fact that about 90 percent of the population was Sunni Muslim provided a religious and cultural unity to these two otherwise disparate approaches to life. Pockets of Christians, who were mostly Greek Orthodox, often played a significant role in economic matters and some acted in important liaison capacities with the Ottoman government. Most Christians were also farmers who had in common with their Muslim neighbors a social organization based on tribalism. The region received an important infusion of new population when, with Ottoman approval, a few hundred Circassians moved there from Russia in the late nineteenth century. Even their small numbers made an impact on the small population of Transjordan. These Sunni Muslims contributed talent, vigor, and some innovations without causing significant conflict between themselves and the established inhabitants. Their growth over the following years was steady and they sometimes enjoyed a majority in Amman, which was their most important population center.

Only a self-sustaining group like the Circassians could survive in Tranjordanian society without disrupting it. The indigenous resources were simply inadequate to support any considerable population growth that was unable to sustain itself. This essentially subsistence economy could not generate the revenue requirements of a modern state. No appreciable part of the population could be free from ordinary work, especially food production, to serve in an administrative or military capacity. Likewise, no significant number of the inhabitants could engage in anything beyond rudimentary manufacturing. The mineral resources of phosphate and magnesium in the Dead Sea area and the desolate southwestern region required capital, roads, heavy equipment, and transportation that were unavailable.

The lack of a political identity and heritage that might overcome the intrinsic economic weaknesses also augured ill for nationhood. Each tribe was self-governing and only related to its neighboring tribes in traditional ways whenever necessary. Tribal jealousies virtually precluded the possibility of accepting the centralization of power that might elevate one tribe above the others. For four centuries the region related to the central government in Istanbul only marginally through the regional governor at Damascus. Some small Turkish military outposts and a few tax collectors constituted Transjordanian intercourse with Ottoman officialdom.

Ottoman construction of the Hijaz railway through Transjordan in the early twentieth century had significant repercussions. This first major Ottoman capital investment in the region employed a number of locals and connected the region directly to Damascus in the north and Medina and Mecca in the south. Developments on either end of the railroad were likely to affect the relatively unimportant Transjordan in the middle. The Ottoman Empire ended too soon after the completion of the railroad to have a significant impact on how the Ottomans related to Transjordan. The railroad, which reached Amman in 1903, however, gave that town of less than 5,000 an importance that helped impel it, rather than Salt, to become the future capital of Transjordan. Salt, which is fifteen miles west of Amman, had been the Ottoman administrative center and long enjoyed a larger, more diversified population and economy than Amman. Indicative of its stature, a Greek Orthodox Christian resident of Salt, Said Abu Jaber, represented the region in the Ottoman legislature after the restoration of the constitution in 1908.

Transjordan's north-south railway link was of both political and religious importance. Since it constituted the southern part of the Ottoman *Vilayet* of Syria, it had a long affiliation with Damascus. Official business flowed south throughout Transjordan from Damascus. Trade, business, and travel tended to follow the same path. While there was trade and other relations with Jerusalem and Nablus and the surrounding area, relations with the West Bank were considerably less significant. Kinship and religion sustained a close relationship with the Hijaz. Many of the southern tribes of Transjordan had originated in the Arabian peninsula and they continued to have both good and bad relations with tribes in the northern Hijaz. Transjordanian Muslim pilgrimages to Mecca and Medina in the Hijaz also kept relations between the two regions active. The Ottomans, in fact, constructed the Hijaz railway primarily as a means of facilitating the pilgrimage for both financial and religious reasons. Even given the Transjordanian kinship with Hijazi tribes, its relationship with the Hijaz was largely related to religion like other Muslim communities in the region. Otherwise, politically and economically, Transjordan was affiliated with Damascus.

IRAQ

Modern Iraq lies in the center of the Fertile Crescent, which in ancient times was commonly known as Mesopotamia. In contrast with the adjoining mountains and deserts, it seemed like a Garden of Eden even though the life-giving Tigris and Euphrates rivers could be as treacherous as they were nourishing. Its bounty attracted a series of empires, which built civilizations from at least 4000 B.C. Sumerians, Akkadians, Babylonians, Assyrians, Chaldeans, Persians, Macedonians, Parthians, and Sassanid anchored their empires in Mesopotamia and reached out for additional conquests. Although it provided the potential for the luxury associated with it, the area experienced frequent decay and the return to nomadism when a strong central authority did not exist to coordinate control of the raging rivers at flood time, and provide supervision for irrigation much of the year when there was no rain. Gertrude Bell, the distinguished British civil servant, said in 1926: "This is a country of extremes. It's either dying of thirst or it's dying of being drowned." Whether it is the result of the weather and/or its tumultuous history, Iraq has a reputation for political and social extremes, as well. It has a political and social history of divisiveness and dramatic change through violence.

Despite its long history, modern Iraq's values, institutions, and customs derive almost exclusively from its Islamic and Arab heritage. While Iraq came under Islamic control by the middle of the seventh century, the fourth Caliph, Ali, left a special indelible impression on the southern half of Iraq as the center of the Shiah sect. In 750 the Abbassids gained control of the caliphate and moved the capital of Islam from Damascus to Iraq, where by 766 they built the new capital city of Baghdad, which soon became the envy of the world because of its wealth, influence, and learning. The prosperity and spirit of toleration that prevailed in Baghdad inspired people working in materials, words, and ideas to perform their arts to the fullest. Baghdad scholars from various religious and ethnic backgrounds transformed existing Greek, Persian, and Arabic knowledge and concepts into a rich Islamic culture, which was essentially Arabic even though ethnic Arabs often participated mainly as patrons.

Invasions from the middle of the tenth century caused a steady decline in Iraq largely because, as cities were sacked and as central authority weakened, the countryside fell into decay. A Mongol attack on Baghdad in 1258 nearly devastated the entire region and the 1401 attack by Tamerlane administered the *coup de grace*. By the sixteenth century Iraq became the focus of a war between the Ottoman Turk and Persian empires, which the Ottomans finally won in the mid-seventeenth century. This prolonged conflict colored Iraqi history from that time as the Sunni Ottomans and their Arab fellow-believers resisted and feared attacks from the Persian Shiah on their border. Sunni-dominated post-Ottoman governments in Iraq have generally shared that view.

Ottoman Iraq

Ottoman conquest of Iraq was more the elimination of Persian rule than an assertion of Ottoman rule. Other parts of the empire received the attention of the usually overextended Ottoman bureaucracy. Iraq, therefore, primarily served as a buffer against hostile eastern neighbors. Nomadism spread and the urban areas lapsed into penury. Baghdad, for instance, which had supported a population of more than a million in the tenth century could muster no more than 90,000 souls in at the end of the eighteenth century. Early in the eighteenth century the Ottoman government adopted the use of Mamluk rule to rectify the situation. The martial law of the trained slave-administrators restored order and a partial revival of prosperity to the urban areas, but the tribal shaykhs prevailed in the countryside with Mamluk consent. Their more than a century of domination in Iraq never extended to the northern mountains with the long-lasting result that the predominantly Kurdish region felt no kinship with its southern Arab neighbors. The Kurds identified with the strongly Ottoman city of Mosul, which in turn focused its significant trade and cultural relations toward Istanbul and Aleppo, rather than toward Baghdad and Basra.

In 1831 Sultan Mahmoud II decided that the successful Mamluks, who had developed some gifted leaders, were much too independent of Istanbul control. Mamluk success, however, made Iraq more appealing as a source of additional Ottoman revenue and worthy of direct Ottoman rule. Mahmoud's military expedition destroyed the Mamluks in 1831 and Iraq returned to direct Ottoman rule under governors whose venality, incompetence, and occasional stupidity remain legend in Iraq. Ottoman military ability extended central authority to the countryside and into the Kurdish regions. Central to Ottoman policy in Iraq, in fact, was a concerted effort to destroy the power of the tribal shaykhs through a combination of force, extension of the bureaucracy to the countryside, and the implementation of individual land titles to both the shaykhs and their tribesmen.

Influence of Midhat Pasha

One Ottoman governor, Midhat Pasha, developed a reputation for excellence and constructive service that preserved a place of honor for him even after the Ottomans lost Iraq. He established the foundation for modern Iraq in his brief term as governor from 1869 to 1872. Midhat was, after all, one of the chief architects of the Tanzimat movement and its most fervent implementor as he had demonstrated earlier in Bulgaria. He used his full authority and passion for modernization to transform Iraq into a more modern society through his attention to economic development and his encouragement of education, information, centralization, and consultation.

In keeping with the Tanzimat format Midhat created local councils in the urban areas to advise professional administrators on their needs and to make Iraqis feel a part of the governing process. These councils, which many traditionalists resented as threats to their authority, also allowed Ottoman officials to inform local notables of the Porte's intentions. Midhat's most enduring and significant contribution, however, was in education even though he only established four schools during his tenure. They were the first publicly supported, secular schools in Iraq that were accessible to students of all religious and economic backgrounds. Graduates of these schools, and others that were established over the next forty years, provided the Ottoman Empire and the Hashemite regime that succeeded it with some outstanding military officers and civilian administrators.

Midhat's application of the Ottoman Land Law of 1858 had the desired effect of settling many of the raiding, warring, nomadic pastoral tribesmen as agrarian cultivators. Unfortunately, many tribesmen failed to claim land in their own names in fear that an individual identity would lead to taxation and conscription into the Sultan's army. Their reluctance to utilize the Ottoman Land Law cost their entire class dearly as the shaykhs and urban investors laid claim to a large portion of the arable land and suppressed the formerly proud warriors into sharecroppers, who paid 40 to 60 percent of their production to the landowners. These recently created landless masses would be ineligible to vote in the future constitutional governments in which the franchise was based upon land ownership.

The continuation of Midhat's policies after he returned to Istanbul testifies to his success. Iraq, more than any other Arab part of the Ottoman Empire, entered the mainstream of Ottoman modernization. Foreign Christian missionary activities were far less common in Iraq than they were in Syria, Lebanon, or Palestine; as a result, government-sponsored education in Turkish was the only route for students who wished to improve their conditions. Desire for education beyond high school led ambitious Iraqis to Istanbul, where advanced military training was the specialization most available to them. As a result, an inordinately high percentage of the Arab Ottoman officers were Iraqis, which helps explain why Iraqi officers played such a strong role in the Arab Revolt and became attached to Feisal, their future monarch.

By 1914, Iraq was quite different from 1831 when the Ottomans had reasserted their authority. Its population had almost doubled during that period. Iraqi cities such as Baghdad, Basra, and Mosul were significant centers of trade and intellectual activity. The country was not only able to feed itself but had surplus grain to export. Steamboat travel, telegraph connections, and postal service connected Iraq with the outside world. Newspapers, which began in 1869 under Midhat Pasha, also helped establish a sense of Mesopotamian unity to replace the former prevalence of localism. Like most of the Ottoman Empire, however, the predominantly cottage and small artisan manufacturing of Iraq actually declined during this period in the face of foreign competition, especially from Great Britain. British influence on Iraqi import and export trade emerged slowly from 1640 and, in fact, became dominant from the major trading stations at Basra and Baghdad by the close of the eighteenth century.

Iraq's Borders

If the Great Powers, which determined Iraq's structure in the post-World War I period, performed admirably in establishing a political system that could meet the nation's needs, there is little defense for the boundaries they drew. Iraq's essentially landlocked position made some sense at the time, since Britain controlled both Transjordan and Palestine and had a good working relationship with the French in mandatory Syria-Lebanon because of their mutual interest in Iraqi oil. Mandatory Iraq, thus, had access to the ports of Haifa on the Mediterranean and Aqaba on the Gulf of Aqaba, with plans for British-built roads and railroads in between.

While the Uqair Conference of 1922 determined the border with the developing Saudi kingdom, the very contentious border with Turkey from Mosul north only solidified on July 18, 1926 after years of border conflicts and League of Nations arbitration. Under heavy British pressure the League appended the former Ottoman *vilayet* of Mosul, with its heavily Kurdish population and large oil reserves, to Iraq. The Sykes-Picot agreement ceded it to France, but British occupation of the region at the end of World War I allowed Britain to claim its strategic and mineral benefits in behalf of Iraq. Iraqi sentiment in behalf of acquiring Mosul became so strong that ratification of the Anglo-Iraqi Treaty of 1924 was contingent upon British success in delivering Mosul to Iraq in the negotiations with Turkey. The British, of course, were equally interested in keeping the Mosul-Kirkuk oil under their control in Iraq.

Even worse than the above restrictions, Iraq's meager outlet to the Gulf was inadequate and ill-conceived for a mandatory entity that Great Britain and the League were preparing for independence. Iraq had no port on the Gulf and the only port that could serve international shipping was 120 miles inland at Basra on the Shatt al-Arab. The natural port for Iraq was Kuwait City; however, the British kept Kuwait under separate control through its treaty affiliation with the al-Sabah family, which had prevailed in that shaykhdom since the middle of the eighteenth century. Kuwait, like Iraq, had been part of the Ottoman Empire until the British took it under unofficial protection with Ottoman consent in 1913 and official protection in 1914 when the two parties became belligerents during World War I. Iraqis neither understood nor forgave Britain or the League of Nations for excluding Kuwait in the Mesopotamian mandate. By excluding Kuwait, they had prevented it from becoming part of an independent Iraq. In Iraqi eyes, the al-Sabah family was no more distinguished than other tribal chieftains in southern Mesopotamia, although they did have a strong affiliation with Gulf coastal tribes and the interior tribes in the northeast sector of the Arabian peninsula.

THE ARABIAN PENINSULA

From a historical perspective, the severe climate and sparsity of resources prevented all but the southwest part of the Arabian peninsula from supporting a significant level of population. Consequently, it has been of marginal political and economic importance through the ages. Its distinction as the birthplace of Islam is a major exception for this predominantly desert region. Even the success and spread of Islam was probably dependent upon transferring its center from the Hijaz to Damascus and Baghdad, where communication was much easier because of the great population and resource centers of Asia and Africa.

The Gulf Region of Arabia

Although the Gulf provided a vital link between southwest Asia and the Far East, it had never prospered. Interesting archaeological evidence, however, indicates that the region had a prolonged period of human habitation even though it was never heavily populated. Approximately one million people lived along the entirety of its shores and their immediate environs early in the nineteenth century. There was no substantial change in the size of the population of the Gulf region until well into the twentieth century. A plentiful supply of seafood from its salty waters could not overcome the serious shortage of fresh water for agriculture, animal husbandry, and human needs. Besides seafood, the Gulf residents could produce enough meat and animal products, dates, fruits, and some vegetables for their sustenance. The region imported coffee, tea, spices, rice and other grains primarily from India, upon which it relied for most of its commerce. In fact, the Gulf was at least as culturally related to India as it was to the interior of Arabia and Mesopotamia in everything other than religion.

Considerable political fluidity prevailed on the eastern shores of the Arabian peninsula as strong individuals and families often achieved prominence they could not sustain. Confederations also emerged that were, in time, subject to internal disorder and interference from forces beyond the region. In fact, favorable commercial and military arrangements with foreign allies became a necessary prerequisite for any regional entity to achieve any substantial period of economic and political success.

Oman, which generally encompassed the southeast corner of the Arabian peninsula, was the dominant regional power by the beginning of the nineteenth century. Most agree that the Omani port of Muscat at least equalled the trade and wealth of all the other ports on the eastern coast of the peninsula during the first couple of decades of the century. Strong families emerged in Ra's al-Khaima, Sharja, Abu Dhabi, and Dubai on the Gulf shore that severed their towns and the surrounding areas from Omani control. They soon commanded a share of the trade and power that Oman had formerly enjoyed. Bahrain, a crucial pearl-rich island in the west central Gulf, and Kuwait on the northwest coast also developed as rivals to contest Oman's previous domination of power and wealth in the Gulf. The *Wahhabi* religious fundamentalist movement, which was centered in Najd and Qatar, provided additional ferment to the region, which was becoming increasingly chaotic.

The often violent competition among the contentious elements was sufficiently harmful to all parties that they accepted Great Britain as an intercessory power to provide all with military protection and the adjudication of disputes. The British introduced their Trucial system to serve these functions in the 1830s; it would remain in place, with occasional modifications, until member shaykhdoms received their independence in the 1960s and 1970s. After Egyptian military efforts subdued the *Wahhabi* movement by the late 1830s, eastern Arabia experienced a more tranquil period.

Pax Britannica prevailed as much in the Gulf region as any place else in the late nineteenth century. Britain's posture of dominating without ruling the region did not present either a real or emotional threat to any possible opponent. Its military strength prevented any other entity from serious consideration of expanding at the expense of their neighbors. The Ottoman and Persian empires were in no condition either to assert their own claims to the region or to challenge Britain's domination. The presence of a significant Persian population on the eastern shore of the Arabian peninsula and on the islands in the Gulf obligated Persia, or elements in Persia, to make occasional claims to those territories. This was particularly true in relation to the islands of Bahrain, Abu Musa, and Tunbs. Persia's inability to protect its sovereignty against Russian and British intrusion provides adequate explanation for why Persia made essentially perfunctory claims and, like the small shaykhdoms, accepted British dictates.

The truth is that by the second half of the nineteenth century, the importance of the Gulf had declined to the point that virtually no one outside of the immediate region cared about the Gulf area. The opening of the Suez Canal in 1869 contributed to this diminution because it provided a direct sea route between the East and West. The new steamships of European ownership transported all large ocean-going cargos and passengers. The reliable *dhows,* which had customarily plied the seas between Arabia and Africa, and between Arabia and India, were relegated to service along the coast or to commercial activities of minor importance. Britain had actively pursued policies that established its predominance in the Gulf but it enjoyed that status primarily by default. There was neither knowledge nor suspicion that the region possessed vast quantities of petroleum and gas that would make control of it vital to a new way of life in the twentieth century.

The Emergence of Saudi Arabia and Hashemite Hijaz

Early in the twentieth century the Al-Saud and Hashimi families took initatives that would reshape the Arabian peninsula and the entire Arab world. Abdul Aziz Ibn Saud soon established a nation under his control that encompassed three-fourths of the Arabian peninsula. In the process of forming his kingdom, he eliminated the Hashemite Kingdom of the Hijaz that Sharif Hussein al-Hashimi had established during World War I. However, the Hashemites, who had begun their rise in the Arabian peninsula, had positioned themselves during World War I to provide the monarch of a short-lived kingdom in Syria and the monarchies of the two new Arab states of Iraq and Transjordan.

On January 15, 1902, Abdul Aziz Ibn Al-Saud and fewer than forty companions seized the fortress of Musmak in the town of Riyadh, which was to become the capital of the Kingdom of Saudi Arabia thirty years later. During the intervening years, his success and style in solving regional and international problems established his reputation as one of the most significant figures in the modern Middle East. Abdul Aziz was a member of the Al-Saud family that, in alliance with the *Wahhabi* movement, had emerged as a vital force in the Najd and eastward a century earlier. Al-Saud success expanded their territories from the capital of Riyahd and soon collected tribute from most neighboring shaykhdoms, including the powerful Oman. Al-Saud influence continued after Egyptian efforts eliminated most of their *Wahhabi* allies and drove that movement underground. The Rashid clan, which was centered 350 miles to the north in the town of Hail, had forced him and his family out of Riyadh in 1891. The Al-Sauds had lived in refuge in Qatar and Kuwait until the twenty-one-year-old Abdul Aziz regained their traditional center of power.

It appeared that control over the small oasis town of Riyadh actually proved little and gained little more than family honor unless Abdul Aziz could do much more against overwhelming odds. Of their neighbors, only members of the Al-Sabah family, which ruled Kuwait, were friendly to the Al-Sauds. The entire Arabian peninsula was ostensibly part of the Ottoman Empire, although the Ottomans had never established their authority in the interior of Arabia. The Ottoman government relied upon the Rashids to protect its interests in the Nefud, Hasa, and Najd provinces. But the limited resources and communications of the Ottomans forced them to restrict their ambitions to preventing forces patently contrary to their interests from arising in the region, which had too few people and too few proven resources to merit greater attention.

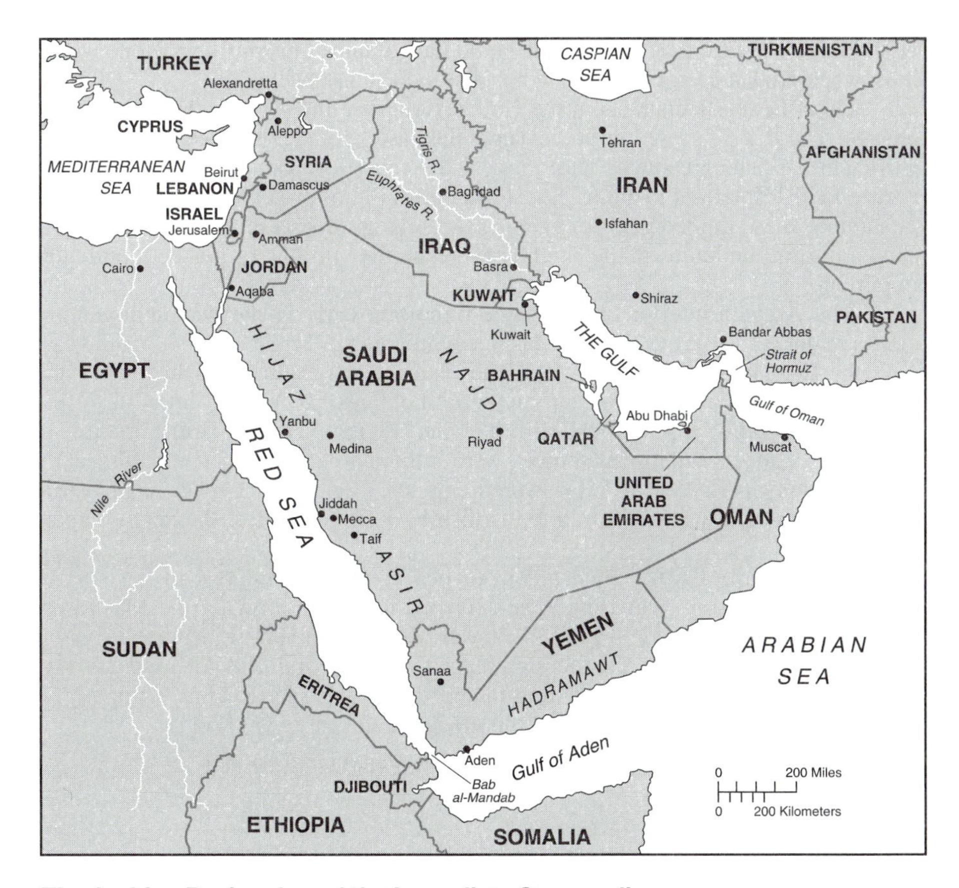

The Arabian Peninsula and the Immediate Surroundings

Great Britain was the real power in the region, as it had been since it had replaced the Portuguese and the Dutch in the eighteenth century. The British enjoyed good relations with all of the coastal shaykhs of the Gulf and with the Rashids. The British had also led Western European efforts to prevent the dissolution of the Ottoman Empire since the middle of the nineteenth century. Britain's conflicts with Germany, which had made significant economic and military inroads into the Ottoman Empire at the turn of the century, precluded Britain from giving succor to someone like Abdul Aziz, whose desires might be contrary to Ottoman interests.

From 1908, when Sharif Hussein Al Hashimi became the Turkish governor of the Hijaz, Abdul Aziz had to contend with a formidable regional foe whose ambitions were a match for his own. Sharif Hussein enjoyed the benefits of governing an indigenously more prosperous region, which also enjoyed the income from pilgrims from throughout the Muslim world. Hussein was a Turkish official until 1916, when he led the Arab Revolt against the Ottoman Empire. Following that, he was the fulcrum of British policy in the Red Sea and the interior of Arabia. Few would have wagered that Abdul Aziz could have retained his position. None would have wagered that he could improve his position against such odds.

Great Britain's interests in the Gulf region were the greatest deterrent to any change. The British shared with the Turks the basic attitude that the status quo was sufficient. British agreements with most of the coastal shaykhs were meant to help secure British interests in India. Subsidies and military protection for the shaykhs guaranteed these limited goals of keeping the strategic coasts in friendly hands. The sands and the bedouin of the interior were neither militarily nor economically important.

The Arabian interior only became important early in the twentieth century after a major oil strike occurred at Masjid es-Suleiman in Persia in 1908, seven years after the Englishman William d'Arcy had obtained the exclusive right to find and market oil in Persia. Since Britain's imperial holdings had yielded little oil to that date, the possibility of additional oil in the Gulf region increased British interest in all parts of Arabia. Additional sources were important because Britain had recently begun to convert its fleet to oil-powered engines. Germany's growth in industrial and naval strength further spurred the British to desire control of the newly important fuel.

By 1914 the British government owned controlling interest in the Anglo-Persian Oil Company, which had been formed in 1908 following the Masjid es-Suleiman discovery. In 1911 and 1913 the British government signed exclusive oil concession agreements with the shaykhs of Bahrain and Kuwait respectively. Private British interests already dominated the Turkish Petroleum Company in Mesopotamia. Oil had increased the importance of the entire Gulf region.

YEMEN

Historically, southwestern Arabia has been the most prosperous part of the subcontinent. This was due in no small part to the presence of an adequate supply of fresh water, which other parts of the peninsula lacked. Regular rainfall, mountain streams, and the capacity to retain seasonal rains for agriculture provided the region with a food supply for a significant population. Its location on a major sea also provided the region with the benefits of an often vibrant international trade. Ready access to South Asia and East Africa contributed to South Arabia's reputation in antiquity as *Arabia Felix*, Fertile Arabia. Consumers throughout the entire Mediterranean region assumed that all the wonderful products they received from The Yemen originated there, while, in fact, Yemeni merchants often served merely as middle men. For multiple reasons, therefore, the region held a special fascination for people within and beyond its physical confines.

Yemen's location at the entrance to the Red Sea, at the northwest-most portion of the Arabian Sea of the Indian Ocean, made it the perfect entrepot for providing the West with the exotic commodities of the Orient. The fact that the highly prized frankincense and myrrh actually originated in Yemen prevented its reputation for fine things from being totally spurious. A general lack of safety for navigation on the Red Sea was also beneficial to Yemen, as goods from the Orient often could travel more safely overland to their northern destinations.

"The Yemen" is a roughly rectangular area about eight hundred miles long and four hundred miles wide on the southwest side of the Arabian peninsula. This identity has prevailed through the centuries, despite the fact that it has seldom been under a single jurisdiction. The predominantly mountainous terrain is perfectly suited for the many tribes living there to preserve their independence. Local kingdoms, and even empires, flourished at times only to disintegrate under a combination of internal and external pressures. Persian, Roman, Egyptian, and Ethiopian emperors periodically exercised some level of control over Yemen before losing their hold, more often than not to assertive indigenous rulers. In modern times the Ottoman and British empires claimed jurisdiction over parts of Yemen with a minimum of conflict between them and a general recognition that much of Yemen was either ungovernable or not worth the effort.

Yemen's diversity, as well as its complex tribal structure, lends depth to its peculiar character. Life along the Red Sea coast is akin to that in Africa; residents in the high mountains of North Yemen have no regional parallel, the arid but irrigated Hadramaut has a way of its own, and the eastern region subsists in the sparsity incumbent upon the land adjacent to the Rub al-Khali, or Empty Quarter. Large numbers of Jews migrated to Yemen after their expulsion from Palestine in the first century. They thrived in Yeman and, for a short time in the sixth century, they expanded beyond the region. A small Christian community enjoyed brief periods of prominence and provoked outside interference on their behalf especially from Ethiopia and Egypt. The uniqueness of Yemen allowed the survival of Zaidi Shiahism that would assure the continuation of Yemen's distinction of being unlike anyplace else on earth.

Zaid, the grandson of Imam Hussein, inspired a separate branch of Shiahism after his martyred death in 740. While Zaidism soon attracted converts from Iraq to the Hijaz, it only thrived in the mountains of North Yemen. It was not until the last decade of the ninth century, however, that Yahya al-Rassi established the first Zaidi state with its capital at Sanaa. For long periods over the following centuries, no Zaidi state existed anywhere in Yemen. Conventional Sunni Islam, often under foreign influence, dominated the region and suppressed Yemen's unique form of Shiahism. This persecution aided Zaidism's identification, even among Yemeni Sunnis, with Yemen's desire for independence. During a period of resurgence in the second half of the seventeenth century, Zaidism actually spread over the entirety of Yemen before local insurgencies pushed it back to its mountain fastness surrounding Sanaa.

Zaidism differed from other variations of Shiahism in several ways and was closer to Sunni belief than the other Alid approaches to Islam. For instance, there was no belief in *The Madhi*. The Zaidi Imam was elected and reigned in his time. Candidates had to descend from Ali, but proximity to the First Imam was unimportant. Instead, religious qualifications, moral purity, and leadership ability were supposed to be the primary considerations for conferring the Imamate upon someone from a fairly broad pool of candidates. Periods of virtual hereditary succession occurred, but, since this type of succession did not comply with Zaidism's highest ideals, improperly elected Imams could expect dissent, opposition, and justification for rebellion. Frequent armed conflict among the Zaidis in North Yemen spilled over into the affairs of the Sunni majority on the shore, and to the southern and eastern parts of Yemen.

Although blessed with more fresh water than other parts of Arabia, Yemen's reputation as a land of plenty depended upon its commerce in commodities from the far Orient. Once the Romans discovered the source of Yemen's exotic goods in the second century, they soon also discovered how to reach India without hugging the southern shore of Arabia. Romans and their successor societies contrived successful attempts to eliminate the Yemeni middlemen to the steady detriment of Yemen's economy. Cultivation of coffee, which was centered in Mocha, had revived Yemen's uniqueness during the later half of the first millennium. However, by the time it became a popular beverage in the Mediterranean region in the sixteenth century, Europeans had established direct trade with the far Orient. Near the end of the seventeenth century the Dutch established coffee cultivation in Java and the Portuguese later spread it to South America. Yemen's subsequent commercial decline relegated its primary importance to strategic and logistical concerns of distant nations that desired bases in the region.

The Ottomans incorporated Yemen into their empire in the early sixteenth century, but the Zaidi Imam, Muayyad Muhammad, ousted the Ottomans a century later as he achieved the apogee of Zaidi success in Yemen. While the Ottomans withdrew in 1636, they continued to regard Yemen as part of their empire. In less than a century, local insurgencies pushed the Zaidis back to North Yemen and the British and Dutch usurped most of the lucrative trade associated with Yemen.

Britain's Seizure of Aden

Yeman's modern shape emerged early in the nineteenth century when Great Britain became actively interested in Aden. This small, strategic peninsula, which has two major protected harbors, lies approximately one hundred miles east of Bab al-Mandab, the southern entrance to the Red Sea. It had the added appeal of being an ideal coaling station for Britain's steam-driven naval and merchant fleets. Following mutual, amicable attempts to arrive at a satisfactory arrangement, the British finally seized Aden from the Sultan of Lahij, who governed the area immediately adjacent to the peninsula, on January 19, 1839. From this base Britain gradually established the only significant general authority over South Yemen, although it primarily limited its efforts to protecting the Aden harbors and access to the Red Sea. In pursuit of the latter goal Britain seized Perim Island in 1857. Situated in the middle of the Bab al-Mandab, the island was essentially Britain's Gibraltar of the Red Sea. Britain's initial interest in Aden increased exponentially once the Suez Canal opened in 1869. From the 1870s Britain steadily established agreements with South Yemen rulers to extend a protectorate over the entire region. A combination of Britain's vital support for the Ottoman Empire's resistance to Russian aggression and Ottoman preoccupation with other problems minimized Anglo-Ottoman conflict in Yemen. In fact, in the Anglo-Ottoman Convention of March 9, 1914, which addressed all areas of mutual concern between the two empires on the Arabian peninsula, the Ottomans acknowledged British hegemony in South Yemen.

The withdrawal of Muhammad Ali's Egyptian forces from Yemen in 1840 initiated renewed conflict among ambitious local leaders. The Ottomans reasserted their claims in 1849 through a Zaidi imam of their choice, but irate Zaidis led a general resistance to Ottoman ambitions. Beginning in 1871 the Ottomans established a modicum of control over North Yemeni lands that abutted British control in the south, but the Zaidis led a persistent resistance. Imam Muhammad ibn Yahya was particularly effective in resisting the Ottomans after he was elected in 1891. His son, Yahya, continued Yemen's nationalist activities when he succeeded his father as imam in 1904. Yemini opposition was rewarded in the Treaty of Daan in 1911, by which the Ottoman government conceded considerable autonomy to the Imam in the traditional Zaidi region. The loss of Libya to Italy the same year and the problems brewing in the Balkans influenced the Ottoman decision to make concessions in Yemen. While the Ottoman government maintained a presence in North Yemen and continued to regard it as Ottoman territory, its authority was minimal, at best, by the outbreak of World War I.

5

World War I in the Middle East

HISTORICAL TIMELINE

1914
- ⇛ The British purchased a controlling interest (51 percent) in the Anglo-Persian Oil Company in May.
- ⇛ The British recognized Abdul Aziz as the independent ruler of the Najd and its dependencies.
- ⇛ Saad Zaghlul was elected speaker of the Egyptian Legislative Assembly.
- ⇛ Archduke Franz Ferdinand of Austria assassinated in Sarajevo on June 28.
- ⇛ German Declaration of War against Russia on August 1.
- ⇛ Britain announced withholding of shipment on two battleships to Ottoman Empire August 3.
- ⇛ Germany began shipment of arms to Ottoman Empire August 4.
- ⇛ Germany transferred two battlecruisers to Ottoman control on August 11.
- ⇛ Ottomans closed the Straits to all shipping on September 27.
- ⇛ Porte reduced or abolished all special privileges of foreign governments on October 1.
- ⇛ Gold shipment from Germany arrived in Istanbul on October 21.
- ⇛ Russia broke off relations with Istanbul on October 30.
- ⇛ Russian declaration of war on Ottoman Empire November 2.
- ⇛ Russia stated intentions of annexing the Straits and Istanbul in November.

- ⇛ British and French declarations of war against Ottoman Empire November 5.
- ⇛ Britain occupied al-Faw at the mouth of the Shatt al-Arab in November.
- ⇛ Sultan declared Holy War on November 14.
- ⇛ British declared Egypt a protectorate on December 18, deposed Abbas Hilmi, replaced him with his uncle Hussein Kamal, and gave him the new title of Sultan.
- ⇛ British established Zion Mule Corp; corp abolished after Gallipoli.
- ⇛ Persia declared its neutrality in World War I. Russians and British did not honor neutrality. Most Persians supported the German cause and a Persian quasi-government of constitutionalists in Kermanshah declared war on the German side.
- ⇛ British governed most of southern Persia during World War I. However, Russia's problems, and later its revolution, prevented it from governing its northern sphere.
- ⇛ Battle of Sarikamish December 29–January 2. Eighty thousand Ottoman soldiers were lost in the battle.

1915

- ⇛ Ottoman Empire forces crossed Sinai and launched an attack on the Suez Canal in January.
- ⇛ Ottoman reprisals began against Armenians in February.
- ⇛ British first attack on Gallipoli began on February 19.
- ⇛ British and French reached agreement to allow greater land claims for Russia before proceeding with the Gallipoli invasion March 7–15.
- ⇛ Allied forces were severely defeated at Gallipoli in March.
- ⇛ Armenian Nationalist declaration of Armenian Republic in April.
- ⇛ British launched another assault on Gallipoli April 24.
- ⇛ Treaty of London April 25 enticed Italy to join Allies.
- ⇛ Italy entered the war on May 23.
- ⇛ Ottoman Empire removed Armenians from Eastern Anatolia to Syria (June–September).
- ⇛ Sharif Hussein of the Hijaz opened correspondence with Sir Henry McMahon in July.
- ⇛ Executions of Arab nationalist leaders in Beirut and Damascus took place during August.
- ⇛ British moved troops from Basra to Kut al-Amara in September.
- ⇛ Bulgaria entered the war on October 14 as ally of Central Powers in exchange for territory in Eastern Thrace.
- ⇛ A strong separatist movement began in Gilan province of Persia under the leadership of Kuchik Khan.
- ⇛ British made an offer to Sharif Hussein on October 24.
- ⇛ British attempted conquest of Baghdad in November.
- ⇛ Sharif Hussein accepted British offer for an alliance on November 5.

	⇛ Negotiations began in November between Charles Francois Georges-Picot and Sir Mark Sykes to determine the partitioning of the Middle East.
1916	⇛ Allies withdrew from the Dardanelles on January 8–9.
	⇛ British accepted Sharif Hussein's terms on January 30.
	⇛ British suppressed Kermanshah movement of Persia in 1916 and suppressed all German activities in its sector.
	⇛ Sykes-Picot Agreement secretly endorsed by British and French governments on February 4.
	⇛ British occupied Baghdad on March 11.
	⇛ Second Ottoman-German attack on Suez Canal April 23; third attack followed on July 19.
	⇛ General Townshend's forces surrendered on April 29 to the Ottomans at Kut al-Amara.
	⇛ Sharif Hussein declared the beginning of the Arab Revolt against the Ottoman Empire on June 5.
	⇛ Hussein's Arab forces seized Mecca, Jeddah, and the Red Sea coast north to Yanbo June 6–September 22.
	⇛ Sharif Hussein was proclaimed King of the Arabs on October 29.
	⇛ British launched Sinai-Palestine campaign November 15.
	⇛ British recognized Hussein as King of the Hijaz on December 15.
	⇛ British conquest of Mesopotamia was initiated under General Frederick Maude on December 13.
	⇛ Lloyd George cabinet assumed power in Great Britain on December 10.
1917	⇛ Hussein's forces captured Wejh in January.
	⇛ Fall of Erzerum on February 16.
	⇛ Kut al-Amara was reconquered by the British on February 23.
	⇛ Baghdad fell to British March 11.
	⇛ Tsar Nicholas II of Russia was overthrown on March 16.
	⇛ United States entered World War I on April 6.
	⇛ In April, the British government expressed determination to maintain exclusive control over Palestine.
	⇛ Treaty of St. Jean-de-Maurienne on April 19.
	⇛ British cabinet discussions began in June regarding Jewish homeland in Palestine.
	⇛ Allenby took command of Palestine campaign on June 28.
	⇛ Eastern third of Anatolia was under Russian control by the end of summer.
	⇛ Arab forces captured Aqaba on July 6.
	⇛ Woodrow Wilson endorsed the idea of a Jewish homeland in Palestine in October.
	⇛ British forces penetrated Ottoman defenses at Beersheba on October 31.
	⇛ British cabinet approved the Balfour Declaration on October 16.

- ⇛ Balfour Declaration was issued in the form of a letter to Lord Rothschild on November 2.
- ⇛ British forces entered Jerusalem December 11.
- ⇛ Russian troops withdrew from Persia after the Russian Revolution occurred.
- ⇛ State Committee of the Democratic party of Azerbaijan in Persia essentially declared its independence after Russian troops withdrew.
- ⇛ British established their hegemony over most of Persia once the Russians withdrew.
- ⇛ Death of King Hussein Kamel of Egypt. Fuad became king.

1918
- ⇛ Treaty of Brest-Litovsk on March 3.
- ⇛ Batum fell to Turkish control on April 15.
- ⇛ Abdullah-led forces lost the Battle of Turaba in May.
- ⇛ Allies began major offensive against Bulgaria on September 14.
- ⇛ British began campaign to take Damascus on September 19.
- ⇛ British and Arab forces conquered Damascus on September 30.
- ⇛ Bulgarian capitulation on September 30.
- ⇛ Feisal declared Syria independent on October 5.
- ⇛ Committee of Union and Progress sued for peace on October 5.
- ⇛ Committee of Union and Progress cabinet members resigned on October 7.
- ⇛ Small French force landed at Beirut October 7.
- ⇛ Ottoman Minister of War Hussein Orbay arrived at Moudros for negotiations with the British on October 27.
- ⇛ Ottomans signed Armistice of Mudros on October 31.
- ⇛ British suppressed Gilan movement and Ottomans suppressed Azerbaijan movement, but grassroots support and leadership of both were ready to reassert their separatist activities.
- ⇛ British sent a Zionist Commission to Palestine.
- ⇛ On November 7, British and French assured the Iraqis that British occupation was for their liberation and was a necessary step toward Arab self-rule.
- ⇛ Saad Zaghlul formed *Wafd al-Misri* (Egyptian Delegation) and attempted to gain permission to take Egypt's case for independence to the Paris Peace Conference.

1919
- ⇛ Paris Peace Conference convened on January 18.
- ⇛ Creation of League of Nations on January 25.
- ⇛ First Palestinian National Congress, meeting in Jerusalem January 27–February 10 rejected Balfour Declaration and demanded independence.
- ⇛ Zaghlul of Egypt was exiled to Malta in March. Unrest in Egypt forced High Commissioner Allenby to allow Wafd to attend Peace Conference.
- ⇛ Peace conference decided on March 25 to send international commission of inquiry to ascertain aspirations of Near East peoples.
- ⇛ Greek army landed at Izmir on May 15.

- ⇛ Major Saudi and Ikhwan victory over Hashemite forces at Turaba on May 25.
- ⇛ King-Crane Commission began investigation in June.
- ⇛ Treaty of Versailles and League of Nations Covenant signed on June 28.
- ⇛ Syrian National Congress declared independence on July 2.
- ⇛ Anglo-Persian Treaty of August 9 gave Britain control of Persian affairs, which was unacceptable to Persians, Soviets, and Britain's wartime allies.
- ⇛ King-Crane report was completed on August 28.
- ⇛ Turkish Nationalist Congress at Sivas September 4.
- ⇛ National Pact of Turkish Nationalist Movement September 13.
- ⇛ French troops moved into Beirut area October 9.
- ⇛ British withdrew troops from Syria on November 1.

1920

- ⇛ Turkish Nationalists launched a major military campaign in January against the French in Cilicia.
- ⇛ Ottoman parliament in Istanbul endorsed the National Pact on January 28.
- ⇛ Feisal talked with Clemenceau in January.
- ⇛ General Syrian Congress elected Feisal king of Syria and an Iraqi element elected Abdullah king of Iraq on March 8.
- ⇛ Zaghlul and Milner negotiated a relationship between Egypt and Great Britain from March through August.
- ⇛ On March 15 Allies used military force in Istanbul and arrested Ottoman officials suspected of sympathizing with the Nationalists.
- ⇛ San Remo Conference met on April 18.
- ⇛ Disturbances broke out in Palestine in April due to fears of Zionism.
- ⇛ Turkish Nationalists established provisional government with Mustapha Kemal as president on April 23.
- ⇛ San Remo Conference announced on the mandate system on April 24.
- ⇛ Muhammad Khiabani seized control of Azerbaijan on behalf of the Azerbaijan Democratic party in April.
- ⇛ The Turkish delegation first saw the treaty of Sevres on May 11.
- ⇛ Soviet troops entered Persia on May 18 and refused to leave until Britain accepted the termination of the Anglo-Persian Treaty of 1919.
- ⇛ Kuchik Khan declared the creation of the Persian Soviet Socialist Republic on June 4.
- ⇛ Ottoman government, including the Sultan, refused the Treaty of Sevres on June 10.
- ⇛ Premier Hassan Pirniya renounced the Anglo-Persian Treaty and established diplomatic relations with the Soviet Union in June.

- ⇛ General Gouraud demanded on July 14 that Feisal withdraw from Damascus.
- ⇛ France occupied Damascus and expelled Feisal on July 25.
- ⇛ British civilian administration was inaugurated in Palestine on July 1; Sir Herbert Samuel was appointed first high commissioner.
- ⇛ Large-scale hostilities developed in Iraq from August to October in protest of the British mandate.
- ⇛ Sir Percy Cox returned to Iraq in the fall and restored order in part by the establishment of an Iraqi Arab government.
- ⇛ The Greek armies routed the Nationalist forces in Bursa and Thrace from June 23 through July 24.
- ⇛ Ottoman government agreed to the Treaty of Sevres August 10.
- ⇛ Treaty of Sevres created republics for Kurds and Armenia.
- ⇛ French created Greater Lebanon on September 1.
- ⇛ British supported tribal armies in Persia and the Royal Cossack Brigade killed Muhammad Khiabani on September 14 and suppressed the Azerbaijan Democratic Movement.
- ⇛ Abdullah al-Hashimi began to form an army to reestablish his brother, Feisal, as king of Syria in October.
- ⇛ King Alexander of Greece died unexpectedly on October 25.
- ⇛ Abdullah arrived with small forces in Maan in November.
- ⇛ Greek free election on November 14.
- ⇛ Venizelos resigned and went into exile following his election defeat.
- ⇛ Turkish Nationalist Movement Treaty of Alexandropol with Armenian Republic on December 2.
- ⇛ King Constantine returned to Greece on December 19.
- ⇛ Third Palestinian National Congress at Haifa elected an Executive Committee in December, which controlled the Palestinian political movement from 1920 to 1935.
- ⇛ Saudi and Ikhwan forces redefined the borders in the west with Yemen and in the east with Kuwait.

1921

- ⇛ Turkish victory in first Battle of Inonu January 6.
- ⇛ National Assembly adopted its Fundamental Law, which called for parliamentary democracy and universal manhood suffrage, on January 20.
- ⇛ Colonel Reza Khan of the Cossack Brigade, in conjunction with Sayyed Zia, seized power in a *coup d'etat* on February 21.
- ⇛ Supreme Council of the Allies called a special meeting in London on February 21.
- ⇛ Iranian government renounced the Anglo-Persian Treaty and signed a treaty with the Soviet Union on February 26.
- ⇛ Abdullah arrived in Amman on March 2.
- ⇛ Cairo Conference created the Kingdom of Iraq with Feisal al-Hashimi as king on March 12.

- ⇛ The Treaty of Moscow was signed on March 12. In this treaty, the Soviets recognized the Nationalist government as the legitimate government of Turkey and extended it diplomatic, financial, and military aid. The Soviets returned Ardahan and Kars, which they had obtained at the Congress of Berlin in 1878.
- ⇛ Churchill and Abdullah met in Jerusalem and Abdullah received temporary custody of Transjordan after the Cairo Conference.
- ⇛ On March 13, the Turkish Nationalist Movement signed an agreement to remove the Italians from Turkey.
- ⇛ The Second Battle of Inonu took place. Greece launched another offensive on March 23, which Ismet again turned back at Inonu.
- ⇛ Outbreak of disturbances in Jaffa on May 2 against Zionist immigration resulted in the death of 46 Jews and 146 wounded.
- ⇛ British appointed Hajj Amin al-Husseini Mufti of Jerusalem on May 8.
- ⇛ Council of State elected Feisal king of Iraq on July 11.
- ⇛ Plebiscite indicated 96 percent of Iraqis approved Feisal as king.
- ⇛ League of Nations approved mandates for Syria, Lebanon, and Palestine on July 24.
- ⇛ Feisal was coronated as king of Iraq on August 23.
- ⇛ On October 20, the Turkish Nationalist Movement signed an agreement to remove France from Turkey.
- ⇛ France signed the Treaty of Ankara on October 10, which brought diplomatic recognition and peace with France. It pushed the French mandatory border 10,000 square miles south and restored the territory of Cilicia to Turkish control.
- ⇛ France ceded Cilicia to Turkey on October 20.
- ⇛ Haycraft Commission of Inquiry in October attributed the Jaffa disturbances to the magnitude of Zionist mass immigration.
- ⇛ Zaghlul, leader of the Egyptian *wafd,* was exiled to the Seychelle Islands.
- ⇛ Abdul Aziz seized control of Hail, the Rashid capital, in November.

1922

- ⇛ Great Britain recognized Egypt as an independent country on February 28 but continued to rule by martial law until July.
- ⇛ Egypt received a new constitution in April.
- ⇛ Zaghlul and Wafd won an overwhelming majority in the legislature of the new Egyptian constitutional monarchy.
- ⇛ Churchill issued the White Paper on June 2. This paper, which dealt with Palestine, stated the British concept of their obligations to the Zionists; it excluded Transjordan from the Balfour Declaration and the League of Nations mandate; Jewish immigration was not to exceed the economic capacity of a country.
- ⇛ U.S. Congress endorsed the Balfour Declaration on June 30.
- ⇛ League of Nations approved mandates for Syria, Lebanon, and Palestine on July 24.
- ⇛ Fifth Palestinian National Congress at Nablus in August

resolved to implement an economic boycott against the Zionist community.

⇛ Anglo-Iraqi Treaty of October 21 defined the relationship between the two countries. The League of Nations still regarded Iraq as a mandate.

⇛ The British published the first census of Palestine in October, which estimated the total population at 757,182. This included 78 percent Muslim, 11 percent Jewish, and 9.6 percent Christian.

⇛ The National Assembly abolished the Ottoman Sultanate on November 4 and exiled the Sultan to Malta.

⇛ Uqair Conference fixed Iraqi borders with Saudi Arabia in November.

1923 ⇛ Vladimir Jabotinsky resigned from the Zionist Executive in January and vowed to use all means possible to colonize Palestine and Transjordan.

⇛ British recognized Abdullah as Emir of Transjordan on May 25.

⇛ The Lausanne Treaty was signed on July 24 and the Turkish Grand National Assembly ratified it one month later. Mosul question was left unresolved.

⇛ Religious leaders the British expelled from Iraq arrived in Iran in August.

⇛ British mandate for Palestine officially went into effect on September 29.

⇛ Ankara officially became the capital of the Turkish Republic on October 13.

⇛ Reza Khan became premier of Persia on October 28. At his suggestion, Shah Ahmad went on an extended European "vacation."

⇛ Kemal was elected president of the Republic of Turkey on October 29.

⇛ Ismet was appointed prime minister of Turkey on October 30.

1924 ⇛ Turkish National Assembly abolished the Caliphate, exiled the Ottoman family, abolished the Ministries of Religious Affairs and Sharia, and abolished Muslim schools on March 5.

⇛ King Hussein of the Hijaz proclaimed himself Caliph after the Turkish Republic abolished the Caliphate.

⇛ King Hussein of Hijaz denied pilgrims from Najd and the Ikhwan access to the Muslim Holy Places in the spring.

⇛ The Iraqi Constitutional Assembly convened on March 27 and approved the treaty with Great Britain by the smallest possible majority.

⇛ Turkish National Assembly abolished the Sharia courts on April 8.

⇛ Adoption of the Turkish constitution on April 20.

⇛ Reza Khan made his peace with Persian and Iraqi religious leaders from April to October and assured them that he did not support the establishment of a republic in Persia.

- ⇛ Abdullah of Transjordan accepted a British ultimatum in August to retain his position.
- ⇛ Ikhwan forces attacked the city of Taif on August 24 and gained control of the city on September 5.
- ⇛ Assassination of Sir Lee Stack, governor-general of Sudan and *Sirdar* on September 23.
- ⇛ League of Nations approved the Anglo-Iraqi treaty and established the mandate of Mesopotamia on September 27.
- ⇛ The question of Mosul was turned over to the League of Nations on September 30.
- ⇛ King Hussein of the Hijaz abdicated on October 3 in favor of his son, Ali.
- ⇛ *Ulama's* endorsement of Reza Khan in October indicated that religious leaders no longer supported Shah Ahmad.

World War I, by definition, was large in scope if not completely global. Even so, it was largely a European conflict, which produced the humiliation of Germany and the Bolshevik Revolution as the most dramatic results. The European focus was also obvious in the Paris Peace Conference, where European concerns relegated other related issues to inconsequential status. Within twenty-five years after the peace settlement, however, it became obvious that acts of commission and omission on the part of the European Powers in the Middle East during and after the war created problems that no one anticipated at the time. Dissatisfaction with the postwar settlement among numerous groups in the Middle East has kept the region in turmoil and spilled over into the entire world. Central to the problem was the very fact that the Ottoman Empire became a belligerent on the side of the Central Powers.

One could legitimately ask why the Ottoman Empire became involved in a war in November 1914, when it was still confined to the large European Powers. The Ottomans were not party to the entangling alliances, the Ottoman Empire had not engaged in the competition for colonies, it had no industrial production in need of foreign markets, and its archaic military did not threaten the military equation. In fact, the Ottomans' military losses to their own Balkan provinces had left them weak and embarrassed. Additonally, the Ottomans had recently lost control of Egypt and Libya to Britain and Italy. They had lost Crete to Greece. The British had also strengthened their dominant position in the Persian Gulf region of the Ottoman Empire. The Ottomans were strongly under European influence because of the Ottoman Public Debt Administration, the capitulations, and the huge European investments in the entire Ottoman economy and utility infrastructure. Under these circumstances the Ottoman Empire could not realistically pursue visions of grandeur, but could only hope to survive.

However, when the Ottoman nemesis, Russia, allied with Great Britain and France, the Porte's recent defenders, there was reason to believe that Ottoman interests were in jeopardy. Russia would obviously try to extract Anglo-French acquiescence to Russian aggrandizement in the Straits area as a reward for participation in the war against the Central Powers. The Porte could easily believe that its former shepherds were in league with the wolf.

OTTOMANS ALLY WITH GERMANY

Correspondingly, the Porte's relations with Germany had improved in the last couple of decades. Kaiser Wilhelm II had courted Ottoman affection while the other European nations seemed at best to regard the Middle East as prey for easy domination and profits. Germany alone had paid a fair price for its concessions in the Ottoman Empire and neither held nor claimed the right to any Ottoman territory. Germany's influence had also grown after General Liman von Sanders had gained control of Ottoman military planning and restructuring in the fall of 1913. He actually commanded the Ottoman First Army, which had the responsibility of defending Istanbul and the Straits. The German imprimatur was stamped heavily on the Ottoman attempt at military modernization.

Timid Allied assurances to the Ottoman Empire at the outset of the war, Enver Pasha's enthrallment with German military supremacy, adroit German maneuvering, and luck altered the Ottoman commitment from neutrality to alliance with the Central Powers. The Allies, in fact, sought only Ottoman neutrality, while Germany openly sought an alliance. The Allies promised a continuation of the status quo, while Germany offered financial and military aid, as well as the opportunity for the Ottomans to rectify old wrongs and fulfill imperial expansion.

Most members of the Ottoman government and its citizenry thought only of neutrality and a respite from war. They could not conceive that, in view of recent Ottoman losses, another war augured anything but new disasters. Enver Pasha, the war minister, saw the European imbroglio as an opportunity for his country to sever its European bonds, defeat Russia, regain lost territory, and expand to its natural Turanist limits in alliance with the militarily invincible German Empire.

Enver had moved Ottoman interests as close to Germany as he could between the Serajevo assassination on June 28 and Germany's declaration of war on Russia on August 1. In July he received a German promise of military aid to prevent Russia from seizing the vital Straits if war occurred. His fear was realistic because use of the Straits was so vital to both Russian survival and its ability to conduct the war.

Germany committed the agreement to paper on August 2 and began to send arms to Istanbul on August 4. After these actions a Turco-German alliance seemed imminent. These developments and Enver's aspirations and position, however, were inadequate to move his nation to belligerency in 1914 without aid from circumstances that were beyond his control.

Ottoman official and public opinion began to move toward Enver when the British announced on August 3 that they would retain two battleships they had just completed for delivery to Istanbul. The announcement caused an angry outcry in the Ottoman public as Ottoman citizens, including women and schoolchildren, had made great sacrifices to finance this major improvement of the Ottoman navy. Therefore, it must have seemed that providence had intervened when, on August 11, two massive, new cruisers bearing Ottoman names appeared in the Istanbul harbor. Only hours before, they had been German ships in flight before a British fleet. Germany had "sold" them to the Ottoman Empire after they had reached the safety of Ottoman waters.

Continued British naval patrols at the mouth of the Dardenelles led to the German commander of Turkish installations closing the Straits to all shipping on

September 27. Consequently, Russia was isolated from its allies and unable to conduct either normal military or merchant shipping.

On October 1 the Porte reduced or abolished many of the special privileges of foreign governments, which amounted to an abolition of the capitulations. This sequence of Ottoman behavior threatened the Entente war effort and favored the Central Powers. The Porte could expect a declaration of war from either St. Petersburg or London. Enver had, in fact, agreed to declare war on the Entente in return for a substantial gold shipment. After the gold arrived on October 21, the two new cruisers and assorted Ottoman ships staged a raid on Russia's Crimean coast and destroyed many Russian vessels on October 29. Russia broke relations with Istanbul the following day and declared war on November 2. Similar declarations by Britain and France three days later set the Ottoman Empire on a gambler's spree in which only a German victory could prevent disaster.

OTTOMAN WORTH AS AN ALLY

Although militarily weak and hopelessly unprepared with anything other than manpower to fight a modern war, the Ottoman Empire had considerable appeal to recommend it to the Central Powers. Under German supervision it might continue to prevent Russia from receiving assistance through the Straits. This was crucial given Russia's essentially landlocked condition and its own lack of war materiel. The Ottoman desire to expand into the Russian Caucasus and the Russian desire to expand into eastern Anatolia could drain Russian divisions from the German eastern front. Britain would have to commit considerable resources to retain its holdings in, and adjacent to, the Ottoman Empire in the Mediterranean, Egypt, the Persian Gulf, and Mesopotamia.

This distraction of Entente effort could allow German victory in Europe, which was where its real interests lay. A transparent weakness in Ottoman ability to play its role was the absence of a direct line of communication between the Central Powers and Ottoman territory. Bulgaria would have to join the Central Powers to provide the link.

OTTOMANS AT WAR

Two of these expected fronts, in addition to the Straits, opened immediately after the Ottomans entered the war. Britain invaded southern Mesopotamia on November 22 to secure the Shatt al-Arab, the confluence of the Tigris and Euphrates rivers just north of the Persian Gulf. The British rapidly pushed 120 miles north to Basra to establish a security buffer for the newly important oil refineries in Abadan at the northern Gulf.

The Ottomans took the initiative against Russia in November, when their victory in a small battle led to the more ambitious plan for an attack against the Russian Caucasus mountain town of Sarikamish. They believed their fellow Turanists would rise in open rebellion and serve as a Fifth Column for them as the Armenians did for the Russians in the Ottoman Empire. The Enver-led attack in the dead of winter resulted in an icy debacle that lost 80,000 men from December 24 to January 5. The time was obviously too short to test the validity of a possible uprising.

Turco-German strategy early directed its attention to the vital role of the Suez Canal in British logistics and thinking. Since it controlled traffic with the entire Asian, Australian, New Zealand portion of the British Empire, any disruption of it could do inestimable damage to the British economy and war effort. Invaluable though it was, the British believed their naval supremacy assured the Canal's security, because they assumed no attack would come from the uncrossable Sinai.

Djemal Pasha and his German advisers thought differently, however, and after careful planning, chose the cool of winter to cross the Sinai in January of 1915 and launched an attack on February 2. Some of the invaders actually crossed to the western bank before the British repelled them. They had no hope of their division-strength force taking control of the Suez Canal unless the Egyptians arose in large numbers in response to the Sultan's declaration of a *jihad.* Otherwise this tactical foray was designed to do some damage and put fear in the hearts of the British.

While the campaign was unsuccessful, it had lasting results. It gave the Turks and Germans good information on the Sinai for future use and it created an understandable paranoia among the British. The importance of Palestine, from which the attack came, became of paramount importance to British concern for the Suez Canal's safety. This realization altered British policies during and after the war. Nearly 300,000 British troops, with all their accompanying support, guarded the canal for nearly three years before they were of much real value for the invasion of Palestine. Obviously the large number of British troops who guarded the canal could have made a major difference on the Western Front.

THE DARDANELLES CAMPAIGN

The smoke and dust had hardly cleared along the Suez before the British began their own campaign against the Ottomans, which resulted in a physical and morale blow that at least equalled the psychological impact of the Suez attack. Winston Churchill, the First Lord of the Admiralty, concluded that Entente conquest of the Straits would serve the dual purpose of removing the Ottomans from the war and keeping the Russians in the war. Success would also secure British interests from the Suez east and free it to concentrate on the European theater. The acknowledged weakness of Ottoman naval strength and fortifications in the Dardanelles made a strike against the soft underbelly of the Central Powers an inviting prospect. He and his associates believed a modest naval force could accomplish this crucial task.

An Allied fleet began its attack against the Ottoman fortifications of the Gallipoli peninsula on the northwestern shore of the Dardanelles on February 19, 1915. The major improvements of Ottoman artillery under the direction of the German general, Rheinhardt Weber, proved sufficiently formidable to inflict heavy losses and turn the Allies back. One month later, a larger Allied force met even greater devastation. Even the Ottomans were surprised at their success and had been prepared to evacuate Istanbul. The Allies had also been closer to success than they had known because Ottoman munitions were nearly spent when the crippled fleet withdrew.

Too much was already invested and the object was too important, however, for the Allies to accept defeat. By April 24 they again launched an assault with the largest fleet ever assembled, but this time with the objective of landing troops to destroy the Ottoman resistance. During this stage they faced even larger Ottoman forces under the combined command of von Sanders and Mustafa Kemal.

Most of the Allied troops were from the eastern portion of the British Empire. The Australian and New Zealand troops, especially, wrote a story of courage and bravery on the beaches of Gallipoli that few troops ever matched. The Turco-German strategy was to allow the troops to land on the narrow beaches and destroy them. The slaughter raged through the stifling heat of summer and through the frigid winter before the Allies withdrew in January of 1916. Mustafa Kemal, who already enjoyed an outstanding reputation for his efforts in the Libyan and Balkan wars, enhanced his status for his command of the battered but successful Ottoman defense.

Ottoman success was also due in part to Bulgaria's entry into the war on the side of the Central Powers in October in return for Ottoman territory in eastern Thrace. The Bulgarian alliance freed Ottoman soldiers from a defensive posture on the Bulgarian border, and, just as importantly, opened the vital supply lines between Germany and Istanbul.

The abortive campaign had engaged 500,000 British troops and large numbers of ships. Nearly half the British imperial troops were killed or wounded in the campaign, while the Turks suffered close to the same number of losses. Although the importance of the campaign is obvious, it is worth noting that the Ottoman Empire proved worthy of the attention Germany had given to bringing it into an alliance. The Ottoman effort had proven very helpful to the Central Powers as the Gallipoli campaign and the British reinforcements along the Suez Canal had diverted 750,000 Allied troops from the struggle in France in 1915.

THE MESOPOTAMIAN THEATER

In the dark hours of the Gallipoli campaign, the British began another campaign with predominantly Indian troops under the command of the India Office to improve their hold in Mesopotamia. The initial push 150 miles northward in September from Basra to Kut al-Amara met little resistance.

The easy conquest of Kut al-Amara led British policymakers to the faulty conclusion that another drive of roughly the same distance could bring the grand reward of Baghdad. The decision in mid-November to conquer Baghdad corresponded with the British decision to withdraw from Gallipoli. There is little doubt that they sought success in Baghdad as compensation for the loss in the Straits.

However, the Ottomans had strengthened their forces in preparation for a possible British advance. Ottoman preparation, combined with the fact that British forces had moved too far ahead of their supply capabilities, brought heavy losses and retreat back to Kut al-Amara. The Ottomans closed in and besieged the ill-supplied British troops, many of whom were sick, wounded, and close to starvation. Repeated British attempts to relieve General Charles V.Townshend's forces failed from January through April of 1916. The frustrated rescuers suffered from many of the same hardships as the trapped legions and withered under fierce opposition from the Ottoman troops. Townshend surrendered at the end of April, only to see many of his men perish from a forced march and heavy labor. British efforts to advance beyond Basra had cost another 40,000 casualties and only brought additional humiliation to the carnage and embarrassment of Gallipoli.

THE ARMENIAN DISASTER

A major, though less glorious development regarding the Ottoman Empire's Armenian population unfolded during 1915, simultaneously with their costly, but successful, defenses of Gallipoli and Mesopotamia. This large Christian minority of nearly two million people played a major role in the Ottoman administration and economy, as well as providing many of the empire's most capable artisans. Their status increased after the Greek revolution in the 1820s diminished Ottoman trust in its Greek population.

Armenian loyalty, however, fell under suspicion after many in the Armenian community openly aided Russia's invasion in 1877. The dispersal of Armenians throughout Ottoman territory from Istanbul to eastern Anatolia and the existence of a large, quasi-self-governing Armenian province in Russia exacerbated their threat to Ottoman authorities.

Armenian nationalist desires grew steadily during the second half of the nineteenth century in collaboration with their counterparts in Russia. Russia's overt assistance to Ottoman Armenians added to Ottoman concerns regarding Armenian irredentism. The violent Armenian separatist activities in the 1890s increased Ottoman anxiety, which resulted in strong reprisals that curbed overt Armenian actions and drove most of the separatist leaders to Europe or Russia.

Armenian exiles in Europe had demanded the dissolution of the Ottoman Empire at the Young Turk Congresses, and Armenian representatives had demanded a separate Armenian state when the parliament met after the Young Turk revolution in 1908. The fundamentalist Muslim Counterrevolution in 1909, in turn, vented considerable anger and violence against the Armenian community. Many in the Armenian community, therefore, welcomed Nicholas II's promise that the Ottoman alliance with the Central Powers provided Russia the opportunity to liberate the Armenian Christian population.

The Armenian community did not improve its status when it refused government overtures for a strong Armenian commitment to the war effort against Russia. Ottoman authorities believed, in fact, that Armenian assistance on both sides of the border contributed to Russia's victory at Sarikamish, which left a Russian army poised to seize all of eastern Anatolia and link up with the British drive into Mesopotamia.

In the aftermath of Sarikamish, Ottoman authorities began reprisals against Armenians in February 1915, which included removing the populations from entire towns in anticipation of a major confrontation with Russia for control over eastern Anatolia. By April, widespread fear among the Armenian population afforded Armenian nationalists the opportunity to declare the ancient city of Van the capitol of an Armenian Republic. Thereafter, Ottoman arrests of Armenians, including some of the most prominent leaders in Istanbul, became more widespread. At Van, the Armenian defense, which reflected good organization and tenacity, repelled Ottoman attacks until a Russian army entered Van in mid-May. Although a strengthened Ottoman effort finally drove the Russians and the Armenians from Van in mid-July, it lacked the capacity to continue a campaign against the main Russian forces to the north.

From June through September, Ottoman authorities systematically attempted to remove most Armenians from the eastern third of Anatolia to Syria in preparation for the campaign with Russia. Regardless of the intentions of Istanbul authorities related to this removal, the events that followed were disastrous for the Armenians and for Turkish relations with Armenians to this day. As a result of the attitudes of Ottoman officials and commanders in eastern Anatolia; the resentment of the Kurds and other Muslims in the region; the harshness of the terrain; the absence of adequate roads, transportation facilities, food, water, and medicine; and the presence of thousands of children, women, and elderly, tens of thousands of Armenians perished.

Doubtlessly true stories abound of Turkish and Kurdish atrocities connected with this tragedy. The emotions that it engendered seem to have blinded even honest (but partisan) scholars on both sides from rendering an accurate account. A lack of agreement on the number of Armenians in Anatolia, for instance, greatly determines how many need to be accounted for after the war. The inability to know beyond doubt how many of the Armenians withdrew with the Russian troops or settled in Syria and Lebanon confounds tabulation even further. It is only safe to say that the Armenian disaster later had harmful results on the Ottoman war effort itself, and created problems for future Turkish governments and citizens that exceeded any benefits it could have produced in 1915.

ALLIED PLANS TO PARTITION THE OTTOMAN EMPIRE

The Ottoman Empire's unexpected entry into the war not only widened the war beyond all expectations, but shook traditional policies of the members of the Entente Cordiale. Within a week of declaring war on the Ottomans, Russia informed its allies that it expected to annex the Straits and Istanbul. Although France, and especially Britain, had fought wars and expended untold diplomatic efforts to prevent this in the past, their need for Russia's effort against the Central Powers resulted in their rapid consent to the Russian demand.

But since the Anglo-French campaign in Gallipoli had been directed against Russia's prize, it demanded a written guarantee to even broader terms. Russia demanded Istanbul; the Dardanelles; the Sea of Marmora to the Bulgarian border; land adjacent to the Asian shore of the Bosphorus east to the Sakaria River; and the islands of Imbros and Tenedos, which controlled the entrance to the Dardanelles.

In negotiations between March 7 and March 15, France and Britain agreed to these previously unthinkable demands on the condition that Istanbul would become a free port and the Straits would remain open to all commercial shipping. This fulfillment of a centuries-old dream for Russia led it to acquiesce to British and French compensatory demands of Ottoman territory.

The British demanded the right to annex the neutral zone in Persia to their sphere of influence, and vague claims regarding the "emerging Moslem nation in Arabia," which resulted from exploratory conversations the British had held with Sharif Hussein of the Hijaz over the previous months. France demanded Syria, the Gulf of Alexandretta, and Cilicia to the Taurus mountain range.

The imprecision of the Anglo-French portions required further refinement. Official committees and interested groups in both nations drew up shopping lists of Ottoman territories for nearly a year following the agreement with Russia.

French investments, religious institutions, and schools, as well as the diplomatic dominance France had enjoyed in the region for centuries, gave it better claims in the crucial Levant than Britain could muster. The French wanted control of the entire eastern shore of the Mediterranean and its interior; Cyprus; nearly half of the southern shore of the Anatolian peninsula and its interior; and a corridor into Asia to the Persian border, including the Mosul oil fields in upper Mesopotamia.

Britain wanted to secure an uninterrupted land link between the Mediterranean and its holdings in Mesopotamia and the Gulf, in addition to the demands it had made earlier meetings. Both Britain and Russia, however, were unwilling to allow France unilateral control over the Holy Land in Palestine by the time Charles Francois Georges-Picot for France and Sir Mark Sykes for Britain began their negotiations in November 1915.

SYKES-PICOT AGREEMENT

Britain gained direct control over Mesopotamia from just north of Baghdad south to the Persian Gulf and along the western shore of the Gulf. It received indirect control over Arab territories that stretched eastward from the Sinai border past the Kirkuk oil fields in northern Mesopotamia to the Persian border.

France obtained direct control of Cilicia and the eastern shore of the Mediterranean south to Acre. Its area of indirect control stretched east of this acquisition past the Mosul oil fields to the Persian border and abutted the British zone of indirect control in the south.

Skyes and Picot proposed an internationalized Holy Land in Palestine under Russian-British-French supervision, but Britain received the ports of Haifa and Acre, and the right to construct a railway from Haifa to Baghdad. Each portion would assume their fair share of the Ottoman debt; each party would enjoy free access to all ports; unrestricted trade would flow through the entire region; and they agreed to share the water resources.

The British and French governments secretly endorsed the Sykes-Picot Agreement on February 4, 1916 and the authors personally took it to St. Petersburg a month later, where they received Russian approval after agreeing on its outright annexation of northeastern Anatolia. As with most Great Power negotiations in the late nineteenth and early twentieth centuries, only a limited circle within the signatory governments were aware of the terms of this agreement, which expressed the war aims of each in the Middle Eastern theater.

ITALY JOINS THE ALLIES

The Entente's attempts to convince Italy to join their alliance required concessions of Ottoman territories to placate the Italian desire for an empire. Italians had enjoyed trade and other relations with the Ottomans long before any of their European colleagues, but modern Italy had only recently reentered the Ottoman markets and made significant investments there. The Entente began serious talks with Italy after they had established their general agreement for dividing the Ottoman Empire among themselves. Their offer to Italy in the Treaty of London on April 25, 1915 was vague, since the Sykes-Picot Agreement was still ten months from completion.

The promise of sovereignty over Libya and the Dodecanese Islands, which it already held, and territory in the Adalia region helped induce Italy to enter the war in May. Italian pique over learning that the Big Three had established a specific arrangement of some kind moved its allies to define Italian rewards specifically. On April 19, 1917, nearly two full years after the Treaty of London, the British and French signed a supplementary Treaty of St. Jean de Maurienne. The Italians received a combination of direct and indirect control over the southwestern half of the Anatolian peninsula, beginning at Boursa and extending through Konia and Antalia, east to the French claims in Cilicia. These were generous rewards for a junior partner even though Greece had reason to believe that much of this same area would be its still undefined reward.

Collectively the various agreements among the Allies left only the northcentral portion of the Anatolian peninsula unclaimed by the spring of 1917.

GREAT BRITAIN COURTS THE ARABS

However, this complex, far-flung war required many actors whose essentially cameo performances might lead to victory. The strained resources of the Allies moved them to seek any alliance that might help their cause. This search helps account for Britain's accepting the overtures for an alliance with Sharif Hussein of the Hijaz after refusing him any response before the war began. Hussein al-Hashimi, who became the Ottoman Governor of the Hijaz after the Young Turk revolution, doubted the stability of his position once the Young Turks began their "Turcification" policies. His kinship with the Prophet Muhammad and his custody of the holy cities of Mecca and Medina seemed to qualify him as the most likely catalyst for the still desultory Arab nationalism. It was hoped that he would rally the Arabs against their Turkish overlords.

Hussein might well have either sat out the war or confined his role to calling for a *jihad* of the world's Muslims to join the Sultan's cause. He seems to have sensed, however, that the time was opportune to play an historic role and restore Islam to Hashimi and Arab leadership. Realization of this dream was more likely if his family ruled an Arab state, which included the Islamic Holy Cities, Damascus, and perhaps Baghdad. His ambitions were grist for a British desire to prevent the Central Powers from using Hussein's bailiwick on the eastern shore of the Red Sea to impede or prevent their use of that vital waterway. His potential role as the leader of a general uprising of the Arabs against the Turks recommended him almost as much. Or, if Hussein were only capable of engaging the Ottoman forces in the Arabian peninsula, it was sufficient to justify considerable British attention and concessions.

The British courted an Arab rebellion from the second month of the war, but Hussein restrained his response until July 1915, when he opened a correspondence with Sir Henry McMahon, the British High Commissioner in Cairo, who was under close instructions from London. Interestingly, Sir Mark Sykes worked closely on McMahon's negotiations with Hussein while he was also engaged in shaping an agreement with France. Sykes' familiarity with British promises to France moved McMahon to inform Hussein that Britain could not agree to an Arab state that encompassed all the Arab territories of the Ottoman Empire.

McMahon's letter to Hussein on October 24, 1915 conveyed Britain's offer, which Hussein finally accepted on November 5, although he continued to express his dislike of the unclear areas it excluded for France. McMahon's letter excluded the districts of Mersin and Alexandretta, as well as the areas west of Damascus, Homs, Hama, and Aleppo, on the grounds that they were not "purely Arab." Since Damascus was the southernmost checkpoint in this restriction, Hussein had reason to believe everything south of a line from Damascus to the Mediterranean shore, in other words, Palestine, was part of the British promise. The next paragraph alluded to British limitations related to "her ally, France," but in no way implied that French demands exceeded the narrow strip of territory along the Mediterranean coast from Mersin to Sidon or, at most, south to Tyre. Britain agreed to defend the Muslim Holy Places, but tied the "Arabs" to an exclusive British monopoly on "advice and guidance." The final significant point was British insistence upon a "special administrative arrangement" in the *vilayets* of Baghdad and Basra, which presumably meant the entire area between the two in southern Mesopotamia. The letter never mentioned a "state" or "nation," while it referred to "forms of governments in those various territor*ies*" (italics mine).

Seven months after his formal acceptance of British terms, Hussein declared a revolt against the Ottomans on June 5, 1916. He was acclaimed King of the Arabs on October 29, but British recognition of his new royal status on December 15 referred to him as King of the Hijaz! Britain, in fact, recognized Hussein's sovereignty only in that one limited region where its agreements did not conflict with either the Entente Powers or Ibn Saud, King of the Najd, and other shaykhs.

Hussein and his sons must have believed, however, that their military efforts were in pursuit of a single Arab kingdom exclusive of the Levant coast and lower Mesopotamia. Abundant British gold, as well as military advisers under the command of Colonel C.E. Wilson kept a small, but effective, Arab army in the field. No general Arab uprising ever occurred for several reasons: fear of Ottoman retaliation; Hussein's apparent reluctance to include tribes not personally loyal to him; jealousy of Hashimi ascendancy; and the absence of a real sense of modern nationhood among the Arabs.

These obstacles did not diminish the value of the Arab efforts to the British and the Hashimis, nor the damage to the Ottomans and the Central Powers. Hussein's forces quickly seized Mecca, Jiddah, and the Red Sea coast north to Yanbo from June 6 to September 22. In January 1917, they captured the coastal city of Wejh, which was two hundred miles further north. By this time, Feisal had emerged as the dominant Arab military leader. Medina remained under Ottoman control but since the Arabs had destroyed its rail communications, the Medina garrison was ineffective. The Arab thrust northward climaxed with the capture of Aqaba on July 6, 1917 and placed the Arabs in a position to serve as auxiliaries to Allenby's invasion of Palestine, which parallelled a successful British advance to northern Mesopotamia.

BRITISH INTEREST IN PALESTINE

Besides the normal unfolding of the British war effort in the Middle East, Palestine had acquired increased stature in British plans because it served as a base for a second Turco-German attack on the Suez Canal in August 1916. By April 1917 the British became determined to maintain exclusive control over Palestine after the war, primarily because of its strategic proximity to the Suez Canal. The Ottoman mobilization in Palestine for their attacks on the canal during the war confirmed

British attitudes toward Palestine's strategic importance. While the British decision was contrary to both the Sykes-Picot and the Hussein-McMahon agreements, the British informed only the French of their intentions. British forthrightness with France on this issue manifested their unshakable determination to govern Palestine after the war.

The British visualized some kind of protectorate arrangement over postwar Palestine, since they had neither a legitimate prior claim to the territory, nor an affiliation with any of its inhabitants that could justify British presence. France, by contrast, had a long-standing affiliation with the Christians of Greater Syria, and Russia had a close association with the Armenians and the Orthodox Christians of the entire region.

British desire to control Palestine and to cultivate a symbiotic relationship with a strong population segment in the region, therefore, converged with Zionist desires to build on their small but sophisticated foundation in Palestine with the recognition and assistance of a Great Power. Ordinarily, the relationship between a Great Power and a small interest group merits little more than a footnote in the account of a global conflict. The Anglo-Zionist relationship, however, had repercussions long after the war which dwarfed the significance of events which seemed much more important at the time.

The fact that the Allied war effort was less than promising when the Lloyd George cabinet assumed power in December 1916 added a note of urgency to British willingness to assist Zionism. Russia was on the verge of collapse, and when the tsar fell in March 1917 it became even more questionable whether the provisional government would or could continue the war. The United States was still neutral, and even after it entered the war in April 1917, it was months before American entry began to make a difference. The Allies were only holding their own on the western front, so it was problematical as to whether the untried Americans could compensate for the loss of the diversion of an eastern front in the event that Russia, indeed, withdrew from the war. The Central Powers could win the war in Europe under these circumstances.

Only in the apparently minor theater of the war between the British and the Ottomans did success appear obvious. British troops swept north through Mesopotamia toward Baghdad, while the British-funded Arab revolt steadily pushed the Ottomans out of the Arabia peninsula. The British were preparing a campaign to secure the Sinai and Palestine. Victory in the Near East, however, would be hollow, if not worthless, should Europe fall under German domination.

GREAT BRITAIN AND ZIONISM

The Allies needed every possible shred of international military, financial, and moral support they could muster to win the war. The *diaspora,* which was a plague to the Jews, gave them appeal in these circumstances, because they were spread all over the Christian world, where it was commonly believed that they possessed great wealth and wielded even greater influence. The Zionist movement had given the Jews a network of communication and a unity of purpose, which the British government believed could help win the war and secure Palestine under British influence for the future.

Zionism was badly in need of assistance during the war. Ottoman authorities had curtailed most Zionist activities in Palestine after the war began. Zionist public organizations, schools, newspapers, clubs, and the Anglo-Palestine Bank were closed, and manifestations of Zionist nationalism such as their flag, stamps, and script were abolished. Zionist leaders, including Ben-Gurion and Ben-Zvi, who protested the Ottoman scrutiny of Jewish land titles, were forced into exile. The Jewish population declined from 85,000 to 65,000 as a result of exile, but mostly from voluntary emigration in the face of the terrible hunger and hardship that all occupants of Palestine suffered during the war.

Despair of ever achieving a working relationship with the Ottomans led many of the exiles to open support of the Allied cause. They joined the Zion Mule Corp, which the British established in Egypt in 1914, under the command of a British officer, Colonel John Patterson. They saw action in the Gallipoli campaign, after which the Zion Mule Corp was abolished.

The World Zionist Organization maintained a firm neutrality during the war and moved its main operations to neutral Copenhagen. Jews generally supported the policies of their countries of residence, regardless of whether they were involved in the war or neutral. Russian Jews, in particular, feared any indication of an attitude that would provoke government reprisals. The permeating effects of the war throughout Europe, and the inhospitable conditions in Palestine, dissuaded migration to Palestine during the war.

Zionists in Great Britain had greater freedom to continue their activities than Jews in most other countries, without causing suspicion or retaliation. Their freedom hardly seemed auspicious, since British Jews were notably quiescent in the Zionist movement. The Jews who had been in Britain for generations had full rights and liberties and many were, in fact, well placed in business and the professions. Recent Jewish immigrants, who might have been more inclined to support Zionism, lacked money, influence, and familiarity with the British political system.

Chaim Weizmann, a Russian Jew who had been educated in Switzerland, was an exception. An articulate, physically imposing figure of a man, Weizmann became the president of the English Zionist Federation. This gifted chemist on the faculty of the University of Manchester contributed to the British war effort by helping develop essential new naval explosives. His renown provided him easy access to the highest echelon of British politicians and publishers. The intercession of Sir Herbert Samuel, a noted Zionist, accelerated his intimate acquaintance with Lloyd George, Robert Cecil, Winston Churchill, and the editors of both the *London Times* and the *Manchester Guardian.* As early as 1906 he had convinced Arthur Balfour of the need for a Jewish homeland in Palestine. He was also on close terms with government Middle East specialists such as Mark Sykes, David Ormsby-Gore, and Leopold Amery. Weizmann acknowledged that the guidance and advice of Sykes were greatly responsible for his success with the British government in behalf of Zionism.

The Lloyd George cabinet, largely through the work of Sykes, began working toward some kind of agreement with British Zionists soon after its members took office near the end of 1916. The cabinet discussed issuing a statement in support of Zionism as early as June 1917, and Balfour, the Foreign Minister, invited Lord Walter Rothschild and Weizmann to draft a statement for cabinet consideration. Once debate began in the cabinet in July, Sir Edwin Montagu, the only Jew in the cabinet, opposed it. He and other anti-Zionist Jews, such as C.G. Montefiore, the president of the Anglo-Jewish Association, opined that such a statement called the loyalty of Jews to their government into question. The anti-Zionist Jews asserted that sympathy for the proposed statement was confined to Jews of foreign birth who desired a homeland in Palestine. They further maintained that Palestine was too small to accomodate the world's Jews, many of whom had no desire to leave their countries. Lord Curzon also doubted that Palestine could absorb a significant additional population.

Meanwhile, the Zionists were encouraged to inform the Allies of Zionist desire to migrate to Palestine under British protection, in order to assuage the fears of some that the British were using the movement to acquire control of Palestine. Sykes guided Nahum Sokolow, the leader of the Zionist Organization of London, through the diplomatic channels of the Allied capitals and the Vatican, where he obtained their unanimous consent.

Montagu, as the spokesman for the anti-Zionist Jews, continued to block acceptance in the cabinet, where the other statesmen, along with their Zionist allies, were becoming impatient. These supporters arrived at a consensus that the endorsement of President Wilson of the United States could justify overriding the opposition's objections. Justice Louis Brandeis and other leading American Zionists persuaded Wilson's confidant, Colonel Edward House, of the efficacy of their proposal. The House, in turn, obtained the President's approval. Receipt of his consent on October 16 accelerated cabinet approval of a carefully worded statement.

THE BALFOUR DECLARATION

On November 2, 1917 Balfour issued the simple, provocative, and singularly influential statement to Lord Rothschild in the form of a personal letter. The care in drafting, and the plans for exploiting the propaganda value of the statement, assured the maximum impact throughout international Jewry. The combined prefatory and closing remarks of fifty words encased the following declaration:

> His Majesty's Government view with favor the establishment in Palestine of a national home for the Jewish people, and will use their best endeavors to facilitate the achievement of this object, it being clearly understood that nothing shall be done which may prejudice the civil and religious rights of the existing non-Jewish communities in Palestine, or the rights and political status enjoyed by Jews in any other country.

The last phrase was appended to earlier drafts to allay the fears of contented Western Jews, who visualized that the creation of a Jewish home could justify wholesale shipment of Jews to their new "home." Whether intended or not, the failure to mention the protection of the majority Arabs' civil and religious rights specifically, gave rise to the accusation that the British government and the Zionists regarded the Arabs as worthless of mention.

While the needs of the war and the strategic considerations have been discussed as motivations for the British promulgation of the declaration, there were also genuine humanitarian concerns; a desire to right old wrongs; and an expression of Protestant millenarian belief that Christ would only return when the Jews reinhabited Solomon's temple. Failure to consider the aspirations and feelings of the Arabs in the formulation and proclamation of the document also manifested a callousness toward them, which no amount of later reassurances could disguise.

This laconic note quickly reached millions of Jews through its publication in newspapers and leaflets. While some Western Jews were only mildly interested, or even hostile to the Balfour Declaration, eastern European Jews greeted it with jubilation. Their overwhelming enthusiasm assured Britain of support for its war effort, and rekindled hope in many that an ideal life in Palestine was still possible.

The declaration came too late to help the war effort substantially, because the U.S. had entered the war in April, and the Bolshevik revolution removed Russia from the war before most Russians learned about it. It did, however, spark the creation of a Jewish battalion in the British army, which was composed of veterans of the Zion Mule Corp and volunteers from throughout Jewry. The Zionists were again under the command of Colonel Patterson, with Vladimir Jabotinsky as his aide and Ben-Gurion and Ben-Zvi as officers. It had more symbolic than military significance, because by the time it was ready for mobilization, there was little but patrol duty remaining in the Palestine theater.

After General Allenby's army entered Jerusalem in December, new leaflets were dropped from planes in Germany and Austria, urging the Jews to aid the Allied cause. The leaflets declared that the Allies had liberated Palestine from the Turks for the specific purpose of giving it to the Jews to reestablish Zion. Since there were more than fifteen million Jews in the world, it was little wonder that Arabs in Palestine and elsewhere questioned the motives of both the British and the Zionists.

Arab unrest was sufficient to induce the British government to send a Zionist Commission to Palestine early in 1918, in part to convince the Arabs of the compatibility of Zionism and Arab aspirations. Weizmann led the commission, which demonstrated considerably more interest in informing British military and civilian officials from Cairo to Amman of British commitment to the establishment of Zionist immigration and institutions. Another task was to make preparations for the establishment of a Jewish university and hospital in Palestine. The commission and sympathetic British officials were disturbed by the intensity of Arab opposition to their plans for a Jewish homeland.

Since Palestinian Arabs had until recently been under Ottoman authority, it would have been difficult to obtain adequate Anglo-Zionist consultation with Palestinians on their plan. This impediment, plus preoccupation with the complicated mechanics of arriving at a solution, as well as a measure of callousness, led to neglect of the possible Arab obstacle to fulfilling the Zionist dream and British imperial desires. Centuries of Arab submission under Ottoman authority made them easy to overlook. Arabs, however, had made progress toward their own sense of nationalism by the outbreak of the Great War. Arab subservience within the Ottoman Empire; Western preoccupation with the international tension prior to the war; and the struggle for survival during the war, had obscured the only recent emergence of Arab nationalism.

THE CAMPAIGN IN ARAB LANDS

The British two-pronged attack upon the Arab areas of the Ottoman Empire early in 1917 proved an interesting test of Arab attitudes and nationalism. Would the Arab population rise to meet the Christian armies as liberators and assist in the cause?

Would smoldering Arab nationalism achieve cohesion to establish an Arab nation? Would Arab determination for nationhood be strong enough to overcome the restrictions that Entente agreements placed upon it?

General Frederick Maude initiated a British conquest of Mesopotamia in October 1916 and retook Kut al-Amara by the end of February 1917. This renewed British effort was as overprepared as the spring campaign in 1916 was underprepared. Baghdad fell easily to the British on March 11, 1917, but the unclear goal for further penetration, coupled with the disintegration of the Russian army in Persia following the Russian revolution, left the British forces stagnant. Nearly 500,000 British troops sat out the remainder of the war in this position, awaiting an Ottoman counterattack.

Plans for a major Ottoman effort in Mesopotamia were, in fact, ready for implementation when Allenby's success in Palestine diverted the entire spectrum of Ottoman capabilities to that theater. The large number of British troops in Mesopotamia fought no more serious engagements, but were in a position for an uncontested march to Mosul after the Mudros armistice. Britain's overwhelming strength in the region left no doubt that it had won the Middle East theater of the war and underscored Britain's claim for the Mosul area, even though France was supposed to receive it under the provisions of the Sykes-Picot Agreement.

Britain's invasion of Palestine from the Sinai through Gaza met much stiffer resistance despite the softening effect Feisal's army had upon the interior from his base in Aqaba. The campaign in Palestine began under General Archibald Murray's command only a month after the Mesopotamia drive began, but British forces suffered heavy losses and no success. Allenby relieved Murray, whose caution was legendary. The new British commander's superior strategy exceeded the declining morale and supplies of his Turco-German counterparts, who were conducting their campaign for a rapidly withering Ottoman Empire. Careful deception led the Ottomans to expect a renewed attack on Gaza, but Allenby penetrated the weaker defenses further east at Beersheba on October 31. British forces faced resistance, but had little difficulty entering Jerusalem on December 11, 1917 to earn Allenby the distinction of being the first Christian conqueror of the City of Peace since the crusades.

Allenby planned and prepared for several months before he opened an offensive to destroy the last vestiges of Ottoman forces in Greater Syria and capture Damascus. Liman von Sanders personally organized the Turco-German defense with the benefit of the forces that had been destined to thwart the British advances in Mesopotamia. Allenby's preparations, which included increased activities of Feisal's army in the Jordan Valley, appeared to indicate he would attack from the east, but he attacked closer to the coast on September 19, 1918. His brilliant strategy shattered the Ottoman forces, many of whom fled in a steady stream toward Anatolia.

The obvious disarray of the Ottoman armies finally inspired something akin to an open Arab uprising after the British success in northern Palestine. Feisal's army also displayed a definite urgency to beat the rush of British forces to Damascus, where Arab nationalist vigor resulted in open rebellion. By the time British imperial forces and Feisal's army reached Damascus on September 30, 1918, there was no Ottoman resistance. The Arab army received the honor of being the first of the victorious forces to enter the coveted center of past Arab glory.

British and Arab forces proceeded to occupy the other Syrian cities before the end of October. A small French military contingent landed in Beirut to stake out their claim to lands they believed they had earned on the Western Front and through centuries of religious, cultural, and economic cultivation in the Middle East.

CAMPAIGN IN THE TRANSCAUCUSUS

The decisive British victories in Mesopotamia, Palestine, and Syria were due in no small part to Russia's distractions of Ottoman forces to eastern Anatolia. General Nicolai Yudenich opened his campaign in the dead of the bitter Transcaucusus winter during January 1916 with the initial objective of seizing the apparently impregnable fortress city of Erzerum. The dramatic Russian efforts to scale the heights, which provided its natural defense, caught the Ottomans by surprise and established an atmosphere of panic that did not cease before Russian troops destroyed Ottoman resistance in the entire region. Erzerum's fall on February 16 led to a rapid Russian conquest of the eastern third of Anatolia by the summer of 1917.

The simultaneous outbreak of British attacks in Mesopotamia and Palestine prevented the Ottomans from bringing reinforcements from the east to use against the Russian threat to the Turkish heartland. Also, unlike in the Arab areas, the Armenians gave their support to the Russians from the beginning by providing information, supplies, and soldiers. The Armenians, of course, did not know that Russia had reneged on its promise of an independent Armenia and had gained Entente approval of outright annexation of eastern Anatolia to the Russian Empire.

Revenge against the Turkish atrocities of 1915, however, was adequate motivation for Armenian fury. Turkish soldiers and civilians alike suffered unspeakable retaliation from the Armenians who entered the wake of the Russian advance. Deaths and casualties inflicted upon Ottoman soldiers from Russians and Armenians, as well as wholesale desertions, reduced the Ottoman army by half before the Russian revolution ended the Russian effort in Anatolia. Even the Turkish soldiers who were fleeing from the Arab areas had to pass through the gauntlet of vengeful Armenians as they tried to find sanctuary from death on all sides.

However, in the midst of this Ottoman despair, the successful Bolshevik revolution against the provisional government in Russia rekindled Turkish motivation and provided an additional moment of glory for the Ottoman government. The Bolshevik publication of the secret Entente treaties left no reason for Turks to believe there would be any kind of Turkish government if the Allies won. No amount of Allied reassurances could convince the Turks that there would be a Turkish state. They were, therefore, no longer fighting for honor before some kind of peace arrangement; they were fighting for their national survival. Only a challenge of this magnitude could have rallied any of the population, which faced widespread hunger, if not starvation; epidemics; bad news from all Central Power fronts; and hard times in general.

The monumental Bolshevik concessions at Brest-Litovsk on March 3, 1918 not only renounced Russia's claims in Anatolia, but withdrew Russian support for the Russian provinces of Armenia, Georgia, and Azerbaijan. While the regrouped and revitalized Ottoman army in Anatolia was weak, it was more than a match for the irregular forces these areas could muster. A wave of hope spread through the Turks that Enver's goal of uniting the Turks across the Caucusus into Afghanistan was still possible. Territorial acquisitions in that region would more than compensate for losses in the lands of the Arabs.

Desperation among the Armenians on both sides of the border, along with that of the Georgians and Azerbaijanies, at least matched Turkish hope. Word of the general terms of Brest-Litovsk leaked out during the three months of negotiations and led the endangered provinces to expect the worst. On the common bond of fear, these three otherwise largely incompatible nationalities formed the Transcaucusus Republic, with its capital in the Georgian city of Tiflis.

As the Russians withdrew, the Turkish armies began their resurgence and recovered the Armenian-populated territories within the Ottoman Empire. From February to April Erzincan, Van, Kars, Ardahan, Erzerum, and Batum again fell under Ottoman control. When the Black Sea port of Batum, which had been under Russian control since 1878, fell on April 15, a German-sponsored attempt at negotiations also failed because of the magnitude of Turkish demands. Germany's intentions of seizing the same strategically and economically important region hardened Turkish inflexibility. The oil fields in the Caspian area of Baku, along with the pipeline that stretched to Batum, were worthy prizes to stimulate strong competition between the two allies.

The Turks had the advantage of an army in the area and an indigenous Azerbaijani Muslim element to aid their cause. Turkish forces proceeded to sweep through Georgia and Armenia to link up with the Azerbaijani for a successful assault on Baku, which fell on September 15. With this thrust, the Transcaucusus from Batum to Baku was under Ottoman control for the first time since the end of the 1877–78 Russo-Turkish war. Turks on the scene could feel that some good had finally resulted from four years of death and destruction.

OTTOMAN LOSSES IN THE WEST

Hundreds of miles to the west, however, the Ottoman capital was in danger for the first time since the Gallipoli campaign. Allied forces in Greece finally opened a major offensive against Bulgaria on September 14, which resulted in Bulgarian capitulation on September 30. The fall of Bulgaria cut Istanbul off from vital German supplies and made continuation of the Ottoman war effort impossible. The Committee of Union and Progress cabinet sued for peace on October 5 and resigned on October 7. Only with great hesitation did Marshall Ahmet Izzat Pasha agree to form a government to face the anticipated severe demands of the victorious Allies.

Britain's utilization of over two million men against the Ottomans during the war determined that it, exclusive of its allies, would dictate the terms and accept the surrender of the Ottomans. It was well situated to achieve its goals. British troops moved north from Baghdad to the oil-rich area of Mosul. The British navy had controlled the entrance to the Dardenelles for some time. Once British troops moved adjacent to Istanbul in Thrace, Britain allowed armistice procedures to begin under circumstances of British strength that neither its allies nor the Turks could deny. President Wilson also acknowledged British ascendancy by refusing to reply to Turkish requests that he arrange terms.

THE ARMISTICE OF MUDROS

Britain assigned Admiral Arthur Calthorpe, commander of the Aegean fleet, the honor of conveying the conditions of surrender. He chose Mudros, on the island of Lemnos, as the place to meet the Turkish delegation. However, the Turks initially sent General Townshend, whom they had captured at Kut al-Amara in 1916, to present their requests. The Turks hoped that his British colleagues would be more lenient. The stern British refusal of the Turkish proposals indicated the reception that the Turkish delegation, under Minister of War Hussein Orbay, received when it arrived on October 27.

Calthorpe did not budge from his instructions and on October 31 the Turks signed the Armistice of Mudros. In short, all of the Ottoman Empire was subject to Allied occupation and use for Allied operations against the Central Powers. The Turks were further obligated to bear all the expenses of Allied activities. Along with occupation the Turks were forced to accept a litany of demands that stripped them of any semblance of sovereignty.

The gamble that had begun almost exactly four years earlier had failed. The ambitious CUP not only lost the Ottoman empire, it also lost the Turkish heartland. There was no solace in the fact that an archaic empire, which many had thought was "sick" for a century, found the will and ability to come within eleven days of remaining in the war as long as the modern German Empire, which many regarded as invincible.

MIDDLE EAST PEACE SETTLEMENT

Great hope and expectation prevailed when the Paris peace conference convened on January 18, 1919. For a full year, there was a widespread belief that Woodrow Wilson's Fourteen Points guided the Allies' war objectives and would guide the peace settlement. The Conference's unanimous decision to create the League of Nations at the end of its first week enhanced the belief that a few large, European nations would not dominate the future as they had the past. The principle of "self-determination" would allow ethnic groups in Europe and the Middle East to form their own nations with the blessing and protection of the international community. Understandably, therefore, representatives from almost every Eurasian ethnic group appeared in Paris to present their cases. The absence of representation from the vanquished nations seemed to assure success for peoples formerly subsumed in the great empires.

Almost immediately, however, the Big Four of Great Britain, France, Italy, and the United States seized control and shaped the world through a process of compromise and self-interest that belied the lofty aspirations they publicly articulated during the war and when the conference began.

Financial strain and war-weariness among the Allies help explain unjust acts of omission and commission at the conference and the failure to implement all of their agreements. But the tenacious insistence of France to obtain protection from Germany goes much further in explaining why a settlement for Europe received most of the time, energy, and attention of the conference. The fact that the Middle East region remained volatile for several years, while Europe was relatively calm, is also an important consideration.

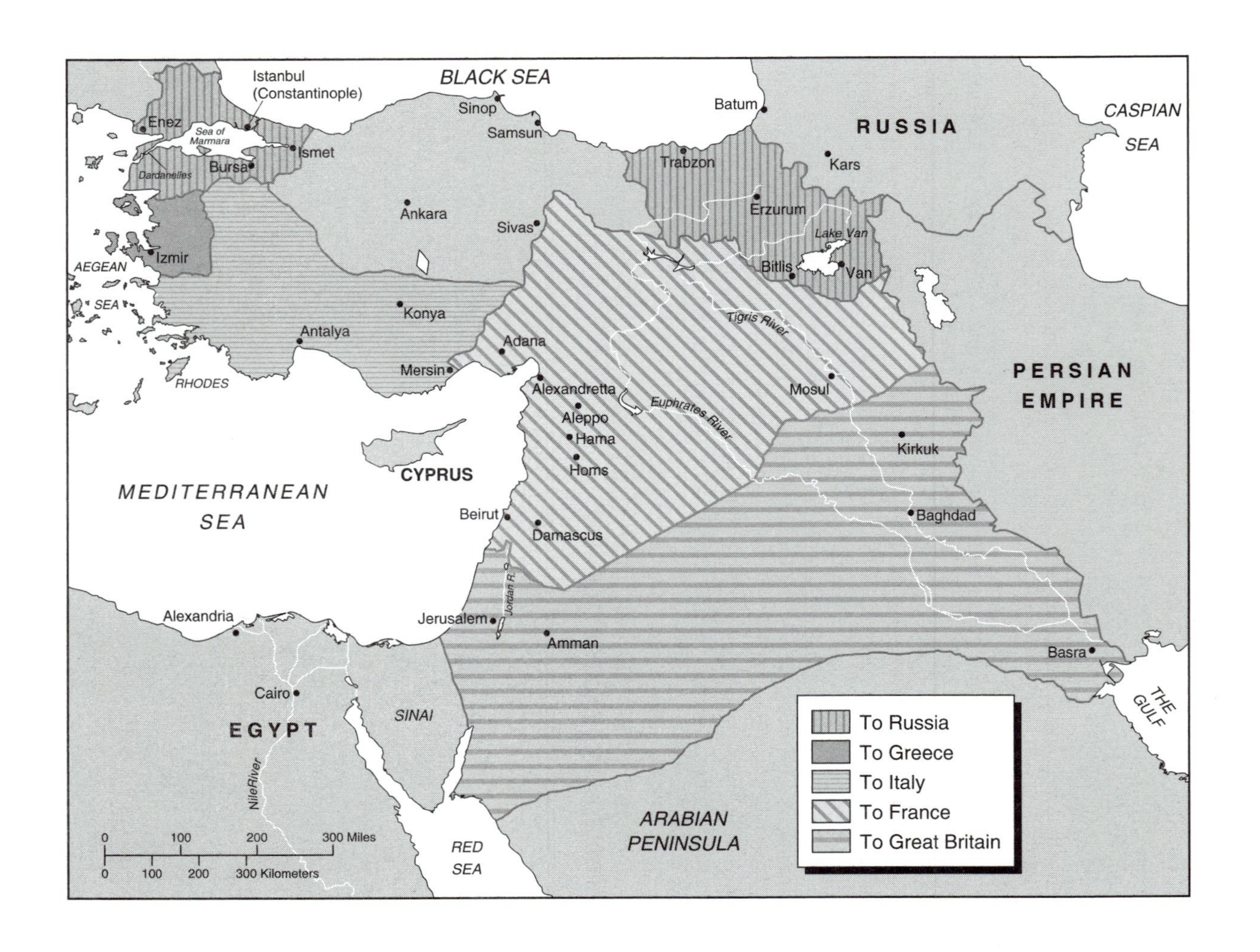
Istanbul (Constantinople)
BLACK SEA
Sinop
Samsun
Batum
RUSSIA
CASPIAN SEA
Enez
Sea of Marmara
Ismet
Bursa
Dardanelles
Trabzon
Kars
Ankara
Sivas
Erzurum
Lake Van
Izmir
AEGEAN SEA
Bitlis
Van
Konya
Antalya
Tigris River
Adana
Mersin
RHODES
Alexandretta
Mosul
PERSIAN EMPIRE
Euphrates River
Aleppo
Hama
Homs
Kirkuk
CYPRUS
MEDITERRANEAN SEA
Beirut
Damascus
Baghdad
Jordan R.
Alexandria
Jerusalem
Amman
Basra
Cairo
SINAI
EGYPT
THE GULF
Nile River
To Russia
To Greece
To Italy
To France
To Great Britain
ARABIAN PENINSULA
RED SEA
0 100 200 300 Miles
0 100 200 300 Kilometers

THE POSTWAR SITUATION

British military control over the Middle East from Egypt in the west to Afghanistan in the east; north to Anatolia; and south to the northern reaches of the Arabian Peninsula was the most significant political reality in the postwar period. This presence defined British interests: in the Suez Canal, with Palestine as a buffer; the Mosul and Kirkuk oil fields in northern Mesopotamia; and from Baghdad south to the Gulf, in order to protect Persian oil fields and communications links to the Far East. The British had carefully positioned their forces in this configuration in order to impose their will upon the region. This position did not conform with agreements they had made with the French and the Arabs during the war.

France had no military presence in the Levant until a small number of French troops, under the leadership of General Henri Gouraud, replaced the British on the coast around Beirut on October 9, 1919. Gouraud's status as Allied Commissioner was a foreshadowing, however, that the Allies might implement the Sykes-Picot agreement the Bolsheviks had published for the world to see. The Arab army in Damascus under Feisal would be no match for this French force if it received some reenforcement.

The unwillingness of Britain, France, and Italy to follow Wilson's suggestion to participate in an investigatory commission to the Levant in the spring of 1919 further indicated that the Europeans had a separate agenda. The commission was supposed to study the people and situation in the eastern part of the Ottoman Empire to determine the best way to fulfill League of Nations principles. Instead, two Americans, President Henry C. King of Oberlin College and an industrialist, Charles R. Crane, led an American delegation to the region. Their findings were instructive, even though the favorable attitudes they reported from the region toward the United States and Great Britain might reflect a desire on the part of their informants to please their American guests and the British occupying forces. The unfavorable comments they reported toward the French call into question whether the British allowed the commissioners free access to the many friends France had developed over centuries in the region.

The King-Crane Commission recommendations were available for consideration on August 28, 1919. Interestingly, its conclusions conform closely with the Sykes-Picot boundaries rather than the Hussein-McMahon agreement or a fresh alternative. While the Sykes-Picot agreement seems to have provided them a foundation, King and Crane's reflections of Levantine attitudes suggested the possibility and justiciability of Arab self-government in the near future.

Unlike a report the Syrian National Congress submitted to the commission, King and Crane assumed there would be League mandates in the Arab region. Their report, however, reflected the foremost Arab desire for a single mandate over all of Syria if there had to be one. This, the report urged, was the desire of the people in the region who opposed smaller and unnatural units. The Arabs pleaded for the incorporation of Lebanon into the same mandate for economic and cultural reasons and to assure the best participation of Christians in regional affairs. The latter suggestion probably reflected Orthodox Christian views, since in such an arrangement they would have considerably outnumbered the Maronites who had dominated Mount Lebanon under European protection since 1861. The commission praised Emir Feisal as unquestionably the most popular and capable choice to head the Syrian state.

The report confessed that its members were favorably disposed toward the Zionist homeland concept when they began their investigation, but had concluded that there must be "serious modification of the extreme Zionist program for Palestine of unlimited immigration of Jews, looking finally to making Palestine distinctly a Jewish state." It reported that opposition to Zionist immigration was the single issue that inhabitants of Syria and Palestine agreed upon most. The report further stated that British military officials in the region predicted that the implementation of the Zionist program would require at least fifty thousand troops "to initiate the program." It closed with the observation that giving up the idea of a "Jewish commonwealth" would allow the incorporation of Palestine in the Syrian state.

The Paris Peace Conference had nearly completed its work and the Germans had already signed their treaty two months before the American administration received the King-Crane report. By that time the United States had defaulted any significant role in the peace process and did not bother to make the King-Crane report available for consideration. As the later arrangements clearly attest, the members of the conference ignored Arab concerns the report reflected when they made the final peace settlement.

THE SAN REMO AGREEMENT

Nearly ten months after the Germans signed the Treaty of Versailles the Allies met at San Remo on the Italian Riviera to shape a final settlement for the Middle East. They intended to submit this settlement plan to the League of Nations for approval. Many talks and negotiations among the Allies to determine the fate of the Ottoman Empire occurred in the intervening time, but so did the influx of occupying armies and a significant armed Turkish resistance.

The British and the French dominated at San Remo because of American disarray over its international role and the diminished stature of Italy. British and French plans for the Middle East, however, were on the verge of disintegrating when they convened at San Remo on April 18, 1920. A Syrian national Congress had elected Feisal as their king on March 8 and nominated his brother, Abdullah, as king of Iraq. Serious Arab riots had just broken out in Palestine. Egyptians were restless because of their failure to receive a recognition of independence and over continued British occupation. Lower Mesopotamia was far from being tranquil and was actually on the eve of rebellion. Mustafa Kemal's Nationalist Movement was growing in strength in Anatolia and moving toward a friendly relationship with the Soviets. Military and civilian personnel wanted to return home to normal lives after years of war. Their governments were financially strapped and there was a growing distaste for the financial and moral burdens of empire in a wide spectrum of their citizenries.

The Anglo-French deliberations at San Remo reached an agreement that pleased only the British. It was, however, the best deal France could obtain from its ally and shaped both the Treaty of Sevres with the Ottomans and the subsequent mandate system under the auspices of the League of Nations. While more than two years would pass before this arrangement would become official League policy, it served as provisional justification for Britain and France to govern most of the Arab lands in southwest Asia.

At the conclusion of the San Remo conference on April 24, the Arabs of the

Ottoman Empire learned that the Great Powers planned to retain dominion over their region through a new device called a mandate. The Powers justified this approach on the assumption that the Arabs were insufficiently prepared to govern themselves without passing through a stage of European tutelage. The full details of the mandatory arrangement took until 1922 for Syria and Palestine and until 1924 for Iraq but the British and French began to exercise their authority immediately after San Remo and the Arabs began to react to their perceived injustice.

Since British forces already occupied their newly authorized areas they only had to deal with the uprisings that occurred after the announcement of the San Remo agreement. France, however, had to move inland from its coastal base and oust the newly elected Arab government in Damascus and establish its physical control over a considerable area. General Gouraud built up his forces after San Remo and on July 14 demanded that Feisal withdraw from Damascus. Feisal understood that his forces and his capital could not withstand a French assault so he reluctantly agreed to the ultimatum against the advice of some of his close associates. He withdrew to Palestine with most of his limited forces while elements of his army resisted the French, who captured Damascus on July 25. The French soon established control over its mandatory acquisition whose boundaries were still undefined.

THE TREATY OF SEVRES

A formal acknowledgment of the Allies' agreement of San Remo occurred when the non-functioning Ottoman government agreed to the Treaty of Sevres on August 10, 1920. Needless to say, the Allies dictated these terms in the same manner that they dealt with the other defeated Central Powers. The total effect of the treaty's terms deprived a severely truncated Turkey of its sovereignty as the Allies divided most of the Ottoman territory among themselves and obtained the right to supervise Turkish activities in the small territory it retained. The Allies, for instance, would control the Turkish budget and its expenditures; they also reimposed the capitulations the Ottomans had rescinded at the outbreak of the war. Only about one-third of north central Anatolia remained unfettered with some type of European occupation under uncertain terms for an uncertain time. The Powers controlled Istanbul and the entire length of the Straits from the Black Sea to the Aegean Sea as an internationalized area in which only the Allies could have military forces.

The Allies divided the remainder of the Ottoman Empire among themselves. Greece obtained the vital shipping and industrial center of Izmir and surrounding territories, which they hoped would be a base for expansions over much of western Anatolia. It also acquired an outright annexation of Eastern Thrace, the Gallipoli peninsula, the major islands of Imbros and Tenedos with the adjacent smaller islands, and the Dodecanese Island chain. Italy received about one-third of Anatolia from Brousa south to the Mediterranean and east to the French zone. The French acquisition began at Mersin in the west and stretched to within sixty miles of the Black Sea in the north and over to a proposed independent Armenia in the east. This French-controlled area of Cilicia adjoined the French mandate in Syria and provided them dominion over the northeastern Mediterranean centered on the vital port of Alexandretta. The nature of French and Italian authority was murky, but if left unperturbed they clearly could impose their wishes upon the regions.

The Sevres documents completed disposal of the Turkish heartland by timidly addressing the nationalist aspirations of the Armenians and Kurds in eastern Anatolia. The Ottoman government consented to an independent state of Armenia in easternmost Anatolia. President Wilson would define the borders of this new state in the future. The treaty also provided for an even more vaguely delineated autonomous Kurdistan, which was a status short of nationhood. Both troubled groups would need international assistance to transform these promises into nations.

The Ottomans relinquished sovereignty over their Arab lands and recognized both the independence of the Hashemite Kingdom of the Hijaz and League of Nations authority to dispose of the Fertile Crescent. In conformity with the San Remo agreement, France received the right to establish a mandate over Syria. Contrary to the Sykes-Picot agreement, this smaller acquisition confirmed the British claim to the oil-rich Kurdish area of Mosul and Kirkuk. The British acquired a mandate over Mesopotamia and Palestine, but most of these borders were still undefined. It was, for instance, unclear where Palestine ended and Mesopotamia began, and, for that matter, where mandatory Syria and Mesopotamia met. No border yet existed in the vast desert between the emerging Kingdom of Saudi Arabia and mandatory Mesopotamia. Adding to the confusion was the unsettled question of former Turkish and German ownership in the oil interests of the Mosul-Kirkuk region over which both France and the United States asserted claims.

Despite their differences, Britain and France managed a great deal of cooperation and agreed upon the free flow of trade and peoples between their mandatory territories, as well as a mutually beneficial management of the region's vital water resources. They planned for interconnecting railroads and France agreed to allow the British to construct oil pipelines through Syria from northern Mesopotamia to the Mediterranean.

The mandates clearly stated that the British and French had custody over Mesopotamia and Syria to establish order; protect religious and civil rights; eliminate brigandage, crime, and drugs; and develop an institutional infrastructure to prepare the areas for self-government.

There was no mention of preparation for self-government in the British mandate over Palestine. This was not an oversight, but a means of giving the British full latitude for assisting the Zionist movement to establish a "national home" in Palestine, although neither international law nor common usage defined this new term. The mandatory document contained a verbatim quote of the last half of the Balfour Declaration. Britain, thus, had the internationally sanctioned task of promoting Zionist immigration and settlement in Palestine while assuming the almost impossible responsibility of guaranteeing the "civil and religious rights" of all peoples under its authority. Article 6 was particularly provocative in this regard because it specified that British mandatory authorities must facilitate the "close settlement" of Jews in Palestine. This provision led to the sometimes forceful removal of Arabs from lands to allow an uninterrupted Jewish culture to prevail area by area.

Article 25 of the mandate proved to be crucial for British policy that frustrated Zionist ambitions. Its reference to "the territories lying between the Jordan and the eastern borders of Palestine" established that Palestine reached to some indefinite place east of the Jordan river. The Balfour Declaration, after all, had promised the Zionists a national home "in Palestine." Zionists, therefore, assumed in 1917 and later that all of Palestine was legitimately available for their settlement by both the promise of the Balfour Declaration and, especially, the preamble of the British Mandate for Palestine. This article, however, authorized the British with League consent "to postpone and withhold application of such provisions of this mandate as he [Britain] may consider inapplicable to the existing local conditions" and make changes "suitable to those conditions." The British exercised this option when it created the Emirate of Transjordan and thereby relegated Zionist settlement to the area west of the Jordan River.

The war and its aftermath was apparently over because the Treaty of Sevres made peace with the Ottoman government and settled all but some border adjustments and petroleum rights among the Allies. These tidy arrangements, however, depended upon cooperation from the occupied residents of the former Ottoman Empire. War weariness and financial strain limited the ability and will of the Allies to sustain their acquisitions in face of determined Turkish and Arab resistance.

The humiliating terms for the Ottomans raised the possibility that even such a hopeless government might reject the treaty, despite the Allied presence in Istanbul. The growth of the Nationalist Movement under Mustafa Kemal presented the further possibility that the government in Istanbul could not make a treaty acceptable to most Turks. There was also a serious question of whether the Allies were capable of forcefully imposing their wishes upon Turkey.

Arab unrest forced the British to make some important adjustments to the San Remo and Sevres arrangements. Both British mandates experienced widespread violence that threatened British ability to retain control. This was especially true in Mesopotamia, where the scale of the uprising was great enough to entail an unacceptable financial outlay even though the British had the military strength to prevail. A change in British policy was also due in part to an element of British officialdom that regretted the failure to treat the Arabs better in the peace settlements.

While the British contended with Arab uprisings in Mesopotamia and western Palestine, a new threat appeared in the middle. Abdullah Hashimi, the son of Sharif Hussein, gathered a small tribal army and travelled northward from the Hijaz to regain Syria for his brother Feisal. The British feared this more formal movement under Hashimite leadership could lead to a massive Arab uprising throughout the French and British mandates.

Under these circumstances, a more amicable agreement with the Arabs was necessary in order to salvage something from the Middle East peace, because all the plans for Turkey were also falling apart. Kemalist forces had recently won the First Battle of Inonu and only a Greek army stood between them and control of Turkey. Indicative of the Turkish nationalist success was the reality that, within a week before the Cairo Conference met, Kemal's government had pressured Italy into withdrawing its claims in Anatolia and had signed a major treaty with the Soviets.

THE CAIRO CONFERENCE

Winston Churchill, the colonial secretary, convened a group of Arab specialists in Cairo in March 1921. T.E. Lawrence, who had worked closely with Feisal and the Arab revolt, and Gertrude Bell, who was renowned for her knowledge of people and circumstances in Mesopotamia, helped convince Churchill to give most of the

British mandatory areas at least the appearance of self-rule. Toward this end, the Cairo Conference decided to make Feisal the king of Iraq in Mesopotamia as compensation for his contribution in the war and his loss of the Syrian throne. The conference created the emirate of Transjordan from the east bank of the Jordan River to the western border of Iraq for Abdullah to rule. The fact that neither newly elevated ruler had any previous affiliation with their new realms did not deter the British, because both were direct descendants of the prophet Muhammad and both had been prominent figures in the Arab revolt against the Ottomans.

These were momentous changes even though the basic British territory did not change and the League of Nations still regarded the two new Arab states as mandates. Also, Iraq and Transjordan remained almost totally under British guidance and control. However, both states retained their basic configurations long after the mandate system passed. And, since the League had not yet approved the mandate for Palestine, the special provisions that related to British obligations to the Zionist movement did not extend to Transjordan.

These developments, along with the French creation of a Greater Lebanon from the Syrian mandate in September 1920, established the basic border alignments of the northern Arab states that endured with little modification until full independence and beyond. It would, however, take decades before most people within these new entities identified with their states and ceased dreaming of variations of a larger Arab state or states. In the meantime, they faced their more immediate challenge of divesting themselves of their mandatory overlords, whom they regarded as thinly disguised colonial imperialists.

6

Kemal Ataturk and the Turkish Nationalist Movement

HISTORICAL TIMELINE

1918 ⇛ Mudros Armistice on October 30, 1918.

1919 ⇛ Greek army landed at Izmir on May 15.
⇛ Nationalist congress met in Sivas on September 4.

1920 ⇛ Nationalists launched a major military campaign in January against the French in Cilicia.
⇛ Ottoman parliament in Istanbul endorsed the National Pact on January 28.
⇛ On March 15, Allies used military force in Istanbul and arrest Ottoman officials suspected of sympathizing with the Nationalists.
⇛ Kemal's election as president of the new Turkish parliament on April 23 at its new capital of Ankara.
⇛ The Turkish delegation first saw the treaty of Sevres on May 11.
⇛ Ottoman government, including the Sultan, refused the Treaty of Sevres on June 10.
⇛ The Greek armies routed the Nationalist forces in Boursa and Thrace from June 23 through July 24.
⇛ King Alexander of Greece died unexpectedly on October 25.
⇛ Greek free election on November 14.
⇛ Nationalist Movement Treaty of Alexandropol with Armenian Republic on December 2.

⇛ King Constantine returned to Greece on December 19.
⇛ Venizelos resigned and went into exile following election defeat.

1921 ⇛ Greek army launched its attack to liquidate the Turkish Nationalists on January 6.
⇛ National Assembly adopted its Fundamental Law : Parliamentary democracy and universal manhood suffrage on January 20.
⇛ First Battle of Inonu January 6-10.
⇛ Supreme Council of the Allies called a special meeting in London on February 21.
⇛ In the Treaty of Moscow, which was signed on March 12, the Soviets recognized the Nationalist government as the legitimate government of Turkey and extended it diplomatic, financial, and military aid. The Soviets returned Ardahan and Kars, which they had obtained at the Congress of Berlin in 1878.
⇛ At the Second Battle of Inonu, Greece launched another offensive on March 23, which Ismet again turned back at Inonu.
⇛ Battle of Sakkaria August 24–September 16.
⇛ France signed the Treaty of Ankara on October 10, which brought diplomatic recognition and peace with France. The treaty pushed the French mandatory border ten thousand square miles south and restored the territory of Cilicia to Turkish control.

1922 ⇛ Battle of Afion-Karahissar lasted from August 18 to August 30.
⇛ In September–October the Nationalists adopted an official policy of expelling the entire Greek population.
⇛ The Armistice of Mudania on October 3 provided for the Greeks to withdraw to Western Thrace.
⇛ National Assembly abolished the Sultanate on November 4. The Sultan was exiled to Malta.
⇛ Lausanne Conference began on November 22.
⇛ Official announcement of the formation of Kemal's People's Party on December 6.

1923 ⇛ The Lausanne Treaty was signed on July 24 and ratified by the Grand National Assembly one month later.
⇛ Ankara officially became the capital of the Turkish Republic on October 13.
⇛ Kemal was elected president of the newly declared Republic on October 29.
⇛ Ismet was appointed prime minister on October 30.

1924 ⇛ Friday was declared a legal holiday on January 5.
⇛ Abolition of Caliphate, exiling of Ottoman family, abolition of Ministries of Religious Affairs and Sharia, abolition of Muslim schools on March 3.
⇛ Abolition of Sharia courts on April 8.
⇛ Adoption of Turkish constitution on April 20.
⇛ Question of Mosul turned over to the League of Nations on September 30.

1925 ⇛ Kurdish rebellion began on February 11.
⇛ Law for the Maintenance of Order was passed on March 4.
⇛ Use of fez was outlawed on November 25.
⇛ Abolition of religious orders and closing of their facilities took place on November 30.
⇛ League of Nations ruled in favor of Great Britain on the Mosul question on December 16.
⇛ Adoption of international clock, time, and calendar on December 26.

1926 ⇛ New Civil Code was adopted on February 26.
⇛ New Obligations Code on March 8.
⇛ New Penal Code on March 13.
⇛ New Commercial Code on June 28.

1927 ⇛ Kemal's six-day, (thirty-six-hour) speech at People's Party congress in November.

1928 ⇛ Designation of Turkey as a Muslim nation was deleted from the constitution on April 10. Oaths thereafter were taken to the constitution and not to God.
⇛ Adoption of Western form of Arabic numbers on May 24.
⇛ Adoption of Latin alphabet on November 3.

1929 ⇛ Expiration of the Law for the Maintenance of Order.

1931 ⇛ All instruction in schools had to be in Turkish and had to be taught by Turks after March 31.

1934 ⇛ Implementation of the compulsory use of surnames on June 21.
⇛ Kemal received new surname of Ataturk on November 24.
⇛ All members of the clergy were forbidden to wear distinctive clothing away from their premises on December 3.

1935 ⇛ Women received the right to vote on February 8.
⇛ Sunday replaced Friday as official weekly holiday on May 27.

1936 ⇛ Turkey received permission to fortify the Straits at the Agreement of Montreux on June 20.
⇛ France promised Syria to include Hatay in an independent Syria on September 9.
⇛ Turkey insisted that Hatay be independent on October 9.

1937 ⇛ Arabs gained ascendancy in government of Hatay on November 29.

1938 ⇛ Turks gained control of Hatay through new election on July 21.
⇛ Death of Ataturk on November 10.

1939 ⇛ France conceded Hatay to Turkey in return for a non-aggression pact on July 23.

The Allied victory was so decisive and the Ottoman situation was so dire that the latter felt it had no choice but to accept the Mudros Armistice on October 30, 1918. Since its terms were so harsh there was no reason to believe Allied demands in a final peace settlement would be anything short of brutal to the once proud empire. Turks seemed, however, to have had little trouble accepting the prospect of losing their Arab lands much as they had lost the Balkan region in 1912-1913. They regarded their behavior during the war and armistice proceedings as honorable enough to retain control over the Turkish heartland in Anatolia after a brief period of British and French occupation until they could sign a permanent peace. Mustafa Kemal, a Turkish nationalist and a respected Ottoman general, initially accepted the responsibility of supervising the demobilization of a large portion of the Ottoman army.

All Turks, and especially Mustafa Kemal, were shocked, therefore, when on May 15, 1919 a large Greek army landed at Izmir, which had a large ethnic Greek population. Since Greece had not fought the Ottomans during the war, the arrival of a Greek army could only mean that the Allies planned some unexpected dismemberment of Anatolia as well. The Greek invasion transformed Kemal from a dutiful, cooperative demobilizer into a passionate remobilizer of existing Turkish forces and a recruiter of new troops to resist the entirety of the Allies' schemes.

THE BEGINNING OF THE NATIONALIST MOVEMENT

Kemal, who had been in Sivas in central Anatolia when he learned the news of the Greek invasion, issued a call for a Turkish congress to meet in that city on September 4. In the meantime he actively organized every possible person and military-related item to wage a resistance to expel all foreigners from Turkish soil. Military men and civilians from all over Anatolia soon heeded his call to arms and made their contributions. Soldiers ceased turning in their weapons and in some places regained possession of guns and ammunition they had relinquished earlier. Some politicians escaped Istanbul to join Kemal and his new Nationalist party in the interior. The apparent fruitlessness of their cause worked to the Nationalists' advantage because it grew up fairly rapidly but in something near obscurity. The Allies were preoccupied with demobilizing after a soul-rendering and expensive war; they were working through the disquieting process of formulating a complex peace for many nations spread out over thousands of miles. Since the other nations stripped their occupation forces in Anatolia to a minimal level, only the Greeks seemed concerned about the Nationalist movement's growth. As a result, only the Greeks were in a position during the summer of 1920 to counter the Nationalists' effort to resist the humiliating terms of Sevres.

The Nationalist-led congress met in Sivas on September 4, 1919 and adopted the National Pact, which opposed foreign occupation of Turkish territory minus the former Arab areas. It renounced the capitulations the armistice had reimposed. It also created a Grand National Assembly and denied the validity of the Ottoman Parliament in Istanbul.

MILITARY AND DIPLOMATIC VICTORIES

In January of 1920 the Nationalists under Kemal launched a major military campaign against the French in Cilicia. Their overwhelming success had the immediate effect of tempering French desire to hold the region. It also sparked acts of violence from Turkish troops as far west as Gallipoli and in Istanbul. The Nationalist movement was impressive enough to move the Ottoman parliament in Istanbul to accept the National Pact on January 28, although it did not vote itself out of existence. Allied officials were concerned enough by March 15 to use overt military force in Istanbul and arrest Ottoman officials suspected of sympathizing with the Nationalists. The Allies transported the arrested officials to Malta for incarceration. These were hardly propitious developments for the Allies as they moved toward a final determination of the Ottoman territories.

The success of his upstart movement easily led to Kemal's election as president of the new Turkish Grand National Assembly on April 23 at its new capital of Ankara, which was two hundred miles east of Istanbul. This important step in Turkish nationalism occurred one day before the Allies concluded their meeting at San Remo and one month after the Syrian Congress elected Feisal as its king.

The surprising zeal and strength of the Nationalists relative to the Allied military presence made a successful imposition of the Treaty of Sevres upon a supposedly prostrate Turkey more difficult, if not impossible. It was clear, however, that no Allied member was interested in increasing its military contingent in Anatolia.

The Turkish delegation first saw the treaty on May 11 and refused to sign it. The situation became even more dramatic when the entire, hitherto passive Ottoman government, including the Sultan, refused the document after its official presentation on June 10. The Ottoman military commander's declaration of allegiance to the Nationalists accompanied a general Turkish outcry of rage. Ottoman soldiers streamed to join Kemal, who decided to launch a military attack upon the weak Allied forces in Istanbul. This seemed incontinent behavior for a "sick man."

WAR WITH GREECE

In response to this threat, Allied authority Lloyd George invited the Greek government, which had the only capable military force in Anatolia, to repel the Nationalist assault. From June 23 to July 24 the Greek armies routed the Nationalist forces in Boursa and Thrace and inflicted severe casualties on both Turkish troops and civilians. Venizelos, the Greek Prime Minister and architect of Greek acquisitions during the peace talks, had not only saved the treaty but seemed to have elevated Greece to a stature unknown since the Byzantine Empire. The Greek triumph caused some concern among the Allies, but the Italians and French had renewed hope they could keep their zones of domination in Anatolia, which the Nationalists had threatened a mere month earlier.

Greek developments took a dramatic turn when King Alexander died unexpectedly in late October 1920. He and his royalist supporters had not been a factor in shaping Greek policies since 1917, although there was good reason to believe that most Greeks were committed royalists. Venizelos was sure, however, that his government's dramatic success and the acquisition of a new empire had lessened royalist ardor, so he allowed a free election. But the royalists won a decisive victory in November. King Constantine, whom the Allies had exiled in 1917 for his unwillingness to commit to the Allied cause, returned on December 19, 1920. Venizelos, who had thought his position was safe after his triumphs, resigned and went into exile.

The formerly passive king not only became an enthusiastic advocate of keeping Venizelos's acquisitions but also of pushing Greek possessions even further and destroying the Nationalist movement. There is no reason to believe subsequent Greek policy was any different from the one Venizelos would have pursued, but

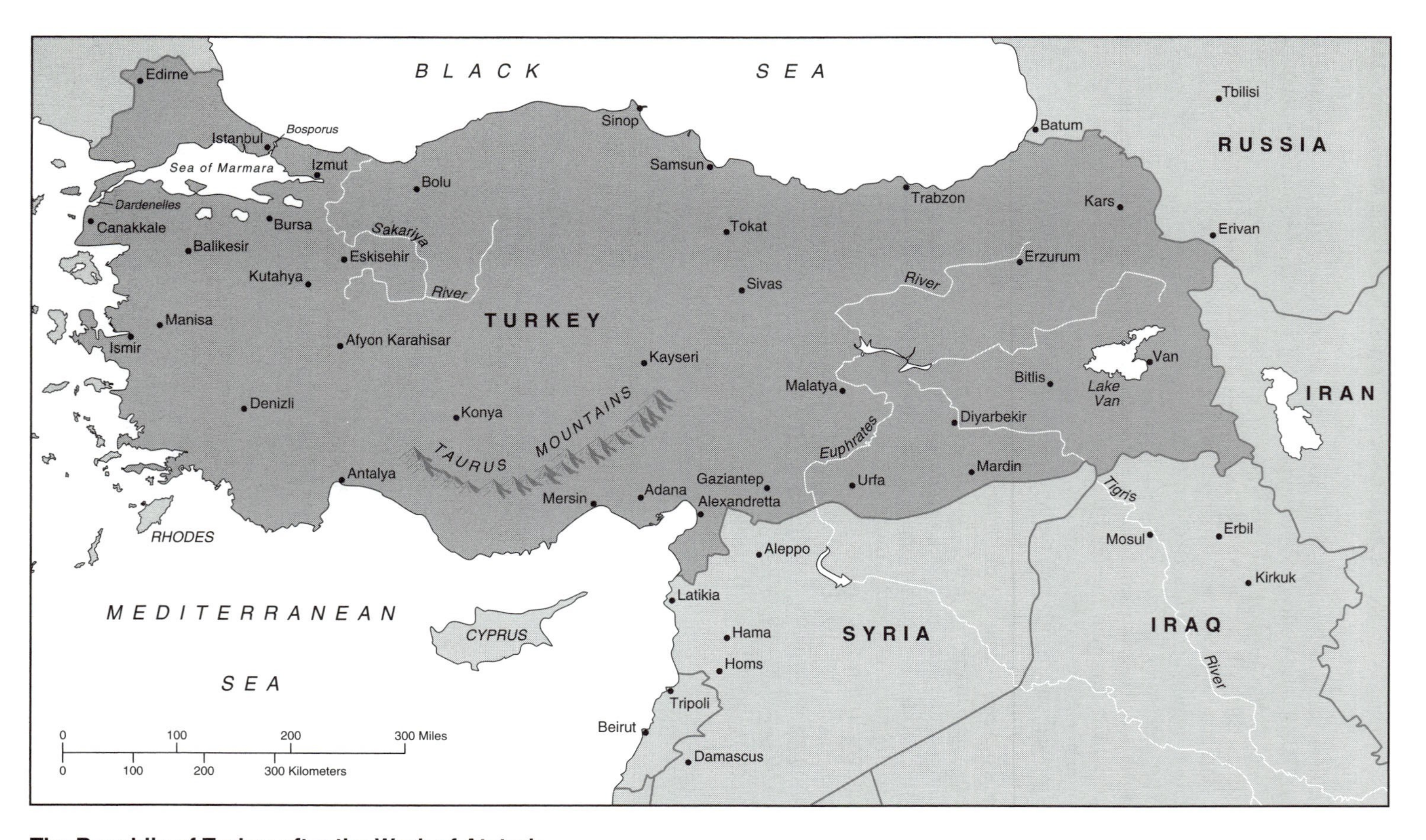

The Republic of Turkey after the Work of Ataturk

there was no doubt that the majority of troops in the trenches felt better fighting on behalf of their king.

The Nationalist movement, however, which lost the July 1920 campaign to the Greeks, was much stronger nearly six months later. It had all but eliminated significant Turkish opposition, primarily from religious traditionalists. It had pushed back the Armenian republic's borders from Kars and forced it to accept a treaty of peace at Alexandropol on December 2, 1920. The new Soviet regime was courting the Nationalist movement. The National Assembly had adopted its Fundamental Law on January 20, 1921, which promised a parliamentary democracy with universal manhood suffrage. Of foremost importance, the Nationalist's military capability was also greatly improved.

The emboldened Greek army, which enjoyed a two-to-one numerical advantage and superior armaments, launched its attack to liquidate the Nationalists on January 6, 1921. The Nationalist commander, Ismet Pasha, seized the initiative at Inonu where the Turks inflicted surprisingly large casualties upon the Greek army and turned back the attempted advance. Ismet's victory at Inonu prompted the Supreme Council of the Allies to extend an invitation for the Nationalists to attend a special meeting in London on February 21. The invitation was a recognition of the Nationalist's strength and importance, as well as an acknowledgment of the changed situation. Greece, however, was unreceptive to the conciliatory posture of the Nationalists at the meeting and determined to fight alone if the Allies continued to waver.

These developments moved the Soviets to action. They had, of course, only recently had their own problems with Allied occupation. In the Treaty of Moscow on March 12, 1921 the Soviets recognized the Nationalist government as the legitimate government of Turkey and extended to it diplomatic, financial, and military aid. Just as importantly, after the treaty with the Soviets, Kemal could concentrate his forces upon the Greeks and not worry about Russian aggression. The Soviets demonstrated their sincerity even further by returning Ardahan and Kars, which they had obtained at the Congress of Berlin in 1878.

Greece launched another offensive on March 23, which Ismet again turned back at Inonu. Ismet's victories assured him a place in the hearts of his countrymen just below that of Kemal and helped convince all but the British to abandon the Greeks and make peace with the Nationalists. The Allies' Supreme Council adjourned in June after Greece refused its offer to mediate with the Nationalists.

In fact, in July, revitalized Greek forces accompanied by King Constantine advanced into the interior of Anatolia from their base in the Afion-Karahissar region. Kemal withdrew and chose to defend against the Greek advance along the Sakkaria River. Turks made enormous sacrifices of their worldly goods to finance the campaign and volunteers streamed to join Kemal at Sakkaria. The Greek attack on August 10 initiated three weeks of fierce battle in which each side sustained casualties of about one-third of their original strength. Kemal's brilliant move at the right moment, however, brought a Turkish victory and set the Greek army into retreat.

Nationalist victories separated Italy and France from the Alliance and each sought accommodations with the emerging Turkish republic. Both had significant economic concerns in Anatolia and neither had the financial ability nor the will to enter a sustained war against an aroused and inspired Turkish population. On March 13, 1921 Italy secretly agreed to withdraw its forces and claims after the Second

Battle of Inonu. Following the Nationalist victory at Sakkaria, France shocked its British ally by signing the Treaty of Ankara on October 20, 1921. This treaty was more important than the Treaty of Moscow because it not only brought diplomatic recognition and peace with France, it also pushed the French mandatory border ten thousand square miles south and restored the territory of Cilicia to Turkish control.

In the fall of 1921 the Nationalists faced only a Greek army in western Anatolia and the diplomatic posture of Great Britain, which still commanded a diminished role in Istanbul. The Nationalist movement became stronger during the next year as it could concentrate on one front and utilize weapons the Italians and French left behind as well as those they received from the Soviets. Kemal struck in the middle of August 1922, when the Greek forces at Afion-Karahissar were weakened following their abortive attempt to seize Istanbul, only to have the British turn them away with diplomatic pressure and the threat of naval retaliation. After considerable subterfuge, Kemal attacked the heart of Greek defenses, which broke quickly. Within a few days the remnant of the Greek forces fled toward Izmir and wreaked havoc on innocent civilians in the process.

The Greek population in western Anatolia feared drastic retaliation from the pursuing Nationalist forces. Tens of thousands of Greeks, who descended from Greeks who had lived in the region from antiquity, left their homes for the perceived safety of the coastal city of Izmir. Anxiety among the Greeks, accompanied by some violence from Turkish civilians and troops, set off a panic among the Greeks, who rushed to board ships to transport them to Greece. Greek naval and civilian ships and boats conducted one of the most extensive evacuations in history. Before the entire evacuation process ended, ships from several nations played a role. In the midst of the Greek exodus and Turkish retaliation fires burned out of control in the city of Izmir. With the breakdown of order and cooperation, the uncontrolled fires turned Izmir into an inferno that destroyed two-thirds of the city.

Faced with the inability to house and care for the flood of refugees, the Nationalists seized upon Greek fear and adopted an official policy of expelling the entire Greek population in September and October. Close to 1,500,000 Greeks left the land of their birth and crossed the Aegean to live with their blood kin. Greece responded in kind and expelled about 500,000 ethnic Turks and other non-Greeks, who had to find new homes in the new Turkish state. At the expense of two million disrupted lives, both Greece and Turkey began the postwar era as essentially ethnically homogeneous nations.

While no Greek forces remained in Anatolia, other Greek forces were reorganizing across the Sea of Marmora in Thrace. Moreover, a military coup against King Constantine, along with recent executions of Greek officers and officials, who had allowed the Nationalist Movement's victories, indicated that Greece intended to fight. Kemal's forces, thus, faced a difficult dilemma, because pursuit of the Greek army into Thrace would put the Nationalists in conflict with Great Britain, which still adhered to the full provisions of the Treaty of Sevres.

All concerned realized that the Nationalist forces had won and overturned the post-Great War agreements. Therefore, they had to find a way to negotiate a settlement that reflected the new reality. French intercession led to an Anglo-Turkish meeting at Mudania on the shore of the Sea of Marmora on October 3. The Armistice of Mudania provided for the Greeks to withdraw to Western Thrace, while an Allied force administered the area until an international treaty could recognize the reestablishment of Turkish control.

LAUSANNE CONFERENCE

The parties agreed upon a conference in Lausanne, Switzerland to settle all outstanding issues. When the Allies issued an invitation for both the Porte and the Nationalists to send delegations, the Grand National Assembly abolished the Sultanate on November 4, 1922. The caliphate, which Sultan Vahid-ed-Din did not hold, remained an official Turkish office until March 3, 1924. The Sultan's exile to Malta seemed to have ended the last institutional vestige of the Ottoman Empire and left Mustafa Kemal and the Nationalist Movement as the undisputed government of the Turkish nation.

The Lausanne Conference began on November 22, 1922 with the Soviets participating for the first time in an important international deliberation. Lord Curzon, who remained Foreign Minister in the new Bonar Law cabinet, and Ismet Pasha, now known as Ismet Inonu, were the dominant figures at the conference. The small, quiet Turk nearly drove the gigantic and histrionic Englishman to distraction with an exaggerated emphasis upon his poor hearing as well as his unwillingness to compromise on Turkish vital interests.

Since Turkey had already defined most of its borders through negotiations or war, much of the deliberation dealt with the disposition of the Straits; the Ottoman Public Debt; restructuring international relations with Turkey in the absence of the capitulations; and the Mosul question. The conference agreed that the Straits should remain open to all commercial shipping in both peacetime and wartime. They would also remain open to all naval shipping in time of peace with the provision that no foreign naval presence could exceed Russia's Black Sea fleet. Further, the Straits would remain demilitarized for fifteen kilometers on either shore.

Ismet allowed the conference to recess for nearly three months beginning February 4, 1923, rather than concede to anything approaching the kind of stranglehold foreign nations had enjoyed upon the Ottoman economy prior to the beginning of the world war. When it reconvened on April 23, 1923 Ismet obtained agreement that the new Balkan states should accept responsibility for their portion of the Ottoman debt. Foreign countries did not regain the extraordinary economic and judicial concessions they had formerly enjoyed. While Ismet was unable to obtain reparations from the Greeks for damage they inflicted while in Anatolia, he obtained an admission of guilt from them for the damages. Turkey refused to accept the need for any kind of League of Nations supervision to protect minorities within its borders on the grounds that it represented an infringement on Turkish sovereignty. It did allow international assistance in obtaining land of equal value to that which Turkish refugees had left in Greece. The Mosul question remained unresolved for later bilateral deliberations between Turkey and Great Britain, which held it as part of the Mesopotamian mandate.

The Lausanne Conference illustrated that Mustafa Kemal and his Nationalist Movement had forged a viable, independent nation out of a remnant of the Ottoman Empire. At Lausanne it had met with other nations as an equal and had no more restrictions on its internal affairs than any other country had to accept. The new state had the same protection under international law as other nations. The Lausanne Treaty was signed on July 24, 1923 and the Grand National Assembly ratified it one month later. The Allies withdrew immediately and the former "Sick Man" was on its own, albeit significantly altered from how it began the Great War.

THE REPUBLIC

Freed from both the Allied occupation and the constrictions of the Sultanate, the Turkish Nationalist Movement initiated a modernization program that its Tanzimat predecessors would have envied. Their total control enabled the Kemalists to proceed without serious fear of either internal or external interference. In truth, almost every change sprang from the iconoclastic mind of Kemal, who was very familiar with Western ideologies, but tailored his program to the unique situation in Turkey. Need, rather than ideology, dictated the revolutionary approach the Kemalists pursued, free from consideration of precedent. Their basic test for all new policies was whether the changes could make Turkey stronger and guarantee its sovereignty. Kemal tended to equate "civilized" institutions and behavior with Western practices, which he wished to emulate. Conversely, his low regard for everything Ottoman and Islamic helped identify institutions and practices for eradication.

The constitution of the new state proclaimed it a republic on April 20, 1924, but it was in practice a totalitarian state under Kemal and his People's Party. It experimented with an officially sanctioned opposition party for four months in 1930, but it "voluntarily" ceased when reactionary forces flocked to it. From February through April of 1925, a Kurdish rebellion under the leadership of Shaykh Said of Palu justified the use of martial law that stayed in effect until 1929. Government under this Law for the Maintenance of Order restrained the many elements that regarded Kemalist changes as appalling. But even the absence of constitutional restraints cannot account for the generally passive response of Turks to the monumental transformation of their country. In part, many of Kemal's innovations were logical extensions of Tanzimat principles that had existed for three generations. Also, few could deny the "Gazi" a free hand to shape the state he had rescued from certain destruction. This title, which he adopted after the battle of Sakkaria in 1921, sufficed to accord him adequate distinction until the Turkish parliament proclaimed him "Ataturk," Father Turk, in November 1934.

The Gazi characteristically approached every issue forthrightly, with little concern for subtlety. While he had great concern for his people, he believed that their long subservience under Ottoman domination had not prepared them for quick comprehension of either their new status, their new opportunities, or the means of reaching their potential as a nation. He loved to assume the role of teacher, as he did in his attack upon the fez and in behalf of the Latin alphabet, to emblazon his convictions upon the minds of his countrymen. In this vein, he obtained National Assembly consent to move the capital to Ankara on October 13, 1923. This move would emphasize that virtually nothing of the new republic was connected with the Ottoman past. In his typically pedagogical manner, Kemal explained the significance of forsaking sophisticated Istanbul for rustic Ankara.

The National Assembly unanimously elected him president on October 29, 1923, just as it would continue to do until his death. The next day he appointed Ismet as Prime Minister, a position he would retain until October 1937, except for a three-month respite in 1924-1925. This assured the new regime uninterrupted continuity to impose its will upon the nation. The cabinet was responsible to the president, who was responsible to the constitution, which reflected the thinking of the president.

SECULARIZATION OF THE STATE

The Gazi's vision for Turkey was predicated on it becoming a productive nation with a fair opportunity for all citizens to reach their potential and thereby increase Turkey's prosperity and strength. None should enjoy an advantage because of rank, gender, religious affiliation, or any other distinction. He desired, as much as possible, to make Turkey an economic and cultural extension of Europe. While he, like many Turks, resented Europe's former hold on the Ottoman society, he wished to emulate the European practices that had made them strong, rather than reject them. Toward this end, many crucial changes needed to occur to synchronize Turkish practices with the Europeans. He implemented other changes simply because they appeared to be compatible with European behavior and differed from Ottoman custom.

The Assembly's declaration of Friday as a legal holiday for everyone in Turkey on January 5, 1924 at first glance seems like a frivolous early act of the new republic. Kemal regarded it as much more. It provided Turks an official day of rest in partial conformity with the widespread European weekend. It was easier to implement it on Friday, since that was the day religious Muslims reserved for prolonged religious activities. It pressured the non-Muslims to rest on the same day as their Muslim brethren. After other laws had sufficiently reduced Muslim resistance, he changed the official day of rest to Sunday on May 27, 1935 in full compliance with European practice. Thus, Turkish banks, businesses, and government offices shared the same operating hours, to the considerable benefit of their complex intercourse.

Fulfillment of his dream could not occur while the Islamic law prevailed. Kemal began by destroying the Islamic institutions and replacing them with secular institutions as rapidly as possible. In doing so, he avoided constructing parallel institutions, which the entrenched forces could criticize and impede. The Assembly abolished the Caliphate on March 3, 1924 and ordered the exile of all remaining members of the Ottoman ruling family. On the same day, it abolished the Ministry of Religious Affairs, the Ministry of the Sharia (Islamic Law), and closed all Muslim schools. A little more than a month later, it abolished the Islamic courts on April 8. From that point, Turks had no choice but to depend on the secular apparatus of the state in such vital matters as marriage, divorce, and inheritance, which had always been under the exclusive jurisdiction of Islamic authorities.

Kemal's attack upon the use of the fez demonstrated that his virtually nihilist approach did not flinch from any issue. Many might assume this was too small an issue to merit the attention it received from such a great man, who was engaged in so many great matters. Kemal, however, regarded his policy of abolishing the use of this traditional Ottoman head covering as more than symbolic in the necessary transformation of Turkey. He went so far as to publicly humiliate innocent traditionalists to make his point that modern, civilized people did not wear the offensive anachronism. The law that forbade the use of the fez on November 25, 1925 specified that Turks should wear hats with brims. This gives a better indication of Kemal's real intention, because Muslims simply could not keep their head covered with their brimmed hats when they bowed to pray. Without outlawing religion, he found ways to make religious practice both unfashionable and inconvenient.

Five days after abolishing the use of the fez, the Assembly abolished all religious orders and closed their facilities. Ottoman authorities had already greatly restricted the dervishes and other religious orders, but this law administered their *coup de grace.* The regime discouraged Islamic observance further by restricting the use of distinctly Islamic clothes to certified religious functionaries. The thrust of this policy reached maturity when the Assembly outlawed distinctive religious garments for the clergy of all religions outside of their religious properties on December 3, 1934.

Traditionalists received another shock on December 26, 1925 when the Assembly officially adopted the international clock and method of time designation, as well as the Gregorian calendar of the West. This facilitated relations with the non-Muslim world and removed the confusion that occurred from making the calculations necessary to conduct all kinds of ordinary business. It also consigned into obscurity a considerable body of Islamic experts, who had traditionally reigned over these mysteries. These apparently administrative modifications distanced Turkey further from the international Muslim community to the consternation of traditionalists within Turkey and abroad. Simple folk did not appreciate Kemal imposing his will upon God's time and calendar.

The logical corollary of abolishing the Sharia occurred in 1926, when the Assembly approved various secular law codes to replace traditional Islamic law. This entire approach was an abomination to traditionalists, who regarded God's law as the only law. Traditional Islam, after all, had always insisted that state and religion were inextricably united under God's unchanging law. But the new codes originated in the secular societies to Turkey's west in response to the mundane needs of mankind's modern, temporal society under constitutional law. Thus, from February through June, the Turkish republic adopted civil codes, financial obligations, penal guidelines, and commercial codes of mostly Swiss and German origin. This massive legal revolution occurred with little outward resistance, in sharp contrast to the response Tanzimat administrators had received for much more modest changes.

A law of April 10, 1928 acknowledged the obvious when it deleted the portion of the constitution that declared Turkey a Muslim nation. An accompanying amendment excluded an oath before God as part of the acceptance of public office. Turks were, thus, answerable to the law of the land, regardless of the provisions God might have for malfeasance or impropriety.

Kemalism proceeded on its revolutionary course in 1928 when the Assembly adopted the Western form of Arabic numbers and replaced the Arabic alphabet with the Latin alphabet. The Arab numbers of the Orient were considerably different from their Western counterparts and caused confusion in relations between Turkey and the West. Although this was a significant change on May 24, 1928, it did not evoke the anathema of some of the other changes and had some obvious benefits. The adoption of the Latin alphabet on November 3 was quite a different matter. The entrenched, literate Turks were comfortable with the modified Arabic alphabet for writing in Turkish. Those who had not studied Western languages, however, were not familiar with the Latin alphabet. The adoption of it, therefore, effectively rendered them illiterate. In addition, the Latin alphabet was, in their perception, unquestionably of Christian origin, while Arabic and its alphabet were the instruments of God's expression as He had revealed in the Holy *Quran.* Kemal's realization of the provocative nature of this change prompted him to make his most concerted public effort to obtain its acceptance. Again, his main argument was that since the "civilized" world used the Latin alphabet, Turkey should also. In addition, he maintained, the Latin alphabet was more compatible with Turkish phonics and would accelerate achievement of the goal of eradicating the widespread illiteracy of Turkey. His relentless effort in conveying the efficacy of the new alphabet earned him the designation of "Chief Instructor of the School of the Nation" from the cabinet on November 11. This successful change in the alphabet functionally and culturally united Turkey with Europe more than any of Kemal's other changes. At the same time, it almost callously relegated to illiteracy some formerly educated people who's high culture, for most practical purposes, disappeared when Kemal's signature changed the law of the land.

Additional efforts to sever Turkey from its Ottoman past forbade the study of Arabic and Persian in the fall of 1929. All primary students were prohibited from attending private schools and were compelled to receive their initial education in government schools. This effort to create a homogeneous new generation of Turkish citizens inspired a law on March 31, 1931 that specified that all instruction had to occur in the Turkish language under Turkish instructors.

The June 21, 1934 law that made the adoption of surnames compulsory initially resulted in more confusion than trauma. Its aim, of course, was to eliminate the greater confusion that arose from so many people in any particular situation having the same, single first name and no surname. The records of a modern state required considerably more specificity than first names alone provided. Each family, thus, had to adopt a surname and register it with government authorities. The Assembly bestowed the surname "Ataturk" upon Kemal at this juncture with the provision that no one else could ever use the name.

Kemalists were strong advocates of equality for women from early in their movement, largely in recognition of the important role women played in the success of the Nationalist Movement. The abolition of polygamy was an important step in improving the status of women and providing them with additional security. Resistance to change in this sensitive area prevented as many changes as the Gazi and other nationalists desired. Their prohibition of veiling was impossible to enforce since many women, especially in villages, regarded the practice more a demonstration of modesty than a fulfillment of religious obligation. Education for women increased and women began to enter the professions and public employment at a significant rate. The Assembly finally granted women the right to vote on February 8, 1935, although there were indications it would have done so earlier, except for the pronounced opposition such a revolutionary change faced.

The collective effect of the Kemalist changes in Turkey were monumental. The destruction of the old order and the indefatigable efforts of Ataturk created a nation entirely different from the society it replaced. Many of the changes were more a difference in scope than in kind, as the Tanzimat reformers and the Young Turks had attempted to accomplish the same goals. The absence of traditional religious obstruction and the overpowering strength of Ataturk's personality and political power helped him succeed where others had failed. The task was easier because the Turkish Republic was smaller and considerably less ethnically and religiously complex than its Ottoman predecessor had been. The republicans also had the advantage of modern, rapid communication and transportation that surpassed the dreams of the Tanzimat reformers.

Turkey was decidedly different and definitely more secular by the time of the Gazi's death on November 10, 1938. It had cast its lot with the West, rather than with the Orient. Turks and everyone else, therefore, judged it in comparison with its

European neighbors. Turkey proved to have fundamental weaknesses in resources, technology, capital, and educational development that no amount of central management could develop to match the Great Powers to its north and west. The government in the central location of Ankara could not effectively reach into the nation of small villages and farmers and impose a way of life that lacked familiarity and appeal. It was extremely difficult to overcome centuries of custom and habit. A major weakness of the Kemalist approach, in fact, was its failure to develop a strong agricultural base in a concerted effort to meet its manufacturing needs within its own borders. While Ataturk's unbridled nationalism was hardly xenophobic, it led, with considerable success, to a commitment to preventing Europeans from obtaining dominion over the republic like the Ottoman Empire had experienced. Turkey was sovereign and enjoyed a strong sense of its unique identity. Its strategic location, alone, assured it of a continued level of importance other nations had to consider in their strategic planning.

THE PROBLEM OF HATAY

Toward the end of Ataturk's life, he succeeded in obtaining from France the vital, northeastern port of Alexandretta and the surrounding province of Hatay. This was a source of continued consternation for Syria. Syria's cause for trepidation was because it resented French approval of Turkey's annexation of Cilicia in 1921, since it had originally been part of the French mandate of Syria. The vital water resources and agricultural base of Cilicia had always been culturally and economically affiliated with Greater Syria. Therefore, Syrians regarded it as a natural part of their developing modern state.

France had retained Hatay as part of their mandate over Syria, but administered it as a separate province in large part because the population was almost evenly divided between Turkish and Arabic inhabitants. Hatay became an issue of contention when France negotiated a treaty with Syria on September 9, 1936. The treaty promised to include the province in an independent Syrian state. The impending independence of Lebanon, which France had separated from the Syrian mandate in 1920, would deny Syria unquestioned access to the vital port of Beirut. The port of Alexandretta, therefore, was of particular economic and strategic importance to Syria, regardless of Syrian concerns for national pride and the prospect of losing additional Arab population.

Hatay was, of course, important to Turkey, because it could provide a needed port for the eastern portion of the elongated republic, which was not blessed with good roads to serve commerce with its western ports. Also, Ataturk's reputation for retaining all Turks under the republic's jurisdiction was at stake. Turkey had a decided advantage in presenting its case to France because Turkey's policy in a likely Franco-German war surpassed anything the still dependent Syria could offer.

Turkey took the initiative and asked for a League of Nations ruling on the matter of Hatay, since France could not legally dispose of the matter unilaterally, as it had jurisdiction of the area by League authority. To the satisfaction of Turkey and the bewilderment of Syria, the League of Nations recognized the autonomy of the province under continued French control on May 29, 1937. France, however, allowed the Arab majority to dominate the new government of Hatay and engendered Ataturk's wrath. He forced France to hold a new election on July 21, 1938 in which the Turkish population prevailed. Having narrowly escaped falling under Arab domination and possible annexation to Syria, the new Turkish government in Hatay, with encouragement from Ankara, petitioned for union with Turkey. Neither France nor the League of Nations were in a position to deny the momentum on behalf of Turkey's annexation of Hatay. In fact, the League was in disarray from defections and because of its inability to cope with Axis and Japanese aggression. French concern for its safety from Hitler's Germany caused it to seek an accommodation with Turkey. The fact that France had never ratified the 1936 treaty with Syria prevented it from entering into legally binding contradictory treaties.

Franco-Turkish negotiations that had begun before Ataturk's death resulted in a nonaggression pact between them on June 23, 1939. Turkey extracted French approval of Turkey's annexation of Hatay as an inducement to join the pact. The Gazi's groundwork, which led to annexation of an additional acquisition for Turkey, symbolized his continued influence from his grave.

Turkey under Ataturk had tied its fate to the West and paid scarce attention to its Arab neighbors. Interestingly, it developed close relations with its Balkan neighbors with whom it had less of a religious connection. The secular nature of Republican Turkey does not explain this somewhat peculiar development, because secular forces prevailed in the Arab areas as well. Despite their shared heritage with the Ottoman and Islamic past, they had little reason in the immediate aftermath of the Ottoman demise either to work together or against each other to any significant extent. Neither produced much for exportation, nor could either one afford much importation. Both areas had different degrees of dependence upon the West, while they struggled to maintain their national identities from positions of weakness. Turkey's defined borders and more uniform cultural and institutional solidity allowed it to deal with the West on a more equitable basis than the fragmented Arabs. Also, Turkey remained aloof from the question of Zionism, which tormented Arab relations with the West and among themselves. The modern Osmanlis could purposefully pursue the course the upstart Nationalist Movement had charted when it decided to defy the victorious Allies and all odds at Sivas in 1919.

7

Palestine to 1945

HISTORICAL TIMELINE

1919
- ⇛ First Palestinian National Congress, meeting in Jerusalem January 27–February 10 rejected the Balfour Declaration and demanded independence.
- ⇛ Peace conference decided on March 25 to send international commission of inquiry to ascertain aspirations of Near East peoples.
- ⇛ Henry C. King and Charles R. Crane, U.S. members of an international commission of inquiry, proceeded to Near East alone in June after the failure of Britain and France to join the commission.
- ⇛ Treaty of Versailles and League of Nations Covenant were signed on June 28.
- ⇛ General Syrian Congress, including some Palestinian delegates met; they rejected the Balfour Declaration on July 2.
- ⇛ Report of King-Crane Commission of Inquiry August 28.

1920
- ⇛ General Syrian Congress proclaimed independence of Syria, Lebanon, Palestine, and Transjordan, with Prince Feisal as king on March 8.
- ⇛ Disturbances broke out in Palestine in April due to fears of Zionism.
- ⇛ British removed Musa Kazim Pasha al-Husseini, mayor of Jerusalem.

⇛ San Remo Peace Conference assigned Palestine a Mandate to Britain without consent of the Palestinians April 25.
⇛ British prevented Second Palestinian National Congress from convening in May.
⇛ British civilian administration was inaugurated on July 1; Sir Herbert Samuel was appointed first high commissioner.
⇛ British Mandatory authorities set a quota of 16,500 Jewish immigrants for first year on August 26.
⇛ Third Palestinian National Congress at Haifa elected an Executive Committee in December, which controlled the Palestinian political movement from 1920 to 1935.

1921 ⇛ Fourth Palestinian National Congress at Jerusalem decided in a meeting from May to June to send a Palestinian delegation to London to explain Palestinian objections to the Balfour Declaration.
⇛ Syrian-Palestinian conference in Geneva discussed regional concerns regarding the mandate system.
⇛ Outbreak of disturbances in Jaffa on May 2 against Zionist immigration resulted in the death of 46 Jews and 146 wounded.
⇛ British appointed Hajj Amin al-Husseini Mufti of Jerusalem on May 8.
⇛ Haycraft Commission of Inquiry in October attributed the Jaffa disturbances to the magnitude of Zionist mass immigration.

1922 ⇛ Second Palestinian Delegation to London in February rejected Balfour Declaration and demanded national independence.
⇛ Churchill issued a White Paper on June 2 dealing with Palestine. The White Paper stated the British concept of their obligations to the Zionists; it excluded Transjordan from the Balfour Declaration and the League of Nations mandate; it dictated that Jewish immigration was not to exceed the economic capacity of Palestine.
⇛ The U.S. Congress endorsed the Balfour Declaration on June 30.
⇛ A League of Nations Council approved the mandate for Palestine on July 24.
⇛ The Fifth Palestinian National Congress at Nablus in August resolved to implement an economic boycott against the Zionist community.
⇛ The British published the first census of Palestine in October, which estimated the total population at 757,182. This included 78 percent Muslim, 11 percent Jewish, and 9.6 percent Christian.

1923 ⇛ Vladimir Jabotinsky resigned from the Zionist Executive in January and vowed to use all means possible to colonize Palestine and Transjordan.
⇛ British mandate for Palestine officially went into effect on September 29.

1925 ⇛ Jabotinsky formed the Revisionist party to colonize Transjordan and Palestine.
⇛ Palestinians began a general strike in March to protest Lord Balfour's visit to Jerusalem.
⇛ Sixth Palestinian National Congress convened in Jaffa in October.

1928 ⇛ Seventh Palestinian National Congress convened in Jerusalem in June.
⇛ First attempt by a group of Jewish religious leaders to change "status quo" at the Wailing Wall September 24.
⇛ Islamic Conference, which met in Jerusalem in November, demanded the protection of Muslim property rights at the Wailing Wall.

1929 ⇛ Beginning on August 23, Palestinians rioted in several towns in response to Zionist demonstrations at the Wailing Wall. Arabs killed 133 Jews and wounded 339; British military inflicted most of the damage on Palestinians, which left 116 killed and 232 wounded.
⇛ Palestinian conference convened in Jerusalem in October to adopt a policy following the Wailing Wall problems.

1930 ⇛ League of Nations Council appointed a commission on January 14 to investigate the conflicting claims of Palestinians and Jews at the Wailing Wall.
⇛ Shaw Commission report on 1929 problems in Palestine. Attributed the violence to Arab fear of the magnitude of Zionist immigration.
⇛ Fourth Palestinian Delegation went to London. British refused to remedy their complaints against the growth of Zionist community in Palestine.
⇛ Fourth Palestinian Delegation to London announced in May that the British had rejected their demands for redress against Zionist expansion and the continuation of the British mandate.
⇛ Jewish Agency for Palestine was enlarged to include both Zionists and non-Zionists from many countries.
⇛ Sir John Hope-Simpson reported in October that there was no room in Palestine for additional Zionist immigration.
⇛ British Colonial Secretary, Lord Passfield, issued a White Paper that reflected the conclusions of Hope-Simpson.
⇛ International Wailing Wall Commission confirmed Muslim property rights at Wailing Wall and recommended a return to the *status quo*.

1931 ⇛ Prime Minister Ramsay MacDonald's letter to Chaim Weizman on February 14 virtually retracted Lord Passfield's White Paper on Palestine.
⇛ General Sir Arthur Wauchope succeeded Sir John Chancellor as high commissioner in October.
⇛ The second British census of Palestine showed an increase of

population to 1,035,154, of which 73.4 percent were Muslim, 16.9 percent were Jewish, and 8.6 percent were Christian.
⇛ Lewis French, British director of development for Palestine, issued his report on land dispossession of Arabs in December.
⇛ Out of concern for Palestine, 145 delegates from all over the Islamic world attended a conference in Jerusalem in December.

1932 ⇛ Istiqlal (Independence) party became the first legal political party in Palestine on August 2.

1933 ⇛ Arab Executive Committee expressed new alarm in March about the increased scale of Zionist immigration.
⇛ British issued a statement on July 14 for a new plan to resettle displaced Palestinian farmers.
⇛ Arab Executive Committee called for general strike in October and disturbances broke out in the main towns.

1934 ⇛ Sir William Murison's special commission on Palestine reported in February on the cause of the 1933 uprising.
⇛ Defense party was founded on December 2.

1935 ⇛ Palestine Arab party was founded on March 27.
⇛ Reform party was founded on June 23.
⇛ National Bloc party was founded on October 5.
⇛ Revisionists quit World Zionist Organization in October to form the New Zionist Organization to "liberate" Palestine and Transjordan, by force if necessary.
⇛ Dissident Haganah members founded Irgun Zvai Leumi (National Military Organization) in October; Jabotinsky was named Commander in Chief.
⇛ British discovered a large quantity of arms at Jaffa, which the Zionists had smuggled from Belgium.
⇛ Joint resolution from Palestinian political parties to the British High Commissioner on November 25 requested cessation of Zionist mass immigration and land acquisition. Resolution also requested the establishment of a government on the basis of proportional representation.
⇛ British high commissioner of Palestine proposed on December 21 the establishment of a twenty-eight-member legislative council with Palestinians holding only fourteen seats, which the Palestinian leadership accepted in principle.

1936 ⇛ Pro-Zionist members of the British House of Commons defeated the proposal for a legislative council for Palestine on March 25.
⇛ Palestinians created National Committees in all larger towns from April 20 to April 30.
⇛ Leaders of all five Palestinian political parties called for a general strike on April 21.
⇛ Leaders of the Palestinian political parties were constituted as the Arab Higher Committee on April 25.
⇛ Conference of all National Committees in Palestine in

Jerusalem on May 8 called for no taxation without representation. The Great Rebellion, commonly called the General Strike, began.

⇛ British moved reinforcements into Palestine on May 11.

⇛ British appointed a Royal Commission on May 18 to investigate the cause of the rebellion in Palestine.

⇛ Palestinian civil service and judiciary personnel protested to the high commissioner on June 30 against his pro-Zionist policies.

⇛ Fawzi al-Qawukji entered Palestine on August 25 with 150 volunteers from Arab countries to participate in the uprising against Britain.

⇛ Arab higher committee accepted appeals by kings of Saudi Arabia and Iraq, and the emir of Transjordan, to call off the General Strike on September 22.

⇛ Arab Higher Committee declared an end to the General Strike on October 11.

⇛ Lord Peel's Royal Commission arrived in Palestine on November 11.

1937 ⇛ Peel Commission report of July 7 concluded that the underlying cause of the disturbances was an Arab desire for independence and the Arab fear of the establishment of a Jewish national home in Palestine. The report recommended termination of the Mandate and partition of Palestine.

1939 ⇛ The British issued the White Paper restricting Jewish immigration to a total of 75,000 over the next five years and protection of Palestinian land rights from purchases by Zionists. Palestine to be granted independence in ten years.

1940 ⇛ British had subdued most Zionist resistance and illegal immigration. Few Jews were able to escape Nazi-held portions of Europe.

1941 ⇛ Zionists formed Palmach, a highly trained military strike force.

1942 ⇛ The Biltmore Program in 1942 called for a "Jewish Commonwealth" and signalled the switch from Great Britain to the United States as the primary supporter of Zionism.

1943 ⇛ Stern Gang renewed attacks on British personnel.

1944 ⇛ Menahem Begin's *Irgun* began the systematic destruction of British administrative centers. Stern Gang (*Lehi*) assassinated Lord Moyne on November 6.

1945 ⇛ Zionist leaders had *Irgun* and *Lehi* under control to prevent violence against the British. Chaim Weizmann went to Palestine to plead for Zionists to cooperate with the British to achieve a peaceful accommodation.

Frequently as people of many stations use the term "Palestine," they seldom understand how imprecise it is. For most people this vagueness is of no importance. For others, however, their very legitimacy as individuals and nations is at stake in its designation.

A myriad of empires over thousands of years left differing degrees of influence in this center of mankind's longest experience with civilization. There was, therefore, little ethnic or racial purity in a land where Semites, Hittites, Egyptians, Canaanites, Philistines, Greeks, Hebrews, Assyrians, Chaldeans, Persians, Macedonians, Romans, Byzantines, Arabs, Christian crusaders, and Turks had ruled from brief periods to centuries. Different laws and customs prevailed and perished in the wake of new conquerors. Dominant languages also came and went. Even the terrain alternated between lush abundance and barren infertility, according to particular stewards' abilities to manage it. However, as important as the area was at times, it was almost always subsumed in a larger entity and enjoyed no significant separate identity.

There was certainly an abundance of religious practice and creativity, as well. Everything from animism to monotheism enjoyed legal protection and exclusivity at one time or another. In fact, the lineal development of the three great monotheistic religions of Judaism, Christianity, and Islam in the region confounded, rather than clarified, the picture. All acknowledged Abraham as their father. Like greedy sons, however, they fought for his exclusive blessing and over his patrimony. Control of land, and more importantly, specific sites of land, became the prize each sought to sanctify their legitimacy and superiority. The quest to control Jerusalem, the City of Peace, became the quintessential prize.

CULTURAL UNITY UNDER ISLAM

Arab conquest in the seventh century substantially homogenized Palestine and the surrounding area both linguistically and religiously. First their language, Arabic, then their religion, Islam, became the language and religion of all but a few. A small percentage of Christians, and a larger percentage of Jews, retained their religious identities while nearly all of each group embraced the Arabic language. Pockets of Jews and Christians remained, but, otherwise, centuries of Arabic-Islamic hegemony erased most of the dross from the variegated past.

Four centuries of Ottoman Turkish rule provided even further continuity as the Turks were also Sunni Muslims and did not attempt to supersede the language of their Prophet. Better still, the Ottomans gave the area very little special attention for, in the nineteenth century, parts of it were situated in three different administrative districts centered in Damascus, Beirut, and Jerusalem. This fairly unimportant part of the vast empire possessed no particular economic or strategic significance. The one distinction it had for the Ottomans, if any, was that it had a tradition of being generally tranquil.

While this benign Turkish neglect allowed continuity, it also allowed decay. The absence of an attentive central authority in the nineteenth century did not provide adequate encouragement or safety for productivity to prosper. The classic pattern followed, as warrior herdsmen subdued sedentary fields and towns. In some areas of Palestine, fields fell fallow and markets dried up for agricultural products and manufactured goods. Traditionally productive farmlands and their adjoining towns along the northern coast and in the northern plains fell into disuse. Damp lowlands became unmanageable swamps. Prosperous farms went untended in face of bedouin brigandage and untenable demands for protection. A disproportionately high percentage of the population, therefore, resided in the rocky, less fertile highlands of central Palestine. Despite its potential, the Land of Milk and Honey could provide only a meager subsistence for most of its limited population under these circumstances.

Conversely, in the Gaza region, where there was a strong working relationship between the bedouin tribesmen and the peasant farmers, considerable prosperity occurred by the late nineteenth century. The Jaffa region, which was famous for its oranges (which the inhabitants called "Palestine's gift to the world"), also prospered and exported most of its production.

Turkish cadastral reform in the Land law of 1858 exacerbated the land situation in areas of less security. Understandably, the reforming Ottoman government wanted to know the details of land ownership and its potential for producing revenue. Customarily, however, Palestinians worked family-owned land, which was not legally registered in individual names. Many Palestinian residents, therefore, like their counterparts in the empire, feared that registration of their lands with the government would lead to higher taxes and impressment in the Ottoman army. Alert members of the landed and merchant classes, again, as elsewhere, "volunteered" to register the land and obtained the right to dispose of it and its tenants as they saw fit. Their avarice often drove even more struggling peasants from the land and made life miserable for many who remained.

The encroachment of nomadism and the decline of agriculture in naturally fertile areas, along with the acquisition of large holdings in the hands of a few, had important results. Many important landholders, for instance, had no family connection with the tenants of their lands. Many of the absentee landowners, in fact, lived far away in Damascus or Beirut. They only knew that their sometimes vast holdings produced marginal revenues. Further, they often had little sense of moral obligation to provide a means of earning a living for their tenants. They were, therefore, willing, if not eager, to sell their lands to anyone who offered them a good price.

WHAT IS PALESTINE?

Confusion about Palestine derives in no small part from the fact that Palestine had neither political nor geographical definition prior to the twentieth century. It still does not. There was never a Palestinian state. Whatever Palestine was, and wherever it was, generally depended upon individual interpretation. Different portions of the general area had some kind of designation as "Palestine" during the centuries of Roman and Byzantine rule. As part of these empires, the function of the areas variously delineated as "Palestine" changed haphazardly, as did its boundaries, to accommodate local rulers and administrative needs. Beginning with the era of Arab-Islamic rule, Palestine was considered part of *Bilad al-Sham,* or Greater Syria.

Jews of the diaspora preferred "Eretz Israel," Land of Israel, and eschewed the use of the term Palestine, which did not recognize their claim to the land as their gift from God. Western Christians, who fought crusades to liberate it from Muslims, generally referred to the region as the Holy Land and actually held a great deal of the region as the Latin Kingdom of Jerusalem, not Palestine, for two centuries.

The people who lived there had little reason to think of themselves as Palestinians until the beginning of the twentieth century. All of them were Ottoman subjects and for centuries any specific identification was usually confined to family and religious affiliation. The predominantly Arab population knew they were not Turks, but since most were Sunni Muslims, they historically did not differentiate between themselves and their Turkish fellow believers. In addition, until the twentieth century, there was no significant Arab nationalism with which they could identify. The roughly 15 percent Christian Arab population preserved both their freedoms and limitations through compliance with Ottoman traditions. They, too, had no viable alternative identity, although the Christian Western nations interceded on behalf of all Ottoman Christians throughout the nineteenth century. The situation of the smaller Jewish population was similar to that of the Christian Arabs, except there was no Jewish state anywhere to protect or succor it.

Zionists had the clearest concept of the area the Christians called Palestine. For them "Eretz Israel" reached from the Sinai peninsula to the north central Euphrates area east of Damascus; the furthest extent of King David's conquests about 1000 B.C. No Israeli state, before or since, equalled David's brief territorial expansion. No Israeli state of any kind existed from 135 A.D. to 1948. But the halcyon borders in David's time were the perimeters most Zionists envisioned as the land the Balfour Declaration of 1917 promised them as a "national home." The League of Nations mandate seemed to imply that Palestine, indeed, extended to somewhere near the Euphrates, because Article 25 referred to "territories lying between the Jordan and the eastern borders of Palestine."

Britain's creation of the Emirate of Transjordan in 1921, therefore, was a major blow to Zionist plans. Many, however, never altered their goals and most continued to regard Transjordan as an integral part of their patrimony. But, in fact, the British had defined Palestine for modern purposes as the land east of Egypt's Sinai peninsula, south of French mandatory Syria and Lebanon, and west of Transjordan along the west bank of the Jordan River straight southward to the northern tip of the Gulf of Aqaba.

Regardless of previous attitudes, the indigenous population within these new borders rapidly assumed the identification of "Palestinian." While many Palestinians before this time might have accepted the label of Syrian, French control over Syria and British control over Palestine made identification with Syria less viable. Some Palestinians did, however, increase their hope for a Greater Syrian Arab state at the end of the mandate nightmare. As the King-Crane findings and other evidence indicates, most Arabs in the region envisioned an affiliation with Damascus in the absence of their Turkish overlords. No Palestinians had a sense of being Lebanese and, in fact, most regarded Lebanon, like Palestine, as a part of Syria. Palestinian Arabs had no sense of affiliation with Transjordan and its dusty capital of Amman. The sparse population of that emirate was, after all, primarily bedouin nomads, while the Palestinians were mostly farmers and town dwellers. Affinity with Iraq was equally untenable as it was hundreds of desert miles to the east and less well developed than the western Levant.

Nearly half of the 10,000 square miles of Palestine is barren and unable to support substantial population without extraordinary efforts to supply it with water. Like the area to its north on the eastern Mediterranean Sea, most of the coastal area of Palestine is fertile and extends eastward to the northern Jordan River valley in the east. In this area, large-scale farming of a wide variety of crops, including citrus, is possible and lends itself to the use of the most modern machinery. The central highlands are rocky but provide a favorable condition for grapes, olives, and small-scale farming of grains and vegetables. There is ample water for a modest population that generally must rely on hand tools and animal power to cultivate the crops. The Jericho region in the Jordan River valley, which is the lowest place on earth, enjoys a tropical climate that is particularly good for the cultivation of dates and bananas. From just east of Jerusalem to the Dead Sea is an area of rugged wasteland that can sustain a handful of nomads and their flocks. The Negev desert, which constitutes nearly 40 percent of modern Palestine, stretches south of Beersheba to the Gulf of Aqaba. Though arid, it produces a considerable amount of grain and sustains a surprising number of nomads and their livestock.

POPULATION

There is evidence that Palestine was more hospitable to human habitation in the past, before deforestation and erosion became widespread in the interior and before large areas near the coast turned into swamps. Some estimates put the population as high as four million in the early centuries of the Christian era. Scholars agree, however, that the population was between 600,000 and 700,000 in the early twentieth century. However, inadequate data and political concerns about the size and ethnic composition of the population makes arriving at an exact figure both impossible and problematical.

The deprivations of war, coupled with famine and locusts, caused a decline in the population during World War I. The decline was most pronounced among the fairly recent Zionist immigrants who had entered Palestine in the First Aliya after 1881. About 60,000 Jews entered Palestine from 1881 to 1914, which brought their total number to about 85,000. By the end of the war most authorities agree that, largely as a result of emigration, the Jewish population was about 65,000. Even with their decline, by 1914, Jews were probably a majority of the small population of Jerusalem. They were a significant proportion of the residents of the largely Christian coastal city of Haifa and they constituted nearly all of the residents of the new city of Tel Aviv in the suburb of Jaffa. As a result of the hardships of war, famine, and disease, the Arab population decline nearly matched the Jewish decline in absolute numbers. This figure, of course, did not represent as high a proportion of their numbers as the Jewish decline.

Palestine experienced a dramatic growth of population following the Great War. The nature of the increase, however, is cause for considerable controversy among people who agree on the approximate numbers. There is neither mystery nor controversy over why and how the Jewish population grew. The questions arise over why the Arab population increased from between six and seven hundred thousand in 1919 to just under one million by 1936. Arabs and their supporters claim that the increase resulted naturally from greater security, an improved economy, and better health and nutrition. Zionists and their supporters claim that the Jewish-inspired increase in the standard of living in Palestine attracted a large number of Arabs from the surrounding region. If, in fact, this were the case, the later displacement of migrant Arab workers was less onerous than if such displacement occurred primarily among indigenous Palestinian Arabs.

Jewish immigration quickly thrived under the protection of the League of Nations and Great Britain. It also benefited from an emboldened, well-organized, and well-financed Zionist Organization. Jewish settlers poured into Palestinian cities and the populations of rural Zionist settlements increased at an unprecedented level. Jewish population in Palestine grew from the roughly 65,000 in 1919 to about 400,000 by 1936. Although the increase was impressive, Jews remained a decided minority of the population and probably owned about 5 percent of the land. Their hope of becoming a majority and acquiring a larger amount of the land depended on continued League and British willingness and ability to curb Arab resistance to Zionist efforts.

THE BRITISH MANDATE

Great Britain established a civilian government in Palestine on July 1, 1920, even though the League of Nations mandate did not officially go into effect until September 29, 1923. This boded ill for Palestinian and Pan-Arab nationalists because it indicated that the British intended to implement an enduring presence as they had announced two months earlier at San Remo. The intensity of anti-Zionist riots in Jerusalem, however, on the occasion of the Nebi Musa celebrations shortly before the San Remo meeting, signaled that both the Jews and the British would meet with strong Arab opposition. The British removed Musa Kazim al-Husseini as mayor of Jerusalem following the riots and placed Raghib al-Nashshashibi in that office. The fervently nationalist al-Husseini family provided a consistent and uncompromising leadership of Palestinian opposition to the British and Zionists throughout the mandate period. Hajj Amin al-Husseini, whom the British appointed to the powerful position of Grand Mufti of Jerusalem in the spring of 1921, led Palestinian anti-mandatory efforts until his exile in 1937.

Palestinian hopes grew even dimmer when the French expelled the newly elected king of Syria, Feisal, from Damascus on July 24. France and Britain seemed equally well ensconced in their respective mandates where they could perpetuate the inability of the Arabs to coordinate a resistance.

Although Sir Herbert Samuel, the first high commissioner of Palestine, was a Jew, he apparently made every effort to treat Arabs and Jews fairly. His and the British role in general was, however, virtually impossible from the beginning. How could they assist the Zionist to construct a "national home" and also protect the civil and religious rights of the Arabs, which by the parlance of the day must have included their right to self-government?

British rule was not altogether bad for Palestinian Arabs, as they provided health and agricultural services that exceeded those of any previous rulers. Government construction of barracks, offices, housing, roads, harbors, pipelines, airports, and other vital facilities provided work and income for many Arabs. Some Palestinians set themselves apart as they learned to operate motorized vehicles. A combination of British and Zionist activities inaugurated an economic boom in Palestine until the Great Depression ended it there as elsewhere. Some Palestinians, thus, prospered while others lost their livelihoods to Zionist expansion.

Life for certain elements of Palestinian society, in fact, mirrored that of their counterparts in the Western world. A wide variety of professional organizations, sports clubs, YMCA's (and their Muslim equivalent), Boy Scouts, and musical organizations thrived. The construction of a surprisingly large number of elegant homes also indicated a pronounced prosperity. While the British did little to foster public education, more than four hundred public schools existed in Palestine by the end of the mandate. Private schools of various kinds, usually under the sponsorship of religious institutions, including some for girls, grew in numbers and sophistication. The Arab College in Jerusalem earned international respect for its well-designed curriculum and the quality of its graduates. Thus, Palestinians demonstrated an early affinity for education for which they later became famous.

ARAB RELATIONS WITH THE MANDATE

High Commissioner Samuel's attempt to obtain Arab participation in an advisory council failed. The Arabs adopted the tact of noncooperation from the beginning, on the principle that cooperation was de facto recognition of the legitimacy of both the Zionist movement and the mandate. The Palestinian Arab posture never changed. Consequently, throughout the mandate they had only the government services the British provided. Perhaps more importantly, they gained no experience in a centralized governing process, while they became very adept as a subverting opposition.

On balance the Palestinian Arabs demonstrated good political awareness and ability, although their ultimate failure against overwhelming foes often leads observers to think otherwise. But within six months of Samuel's appointment the Palestinians transformed their Syrian-oriented Palestinian National Congress (PNC) into an effort to confront the British and the Zionists in Palestine. Muslims and Christians cooperated fully and religious concerns never impeded their efforts. The twenty-four-member Arab Executive of the PNC gave them continuity for action. The PNC drafted numerous resolutions against all aspects of the mandate's mission and policies, and sent numerous delegations to international capitals, especially London, to represent their views. It played a role in coordinating resistance to the British and the Zionists within Palestine and with neighboring Arab states, which were also under British and French domination.

Political parties developed but they had little opportunity to function in the absence of a legislature that could pass binding laws. Interestingly, the Istiqlal (independence) party was decidedly the first (August 1932) to emerge and the only one that functioned as a true political party. It and its counterparts by the same name in Syria, Lebanon, and Iraq never wavered from their primary goal of an immediate end to the mandates. The other four parties emerged more than two years later primarily as structural embossment for the personal following of the families who created them: National Defense, al-Nashashibi (1934); Palestine Arab, al-Husseini (1935); Reform, Khalidi (1935); National Bloc, Salah (1935). There was also a tiny Palestinian Communist Party that cooperated with their tiny Jewish counterpart and other Jewish leftists.

Palestinian resistance always revolved around the dynamic leadership of Hajj Amin al-Husseini. As Grand Mufti, he also became the president of the Supreme Muslim Council in December 1921. These two major offices, which the British bestowed upon him within a few months' time, gave him stature and finances that no other Palestinian figure could match.

In the absence of judicial recourse on the mandatory or international levels, Palestinians frequently vented their frustrations in violence. Over the years of the mandate, a pattern developed of heavy Zionist immigration, followed by Arab pleas for relief, followed by British silence, followed by Arab violence, followed by British study commissions and concessions to Arab violence, followed by Zionist pressures upon Whitehall, followed by British reinstatement of former pro-Zionist policies. It began with the Nabi Musa riots in the spring of 1920 and the Jaffa riots a year later, after the Cairo Conference had ended any apparent possibility of Hashemite-led relief to the mandate. The Haycroft Commission documented Arab fears of Zionist expansion that had already increased their numbers past those of the Palestinian Christians.

Winston Churchill's White Paper in June 1922 tried to please both the Zionists and the Arabs, because each group feared British intentions. The document assured the Arabs that Britain did not endorse Zionist intentions to make Palestine "as Jewish as England is English." Instead, it stated, the kind of self-government Jews enjoyed in their population centers, along with their other institutions and the use of Hebrew, were all the British intended to implement toward the creation of a national home "in Palestine" not of Palestine. For the Zionists, the document maintained that Britain and the international community recognized the historical connection of Jews to Palestine and that their National Home there was "of right and not on sufferance." While this reassured the Zionists, they were newly alarmed that Churchill promised the Arabs to limit Zionist immigration to "the economic capacity of the country at the time to absorb new arrivals." Zionists held this view because they knew their resources and desires could increase the economic capacity of Palestine far beyond what any other people could imagine.

LAND AS THE CENTRAL ISSUE

Throughout the 1920s Zionist immigration, under British constraints, proceeded too slowly for most Zionists and too rapidly to satisfy any Arabs. Even Chaim Weizmann advocated Zionist behavior that the British found too adventurous. Vladimir Jabotinsky, however, emerged as the leader of an element of Zionists who refused to accept the Jordan River as the eastern boundary of Palestine. He formed the Revisionist party in 1925 to abolish all restrictions on the in-gathering of Jews. Jabotinsky advocated the use of all means, including violence, to implement Zionist ideals. Attempts by his followers to abolish the restrictions Britain enforced near the Wailing Wall led to a major confrontation between Jews and Arabs at that holy site in August 1929. This ignited the largest uprisings of Arabs against Jews since the mandate had begun. Arabs inflicted nearly 500 Jewish deaths and casualties, primarily in Jerusalem and Hebron. British forces and Zionists killed and wounded about 350 Palestinians.

League of Nations, Arab, and Muslim investigations ensued, along with two British studies by the Shaw Commission and Sir John Hope-Simpson. The two British studies agreed that Palestinian fear of dispossession of their land was the central Arab grievance. As a consequence of these investigations Lord Passfield, the British colonial secretary, issued a White Paper on October 20, 1930, that shocked the Zionists. It implored the Zionists to make major alterations in both their actions and rhetoric to ease the documented causes for Arab concern. Decisive Zionist appeals to their supporters in Britain and the United States produced a reversal of British policy when Prime Minister Ramsay MacDonald issued a public letter on February 14, 1931, stating that there was no change in British commitment to Zionist immigration or land acquisition in Palestine. Near the end of this long letter, the otherwise conciliatory missive cautioned that the British government was "bound to have regard" for the displacement of Arab labor. By this time, Jews outnumbered Christians two to one and constituted about 17 percent of the Palestinian population.

British mandatory authorities understood from the outset that land—its ownership and use—was crucial. After all, land provided a direct or indirect source of income and employment, as well as honor and identity, for most Palestinians. The anticipated influx of Zionist immigrants placed their highest priority on the acquisition of land, which they intended to work with their own hands. However, the British mandatory government, as the successor of the Ottoman government, owned approximately 70 percent of the land. Religious institutions of all kinds had acquired a significant amount of land over the centuries. Someone seemed to make some part of their living from all but small, hopelessly desolate tracts. While considerable amounts of arable and potentially arable land was unused, areas of heavy use seemed to have a maximum population.

Early British regulations attempted to control all land transactions. No doubt the desire to protect essentially helpless tenant farmers and laborers from dispossession guided British concerns and policies. They were, however, also aware of the problems a significant number of homeless, unemployed people could have in Palestine and throughout the Arab world. It was impossible for even the expanded economy that resulted from fresh British, Zionist, and Arab capital to absorb massive migrations from the fields. Housing in urban areas for large, extended agrarian families, composed of twelve- to fifteen-member nuclear families, was impossible.

Regulations to protect agrarian cultivators in 1920, 1921, 1929, 1931, and 1933 were largely unsuccessful. Arab sellers and Zionist buyers had too many ways to circumvent an overworked mandatory bureaucracy and a powerless peasant class. Interestingly, however, these attempts to address the problem corresponded with intense Arab outbursts against developments in Palestine.

INCREASED IMMIGRATION AND VIOLENCE

The first years of the worldwide depression retarded the rate of growth of Zionist immigration, but Hitler's rise to power in 1933 created a new urgency among Zionists to accelerate migration to Palestine. The German Jews who sought refuge there were also considerably better capitalized, better educated, and more skilled than earlier immigrants from eastern Europe. An already difficult situation rapidly became explosive.

Intensified Zionist immigration in 1933 caused major new disturbances among the Arabs and correlated with the most pronounced British efforts to protect Arabs from becoming landless. A British investigatory commission followed, under the leadership of Sir William Murison, as the British tried to reconcile their obligations in Palestine with international pressure to allow more Jews to immigrate. At the same time, the German and Italian governments increased their anti-British and anti-French appeals to receptive Arab audiences throughout the Arab world. For the first time since the end of World War I, Palestinians and other Arabs began to feel that they could find international assistance.

Palestinian Arab leaders also indicated a greater willingness to participate in the political structure while they still enjoyed a majority. This, no doubt, helps explain the formulation of the Palestinian political parties in rapid succession from December to October of 1934–35 (see page 172). The considerable talk about a Palestinian legislature following the Passfield White Paper gradually appealed to the Arabs and caused concern among the Zionists who were still a decided minority. Evidence of large-scale Jewish arms transactions in October 1935, along with the Revisionists' withdrawal from the World Zionist Organization and the founding of the Irgun, signalled a possible new round of greater violence. However, when pro-Zionist elements in London scuttled a proposed legislature for Palestine in the spring of 1936, cause for Zionist violence seemed to subside.

In a situation where both sides increasingly believed the stakes were all or nothing, success for Zionists could only mean failure for Arabs. National Committees sprang up in every sizable Arab community. An Arab Higher Committee, composed of the leaders of the political parties with Hajj Amin al-Husseini presiding, called for a general strike April 21, 1936. Their objective was to bring the economy and government of Palestine to a halt and gain redress of their grievances since all else had failed. On May 8, a conference of the National Committees met in Jerusalem and issued the time honored slogan of modern revolutions: "No taxation without representation."

Widespread Arab violence from May into November accomplished the goal of disrupting normal life in Palestine. No element, including Arab areas, escaped the effects. British installations of all kinds, but particularly far-flung utilities such as roads, phone lines, pipelines, and trains, suffered devastating damage from a small and meagerly armed Arab force. Many Zionists' farms and factories perished or experienced reduced production. Large numbers of Arabs had no income as they joined the boycott, while those who refused to comply suffered repercussions from fellow Arabs who regarded failure to conform as treason.

Both aggressive and passive Arab actions were enough to create havoc, but they were inadequate to achieve success. After a hesitant beginning, the British used the force at their disposal to confine and then render armed resistance harmless. In the meantime, they imprisoned Arab leaders and collectively punished the entire populations of the strongest centers of suspected Arab violence. Upon the advice of the governments of Saudi Arabia, Yemen, Iraq and Transjordan in early October, the Arab Higher Committee officially ended the strike, which soon subsided.

The British appointed another in a succession of apparently interminable commissions to investigate problems in Palestine at the outset of the General Strike, but did not allow it to begin its work until the strike ended six months later. Two months of investigations and six months of deliberations later, the Peel Commission Report issued an unusually candid report. It frankly related several possible solutions that had been recommended by various interested parties. It proceeded to dismiss them all as contrary to the interest of one of the major parties. According to the report, no viable state could include the diametrically opposite Zionists and the Arabs. It characterized the conundrum of Palestine as a conflict of "right against right."

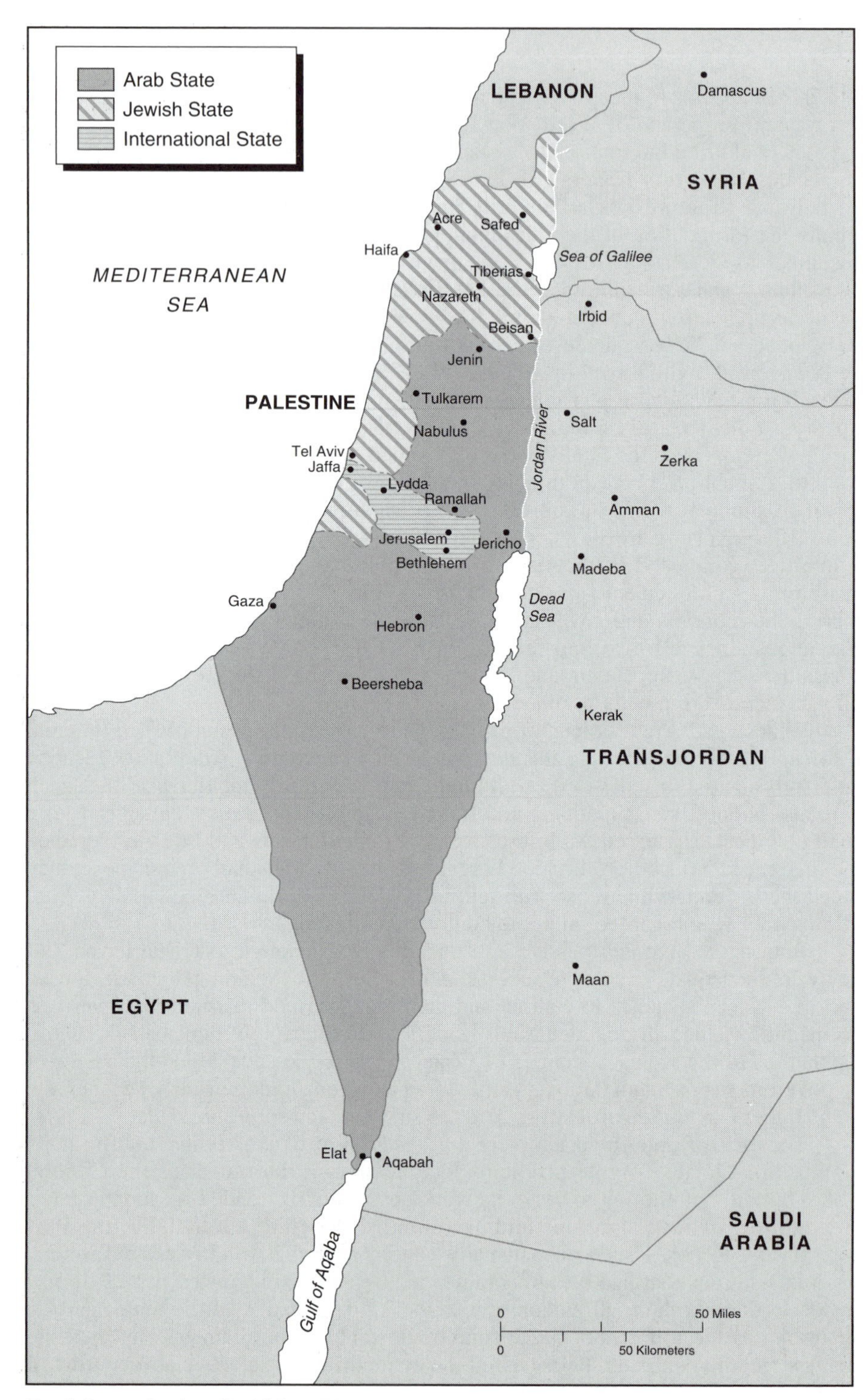

Peel Commission Partition Plan, 1937

PARTITION POSSIBILITY

In a bold departure, the report advocated partition of Palestine into two sovereign states, with Britain maintaining a mandate over the Holy Places around Jerusalem and a corridor to the sea at Jaffa. It proposed a Zionist state of about 20 percent of Palestine in the northwest quadrant where most of the 400,000 Jews lived, but where the Arabs owned nearly 80 percent of the land. The one million Arabs in the remainder of Palestine would merge with the Emirate of Transjordan.

The vast majority on both sides rejected this solution, which also violated Britain's obligation to the world community. Significant debate occurred, however, in both camps about the possibility of at least negotiating for better terms. Zionists deemed the area too small to accomplish their goals, especially because of Nazi persecutions. Arabs regarded any loss of their land intolerable and condemned this plan that incorporated Arabs, Arab-owned land, and nearly 80 percent of the best citrus area in a Zionist state.

Developments in Palestine precluded the necessary protracted negotiations that could lead to a compromise version of the Peel recommendation. At the end of September 1937 the British took decisive precautions against expected violence. They dismissed Hajj Amin as president of the Supreme Muslim Council and he fled to Lebanon. Most members of the Arab Higher Committee were arrested or fled. Renewed Arab violence brought unprecedented British reprisals similar to those they had used in 1936, with the added practice of blowing up the homes of suspected activists. Arab violence against nonparticipants in the uprising was more pronounced than before. Pro-Palestinian groups held formal conferences in Bludan, Syria in September 1937 and in Cairo in October 1938. Jews in neighboring Arab states suffered attacks and endured major demonstrations against developments in Palestine.

Few Palestinians could regard Britain as an arbiter in the conflict because, while it used appalling force and restrictions on the Arabs, the Zionists' communities thrived. The British had, in fact, placed more restrictions on Zionists' immigrations since 1936 than at any time during the mandate. However, British forces protected Zionist settlements and allowed the Zionists to expand their own defense capabilities. New Zionist settlements developed under this protection in anticipation that some permanent resolution might result from the all-out war that prevailed until January 1939.

The severe British measures could not subdue the Palestinians at a time when Nazi successes made British interests in Europe more grave and in need of their undivided attention. Another Royal Commission, dubbed the Woodhead Partition Commission, recommended in the fall of 1938 that partition simply could not work in Palestine. By that time, this conclusion was more favorable to the Arabs, since most of the Zionist leadership, except the Revisionists, were inclined to accept a limited Zionist state. But recent developments greatly diminished Zionist influence just when the plight of German Jews increased. Also, Hitler's success at Munich a few weeks earlier augured as much for war as it did for peace. Arabs and Muslims were in a better position to determine Britain's performance in a war than the Zionists were. Facing failure in Palestine and the prospects of war with Germany, Britain, in desperation, decided to convene a Zionist-Palestinian conference in London to determine if the three principals could find a solution.

Britain's invitation for delegates from Egypt, Saudi Arabia, Yemen, Transjordan, and Iraq to attend the conference, over Zionist opposition, indicated a British tilt to appease the Arabs. They even released members of the Arab Higher Committee from incarceration, but refused to allow Hajj Amin, who was in Lebanon, to attend the conference. The British never relented in regard to the Mufti but he managed to block British attempts to impose a more pliable al-Nashashibi-dominated delegation upon the Palestinians. There were, in fact, by this time bitter feelings between the two leading families and their followers, with the al-Husseinies in command of the dominant hardliners, while the al-Nashashibies had gravitated closer to the British and their client, the Emir Abdullah of Transjordan.

The entire Arab delegation planned their strategy in Cairo before continuing to the conference in London, which opened on February 7, 1939. Britain had to negotiate separately with the two delegations because the Arabs refused to convene with the Zionists. Clearly, the Arabs had the stronger influence, even though both American and British delegates joined the predominantly Jewish Agency Zionist delegation. The Arabs forced the British to review their entire relationship with the Arabs dating back to the Hussein-McMahon agreement. The British admitted, contrary to all previous British interpretations, that the Hussein-McMahon correspondence gave Arabs reason to believe that Palestine would also be independent. This admission helped harden Arab insistence that justice dictated both an end to the mandate and the creation of the Jewish National Home. Obviously, the Zionists could not accept the Arab demands. In face of the continuing irreconcilable postures, the conference disbanded on March 17.

Two months later, on May 17, the British rendered their conclusions in a White Paper that reflected a compromise that Iraq, Egypt, and Saudi Arabia suggested, no doubt, in consultation with the Palestinians. The document acknowledged Arab reason to believe Palestine would be self-governing after World War I, and that the British government had always intended to allow self-government to evolve in Palestine. Britain, however, had a League of Nations mandate to assist the development of a National Home for Jews in Palestine. The British position, therefore, was to implement a constitution over the next ten years to include all residents of Palestine. In the event this procedure proved impossible, the British proposed referring the issue to the League. In the meantime, Britain proposed a policy that was designed to reduce Arab concern that Zionist immigration would lead to Zionist domination. Britain would allow 75,000 Zionist immigrants over the next five years, after which any additional immigration would require Arab consent.

Implementation of this policy spelled the end of Zionist intentions of pouring Jews into Palestine to create a Jewish majority. The 400,000 Jews in Palestine, augmented by 75,000 future immigrants, had no hope of surpassing the one million Arabs with their traditionally high birthrate. Arab resistance, thus, seemed to have won.

THE ZIONIST COMMUNITY

Zionists immediately appreciated the significance of the brief and apparently innocuous Balfour Declaration. By the time of his death, Herzl had convinced most Zionists, including his severe critics, of the efficacy of gaining international legitimacy. Balfour's endorsement of Zionism, in behalf of the most powerful empire on earth, was the first vital step. It complied with Herzl's insistence that Zionists should operate totally within the law and openly conduct their business for all to see and understand.

The diminished Jewish population in Palestine at the end of the war still enjoyed the benefit of nearly four decades of Zionist organization and institutional development. Zionists were well positioned to build upon this progress with British support and the strong endorsement of the League of Nations. The Jewish community in Palestine, with its extensive and sophisticated international Zionist Organization, essentially became self-governing during the British mandatory period. This was a stark contrast with the Palestinian Arabs, who were unable to sustain viable leadership or institutional development during that period. Long before the mandate ended, Palestinian Arab leaders were in exile. Throughout the mandate, Arabs basically had the benefit of such institutions and services as the British deigned to provide. Similar circumstances prevailed among their more modern Arab brethren in Syria, Egypt, Iraq, and Lebanon, who abhorred their fate, while the international community, through the League of Nations, endorsed the advancement of the Zionist cause.

The World Zionist Organization, which began in 1897, coordinated Zionist activities from Geneva. Soon after the British conquest of Palestine the organization had a base of operation there and the League mandatory document recognized it as the official Zionist body to work with Great Britain to establish a Jewish national home. The Jewish Agency for Palestine, which came into existence in 1929, was a parallel organization that began as a means to accommodate support from Jews who supported some kind of Jewish homeland in Palestine but could not endorse the creation of a Jewish nation. The president of the Zionist Organization also presided over the Jewish Agency and their leadership personnel became increasingly the same. Zionists quickly dominated the Jewish Agency and it became the most visible instrument for implementing Zionist policies in Palestine. Membership dues and additional contributions provided financial support for the Zionist Organization. Considerable revenue went into the National Fund for the specific purpose of purchasing land in Palestine.

Zionist affairs in Palestine began as an extension of Zionist Organization policies, but evolved into a closer relationship with the Jewish Agency that had the specific role of implementing a national home. This distinction is vital for understanding later rifts that revolved around differences between Zionists living in Palestine and their supporters abroad. By the mid-1930s Palestinian Zionists, under the leadership of David Ben-Gurion, chafed at the slower pace toward statehood that Weizmann-led European and American Zionists often championed. Pressure from even less patient Palestinian Zionists influenced Ben Gurion's assertiveness, as did his conception that Zionism might only have support from Britain for a limited period.

Immigration of settlers was one vital area of their development that Zionists could not control. They could only influence immigration through pressure upon the British. While the mandate obligated the British to assist the development of a Jewish national home, it established no timetable. Britain, therefore, controlled the flow of Zionist immigration according to the vagaries of Arab resistance and its own national interests.

Procedurally, Britain periodically decided on Zionist immigration quotas and, in turn, allowed the Jewish Agency to distribute the visas to whomever it wished. Zionist need to establish a profound presence, and ultimately a state, in a largely unproductive land determined the choice of immigrants. Consequently, Jewish immigrants were usually young, virile, talented individuals who possessed the skills necessary to build a nation in a physically and politically hostile environment. Humanitarian concerns, however, prevented all immigrants from conforming with this profile.

Zionists had considerable experience in self-government from the earliest days of the mandate. In fact, considerable foundation remained from their prewar experience under the Ottomans. Arab refusal to serve in any government with the Zionists had assured there would be no mandatewide government in Palestine that included both Zionists and Arabs. Britain's self-imposed and internationally sanctioned obligation to create a Jewish national home also gave Zionists control over most of their affairs. Further, the mandate's provision for "close settlement" of Jews in Palestine clustered Jews in limited areas that encouraged nationlike intercourse in all their activities.

The creation of a formal Zionist self-government corresponded with Britain's establishment of a civilian government to replace a military government for Palestine in 1920. A liberal franchise allowed most Zionist residents to vote for an elected assembly, which chose members of the legislature to form a national council. This council essentially served as a cabinet. The Zionist structure was usually called a quasi-government, because its various departments shaped and implemented the regulations and institutions that governed the Zionist community. Besides an internal police force, there was a defense force called the Haganah, from the early days, which grew in numbers and sophistication as Arab opposition increased.

ZIONIST DIVERSITY

The Zionist community, which most outsiders regarded as monolithic, actually contained considerable diversity and endured internal conflicts. Their common bond of establishing a Zionist state could not overcome disagreements that arose from linguistic, cultural, and educational differences, as well as from their divergent views on the nature of the proposed state. Immigrants, after all, came from many regions of the world. While a strong majority of approximately 75 percent were Ashkenazim from Europe, their diverse backgrounds and goals defied a homogeneous profile. Their numbers and talents, in addition to their abilities to deal with their European and American benefactors, assured their predominance. Centuries of unique experiences among the roughly 10 percent Sephardic Jews from the Mediterranean countries produced significant differences among themselves, and between them and Jews from other regions. Oriental Jews, mostly from Yemen, provided even further diversity.

Most Zionists agreed that their society and future state should be socialist. They further agreed that most citizens should engage in primary production in either manufacturing or farming. The fact that most immigrants had to rely upon communal funds from world Jewry reduced the onus of individuals lacking personal capital, and allowed all to enjoy stature commensurate with their efforts and talents, while it also promoted socialism. Their monumental challenges of building a new society in a region where most of the residents resented their presence made any divisive cleavages over the precise nature of their socialist society a luxury they could not often afford.

The General Federation of Jewish Labor's domination of economic and labor policies from the outset made most debate academic. This strongly socialist organization, which was better known as the Histadrut, owned a majority of the factories and farms and established working conditions and wages for about three-fourths of the Zionist workers. A similar predominance in educational, financial, and cultural affairs assured the Histadrut's role in shaping the emergent Zionist society.

The Labor party's control of the Histadrut explains its ascendancy in the complex sphere of Zionist politics, where a plethora of parties, each of which stressed party loyalty, became hallmarks of the Zionist experience in Palestine. Small, even tiny, parties contested for seats in the legislature alongside relative giants such as the Labor party. Citizens voted for party platforms and the parties then decided on which members would hold office. Large as the Labor party was, it had to rely on coalitions with smaller parties to form a workable majority in the elected assembly, which evolved into the Knesset. Cabinet members from the small parties could usually obtain some degree of implementation of their policies by threatening to withdraw from the cabinet. This check upon the "tyranny of the majority" established a mosaic in Palestinian Zionist policy instead of the monochromatic hue that the Ashkenazim-Labor preponderance seemed to dictate.

Under the leadership of David Ben-Gurion, Labor's pragmatic approach to the struggling movement's challenges could never satisfy its more ideological opponents, who had no hope of prevailing. The small Agudist movement, for instance, opposed the fundamental approach of modern Zionism, because these religious traditionalists believed that God had destroyed ancient Israel out of dissatisfaction with Israeli behavior. Only God, not the secular Zionists, could restore Israel. On the left, the small communist movement contradicted the essence of Zionism because it insisted on including Arab workers as full citizens in the socialist experiment in Palestine. The numerous parties in the middle could influence Zionist policies more than the extremists but they, too, could never lead.

It was never as easy to rule out the emergence of the Revisionists under the leadership of Vladimir Jabotinsky. Although never very large, this movement was willing to identify problems and offer solutions that the pragmatic Labor party eschewed. Revisionists abhorred the truncated Palestine open to Jewish settlement. They resented British presence in Palestine nearly as much as the Arabs did, because they believed an unfettered Zionism must, and could, create a Jewish state sufficient to accommodate all Jews who wished to be part of it. Jabotinsky cared less about any right Jews had to live in their own nation than about a need his people faced. He occasionally admitted that fulfillment of his goals would cause hardship for a small percentage of the greater Arab population of the region, but that their deprivations paled into insignificance compared with the dire needs of long-persecuted world Jewry under new attack from Hitler's Germany. He advocated the use of all means, including violence, to remove British, Arab, and even Jewish, impediments to the earliest creation of a Jewish state.

Developments throughout the 1930s created more pronounced conflicts among Zionist leaders. Increased Arab unrest and violence, which caused the British to vacillate and increased pressure on European Jewry, infused an urgency for each faction to fulfill its agenda. By the mid-1930s, however, Weizmann, Ben-Gurion, and Jabotinsky no longer talked of a National Home but had in common a commitment to establishing a Jewish state. Weizmann and Ben-Gurion agreed on a Zionist state in mandatory Palestine, but the former was confident that diplomacy and moral appeal could achieve that goal. Ben-Gurion, who was better attuned to Arab hostility and British imperial needs, increasingly advocated an increase in Zionist strength that would quell the Arabs and Britain into submission. In addition, he always had to deal with the relentless Revisionist's appeal in Palestine and abroad.

The British expulsion of Jabotinsky from Palestine did not reduce his influence because he remained in the World Zionist Organization and unabashedly called for a Jewish state on both sides of the Jordan River in 1931. His assertiveness embarrassed both Weizmann and Ben-Gurion, both of whom followed a more diplomatic route toward the same end. Jabotinsky withdrew from the World Zionist Organization in October 1935 and started his own New Zionist Organization to accelerate the creation of a large Jewish state. Soon thereafter, for the same reason, he weaned a dissident element of the Haganah over to his command as the Irgun Zvai Leumi.

ZIONIST RESPONSE TO ARAB VIOLENCE

The 1936 Arab uprising, Hitler's success, and the Peel Commission report temporarily drew Weizmann and Ben-Gurion closer together, as both of them and a majority of the Zionist Organization endorsed a partition of Palestine that would establish a small Zionist state. They concluded that some kind of Jewish state was better than nothing and they were confident that Zionists could expand the limited borders through further diplomacy and action. However, the collapse of a peaceful partitioning possibility by the fall of 1937 moved most Zionist elements to greater militancy. The partitioning proposal and debate, after all, had made discussion of a Jewish state, instead of a national home, a legitimate issue. In the fall of 1937 the mainstream of Zionism increased the size and capability of the Haganah while the Irgun began armed attacks on Arabs. The Jewish Agency endorsed the establishment of numerous unauthorized settlements on the assumption that any future Zionist state would conform largely to areas where there was a significant Jewish presence. The intensity of the Arab uprising in 1937 led the British to increase the size and armaments of the Zionist constabulary, which also constituted much of the Haganah, to defend the Zionist community. The failure of the London Conference in March 1939 accelerated the Haganah's growth toward a real national army as the National Council made registration compulsory for all men and women between the ages of 18 and 35 in May and Ben-Gurion established a general staff in August. By then it had an effective force of nearly 20,000 with a command structure and recruitment procedure for additional growth.

ZIONIST CONFLICT AND COOPERATION WITH GREAT BRITAIN

Arab hostility was the obvious target of Zionist military preparedness, but there was no denying Zionist differences with Great Britain. In fact, Britain's attempt to enforce the immigration restrictions of the White Paper drove the Zionists to engage in large-scale illegal immigration. The Jewish Agency called the White Paper a "surrender to Arab terrorism" and pledged to "fight rather than submit to Arab rule." It further stated that the Jews would "never accept the closing to them of the gates of Palestine nor let their national home be converted into a ghetto." Still, with the impending war, which Ben-Gurion had predicted five years earlier, the Zionists faced a tremendous dilemma. Ben-Gurion, in his inimitable manner, resolved it by saying that the Zionists would "fight with the British against Hitler as if there were no White Paper, and fight the White Paper as if there were no war."

Circumstances, however, dictated that mainstream Zionists, including Ben-Gurion, had to work more closly with the British than the strident remark indicated they should. From early in World War II large segments of European Jewry came under the same brutal treatment that had formerly been confined to those in Germany. Most of the entire Arab world supported the Axis effort as a means of ending Anglo-French dominion over their lands. As if these were not challenge enough, radicals, under the leadership of Menachem Begin and Abraham Stern, threatened to destroy all peaceful relations between the Zionist movement and Great Britain, which offered the only hope of destroying Hitler before the United States entered the war.

ZIONISM DURING WORLD WAR II

Ben-Gurion seized the leadership of Zionism during the war and subdued the efforts of those under the leadership of Weizmann, who resisted forthright attempts to create a Zionist state, and those under the leadership of Jabotinsky, who intended to use overt violence against the British to create a Zionist state immediately. After establishing his control over the Jewish Agency in Palestine, Ben-Gurion imposed his policies upon both the Haganah and the Histadrut, the other two most important institutions in the Zionist community. His personal will and his ability to use the political structures of the Zionist institutions propelled him into a position to shape Zionism more than any other individual.

Ben-Gurion and most other Zionists attempted to have a high level of separate Jewish military presence in the war effort for both political and military reasons. Such participation would be in stark contrast to the Arab sympathy for the Axis. It would also serve the double purpose of striking a blow against Hitler and providing vital military experience for the expected confrontations with the British and the Arabs after the war. The British, however, resisted the formation of separate Zionist units until 1944 but allowed individual Jews to join other units. The Haganah, in fact, became increasingly professional during the war and a highly trained strike force, called the Palmach, developed in 1941 to resist a possible German invasion of Palestine. It also developed a sophisticated intelligence branch for use against the Axis, the British, the Arabs, and radical fringe Zionists. The Palmach actually gained some military experience in 1941 when its members helped the British overthrow the Vichy regimes in Lebanon and Syria. Jews from all over the world gained vital experience in the armies of their respective nations and Zionists in the Jewish Brigade gained unique logistical knowledge that served their interests later.

Allied war needs were a boon to the Zionist economy in Palestine and especially for the Histadrut factories and farms. Large-scale production of food and manufactured goods on an unprecedented level helped prepare the Zionists for their own future war and allowed them to live on their own.

The broadest spectrum of Zionists made every effort to circumvent the White

Paper restrictions on immigration after its announcement and during the first two years of the war. By 1940, however, British countermeasures became more effective and after 1941 there was virtually no means of relieving the millions of Jews confined within the Third Reich. British and Zionist short-term concerns were similar enough to encourage increased cooperation. Even the Irgun ceased its attacks upon the British until Begin took command in 1943. There was, however, no overlooking the long-range disparity between British and Zionist goals.

ZIONIST RELATIONS WITH THE UNITED STATES

Having concluded that British needs and intentions were in many respects contrary to the needs and goals of Zionism, Ben-Gurion nurtured the growing support for Zionism in the United States. This was especially true after 1942 when the Axis threat to the Middle East disappeared and increased knowledge of the fate of European Jewry under the Nazis became more widespread. The Biltmore Program, which resulted from the May 1942 American Zionist conference at the Biltmore Hotel in New York, signalled a new direction for Zionism and its relationship with the United States. It openly advocated a "Jewish Commonwealth" and urged both the American government and U.S. public to work toward its realization. Broad American zeal for Zionism soon surpassed support the movement had received in England. American funds from all sectors were soon available for the Zionist cause and by 1944 both major political parties in the United States, as well as both houses of Congress, most state legislatures, the biggest labor organizations, and various Christian groups passed resolutions in support of the establishment of a Jewish state in Palestine. Thus, Zionism, which many American Jews still opposed, became a compelling central issue in American domestic and foreign policy. It also became a major source of conflict between the United States and its wartime ally, Great Britain.

ZIONIST CONFLICT WITH GREAT BRITAIN

American support increased just at the time that Anglo-Zionist relations hit a new low because of Irgun and Stern Gang (Lehi) activities. The followers of Abraham Stern, who specialized in assassinating British officials, renewed their attacks on British personnel in the summer of 1943, even though British police had killed Stern in 1942. Begin's Irgun began systematically destroying British administrative centers in February 1944. But Lehi's assassination of Lord Moyne on November 6, 1944, in Cairo was their most notorious success and forced a showdown. The British informed the Zionists in no uncertain terms that the death of this cabinet minister was beyond acceptable bounds. Even Churchill, who had always supported Zionism, threatened to withhold all support after the death of his friend. While both militant groups came under attack from the British and mainstream Zionists, the British scrutiny of the radicals' activities caused them to have increased concern for the entire Yishuv's military capability, which had increased during the war with British assistance. Largely as a result of the Yishuv's efforts both Lehi and the Irgun were subdued before the end of the war. Ben-Gurion and members of the mainstream believed the end of the war was the time to make their move for an independent Zionist state.

Weizmann was a gradualist until the end of the war and he used his presence in London as the President of the Jewish Agency to assure the British of modest Zionist demands for the establishment of a small Israel west of the Jordan in a reasonable time frame. In an extended trip to Palestine early in 1945, when allied victory in Europe seemed assured, he still received appreciative audiences for his gradualist approach, although Ben-Gurion was determined that Palestine would become a Jewish state that would absorb a massive transfer of the world's Jewish population immediately after the war.

Churchill's wartime government had come to a more sympathetic posture toward the creation of a small Zionist state through a combination of the gentle prodding of Weizmann, the Zionist war effort, and a realization of the magnitude of the Nazi holocaust. Palestine's strategic importance to Great Britain was, however, probably even greater than before due to the impending independence of most of the Arab states. Weizmann's approach, therefore, was more appealing to the British as it presumed a considerable evolutionary period that allowed for reasonable postwar considerations and adjustments. The impatience of the Zionists in Palestine and their American supporters would test whether the Weizmann-British relationship that stretched back to early World War I would prevail at the end of World War II.

8

The Arab Region: 1914–1940

HISTORICAL TIMELINE

1914 ⇛ Anglo-Ottoman Convention on March 9 settled questions between them on the Arabian peninsula.

⇛ British recognized Abdul Aziz as the independent ruler of the Najd and its dependencies.

⇛ Saad Zaghlul was elected speaker of the Egyptian Legislative Assembly.

⇛ Britain announced withholding of shipment of two battleships to Ottoman Empire on August 3.

⇛ British and French Declarations of War against Ottoman Empire November 5.

⇛ Britain occupied al-Faw at the mouth of the Shatt al-Arab in November.

⇛ Sultan declared Holy War November 14.

⇛ British declared Egypt a protectorate on December 18, deposed Abbas Hilmi, replaced him with his uncle Hussein Kamil and gave him the new title of Sultan.

1915 Sharif Hussein of the Hijaz opened correspondence with Sir Henry McMahon in July.

⇛ Large-scale executions of Arab nationalist leaders in Beirut and Damascus during August.

⇛ British moved troops from Basra to Kut al-Amara in September.

⇛ British made an offer to Sharif Hussein on October 24.
⇛ British attempted conquest of Baghdad in November.
⇛ Sharif Hussein accepted British offer for an alliance on November 5.
⇛ Negotiations began in November between Charles Francois Georges-Picot and Sir Mark Sykes to determine the partitioning of the Middle East.

1916 ⇛ British accepted Sharif Hussein's terms January 30.
⇛ Sykes-Picot Agreement was secretly endorsed by British and French governments on February 4.
⇛ British occupied Baghdad on March 11.
⇛ Second Ottoman-German attack on Suez Canal April 23; third attack followed on July 19.
⇛ General Townshend's forces surrendered on April 29 to the Ottomans at Kut al-Amara.
⇛ Sharif Hussein declared the beginning of the Arab Revolt against the Ottoman Empire on June 5.
⇛ Hussein's Arab forces seized Mecca, Jeddah, and the Red Sea coast north to Yanbo June 6–September 22.
⇛ Sharif Hussein was acclaimed king of the Arabs on October 29.
⇛ British launched Sinai-Palestine campaign on November 15.
⇛ British recognized Hussein as king of the Hijaz on December 15.
⇛ British conquest of Mesopotamia was initiated under General Maude on December 13.

1917 ⇛ Hussein's forces captured Wejh in January.
⇛ Kut al-Amara was reconquered by the British on February 23.
⇛ Baghdad fell to the British on March 11.
⇛ Tsar Nicholas II of Russia was overthrown on March 16.
⇛ United States entered World War I on April 6.
⇛ The British government expressed determination to maintain exclusive control over Palestine in April.
⇛ British cabinet discussions began in June regarding Jewish homeland in Palestine.
⇛ Allenby took command of Palestine campaign on June 28.
⇛ Arab forces captured Aqaba on July 6.
⇛ Woodrow Wilson endorsed idea of Jewish homeland in Palestine in October.
⇛ British forces penetrated Ottoman defenses at Beersheba October 31.
⇛ Balfour Declaration was issued in the form of a letter to Lord Rothschild on November 2.
⇛ British cabinet approved the Balfour Declaration on October 16.
⇛ British forces entered Jerusalem on December 11.
⇛ Death of King Hussein Kamal of Egypt. Fuad became king.

1918
- ⇛ Abdullah-led forces lost Battle of Turaba in May.
- ⇛ British began campaign to take Damascus on September 19.
- ⇛ British and Arab forces conquered Damascus on September 30.
- ⇛ Feisal declared Syria independent on October 5.
- ⇛ Small French force landed at Beirut on October 7.
- ⇛ British sent a Zionist Commission to Palestine.
- ⇛ British and French on November 7 assured the Iraqis that British occupation was for their liberation and a necessary step toward Arab self-rule.
- ⇛ Saad Zaghlul formed *Wafd al-Misri* (Egyptian Delegation) and attempted to gain permission to take Egypt's case for independence to the Paris Peace Conference.

1919
- ⇛ Paris Peace Conference convened January 18.
- ⇛ Creation of League of Nations January 25.
- ⇛ First Palestinian National Congress, meeting in Jerusalem January 27–February 10 rejected Balfour Declaration and demanded independence.
- ⇛ Zaghlul of Egypt exiled to Malta in March. Unrest in Egypt forced High Commissioner Allenby to allow Wafd to attend peace conference.
- ⇛ Peace conference decided March 25 to send international commission of inquiry to ascertain aspirations of Near East peoples.
- ⇛ Major Saudi and Ikhwan victory over Hashemite forces at Turaba on May 25.
- ⇛ King-Crane Commission began investigation in June.
- ⇛ Treaty of Versailles and League of Nations Covenant signed June 28.
- ⇛ Syrian National Congress declared independence July 2.
- ⇛ King-Crane report completed August 28.
- ⇛ French troops moved into Beirut area October 9.
- ⇛ British withdrew troops from Syria on November 1.

1920
- ⇛ Feisal talked with Clemenceau in January.
- ⇛ General Syrian Congress elected Feisal king of Syria and Abdullah king of Iraq on March 8.
- ⇛ Zaghlul and Milner negotiated a relationship between Egypt and Great Britain from March through August.
- ⇛ San Remo Conference met on April 18.
- ⇛ Disturbances broke out in Palestine in April due to fears of Zionism.
- ⇛ San Remo Conference announced on the mandate system on April 24.
- ⇛ General Gouraud demanded on July 14 that Feisal withdraw from Damascus.
- ⇛ France occupied Damascus and expelled Feisal on July 25.
- ⇛ British civilian administration inaugurated in Palestine on July 1; Sir Herbert Samuel appointed first high commissioner.

⇛ Large-scale hostilities developed in Iraq from August to October in protest of the British mandate.
⇛ Sir Percy Cox returned to Iraq in the fall and restored order in part through the establishment of an Iraqi Arab government.
⇛ French created Greater Lebanon September 1.
⇛ Abdullah al-Hashimi began to form an army to reestablish his brother, Feisal, as king of Syria in October.
⇛ Abdullah arrived with small forces in Maan in November.
⇛ Third Palestinian National Congress at Haifa elected an Executive Committee in December, which controlled the Palestinian political movement from 1920 to 1935.
⇛ Saudi and Ikhwan forces had redefined the borders in the west with Yemen and in the east with Kuwait.

1921 ⇛ Abdullah arrived in Amman on March 2.
⇛ Cairo Conference created the Kingdom of Iraq with Feisal al-Hashimi as king on March 12.
⇛ Churchill and Abdullah met in Jerusalem and Abdullah received temporary custody of Transjordan after the Cairo Conference.
⇛ Outbreak of disturbances in Jaffa on May 2 against Zionist immigration, which resulted in the death of 46 Jews and the wounding of 146
⇛ British appointed Hajj Amin al-Husseini Mufti of Jerusalem on May 8.
⇛ Council of State elected Feisal king of Iraq on July 11.
⇛ Plebiscite indicated 96 percent of Iraqis approved Feisal as king.
⇛ League of Nations approved mandates for Syria, Lebanon, and Palestine July 24.
⇛ Feisal coronated as King of Iraq on August 23.
⇛ France signed the Treaty of Ankara on October 10. This treaty brought diplomatic recognition and peace with France; it pushed the French mandatory border 10,000 square miles south and restored the territory of Cilicia to Turkish control.
⇛ France ceded Cilicia to Turkey October 20.
⇛ Haycraft Commission of Inquiry in October attributed the Jaffa disturbances to the magnitude of Zionist mass immigration.
⇛ Zaghlul, leader of the Egyptian *wafd,* was exiled to the Seychelle Islands.
⇛ Abdul Aziz seized control of Hail, the Rashid capital, in November.

1922 ⇛ Great Britain recognized Egypt as an independent country on February 28 but continued to rule by martial law until July.
⇛ Egypt received a new constitution in April.
⇛ Zaghlul and *Wafd* won overwhelming majority in legislature of the new Egyptian constitutional monarchy.
⇛ Churchill issued White Paper June 2 on Palestine. The White Paper stated the British concept of their obligations to the

Zionists; it excluded Transjordan from the Balfour Declaration and the League of Nations mandate; Jewish immigration was not to exceed the economic capacity of a country.
⇛ U.S. Congress endorsed Balfour Declaration on June 30.
⇛ League of Nations approved mandates for Syria, Lebanon, and Palestine July 24.
⇛ Fifth Palestinian National Congress at Nablus in August resolved to implement an economic boycott against the Zionist community.
⇛ Anglo-Iraqi Treaty of October 21 defined the relationship between the two countries. The League of Nations still regarded Iraq as a mandate.
⇛ The British published the first census of Palestine in October, which put the total population at 757,182 with 78 percent Muslim, 11 percent Jewish, and 9.6 percent Christian.
⇛ Uqair Conference fixed Iraqi borders with Saudi Arabia in November.

1923 ⇛ Vladimir Jabotinsky resigned from the Zionist Executive in January and vowed to use all means possible to colonize Palestine and Transjordan.
⇛ British recognized Abdullah as Emir of Transjordan on May 25.
⇛ Religious leaders the British expelled from Iraq arrived in Iran in August.
⇛ British mandate for Palestine officially went into effect on September 29.

1924 ⇛ King Hussein of the Hijaz proclaimed himself Caliph after the Turkish Republic abolished the Caliphate.
⇛ King Hussein of Hijaz denied pilgrims from Najd and the Ikhwan access to the Muslim Holy Places in the spring.
⇛ The Iraqi Constitutional Assembly convened on March 27 and approved the treaty with Great Britain by the smallest possible majority.
⇛ Abdullah of Transjordan accepted a British ultimatum in August to retain his position.
⇛ Ikhwan forces attacked the city of Taif on August 24 and gained control of the city on September 5.
⇛ Assassination of Sir Lee Stack, governor-general of Sudan and *Sirdar* on September 23.
⇛ League of Nations approved the Anglo-Iraqi treaty and established the mandate of Mesopotamia on September 27.
⇛ The question of Mosul was turned over to the League of Nations on September 30.
⇛ King Hussein of the Hijaz abdicated on October 3 in favor of his son, Ali.

1925 Jabotinsky formed the Revisionist party to colonize Transjordan and Palestine.

⇛ Palestinians began a general strike in March to protest Lord Balfour's visit to Jerusalem.
⇛ Druze-led general uprising in Syria began July 18,1926.
⇛ French established Republic of Lebanon within the Syrian mandate.
⇛ Sixth Palestinian National Congress convened in Jaffa during October.
⇛ Ibn Saud conquered Mecca on December 10.
⇛ Ali abdicated on December 10, 1925, and joined his brother Feisal in Iraq.
⇛ League of Nations ruled in favor of Great Britain on the Mosul question on December 16.
⇛ Adoption of international clock, time, and calendar in Turkey on December 26.

1926 ⇛ In January Ibn Saud proclaimed himself king of the Hijaz in the Great Mosque of Mecca .
⇛ Charles Dabbas was elected president of Lebanon.
⇛ French created the Republic of Lebanon on May 23.
⇛ Iraqi borders were fixed with Turkey on July 18.

1927 ⇛ A conference between Abdul Aziz and 3,000 Ikhwan in January failed to resolve their differences.
⇛ Major oil discovery at Kirkuk in Iraq.
⇛ Saad Zaghlul of Egypt died in August.
⇛ A band of Ikhwan slaughtered the British workmen who were building a British police post in September within the Iraqi border; Ikhwan carried out other unauthorized raids.
⇛ Anglo-Iraqi treaty on December 14 reduced British control and contained British promise to sponsor Iraq into League of Nations by 1932. Iraq did not ratify the treaty.

1928 ⇛ Anglo-Transjordanian Agreement on February 20.
⇛ Prime Minister Mahmoud of Egypt suspended the constitution for three years.
⇛ Hasan al-Banna formed the Muslim Brotherhood.
⇛ Seventh Palestinian National Conference convened in Jerusalem in June.
⇛ Zionist religious leaders began efforts to change the status quo at the Wailing Wall on September 24.
⇛ Islamic Conference in Jerusalem during November. Members of the conference demanded protection of Muslim property rights at the Wailing Wall.

1929 ⇛ Ikhwan, under leadership of Sultan Ibn Bijad, attacked fellow Ikhwan in Hasa in February.
⇛ Turkish Petroleum Company renamed Iraq Petroleum Company.
⇛ Abdul Aziz defeated major Ikhwan force at Sibilla on March 30.
⇛ Lebanese president's term of office set at six years nonrenewable in April.

⇛ Beginning August 23, Palestinians rioted in several towns in response to Zionist demonstrations at the Wailing Wall. Arabs killed 133 Jews and wounded 339; British military inflicted most of the damage on Palestinians, which left 116 killed and 232 wounded.
⇛ Palestinian conference convened in Jerusalem in October to adopt a policy in the wake of the Wailing Wall problems.
⇛ By the end of the year, Abdul Aziz was the undisputed ruler of Saudi Arabia.

1930s–1950s ⇛ Extensive work of Sati al-Husri to foster Arab nationalism primarily through modern secular education.

1930 ⇛ League of Nations Council appointed a commission on January 14 to investigate the conflicting claims of Palestinians and Jews at the Wailing Wall.
⇛ Shaw Commission report on 1929 problems in Palestine. Attributed the violence to Arab fear of the magnitude of Zionist immigration.
⇛ Fourth Palestinian Delegation went to London. British refused to remedy their complaints against the growth of Zionist community in Palestine.
⇛ Syria adopted a constitution on May 22 and became a republic.
⇛ Anglo-Iraqi treaty of June 30 defined new relationship between the two countries. Iraq apparently sovereign.
⇛ Jewish Agency for Palestine was enlarged to include both Zionists and non-Zionists from many countries.
⇛ Sir John Hope-Simpson reported in October that there was no room in Palestine for additional Zionist immigration.
⇛ British Colonial Secretary, Lord Passfield, issued a White Paper that reflected the conclusions of Hope-Simpson.
⇛ Ismail Sidki Pasha became prime minister in Egypt until 1933 and imposed a new constitution that kept the Wafd out of power.
⇛ An international Wailing Wall Commission's report in December confirmed the rights of Muslims in the area of the Wailing Wall.

1931 ⇛ Prime Minister Ramsay MacDonald's letter to Chaim Weizman on February 14 virtually retracted Lord Passfield's White Paper on Palestine.
⇛ Iraq began to receive £400,000 annually on oil concessions.
⇛ Creation of *Ahali* organization in Iraq.
⇛ Death of Sharif Hussein, former King of the Hijaz, on June 4.
⇛ General Sir Arthur Wauchope succeeded Sir John Chancellor as High Commissioner of Palestine in October.
⇛ The second British census of Palestine showed an increase in population to 1,035,154, of which 73.4 percent were Muslim, 16.9 percent were Jewish, and 8.6 percent were Christian.
⇛ Lewis French, British director of development for Palestine, issued his report on land dispossession of Arabs in December.

⇒ One hundred and forty five delegates from all over the Islamic world attended a conference in Jerusalem in December out of concern for Palestine.

1932 ⇒ Lebanese census on January 31.
⇒ French Commissioner, Henri Ponsot, suspended the Lebanese constitution on May 10.
⇒ Dabbas remained in the Lebanese presidency for six extra months after suspension of the constitution.
⇒ Antun Sa'ada founded Syrian Nationalist Party.
⇒ Istiqlal (Independence) Party became the first legal political party in Palestine on August 2.
⇒ Abdul Aziz assumed the title of King of Saudi Arabia on September 18.
⇒ Iraq admitted to League of Nations on October 3. First Arab country to receive recognition of independence.

1933 ⇒ Abdullah Bayhum took over executive powers in Lebanon following Dabbas's resignation on January 2.
⇒ Habib al-Sa'd performed ceremonial powers of the Lebanese presidency for one year beginning January 31.
⇒ Arab Executive Committee of Palestine issued a strong statement on continued Zionist immigration.
⇒ In May Abdul Aziz signed an oil concession with SOCAL for an initial loan of £30,000. This was followed by a £20,000 loan eighteen months later and a £5,000 annual rental. SOCAL had what many believed was a worthless concession.
⇒ British made a new effort on July 14 to resettle displaced Palestinians.
⇒ King Feisal of Iraq died on September 8. Ghazi became king.
⇒ Palestinian Arab Executive called for a general strike in October and demonstrations began in the main towns to protest Zionist immigration.
⇒ Brutal suppression of Assyrians in Iraq.
⇒ French suspended Syrian and Lebanese constitutions on November 24.
⇒ Iraqi oil pipeline completed to Mediterranean Sea.
⇒ Great Britain and North Yemen signed the Treaty of Sanaa, which established borders between North and South Yemen.

1934 ⇒ Sir William Murison's special commission on Palestine reported in February on the cause of the 1933 uprising.
⇒ Defense party founded in Palestine on December 2.
⇒ Treaty of Taif established borders between Yemen and Saudi Arabia.

1935 ⇒ Palestine Arab party founded March 27.
⇒ Reform party of Palestine founded June 23.
⇒ Death of Ali, former king of the Hijaz.
⇒ Major riots in Egypt in opposition to British military build-up to counter Italian and German activities.

- National Bloc party of Palestine founded October 5.
- Revisionists quit World Zionist Organization in October to form the New Zionist Organization to "liberate" Palestine and Transjordan by force if necessary.
- Creation of the League of National Action in Syria.
- Dissident Haganah members founded *Irgun Zvai Leumi* (National Military Organization) in October; Jabotinsky named Commander in Chief.
- British discovered a large quantity of arms at Jaffa, which the Zionists had smuggled from Belgium.
- Joint resolution from Palestinian political parties to the British high commissioner on November 25 requested cessation of Zionist mass immigration and land acquisition. Resolution requested the establishment of a government on the basis of proportional representation.
- On December 21, the British high commissioner of Palestine proposed the establishment of a twenty-eight-member Legislative Council with Palestinians holding only fourteen seats, which the Palestinian leadership accepted in principle.

1936

- Uprising in Syria, Lebanon, Egypt, and Palestine in January.
- Emile Edde elected president of Lebanon in January.
- Pro-Zionist members of the British House of Commons defeated the proposal for a Legislative Council for Palestine on March 25.
- Death of King Fuad of Egypt on April 28. Farouk became king.
- Pro-Zionist members of the British House of Commons defeated the proposal for a Legislative Council for Palestine on March 25.
- Palestinians created National Committees in all larger towns from April 20 to April 30.
- Leaders of all five Palestinian political parties called for a general strike on April 21.
- Leaders of the Palestinian political parties constituted as the Arab Higher Committee on April 25.
- Conference of all National Committees in Palestine in Jerusalem on May 8 called for no taxation without representation. The Great Rebellion, commonly referred to as the General Strike, began.
- British moved reinforcements into Palestine on May 11.
- British appointed a Royal Commission on May 18 to investigate the cause of the rebellion in Palestine.
- Palestinian civil service and judiciary personnel protested to the High Commissioner on June 30 against his pro-Zionist policies.
- Fawzi al-Qawukji entered Palestine on August 25 with 150 volunteers from Arab countries to participate in the uprising against Britain.
- Anglo-Egyptian Treaty on August 26 established a new relationship between two apparently sovereign nations.

⇛ Franco-Syrian treaty to replace mandate September 9.
⇛ France promised Syria to include Hatay in an independent Syria on September 9.
⇛ Arab Higher Committee accepted appeals by kings of Saudi Arabia and Iraq, and the emir of Transjordan, to call off the General Strike on September 22.
⇛ Turkey insisted that Hatay be independent on October 9.
⇛ Arab Higher Committee declared an end to the General Strike on October 11.
⇛ Lord Peel's Royal Commission arrived in Palestine on November 11.
⇛ French Commissioner de Martel negotiated a Franco-Lebanese treaty in the spring, but France never ratified it. Lebanon ratified it on November 13.
⇛ Pierre Gemayel formed Kata'ib (Phalange) political party in November.
⇛ General Bakr Sidqi *coup* in Iraq on November 29. The first Arab military *coup*.
⇛ SOCAL sold half its interest in the Saudi oil concession to Texaco.

1937 ⇛ President Edde of Lebanon appointed Khayr al-Din al-Ahdab as first Muslim Prime Minister in April.
⇛ Peel Commission Report on July 7 stated that Arab fear of Zionist expansion caused problems in Palestine. It recommended termination of the mandate and partition.
⇛ Saadabad Pact, a nonaggression agreement, among Iran, Turkey, Iraq, and Afghanistan on July 8. Agreement gave Iran better navigation privileges in the Shatt al-Arab.
⇛ Overthrow and death of General Sidqi of Iraq on August 17.
⇛ Woodhead Commission Report on November 9 addressed the feasibility of partition.
⇛ Arabs gained ascendancy in government of Hatay on November 29.
⇛ Aden became a British Crown Colony.

1938 ⇛ On March 3, Well #7 spewed forth the first evidence of the largest oil reserve in the world in Saudi Arabia.
⇛ Turks gained control of Hatay through new election on July 21.
⇛ Egypt hosted largest Arab congress on the problem of Palestine in October.
⇛ Trial in November of the "Fifty-Three," who later developed the Tudeh Party in Iran.

1939 ⇛ King Ghazi of Iraq died in an automobile accident April 4. Four-year-old Feisal II became king and his uncle, Abd al-Ilah, became regent.
⇛ In May, Caltex shipped the first load of Saudi oil out of the new port of Ras Tanura.
⇛ British White Paper on Palestine on May 17 limited Jewish

immigration to 75,000 over five years and provided for Palestine to be independent in ten years.
⇛ France conceded Hatay to Turkey in return for a nonaggression pact on July 23.
⇛ France declared war on Germany on September 3; France renounced Franco-Syrian treaty in November. There was an uprising of protest in Syria.
⇛ French Commissioner Puaux suspended the constitution of Lebanon and Syria on September 21.
⇛ Hajj Amin al-Husseini arrived in Baghdad in October.
⇛ Zaki Arsuzi created the Arab Nationalist party in Syria.
⇛ Prominent Egyptian leaders were jailed for their support of the Axis war effort.
⇛ Middle East Supply Center was headquartered in Cairo.
⇛ Fritz Grobba, Germany's Minister to Iraq, moved German propaganda operations from Iraq to Iran after the beginning of World War II.

1940 ⇛ Paris fell to Nazis on June 14.
⇛ General Henri Dentz, representing the Vichy government, became Commissioner of Syria and Lebanon on June 17.
⇛ Zaki Arsuzi created *al-Baath al-Arabi.*

A change in masters or foreign occupation was nothing new for Greater Syria and the Fertile Crescent, although nearly four centuries had passed by the time it happened at the end of World War I. Most people in this Arab speaking region had few regrets that the war had ended Ottoman, and therefore Turkish, domination. However, they soon found themselves victims of a foreign occupation that was supposed to be for their benefit. The newly formed international organization called the League of Nations authorized two European states to govern the entire area, supposedly in preparation for Arab self-government. There was, in fact, no precedent for stewardship of this magnitude. People of the region could not understand why they should be singled out for such special treatment. Their sense of Arab identity had been slow to arise in the face of omnipresent Ottoman domination for such a prolonged time. But during the last stages of the war and its immediate aftermath, Arab nationalism grew rapidly. There was a profound desire among the Arabs for immediate self-government in compliance with the promises the Entente Powers had made during the war.

Egypt's case was different, since British occupation had existed there for nearly four decades by the end of the war, which promised to fulfill astute Egyptians' worst nightmare that the absence of the Ottoman Empire removed all restraint upon complete annexation to the British Empire. Again, Egyptians had reason to believe that the stated war objectives of the Entente Powers and the United States would bring them independence after the war. No nation at the Paris Peace Conference could pretend to have a better claim to independence than Egypt, with its long and illustrious history. It defied comprehension that the international community assured freedom for places like Czechoslovakia, Yugoslavia, and Albania, while it acquiesced to Egypt languishing under continued British occupation. Or, closer to home, were Nejd and Hijaz more capable of self-government

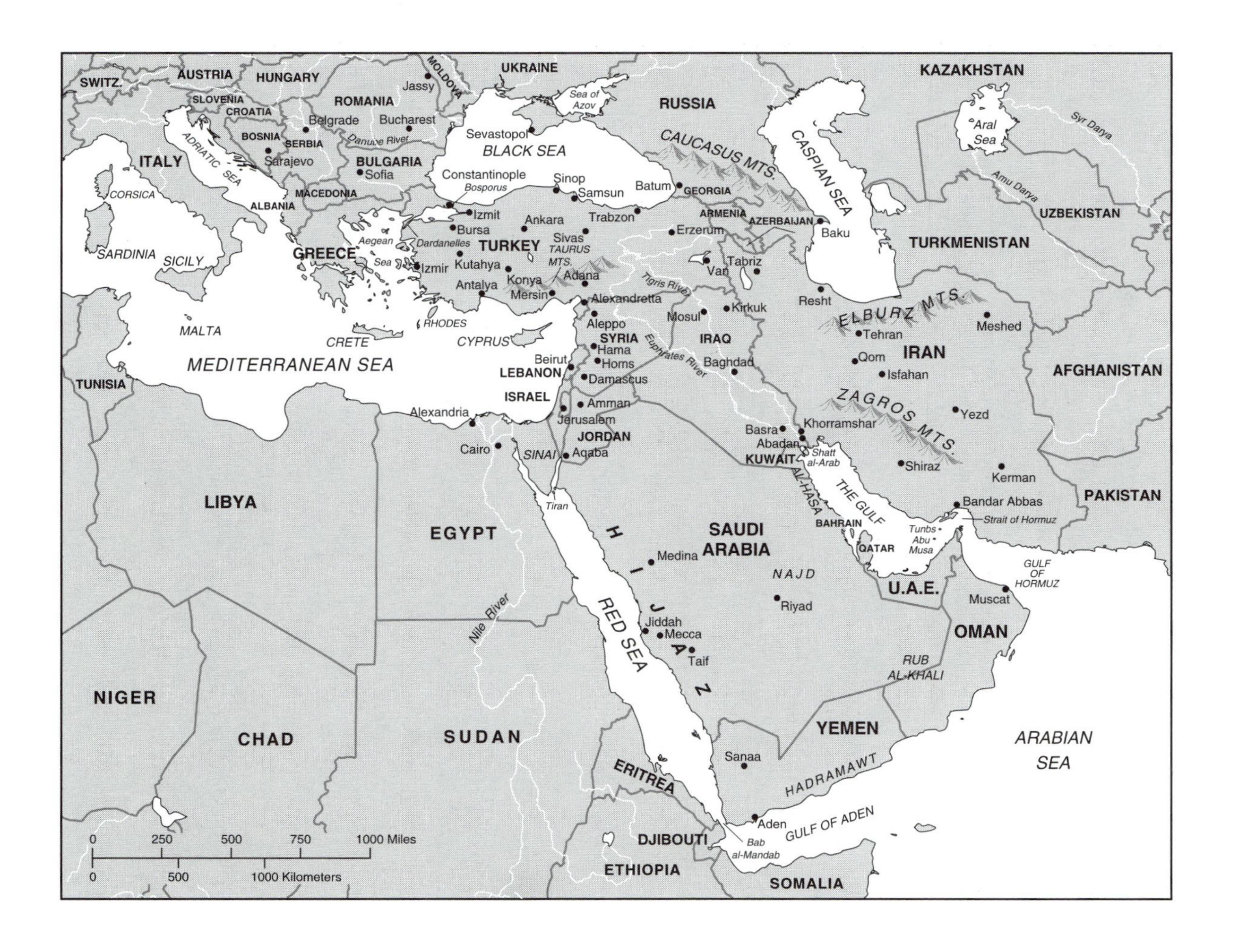

SWITZ.
AUSTRIA
HUNGARY
MOLDOVA
UKRAINE
KAZAKHSTAN
SLOVENIA
CROATIA
ROMANIA
Jassy
Sea of Azov
RUSSIA
Aral Sea
Syr Darya
Belgrade
Bucharest
BOSNIA
SERBIA
Danube River
Sevastopol
BLACK SEA
CAUCASUS MTS.
CASPIAN SEA
Amu Darya
ITALY
ADRIATIC SEA
Sarajevo
BULGARIA
Sofia
Constantinople
Bosporus
Sinop
Samsun
Batum
GEORGIA
UZBEKISTAN
CORSICA
MACEDONIA
ALBANIA
Izmit
Ankara
Trabzon
ARMENIA
AZERBAIJAN
Baku
Bursa
Erzerum
TURKMENISTAN
SARDINIA
SICILY
GREECE
Aegean Sea
Dardanelles
TURKEY
Sivas
TAURUS MTS.
Izmir
Kutahya
Van
Tabriz
Konya
Adana
Antalya
Mersin
Tigris River
Alexandretta
Kirkuk
Resht
ELBURZ MTS.
Meshed
MALTA
RHODES
Aleppo
Mosul
CRETE
CYPRUS
SYRIA
IRAQ
Tehran
Hama
Euphrates River
Qom
IRAN
MEDITERRANEAN SEA
Beirut
Homs
Baghdad
Isfahan
AFGHANISTAN
TUNISIA
LEBANON
Damascus
ISRAEL
Amman
ZAGROS MTS.
Yezd
Alexandria
Jerusalem
Khorramshar
Basra
JORDAN
Abadan
Cairo
SINAI
Aqaba
KUWAIT
Shatt al-Arab
Shiraz
Kerman
AL-HASA
THE GULF
LIBYA
Bandar Abbas
PAKISTAN
Tiran
Strait of Hormuz
BAHRAIN
EGYPT
SAUDI ARABIA
Tunbs
Abu Musa
QATAR
Medina
HIJAZ
GULF OF HORMUZ
NAJD
U.A.E.
Muscat
Riyad
Nile River
Jiddah
Mecca
OMAN
Taif
RED SEA
RUB AL-KHALI
NIGER
CHAD
SUDAN
YEMEN
ARABIAN SEA
Sanaa
ERITREA
HADRAMAWT
Aden
GULF OF ADEN
0 250 500 750 1000 Miles
DJIBOUTI
Bab al-Mandab
0 500 1000 Kilometers
ETHIOPIA
SOMALIA

than Egypt? Egyptians, like the residents of Greater Syria and the Fertile Crescent, soon expressed a strong skepticism of the ultimate purpose of the League of Nations.

Arabs, who could accept the time-honored principle that the vanquished usually suffer while the victors enjoy the spoils, had even greater difficulty understanding how the League of Nations could justify the imposition of a potentially large number of alien people upon the region. Their resistance to the influx of Zionists under League protection was almost instantaneous and universal. Such an unwanted infusion of Europeans was only possible because of the overwhelming military support the Zionists enjoyed. Resistance to the legitimacy of Zionist migration to Palestine became a *cause célèbre* for almost all Arabs, Christian and Muslim alike. If there was any truth to the mandate system, the European nations would withdraw from the region at some point in the near future. However, millions of Zionists would be there forever, as a constant reminder of how the Europeans took advantage of Arab weakness to establish a European outpost in the heartland of the Arab world.

The Arabs had very limited means of resisting either the short- or long-range objectives of their European masters. Their sense of personal and national dignity compelled them to resist, nevertheless. They persisted in their struggle under the inspiration that their cause was just and in hope that the League of Nations would change its policy, or some powerful outside benefactor would help them defeat their foes, or that they could develop their own capacity to free themselves. The likelihood of the latter possibility seemed slight in view of the strength of their oppressors, which could curtail Arab efforts of self-determination.

SYRIA

After experiencing the deprivation and devastation of World War I, Syrians witnessed the terrible condition of the Ottoman forces as they withdrew from the Levant. The arrival of the strong, modern British army indicated that a new era was at hand. Much more encouraging was the presence of the victorious Arab army in Damascus, where Lawrence said the city "went mad with joy" when it arrived on September 30. In the last weeks of the war Syrian Arabs, indeed, became convinced that independence was not only possible, but would immediately follow a brief postwar occupation, while the British army and the token French force prepared for departure. Knowledge of the Arab war effort, Wilson's Fourteen Points, the Hussein-McMahon agreement, and recent Anglo-French affirmations on behalf of Arab independence outweighed recent revelations that the British and French had agreed to divide Arab territory between them. As the war ended, they could not take the Zionist threat seriously, since Arab participation in the divestiture of Palestinians from their land to provide homes for Jews was unthinkable.

The immediate actions of the Arab government, with its capital at Damascus, indicated that it was genuine and that it was free from foreign control. Feisal, as governor, declared the Arab Syrian Government independent on October 5, 1918. He established a broadly based government of rural and urban, Christian and Muslim officials from all over Greater Syria. The new government utilized the wealth of educated Syrians to propose plans for shaping a nation. The use of Arabic language, education, health, agriculture, industry, and the transportation infrastructure received special attention. Many new schools began to operate immediately, but most matters required the establishment of a revenue system and a legislative process.

Feisal attended the Paris peace talks, where he obtained further evidence that Britain and France intended to occupy Arab territory. At his suggestion Great Britain and the United States agreed to sponsor an international inquiry into the disposition of Syria. British and French opposition to an inquiry left the study to two Americans, Henry C. King and Charles R. Crane. Syrians assumed the King-Crane commission was an opportunity to present their case to the world.

King, Crane, and their associates witnessed a surprising amount of Syrian unity, expressed in the form of a legislative resolution to augment their many individual interviews. Elections for a Syrian National Congress in the spring of 1919 produced a generally well-educated assembly from Greater Syria, including Palestine and Iraq. By July 2 this unquestionably representative body presented its demands for an independent constitutional monarchy in Syria, a similar state in Iraq, and the termination of Zionist activities in Palestine. This declaration of independence, like Feisal's earlier one, was in behalf of Greater Syria, as it specifically rejected any form of partition and mandates. The presentation of the resolution was clinical and legalistic, rather than militant, since much of Syria remained under British occupation and French military strength along the coast was growing daily. The French increased their numbers in anticipation of establishing their mandate, but also in response to several revolts in northern and western Syria in support of the government in Damascus.

When the British withdrew their forces into southern Syria (Palestine) at the beginning of November, only the French stood between the Syrians and independence in the north. Kemalist activities in French-claimed Anatolia gave reason to hope a joint Kemalist-Syrian effort could expel France from the entire region. Feisal chose direct negotiations with France, however, and efforts to form an alliance with Turkish nationalists never materialized. Some Syrian nationalists resented the fact that Feisal was talking to Clemenceau in January 1920, during the very period of time that Kemalist forces were loosening the hold of France on Cilicia. France, which wanted Syria more than it wanted Cilicia, and which enjoyed a military advantage against the Arabs, did not budge. After that, it was obvious that the Syrians had no recourse with any part of the international community to prevent the mandate.

Feisal convened the Syrian Congress again. On March 8, it endorsed his proclamation of the Kingdom of Syria. Twenty-nine Iraqi members in attendance announced Abdullah, Feisal's older brother, as their king. Neither France nor Great Britain recognized Syria's independence as they were, in fact, making the final arrangements to meet at San Remo to culminate their mandate plans. Their announcement of the mandates on April 24 set off demonstrations throughout the Arab world, including Lebanon. Vows to fight abounded while the French built up their forces. General Gouraud, the French commander, issued an ultimatum to the Syrian government on Bastille Day. Feisal decided not to fight against the overwhelming French force, but some of the Syrian nationalists bloodily challenged the French at Maysalun pass. By July 25, Damascus was under French control and Feisal soon withdrew to Palestine. France proceeded to establish its mandate, but the dream of an independent Syrian state, stretching over the entire region, persisted.

The French Mandate

It is fashionable to talk about the prevalence of family, clan, tribal, and confessional allegiance in Syria and the absence of any significant sense of nationhood. That was undoubtedly true in the centuries of Ottoman domination, when non-Arabs governed the region from Istanbul more than a thousand miles away. Too many of the observations about narrow provincialism come from that period or immediately following the Ottoman demise. French mandatory authorities predicated their policies on the strong provincial feelings and pursued an approach of divide-and-rule, which they believed would serve French goals by preventing Syrian unity. The collective political activism throughout Syria soon after the beginning of the French mandate, however, provides a stark contradiction to those who wish that Syria, and the concept of Greater Syria, would disappear.

Efforts to construct, or reconstruct, Greater Syria were almost as contentious a problem between World War I and the early 1950s as the problem of Palestine. Indeed, in the early years for most, and in the later period for many, reunion of Palestine with the rest of Greater Syria was an integral part of expelling both the British and the Zionists. The passage of time and stark political realities diminished the appeal for most to reunite with Syria. Nothing, however, seemed to diminish Syrian desires to regain its lost provinces.

In addition to the Syrian heartland falling under French control, Syrian nationalists had to endure drastic dismemberment of their state. The British controlled all of southern Syria, which it divided into two pieces when it created the Emirate of Transjordan in 1921 and kept the remainder of Palestine as an open-ended mandate in which it assisted in the creation of a Jewish "national home." France separated Mount Lebanon from Syria in 1920 and gradually developed it into a separate republic in 1926. However, this new Lebanon increased to three times its former size when France gave it the coast from just north of Tripoli to north of Acre. This denied Syria control over its best port at Beirut. The largely Sunni population of that region resented their forced incorporation into Maronite-dominated Lebanon. The Shiah-populated regions south of Mount Lebanon and east through the Biqa valley deprived Syria of land and people.

French Rule

Further dismemberment followed as France pursued a policy of divide-and-rule. Between 1920 and 1923 Damascus, Aleppo, Latakia, Jebal Druze, Alexandretta, and Jazira all became distinct districts of the French mandate among which the French provided the only unity. None of these entities were capable of becoming viable states and their separation was hardly an advisable intermediary step toward establishing self-government. France, of course, had its own national agenda, including the acquisition of the oil fields in northern Iraq. In 1921 France agreed to allow the emerging Republic of Turkey to acquire thousands of square miles of grain-producing territory and vital water resources in Cilicia, which Syria regarded as its own.

French mandatory practices were provocative in Syria for other reasons. Far from providing the gentle, enlightened guidance toward self-government that the League of Nations envisioned, France implemented martial law. True, the Syrians refused to cooperate, but France made clear from the beginning that it would make and administer all laws and policies in Syria. Syrian officials at all levels were appointed by the mandatory authority and expected to carry out the often unpopular policies their French superiors or counterparts dictated. The French practice of having a French official for every Syrian official was both humiliating and expensive. Although Syria and Lebanon were separated, the French mandatory system placed them in a single customs union and tied their common currency to the French monetary system. French companies owned or controlled almost all of the important facilities and businesses in Syria. The French language, and French literature and history, became compulsory in the schools to the neglect of Arabic, Arabic literature, and Arab history. Minorities received favored treatment in the appointment to government positions and the military as a means of preventing the natural leaders of Syria from emerging.

Throughout the mandate period, something of a contradiction existed in the relations of different districts, which were sometimes "states," of dismembered Syria. The separate states, especially Jebal Druze and Latakia, alternated between active, and even violent, support of Syrian unity and resistance to unification under Damascus authority. Central authority during this period, however, meant French authority, in whatever way it was filtered through Syrian functionaries.

The absence of any single figure around whom Syrians could rally allowed the French policy of playing different regions against the others to succeed. Feisal came closest to offering a focus of Syrian nationalism, but he was fully occupied in Iraq, where he had neither the freedom nor the resources to lead the Syrians. His early death in 1933 reduced the viable Hashemite alternative, because far fewer Syrians regarded Abdullah in Transjordan or Feisal's immediate successors in Iraq as highly as they revered their first modern leader.

French "success" in Syria, however, was painful for all parties, because Syria remained in turmoil that varied from a silent seething to overt rebellion. French conflict with the Jebal Druze in 1925 flared into a nationwide uprising that lasted nearly two years. Sultan Atrash, a Druze, was an unlikely leader for a predominantly Sunni nation, but prominent Muslims and Christians of the People's Party helped him coordinate an impressive uprising that threatened the French ability to hold Syria. The leaders finally took refuge in Transjordan, where they attempted to persuade Abdullah to assist them. Abdullah was, of course, receptive but the British prevented overt Transjordanian participation. The availability of safe haven for Syrian rebels in British-controlled Transjordan and Palestine constantly strained relations between France and Great Britain throughout the entire mandate period.

Republic under the Mandate

The National Bloc party assumed the leadership in Syria following the demise of the People's party once the 1925–1927 rebellion subsided. Even this coalition of Syria's privileged classes expressed nationalist ardor the French could not contain. One advantage they provided for the French was an inclination to develop Syria into a republic, rather than to look to either branch of the Hashemites for leadership. National Bloc insistence on the unification of all of Syria, including Lebanon and southern Syria, into a sovereign state ensured a continuation of poor relations between the Syrians and France. Agreement upon a constitution in 1930 did not bring tranquility. Syrian agitation for independence and for a treaty to replace the mandate was unacceptable to France. The French were having major problems with a restive population in Lebanon as their 1932 election approached. The Depression had reached an already unhealthy Middle East economy. The new force of the Syrian Nationalist Party under Antun Sa'ada emerged in 1932 to agitate for the union of Lebanon and Syria. France suspended the constitutions of both Syria and Lebanon in 1932. Feisal's death in 1933 set off demonstrations in memory of the promise his leadership had offered a united Syria from 1918 to 1920.

A rebellion similar to the one in 1925 erupted in January of 1936 and brought normal activities to a halt throughout the country. Violence soon followed in Egypt, Palestine, and Lebanon, along with a coup in Iraq, to present Anglo-French control of the Arab world with its greatest challenge. Axis propaganda and political success inflamed the region, which had long-standing grievances against foreign domination. The bold and assertive actions and demands of the Zionists in Palestine moved even the elements that were normally uninvolved to activism.

French mandatory officials of Leon Blum's new Popular Front Socialists entered serious negotiations with Syrian leaders in the early spring of 1936, after military efforts restored something close to normal life. On September 9 they agreed on a treaty similar to the Anglo-Iraqi treaty of 1930, which would recognize Syrian independence. However, France retained a military presence, strong influence over all aspects of Syrian monetary and business policies, and continued exclusive French guidance over Syrian politics and diplomacy.

The Syrian government and parliament of President Hashim al-Atasi, who had been Feisal's Prime Minister, approved the treaty, because, while it authorized a demeaning French interference, it ostensibly recognized Syrian independence. The treaty, however, required the ratification of France to constitute a binding new relationship.

The illusion of independence; fascination with, and assistance in, the Palestinian uprising; the end of the Depression; and concern for Hashemite interference kept the Syrian government benignly occupied until 1939. Meanwhile, France neither ratified nor rejected the treaty, but coerced the Syrian government into making embarrassing concessions.

In 1939 developments outside of the region altered French relations with Syria. Fear of war with Germany led Edouard Daladier's government to conclude a nonaggression pact with Turkey on June 23. In return for Turkish neutrality, France ceded the Syrian province of Alexandretta to Turkey. The resolution of this problem, which had been brewing for two years, was a major blow to Syrian pride and deprived Syria of essential territory and a vital port. The French government, which had turned further to the right in October 1938 after the Munich Conference, was overwhelmed with strategic concerns throughout 1939. France declared war on the Third Reich on September 3 and in November Daladier's government finally renounced the 1936 treaties with Syria and Lebanon.

The French government's announcement ended all illusions of Syrian independence. Violence and demonstrations erupted in Syria and Lebanon as outraged citizens struck out against continued French occupation and the naive governments the French had so easily duped. The magnitude of the eruption forced High Commissioner Gabriel Puaux to suspend both constitutions and assume direct French rule by decree. When Paris fell in June 1940, a French Vichy official, General Henri Dentz, replaced Puaux and continued to govern both countries by martial law.

LEBANON

In accordance with the Sykes-Picot Agreement, France occupied Mount Lebanon and the surrounding area late in 1918 and received Allied consent to mandatory control at San Remo in the spring of 1920. On September 1, 1920 France officially separated Lebanon from its larger Syrian mandate and created new boundaries, to include the predominantly Muslim coastal cities and the Biqa valley. The French High Commissioners for Syria and Lebanon established a Representative Council for Lebanon that elected its own president.

Lebanese agitation for even greater control of their affairs, coupled with the large uprisings in Syria, led High Commissioner Henri de Jouvenel to accept a Lebanese constitution and create the Republic of Lebanon in 1926. Lebanon's new status did not diminish French authority because France retained control of Lebanese monetary policies and foreign affairs; and the High Commissioner had the right to veto legislation of the Lebanese Chamber of Deputies. French authorities participated at all levels in policymaking and administration of the new republic. The *services speciaux,* supposedly information officers, were particularly obtrusive since they represented the eyes and ears of the French throughout Lebanon.

The constitution distributed seats in the Chamber of Deputies by confessional designation and allowed each religion representation commensurate with its proportion of the entire population. The Chamber of Deputies in turn elected the president, whose initial term of three years was altered in 1927 to a six-year, non-renewable term. There was an understanding that the president would be Christian, but the office was not yet restricted to the Maronite sect. Charles Dabbas, who was Greek Orthodox, became the first president and served two consecutive terms until 1932. He usually appointed prominent Maronites to serve as prime ministers, in part because most of the natural Muslim leaders refused to acknowledge the validity of Lebanon detached from Syria.

Dabbas's second term was troublesome as the Depression hit Lebanon. Lebanese struggled with the French for greater control over their affairs; Lebanese continued to differ over affiliation with their Arab neighbors; and the Maronites were split over who should succeed Dabbas. The French favored Emile Edde, a Maronite, whose fervent support for the French mandate and Christian control of Lebanon made his candidacy untenable to some Maronites and to almost every other group. Bishara al-Khoury, another Maronite, was much more acceptable to the wider spectrum of the Lebanese population because of his attempts to accommodate the needs of all Lebanese in the new state. Al-Khoury's commitment, however, to an Arab Lebanon that could maintain good relations with the greater Arab world, was unacceptable to the French. Al-Khoury could have won the upcoming election in 1932; Edde could not. Edde and his supporters blocked al-Khoury's election by withholding their support. When the Muslim president of the Chamber of Deputies, Shakyh Muhammad al-Jisr of Tripoli, presented himself as candidate for the presidency, the French commissioner, Henri Ponsot, saw no alternative to dissolving the Chamber of Deputies and suspending the constitution.

Since the presidential election was impossible, Ponsot appointed Dabbas to continue in office. Dabbas resigned after six months and the Commissioner placed executive powers in the hands of a Beirut Muslim, Abdallah Bayhum, who received the title of Secretary of State. The Commissioner then appointed a Maronite septuagenarian, Habib al-Sa'd, as president, to perform ceremonial functions.

Syrian Nationalist Party

Firm French control did not diminish the frustration of the various groups. The constant Muslim dissatisfaction at French and Lebanese Christian domination simmered but did not significantly erupt. An interesting coalition, however, called the Syrian Nationalist Party, which transcended religious delineations, developed in 1932 under the leadership of Antun Sa'ada, a Greek Orthodox. The party's raison d'etre was to confirm, within modern boundaries, a nation of Greater Syria that it contended had always existed, even when submerged in dominant empires. That nation included the regions of the Syrian-Lebanese mandate, Palestine, Transjordan, Iraq, and Cyprus. Sa'ada maintained that the religious and ethnic complexity of this natural political and economic entity could only fulfill its role by separating religion and politics. His generally well-educated followers were well organized and committed to accomplishing what they regarded as an historical mission. This party's activities, along with Muslim resistance, required diligent French efforts to sustain a separate Lebanon.

Unrest and Instability

In 1936 there was intense Arab unrest throughout the Middle East and the Palestinian and Syrian revolts against their respective mandatory Powers threatened to spill over into Lebanon. French Commissioner de Martel, without restoring the constitution, convened the Chamber of Deputies to conduct a presidential election to reduce opposition to French rule. The Francophile Emile Edde narrowly won the presidency, but he lacked widespread support even among the Maronites. Lebanese nationalists in the Chamber of Deputies, under the leadership of al-Khoury, demanded restoration of the constitution and a Franco-Syrian treaty to replace the mandate. Egypt and Syria were simultaneously involved in the same kind of negotiations with their occupational Powers. This movement toward treaties, which implied confirmation of national boundaries, spurred Muslims and the Syrian Nationalist Party to open resistance.

The Anglo-Egyptian Treaty went into effect in August, the Franco-Syrian treaty in September, and the Chamber unanimously approved the Franco-Lebanese Treaty on November 13. Lebanese Muslim deputies, who had slowly come to enjoy their role in the smaller Lebanese state, accepted the treaty. Much of the urban Muslim population, however, demonstrated and rioted in protest. The violence did not overturn the Lebanese government's approval of the treaty, which promised French sponsorship of Lebanon into the League of Nations in 1939.

Muslim violence inspired a Beirut pharmacist, Pierre Gemayel, to form a small, well-organized Kata'ib (Phalange) political party. The circumstances, and Gemayel's fascination with the fascist organizations in Spain, Italy, and Germany, moved the Phalangists to adopt a paramilitary approach from its inception.

President Edde demonstrated his appreciation of Khayr al-Din al-Ahdab's role in passing the treaty with France by appointing the Muslim leader prime minister in 1937. Edde's unexpected contribution to improved Muslim-Christian relations acknowledged the need for cooperation among the confessional groups to make Lebanon a viable nation when it would become independent in 1939. It was a gesture toward Sa'ada's advocacy of secularism but inadequate for Lebanese who desired union with Syria. Al-Ahdab's appointment established a precedent for a

Sunni Muslim always to be prime minister. The arrangement signaled a new dependence among Lebanon's political leaders to share political power, economic gains, and influence. The political leaders' commitment to this approach might well have been more a result of selfishness than of nationalism, but it proved a formula for survival for them and their troubled nation for forty years.

TRANSJORDAN

Ironically, Transjordan's future was destined to become intertwined with Palestine, west of the Jordan River, rather than with either the heart of Syria to the north or with the Hijaz to the south. As was the case with other places in the Levant, the vagaries of World War I and the whims of the Western nations superseded historical development, cultural affiliation, and economic logic to create a nation hardly anyone had imagined and almost no one wanted.

Even Abdullah bin Hussein al-Hashimi, the eventual primary beneficiary of the creation of Transjordan, was slow to conceive of the future state when he entered the historical stage. This unquestioned direct descendent of the Prophet Muhammad was the second son and favorite of Sharif Hussein al-Hashimi, who had agreed with the British to generate an Arab revolt against the Ottomans during World War I. Abdullah was a member of the first Ottoman parliament, but became disillusioned with the Turks as they reduced the role of Arabs in the empire and even threatened the traditional authority of his father in the Hijaz. He had explored the possibility of British support for an Arab revolt against the Ottomans seven months before war broke out and more than two years before his father formally agreed to do so. Not the least of his efforts during the war was a persistent attempt to get recognition of his father as king of as much of the Arab world as the British and other Great Powers would accept. This proved good training for his extensive later attempts to obtain royal status on his own behalf.

Abdullah's strong ambitions from very early in his life helped build a poor reputation, because he did not combine his ambition with either hard work or good performance. While he was usually cordial and charming, hardly anyone outside of his immediate circle of friends either respected or trusted him. He frequently seemed unaware of this as he sought aggrandizement for his family and increasingly for himself.

Hashemite Successes, Failures, and Ambitions

Abdullah played an inglorious role during World War I, as he spent most of his time ineptly besieging the Turkish garrison at Medina, which never surrendered. His brother, Feisal, led the successful Arab effort that swept the other Turks out of the Hijaz and marched triumphantly to Damascus. The General Syrian Congress in March 1920 rewarded Feisal, Hussein's third son, with the Syrian throne. It also acknowledged Abdullah as king of Iraq. But neither fulfilled these roles as the French expelled Feisal from Syria in July 1920 and the British declared its mandate over Iraq at San Remo in April.

Hashemite ambitions of ruling the Arab world, as a reward for helping the British win the war and liberating the Arabs from Turkish domination, seemed groundless. Even the Hijaz was in danger of falling to the westward thrust of Ibn

Saud and his Wahhabi supporters. Abdullah's own part in that war resulted in his humiliating defeat at the battle of Turaba in May 1918.

Abdullah, who was always the most assertive Hashemite, refused to accept the fate of his brother and his family. Soon after his brother's expulsion, he began to organize a tribal force in the Hijaz and lower Transjordan to regain the Syrian throne. He established a base at Maan in southern Transjordan toward the end of November 1920. Many of Feisal's supporters had fled to Transjordan and welcomed Abdullah's military initiative, because Feisal only pursued a diplomatic effort in a trip to Europe. Fear that France might assert control over Transjordan as a traditional appendage of Syria heightened Arab concern. This was a realistic concern, since the lines between British and French mandates were not clearly defined. As Abdullah arrived in Amman on March 2, 1921 British experts on the Middle East were converging on Cairo to meet with Winston Churchill, the colonial secretary, who opened the Cairo Conference on March 12.

The Cairo Conference decided to compensate the Hashemite war effort by creating a kingdom of Iraq for Feisal. They were unsure about how to deal with Abdullah to deter his campaign against French occupation of Syria. Churchill, therefore, met Abdullah in Jerusalem after the conference ended and offered him temporary authority in Transjordan, which this Hashemite claimant could use as a base from which to negotiate with France for his elevation to a throne in Damascus. While this suggestion seems fanciful, it fueled Abdullah's ambition to unite all of Greater Syria under his control. This goal became his abiding passion for the rest of his life.

Dependence upon Great Britain

Abdullah's early experience in Transjordan provided him neither fulfillment nor encouragement. The British subsidy was meager and he had virtually no tax-collecting capacity and, for that matter, no revenue base in the population of perhaps 250,000. For months he had no home of his own and was unable to bring his family from the Hijaz. Arab nationalists, mostly Syrians, flocked to Amman and dominated his early government to the consternation of France, Great Britain, and native Transjordanians. But he and the nationalists had a symbiotic relationship as both saw the other as their hope of restoring Arab control of Syria. Within a year, under pressure from all sides, Abdullah eased the nationalists out of the government. However, their continued activities in the safety of Transjordan presented both an internal problem and a source of regional and international tension.

Transjordan became totally dependent upon British diplomatic, financial, and military support. Britain interceded to prevent French retaliation against Transjordan as a center of Arab nationalist activities. The British put down tribal uprisings against Abdullah and forcefully prevented Ibn Saud from extending his expanding kingdom into southern Transjordan. Although the British supported him, they did not clearly define either his role or their relationship with him and Transjordan. Highly placed officials in both the colonial and foreign offices strongly advocated his removal because of personal dislike, charges of incompetence and fiscal irresponsibility, and his relentless pursuit of Hashemite aggrandizement. The British delayed acknowledging him as emir until May 25, 1923, after they had assumed control over the small but effective military force, the Arab Legion. Even this agreement contained conditional clauses that left Transjordan's status undefined. Much to the emir's chagrin, his government remained under the supervision of the British High Commissioner for Palestine, who reported on it to the League of Nations as part of the British mandate.

Abdullah's visit to the Hijaz to perform the *hajj* from June to August in 1924 demonstrated his tenuous hold on power. Most agree that only upon his acceptance of a humiliating set of demands, primarily related to his expenditure of funds, did the British allow him to return to Transjordan. It seems likely, however, that if the British thought they had any alternative to Abdullah, they would have issued their "ultimatum" in Maan, just after he crossed the border, rather than wait until he got to Amman. The truth is that soon after Abdullah assumed authority in Transjordan, the British discovered they needed him as much as he needed them. Although most of his British advisers and supervisors grew to dislike the little Hashemite, his family stature and awareness of world affairs gave Transjordan credibility no native Transjordanian could provide. Also, as an outsider, he could remain aloof from many British conflicts with the tribes. He was the only neutral force in disputes among the tribes and between the British and the tribes. His experience with the complicated diplomacy of the Ottomans, whom he admired, served him well in Transjordan. Little wonder he smiled when the British admonished and instructed him on their expectations, but continued to behave in his own inimitable way.

Hashemite fortunes were crumbling at this time, except for Feisal's success in Iraq. Ibn Saud gained control of Mecca by the middle of October 1924 and forced Hussein and Ali, his heir, into exile. The British refused to allow either Abdullah or Feisal to provide refuge for their father in fear of displeasing Ibn Saud. Thus, the sharif, king of the Hijaz, leader of the Arab revolt, and self-proclaimed Caliph only seven months earlier, lived for six years away from his family and people on Cyprus before the British permitted him to join Abdullah in time to die on June 4, 1931.

Abdullah's subservience to Britain prevented him from giving even verbal support to the major Arab uprising in Syria in the summer of 1925. Increasingly, Arab nationalists lost faith in him as a potential catalyst for their movement. People no longer fled to Transjordan to raise the flag of liberation but to escape the violence in Syria, Saudi expansion in the Arabian peninsula, and the unrest in Palestine.

Transjordan, which remained tied to Great Britain, was in no position to help any part of the Arab world gain independence. Its inability to even come close to meeting the costs of a modern state made it dependent on Great Britain regardless of other matters. Transjordan's situation was no better after it finally reached a formal agreement on its relationship with Great Britain on February 20, 1928, as Britain continued to control finances, military matters, and foreign affairs. The agreement provided for a twenty-one member Legislative Council in compliance with the British stated purpose of developing democratic institutions in Transjordan. However, since they controlled the appointment of the chief minister, who, in turn, controlled all legislation and presided over the legislature, it was clear both inside and outside of Transjordan that the emirate and its emir were puppets of the British.

This sham constitutional structure, like the later one in 1947, indicates the hypocrisy in much of Britain's relationship with Transjordan. From his earliest days, British officials claimed that Abdullah's despotism prevented their support for elevating his status above that of temporary custodian of Transjordan. Similar charges persisted through the years, while they impeded the establishment of representative institutions well past the time the British recognized him as king in 1946.

Attention to Palestine

The Transjordanian emir turned his attention to Palestine after opportunities in Syria and the Arabian peninsula seemed closed to him. However, he never gave up hopes of acquiring either and fostered unrest in both. He even made overtures to become the king of Iraq when Feisal died in 1933 and especially after Ali, his oldest brother, died in 1935. In short, he realized that none of his ambitions were possible until he expanded his base beyond the limitations of Transjordan.

Although he publicly voiced all the expected Arab protests against Zionism, his opposition was neither deep nor sincere. After all, the center of Zionist activities lay outside of his original plans for expansion to the north and south. He even visualized the possibility of a Zionist National Home as part of his larger holdings. Zionist possession of both the capital and expertise he needed was appealing to the impoverished Hashemite. The Zionists welcomed his receptiveness since he was the only Arab leader to do so and because they hoped to find a way to open Transjordan to Jewish immigration, or, at least, to obtain his cooperation in accepting Palestinians who became dispossessed by Zionist land purchases in Palestine. In 1932–1933 he scandalized the Arab world when word leaked out that he had taken money from the Jewish Agency in return for options to purchase land and other concessions in Transjordan. At this juncture, Zionism was perceived as a renewed threat as Hitler's rise to power generated an increased Jewish immigration to Palestine. Abdullah denied accepting money from the Zionists while he continued to accept the payments the Jewish Agency hoped would reward them some day when anti-Zionist sentiments were not as strong in the Arab world.

Increased Zionist immigration in the mid-1930s, however, resulted in the Palestinian general strike and widespread violence in 1936. Abdullah, along with fellow rulers in Saudi Arabia, Iraq, and Yemen managed to broker an end of the strike after six months of violence. Abdullah cooperated with the Peel Commission that investigated the Palestinian uprising and he even offered to take some Jewish settlers in Transjordan under proper restrictions. His role helped ingratiate him to the Jewish Agency and to the British; both rewarded him monetarily for his efforts. His fellow Arabs knew nothing of this, but they uniformly denounced his endorsement of the July 7, 1937 Peel Commission's recommendation of partition for Palestine. This, along with his good relations with Turkey, which seemed on the verge of annexing Alexandretta from Syria, demonstrated his lack of commitment to Arab concerns.

Abdullah's endorsement of partition excluded him as a possible rallying point for Palestinian frustration, which erupted in even greater violence in October 1937. Their own leaders were either under arrest or in exile as the British used major military force, collective punishment, and massive arrests to quell the uprising. When the Woodhead Partition Commission renewed the study of the cause of violence in Palestine, Abdullah again had the dubious distinction of being the only notable Arab to cooperate with it. He suggested that partition was not, in fact, the answer, but that all of Palestine, including a Jewish National Home, should merge with Transjordan. His overall concept was one of the most statesmanlike proposals ever made to solve a near impossible situation. It would have pleased none of the major parties, which therein established its merit. Abdullah, however, enjoyed such low esteem, especially among the Arabs, that his solution was untenable. He did not improve his status when he was also the only Arab leader who openly approved the 1939 White Paper, which the British issued in an attempt to tidy up the Middle East theater in anticipation of a major war in Europe.

IRAQ

A day after declaring war on the Ottoman Empire on November 5, 1914, Britain occupied al-Faw at the mouth of the Shatt al-Arab in its first act of hostility against the Ottomans. Two weeks later, British forces moved 120 miles inland and occupied Basra to protect British lives and property there and provide a better buffer between Ottoman forces and the Abadan refineries across the border in Persia, which were the real British strategic concern. Their first attempt to penetrate to Baghdad in the fall of 1915, in compensation for the debacle at Gallipoli, led to the surrender of General Townshend's army. The British finally swept up the Tigris in the spring of 1917 and occupied Baghdad on March 11. While the area south of Baghdad remained under firm British control, the Euphrates valley to the west, with the Shiah holy cities of al-Najaf and Karbala, experienced little British presence and became the center of resistance to British occupation.

The large number of British officials and predominantly Indian troops was disconcerting to several elements in Iraq, while the Jews, who dominated trade and banking, welcomed them. Shiah Iraqis resented the British presence as non-Muslims. Early adherence to British authority was also slow to develop, in part because some Iraqis could not imagine that the Turks, who had dominated Mesopotamia for over three hundred years, would not return after the war and render retribution to anyone who helped the invaders. Arab nationalists feared the British would remain and impede their independence.

General Maude's proclamation after entering Baghdad, as well as a joint Anglo-French declaration on November 7, 1918, assured the Iraqis that British occupation was only for their liberation and that it was a necessary step toward Arab self-rule. The carefully worded statements masked British intentions of remaining in Iraq as arranged in the Hussein-McMahon and Sykes-Picot agreements. British assurances could not, however, prevent feelings from running high among many in behalf of Iraqi independence. Meanwhile, Iraq remained under British military authority, which reached to the northern city of Mosul within days after the Ottomans agreed to the Mudros Armistice. Iraqis, however, expected the British to leave once the war ended and allow the Arabs to govern themselves in keeping with President Wilson's Fourteen Points and earlier British promises.

Disappointments of the Peace

Iraqi nationalists welcomed the news from Syria after the Syrian National Congress declared Feisal their king on March 20, 1920 and the Iraqis attached to the Hashemite government in Damascus nominated his older brother, Abdullah, as king of Iraq. Iraqis were surprised, therefore, when six weeks later, Britain and

France announced at San Remo on April 24 that Syria would become a French mandate and Iraq, including Mosul, would have the same status under Britain.

With reinforcements in place and British consent, General Gouraud issued Feisal an ultimatum to submit to French authority by July 14. To prevent bloodshed, Feisal consented. This was against the advice of many of his closest advisers. In fact, it disappointed his entire following, many of whom fought valiantly before the French prevailed on July 25. Feisal left the country rather than serve in some reduced capacity under the French.

Much of Iraq began to seethe with anger at British betrayal of Arab independence in Iraq and Syria. Sunnis and Shiah held joint meetings in each others' mosques in Baghdad, and the coffee house debates became occupied with schemes to rid Iraq of British occupation and rule. Large-scale hostilities developed from August to October, which cost the financially strapped British government about £40 million and four hundred lives. British casualties would, no doubt, have been higher except for their liberal use of the RAF, which they employed then and later to strike terror into lightly armed tribesmen. The most severe fighting occurred in Shiah tribal areas surrounding al-Najaf and Karbala of the mid- and lower Euphrates, where British presence had never been strong.

While Shiah resistance resulted from religious and provincial concerns, nationalists in Baghdad, and among the Sunnis in general, only remained quiet in the face of overwhelming British strength. Kurds did not become involved, as they were not interested in Arab nationalism and some pinned their hopes on independence, since the northern border of British mandatory Iraq was still in dispute.

The scale and expense of the 1920 uprising and the mood of the country alerted the British of the need to approach their role in Iraq with great care. Strong elements of the British Parliament and public opinion resisted the acquisition of Mesopotamia, even though specialists assured them that financial benefits abounded and that the Arabs welcomed British rule. The conquest and occupation of Iraq had already cost Britain about £300 million, while the Iraqi uprising and widespread unrest in the region demonstrated Arab revulsion toward British occupation.

British Mandate

The British government countered by returning the widely respected Sir Percy Cox to Iraq, where he quelled the rebellion, in part by establishing an Arab government. This took place in late October, under the presidency of a prominent Sunni religious leader, Abd al-Rahman al-Galiani. The Council of State was composed of religious and landed notables. Sir Percy, as High Commissioner, clearly retained real authority along with the British advisers who shadowed each council member.

A major function of Cox's carefully chosen government was to win approval of a British proposal for a permanent Iraqi governmental structure. Under the guidance of the Colonial Secretary, Winston Churchill, and with Cox in attendance, those attending the Cairo Conference of March 1921 decided to finesse the tender feelings of the Iraqis, the Hashemites, and concerned British opinion by nominating Feisal as king of Iraq and rewarding his brother, Abdullah, with the title of emir of Transjordan. The establishment of monarchies provided a veneer of independence that Churchill and his Arab specialists thought might cause the new and provocative term, "mandate," to fall into disuse.

Semifree Kingdom

Feisal arrived in Iraq and was soon surrounded by Iraqis and some Syrians who had served with him in the Revolt and in Syria. However, he was, at this stage, much more under the tutelage of Cox's secretary, Lady Gertrude Bell, whose understanding of the region and warm rapport with its inhabitants and Feisal fitted her for the singular task of tutoring the royal nominee on the tribal shaykhs and other notables of his new country. Toward this end she arranged audiences with most of the important Iraqi notables, including the Jewish leaders of Baghdad. Oaths of allegiance from notables and the expulsion of Talib al-Naqib, a self-proclaimed candidate, moved the Council of State to elect Feisal on July 11 with the agreement that he would be a constitutional monarch. British authorities arranged a questionable plebiscite, excluding the Mosul area, which was still under contention with Turkey, that showed 96 percent of his subjects approved Feisal's selection. His coronation occurred with full British pomp on August 23, complete with the playing of "God Save the King," since Lady Bell had not yet helped him write an Iraqi anthem.

The new king was the only choice that a majority could regard as anything other than a factional shaykh. While he was only thirty-eight years old, his distinguished lineage from the Prophet, his experience in Istanbul and Mecca, his leadership of the Revolt, his postwar diplomacy in London and Paris, his sincere effort to establish an Arab kingdom in Syria, and his close association with Arab nationalists provided him with credentials no other Arab could match. Also, he possessed a warm charm and quiet wisdom to accompany his natural regal appearance. He tempered his commitment to Arab nationalism with an understanding of Arab limitations in the immediate postwar era due to their diverse outlooks, centuries of disunity, and economic and educational dissimilarities. All who knew him understood that he cooperated with the British out of necessity, as a means of developing his adopted realm for genuine independence. It is difficult to imagine any circumstances that could have forged the modern nation of Iraq, with its large Kurdish minority, which would not have required the interim period of Feisal's reluctant concert with the British.

The coronation of their candidate did not assure Britain of control of Iraq or continued domination of the region. Saadist activities in Egypt; riots in Palestine; Soviet adventures and Reza Khan's coup in Iran; Saudi unification forays in Arabia; Kemalist victories in Turkey; strikes and demonstrations in Syria; and the uprising in Iraq, compelled the British to treat Feisal's government with apparent respect. They, therefore, determined to enter a treaty relationship with the Kingdom of Iraq, while quietly fulfilling their obligations to the League of Nations over mandatory Mesopotamia.

Anglo-Iraqi Treaty

Feisal insisted on a treaty with as much reciprocity as possible, especially on financial points, in view of his limited income. The Council of Ministers accepted a less than satisfactory treaty on October 21, 1922, with the provision that the as yet unelected Constitutional Assembly approve it. The situation was even more awkward because Iraq's borders remained undefined. Iraq, therefore, had no particular status in the League of Nations, whereas that body approved mandates for Palestine, Syria, and Lebanon on July 24, 1922.

Election procedures began after the Council approved the treaty, but border disputes with Ibn Saud, negotiations with Turkey, the departure of Sir Percy Cox, and large-scale resistance to the treaty delayed the elections. A formal treaty of peace between the Powers and Turkey at Lausanne on July 24, 1923 clarified little because it did not settle the Turco-Iraqi question over Mosul. Even promises of better terms later were not enough to entice any combination of delegates to approve a treaty with Britain, which popular opinion still regarded as a mandate. The king finally convened the Assembly in Baghdad on March 27, 1924, where debate proceeded for more than two months amid considerable public outcry. Threats from the British to ask for League of Nations assistance unless the Assembly approved the treaty by June 10 failed to bring results. The prime minister, Jafar al-Askari, coerced a late night quorum of sixty-nine of the one hundred assemblymen to convene, but could still only get thirty-seven to approve ratification. Such was the strained atmosphere of Anglo-Iraqi relations as they began their treaty relationship. A strong sense of Iraqi outrage followed Britain's reoccupation in 1941 and its attempts for a renewed assertion of influence through the Baghdad Pact in 1955.

The absence of significant resistance to either the constitution or the election law allowed approval of both in August. Thus, three full years after Feisal became king, Iraq finally had both a formal permanent government and a formal relationship with the member of the Great Powers the San Remo Conference had assigned to guide Iraq to acceptance into the fraternity of sovereign states. Britain presented Iraq's case to the League of Nations with a promise to that body that Britain would sponsor Iraq's independence as early as possible. The League acquiesced to the thinly veiled mandate on September 27, 1924, but made it clear that both Iraq and Britain were answerable to the League for developments in Mesopotamia and the for behavior of both the tutor and the pupil toward all other nations.

Government Structure

Britain's influence on financial and military matters, as well as the continuation of British advisers in all governmental departments, gave it domination over the policies of the fledgling nation. The king, who reluctantly remained under close British rein, exercised most of his powers through his cabinet, which he could chose, and the parliament, whose membership he could shape through the two-stage system of election. Nevertheless, the controlled constitutional process became the method of government that even the most dissatisfied soon recognized they must penetrate in order to have influence.

Iraq was politically more stable than it appeared during its monarchical period from 1921 to 1958. Fifty-nine different cabinets during that time seems to belie such an observation. All but two of those cabinets, however, obtained their authority from the monarch, who also controlled the electoral process, the composition of the parliament, and the right to call for an election at any time. Even this explains little without also understanding that, although Iraq was apparently authoritarian, there was usually enough freedom of the press to reflect strong dissenting views, and enough electoral freedom to allow the election of ten- to fifteen-percent uncontrolled legislators. Public outcry through either of these means often caused adjustments in the cabinet to place the right ministers in the sensitive ministries to meet the immediate need. The changes usually signalled the beginning of either the diametrically opposite approaches of concession or repression.

More than anything else, these changes reflect the insecurity of the monarchy, which had to contend with the conflicting aspirations of the British, the dominant landed class, the restless and unrepresented urban poor, a frustrated younger professional class with no influence, Iraqi nationalists, dissatisfied minorities, Arab nationalists, and ambitious, often petty, professional politicians. Contemporary and later assessments of King Feisal as "weak" fail to consider these grave, disturbing variables. Characterizations of Nuri al-Said as "tyrannical" are equally questionable.

Most people agree that, for many different reasons, Mesopotamia has only prospered under strong, usually authoritarian, regimes. Blatant authoritarianism was not, however, a choice for Feisal and his successors, regardless of the merit of such an approach. Great Britain was, after all, committed to constitutionalism for Iraq and could not have obtained League of Nations approval for any other kind of government for Iraq. Restricted as it was, constitutionalism prevailed during Iraq's monarchical period except for two brief military dictatorships.

In this context, the constant factor of Nuri al-Said's role under the monarchy makes sense. Otherwise, his ubiquitousness and his frequent status of being in office as premier or foreign minister, or being out of office, but still in control, defies comprehension. He was, in fact, the matrix that held the complex Iraqi political system together. At his will, by persuasion or with overt coercion, Nuri could usually obtain a parliament to match the cabinet of his choice or visa versa.

This unique role evolved out of his long association with Feisal, which dated back to the Arab revolt against the Ottomans, where, as T.E. Lawrence observed, Nuri had demonstrated that he was at his best and was most calm in the most treacherous situations. Feisal trusted and respected him. Nuri respected reality. He was free from ideological predilections and accepted the presence, and even the importance, of Great Britain in Iraq in the formative years of the semi-independent monarchy. His quest was for full statehood for Iraq under conditions that would guarantee its safety from internal and external threats. He appreciated equally the reality of the dominant role of the landed class in Iraq, although he seems to have had a genuine interest in improving the standard of living for the less fortunate. He understood the yearnings of frustrated Arab nationalists, especially the young army officers, but he thought they were impetuous, unrealistic, and naively receptive to demigods. In short, Nuri pragmatically made the best of a bad situation to hold Iraq together with the very strong conviction that the constructive use of its oil revenues could result in a prosperous, educated, and powerful nation. Iraq could then enjoy parity with other nations, escape subservience to any regional foe, and perhaps restore Baghdad to leadership of the Arab world.

Much to the chagrin of Feisal and the Arab nationalists, due to British insistence, the army remained small, and as such, had little influence on policies. The task of keeping order and suppressing rebellion rested primarily with the British and the mercenary Nestorian Christian Assyrian levies that Britain allowed to migrate from Turkey. Significantly, Sunnis filled most of the high positions in the government and military, while Shii, as under the Ottomans, provided most of the soldiers who seldom rose above noncommissioned rank.

The British and the Iraqi government understandably courted the favor of the large landowners, who had direct contact with, and great influence over, the predominantly rural population. Shaykhly interests dominated in the cabinet and the legislature, while the Tribal Disputes Code exempted the vast tribal regions from the central legal system, except in particularly dire cases. Anglo-Hashemite and landed-elite interests became so intertwined that a threat to one became a threat to all. Real political parties did not develop in this arrangement, but nascent, often sub-rosa, parties emerged, particularly among the urban classes under leadership of the intelligentsia. In contrast with the ruling, landed elite, opposition parties and groups all had agendas and some possessed ideologies.

Government expenditures usually favored the agricultural regions where the landed elite prevailed and most of the population resided. Also, Iraq's marginal economy and the reluctance of Iraqis to pay taxes precluded major projects to address social ills that resulted from a steady migration of people from the countryside to the cities. The government's initial attention to the rural areas out of political expediency soon became habit. Governmental benefits to the great landowners caused them to overlook the fact that their aid to the extension of central authority into the hinterlands spelled their demise in the future. Royal and shaykhly disregard for the urban elements fostered frustration and bitterness that threatened them both, especially if combined with well-placed elements of the military.

The Move to Independence

Most politically active and vocal elements in Iraq repudiated any merit of remaining affiliated with either Great Britain or League of Nations supervision. Their strong desire for full independence caused problems for the British and Iraqis who did not share their views. The nationalists ignored the fact that Iraq had come into existence under the new rules of post-World War I and could not acquire international recognition without satisfying the standards of the League of Nations, especially in regard to the protection of Iraqi minorities. Great Britain and the Iraqi government had to meet very specific requirements before the League would approve British withdrawal and welcome Iraq into the family of nations.

Feisal and some of his advisers, especially Nuris al-Said, realized that Iraq was still weak and remained a very socially, ethnically, and religiously fractured society that lacked both an identity and national integrity. They appreciated the necessity of following the international procedures and meeting the qualifications, under British sponsorship, even though other nations had never been subjected to such regulations. Great Britain was, for the most part, a willing partner in accelerating Iraqi independence, largely to escape the financial burden of administering the country. This approach was predicated, however, on establishing a treaty relationship that would guarantee the protection of British oil interests and the right to maintain military bases in an independent Iraq. The shape of the future began to emerge in the Anglo-Iraqi treaty of December 14, 1927 when the British agreed to relinquish some control and promised to sponsor Iraq's membership into the League of Nations by 1932.

Iraq's superior financial situation, along with a reliable governmental structure, helps account for it being the first mandate to gain independence. Its oil assets put it in a class by itself. Iraqis realized this and chafed at the failure of the Turkish Petroleum Company to accelerate oil production. A seventy-five year concession to the oil rights eliminated any reason for British oil interests to concentrate on Iraqi oil that required the construction of more than a thousand miles of pipelines to the Mediterranean ports. Negotiations of rights of way and transit fees with French-

Lower Mesopotamia

mandatory Syria complicated the development of Iraqi oil to export levels. In addition, the oil concessions in Iran were of shorter duration and the oil deposits were convenient to shipping facilities.

Pressure from the League of Nations Mandate Commission moved the Turkish Petroleum Company, which became the Iraq Petroleum Company in 1929, to speed up production. The discovery of a major deposit near Kirkuk in 1927 was perhaps of even greater influence. By 1931 League pressure and the promise for profit led to an agreement that provided Iraq with £400,000 annually while a pipeline across Syria was under construction with a completion deadline of 1936. The pipeline was actually completed by 1934. In the meantime other agreements yielded additional revenue. This new income increased Iraq's ability to demonstrate its capacity for self-government and provided the central government funds to provide services that could quiet some domestic criticism.

Both Great Britain and Iraq manifested considerable desire to convince the international community of Iraq's maturity. British recognition of Iraq's independence was an important step in this process. Iraq had never ratified the treaty of 1927, but Nuri al-Said took personal responsibility for negotiating a more extensive treaty, which the two parties signed on June 30, 1930. The terms of the treaty constituted the conditions under which Britain recognized Iraq's independence. Britain retained the right to maintain military bases in Iraq, transport troops through those bases and over Iraqi territory, and serve as the exclusive source of military advice and materiel for Iraq. In case of war, Britain had the right to defend Iraq and use all necessary Iraqi facilities to achieve that mission. Britain obtained diplomatic precedence in Iraq and the two nations promised to avoid alliances contrary to the other's interests.

Nuri obtained ratification of the treaty and Iraq, thereby, became independent, but the League of Nations neither recognized Iraq's sovereignty nor the end of Britain's obligation toward Iraq as a ward of that body. Nuri studiously mended relations with Iraq's minorities, especially the Kurds, and entered agreements with neighboring Arab states to demonstrate Iraq's tranquility both nationally and internally.

After considerable careful scrutiny, the League of Nations accepted Iraq as a member on October 3, 1932. Thus, Iraq gained full nationhood through an often begrudging adherence to the rules of the international community. Feisal and Nuri gained their triumph through submission to British demands, which many Iraqis regarded as demeaning and limiting. Britain's residual rights under the 1930 treaty remained the most provocative single issue in Iraq's internal concerns until the end of the monarchy in 1958. Feisal's unexpected death on September 8, 1933 denied his kingdom any healing effect his leadership could have offered. It also deprived him of the opportunity to demonstrate his capacity to govern with an increasingly adequate income and free from concern of having to please the British and the League of Nations.

Ghazi

Iraq changed with the ascension of twenty-one year old Ghazi to the throne when Feisal died on September 8, 1933. This young, uneducated monarch preferred the fast life and fast cars over care for the delicate balancing of Iraq's complex political composition under continued British influence. Ghazi, in fact, was a strong

Arab nationalist, who abhorred the patience his father and his father's advisers had demonstrated toward the British. He, like so many young Arabs, deplored continuation of all vestiges of the mandates and, in particular, the imposition of Zionist immigration upon Palestine. His fervent Arab nationalism put him in conflict with the British and elevated his stature among Iraqi youth and the younger elements of the Iraqi officer corps. Understandably, he appalled the British and aroused Iraqi passions when he spoke heatedly in behalf of the liberation of Palestine and also urged the annexation of Kuwait to Iraq. Apart from this provocative role, Ghazi was unable to give direction to Iraq.

His attitudes, however, encouraged the army, and especially the young officers, to become involved in all areas of Iraqi policymaking. The Iraqi army was still small and poorly armed as a result of British policies, but, because of reduced British control after Iraq's independence in 1930, it had more freedom to grow in strength and stature than any other Arab army. From its beginning, Iraq had a strong military tradition, since its first king and the men who shaped the nation during his reign had risen to prominence as military men. In addition, the Prussian approach to the role of the army in society permeated every level of Iraqi education from the earliest days of the new state and especially at the time Ghazi assumed the throne.

An Increased Role for the Army

The Iraqi army's brutal suppression of the Assyrians just at the time Ghazi succeeded his father galvanized the Iraqi public while it outraged much of the world. Iraqi perception of the massacre as a national triumph and the army's commander, General Bakr Sidqi, as a hero, is only understandable by appreciation of the popular belief that the Assyrian levies had been a principle instrument for British control of Iraq. Increasingly, in fact, Iraqis and other Arab nationalists looked to the Iraqi army as the best hope of liberating the entire Arab world from imperialist control and Zionist intrusion. Iraqi officers, like many others in the region, admired Kemal Ataturk's success in Turkey and aspired to emulate him. The army would, however, require fuller development to fulfill this role. Military growth could only occur through commitment on the part of the government to appropriate the necessary funds and unrestricted pursuit of all possible sources of military materiel and training. Most believed that the treaty with Great Britain, which allowed it to maintain bases in Iraq, was inimical to Iraqi and Arab interests. Britain's right to be the exclusive supplier of military advice and materiel guaranteed the continuation of an Iraqi military at a level only capable of suppressing internal uprisings. With widespread support, therefore, the army began to assert itself to support ministers who shared their view of the army and Iraq's destiny to liberate the Arab world, beginning with Palestine.

The army officers, like other elements of Iraq, usually used the constitutional structure, which in many respects they disliked, to institute their agenda. The old politicians simply changed to military patrons and continued to provide most of the leadership in the period from 1933 through 1941 when the Palace lost control and the army chose cabinets. Yasin al-Hashimi, Feisal's first chief-of-staff when he was governor and king of Syria, and Nuri al-Said, Feisal's first chief-of-staff of Iraq, were well suited to play the new game. Yasin, who had substantial credentials because of his opposition to Feisal and al-Said's cooperation with the

British, emerged by 1935–1936 as the man the army could rely upon. Astute observers regarded him as the most capable man in Iraq, but the king did not trust his loyalty and probably feared both his ability and his ambitions. Although he had held several cabinet posts in earlier governments, the army helped him obtain the prime ministership, which he coveted, in 1935. His twenty-month premiership was autocratic, but gave Iraq a strong sense of nationalist direction at the expense of personal liberties and the abolition of all political parties other than his own. This did not disappoint many officers who found democratic institutions cumbersome, indecisive, and subject to great swings of direction. Al-Hashimi even found it advisable to make al-Said his foreign minister in order to curb his rival's independent activities.

Bakr Sidqi's Coup

Iraqi politics took a dramatic turn in 1936 when a former supporter of al-Hashimi, General Bakr Sidqi, seized power, rather than simply influence the king to change the government. This former Ottoman officer of Kurdish lineage was well known for his annihilation of the Assyrians and his suppression of the Shiah tribal uprisings. He was, however, uneasy with the pan-Arabist direction of Iraq and his inability, as a Kurd, to obtain the position of chief-of-staff. He aligned himself with Hikmat Sulaiman, a frequent holder of ministerial position, who, however, had never obtained the premiership. Sulaiman, in turn, had recently aligned with the populist (al-Ahali) party of Kamel al-Chadirchi. This moderately leftist party had in common with General Sidqi a desire to concentrate upon Iraqi, rather than pan-Arab, concerns. Sidqi's personal ambitions and al-Ahali's ideological inclinations gave them common grounds for disliking al-Hashini's authoritarian regime.

This first genuine military coup in modern Arab history only endured from November 29, 1936 to August 17, 1937. The personal brutality of Sidqi and his neglect of Arab issues in behalf of Kurds and other minorities, as well as the al-Ahali threat to traditional vested interests, spelled their doom. Arab nationalist officers killed Sidqi and reestablished commitment to pan-Arab affairs as the test for holding office.

EGYPT

A series of British administrators with the title of High Commissioner held office in Egypt during World War I and worked with the Sultan and his cabinet. British interests and war needs dominated the four-year period. Egypt became the base for British operations in the eastern Mediterranean and southwest Asia. Hundreds of thousands of British troops and other personnel were stationed in, and passed through, Egypt. While some Egyptians prospered by performing services for the British, the war was a hardship on most. Taxes were high, confiscation of necessities for the war were frequent, forced labor and conscription into military service occurred, and the great demand for the limited quantity of goods drove prices sky high. In addition, most Egyptians were not anti-Ottoman and disliked the role they played in the Allied war against their brethren Muslims. Martial law prevented any overt display of Egyptian discontent during the war.

Peace and Dissatisfaction

Egyptian officials and nationalists formulated various plans for liberating Egypt from British control after the war. Saad Zaghlul remained the leader of Egypt's nationalist aspirations and it became clear that no arrangement would be acceptable without his approval. He had no official status to speak for Egypt under the martial law that continued after the war ended, but he insisted that he should lead an Egyptian delegation (*Wafd al-Misri*) to London to present the Egyptian case to Whitehall. His agitation and the unrest it caused led to his deportation to Malta in March 1919. The resulting violence in Egypt forced the new High Commissioner Allenby to free Zaghlul and allow him and the Wafd to take their case directly to the Peace Conference in Paris. Like many other minor delegations, the Wafd obtained no hearing but learned, instead, that President Wilson, the wartime advocate of self-determination, recognized a continued British protectorate in Egypt.

In March 1920, Zaghlul negotiated with Lord Milner, who had been trying to draft a new arrangement between Egypt and Great Britain for nearly a year. Their tentative agreement in August was unsatisfactory to Zaghlul, but actually made more concessions to Egypt than the British government was willing to accept. The level of discontent in Egypt convinced Allenby that independence for Egypt was necessary, although his resentment of Zaghlul's insistence on a virtual British withdrawal and the demonstrations he generated led the High Commissioner to exile the Wafd leader to the Seychelle Islands in December 1921. Allenby, who understood how near the entire postwar arrangement was to falling apart, went to London, where he convinced his government to grant Egyptian independence.

Great Britain announced on February 28, 1922 that Egypt was an independent kingdom, but continued to rule by martial law until July. British and Egyptian officials had agreed upon a constitution in April that was not subject to approval of the legislature. Zaghlul returned from exile and led his party to winning an overwhelming majority of 188 seats in the 215-member Chamber of Deputies. No one else could possibly be the prime minister under these circumstances. The constitution granted most real power to the king, who remained under close British supervision and the army remained under British leadership. Britain's continued hold was the result of a *fait accompli,* rather than any formal relationship with Egypt.

Events soon proved that British power, rather than the new constitution, still governed Egypt. Prime Minister Zaghlul, an uncompromising nationalist, continued to provoke resistance to the British. The assassination of Sir Lee Stack, governor-general of Sudan and *Sirdar,* on September 23, 1924, prompted Allenby to confront Zaghlul with demands for retribution that made clear he held Zaghlul and the Wafd responsible for Stack's death. A shaken Zaghlul agreed to all except those that required recognition of British control over the Sudan. Zaghlul resigned and his successor made some concessions to the British. In new elections, a combination of the conservative parties gained a majority but their members reelected Zaghlul as speaker of the Chamber of Deputies in March 1925. King Fuad, who had succeeded his brother in 1917, dismissed parliament out of resentment of Zaghlul's popularity and the difficulties his activities had caused with Britain. The Wafd won the next election more than a year later but Zaghlul agreed to allow a member of the conservative Liberal party to serve as Premier. Zaghlul died in August 1927.

The constitutional process became moribund as a succession of ministers held office because of their support for the king and the British. Prime Minister Mahmoud, one of the original Wafdists, suspended the constitution for three years in 1928. New elections in 1930 returned the Wafd under Nahas Pasha to power, but the king suspended parliament again because of Wafd opposition to an Anglo-Egyptian treaty, which was the main legislation for consideration. Ismail Sidki Pasha became Prime Minister until 1933 and imposed a new constitution that kept the Wafd out of power. He dictatorially kept order but had no way of achieving parliamentary approval of a treaty with Great Britain.

Axis activities by the mid-1930s inflamed matters throughout the Middle East. Major riots occurred in Egypt in November 1935 in connection with British reaction to Mussolini's aggression in Ethiopia. Egyptians reacted adversely to the build-up of British forces in Egypt following Hitler's invasion of the Rhineland, the Italian invasion of Ethiopia, the outbreak of the Spanish Civil War, the formation of the Axis, and the unrest in Palestine in 1936. King Fuad's death in April required the Chamber of Deputies to meet. In fact, there was already a plan to hold elections in the spring. Sir Miles Lampson had convinced Egyptian leaders that a treaty was beneficial to both Egypt and Great Britain.

The 1936 Anglo-Egyptian Treaty

British negotiations with Nahas Pasha produced a treaty that the new parliament, with a Wafd majority, ratified on August 26, 1936. The Anglo-Egyptian treaty, which implied a contract between equals, seemed to establish Egyptian sovereignty. It abolished the office of High Commissioner and limited British troops to the Suez Canal area for twenty years. A schedule for an end of the capitulations and foreign participation in the judicial system would give Egypt control over these two vital areas of traditional foreign leverage.

ARABIAN PENINSULA

Turkey's alliance with the Central Powers soon after the outbreak of World War I also increased British interest in the Arabian interior. While, in the past, the British had virtually ignored Ibn Saud and insisted on regarding him as a Turkish official in their limited contacts, they began to court his alliance. Within six months after the outbreak of the war, the British recognized him as the independent ruler of the Najd and its dependencies, although a year passed before they sent him any arms. Their main concern was to neutralize Ibn Saud and prevent him from attacking Britain's coastal shaykh allies.

Early developments in the war prevented Ibn Saud and the lands he controlled from gaining any further significance. British Indian forces quickly seized southern Mesopotamia and secured the Persian oil fields and the refinery at Abadan. The Gulf was firmly under British control through its military presence and alliances. Britain understandably relied upon Sharif Hussein to secure its even greater interests on the Arabian Red Sea coast. Ibn Saud lacked both the influence and strategic location that his Hashemite rival enjoyed.

Sharif Hussein had many attributes to recommend him as the best instrument for British policy. He was a Turkish official who had spent many years in Istanbul.

He was a direct descendent of the Prophet, who had governed the Muslim Holy Lands, which controlled much of the eastern coast of the vital Red Sea. Muslims worldwide were much more likely to accept his leadership instead of that of the unknown Ibn Saud, who was also tainted from his association with the fanatical Ikhwan, who were determined to establish *Wahhabism* in the land of the Prophet.

The Ikhwan recognized Ibn Saud as their Imam, although his commitment to the entirety of their position was questionable. The Ikhwan and Ibn Saud were also natural allies because of their mutual hatred of Sharif Hussein, albeit for different reasons. To Ibn Saud, Hussein was a pretentious impediment to his ambitions to control the Arabian peninsula. To the Ikhwan, Hussein was an apostate impediment to their desire to reestablish Islamic purity.

The Ikhwan and Ibn Saud began to reshape the borders and the future of the Arabian peninsula before the peace settlement in Paris ended the war that had bypassed them. Only British threats of reprisals prevented Ibn Saud from following up the major Ikhwan victory over Hashemite forces at Turaba on May 25, 1919. While Britain had betrayed Hussein with both the Sykes-Picot agreement and the Balfour Declaration, he remained central to British policy along the Red Sea. They had not had time to reevaluate the newly emerging situation in Arabia.

In 1919 and 1920, Saudi and Ikhwan forces redefined the borders in the west with Yemen and in the east with Kuwait. Turmoil among the Rashid in the aftermath of Turkish defeat permitted Ibn Saud to plan expansion into the northeastern part of the peninsula. The Ikhwan defeat of the Rashid forces, in November 1921, enabled Ibn Saud to negotiate the surrender of the Rashid capital at Hail without a battle. This northward thrust put him in contact with the newly formed British client states of Transjordan and Iraq. Half of his borders, thus, abutted Hashemite territories.

Ibn Saud's northern borders were not, in fact, defined until he met with Sir Percy Cox at the Uqair Conference in November 1922. Sir Percy, who was probably the most respected foreigner ever to serve in the region, was the British High Commissioner in Iraq. His government's influence in Iraq and Transjordan provided Cox the authority to speak on behalf of those states, although King Feisal was represented at the conference. Placement of the border could not please all the parties, but such was the respect for Cox that all watched while he drew the permanent northern Saudi border. It confirmed Saudi acquisitions from the 1920 expedition against Kuwait and granted Iraq more than Ibn Saud would have preferred. Sir Percy also attempted to solve a major border problem by creating two neutral zones on the border to accommodate the needs of the nomadic herdsmen who customarily roamed freely in the region that now fell in different new states. The Uqair Conference limited Ibn Saud's expansion to the north and the Gulf limited his expansion to most of the east, but no agreements prevented him from shaping the south and the west as he saw fit.

Accumulated hard feelings between Hussein and Ibn Saud surpassed containment by 1924. Hussein had denied pilgrims from Najd and the Ikhwan access to the Holy Places. He had proclaimed himself Caliph after the Turkish Republic abolished the Ottoman caliphate in 1924. Hussein's excesses and restrictions won widespread support from nearly all of the religious leaders in Ibn Saud's realm to justify military operations against the self-proclaimed King of the Hijaz.

In September 1924, an Ikhwan army under the command of Sultan bin Bijad and Khaled bin Luwai attacked Taif, which was well defended under the leadership of Hussein's eldest son, Ali. Recollection of previous Ikhwan slaughter apparently spread panic in Ali's army, which abandoned the city to the torch and pillage of the Ikhwan. The disorderly escape from Taif had led to the destruction of much of Ali's army and had left Hussein defenseless in Mecca. Since Feisal ruled Iraq and Abdullah ruled Transjordan, on October 3, Hussein abdicated in favor of Ali and remained in exile until his death in 1931.

Ibn Saud sent word that Mecca was not to suffer the types of atrocities that had occurred in Taif. The Ikhwan heeded his command and he was able to demonstrate to the world that his control over the Hijaz did not mean the triumph of unbridled Wahhabism. Concern for public opinion, especially in the Muslim world, led Ibn Saud to take Jeddah by siege rather than by the sword. Ali abdicated on December 10, 1925, and joined his brother Feisal in Iraq. Ibn Saud entered Jeddah and accepted its surrender. A month later he announced in the Great Mosque of Mecca that he had taken the title of king of the Hijaz, a title he had criticized Sharif Hussein for assuming.

His conquest of the Hijaz distinguished Ibn Saud as the singular conqueror in the history of Arabia. The test lay ahead to determine whether he could rule the combination of desert raiders, herdsmen, small oasis dwellers and Wahhabi fundamentalists on the one hand, and the considerably more sophisticated Hijazi merchants and traders on the other. Ibn Saud had, however, already proven his extraordinary military and diplomatic leadership abilities in getting to this position.

Difficult as the management of his complex realm was, the Ikhwan provided his greatest challenge. Their grievances were many, but foremost among them were Ibn Saud's allowing the unholy to thrive unharried and unreconstructed in his realm; his close association with the Christian British; and his acceptance of the international boundaries that restricted their fiery proselytism and traditional raids for gain and glory. Sadly, by 1927, he found himself on the brink of a military confrontation with the Ikhwan, who had provided him with many of his military victories and had accounted for much of his success.

A conference that he arranged with 3,000 Ikhwan and the Saudi *ulama* in January 1927 failed to accommodate Ikhwan concerns. In September of that year, a band of Ikhwan slaughtered the workmen who were building a British police post within the Iraqi border to subdue tribal raids. Many more raids followed, which Ibn Saud did not approve but could not end, despite British pressure for him to do so. Instead, he asked the British to relinquish their military build-up of modern weapons against the raids. The problem nearly drove Ibn Saud to despair, but the Ikhwan eased his dilemma in February of 1929, when they turned back in the face of Britain's modern weapons in Iraq and attacked fellow Ikhwan in Hasa. This force under Sultan Ibn Bijad exposed their real motive as plunder rather than *jihad.* Ibn Saud could justifiably attack his stalwart former allies. His army met the armies of two of the foremost Ikhwan leaders, Ibn Bijad and Feisal al Duwish, at Sibilla on March 30, 1929, and administered them a sound defeat. The mopping-up operation took several more months, but Ibn Bijad was captured and ended his life in jail. Feisal al Duwish, who was the most notorious of the modern Ikhwan, sought refuge in Kuwait, where he surrendered to the British. He died in the amicable custody of Ibn Saud, but his name remains anathema in Saudi circles.

In the defeat of the Ikhwan, and the razing of their most important centers, Ibn Saud completed a process of construction through destroying his rivals that had begun when he attacked the Musmak fortress in 1902. He had demonstrated his capacity to evaluate his circumstances and continue inexorably toward increasingly larger goals that fate and his instincts defined. Thus, he was apparently unrivaled in the peninsula from his still backward center in Riyadh. The Turks, the Rashid, the Hashemites, and the Ikhwan had all disappeared and he remained the undisputed ruler of a desert kingdom. His marginal use of motorized vehicles against the Ikhwan had probably made the difference in his final contest with them. This innovation was perhaps symbolic of his capacity to build the future firmly upon a proper mixture of the present and the past. His brashness served him well at times, but most of his successes resulted from patience and from taking advantage of his rivals' follies.

For some years, he held the titles of King of Najd and King of the Hijaz, but on September 18, 1932, he assumed the title of king of Saudi Arabia. The following year he designated his eldest son, Saud, as the crown prince and apparent successor. While this was not normal practice in a society that traditionally chose its own leaders, it befitted Ibn Saud, who had already established other new traditions. His second son, Feisal, became the viceroy of the Hijaz. The widely travelled Feisal was better prepared to deal with the worldly Hijaz than Saud, who had seldom left the Najd, which he governed. In a kingdom that had very little formal structure, the decisions and the revenues were firmly in the hands of the family that bore its name.

The truth was that the Saudis lacked adequate funds to meet their royal obligations to the many tribes and groups who looked to the royal family for favors and hospitality. The Great Depression reduced the number of pilgrims who normally provided an infusion of funds as they performed the *hajj.* The worldwide economic disaster had also reduced the demand for petroleum, which provided income for some of Saudi Arabia's neighbors. Under these circumstances, none of the major oil companies that operated in the region were interested in acquiring additional concessions. British oilmen, who knew the region best, were, in fact, convinced that no oil existed in Saudi Arabia.

Ibn Saud, therefore, welcomed the possibility that his old British friend, Harry St. John Philby, extended in 1932. Philby explained that Standard Oil of California (SOCAL) was interested in purchasing a concession to find and develop oil in Ibn Saud's kingdom. SOCAL had a similar concession in Bahrain and, as a nonparticipant in the cartel of the regional companies, was not obligated to share ownership in such concessions. Once the Anglo-Iraqi Petroleum Company officials realized SOCAL might get the concession, they attempted to prevent the emergence of a rival in the region. But Ibn Saud's demands for a £100,000 loan and a £5,000 annual rental in gold was too high for A.I.P.C. to make more than a cursory effort. SOCAL gained the concession with an initial loan of £30,000, followed by a £20,000 loan eighteen months later, and a £5,000 annual rental. SOCAL had what many believed was a worthless concession, but Ibn Saud had a source of revenue without which he would have been bankrupt.

SOCAL engineers believed that their best prospect for oil was in the Hasa hill known as Jebel Dhahran. They had received the concession in May of 1933, but were not ready to drill in the uninhabited area until 1935. Three years and six dry holes later, SOCAL convinced Texaco to purchase half of the concession to avoid abandoning the Dammam Dome, as they had dubbed Jebel Dhahran. Dammam Well #7 rewarded SOCAL tenacity on March 3, 1938, when it spewed forth the first evidence of the largest oil reserve in the world. By May 1939 Caltex, as the merged companies were then known, shipped the first load of Saudi oil out of the new port of Ras Tanura. The Saudi economy would remain unstable for the next two decades, but it finally possessed a source of unimaginable wealth and staggering challenges befitting the stature of its king who had so often seemed larger than life.

THE GULF

The emergence of a strong, assertive Saudi Arabia shortly after the end of World War I drastically altered the situation on the eastern coast of the Arabian peninsula. The emboldened Saudis were in a better position than ever before to establish a systematic collection from the coastal areas that had periodically paid them tribute. Given the weakness of the coastal shaykhdoms, only the British were in a position to prevent the entire region from falling under Saudi control. Ibn Saud's expansion to the west coast, which led to conflict with the Hashimis in the Hijaz; the Zaidi Imamate of North Yemen; and the Idrisis of Asir, were only temporary interruptions that diverted attention from the Gulf coast. After all, the Gulf, rather than the Hijaz, was the traditional arena of Saud influence, and interest in oil concessions in the Gulf from the early 1920s had increased the value and the appeal of the Gulf for many different parties. Saudi ambitions, therefore, presented a challenge to both the British and the coastal shaykhs, because the Saud kingdom was the first source of threat from the interior since the formation of the Trucial System. This system had emerged primarily to protect the coastal shaykhs from each other. Its orientation to the Gulf only provided for naval protection. Britain, in fact, was not prepared in any sense to commit land troops to prevent landward attacks, except in Kuwait, over which it had an official protectorate, and perhaps in Qatar, which enjoyed near protectorate status. Serious questions arose over Qatar, since the Saudis had strong traditional claims over most of the peninsula, except for the limited area of Doha, where the al-Thanis were under British protection.

The British astutely pursued a course of prevarication to prevent Ibn Saud from annexing the entire area, over which he had both superior claims and the capacity to capture unless the British were willing to confront him militarily. Armed conflict was unwise in view of the many problems the British faced in the entire Arab-speaking region. Also, the British strived to prevent the low-level tension between themselves and Ibn Saud from increasing to avoid the possibility of international arbitration that would have, no doubt, favored Ibn Saud. Their primary concern was to thwart all rivals for oil concessions.

Virtually ceaseless negotiations ensued between British officials and Ibn Saud as the British countered Saudi claims and delayed resolution to multifaceted claims related to tribal territories, traditional tribal alliances, and access to water. The numerous agreements between the Ottomans and the British immediately prior to World War I provided the British much of their justifications, which Ibn Saud consistently maintained had no binding effect upon him. The two parties met similar impasses related to postwar conferences and legal opinions of various British authorities. As Saudi officials became more familiar with the documents that purported to verify the British claims, they became more convinced that Saudi claims and the reality of Saudi political power were superior. Some British authorities reluctantly reached the same conclusions and sought more diligently to maintain the status quo.

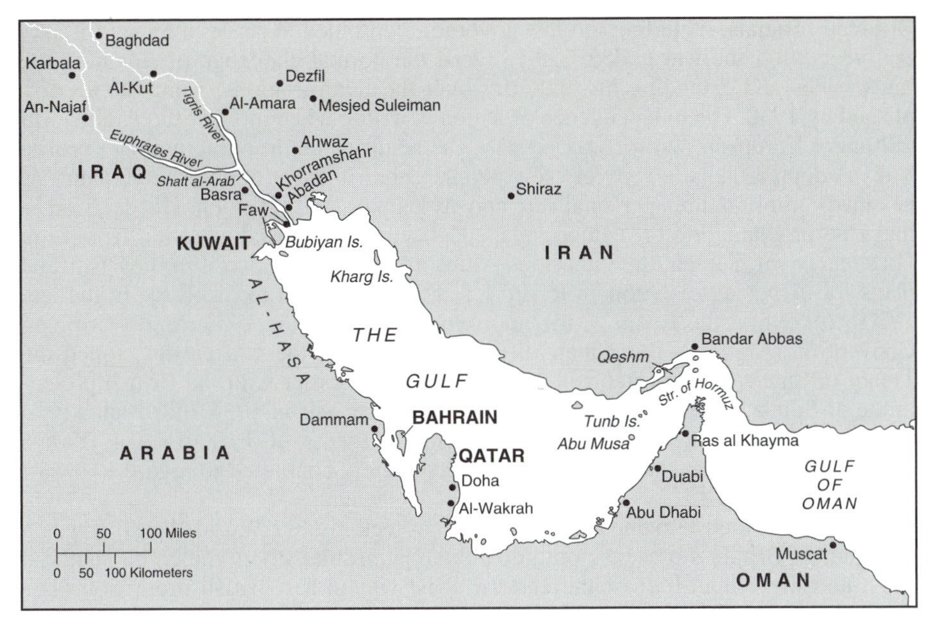

The Gulf

The Gulf shaykhs realized that continued cooperation with the British was their only hope to avoid either Saudi annexation or control. British control over their affairs, therefore, increased with each passing year, the participation of Americans in the oil concessions of Bahrain and Kuwait not withstanding. Even Kuwait, which enjoyed official British protection, suffered an economic boycott from Saudi Arabia.

The Saudis, of course, lacked the resources to engage in a military confrontation, which neither they nor the British wanted. Their pursuit of peaceful solutions yielded some marginal results. Border adjustments occurred, particularly related to Oman and the Hadramawt Protectorate, and ostensibly good-faith discussions continued on all other issues. Without making any significant concessions, the British increased their efforts to establish the best possible relations with Ibn Saud as the threat of war with Germany became more ominous in the late 1930s. Subsequent events dictated that no substantial changes would occur in the Gulf until after World War II.

YEMEN

North Yemen was the one part of their empire that the Ottomans disposed of as they chose at the end of World War I. This was possible because the Ottomans were never dislodged from North Yemen during the war. Imam Yahya, who had forced the Ottomans to accept the terms of the Treaty of Daan, received Ottoman approval to govern the mountainous region of traditional Zaidi control. In fact,

Ottoman officials, including the last governor, continued to serve in Sanaa for several years after the war ended. Yahya faced the normal challenge of subduing the Zaidi tribes and extending his authority over the Sunni regions, which he accomplished by 1930. His independence of action at a time when most of the Arab world fell under European control was, in part, the result of the low international profile Yahya adopted. He allowed very few people either to leave or enter the country as he slowly imprinted his personal rule and style upon North Yemen. His decision to make no proclamation of Yemen independence also deflected attention from him. Fortunately for Yemen, the victorious Allies had never included it in their wartime plans for disposing of Ottoman territories. The British had to use force in the late 1920s to confine the Imam to the approximate area of the 1914 Anglo-Ottoman Convention. After resolving their differences in 1933, the two parties signed the Treaty of Sanaa, which established North Yemen's border with the British protectorate of South Yemen. Yahya's attempts to acquire Asir in 1934 ended quickly in the face of Ibn Saud's superior forces. In the Treaty of Taif in 1934, Yahya acknowledged Saudi control of Asir, but he privately continued to regard it as part of his state.

South Yemen remained under British protection after World War I. It was a vital part of Britain's presence on the Arabian peninsula, where the entire southern coast and more than half of the eastern coast was under British protection. The small peninsula of Aden remained Britain's primary concern, but the adjacent areas required some level of order to assure that Aden met Britain's imperial needs. Consequently, a rudimentary element of British administrators and military officers worked closely with local leaders to settle disputes and provide security. While this measure of control fell far short of providing unity through centralized institutions, it was a silent recognition that South Yemen's many local identities were too strong to overcome without expending more effort than it was worth. Britain's interest in Aden never wavered but its commitment to the remainder of South Yemen was seldom very clear. The lack of a sense of unity within the protectorate, the inability of either North Yemen or Oman to govern it; a desire to prevent Ibn Saud from annexing it; combined with Britain's interest in its strategic importance, finally moved the British to a decisive policy in 1937. In that year it officially became part of the British Empire as the Aden Crown Colony and Hadramawt Protectorate, almost a full century after the British had initially seized the tiny Aden peninsula. Large portions of the Arab-speaking world had experienced direct or indirect British control for over a century, but South Yemen was the only area the British officially annexed. As in the Gulf region, the prolonged British presence exploited the Arab disarray to establish both *de facto* and *de jure* control over Arab lands.

9

Toward Independence

HISTORICAL TIMELINE

1945
- ⇛ League of Arab States charter March 22.
- ⇛ Roosevelt-Ibn Saud meeting February 14.
- ⇛ In April, Truman demanded termination of the provisions of the 1939 White Paper.
- ⇛ Labor government of Attlee-Bevin began in July.
- ⇛ Truman demanded the immediate acceptance of 100,000 Jews into Palestine on August 31.
- ⇛ Zionists increased efforts to smuggle more Jews into Palestine in September.
- ⇛ Zionists attacked Palestine railroad system in 153 places on October 31.
- ⇛ Approval of the Anglo-American Committee of Inquiry November 13.
- ⇛ Quota of Jewish migration to Palestine expired December 30.

1946
- ⇛ British announced on January 30 that they would continue allowing the previous quota of Jewish migration until the Anglo-American Committee finished its study.
- ⇛ Return of Jamal al-Husseini to Palestine in early February.
- ⇛ Report of the Anglo-American Committee of Inquiry May 1.
- ⇛ Truman endorsed Anglo-American Committee report May 1.
- ⇛ Hajj Amin al-Husseini moved to Egypt in May.
- ⇛ Hajj Amin and Jamal were elected to the two highest positions of the Arab Higher Committee on November 22.

- ⇛ Unprecedented Zionist attacks on British first part of the year.
- ⇛ "Night of the Bridges" Zionists destroyed ten bridges June 17.
- ⇛ British arrested large number of Zionist leaders June 29.
- ⇛ Morrison-Grady committee conducted study to determine a compromise between British and American positions throughout July.
- ⇛ Irgun bombed King David Hotel on July 22.
- ⇛ British sent Jewish refugees aboard *Haganah* ship to Cyprus August 12.
- ⇛ Morrison-Grady committee report July 31.
- ⇛ United States rejected and Britain accepted Morrison-Grady report .
- ⇛ Zionists submitted their plan for immigration to Palestine August 6, which Truman accepted.
- ⇛ British officials met with Arab League officials on Palestinian problem policy on September 10.
- ⇛ Truman formally endorsed Zionist plan on October 4.
- ⇛ On October 6, Thomas Dewey, Republican candidate for United States president, called for even higher rate of Jewish migration into Palestine.
- ⇛ Zionist leaders arrested on June 29 and released on November 5.
- ⇛ World Zionist Organization refused to reelect Chaim Weizmann as president in December because of his moderate position on Jewish immigration into Palestine.
- ⇛ Zionists and United States refused to attend London Conference on Palestine scheduled for February.

1947

- ⇛ British submitted Palestine problem to United Nations February 18.
- ⇛ Special session of General Assembly on Palestine question April 28–May 15. Appointed an eleven-member United Nations Special Committee on Palestine (UNSCOP) to recommend a solution.
- ⇛ UNSCOP arrived in Palestine June 14.
- ⇛ *Exodus* ship returned to place of origin July 19.
- ⇛ British executed three Irgunists July 29 and Irgun followed with execution of two British sergeants.
- ⇛ UNSCOP majority report on August 31 recommended partitioning of Palestine.
- ⇛ British announced on September 26 that they would terminate their mandate over Palestine.
- ⇛ General Assembly debate on Palestine from September through November.
- ⇛ General Assembly decision to partition Palestine on November 29 by a 33-to-13 vote.
- ⇛ British announced on December 18 that they would withdraw from Palestine on May 15, 1948.
- ⇛ Two thousand people were killed or injured in Arab-Zionist

conflicts in Palestine during the six weeks following the U.N. vote.

⇛ Irgun carried out extensive attacks against Palestinian Arabs in December.

1948 ⇛ Arab League organized and financed Arab Liberation Army under the command of Fawzi al-Qawaqji January 1.

⇛ Abd al-Qadir al-Husseini became commander of Palestinian guerrillas January 1.

⇛ Haganah concluded major arms deal with Czechoslovakia January 14.

⇛ United Nations appointed a commission to supervise implementation of partition, but violence in Palestine prevented it from conducting its duty.

⇛ Fawzi al-Qawaqji entered Palestine as commander of Arab Liberation Army on March 5.

⇛ United States indecisive in March as to whether it still favored partition. Truman categorically supported it.

⇛ Zionists completed Plan D by March 10. The plan designated the means to neutralize or remove the Arab population from places of special strategic importance on the borders between Zionist and Arab regions of Palestine.

⇛ Zionist offensive to implement Plan D began April 5 with the intention of conquering Jerusalem.

⇛ Irgun conducted massacre of Deir Yassin on April 9.

⇛ Tiberias, Haifa, and Jaffa fell under Zionist control between April 20 and May 6. Most Arabs fled and became refugees.

⇛ Zionists gained control of scores of other Arab areas by the end of April and also moved up to the wall of the Old City.

⇛ Zionists had control of much of eastern Galilee by the middle of May.

⇛ Gush Etzion Bloc surrendered to Transjordanian troops May 14.

⇛ By May 15 Zionists were in control of two northern sectors of the three the U.N. assigned them.

⇛ British withdrew from Palestine on May 15.

⇛ Zionists pronounced the creation of the state of Israel on May 15.

⇛ United States and Soviet Union recognized Israel on May 15.

⇛ Arab League armies entered Palestine on May 15.

⇛ Israel declared creation of Israeli Defense Forces on May 26.

⇛ U.N. appointed Count Folke Bernadotte as official mediator in Palestine on May 20.

⇛ U.N. called for a truce on May 29.

⇛ Count Bernadotte obtained an agreement for the U.N. truce on June 11.

⇛ War resumed on July 9.

⇛ Bernadotte obtained a second truce on July 19.

⇛ *Lehi* assassinated Count Bernadotte on September 17.

	⇛ Dr. Ralph Bunche became U.N. mediator after Bernadotte's death.
	⇛ Hajj Amin al-Husseini announced formation of Government of All Palestine on September 20.
	⇛ Palestinian delegation proclaimed Emir Abdullah King of All Palestine in September and larger delegation proclaimed him King of Greater Syria in December.
	⇛ War resumed on October 15.
1949	⇛ Egypt and Israel began armistice talks on the Island of Rhodes on January 12.
	⇛ Egyptian-Israeli armistice agreement February 24.
	⇛ Lebanon-Israeli armistice March 23.
	⇛ Transjordanian-Israeli armistice April 3.
	⇛ U.N. recognized Israeli independence May 11.
	⇛ Syrian-Israeli armistice July 20.
	⇛ U.N.-appointed Conciliation Commission on Palestine on December 11.
1950	⇛ United Nations-sponsored talks with Arab and Israeli delegations in Lausanne during the spring failed to resolve their differences.

World War II provided the circumstances to end much that began as a result of World War I in the Middle East. At first glance this seems strange since, except for the North African campaign, no major battles occurred in the region and none of the emerging countries were official combatants until the outcome was both clear and irreversible. However, Britain and France, who had shaped the post-World War I Middle East, had been major participants; and both were weaker than they had been for centuries, even though they were on the winning side. The ineffective League of Nations, which had in many respects been the tool of Britain and France, was dead. In short, the old European order had passed and the future belonged to the United States, the Soviet Union, and, to a lesser degree, the new United Nations.

As the war drew closer to an end, Arabs and Jews had even higher hopes than earlier that they would become independent, sovereign states. Both believed their cases were so overwhelmingly just that the international community could not deny their legitimate needs. Jews, for instance, could point to the holocaust as vivid proof of Jewish insecurity in the gentile world. Arabs believed that their endurance of a generation of international tutelage qualified them for sovereignty in the new postwar world order.

ARAB QUASI INDEPENDENCE

From many outward appearances most of the Arabs were already independent. Iraq had become a member of the League of Nations in 1932 after the British recognized its independence in 1930. The British had also recognized Egyptian independence in the Anglo-Egyptian Treaty of 1936. The Free French government, which became the real French government after the war, recognized Syrian and Lebanese independence in 1941. There was no significant dispute that Ibn Saud was King of Saudi Arabia after he assumed that title in 1932. Yemen's borders were fairly stable by 1934, when the British and Ibn Saud recognized its independence. The British White Paper of 1939 promised Palestine, with its strong Arab majority, self-government by 1949. Great Britain recognized the elevation of Transjordan from an emirate to a sovereign kingdom in 1946, ten months after the war ended. Excluding Africa, only the Arab shaykhdoms along the eastern and southern rim of the Arabian peninsula were clearly under foreign control.

Arab affiliation with both the United Nations and the League of Arab States testified further to their independence. Charter membership in the United Nations for Egypt, Iraq, Syria, Lebanon, and Saudi Arabia, was certainly the hallmark of their sovereignty. These nations, along with Transjordan and Yemen, formed the League of Arab States on March 22, 1945, under British guidance, as further evidence that they were free from European and international tutelage. Of special interest is the fact that the charter members of the Arab League granted Palestine full representation in its deliberations and made some of its strongest resolutions on behalf of Palestinian independence. Widespread demonstrations against Zionism in Egypt, Syria, Iraq, and Lebanon during the fall of 1945 indicated that opposition to further Western interference in their affairs through the promotion of the Zionist cause was central to Arab identity and its quest for independence.

British concern for the anti-British sentiments in the Arab world during the war and a realization that the Arab states would receive full independence after the war led the British to suggest as early as 1941 that Arabs should form a structure for cooperation. Britain, after all, had vital military, logistical, petroleum, communication, and transportation interests throughout the Arab world and needed to retain a close working relationship with the emerging Arab nations. This British role as midwife for the Arab League portended ill relations between Great Britain and Zionism.

Despite all the manifestations of independence, there were strong impediments to Arab freedom from colonial status. France, for instance, continued to treat Lebanon and Syria as mandates until British and American pressure forced French military withdrawal in 1946. Iraq remained under a debilitating treaty relationship with Britain that allowed the latter to retain bases in Iraq and interfere in Iraqi affairs if situations contrary to British interests arose. The British retained a strong administrative and military presence in Egypt and continued to control the Suez Canal and defend it with British troops. British mastery of Transjordan was not even thinly disguised and the international community did not recognize it as a member of the United Nations until 1955. More British troops than ever were in Palestine as it increasingly became the logistical, transportation, and communication center for British interests in western Asia and eastward. The Gulf was as much as ever a British lake.

In short, the Arab states were only marginally capable of functioning effectively in domestic or international affairs in the challenging period after the war. Their domestic institutions were weak, nonexistent, or until recently, under the direction of foreigners. Only Egypt had borders its citizens regarded as legitimate. No Arab government enjoyed widespread support from its citizens and, in many cases, citizens owed their allegiance to a government beyond their borders or to a united Arab state that did not exist. Their mandatory overlords had kept them systematically disarmed and denied them any opportunity to acquire either modern military training or modern weapons. They were devoid of connections with international banking and marketing mechanisms that were so crucial in the modern economy. This was especially critical for petroleum producers such as Iraq and Saudi Arabia that had no control over production levels, pricing, refining, marketing, or transportation of their precious resource. Additionally, their recent arrival on the stage of nations prevented them from having either diplomatic affiliations or proven value to individual nations or regional blocks.

Also, Arabs had virtually no means of influencing international public opinion. Few people outside of the Middle East were familiar with Arabs and their culture. Similarly, there was little worldwide realization that the fate of Arabs could influence the daily lives or long-range interests of the world's citizenry. Most people could, at best, conjure up some vague impression of a scattering of camel-riding nomads who practiced a strange religion they believed was quite contrary to their own.

Arabs had, however, potentially very strong allies in important strata of influential nations. Diplomatic, military, business, and scholarly elements in most nations understood the intrinsic value of both the Arabs and the region to their respective fields. This was particularly true in the United States among professionals in the State and War departments and among members of the petroleum industry. They repeatedly attempted to temper the pro-Zionist efforts of the American executive and legislative branches. While such people were not without influence, their insights on the latent potential of the larger Middle East remained unheeded as important decisions unfolded in response to immediate needs and expedient political concerns.

ANGLO-AMERICAN CONCERNS

The scope of the holocaust, of course, intensified the already incendiary situation in Palestine that existed before the war. Zionists were increasingly desperate and increased their moral appeal, while continuing to make an historical claim and call upon the international community to uphold its promises. People worldwide who cared little for Zionism before the war supported Zionism because of the Nazi genocide. Arabs understood that the White Paper might well be overridden and that they might have to bear the burden of Western guilt for European treatment of Jews. Great Britain, destitute from the war, had to withstand pressures from all these fronts while it had to balance its international responsibilities, its national interests, and its limited capacity to manage a situation that would have been difficult even under better conditions. Public pressure in the United States impelled an assertive role in Palestine from a society totally unfamiliar with Middle Eastern affairs.

Conflicting interests of the great powers complicated the situation. This was particularly true between the United States and Great Britain at a time when anything short of their close cooperation left the shaping of events in the Middle East to the irreconcilable views of the Arabs and Zionists. The Soviet Union also threatened to complicate the volatile situation. Soviet resentment of its exclusion from the deliberations led it to look for ways to intercede. Interestingly, Soviet courtship of the Arabs did not meet with outright rejection, although there was a strong assumption in the West that Muslims would be unreceptive to help from avowed atheists. The Soviets also caused concern to both the United States and Great Britain because they could increase the Jewish problem by choosing at any time to release large numbers of Jews, who sought refuge in Palestine, from behind their borders.

The magnitude of any settlement in Palestine was so great, along with the possibility of it happening fairly suddenly, that the Zionists and the Arabs felt compelled to constant vigilance and preparation. Under such circumstances, moderate postures and approaches were unlikely to prevail. The more assertive elements in both camps, therefore, set the standards that the masses had to follow. British and American disarray exacerbated this trend.

THE PALESTINIAN ARABS AND THE ARAB LEAGUE

Even though there was little difference among them regarding their goals, the Palestinian Arabs faced the crucial watershed period with less unity than they had demonstrated in earlier years. Their divisiveness, therefore, was almost solely related to personal and family jealousies over leadership positions. Most of their leadership, after all, had been in exile since 1937. The Palestine Arab party of the al-Husseini family, however, under the leadership of the Mufti, Hajj Amin, and his cousin, Jamal, remained dominant. It relentlessly resisted any compromise in its opposition to all Zionist immigration and land purchases. Likewise, it demanded the end of the mandate and the immediate creation of an independent Arab state. Jamal's return to Palestine in February 1946 and the Mufti's move to Egypt in May assured a continuation of the Palestine Arab party's hard line as the Arab standard. In the view of the Zionists, British compliance in their return to the region indicated a strong British tilt toward the Arabs at the very time the Anglo-American Committee of Inquiry was conducting its investigations. The fact that the two recent exiles obtained the presidency and vice presidency of the new Arab Higher Executive, which officially conducted all Palestinian Arab business with the British, did nothing to diminish Zionist impressions. Palestinian lack of significant military capability reduced their effectiveness. After all, unauthorized possession of a single bullet was a capital offense under mandatory law. In sharp contrast, the Zionists had a large, well-armed military capacity, along with significant foreign capital and sources for additional arms.

Although of recent origin, the Arab League offered the best leadership for the Arabs on all issues, most of which revolved around the final disposition of Palestine. Under the leadership of Secretary General Abd al-Rahman Bey Azzam of Egypt, the League spoke with considerable Arab unity to individual nations, the United Nations, and investigatory commissions. It even managed to mount a modestly financed international public relations campaign on behalf of Arabs under Musa al-Alami, a Cambridge-educated Palestinian. The League held conferences and issued threats of violence and boycotts against Western interests unless Arabs received fair treatment. While their attempts were politically astute, even the collected efforts of the militarily and economically undeveloped Arab nations had marginal influence.

THE AMERICAN ROLE

American entry into Middle Eastern affairs challenged both the Arabs and the British because the Arabs had little experience dealing with the Americans and Great Britain was newly dependent on the United States for postwar recovery. The United States, in fact, became pivotal in shaping postwar Palestine and the Middle East in general, because it became the strongest supporter of Zionism during the war. The strong British sentiment for Zionism faded as Zionist verbal and violent attacks against British personnel, installations, and integrity increased. Also, the British government and public came to resent American pressure on British policy, while it declined any financial or military responsibility to implement a pro-Zionist program that all knew would result in violence.

Roosevelt's meeting with King Ibn Saud shortly before the former's death in April 1945 made him acutely aware of Arab concerns about Palestine. His successor, Truman, had no such personal experience to temper his domestic political considerations and his humanitarian concern for Jewish survivors of the holocaust.

ANGLO-AMERICAN RELATIONS WITH ZIONISM

The Zionists, who were also driven by their sense of desperation and their sense of the justness of their cause, were much better prepared to prevail than their Arab adversaries. Although they no longer enjoyed as much strong governmental and public support in England, increased American governmental, financial, and sentimental support more than compensated for the loss. It meant, of course, that American support must become directed against British policies. By 1945 most Zionists concluded, as the Revisionists had earlier, that Great Britain, rather than the Arabs or the international community, was their real enemy. Accordingly, larger elements of Zionism in Palestine and abroad began to attack the British through illegal immigration, propaganda, and violence.

Zionists had every reason to believe that the new Labor government of Prime Minister Clement Attlee and Foreign Secretary Ernest Bevin would support their cause when it replaced Churchill's government in July 1945. Labor had, after all, always been pro-Zionist. But Labor, faced with the diminished capacity of Great Britain to manage its worldwide obligations, was no less inclined than Churchill to preside over the dissolution of the British Empire. It had to protect British interests in the Middle East while it considered necessary adjustments upon the possibility of ending its long domination of India and elsewhere. Also, the Labor Party only endorsed a limited Zionist presence of a Jewish National Home in a binational Palestine. In particular, Bevin's internationalist trade union background was incompatible with exclusive Zionist domination of Palestine.

The end of the war and the beginning of the White Paper provision for a termination of Jewish immigration without Arab consent was provocative. The Zionists were prepared, however, to capitalize on their experience in organizing illegal immigration during the war if the British insisted on enforcing their 1939 White Paper in the war's aftermath. As much as possible, the British had included the illegals against the White Paper quota during the war. Truman's call for rescinding the White Paper when he took office in April 1945 and again at Potsdam in July complicated the situation further. Also, direct American pressure on the Labor government on August 31 to admit the specific number of 100,000 displaced persons increased the tension between Great Britain and the United States. In the meantime the British had allowed fifteen hundred Jews to enter Palestine each month until December 1945 when it fulfilled the quota of the 1939 White Paper.

On January 30, 1946 the British government announced that it would continue this level of immigration while the Anglo-American Committee of Inquiry conducted its study. It attempted to placate the Arabs with a simultaneous approval of Jamal al-Husseini's return to Palestine. This continuation of the status quo was unsatisfactory to the Truman administration, the Arabs, and the Zionists. All had leverage over British policy. Britain's dire postwar condition was hopeless without American financial and other assistance. Elements in Congress and the executive branch reminded the British of that reality. The Arab League threatened British interests in the Middle East and throughout the Muslim world if British policy responded to American and Zionist pressures. The Zionists could renew their violence against Britain in Palestine.

ZIONIST TERRORISM

The Zionists were in the best position to make good their threats and they did. Their population of about 600,000, compared to the approximately 1,250,000 Arabs in 1945, made anything short of large-scale Zionist immigration unacceptable. Therefore, in the fall of 1945, the Zionist mainstream, under Ben-Gurion and the Haganah, which had grown to about 60,000, moved closer to the Irgun and the Stern Group, which had been hitting British targets since May. A coordinated effort to bring in larger numbers of illegals began in September. The British captured and detained some illegals, only to have a Palmach operation free two hundred by military force in early October. The combined Zionist military organizations demonstrated their ability and determination when their forces blew up the tiny Palestinian railroad system in 153 places on the night of October 31.

THE ANGLO-AMERICAN SEARCH FOR COMPROMISE

Zionist terrorism, American pressure, and Britain's economic condition in the face of the onslaught of winter led to the Labor government agreeing to the announcement of an Anglo-American Committee of Inquiry on November 13. The twelve-man committee of relative unknowns began its work in the European displaced persons camps and made its way to the Middle East for a month of sessions in all the Arab capitals and arrived in Jerusalem during March.

Initially, the May 1, 1946 report of the Anglo-American Committee of Inquiry had the greatest impact on President Truman. Its recommendations for immediate action were similar to those of the Zionists and earlier American investigations and, as such, were reassuring to him. However, the call for the admission of 100,000 Jewish refugees to Palestine was unacceptably provocative for the Labor government of Attlee. None of the many reports on Palestine over the years demonstrated a better understanding of its complexity. Overall, it urged patience, except for its advocacy of the one-time transfer of 100,000 Jewish refugees to Palestine to relieve their unusual plight. Even with this provision, the report's analysis was inimical to Zionism's demands for the immediate creation of a Jewish state.

Thus, Truman only endorsed the call for 100,000 Jewish immigrants into Palestine on the day the report became public, while he denounced British restrictions upon Zionist efforts to transform Palestine into a Jewish state. In a semblance of cooperation with Great Britain, however, he established a Cabinet-level committee to explore a possible Anglo-American policy on Palestine. While he still rejected any American military participation, he did not rule out the possibility of financial and transportation assistance if the British decided to allow 100,000 Jews to enter Palestine immediately. In July, Henry F. Grady went to London on behalf of the president to determine an Anglo-American approach in conjunction with his British counterpart, Herbert Morrison.

The Committee of Inquiry and the subsequent Morrison-Grady deliberations occurred simultaneously with unprecedented Zionist violence against the British mandatory administration. While the Haganah limited its attacks to British efforts to curtail illegal immigration, the Irgun inflicted deaths and casualties on British military and police personnel. There was little indication that the Yishuv objected to the increased terrorism as it had in the past. British endorsement of the Committee of Inquiry's recommendations moved most elements of Zionism to accept violence as their only means to prevail.

THE ZIONIST QUEST FOR STATEHOOD THROUGH VIOLENCE

The Zionists determined to demonstrate to the British that even their force of 80,000 was inadequate to quell Zionist ardor for statehood. On the "night of the bridges," June 17, the Haganah destroyed ten of the eleven bridges it attacked. Thus, its members again demonstrated their command and logistical capability as they had in their concerted attacks on the railway system the previous October.

The British finally responded to the Yeshuv, as the Arab Higher Committee had urged for some months, in the same way it responded to the Arab uprising in 1937. In a massive British military sweep of the Yeshuv, every important office and organ of the Zionist community in Palestine fell under British control. The authorities were armed with warrants for the arrest of leading Jewish Agency officials, including Ben-Gurion, who was abroad. Moshe Sharrett, the principal political officer of the Jewish Agency, was the highest official arrested among the more than 2,700 the British placed in internment camps. The British effort found surprisingly little of the Yeshuv's sizable military hardware and soon released most of the Zionist prisoners after Weizmann interceded, perhaps for the last time, for an agreement of the Haganah to cease military confrontation with the British.

As always, however, Begin and the Irgun did not comply with such agreements. They captured British hostages to prevent punishment of their members under British condemnation to death and decided to carry out the most dramatic attack to date against British occupation. On July 22, Irgun bombs destroyed much of the King David Hotel in Jerusalem, which served as the British mandatory headquarters. More than eighty people died and a similar number were injured nine days before the Morrison-Grady plan became public. The British government issued a formal statement on July 24 that held the Jewish Agency and the Yeshuv responsible for all violence against British personnel and installations. Consequently, the British intensified their efforts to prevent any further growth of the Zionist population in Palestine. When they intercepted the *Haganah* refugee ship, with three thousand illegals aboard, at the end of July, the British announced they would no longer intern illegals in Palestine, but detain them in special camps on Cyprus.

THE MORRISON-GRADY PLAN

The Morrison-Grady Plan of July 31, which resulted from his talks with Grady's British counterpart, satisfied only the British government, although it attempted to follow a course implicit in the Anglo-American Committee of Inquiry report. It proposed a partitioning of Palestine into autonomous Arab and Zionist sectors, with the British retaining sole control as trustee over Jerusalem and the southern third of the mandate. Everything related to the mandate as a whole would remain under British control, but the autonomous sectors could manage their subnational internal affairs. It proposed to allow the 100,000 Jewish immigrants on the condition that the entire package would become policy. It further specified that the United States must transport the refugees to Palestine. In compliance with the Committee of Inquiry's recommendation that the Arab standard of living should improve to match that of the Zionists, it called upon the United States to appropriate $50 million and guarantee that another $250 million would become available for economic development in Palestine.

The United States found the plan unacceptable. The Zionist sector of this plan, for instance, was smaller than that proposed in the Peel Commission of 1937, which the Zionists had deemed insufficient. Britain would have retained control over future Zionist immigration based on the "economic absorbative capacity" of Palestine. The financial obligation it demanded from the United States exceeded American willingness to participate in a process that threatened to scuttle a Zionist state in Palestine. Since it seemed to represent Great Britain's final offer, it essentially ended any possibility of cooperation between the United States and Great Britain before both lost control of the situation.

The British attempted to negotiate with the Arabs and the Zionists in the white heat of these developments in late July. The Arabs initiated the proposed talks, but the Grady-Morrison plan indicated to the Zionists there was no grounds for such a discussion. They submitted their own plan early in August, which soon also became Truman's position on the configuration and structure for Palestine. The Jewish Agency plan called for a Zionist state over two-thirds of Palestine from the southern border of Lebanon to the Gulf of Aqaba. The Arab state would consist of the central highlands, including Jerusalem, to the Jordan River in the east, with a corridor to the sea at Jaffa.

Since neither the Palestinian Arabs nor the Jewish Agency could agree with the British on the agenda or the composition of their respective delegations, British officials met in London with representatives of the Arab League on September 10. The Arab League's insistence on Palestine becoming an Arab state and their demand for an end to Zionist immigration brought a quick suspension of the London Conference.

ZIONIST-AMERICAN COOPERATION

President Truman's public endorsement of the Jewish Agency plan on Yom Kippur, October 4, in his effort to help elect Democrats to Congress, signalled that the United States would not support British efforts to find a compromise. Two days later Governor Thomas Dewey of New York, an emerging Republican candidate for president, said he favored the immigration of "hundreds of thousands," rather than Truman's 100,000 Jewish immigrants into Palestine. In this atmosphere the World Zionist Organization Congress met in Basle, Switzerland in December. It overwhelmingly endorsed the Jewish Agency plan and refused to attend the London Conference to discuss any alternatives. Indicative of its mood, the Zionist Congress left the office of president vacant rather than reelect the moderate Chaim Weizmann. In a major concession to the British, the Congress condemned the Irgun's unprecedented rampage of killing British personnel during November and early December.

BRITISH CONCILIATION AND RESIGNATION

All things considered, British policy was conciliatory to both the Arabs and the Zionists in the face of such adversity at the end of 1946. The British gave freedom and amnesty to most of the individuals in both camps who were in prison or exile. They followed with an invitation for American, Jewish Agency, Arab League, and Palestinian Arab Higher Executive delegations to attend another session of the London Conference. The Jewish Agency refused the invitation but sent a delegation to meet separately with the British. The United States also declined to attend since Arabs and Zionists were not meeting together.

In a final attempt, the British proposed for Palestine to become a binational state after five years of British trusteeship. It agreed to allow 4,000 Jewish refugees to enter Palestine each month over a two-year period, after which the United Nations would determine whether additional Jewish immigration could occur. During the five-year period, the British would help a democratic structure evolve to serve both the Jewish and Arab populations. Both sides found the offer too unsatisfactory to merit further consideration. Great Britain ended the London Conference on February 14 and referred the matter of Palestine to the United Nations.

The British had not decided to abrogate their entire presence or responsibility in Palestine when they requested that the United Nations General Assembly investigate and offer a solution. They had, doubtlessly, reached an impasse vis à vis Arab, Zionist and American obstruction. Equally important, nothing short of the use of brutal strength could restore order in the mandate. The presence of one-tenth of its armed forces in Palestine provided the capacity to subdue both of its hostile populations, but the British never considered this possibility. Instead, military and civilian personnel became barricaded captives in their own compounds in the land they occupied, while the financial, moral, and political price became too high for them to bear alone.

UNITED NATIONS ATTEMPT AT SOLUTION

A special session of the General Assembly convened on April 28 and deliberated until May 15. Its members finally decided on a broadly based, eleven-member United Nations Special Committee on Palestine (UNSCOP) to investigate the situation in the broadest possible terms and recommend a solution. None of the nations

(Australia, Canada, Czechoslovakia, Guatemala, India, Iran, the Netherlands, Peru, Sweden, Uruguay, and Yugoslavia) had a direct interest in Palestinian matters.

The situation in Palestine became worse during the United Nations debates on Palestine. Nearly 12,000 illegal immigrants arrived on the shores of Palestine from the end of the London Conference to UNSCOP's arrival in Palestine in the middle of June. British authorities intercepted most of them and interned them on Cyprus. Each encounter resulted in some degree of violence and further hardened Zionist antipathy toward the mandatory authority. Irgunists carried out dramatic raids and assassinations that drove the British deeper behind their barricades. The Arab community developed a small but openly visible military capacity. The Arab Higher Executive defiantly refused to meet with UNSCOP and impeded the committee's ability to meet with unofficial Arab individuals and groups. UNSCOP received much greater cooperation from Jewish Agency officials and the Jewish community in general.

UNSCOP had, however, the opportunity to witness the Palestine cauldron in microcosm. When the *Exodus* arrived in Haifa harbor with more than 4,500 refugees aboard, the British took it into custody with considerable violence. Hoping to make an example of this ship, British authorities returned it and its passengers to Marseilles, its point of origin, where the refugees refused to disembark. After considerable delay and worldwide attention, the British finally sailed the passengers to British internment camps in Germany. Shortly after UNSCOP left to meet with Arab League members in Beirut, the British executed three Irgunists on July 29 and the Irgun responded by hanging two British sergeants. During their stay in Palestine, some UNSCOP members had attempted to persuade the British to commute the death sentences and avoid the reciprocal violence related to this case.

Eight UNSCOP members submitted their majority report on August 31, 1947, which recommended the partitioning of Palestine into a six-piece jigsaw puzzle configuration. A Jewish state and an Arab state would each have three pieces, with some place of contact among the three pieces of each state. The lines generally conformed to each community's population concentrations, except for the awarding of the entire Negev to the Zionists to provide them room for population expansion and a port at Aqaba. This apparently strange arrangement was predicated upon the assumption that Palestine needed to remain a single economic unit. It also assumed that the United Nations would work with Great Britain and/or other members of the world community to evolve into an integrated socioeconomic unit. Jerusalem and an area around it would be internationalized and placed under permanent United Nations trusteeship.

UNSCOP's members unanimously agreed that the United Nations should immediately address the problem of the 250,000 Jews in displaced persons camps in Europe. Eight members agreed, however, that "any solution for Palestine cannot be considered as a solution of the Jewish problem in general."

THE DECISION TO PARTITION

Vigorous debate on partition ensued in the General Assembly from the latter part of September through November 1947. While Great Britain made it clear that it could not endorse any form of partition, the positions of the Soviet Union and the United States were uncertain. Most assumed that the Soviets would oppose partition to curry favor with the Arab states and to thwart Anglo-American interests in the

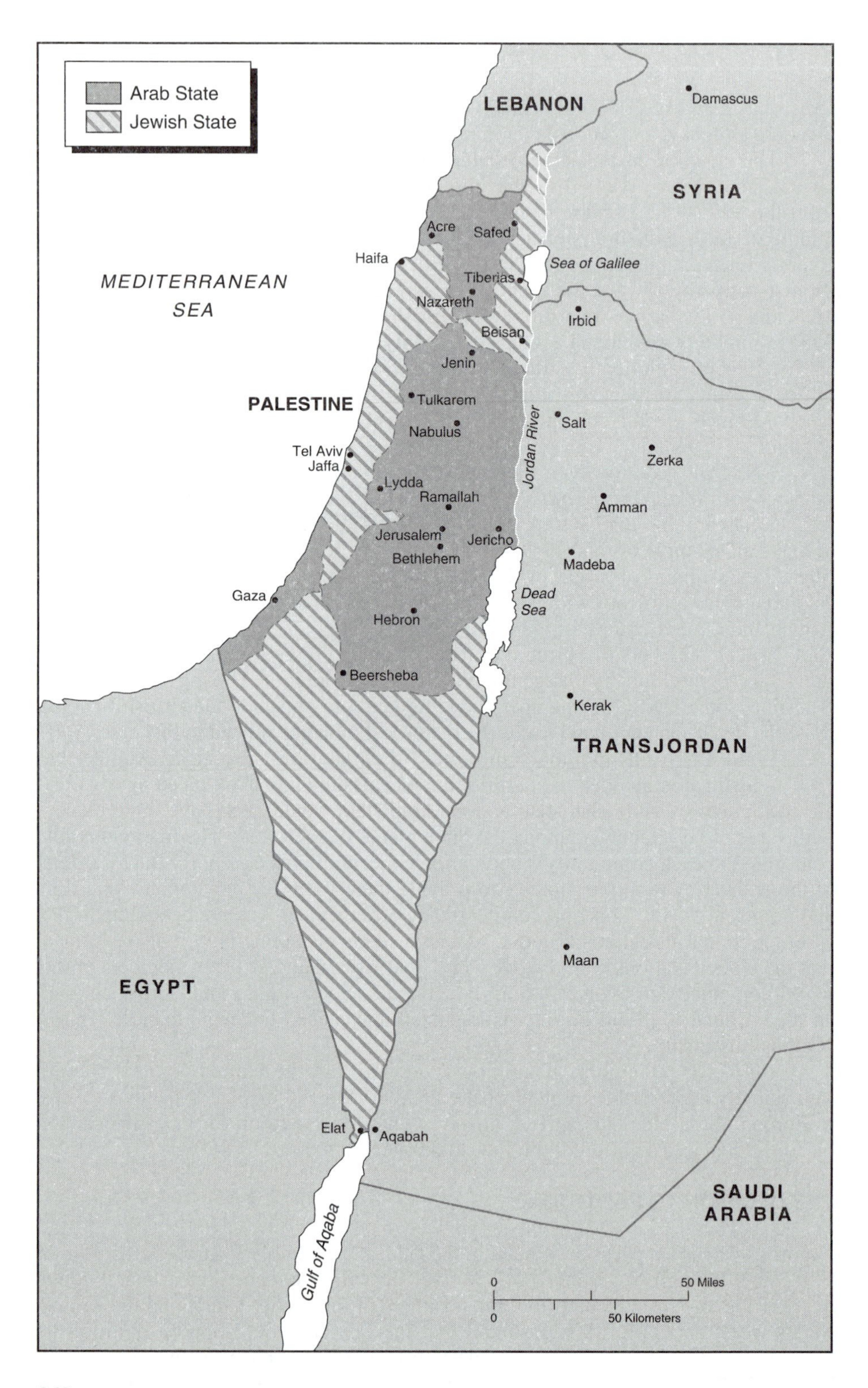
Arab State
Jewish State
LEBANON
Damascus
SYRIA
Acre
Safed
Haifa
Sea of Galilee
Tiberias
MEDITERRANEAN
SEA
Nazareth
Irbid
Beisan
Jenin
PALESTINE
Tulkarem
Jordan River
Salt
Nabulus
Tel Aviv
Jaffa
Zerka
Lydda
Ramallah
Amman
Jerusalem
Jericho
Bethlehem
Madeba
Gaza
Dead
Sea
Hebron
Beersheba
Kerak
TRANSJORDAN
Maan
EGYPT
Elat
Aqabah
SAUDI
ARABIA
Gulf of Aqaba
0
50 Miles
0
50 Kilometers

Middle East and the Muslim world. Also, Zionist activity was unlawful in the Soviet Union. Uncertainty over the American position arose. While Truman, most of Congress, and general public opinion supported a Jewish state, strong voices in the departments of State and Defense, and in business, opposed alienating the Arabs. There was also reason to believe that several smaller states in Africa, South America, and Asia would join the ten Arab and Muslim states in opposing partition, which required a two-thirds majority.

By the time of the vote on November 29, however, a decision in behalf of partition appeared likely. It was fairly obvious, for instance, that the Soviet Union had decided to support partition as the best means of promoting anti-British sentiments in the Arab world. Truman had successfully bypassed the State Department to assure an American vote for partition. In fact, under unprecedented Zionist pressure, American governmental and private sources influenced enough votes to secure a 33-to-13 vote in behalf of partition. Thus, after nearly seventy years of effort, the Zionist movement had international consent to establish its own state. Its nascent state was, however, still subsumed in the United Nations plan for Palestine to remain an economic unit under a continued British mandate until August 1, 1948. The United Nations resolution also provided for a U.N. Commission to work with the British and gradually to assume the role of creating the economic union, establishing fully democratic institutions in each state, and setting up international control over the greater Jerusalem area.

Britain's dislike of partition had not changed. After all, beyond its regional concerns, it was more familiar than any other nation with the difficulty of implementing partition in the inflamed Middle Eastern atmosphere. Further, the United Nations resolution required continued British administration of affairs in Palestine until the United Nations Commission replaced it as the instrument to realize the projected international will in Palestine. The British, therefore, announced on December 18 that they would withdraw from Palestine six months later on May 15, 1948. They refused to work with, or even allow members of the United Nations Commission to enter, Palestine before May 1. This was the only way they could establish beyond doubt any affiliation with the partitioning they opposed.

RESOLUTION BY CONFLICT

After the vote in the U.N., six crucial weeks passed before it established the Commission. Once established, the Commission soon determined that it could not fulfill its mission without military assistance, but during the four month period before Britain's scheduled withdrawal neither the U.N. collectively, nor any individual member, was willing to commit troops to enforce the U.N. resolution. In short, this meant that implementation of the U.N. solution depended upon the willingness of the Arabs and the Zionists to accept it.

For all practical purposes a war between Arabs and Zionists had begun shortly after the U.N. vote on partition. Both the Palestine Higher Committee and the Arab League states, separately and collectively, had made clear that they would use every means possible, including aid from the Soviet Union, to resist partition. The Arab governments, however, were committed to refraining from overt participation in the conflict until the British withdrew. However, arms and personnel had been filtering into Palestine for both the Arabs and the Zionists for some time in anticipation of a military confrontation. In the first weeks after the vote, British forces occasionally interfered in Arab-Zionist conflicts, when about two thousand people were killed or injured. Afterwards, the British, who had been responsible for keeping the peace and who had the only neutral force in the mandate, virtually ignored the chaos around them as they systematically packed up their thirty years of accumulated possessions for an orderly withdrawal.

By the end of December, the level of violence increased as the Irgun carried out dramatic terrorist attacks against dense Arab population centers in Jerusalem and Haifa. In early January, the Arab League organized and financed a multinational volunteer Arab Liberation Army under the command of Fawzi al-Qawaqji. Abd al-Qadir al-Husseini assumed command of the indigenous Palestinian guerrillas. The Haganah concluded a major arms deal with Czechoslovakia and stepped up its own attacks on Arab targets. The ferocity of the many operations on both sides, and the level of commitment to victory of each, convinced everyone that the scale of the conflict could only increase.

As the Palestinian situation unraveled, even the United States no longer remained steadfast in its support of partition. The American ambassador to the U.N., Warren Austin, publicly called for a suspension of partition plans in favor of a U.N. trusteeship on March 19. However, Truman rescinded that suggestion almost immediately. This did, however, demonstrate the division in the highest American leadership over the wisdom of pursuing a partition plan that could only end in war. But matters in Europe also contributed to American vacillation on Palestine. The West Berlin crisis between the Soviet Union and its former western allies by the spring of 1948 drew Great Britain and the United States closer together. Important as Palestine was, it was a secondary concern compared with the possibility of an Anglo-American armed conflict with the Soviet Union over Berlin.

ZIONISTS SEIZE THE INITIATIVE

While the international community grappled for a policy, the Zionist movement, under the relentless leadership of Ben-Gurion, seized the initiative and basically shaped the future of Palestine in April and May. Ben-Gurion, more than any of his colleagues, realized that the Zionists had to forge their nation's boundaries before the British withdrew and the international community obtained full authority to determine the fate of Palestine. He assumed, unlike many other Zionist leaders, that the Arab armies would attack the Zionist state. He convinced others that the partition boundaries were indefensible and that there would never be the peaceful economic unity the U.N. envisioned. This meant, therefore, that the Zionists must forego a defensive posture and utilize large-scale offensive actions to take as much of Palestine as was militarily and politically possible.

The Zionist strategy, called Plan 'D,' was complete by March 10. It called for Haganah forces to seize and secure all lands allotted to the Jewish state; it further called for securing all territory where Jewish settlements existed outside of the partitioning boundaries. In this regard, the acquisition of Jerusalem was the most significant prize and the greatest challenge. Important to the plan was the strategy of bringing all substantial Arab population centers adjacent to the Jewish state's borders under Zionist control in order to deny Arabs bases for operations. In addition to the obvious rewards for such a plan, the more than 800,000 Arabs within the approved state of Israel would have little or no value as a Fifth Column for their Arab brethren. In fact, central to the plan was the intention of creating conditions that would encourage Arabs to flee beyond the borders of the Jewish state.

The Zionist leadership was convinced that the Haganah, along with the Irgun and Lehi forces, could accomplish this goal against the Arab irregular forces without the importation of large quantities of arms and ammunition they had purchased and stored abroad. They would be able to bring such additional materiel in after the British withdrew without fear of it being confiscated and otherwise provoking the British or the international community. Much of this heavier equipment, including armor and airplanes, would be necessary to repel the anticipated attacks from the conventional armies of the Arab League.

The Zionist offensive began on April 5 with the first objective being to conquer Jerusalem. The rough, mountainous terrain to the west of Jerusalem made this a formidable task as the Haganah pushed eastward from the coast. Palestinian irregulars under Abd-al Qadir repelled the offensive but he lost his life in the prolonged battle over Castel, five miles west of Jerusalem. In the midst of this campaign, the Irgun committed an atrocity that helped set off a general panic among the Arab population throughout the emerging Jewish state. In the small village of Deir Yassin three miles from Castel, some 250 men, women, and children perished at the hands of the Irgun, which also committed large-scale mutilations of its victims. Word of the massacre spread very quickly to other Arab communities and made Haganah conquest of major population centers easy as the centers became nearly devoid of their Arab populations. While Menachem Begin denies his forces employed unnecessary brutality at Deir Yassin, he acknowledges that Arab perception of what happened spread "panic" and caused thousands of Arabs to flee before the advancing Zionist forces, "shouting: Deir Yassin." He attributed the fall of many Arab areas to this fear, especially in Tiberius and Haifa. In Haifa, he said, Jewish forces "proceeded. . .like a knife through butter."

Tiberius, Haifa, and Jaffa soon fell under Haganah control. The British withdrew from Tiberius on April 19 and two days later they left Haifa. In both instances Haganah had complete control of the cities within twenty-four hours, as most of their Arab residents fled in panic to Lebanon, Syria, Egypt, or Gaza. In Jaffa, the Arab Liberation Army of al-Qawuqji withstood the joint Irgun-Haganah attack for twelve days, beginning April 24, before it fell. As elsewhere, most of the Jaffa Arab residents fled to Gaza or Egypt.

Throughout April, scores of other battles occurred all over the area designated for a Zionist state. Repeated efforts around Jerusalem resulted in Zionist control of western Jerusalem right up to the walls of the Old City by the end of the month. Continued Arab control of some areas between Jaffa and Jerusalem, however, jeopardized Zionist ability to hold their conquests in the Jerusalem region. Intense fighting around Safed in the eastern Galilee prevented the Haganah from enjoying control of this significant population center until May 12. Beisan fell to Haganah the same day to establish a firm Zionist hold on all of eastern Galilee. Non-Palestinian Arab elements entered the conflict as well during this period. An Egyptian Muslim Brotherhood unit clashed with Zionist settlers at Kfar Darom in the Negev beginning April 10. From May 4, Transjordanian forces fought intermittently with Gush Etzion block settlers just south of Jerusalem until the four settlements surrendered on May 14.

By May 15 the two northern sectors of the Jewish state were firmly under Zionist control with the added benefit of having 300,000 fewer Arab residents than when the conflict intensified in early April. The Haganah had not yet made a concerted effort to penetrate the Negev, although some probing had occurred in the Gaza area by way of preparation. Some Haganah operations in western Galilee, designated for an Arab state, put the Zionists closer to control of the strategic port of Acre and perhaps all of western Galilee. Attempts to bring all adjacent Arab population centers under control did not succeed. Tulkarm, Qalqilyah, Lydda, Ramleh, and Latrun, in the area designated for an Arab state, remained in Arab hands and posed something of a threat. Control over the Jaffa road through the latter three was essential to retain the conquests in west Jerusalem and achieve the even larger goal of obtaining the Old City of Jerusalem.

Numerous discussions and resolutions occurred in the U.N. from the latter part of March through the middle of May. They proved meaningless in the absence of any substantial overt international action in the Palestinian milieu, where two peoples were fighting for their survival. A special session of the General Assembly took no specific action before the end of the mandate. Finally, on May 20, the U.N. appointed Count Folke Bernadotte, the president of the Swedish Red Cross, as its official mediator to restore peace between Arabs and Zionists and to prevent a widening of the war.

FULL-SCALE WAR

Plans of the Arab League countries to use military force to abolish the Zionist menace when Great Britain withdrew proceeded apace. They made numerous supplications to the U.N. to cease partition plans and had, in fact, endorsed proposals for a U.N. trusteeship over Palestine. Despite advice to the contrary from their military advisers, the Arab leaders drastically underestimated the military strength of the Zionists. They assumed that their armies, although weak, could subdue the Zionists. Further, they seemed to have assumed that, through the interference of the U.N., an Arab state as defined in the partition resolution was the worst that could occur from a military effort.

While the Arab countries could agree to strike against Zionist control of Palestine, they suffered divisions that arose from their conflicting ambitions. All resented King Abdullah's apparent intention of annexing Palestine to Transjordan in a first step toward establishing his hegemony over the entire region, including Syria, Lebanon, and Iraq. His Arab Legion, by far the best Arab army, and the favorable strategic position of his troops, caused their concerns to be well founded. Abdullah was also closely associated with both the British and the Palestinians who opposed Hajj Amini's leadership. This also put him in conflict with both the Palestinian guerrillas, under the Mufti's control, and the Arab Liberation Army, which the Arab League financed and controlled. Thus, most of the Arab League states had as much interest in entering the Palestinian conflict to thwart Abdullah as to abolish the Jewish state they regarded as an outpost of Western imperialism.

The British High Commissioner's departure on May 14 sparked a new outburst of violence in Palestine to determine its destiny. In the first minute of May 15, when the British mandate ended, Ben-Gurion announced the independence of the State of Israel. Within ten minutes, President Truman recognized Israel's sovereignty. Military units from Egypt, Syria, Transjordan, Lebanon, Iraq, and Saudi

Arabia moved into Palestine the same day. The U.N. General Assembly met in special session but it took two weeks before it could agree, on May 29, to call for a one-month truce.

The Arab armies enjoyed the momentum of attack and experienced moderate successes on all fronts, the most important of which was the Transjordanian Arab Legion's conquest of the Old City of Jerusalem. They did not, however, enjoy either a united command or mutual trust. Nevertheless, the pressure they put upon the Israeli Defense Forces (as of May 26) limited the besieged state to defensive actions on most fronts. In particular, Israel could make no significant effort to secure the Negev region, which Egyptian forces held. The Israelis' greatest advances occurred in western Galilee when Acre fell on May 17 along with much of the surrounding area. Time favored the Israelis, however, because their heavy equipment began to arrive from overseas and volunteers poured into Israel despite U.N. sanctions against either side improving its military preparedness. By contrast, the Arabs had no means of improving their military situation and, if anything, became even more divided in their purpose.

Count Bernadotte obtained an agreement for the U.N. truce on June 11. The proposal he began to evolve for a peaceful solution was unacceptable to both sides because he suggested that, in recognition of the territorial changes during recent fighting, the Israelis should acquire western Galilee and give up their claim to the Negev. This would have established a fairly compact Israeli state in the most fertile northwest portion of Palestine. However, the Israelis could not accept this denial of the relatively large expanse of sparsely populated territory and the loss of a port on the Gulf of Aqaba for trade with Africa and the Orient. They assumed, after all, that Egypt would not allow them access to those markets through the Suez Canal. In keeping with their long-stated position, the Arabs refused to accept the legitimacy of Israel's claim to any Arab land. All Arab leaders except Abdullah also opposed Bernadotte's belief that the non-Zionist part of Palestine should merge with Transjordan.

Egypt and Syria refused to accept a continuation of the truce largely because they resented both Abdullah's control of Jerusalem and the prospect that he would annex all of the territory designated as an independent Arab state in Palestine. When war resumed on July 9, Israel benefitted from its military improvements and made significant advances, except in the Negev and against the Arab Legion in Jerusalem. Lydda and Ramleh fell, but Arab Legion control of Latrun prevented the Israelis from securing a corridor to the walls of the Old City. Much of western Galilee was under their control. The Israelis, in fact, proved they could defeat the Arab armies if they could prevent a ceasefire or a peace settlement. There was, however, the possibility that the U.N. might not accept extensive acquisitions and impose sanctions that would have made Israel's ability to function untenable. Count Bernadotte was the most visible symbol of this possibility, as even the United States endorsed his proposals. The Israelis had only ten days to obtain their modest gains, because with the threat of U.N. sanctions behind him, Bernadotte obtained a second truce on July 19.

On September 17, the Lehi under Yitzhak Shamir's command shot and killed Count Bernadotte because he was moving international forces toward accepting the exchange of western Galilee for the Negev. Dr. Ralph Bunche, Bernadotte's American assistant, continued the effort of arranging a permanent peace. At this juncture Hajj Amin announced the formation of the Government of All-Palestine, centered in Gaza, on September 20. All Arab League states, except Transjordan, recognized this government. In fact, shortly thereafter, Abdullah convened a contingent of anti-Husseini Palestinian delegates in Amman who pledged allegiance to him. Abdullah summonsed an even larger conference of Palestinians to Jericho in December. This contingent not only recognized him as "King of All Palestine," but acknowledged him as the ruler of Greater Syria. This, of course, expressed his own view of his mission to rule the entire Arab Levant.

TOWARD NEW BORDERS

Israel needed to act decisively to prevent a peace settlement contrary to its goals. Ben-Gurion had assured the Israelis that they enjoyed a decided military superiority because he did not want them to be timid. In the fall of 1948 he solidified all military command when he abolished the separate commands for Palmach units and forced the Irgun to dissolve and submit to the authority of Yaacov Dori, the Chief of Staff of the Israeli Defense Forces (IDF). Both changes were important, especially in light of the near-armed conflict between the IDF and the Irgun during the first truce in June. By mid-October the centralized IDF of about 90,000 troops, with considerable armor and airpower support, dwarfed the decentralized, lightly armed Arab armies of perhaps 50,000.

Israel, however, needed Arab provocation to justify renewing the war it knew it could win. On October 15 Israel seized on an Egyptian indiscretion against the truce to launch a well-planned campaign for control of the Negev. In places the Egyptians proved a worthy foe, but pressure from the international community was Israel's only formidable obstacle. The campaign continued from October throughout December despite U.N. resolutions and a British ultimatum for it to end. During the first week of January, 1949, the Israelis strained their relationship with the British to the breaking point when they shot down five Egyptian-based British planes. By that time, Egyptian losses were extensive enough that they agreed on January 7 to participate in armistice talks. Israel, thus, had control of the Negev, but it was almost the middle of March before its troops established a presence at the northern end of the Gulf of Aqaba. This move convinced King Abdullah to acquiesce to the creation of the Israeli port of Eliat alongside the Jordanian port of Aqaba. His alternative seemed to risk continued war and the likelihood of the Israelis expelling him from the entire West Bank. In June he changed his kingdom's name to Jordan, but he waited until April 25, 1950 to declare the formal annexation of the West Bank.

Israel made other acquisitions when the fighting resumed in October 1949. In Galilee, it dispensed with the Syrian, Lebanese, and ALA armies within three days in the process of annexing the Arab sector of the region, which placed Nazareth within its borders. A large area of the southwestern part of the central Arab sector came under Israeli control in the campaign against Egypt. This was also the fate of the Arab sector along the Palestinian border with the Egyptian Sinai peninsula. Egypt did, however, retain control over the thirty-mile long Gaza Strip where the Mufti had been elected president of the All-Palestine Government on October 1. Neither Iraq nor Transjordan participated in this stage of the war. Abdullah had apparently come to an agreement with the Israelis that enabled him to retain the jointly controlled Hashemite two-thirds of the central sector, including the Old City and East Jerusalem.

AN ARMISTICE WITHOUT PEACE

Only Israel was in a favorable position when the Rhodes armistice talks began on January 12, 1949. Initially, only Egypt and Israel participated, since only their armies were engaged in mortal combat. They signed a permanent armistice agreement on February 24. Four days later, Transjordanian delegates arrived with the authority to speak in behalf of Iraq as well. The Israeli-Transjordanian armistice was not signed until April 3 because Israel was moving its forces into control of Eliat during the intervening period. Lebanon had signed an armistice on March 23. The armistice that finally occurred between Syria and Israel on July 20 left their borders imprecise and in need of further refinement.

These bilateral documents were not peace treaties but merely formal agreements to the cessation of hostilities. They could not be otherwise because none of the Arab states recognized Israel's sovereignty. Thus, the Arab countries remained officially at war with a nation they maintained did not exist.

Israel's acceptance into the United Nations on May 11, 1949 gave it stature and legal protection that would make Arab attempts to abolish it nearly impossible. However, the absence of recognition from the Arab states remained the major impediment to Israel's security and economic development. It had to keep its entire population prepared for war at great financial cost. Lack of Arab recognition prohibited Israel's development of normal trade relations with its regional neighbors and Egypt's prohibition of its using the Suez Canal inhibited trade with much of the world.

Until 1950, there was still hope that Israel's status as an unwelcomed pariah to its neighbors was not a permanent condition. The international community, after all, remained involved in the situation after the armistice. The United Nations appointed a Conciliation Commission on Palestine on December 11, 1949. This commission was composed of the United States, Turkey, and France. It had authority to establish permanent borders, deal with the disposition of Jerusalem, foster economic development and cooperation, and solve the Palestinian refugee problem. The possibility of the commission having some success was based primarily upon the fact that it offered the only hope of the Arabs to achieve through negotiations what they had failed to do through war. If, for instance, they gained no redress, Israel would have increased its size by about one-third over the area allowed by the 1947 partition.

There was strong international sentiment, even from the United States, that Israel should be confined to the 1947 proposal and that Jerusalem should be an international city under U.N. trusteeship. Most also favored the repatriation of the 700,000 Palestinian refugees in Gaza, Lebanon, Syria, Egypt, and in Transjordanian-held Palestine. Attempts to address these problems, however, proved fruitless when the Commission met separately with the Arab and Israeli delegations at Lausanne in the spring of 1949. Direct negotiations could not occur since the Arabs feared that direct negotiations would construe their *de facto* recognition of Israel. Arab insistence on a return to the partition boundaries and a repatriation of the refugees as a prerequisite of further talks was unacceptable to Israel.

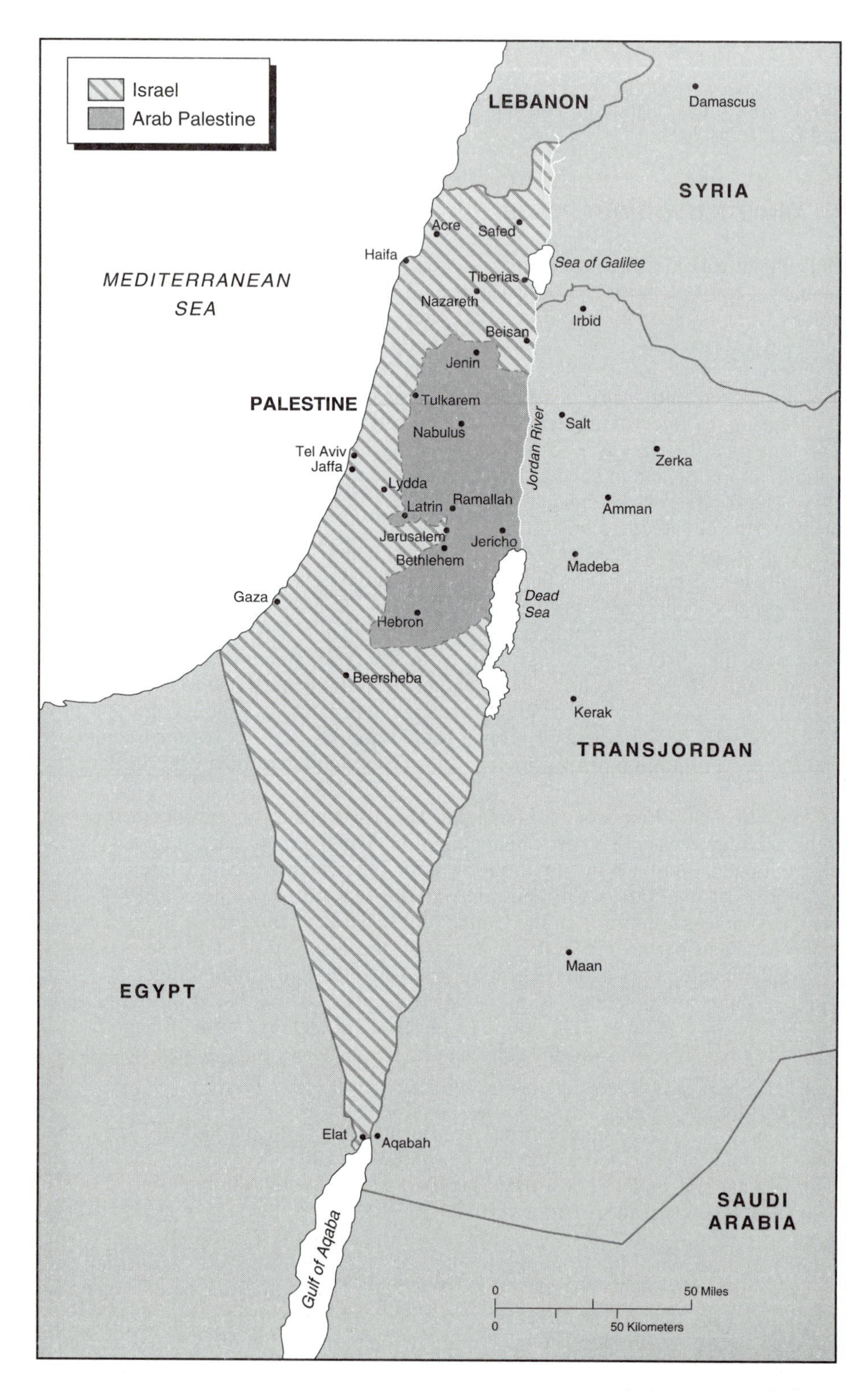
Israel
Arab Palestine
LEBANON
Damascus
SYRIA
Acre
Safed
Haifa
Sea of Galilee
MEDITERRANEAN
SEA
Tiberias
Nazareth
Irbid
Beisan
Jenin
PALESTINE
Tulkarem
Salt
Nabulus
Jordan River
Tel Aviv
Jaffa
Zerka
Lydda
Latrin
Ramallah
Amman
Jerusalem
Jericho
Bethlehem
Madeba
Gaza
Dead
Sea
Hebron
Beersheba
Kerak
TRANSJORDAN
Maan
EGYPT
Elat
Aqabah
SAUDI
ARABIA
Gulf of Aqaba
0
50 Miles
0
50 Kilometers

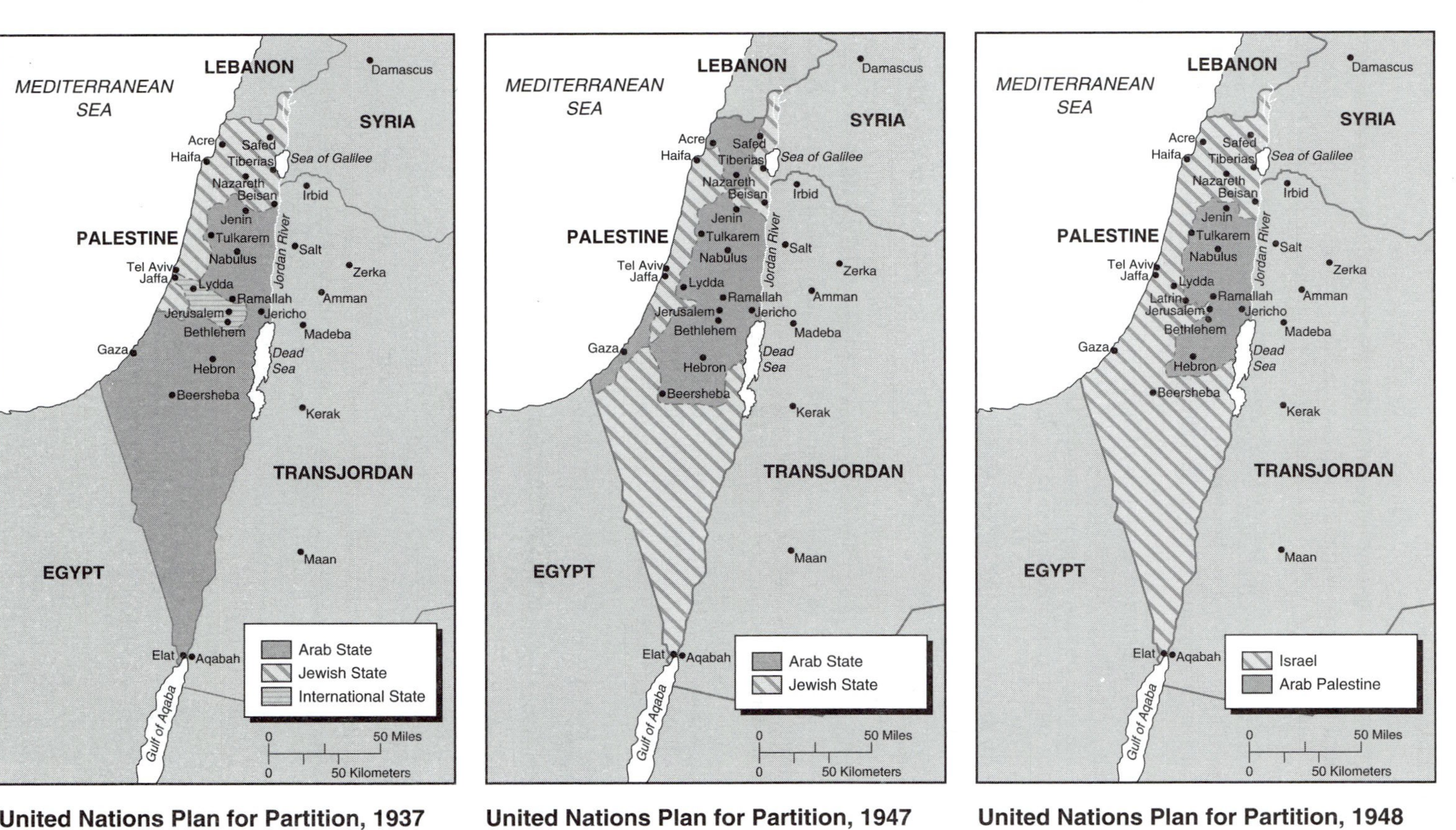

United Nations Plan for Partition, 1937

United Nations Plan for Partition, 1947

United Nations Plan for Partition, 1948

Israel's refusal to budge on any of its positions without recognition from the Arabs, and Arab refusal to negotiate without Israeli concessions, rendered U.N. resolutions meaningless. Having set a pattern for Arab-Israeli relations for decades to come, the Lausanne talks ended.

Therefore, the borders that Israel forged in the war remained intact, although it never defined exactly what its borders were. Zionist plans, after all, had always envisioned an Israeli state much larger than the one the U.N. designated and larger than the one it acquired through the war.

Arab disarray accounted for much of Israel's success in peace as it had in war. No Arab government admitted it had lost the war in Palestine. In fact, since there was still a state of war, there was no defeat. Each pointed to its Arab allies or the conspiracy of international forces to explain the ignoble Arab performance in Palestine. All disliked Abdullah for his expansionist pretensions and his virtual annexation of the West Bank to his kingdom. No Arab government, except Transjordan, enjoyed any credibility after the debacle in Palestine and all were on the verge of collapse from assassination or revolution.

Under these circumstances, the Arabs were in neither the mood nor the position to make any concessions. As they stubbornly stuck to their positions, they and the United Nations had to accept the *fait accompli* of Israel and Abdullah.

The 1948–1949 war in Palestine solidified the creation of the state of Israel; caused the direct or indirect fall of several Arab governments; led to the deaths of several Arab leaders; demonstrated the inability of the United Nations to settle disputes, avoid war, or even arrange an acceptable peace following war; disrupted international economic activities; resulted in about 350,000 Jews leaving their homes in Arab nations; and established barriers between pilgrims and their religious shrines. In this short list of major repercussions, only Israel benefitted since Abdullah was assassinated for his role on July 20, 1951.

Still, the Palestinian Arabs were the major victims of this moderately bloody war. About 130,000 remained within the borders of the new state of Israel where their non-Jewish identity gave them questionable status. Some 700,000 fled to nearby Arab nations with little but the clothes on their backs. While a few escaped with some assets, most huddled in makeshift shelters and relied on the United Nations Relief and Works Agency to care for their basic needs. The majority became political pawns of Palestinian and other Arab leaders. Through both conviction and careful coaching they resolved to remain refugees rather than assimilate into other nations. They did this as a reminder to the world of what had happened to their homeland. Their principal pastime became dreaming of their return to Palestine, much as the Jews had done for two thousand years before the Balfour Declaration had provided them an opening. Despite their own *diaspora,* most Israelis could not feel remorse for the Palestinians because their departure made room for many more Jews to enter Israel. Israelis could never understand why Palestinians could not easily adjust to living among their fellow Arabs. Also, many Jews lost respect for Palestinians because so many had been willing to sell their patrimony in the Promised Land and most had fled rather than fight. Some Arabs shared the same view of the Palestinians.

But Palestine and the plight of the Palestinians remained the focus of Middle East conflict after the world community generally accepted the post-1949 configuration. The legal approach, beginning with the incorporation of the Balfour

Declaration into the League of Nations Mandate for Palestine, failed. The successful use of force allowed Israel and Jordan to expand their borders at the expense of international diplomacy and the Palestinian Arabs. With some under Israeli rule, others under Jordanian authority, and nearly as many in exile, few Palestinians were content with their fate.

Their numbers were too few to predict the continued role they played. They became, however, a symbol of Arab plight, because the creation of Israel seemed to the Arabs the triumph of imperialism over the entire Arab world. Infant Israel, an outpost of the Western world, had defeated the combined Arab armies in the early moments after its birth. In the Arab view, Israel had infinite capital from all over the world to carry out its promise to "make the desert bloom." This success made the proud Arabs appear as inept managers as well as incompetent warriors. Tiny Israel could muster more international support than the Arabs with their vast lands, people, and vital resources.

While Arab leaders, with their close affiliations with the West, could accept this reality, most Arabs regarded the situation as absurd and humiliating. They easily concluded that they had to replace their own leaders as a first step toward preparing themselves to restore their honor through defeating Israel and, by proxy, the forces of imperialism that had created their inability to live with dignity in the modern world.

10

Arab Nationalism

HISTORICAL TIMELINE

1830s–1860s	⇛ The proliferation of European works in translation, especially from the Egyptian, Rifa'a al-Tahtawi, provided an infusion of knowledge and enthusiasm that Egyptian censors could never quell.
1840s–1860s	⇛ Shayhk Nasif al-Yaziji modernized Arabic through extensive poetry in the contemporary idiom. He also wrote on grammar, rhetoric, and logic.
1850s–1870s	⇛ Butrus al-Bustani helped modernize the Arabic language through his dictionary, his encyclopedia, and other extensive writings on the need for Arabs to learn modern science and other knowledge. He strongly emphasized national identity.
1860	⇛ Faris al-Shidyak published the first important newspaper in the Arabic language. He was an important link between Arab and European cultures.
1875	⇛ Creation of the secret society in Beirut that expressed unrest among some Arabs with Ottoman domination.
1871–1879	⇛ Jamal al-Din al-Afghani was in Egypt to help shape pan-Islamic views that inspired Egyptian and Arab nationalists.
1875–1905	⇛ Muhammad Abduh was at his height in his pan-Islamic and Egyptian nationalist activities.
1897	⇛ Muhammad Rashid Rida went to Egypt from Syria to play an

important role in pan-Islamic activities. Enhanced Arab nationalism by insisting on the need for an Arab caliph.

1898 ⇛ Abd al-Rahman al-Kawakibi moved to Egypt from Syria where he began to write and speak on behalf of the need for an Arab caliph.

1905 ⇛ Negib Azoury published his *Le Reveil de la Nation Arabe.*

1909 ⇛ Formation of the Literary Club.
⇛ Formation of *Al-Qahtanyyia.*

1911 ⇛ Formation of *Al-Fatat.*

1912 ⇛ Formation of the Ottoman Party for Administrative Decentralization in Cairo.
⇛ Formation of the Reform Committee in Beirut.

1913 ⇛ Arab Congress convened in Paris on June 18.
⇛ Major Aziz al-Misri formed *Al-Ahd.*

1915 ⇛ Large-scale executions of Arab nationalist leaders in Beirut and Damascus during August.
⇛ Sharif Hussein of Mecca accepted British terms to lead an Arab revolt.

1916 ⇛ Arab Revolt began on June 5.

1918 ⇛ Arab army entered Damascus on September 30.

1920 ⇛ Syrian Congress elected Feisal King of Syria and Abdullah King of Iraq on March 20.
⇛ British and French announced the mandate system on April 24 at the end of the San Remo Conference.
⇛ French occupied Damascus on July 25.
⇛ French expanded borders of Mt. Lebanon to create basic boundaries of modern Lebanon on September 1.

1921 ⇛ British created Transjordan.

1922 ⇛ League of Nations approved mandates for Palestine and Syria.

1924 ⇛ League of Nations approved mandate for Iraq.

1926 ⇛ French created the Republic of Lebanon.

1931 ⇛ Creation of *Ahali* organization in Iraq.

1932 ⇛ Antun Sa'ada created Syrian National Party.

1933 ⇛ King Feisal of Iraq died on September 8.

1930s–1950s ⇛ Extensive work of Sati al-Husri to foster Arab nationalism primarily through modern secular education.

1935 ⇛ Creation of the League of National Action in Syria.

1939 ⇛ Zaki Arsuzi created the Arab Nationalist Party in Syria.

1940 ⇛ Zaki Arsuzi created *al-Baath al-Arabi.*

1943 ⇛ Michel Aflaq and Salah al-Din Bitar created the Baath Movement.

1945 ⇛ Formal announcement of the League of Arab States on March 22.
⇛ Aflaq and Bitar referred to their organization as the Baath Party.

1947 ⇛ Initial congress of the Baath Party on April 4.

1948 ⇛ Creation of the State of Israel on May 15.
⇛ First Arab-Israeli war.

1949 ⇛ Three military coups in Syria.

1952 ⇛ Free Officer Corps coup in Egypt on July 23.

1953 ⇛ Merger of Baath Party with Akram Hourani's Arab Socialist Party.

1956 ⇛ Nationalization of the Suez Canal on July 26.

1958 ⇛ Egypt and Syria merged to become the United Arab Republic on February 1.
⇛ Iraq and Jordan merged to form the Arab Union on February 14.

Arab national consciousness, like most other modern nationalist movements, developed in response to foreign domination. Arab nationalists, however, faced a three-stage challenge. First, they encountered their prolonged subordinate status in the Turkish-dominated Ottoman Empire, which they initially wanted to modify and later desired to escape. After its disintegration during World War I, most Arab areas fell under European domination, which continued until the mid-twentieth century. During these first two stages Arab nationalists concentrated upon justifying what they considered their right and necessity of self-government. Once free from foreign control, Arabs faced the almost equally strong challenge of defining their identity among themselves and establishing the physical perimeters of their nation. Serious questions also arose over the political, social, and economic nature of the state, in addition to determining where it should be centered and to whom the Arabs should entrust their leadership. This latter stage was particularly bedeviling because recognition of the validity of more than one Arab nation was inherently contradictory to the concept of nationalism.

The huge territorial expanse, the religious and ethnic diversity, the disparities in economic development and potential, along with the drastically different experiences of the various portions of the Arab "nation" further confounded attempts to achieve consensus. North African Arabs were, for instance, quite different from their southwest Asian brethren. For that matter, northwest African and northeast African Arabs seemed to have little in common, except in comparison to entirely different people in other parts of the world. In southwest Asia, the Arabs of Greater Syria, with their centuries of intercourse with many of the world's cultures, and the Arabian peninsula Arabs, who had largely remained isolated, were strained to recognize their kinship. Each of these disparate larger regions, with the exception of northwest Africa, however, could make a good case for their region providing the focus of the Arab nation.

The educated elite in all the large cities, which were the centers of nationalist activities, arrived at conclusions about the Arab past and future that the preponderance of the rural population, and the entire Arabian peninsula, did not comprehend.

Their general acceptance of secular precepts and tolerance for Arabs, especially non-Muslims, with questionable Arab credentials caused distress among the less urbane. The general level of sophistication in the entire Levant, where much of the nationalist ideology originated, positioned it at loggerheads with many of the other Arab areas, where traditional approaches and values prevailed. Egypt's uniqueness, because of its cultural continuity from antiquity, its early and intense experiments with modernization, and its peculiar ordeal with British domination, imbued it with its own singular perspective.

The close association of Islam with Arabs also complicated efforts to formulate an agreement on national identity. Prevailing Muslim authorities were inclined to reject concepts and practices from non-Islamic origin. Nationhood intrinsically contradicted the universal nature of Islam both in theory and in practice. Muslim authorities, most of whom had little knowledge of the relatively new concept of nation-state, almost instinctively realized that the modern approach to social organization threatened the status of traditional religion. They were, of course, correct, especially in the proclivity of modern states to supplant religious law with secular law and to demand allegiance to the state above all else. The role of Christian activists in the Arab nationalist movement added to the suspicions of some Muslim authorities. Conversely, some Christian Arab nationalists embraced secular, national government as a better guarantee for their security, rather than depending upon a special relationship between their confessional communities and the Islamic establishment.

The presence of significant clusters of non-Arabs among the predominantly Arab population evoked additional conceptional questions and posed potential problems. Nationalists were compelled to address some means of accommodating groups such as the Kurds, Armenians, Druze, Circassians, Copts, and Jews, who had always lived among the Arabs. Most had distinct ethnic, religious, or linguistic characteristics that distinguished them from the Arabs. Most Christian Arabs did not represent a problem to the Arab nationalists, except for the Maronite Christians, many of whom identified with Western, rather than Arabic culture. These people were unquestionably indigenous to the Arab lands and there was no serious discussion of expelling them. Jews, who entered the region in response to the Zionist movement, were clearly a different matter. Most Arabs, nationalist or otherwise, agreed that the influx of Zionists was an unacceptable violation of regional dignity. Ironically, the perception of a Zionist threat proved to be a unifying factor among Arabs. Opposition to Zionism became the penultimate test of one's Arabism. Ironically, Zionism kept the whole question of Arab nationalism alive.

One of the main questions that arose was "What is an Arab?" From before the time of the Prophet Muhammad, *Arab* designated the traditional nomads. Even the assignment of proportional representation for Arabs in the Ottoman legislature after the adoption of a constitution in 1876 was more the coincidence of Arab speakers with specific land, than a recognition of the Arabs as distinct people within the Muslim *umma*. Otherwise, the Arab population deserved a considerably larger representation, since they outnumbered Turks in the Ottoman Empire. "Arab" began to acquire a broader meaning in the smoldering, strained relations between Arabs and Turks in the late nineteenth century. This innovation surfaced among Christian Arabs, who advocated the adoption of Western constitutional guarantees, and also among prominent Islamic reformers, who were concerned with Turkish stewardship of Islam. As the gulf slowly widened between Arabs and Turks, *Arab* evolved in the early twentieth century to encompass everyone who spoke the Arabic language and identified with the Arab culture. This new approach gained widespread acceptance and had the advantage of linking modern, urban Arabs with their nomadic ancestors, while it also accommodated large numbers of Christians and Druze, who had no significant identification with a culture beyond the region. Vague as the new term was, it also conveyed a specificity that the term "Ottoman" never possessed. It was, however, a simple and adroit means of providing comfort to the widest possible spectrum of the population in the region, which the nationalists aspired to transform into a state.

THE PENALTY FOR SUCCESS

The expansive lands of Arabic speakers were a testimony to former Arab success and glory, just as they were an obstacle to nationalist aspirations. The areas where the Arabic language was dominant closely corresponded to Arabic conquest in the halcyon era of the seventh and eighth centuries after the original Arabs erupted from the Arabian peninsula. It also corresponded to the areas where earlier Semetic languages, in which Arabic is rooted, had deep, traditional roots. This helps explain why the original Arabic conquests were fairly easy and enduring. The dramatic and rapid expansion of the Arabs resulted in a cultural transformation, which spread both Islam and the Arabic language. The empire soon exceeded the capability of a single government in Damascus to control it. This and other results of success led to the emergence of regional dynasties. Even the establishment of a new capital in Baghdad in the middle of the eighth century, under apparent Arab control, signalled the end of Arab domination over the vast empire their conquests had wrought. The inexplicable cosmopolitanism of the Abbasids in Iraq opened all levels of participation and leadership to assertive and forceful individuals, irrespective of their ethnic origin.

This willing incorporation of non-Arabs into the leadership of the Islamic empire, including the caliphate, conformed with the universal message of the Prophet, which did not confine Islam to the perimeters of Arab population or deny its highest offices to believers of any origin. It also established that the vast domain, which resulted from the original Arab conquests, was both Islamic and Arab. The Arabs, in fact, became subsumed in the empire their success created. The spread of the Arabic language and the religion it heralded remained the monument to their triumph. The use of both became second nature to the converts, who embraced both Arabic and Islam and proclaimed devotion to their uniqueness with an ardor that should have pleased the original proselytizers.

Arabic speakers of all linguistic and ethnic origin, as well as many non-Arabic speakers, revered the accomplishments of the original Arabs. The Arabic speakers embraced them as their own triumphs and lost any sense of ever having been anything but Arabs. It was, therefore, fitting that the Arabic language should provide the bond for the millions of Arab speakers, who aspired to resurrect their specific identity in a twentieth-century nation-state. This new political structure, after all, was the modern means of preserving self-esteem and obtaining collective dignity.

Equally compelling was the generally acknowledged tenet that a people without a state in modern times were doomed to perish or endure subservience under some other nation's flag.

SCHOLARLY ISLAMIC CONTRIBUTORS

Egypt's unique experience with British domination from 1882 helped separate it from the larger questions of general Arab nationalism before the mid-twentieth century. This remained true despite the fact that nationalists of almost all persuasions used Egypt as a safe base for planning and publicizing their proposals. There is good evidence that, as many thought, Great Britain encouraged greater Arab nationalism, while it combatted Egyptian nationalism, which was almost exclusively inspired by the desire to expel the British from Egypt.

Some of the major leaders of the Egyptian nationalist movement, however, contributed to the cause of Arab nationalism from its earliest stages by developing acceptable explanations for the compatibility of nationalism with Islam. The erudition of Islamic scholars such as Jamal al-Din al-Afghani, Muhammad Abduh, and Rashid Rida reconciled Islam with nationalism and, almost inadvertently, undermined the validity of the caliphate under Turkish authority. Their emphasis upon the desirability of a more practical Islam, also perhaps against their wishes, reduced resistance to later nationalist concepts that were totally secular.

Al-Afghani was the most important, if for no other reason than that he inspired the others. Probably of Persian origin, despite the name he assumed, he preached his innovative concepts of Islam from India to England. His influence resulted almost exclusively from his teaching and activist political participation, rather than from publishing or obtaining official positions. Political and religious officials, as well as dissidents to both kinds of institutions sought his council, which he was also eager to share. His most effective work, however, occurred in his anti-British activities in Egypt and Persia. He was also an equally formidable foe to supposedly Muslim political leaders if he regarded them as puppets of Western imperialism. Some believe, for instance, that he plotted the assassination of the Khedive Ismail of Egypt and most agree that he successfully inspired the assassination of Shah Nasir al-Din of Persia. His eight years in Egypt from 1871 to 1879 proved to be particularly provocative as this period corresponded with Egypt's financial bankruptcy of Ismail's later reign, which led to Europeans placing Egypt under receivership.

Al-Afghani's concern that the entire Islamic world was falling under European control became the driving force behind all of his activities. He attributed Europe's strength to its superior understanding of modern knowledge and techniques. He surmised that the Islamic world needed modification in every respect to survive. He did not believe that modern science and the use of reason were antithetical to Islam, since much of this knowledge had originated in the Islamic world. However, the West had continued its development while the Islamic world had largely forgotten what the creative early Islamic generations had produced. In al-Afghani's view, authentic Islamic practice required the fullest development of human intellectual faculties to modify the entire Islamic society appropriate to all new developments. Islam, by contrast, tended to regard all change contrary to the milieu of its golden age as unacceptable.

The Islamic world had to become strong or perish. It did not, however, have a single governmental or military instrument through which Muslims could act. It was, therefore, necessary to make the Islamic world stronger region by region. This easily led to justifying the development of strong states. The collective strength of the modern Islamic world would have to result from the strength of the sum of its strong individual states.

Muhammad Abduh was a native Egyptian who confined his emphasis upon reform to Egypt. He worked closely with al-Afghani in Egypt and shared a period of exile with him in Paris. Generally, however, he was able to teach and write about the need for Islamic rejuvenation and enjoy the support of both the British and Egyptian political establishment. In his later years he became Mufti of Egypt and served on the khedive's legislative council.

Abduh supplemented his traditional Islamic education with an extensive study of the major European thinkers. He admired much about European knowledge and appreciated the transformation it had caused in European life and strength. He advocated adapting European developments to Egypt's Islamic society, but he rejected the need for the wholesale adaptation of European practices to Egypt. He predicted that the alternative to such an adjustment would cause the demise of all societies that refused to recognize the inevitable continuation of modern ways and science that had originated in Europe. Like al-Afghani, Abduh believed that Muslims should first know their religion thoroughly in order to understand what to preserve in its original form and which practices, some of which were regarded as Islamic, should fall into disuse.

His contention that Islam was reasonable, and receptive to all that was reasonable, contributed to reducing the monopoly that traditionalist practitioners of Islam had upon Egyptian thinking and education. In his view, no knowledge, from whatever origin, was intrinsically incompatible with Islam. His emphasis upon reason and science led many to question his religious belief, despite the high office and esteem he had as a Muslim. His status made his ideas both respectable and influential.

His contribution to nationalism was related primarily to his concern for making Egypt strong by altering its education and institutions to meet modern needs. He did not, however, approve of the nationalist approach of either Mustafa Kamil or Colonel Arabi, although he suffered exile for finally associating with the Arabi movement. He regarded both of these nationalists as spurious, because they appealed to the grossest instincts of the Egyptian population without regard for the necessary preliminary preparation for independence through education.

Muhammad Rashid Rida was a Syrian Muslim from Tripoli who went to Egypt in 1897 because of his fascination with the teachings of al-Afghani and Abduh. Rida went to Egypt with a sound education in traditional Islamic scholarship. He worked closely with Abduh, since al-Afghani was active elsewhere. His overt attachment to Abduh indicated his predilection to a nontraditional approach to Islam. His "nontraditional" approach, however, was to seek the return of the best of Islam from the earliest times when it manifested its purest attributes.

Rida concluded that Muslims were weak because they had deviated from the essential truth of their religion. He believed Europeans had built their strength on a secular base, but, through the proper approach, Muslims could incorporate modern scientific, political, and social developments without destroying their religious foundation.

Rida's acceptance of much of modern European civilization is all the more remarkable because, unlike al-Afghani and Abduh, he neither studied European literature nor travelled in Europe. His willingness to accept innovation, however, was a testimony to his confidence in Islam and his recognition that Western ways dictated the present and future. He was confident that nearly everything that made Europe strong originated in the Islamic world. Islam could, therefore, deal with it effectively in its modern configuration.

He placed emphasis upon the need for effective and innovative leadership in the caliphate. He wanted reform from the top. This would require the leadership of an Arab caliph, as only someone of Arabic origin could fully understand the original Islam and its later developments in such a way as to be able to differentiate between the essential and the burdensome alien traditions that had become confused with Islam. Achievement of this did not require a separate Arab state, and, in fact, he remained loyal to the Ottoman government until the Young Turks began to expel Arabs from high positions after 1909.

The strident Turkish nationalism of the Young Turks moved Rida to a more overtly Arab nationalist posture. He helped establish the Ottoman Party of Administrative Decentralization in 1912 and played a central role in shaping Arab nationalist efforts in Greater Syria throughout World War I and during the mandate period until his death.

Abd al-Rahman al-Kawakibi, a Syrian of Kurdish lineage, went to Egypt within a year after Rida went there. He arrived at similar conclusions to those of Rida, but expressed a much more overt dissatisfaction with Turkish domination of Islam. His two books, *Characteristics of Tyranny* and *Mecca: Mother of Cities,* criticized the despotic nature of the Ottoman Empire as contrary to the teaching and practice of Islam. He observed that Ottoman despotism had spread ignorance and had affected the religious, civil, and moral character of the entire empire. It was necessary, therefore, to change government policy in order to change the rest of society. But, he pointed out, the Turks could not do this. Like his friend, Rida, he believed Arabs had to regain leadership of Islam to make it whole and rectify the problems of society that helped account for the weakness of the Arab and Islamic world.

Islam needed an Arab caliph, but he advocated that the leader should have only spiritual duties, except in the Hijaz, and that the leader should remain aloof from temporal affairs that corrupt religion. Preferably, the caliph should come from the family of the Prophet that still lived in the Arabian peninsula, where Islam remained purest because its inhabitants understood its precepts. This was unquestionably an Arab-nationalist, even Pan-Arabist, position. It ascribed a moral, and perhaps intellectual, superiority of Arabs over Turks. These ideas proved beneficial in validating the central role of the Hashimite family in the Arab revolt against the Ottoman Empire and the continued struggle of Arabs to free themselves from European control.

NATIONALISM IN THE FERTILE CRESCENT

Although the borders that originated during the mandate period endured, the synthetic nature of the states they defined failed to produce a widespread sense of identity or loyalty among the citizens within the new states. Hardly anyone regarded them as permanent and virtually no one regarded them as sacrosanct. Most Lebanese,

Palestinians, and Transjordanians sought union with Syria. A significant element of the Syrian population desired union with Iraq. Some Iraqis, especially the Kurds, aspired to have their own state or preferred union with Turkey. Some southern Transjordanians favored union with either the Hijaz or the regime of Ibn Saud. All of the governments, except that of Lebanon, actively attempted to annex areas beyond their borders. There was also little doubt that the Zionists also yearned to expand their borders beyond the tiny area in which the League of Nations recognized that they could legally develop a "homeland."

Not surprisingly, this emotional flux inspired almost every conceivable configuration for the Fertile Crescent. This region gave rise to the fullest possible conceptional definitions of the Arab nation. There was little consideration in these early stages of including either the Arabian peninsula or north Africa, including Egypt, in the Arab state. Most believed that those regions, which were also Arabic speaking and predominantly Muslim, were functionally incompatible with the greater Fertile Crescent.

Scholarly controversy abounds over the question of the exact origin of an Arab nationalist sentiment, which in time became the most important force in modern Arab life. The willingness of some to dismiss its earliest expressions as a manifestation of Christian provincialism in league with European Powers seems as unfounded as those who regard them as the unquestioned embryo of the mature movement. It is likely, in fact, that all discussion of a significant difference between Arabs and other peoples of the Ottoman Empire, especially the Turks, contributed to the erosion of both Ottoman and Islamic unity to spawn an interest, and then a commitment, for Arabs to develop an independent identity.

Since the Arabic language ultimately became the primary credential for certifying an Arab identity, it is essential to acknowledge the contributions of three Syrian Christian scholars in arousing Arab interest in their language as a viable instrument for modern written expression in the middle of the nineteenth century. Muslims could not have demonstrated any greater pride than Nasif al-Yaziji, Faris al-Shidyak, and Butrus al-Bustani expressed for the language as a result of their study of classical Arabic works that dealt with either Islamic or secular topics. Their enthusiastic expression of the need for its revival was addressed to Arabs of all faiths. Ironically, a considerable amount of their activity occurred in their efforts to assist American Protestant missionaries find the most effective means of reaching the Arabs with their religious and educational messages. The arrival of printing presses in the Arab-speaking world at the same time opened both the past and the future to literate Arabs, whose numbers increased steadily. The proliferation of European works in translation, especially from the Egyptian, Rifa'a al-Tahtawi, provided an infusion of knowledge and enthusiasm Ottoman censors could never quell.

The brief Ottoman experiment with constitutionalism in 1876–1877 increased Arab hope only to bring eventual frustration. Many Arabs were familiar with Western constitutional concepts by that time through their increased educational opportunities. The entire *Tanzimat* program had acknowledged a need for change in the Ottoman Empire. Failure to implement change rapidly enough kindled separatist attitudes among some of the educated Arabs, who were imbued with a stronger sense of their past and knowledge of more equitable societies to their west. The failure of the new constitutional period under the Young Turks to bring redress ignited an increase in Arab displeasure under an overtly Turkish regime. Educated Arabs, after all, had been among the most enthusiastic supporters of the Young

Turk advocacy of constitutional government. It was not surprising that some of them pursued activities that would either require more liberties for Arab areas or lead to confrontation.

The subsequent clashes between Arab activists and Ottoman officials cannot be dismissed as frivolous and unimportant. The fact that these clashes did not result in the creation of an Arab nation is irrelevant to their role in establishing additional groundwork for later developments. The fact that the most committed activists kept their organizations secret and that many of them suffered execution for their efforts indicates how seriously both they and the Ottoman officials regarded these activities. The participation of Christians, Muslims, and Druze verifies these activities as nationalist, rather than confessional. They had in common a sense of being Arabs under a governmental structure that did not provide them either with fair treatment or with the fullest opportunities to develop either as individuals or as a collective entity.

The nature of the Arab organizations varied but they had a recognition of Arab identity in common. The Literary Club, which was founded in 1909, soon after the counterrevolution failed, was the first major organization to serve Arab interests. Its activities were open and apparently sufficiently innocuous to be centered in Istanbul. The thousands of members of the Literary Club were primarily from the Fertile Crescent, where there were local chapters of the organization. *Al-Qahtaniya* came into existence at about the same time, but its secret and small membership indicated a more political agenda. Under the leadership of Major Aziz Ali al-Misri, this organization adopted a method of selecting its members and maintaining its security that became the model for most successful Arab political organizations that followed. Members knew very few of their fellow conspirators, all of whom had to have a sponsor and satisfy strict standards of commitment. Military officers composed a large portion of the membership, which sought autonomy for Arabs within the empire, similar to the arrangement the Hungarians acquired within the Austrian Empire in 1867. It disbanded out of fear that Ottoman officials had penetrated its security; however, its members remained active and the Ottoman Party for Administrative Decentralization adopted its principal platform from the safety of Cairo in 1912.

Al-Fatat began in Paris in 1911 among Muslim students and remained predominantly a Muslim organization. It screened its members in much the same way as *al-Qahtaniya* and thereby ensured that its membership would remain small even after it moved to Beirut and then to Damascus. This organization sought independence for the Arab regions of the Ottoman Empire without any intermediary step such as autonomy and special administrative considerations. It convened an Arab Congress in Paris on June 18, 1913, to which most of the other organizations sent delegates. The failure of the congress to accomplish any notable results does not discredit it, as some would claim. Ottoman officials were sufficiently concerned to make a strong protest to the French government for allowing the conference and perhaps assisting the Arab organizers. The Ottoman government also thought it a serious enough threat to negotiate with its leaders and promise to grant major concessions to the Arabs in keeping with decentralization concepts that remained the predominant goal of the more august Arab activists. Using tactics similar to those the Ottomans had used against the Young Ottomans, they also offered governmental positions to some activists, who believed they had gained entree for improving the status of Arabs within the empire.

A multiconfessional organization called the Committee of Reform originated in Beirut toward the end of 1912 as essentially a Fertile Crescent branch of the Cairo-based Decentralization party, whose membership was also primarily from the Greater Syria region. It actually attempted to hold meetings in all the larger cities to demonstrate popular sentiments to the Ottoman government and to arouse a popular following. The predictable Ottoman suppression of the movement in April led to demonstrations and arrests, followed by more demonstrations, which the authorities ended through releasing prisoners and making concessions. These events formed the backdrop for the Arab Congress that met in Paris one month later.

The persistence of the Arab activists helps account for the larger concessions the Ottoman government made to the Arab Congress, although they apparently never intended to keep the agreement. They felt compelled to give the appearance of meeting Arab demands to prevent further Arab development. The organizing groups were still small in number and had only begun to seek popular support. No Arab group had reached the point of seeking support from a foreign nation and they had taken no significant steps toward developing their own military option. The Ottoman authorities were aware, however, that some Arab officers were actively involved in the budding Arab nationalist cause.

Major Aziz al-Misri, in fact, had organized a group of more than three hundred Arab officers into *al-Ahd* (The Covenant) at the end of 1913, when it became obvious that the Ottoman government did not intend to implement its promise to establish Arab autonomy. Whether on mere suspicion or on real evidence, despite the officers' attempt to keep their small organization secret, Ottoman officials arrested al-Misri and sentenced him to death. This was not the reaction of a government that believed the Arab nationalists were a mere nuisance. The public reaction was strong enough that, combined with international pressure, the Ottoman authorities released al-Misri and allowed him to return to his home in Egypt. He remained an Arab activist for the rest of his life and helped inspire and organize the Free Officer movement that overthrew the Egyptian monarchy in 1952. After initially accepting the position, he refused to serve as chief of staff of the Arab Revolt under the Sharif of Mecca, because he still sought Arab autonomy rather than independence. However, fellow members of *al-Ahd* provided most of the professional Arab officer leadership of that movement and played prominent roles in all the future Fertile Crescent states.

THE EFFECT OF THE WAR

World War I provided an unexpected opportunity for Arab separatists to alter their approach and launch a frontal attack on the Ottoman government in an effort to achieve independence. There had been no preparation for this new and drastic direction for their frustrations. Serious Arab dissatisfaction with Ottoman policies, after all, had only recently arisen. The limited numbers of those involved in quasi-nationalist activities had confined their conceptional development and limited political activities to seeking constitutional guarantees and the right to use Arabic in educational and administrative institutions. The Arab activists expressed Arab discontent, rather than desperation. A more critical stage in Arab-Turkish relations had emerged less than a year before the war erupted; the formation of *al-Ahd* conveyed the increased cleavage.

In many respects the war hindered opportunities to cultivate a broad base of popular support for either autonomy or independence. Normal civility, which had always existed between Arabs and Turks, vanished. With it went the opportunity for typically prolonged discussions to make adjustments. The Ottomans had always depended more on accommodation, rather than force, to hold their vast lands together. The outbreak of the most violent war the Ottomans had ever faced denied both the Turks and the Arabs the luxury of discussion. In this atmosphere, Arabs could not engage in either demonstrations or boycotts to win concessions. Arab activists, whom the Turks could regard as troublesome during peace, became seditious and traitorous once war began. Arab army officers had no time to engage in conspiracies while they were fulfilling their military duties for the government. Also, predominantly Arab military units moved to the frontiers under attack, primarily in Gallipoli and Iraq, and were unable to provide either the threat or reality of force to gain political goals. Martial law and the deprivations of the war made survival the principal concern of the Ottoman Empire's Arab population. Religious authorities had little difficulty convincing most Muslims that the Islamic caliph and heartland were under attack by forces that presented mortal danger from unbelievers. Once the caliph declared a *jihad,* the discontent for most Muslim Arabs became a minor concern. Any who thought otherwise could expect little following after the large-scale executions of mostly Muslim political activists in Beirut and Damascus in August 1915 and also in May 1916.

The Arabian peninsula became the only possible center for Arab discontent to develop further during the war, since circumstances prevented a popular Arab uprising. Even in the relative safety of the Arabian peninsula, a nationalist movement required collusion with a foreign power to provide finances, arms, and military assistance if it were going to be anything more than symbolic. The eventual British assistance made the Arab Revolt a meaningful part of the Allied war effort against the Ottoman government and provided the Arabs an opportunity to define their future. After the Arab army entered Damascus in September 1918, the circumstances of both the Turks and the Arabs ended any consideration of their future affiliation. The Arabs could govern themselves if the British left.

Emir Feisal consolidated his position from his base in Damascus with the broadest possible appeal to the people of the entire Fertile Crescent. His origin in the Arabian peninsula provided him with sound Arab credentials. His repeated use of the term "Arab," however, indicated that he used it to refer to the people of all faiths who lived in the region and spoke the Arabic language. A significant percentage of the people he cultivated and addressed as Arabs were Christian, Jews, Druze, and members of schismatic Islamic sects. While relatively few Arabs had participated in the military effort, the fruits of victory obviously belonged to all Arabs of the Fertile Crescent. Hashemite ascendancy blurred significant differences in defining the new situation more precisely. The Syrian Congress, which had a Jewish member, and which elected Feisal as King of Syria and Abdullah as King of Iraq in March 1920, contained representatives from the entire region. The father of the two new monarchs remained King of the Hijaz. The older brother, Ali, was the heir to that throne. Ibn Saud was well on his way to establishing his control over most of the remainder of the Arabian peninsula. From all appearances, therefore, Arabs had established their control over the Arab lands, which still contained some British and French occupation forces, but their governments had promised to leave the Arab lands after defeating the Ottoman Empire.

The announcement of the mandates on April 24, 1920 crushed this Arab arrangement and provided Arab nationalists with a greater challenge than the Ottomans had presented. The Arab nationalists faced overwhelming military forces and the concerted efforts of the entire League of Nations. Their one advantage at this stage was a commitment to full independence with broad popular support, rather than the half-measures that had been under consideration before the war without much public knowledge. Fertile Crescent Arabs began to have more in common with their North African brethren, because they were, for the first time, also under occupation by European nations. It became increasingly difficult for one region to gain its freedom without cooperation with the others. Their collective plight inspired new definitions of a larger Arab nation that helped make anything smaller seem provincial and self-serving, if not treasonous.

THE GRADUAL MOVE TO UNITY

The transformation of Arab nationalism from belief in some kind of confederation of regional Arab states to an unwillingness to accept anything short of total unity was gradual. The marked differences among the various major Arab regions were the most obvious reason that most Arab nationalists did not consider the creation of a single state. In addition, each of the specific regions was initially too preoccupied with obtaining independence from its particular foreign occupation to address the larger issue.

The long-standing advocacy of a Syrian state on the part of most of the early nationalists provided an even greater impediment. This was understandable since the largest percentage of the nonmilitary Arab activists were residents of Greater Syria. Damascus appealed to them as the natural capital of the Arab state of their vision because of its connection with Arab glory under the Ummayads and because it had been the capital of the short-lived Arab kingdom following World War I. Baghdad, by contrast, did not enjoy similar appeal and most Arab nationalists in the immediate post-World War I period did not even envision the union of Syria and Iraq, as the creation of two separate kingdoms in 1920 attests. Greater Syria, as then defined, was more sophisticated, more modern, and economically and educationally more developed. Attention not only to French occupation, but its policy of dividing the small Syrian mandate into autonomous provinces, was more than enough to occupy their energies. The challenge of restoring even mandatory Syria to a single unit kept alive the belief that Syria was a natural entity whose diverse population could cooperate in a nonconfessional, constitutional, modern state.

The growing independence of Lebanon under French protection became an overriding concern for Greater Syrian advocates. The expansion of Mt. Lebanon's borders in 1920 and the creation of a separate Lebanese Republic in 1926 boded ill to Syrian nationalists, who had already experienced the separation of Palestine and Transjordan from the Arab state they had envisioned since the later years of the Ottoman Empire.

Many of the ideas of Antun Sa'ada were not new, therefore, when he created the Syrian National Party in 1932, because others had defined much the same borders of the Greater Syria his party militantly tried to establish. Others had also advocated a total separation of religion from national policy or qualification for holding public office, but perhaps none had been so unequivocal on that issue.

There was, however, no precedent for the tight political structure he created, which owed complete allegiance to him and to his secular philosophy. Many supporters of the same basic territorial concept for a Greater Syria perceived Sa'ada and his party as a threat. Party members were generally well educated and relentless. The party was effective, in stark contrast to other parties, which were almost invariably loose confederations of interest groups that were built around the often selfish concerns of individuals or families. Sa'ada's Greek Orthodox background seems to have discredited his leadership even among secularly oriented Muslims. His detractors also accused the Syrian National Party of being a socially conservative movement that served European interests.

The perceived threat of the Syrian National Party arose at the time Iraq received its independence in 1930 and became the first Arab nation to gain admission into the League of Nations. It also corresponded closely with increased Zionist immigration into Palestine and with Emir Abdullah's unabashed attempts to extend his control to Syria following Feisal's death in 1933. Iraq, under its young king, Ghazi, offered hope to nationalists who feared these developments. Ghazi, in fact, had considerable Arab-nationalist inclinations. He allowed the army, which contained strong nationalist sentiments, to become more involved in politics. He reigned over the first Arab nation to have control over its internal policies, although it remained heavily under British influence in foreign and military affairs. The educational program of Iraq became its most notable manifestation of independence, which also made it the new center of Arab nationalist activities. Under German inspiration, Iraq's educational institutions from the primary level to the University of Baghdad proselytized a chauvinistic nationalism that soon developed into advocacy of Pan-Arabism. Iraqis, thus, broadened the scope of existing nationalism to encompass the entire Arabic-speaking world. Their effective presentation of this bold, new ideology put nationalist concepts of lesser scope on the defensive. The burden of proof rested on regional nationalists to defend plans that limited Arab nationhood to anything less than its greatest potential and glory.

Almost all authorities agree that Sati al-Husri, the Dean of the School of Law at the University of Baghdad, was the driving force behind popularizing Pan-Arabism. More than that, he provided a philosophical defense of Pan-Arabism, which he derived from his careful study of the German nationalists, particularly Herder and Fichte. Like them, he emphasized that love of a language and use of the same language determines national identity, regardless of whether the language exists in any state or in a number of different states. In short, he vigorously maintained that all Arabic speakers constituted a single nation and admonished the advocates of regional Arab states to cease support for their petty schemes. His Syrian lineage, his Yemeni birth, his broad European education, his extensive service to the Ottoman government, his high positions first in Feisal's Kingdom of Syria and then in his Kingdom of Iraq provided him strong credentials to buttress his august academic position. The fact that he had learned Arabic as a second language, having been reared on Ottoman Turkish, demonstrated the close association of language and national identity. He confined his activities to the promotion of nationalist education throughout the Arab world, in which he also emphasized the role of history as the second most important ingredient of nationalist identity. Although he defined the new perimeters of the Arab nation, he never addressed the major question of its governmental structure.

THE BAATH

A new movement evolved in Syria during the 1940s that offered the first specific plan for uniting the entire Arab-speaking world into a nation state. Although it always remained small, nearly tiny, it resulted from a merger of Zaki Arsuzi's *al-Baath al-Arabi,* Michel Aflaq and Salah al-Din Bitar's *Harakat al-Baath al-Arabi,* and Akram Hourani's Arab Socialist Party. The relationship among these three groups and their leaders was often strained, as each attempted to dominate the movement. By the mid-1950s, however, the Baath (Resurrection) party had a strong identity under the leadership of Aflaq and Bitar and asserted a militant Pan-Arabism with the motto of "One Arab Nation, One Immortal Mission."

Aflaq, a Sorbonne-educated Greek Orthodox Christian from Damascus, became the acknowledged ideologist of the movement. He refined the party's beliefs into a comprehensive ideology, accompanied by an organizational structure, which became an incontrovertible dogma. In short, the Baathists worked zealously to extend their beliefs and organization into the beliefs and government of a united Arab state. The party's uncompromising egotism made genuine cooperation with all other entities, which it regarded as inferior, impossible. Partnerships they might deign to enter could only be temporary until the Baathists could prevail. While Baathist goals corresponded closely with the developing *Zeitgeist* of the Arab world, other groups and individuals usually refrained from cooperating with them.

The fact that the Baathists usually had to operate clandestinely, sometimes even in Syria, and almost always in the rest of the Arab world, added to their fearsome reputation. Their need for secrecy even prevented members from knowing who belonged to the party. Also, it was not always clear who was the most powerful member of a particular segment of the party, despite its decisive hierarchial structure. Any member, however minor he might appear, could be the National Command's direct link to a local unit of the party. This, too, was essential to their security system, which required the few at the top to have full confidence in the loyalty and actions of the entire rank-and-file of the party, each of whom was carefully screened for membership and required to pass through a prolonged probationary period. This approach combined techniques *al-Fatat, al-Qataniya,* and *al-Ahd* had used in Ottoman times and the more modern methods of the communists to assure secrecy.

The Baathists conspired to evolve their party structure into the government of the entire Arab world, from each neighborhood to the national capital in Damascus. While they desired rapid success, their elitist approach to membership and the necessity for secrecy dictated slow growth. Confidence in their inevitable success and methodology allowed little deviation from the master plan. Circles of three to seven members constituted their smallest organizational unit, which they believed would evolve into neighborhood governments. Three to seven Circles constituted a Division to organize a slightly larger area. The exact amount of territory any of these units would cover depended on the number of party members in an area. Two or more Divisions comprised a Section and two or more Sections constituted a Branch. The Branch was a particularly crucial level in the organization, as it usually encompassed a whole city, a whole province, or perhaps represented the largest Baathist unit in an entire Arab state if the membership were sparse. Otherwise, in Baathist nomenclature an existing Arab state was a Region. A Regional Command, thus, existed in every state or Region that was under the direct control of the National Command.

The National Command approved, created, and controlled all component parts of the Baathist party structure as it evolved, in anticipation of replacing the existing governments, which the Baathist regarded as reprehensible. Aflaq, as Secretary General, presided over this executive committee of thirteen members, which exercised all final authority. Little could occur at any lower level without the National Command's specific approval. The National Command spoke for the party, approved all publications, and decided which regional and international organizations and states were friends or foes. Needless to say, this omnipotent committee administered all of the party's financial matters.

The centralization of National Command power in the party portended the totalitarian control it intended to exercise over a unified Arab state. The Baathists brazenly asserted that they, and only they, knew what was best for the Arabs and that the party was the only means of making the dream of an Arab state a reality. The party intended to give the Arabs liberation, unity, and socialism. Liberation referred first and foremost to severing all vestiges of control of nations from outside of the region, but it also required the abolition of Arab regimes and loyalties connected with foreign nations. Unity dictated the abolition of all existing states in the Arab-speaking world and the creation of a single Arab state under the full leadership of the Baath. The early definition of Baathist socialism was far less clear and seems to have become a major tenet of the party to satisfy the demands of Hourani and his agrarian based Arab Socialist Party. Aflaq certainly did not advocate state ownership of all property and industry, but he said the Baathist state would "guarantee equality and economic justice among the citizens." He was familiar with Marxist communism, which, of course, he rejected, because its internationalist presumption was antithetical to Baathism, whose *raison d' etre* was the fulfillment of pan-Arab nationalism. The fact that Baathists and communists appealed to many of the same people was all the more reason for the Baathists to establish an ideological distance between the two movements on economic matters.

The Baathists doubtlessly provided a clear vision for the scope and structure of Pan-Arabism. Just about every regional and international group and nation attempted to prevent their success, since Baathist triumph portended the annihilation of everything else. This opposition and their restricted membership largely explains the Baathist's inability to elect even their most prominent members to office. It is understandable that the Baathists would come to rely on *coups d'etat* to obtain control and implement their plan. Even this was not a strong possibility in the 1950s, because the party initially had been committed to keeping the military out of politics. Few of even the earliest recruits of the Baathists who had entered the military, therefore, had advanced to significant command positions in the military. By the mid-1950s, however, the Baathist frustration with remaining out of power inclined them to utilize a non-Baathist military man if he shared their vision of uniting all Arabs into a single state.

ISLAM'S OBSTRUCTION TO ARAB NATIONALISM

Imaginative Arab nationalists attempted to eliminate Islamic concerns about the threat of nationalism to the welfare of the Islamic religion that could also make Christian Arabs comfortable in a predominantly Muslim state. They did so by extolling Muhammad as the quintessential Arab. They explained that he had laid the foundation centuries earlier to inspire modern Arabs to resurrect their glorious achievements of the past in a single state to provide a glorious future. Abd al-Rahman al-Bazzaz and Michel Aflaq were at the forefront of this approach. They essentially glossed over his role as a prophet and emphasized his Arab identity, while they also stressed that the spread of Islam was primarily the spread of Arab virtues and culture. For Muslims, who were generally skeptical about Arab nationalism, this argument correlated nicely with the growing belief that Arabs had to regain their central role in Islamic leadership to restore its vitality. Christians, except for the most Islamophobic, could more easily accept this veneration of Muhammad, which was almost always accompanied by a strong emphasis on the practical advantages of the Arabs having a single state in the modern world. The fact that none of the more notable nationalists manifested particularly strong religious inclinations also helped win significant portions of the Arab Christian population to the nationalist banner.

The absence of Islamic vigor in much of the Arab world also aided the spread of nationalism among the younger generation of Arabs of all religious confessions. Without outwardly blaming religion for their plight, the younger Arabs associated traditional Islam with the other prevailing institutions of the Arab world that had allowed the political, military, economic, and educational decay, which led to their inability to resist foreign domination. As the youth became more politically involved, primarily through demonstrations, they became increasingly irreligious. Generally, young Christian, Muslim, and Druze Arabs could cooperate in the streets, the coffeehouses, and on campuses in their new quasireligion of Arab nationalism. As the fever of Arab nationalism spread, there was little doubt of its secular nature. For the youth, there was the exciting possibility that a vigorous secular Arab state would provide them more opportunity than existed under the leadership of older men, many of whom wore the clerical garments of one of the region's religions.

EGYPT AND PAN-ARABISM

For centuries there was no reason to think of Egypt as Arab, since it was so clearly Egyptian, despite the dominance of Arabic and Islam. Muhammad Ali's military forays into Arab lands had undoubtedly been in behalf of his dynastic, rather than Egyptian, interests. Arabi, Abduh, Mustafa Kamil, Taha Husain, and Zaghlul, all of whom were Egyptian nationalists, rejected a possible affiliation of Egypt with a larger Arab nation. Other reasons for their hesitation aside, the continued, although marginal, association of Egypt with the Ottoman Empire provided a legal deterrent to Great Britain's establishing title to the country. None of them were willing to accept the concept that the use of the same language and belief in the same religion constituted an adequate base for nationhood between countries or regions with dissimilar histories and traditions. Egyptian pride in their uniqueness prevented them from conceiving of union with other Arabic-speaking regions on an equitable basis. The annexation of the Sudan, which simply meant the expansion of Egyptian control, was not a similar type of compromise.

Arab nationalists, who rejected the Pan-Arab concept, reciprocated the prevailing Egyptian belief that Egypt was not an Arab country. Egypt, for instance, did not fit the schemes of either of the two Hashemite plans or the Syrian National

Party. The focus of Arab nationalist efforts in Baghdad after Iraq became independent in 1930 caused particular friction between Baghdad and Cairo. The government of Iraq, which was not particularly nationalist, recognized Egypt as its principal rival for leadership of the Arab world. While Egypt generally ignored the possibility of merging its identity with a larger Arab state, it was Arab enough to oppose Hashemite and Iraqi aggrandizement. Even this level of Egyptian participation in Arab affairs indicated its crucial role in the Arab world. Additionally, Egypt became drawn into Arab affairs because it shared similar feelings about Palestine and Zionism with the other Arab states. Egypt's central role in the Arab League, with it headquarters in Cairo, kept it in the forefront of pan-Arab affairs and provided a pattern of behavior and thinking that prepared the way for Egypt's acceptance of leadership of Pan-Arabism in the eyes of Egyptians and other Arabs.

Egypt was, however, too vital to the Pan-Arabists for them to allow it to confine its role to that of a supporter of general international Arab concerns. Sati al-Husri and the Baathists, especially, concentrated on incorporating Egypt into the heart of the Arab nation of their dreams. Al-Husri, the foremost spokesman for uniting all Arabs into a single state, expended considerable effort in establishing Egypt's Arab credentials. His romantic attachment to Arabism also never caused him to ignore essential political realities. He appreciated the knowledge, wealth, and sophistication Egypt could offer an Arab state. Egypt was, in fact, vital to nationalist fulfillment. If doubters accepted his principle hypothesis that language constituted the crucial link for nationhood, they would have to agree with him that Egypt was an Arab society and the potential linchpin of the Arab nation. For the Baathists, Egypt was central to their desire to unite all Arabic speakers into a nation. Their lack of success in obtaining power through constitutional means compelled them to enter a partnership with Nasser, who already enjoyed the popular appeal and charisma they lacked. He, they believed, was the great leader some elements of the nationalist movement had been seeking since al-Afghani had sought a "great man" to throw off imperialism. Nasser was all the more appealing to the Baathists because he lacked an ideology, which they were eager to provide.

Nasser, whose initial concerns were confined to the welfare of Egypt, developed into such a regional force that he had little choice but to accept the mantle of Arab leadership. His mastery of Egypt after 1955 made it possible for him to convince most Egyptians that they were, in fact, Arabs. The nature of Nasser's domination over the Arab masses, however, meant that the other Arab areas would basically be annexed to him and Egypt, if an Arab nation materialized under his leadership. Egyptians had never opposed an Egyptian empire; they had only resented having to acknowledge that non-Egyptians could enjoy parity in an Egyptian state. In this respect, the apparent Egyptian acceptance of Arab nationalism under Nasser had not actually changed.

By the mid-1950s three generations of Arabic-speaking people had been exposed to a steady stream of events and ideas that gave the vast majority of them a sense of being different from all other peoples. Their increased awareness of the glory their forebears had experienced in the distant past contrasted sharply with their collective sense of their own inability to meet the challenges of their present circumstances. Having shared the experience of foreign occupation and domination, they developed a sense of kinship that either had not existed in the past or had not seemed to have much significance. The desire to right the old wrongs and forge a new future encouraged the growth of the closest possible cooperative effort. No possible confederation offered a prospect for success that equalled or surpassed a united effort through total political union. Advocates of this pan-Arab position enjoyed the support of this logic, along with an aroused, vociferous mass following. More cautious souls could only offer substitute approaches at the risk of their lives and reputations. Having established total unity as their highest goals, the majority of the Arab population had little patience with the reticent elements which unity threatened, or with those who believed that practical considerations rendered beliefs in total unity quixotic.

11

Iran

HISTORICAL TIMELINE

1909–1925 ⇛ Reign of Ahmad, who was twelve years old when he assumed the title. Abd al-Qasim was regent until Ahmad assumed full powers of his position on July 21, 1914.

1911 ⇛ Government hired Morgan Shuster, an American, as treasurer-general in May. Shuster was efficient and unswerving in his duty to Persia as a national unit.

⇛ Muhammad Ali invaded from Russia on July 11 in an attempt to regain his throne. He received little support and met defeat by October.

⇛ The British and the Russians asserted themselves much more strongly from November on. Russian pressure caused dismissal of Shuster on December 25 and extracted a promise from the Persians not to hire foreigners without Russian approval.

⇛ This Russian interference essentially ended the constitutional experiment, but support of constitutional government was as strong as before the suppression.

1912–1913 ⇛ There was effectively no central authority or executive, as the British and Russians ruled much of Persia. The Regent fled to Europe in May 1912 and Ahmad did not begin to function as the monarch until July 21, 1914.

1914 ⇛ The British bought controlling interest (51 percent) of the Anglo-Persian Oil Company in May.

⇛ Persia declared its neutrality in World War I. Russians and

British did not honor neutrality. Most Persians supported the German cause and a Persian quasigovernment of constitutionalists in Kermanshah declared war on the German side.
⇛ British governed most of the south during the war, but Russia's problems, and later its revolution, prevented it from governing its northern sphere.

1915 ⇛ A strong separatist movement began in Gilan under the leadership of Kuchik Khan.

1916 ⇛ British suppressed the Kermanshah movement in 1916 and suppressed all German activities in its sector.

1917 ⇛ Russian troops withdrew after the Russian Revolution occurred.
⇛ State Committee of the Democratic Party of Azerbaijan essentially declared its independence after Russian troops withdrew.
⇛ British established their hegemony over most of Persia once the Russians withdrew.

1918 ⇛ British suppressed Gilan movement and Ottomans suppressed Azerbaijan movement, but grassroots supporters and leadership of both were ready to reassert their separatist activities.

1919 ⇛ Anglo-Persian Treaty of August 9 gave Britain control of Persian affairs, which was unacceptable to Persians, Soviets, and Britain's wartime allies.

1920 ⇛ Muhammad Khiabani seized control of Azerbaijan on behalf of the Azerbaijan Democratic party in April.
⇛ Kuchik Khan declared the creation of the Persian Soviet Socialist Republic on June 4.
⇛ Premier Hassan Pirniya renounced the Anglo-Persian Treaty and established diplomatic relations with the Soviet Union in June.
⇛ Soviet troops entered Persia on May 18 and refused to leave until Britain accepted the termination of the Anglo-Persian Treaty of 1919.
⇛ British supported tribal armies and the Royal Cossack Brigade killed Muhammad Khiabani on September 14 and suppressed the Azerbaijan Democratic Movement.

1921 ⇛ Colonel Reza Khan of the Cossack Brigade, in conjunction with Sayyed Zia, seized power in a *coup d'etat* on February 21.
⇛ The new government renounced the Anglo-Persian Treaty and signed a treaty with the Soviet Union on February 26.
⇛ Reza suppressed nationalist movement in Khorasan. In so doing, he eliminated Muhammad Taqi Pesyan, his only possible rival as the military leader of Persia.
⇛ Soviet troops left Gilan on September 8 and government troops destroyed the faction-rent Gilan Movement.

1922 ⇛ Premier Ahmad Qavam hired Dr. Arthur C. Millspaugh as treasurer-general.

⇛ British and Soviets prevented American firms from obtaining an oil concession in Persia.
⇛ Reza and government troops established control over Kurdistan.
⇛ Serious military efforts against the tribes began to bring them under control

1923 ⇛ Reza Khan became premier on October 28. At his suggestion Shah Ahmad went on an extended European "vacation."
⇛ Religious leaders expelled by the British from Iraq arrived in Iran in August.

1924 ⇛ Reza made his peace with Persia and Iraqi religious leaders from April to October and assured them he did not support the establishment of a republic in Persia.
⇛ *Ulama's* endorsement of Reza in October indicated that religious leaders no longer supported Shah Ahmad.
⇛ Reza launched a military campaign in October against Shaykh Khazal of Khuzistan, whom most Iranians believed would have British military support.
⇛ Reza went on a pilgrimage to Iraqi holy shrines in mid-December after subduing Shaykh Khaz'al.

1925 ⇛ Reza returned to Tehran on January 1 to a hero's welcome there and in most other urban areas.
⇛ Majlis awarded Reza with title of Commander in Chief on February 14.
⇛ Conscription Law was passed in May.
⇛ Funding began for railway system.
⇛ In September Shah Ahmad expressed a desire to return to Persia out of fear that the institution of monarchy was in jeopardy.
⇛ Majlis granted Reza dictatorial authority on October 31.
⇛ A constituent assembly offered Reza the throne. He took an oath of office on December 19.

1926 ⇛ Reza Shah's coronation took place on April 25.

1927 ⇛ Reza dismissed Dr. Arthur C. Millspaugh as treasurer-general.

1928 ⇛ Uniformity of Dress Law was passed.
⇛ Civil Code, which had been temporary in 1926, became permanent. Most jurisdiction passed from religious courts to secular courts.

1929 ⇛ Imperial decree allowed the Ministry of Education to define status of religious students and teachers.

1930 ⇛ Another imperial decree mandated the Ministry of Education to dictate the curricula for religious schools.
⇛ Reza established the National Bank.

1931 ⇛ Law was passed that confined religious jurisdiction to marriage, divorce, and guardianship.

⇛ All cases referred from state court and decisions subject to review.
⇛ Communist party outlawed.

1932 ⇛ Registration of Documents and Property Laws transferred these important and lucrative functions from religious to secular courts.
⇛ Cabinet unilaterally cancelled the British oil concession on November 28.
⇛ Abolition of all political parties.

1933 ⇛ New oil concession with Britain on April 29 provided more income and a more accurate accounting of Persia's share of the profits.
⇛ Taqi Arani reestablished a Communist party in Iran.

1934 ⇛ A new Endowment Law placed supervision of *waqfs* under government control.
⇛ Creation of the University of Tehran.

1935 ⇛ Reza officially changed the name of Persia to Iran on March 21.
⇛ Establishment of the Persian Academy to purge words of foreign origin from Persian language.
⇛ Royal decree required Iranian men to wear Western-style brimmed hats.

1936 ⇛ Law requiring all judges to have a law degree (eliminating most clergy).
⇛ Major increase in various categories of relations with Germany.

1937 ⇛ Iran-Iraq agreement was signed; it provided Iran with better navigation rights in the Shatt al-Arab.
⇛ Saadabad Pact, a nonaggression agreement, among Iran, Turkey, Iraq, and Afghanistan was signed on July 8.

1938 ⇛ Trial in November of the "Fifty-Three." These individuals later developed the Tudeh party.

1939 ⇛ Fritz Grobba, Germany's Minister to Iraq, moved German propaganda operations from Iraq to Iran after the beginning of World War II.

1941 ⇛ Leaders of Rashid Ali *coup* and Hajj Amin al-Husseini fled to Iran on May 30 after the British suppressed their movement in Iraq.
⇛ On July 19 and August 16, the British and Soviets demanded the right to use Iranian facilities for their war efforts.
⇛ The Anglo-Soviet invasion of Iran on August 25 was intended to establish a transportation link from the Gulf to the Soviet Union.
⇛ Reza Shah abdicated on September 16.
⇛ Muhammad Reza assumed the throne on September 17.
⇛ Formation of Tudeh party on September 29.

1942 ⇛ Britain and Soviet Union agreed on January 29 to withdraw

their troops from Iran. This took place six months after the cessation of hostilities of World War II.
⇛ Colonel H. Norman Schwarzkopf became commander of Iran Gendarmerie.
⇛ A regional Kurdish independence movement, centered in Mahabad, began under the leadership of Qazi Muhammad.

1943 ⇛ United States forces entered Iran on January 1.
⇛ Dr. Arthur C. Millspaugh returned to Iran to become treasurer-general.

1944 ⇛ Reza Shah died on July 26 in Johannesburg.
⇛ Indications that American companies might obtain an oil concession in Iran prompted the Soviets to demand one for themselves.

In the aftermath of the dissolution of the Majlis in 1912, Russia and Great Britain effectively governed Persia, while the Bakhtayari enriched themselves in the limited areas they controlled on behalf of the central government. When the regent, Abd al-Qasim, fled to Europe in May 1912, there was no executive authority to convene a new Majlis. This hiatus continued until July 21, 1914 when Ahmad reached his majority and assumed full royal authority. The presence of an executive, however, was not enought to overcome Persia's problems. The outbreak of World War I shortly thereafter compelled the Russians and the British to administer Persia to fulfill their wartime needs.

Ahmad Shah declared Persia's neutrality in the war, but none of the parties respected his position. Ottoman forces entered Azerbaijan and held Tabriz for several months before the Russians expelled them from the city. German assistance to the tribes in the southwest forced the British to withdraw from much of their territory until 1916. Many elements in Persia, in fact, hoped a Central Powers triumph in the war would bring Persia's liberation. Clever Ottoman propaganda in behalf of Islamic goals in the war won support from Persian Moderates, while Germany cultivated a close relationship with the Democrats. After the Majlis met in January 1915, the new Persian government signed a treaty with Germany to become a belligerent. When Anglo-Russian pressure forced that cabinet out of office, a coalition of Moderates and Democrats met at Qumm and signed another agreement with Germany before they were forced to withdraw to Kermanshah, where they mounted a short-lived military effort under the leadership of Muhammad Taqi Pesyan.

Prime Minister Muhammad Vali Sepahdar, who had survived in government since the overthrow of Muhammad Ali, agreed to a formal Anglo-Russian military occupation in June 1916, although the Majlis refused to ratify the agreement. Sepahdar also granted a Russian, Akaky M. Khoshtaria, an oil concession in the northern provinces as a means of placating the Russians for the British concession in the south. While the Majlis also refused to ratify this concession, it laid the basis for later Russian claims to the right to explore for oil in northern Persia.

The Anglo-Russian agreement with Sepahdar was not equally beneficial to the two Great Powers. Great Britain quickly capitalized on the new arrangement and solidified its hold on southern Persia after it created the South Persian Rifles in 1916. It subdued the tribes, expelled German influence, terminated the pro-German

Persian quasigovernment in Kermanshah, and secured its vital oil resources. These accomplishments laid the foundation for asserting British control of Persia after the Russian Revolution in 1917. Russia's plight during the war prevented it from diverting the necessary forces to exploit its long-awaited legal domination of northern Persia. Russia's weakness allowed the tribes and the independence movements to emerge in the northern sector, which posed a threat to both the British and the moribund Persian government.

Nationalist movements in the northern provinces of Azerbaijan and Gilan provided some hope to Persians that they could develop a base from which to expel foreign influence and change the ineffective central government in Tehran. A small but effective movement developed in the jungles of Gilan, on the southern shores of the Caspian Sea, in 1915 offered the greatest hope. It protected its citizens' lives and thwarted both the Russian and Tehran tax collectors. The venerable leader, Mirza Kuchik Khan, based his movement on sound peasant support, but his commitment to limited local needs and respect for Islam and private property also obtained support for his *Jangali* movement from intellectuals, clergy, merchants, and landowners. Affiliation with the Ottomans during the war improved its effectiveness and did nothing to diminish its reputation for pursuing nationalist objectives. A movement in Azerbaijan under the Democrat cleric, Muhammad Khiabani, did not begin until Russian troops withdrew during the Russian Revolution. Its original program expressed strong grievances against Tehran for maltreatment of Azerbaijan and the inability of the central government to protect it from foreign domination. The State Committee of the Democratic party of Azerbaijan also enjoyed widespread initial support since it advocated goals most Persians could endorse. British occupation of Gilan and Turkish occupation of Azerbaijan in 1918 temporarily prevented both movements from playing effective roles.

BRITISH HEGEMONY

Ironically, many Persians discovered that the absence of Russian influence over their affairs was not necessarily advantageous. The Persian government and much of Persia's territory fell under direct British control once they no longer had to honor Russia's privileges. Since British pressure prevented Persia from officially recognizing the new Soviet regime, normal trade relations virtually ceased between the two nations. This was especially harmful to Persia, and the northern provinces in particular, because Russia was Persia's primary trading partner and work forces had passed freely across the two borders despite their numerous conflicts. Informed Persians had, in fact, sought for some time to develop an affiliation with a third country to ameliorate the Anglo-Russian condominium over their country. After the Russian Revolution, the British unabashedly asserted their hegemony over Persia with the willing support of a pliable central government.

The British, however, surpassed acceptable bounds when Lord Curzon concluded the Anglo-Persian Treaty of 1919 on August 9. By the agreement, which the Majlis never ratified, the British offered Persia a substantial loan in return for the exclusive right to shape Persian financial, trade, and military affairs. Most of the international community, including Britain's wartime allies, regarded the

British diplomatic *coup* as unwarranted and tasteless. Persian activists, other than those who stood to benefit from the treaty, realized the need to act in concert and seek Soviet assistance to avoid becoming a vassal state of the British Empire. Cooperation with the Soviet regime became even more appealing when it renounced the numerous concessions its tsarist predecessor had extracted from Persia with British consent.

The Azerbaijan and Gilan movements resurfaced to lead opposition to Britain's hegemony in Persia. Muhammad Khiabani seized control of Azerbaijan in April 1920 in behalf of the Azerbaijan Democratic party and declared his government the legitimate government of Persia. He carefully avoided any semblance of separatism for his movement, which expressed concerns for the greater needs of the nation, but emphasized the concerns of his province. Central to his appeal was the avowed purpose of restoring normal economic relations with the Soviet Union. In doing so, the Azerbaijan movement resisted any overt affiliation with either the Soviet government or with the communist movements in Persia or the Soviet Union. Meanwhile the Gilan movement of Kuchik Khan fell under the increased influence of Ehsanollah Khan, an Azeri anarchist, and the Bolshevik-affiliated Adalat Party composed of Persians centered in the Russian Caucasus. Adalat soon changed its name to the Communist Party of Persia. Kuchik, who was never a communist, accepted Soviet overtures for help and agreed to establish the Persian Soviet Socialists Republic in Gilan on June 4, 1920. The arrival of Soviet forces in Gilan on May 18, after ousting the British from Baku in the Soviet Union, had been an added incentive. Other outside elements joined the original Jangali movement and created a situation both Kuchik Khan and most of the population found uncomfortable. The Gilanis, who had their own Persian dialect and traditional Islamic values, resented the arrival of Azeris, Kurds, Armenians, and Russians who forcefully implemented a full gamut of Bolshevik methods and ideas. Even the peasants refused to accept land that the communists had confiscated from private landlords. Needless to say, the traditional clerical, bazaari, and landlord support for the Jangali movement rapidly withered away after the onslaught of the outside influence. The Jangali movement, therefore, had collapsed from within before it confronted a revitalized government effort to destroy it. The combined Jangali and Soviet forces, however, were adequate to withstand British and government efforts to dislodge them. The poor performance of the Cossack Brigade against the Gilan movement led to successful British pressure to dismiss the unit's Russian officers and replace them with Persian officers.

The prospect of the Soviets capitalizing on anti-government and anti-British sentiment in the north and using the Gilan base for a major operation in Persia stimulated government activity and British concern. The pro-British Prime Minister Vossugh al-Dowleh was dismissed in June shortly after the creation of the Gilan Soviet. Hassan Pirniya, who had strong constitutionalist credentials, formed a new government. Pirniya renounced the Anglo-Persian treaty, dismissed British advisers from the government, and established diplomatic relations with the Soviet Union. British pressure on Persia, especially related to Persian military leadership, led to Pirniya's resignation in November and the appointment of the pro-British Sepahdar-i Rashti to the premiership. Britain's strong hand had also mobilized a Kurdish and Shahsavan tribal attack upon the Azerbaijan independence movement, and terminated that threat, which was punctuated by the death of its leader, Muhammad Khiabani, on September 14, 1920 in the hands of members of the Cossack Brigade.

Resistance to the Anglo-Persian treaty impaired the central government's ability to function. This was reminiscent of the period from 1912 to 1914 when Persia had no executive because of the absence of the regent. British authorities, however, refused to withdraw consideration of the treaty. Few Persians were willing to serve in a government so closely tied to Britain and no Majlis could be convened that would ratify it. Soviet forces refused to leave Persian soil unless Persia rescinded the treaty, while Persia lacked the military ability to expel either the Soviets or the British. A broad spectrum of Persian sentiment welcomed the Soviet presence because it offered the best hope of eliminating Britain's dominance. Much of the Persian concern resulted from the economic hardship the interruption of normal relations with Russia caused, but nationalist sentiment chafed even more from British influence.

REZA KHAN'S COUP

Persia's resurgence as an independent nation began on February 21, 1921 when Colonel Reza Khan of the Cossack Brigade carried out a *coup* in conjunction with a civilian, Sayyed Zia al-Din Tabatabai, who became premier. The nation was too weak and too closely tied to British interests, especially in all matters related to the Anglo-Persian Oil Company, to be able to escape all foreign influence. Colonel Reza Khan would, however, end the virtual anarchy that had prevailed since the beginning of the constitutional period. This would be a step toward establishing national institutions and national policies to replace the numerous enclaves of provincial and foreign rule. His personal greed and suspicion would in time tarnish his reputation, but few could doubt that he was a Persian nationalist who aspired to create a sovereign state free from foreign control and devoid of local despotic individuals and groups.

In an era when nations had recently mustered millions into their armies, the approximately seven-thousand-strong Cossack Brigade was not a significant military force. It was, however, superior to both the ill-paid government conscript units and the tribal bands of numerous local chiefs. Under proper authority, it had the advantage of legitimacy over foreign troops, whose justification for being on Persian soil was based largely on a claim of providing order that the central government could not provide. It is not coincidental that the Cossack Brigade played an important independent role at this juncture in Persian history because it had only been under Persian command for a few months prior to the *coup*. Russians had commanded it from its inception in 1879 as a praetorian guard to protect the shahs and carry out their direct orders. Since British pressure had caused the dismissal of the Russian officers and Sayyed Zia was pro-British, some contemporaries and later critics regarded the *coup* as the latest British ploy to retain control.

The new government renounced the Anglo-Persian treaty and within five days of taking office signed a treaty with the Soviet Union that Pirniya had negotiated in his short-lived period in office. There are indications that Britain understood, and perhaps begrudgingly endorsed, this approach, which it had so vehemently opposed three months before. This change in British attitude resulted from a realization that Persians would continue to impose paralysis upon the government until Britain's role was reduced and normal commercial relations resumed with the Soviet Union. Britain faced major uprisings in all the Arab territories under its control at that time and Ataturk was dismembering the Allies' plans for the Ottoman Empire. A rapid and peaceful resolution of the stalemate in Persia, which portended additional conflict, was in Britain's best interest. Disbanding the Persian Rifles helped move the Soviets to withdraw their troops from Gilan after Persia agreed to terms with the Soviets. With the exodus of the British and Russian armies, Persia was finally free from foreign occupation.

There was little to criticize in the agreement, since the Soviets renounced the special commercial privileges Russia had enjoyed since the Treaty of Turkumanchai of 1828, relinquished its capitulation agreement, forgave the outstanding loans to the Persian government, and abandoned all special concessions related to Persia's public utilities and infrastructure. The Soviets also agreed to withdraw their troops, but obtained the right to reintroduce them if other foreign troops ever entered Persia and posed a threat to the Soviets or their allies. Persia also had to promise never to allow other foreigners to acquire the concessions the Soviets abandoned.

Sayyed Zia only lasted three months as premier before his high-handed approach discredited him in most reformist circles. (He had never had any credibility with the more conservative elements.) Ahmad Qavam, whom Sayyed Zia had recently forced from his post as the very capable governor of Khorasan, brought good constitutionalist credentials to the premiership. Since he had been a strong supporter of Shuster, all knew he opposed British influence and leaned toward replacing British advisers with Americans. With Majlis approval, he and Muhammad Mossadegh, the finance minister, began to pursue American assistance in remedying Persia's financial plight. As a result of this approach the government hired Dr. Arthur C. Millspaugh, a financial expert of the United States Department of State, to the position Shuster had held as treasurer-general. His diligence in collecting taxes and reorganizing Persian finances after he assumed his cabinet-level office in 1922 provided the government solvency, although most Persians disliked his uncompromising manner and blunt personality. The cabinet and the Majlis attempted to break Britain's monopoly on Persian oil production by granting a concession in the northern provinces to the American firms of Standard Oil and Sinclair. Opposition from the British and Soviets, along with the American government's hesitation to offend Britain, prevented the American firms from gaining the concessions.

With a reputable government in place, a reliable means of collecting revenue established, and foreign occupation terminated, the suppression of provincial dissidents was the main challenge to the central government. Shah Ahmad remained the titular head of state, but he was at the mercy of a cabinet that had a working relationship with the Majlis and Reza Khan, who had begun to extend his authority over the entire army and gendarmerie. There is little wonder that some began to express interest in transforming Persia into a republic.

REZA SOLIDIFIES CONTROL

Reza Khan, who had only been Army Commander under Sayyed Zia's government, also became War Minister in Qavam's cabinet. Although he faced resistance, he obtained control of additional revenues to fund the extension of his authority over the gendarmes, which had formerly been under Swedish and British command. By 1925 he had a respectable army of 40,000. No tribal armies could repel a determined effort of the revitalized national army, which received good rations and regular pay for the first time in decades. The tribes would feel the full brunt of Reza's forces, since the movements in the northern provinces were under control by the end of 1921. Reza and Qavam dealt severely with the constitutionalist, but nonseparatist, movement of the revered nationalist, Muhammad Taqi Pesyan, who had gained control of Khorasan earlier in 1921, when he had removed Qavam from that governorship on Sayyed Zia's orders. Pesyan, who had led the nationalist army in Kermanshah during World War I, was the one possible alternative to Reza's command of the Persian army. Pesyan's death provided Qavam revenge and removed Reza's rival. The Jangali movement in Gilan, which had all but disintegrated from internal strife by the end of 1920, was moribund by the time the Soviet forces withdrew in October 1921. Reza's Cossacks routed the remaining Jangalis and Khuchik Khan froze to death while in retreat. Khiabani's movement in Azerbaijan had ended with his death in the fall of 1920, although the Kurds under the adventurous Simitko were not brought under control until 1922.

Beginning in 1922, Reza's successful military effort to subdue the tribes enhanced his reputation for establishing order out of chaos and increased his stature in civilian affairs. Cabinet changes reflected his wishes and he used his influence and the army's presence throughout the nation to elect a new Majlis that was more attuned to his vision of what Persia should become. The Fourth Majlis had been heavily under the influence of the Reformist party, which was essentially the former Moderate Party. The Fifth Majlis, which he helped shape, met in January 1923 with a strong Socialist party contingent, which was basically the renamed former Democrat party. The Socialists, along with the Progress party, represented by Western-educated delegates, gave Reza the legislature he wanted. His hand in shaping the new legislature signaled that he no longer favored the conservative elements, with their strong religious sentiments, who had provided his strongest initial support. The former Democrat, Mustofi al-Mamalek, who had signed the agreement with Germany to declare war on the Entente Powers in 1915, began the session as premier and introduced a body of legislation that the Democrat *anjumans* had advocated since the early constitutional period.

The legislation of this new coalition was uncomfortable at best for most of the Reformists and offensive to almost all clergymen and their followers. Particularly troublesome were the proposed laws to establish universal conscription, abolish titles of nobility, and replace the Islamic calendar with one that dated back to Persian antiquity. Laws that required the adoption of family names, established a uniform system of weights and measure, and reduced the court's budget were less threatening. While most could applaud the government's attempt to finance a major railroad construction program without resorting to the use of foreign loans, the nation of tea drinkers resented the taxes on tea and sugar to pay for it.

Reza became premier on October 28, 1923, while he remained the war minister and army commander. At his "suggestion," Ahmad Shah left for an extended vacation to Europe a few days later, leaving Reza in control of the highest leadership positions. As yet there had been no direct attacks upon the monarchy, but Reza did not discourage additional expressions in behalf of a republic with him as president. This was in emulation of Ataturk, who became president of the Turkish republic the same day Reza became premier. Developments in the new Majlis had already begun to galvanize religious leaders of all ranks and their followers before two leading Iraqi *mujtahids* (venerable authorities on Shiah Islam) journeyed to Qumm in the late summer of 1923. They were members of the *ulama* of Najaf (highest rank of *mujtahids* who rendered decisions on Shiah belief and practice) whom the British had expelled because of their opposition to the establishment of a constitutional monarchy in Iraq. Believers saw Islam simultaneously under attack in Turkey, Iraq, and Persia. Shah Ahmad's attempt to capitalize upon the fear this engendered was no small reason Reza sent him on his one-way vacation.

The Republic of Turkey abolished the Caliphate, the Ministry of Religious Affairs, the Sharia courts, the Muslim schools, and exiled the remainder of the Ottoman royal family on March 3, 1924. This aroused major religious unrest in Persia under the leadership of the Iraqi exiles and the indigenous Persian *mujtahids.* Reza was not strong enough to withstand a major religious uprising and he needed clergy support if he was going to take advantage of the shah's possibly permanent departure. He hurried to Qumm and reassured the *mujtahids* that he was the same firm believer who had flagellated himself to impress them during the Ashura celebration in 1921. Reza ingratiated himself further to the Iraqi clergymen when he interceded with the British to allow them to return to Iraq in April for which he provided a military escort. Elements of the Persian clergy remained suspicious of him and interpreted his favoritism to the Iraqis as a carefully crafted plot between him and the British. Reza, however, obtained an unqualified endorsement for his government in October 1924 from the Iraqi *ulama* at Najaf. This endorsement effectively implied that Shah Ahmad no longer deserved the loyalty of the faithful. His solicitous attention to the clergy had paid huge dividends, which justified abandoning any intentions of creating a republic. Since he had no intention of relinquishing the power he had amassed, and the creation of a republic was so unpalatable to Islamic traditionalists, he began to move toward becoming a monarch.

Shaykh Khazal of Muhammara in Khuzistan provided an opportunity for Reza to enhance his reputation and seal his ascendancy over the shah. The Shaykh, who controlled much of the territory of the British oil fields, resisted efforts of the central government to extend control over affairs in his province. He posed as a strong supporter of the shah, the constitution, and the clergy in an effort to justify his unwillingness to obey Reza, whom he portrayed as an interloper. The British, who had prospered from their relationship with Shaykh Khazal, increased their military presence in the Gulf and rumors spread that Khuzistan might merge with its fellow Arabs in British-dominated Iraq. Although Persia as yet received little income from the oil in this western province, it could no longer allow Shaykh Khazal such quasi independence or allow him to secede. The British, in fact, realized that the new strength of the central government negated their long-standing relationship with Shaykh Khazal and provided the kind of stability for Persia they had sought for decades. They had no intention, therefore, of assisting the shaykh.

There was, however, widespread belief that Reza would confront the British when he launched a military expedition against the recalcitrant shaykh in October 1924. Anxiety was high throughout the nation as Reza's troops advanced to subdue the rebellious Arab province. The fact that the campaign was virtually bloodless did not diminish the magnitude of the victory. Reza, who had joined his forces after they had established their control, could accept full credit for the notable triumph. The British took Shaykh Khazal into custody shortly after his defeat and sent him to Tehran, where he managed to live out his natural life under dignified house arrest. In the middle of December, Reza went straight from his victory to a well-publicized pilgrimage to the holy shrines of Najaf and Karbala in Iraq. On January 1, 1925 Reza returned to Tehran to unprecedented acclamation in most population centers of the nation. The Majlis rewarded him in February 14 with the title of Commander in Chief of the Army, which had always been reserved for the monarch. The death of former Shah Muhammad Ali, who was in exile in Russia, in February helped ignite the entire question of the fate of the monarchy. Monarchists feared that the Qajar dynasty might end unless Shah Ahmad, who was in Paris, returned soon. Indications that he had such intentions had circulated from the beginning of the crisis with Shaykh Khazal and he confirmed such intentions in September 1925.

The Majlis officially deposed Shah Ahmad on October 31 and invested Reza Khan with all executive authority, which effectively gave him dictatorial power. Sitting as a Constituent Assembly, the Majlis offered Reza Khan the throne by a majority of 80 to 5. Other changes in the constitution established the line of succession in his recently acquired family name of Pahlavi and specifically excluded the Qajars from future consideration as monarchs. Thirty legislators, mostly Socialists, abstained from voting since they favored a republican form of government. Reza Khan took the oath of office on December 15 and pledged his support for the constitution and Shiah Islam. He formed his first cabinet on December 19 with Muhammad Ali Faroughi as his first prime minister.

Shah Reza placed the crown on his head with his own hands at his coronation on April 25, 1926. His short speech on that occasion was deceptive in that the first third of it emphasized his high regard for Islam. He also invoked the support of the Twelve Imams in the remainder of his address, which left little doubt of what he intended to accomplish. Reza stated that the needs of "fundamental reform of the country. . .leave no time for contemplation and laxity." There was little reason to believe consultation would be part of his approach when he said "that my views may be implemented as I expect." There was broad support for his ascension to the throne because he had established stability and promised to bring prosperity. The last several Qajars could not claim such accomplishments. Other speakers at his coronation also began to emphasize that the nation again had a true Persian ruling family in contrast to the Turkoman lineage of the Qajars. This became a major theme of the Pahlavi monarchs as they tried to establish a link between the nation and themselves with ancient Persia. They began to regard the Islamic period, with its inferior Arab influences, as an aberration.

Assessments of Reza vary widely and often reflect more the attitudes of the assessor than the subject of their evaluation. The qualities that made him a good military officer did not prepare him for much of the prevarication that permeates politics and diplomacy. His lack of education and almost total lack of familiarity with foreign nations caused him to focus on his own nation, which he knew better than most shahs. After all, he had not been reared in the isolation of a royal palace, but had spent much of his life among soldiers in both the countryside and cities of Iran. Unlike other shahs, he retained a senior officer's propensity to travel tirelessly and inspect the manner in which his subordinates implemented his orders. He had seen the chaos that prevailed in the two decades before he obtained power and he possessed an astute ability to determine the causes for genuine discontent as distinguished from personal and ideological aspirations he regarded as incompatible with national interests.

The exceptionally tall man with the haunting face was primarily a nationalist. As such, he was committed to strengthening his nation against disintegration from within and subservience to foreign influence. Affairs in his own country were sufficiently demanding to occupy his tremendous capacity for work and he never possessed adequate military or financial strength to consider expansion beyond his own borders. Devoid of any particular ideology, he adopted practical solutions to the blatantly obvious problems his nation faced. Coincidentally, his conclusions usually conformed with those of the Democrats, Socialists, and Progressives, who stressed the need for modernization through the adoption of many Western practices. Unlike them, he regarded the cumbersome approach of representative deliberation as too slow and open to attack from entrenched interests. He was not insensitive to the distress his policies inflicted upon religious traditionalists or those who preferred a liberal approach, but he believed that the problems of the nation required the specific changes he forcefully imposed. It is even possible that the fortune he amassed was due in large part to his desire to keep industrial and agricultural experimentation and development on his own estates, where the managers were directly responsible to him. He measured his worth and that of others by results rather than wealth or title and behaved modestly in every aspect of his life except for his exercise of power, which he regarded as a duty. Anyone who expected something different from his leadership was disappointed.

POLICIES TOWARD THE TRIBES

There seemed no gentle alternative for dealing with the tribes who seldom had been under direct royal control. Reza's predecessors, including the British and the Russians, had frequently allied with some tribes to subdue others, who, in turn, obtained concessions for their services. Such an approach did not appeal to Reza, who visualized a centralized nation in which all its peoples would be attuned to the same goals and would be willing to sacrifice personal preferences for the benefit of the nation. Local, medieval fiefs and privileges were incompatible with this vision, as were the unwillingness to pay taxes, resistance to national military service, and the use of distinctive clothing and languages. The tribes understandably attempted to resist Reza's policies, which threatened to destroy their unique and treasured identities. To his credit, Reza treated all who resisted with equal severity in pursuit of his effort to make them conform with his policies. Almost all in time experienced his wrath, which they were helpless to resist with anything but sullen compliance.

Tribal levees faced the modernized army that grew in sophistication to include armored vehicles and airplanes. The government's capacity to build roads into tribal lands reduced the tribesmen's ability to resist militarily and maintain a normal life. Successful government campaigns resulted in the death of many tribal leaders and the removal of others to Tehran where they served as virtual hostages to assure the proper behavior of their kin. Most agree that the suppression of the tribes was both ruthless and brutal beyond the level necessary to guarantee their tranquility. Reza was committed, however, to destroying their way of life to prevent them from ever presenting a challenge to the government's ability to function in all regions of the nation. After defeating them militarily, the government usually attempted to convert the traditional herdsmen into sedentary farmers, but it could never provide adequate instruction and supplies to make this a viable approach or reduce the hardship it engendered. Consequently, the pacification succeeded in eliminating the tribes as a disruptive force before the end of Reza's reign; however, many suffered debilitating indignities and sickness in the new society, which had no constructive role for them and treated them as backward primitives.

ASSAULT UPON THE CLERGY

Reza Khan initially needed and sought the support of the clergy and demonstrated sensitivity toward their views, especially in withdrawing his support for a republic. His commitment to secular modernization, however, required the adoption of policies that first threatened, and later destroyed, most of the influence of the clergy. As with all of his other major policies, he implemented restrictions upon the clergy that leftists of various persuasions had advocated during the constitutional period. Reza apparently accomplished the kind of royal control over the law, education, taxation, and religious-owned land in less than two decades that European monarchs had required centuries to achieve. The similar reduction of religious authority in Turkey under Ataturk provided him with a contemporary model and inspiration for his assault upon the clergy. No element of society had better cause for resenting him and his regime, although decades would pass before the right opportunity would arise for the clergy to reassert itself to its traditional role as the source for spiritual direction for the nation.

Bona fide clergymen retained many of their traditional rights and privileges throughout his reign. The identification of who had the right to claim the status of clergyman, therefore, was central to much of Reza's often hostile relationship with the clergy. He insisted that the state would define and certify clergymen, just as it attempted to administer everything else of importance in the newly defined nation, where the state itself seemed to be the new religion.

The Conscription Law, which many Democrats had advocated for years, became law in May 1925 and caused the first major conflict between the then prime minister and the clergy. While the law exempted full-time clergymen, as well as all full-time secular and religious students of conscript age, it specified that the government had the authority to validate all exemptions. This was the first time that the state, rather than the religious authorities, had the right to define who was a clergyman. Religious authorities resented the obvious implications of this law, which they also opposed because they realized that military training was one of the principal conduits for transmitting non-Islamic beliefs and practices into society. The

Uniformity of Dress Law of 1928, which required all subjects to adopt the use of Western clothing, also exempted all full-time clergymen and religious students. Again, government examiners had the right to determine who met the qualifications for clerical status. This provided the government with an excuse for examining the qualifications of almost every clergyman. Many of the uneducated rural *mullas,* in particular, lacked adequate formal training to withstand such scrutiny. Religious men who had no affiliation with a particular mosque or school were at the mercy of the examiners. The law offended most religious authorities even further because it forbade women to wear the veil, which had become a customary manifestation for Muslim women to demonstrate their Quaranic-dictated modesty. An imperial decree in 1929 supplemented the government's control even further when it gave the Ministry of Education the authority to examine religious students to determine whether they met national standards to qualify as either a religious student or a teacher. In a natural progression of bringing religious education and certification under state control, the Ministry of Education dictated the basic curriculum of the religious schools in 1930.

The regime's erection of a secular legal system struck at the very heart of the clergy's role in society, since by tradition an Islamic society should be totally under the jurisdiction of the *sharia,* God's law. The fact that Ali Akbar Davar, the Swiss-educated jurist, led the Ministry of Justice with such obvious talent resulted in success and made the innovations less assailable. The "temporary" new Civil Code of 1926 became permanent in 1928 and began a process of transferring most legal authority from religious to secular government jurisdiction. In 1931 a law confined religious jurisdiction to cases related to marriage, divorce, and guardianship. Even these cases required the specific referral from a state court and placed all religious courts under supervision of the Attorney General. Decisions of the religious courts, which were forbidden to pass sentences, were subject to review from the state courts. The Registration of Documents and Property Laws in 1932 removed this formerly lucrative function from religious courts and transferred it to secular courts. This was a major financial blow to the clergy, which increasingly experienced a state-inflicted reduction of its income from many traditional sources. Clergymen were essentially eliminated from serving as judges when the 1936 law required all judges to have a law degree from either the University of Tehran or a foreign law school.

The Endowments Law of 1934, which placed supervision of the *wqafs* under government control, administered the *coup de grace* to clerical independence. These religious-owned properties had traditionally been free from government control and taxation. While all of them were supposed to conduct religious-related education and welfare functions, they were the principal source of income and a major base for influence of the clergy. Each was uniquely designed to perform specific functions that its charter defined. They varied in size and nature from huge estates to small plots of land, from small mosques to massive centers for training the clergy in the esoteric points of Islamic theology and law, but most were small religious schools, clinics, and even businesses. While they were invariably endowed to do God's work, many had become defiled in human hands and had failed to fulfill their lofty missions. The Endowment Law authorized secular authorities to scrutinize the actual performance of all *waqfs* and confiscate any which deviated from their prescribed objective. Government officials, thus, had license to place all *waqfs* under close investigation and surveillance. Failure of religious schools to meet government inspection led to many becoming part of the public school system. Other confiscated religious properties enriched the monarchy and its friends, many of whom had deservedly poor reputations.

The practice of religion under Reza and his son, Muhammad Reza, became an inconvenience on earth, regardless of the reward it could offer in heaven. Pilgrims often could not obtain permission to fulfill their obligatory pilgrimages to the shrines in the Hijaz and Iraq. The government forbade the elaborate and emotional passion plays and orations related to the death of the Imams Ali and Hussein, which male believers accompanied with public self-flagellation and acclamation of their sorrow for their martyred leaders. Believers witnessed the public humiliation of religious men, while the shah adorned public places with his carved image in abject violation of Islamic law. For sensitive people of faith, the nation appeared to have converted into a servant of Mammon. While intellectually inclined youth had formerly sought fulfillment in religious education, the new generation sought a secular education to prepare to serve the shah's government or to enter private enterprise. The shah's decree in 1935 that all men should wear the Western-styled brimmed hat was intrinsically demeaning, but it also symbolized the entire confrontation between the West-struck shah and his traditionally oriented subjects. The brim prevented them from bowing to the ground in humiliation before their God, but it allowed them to keep their heads erect in pursuit of constructing a Westernized society Reza created.

FINANCIAL DEVELOPMENTS

Reza was determined to avoid Persia's financial dependence upon foreign sources, which had prevailed in the past. In his early months in office, failure to obtain a loan from the United States, which he regarded as a safe source, helped him remain relatively true to this goal. His dismissal of Millspaugh in 1927 was a manifestation of his determination to eliminate foreign financial control, because he recognized the American was committed to his duties and had performed well. Millspaugh's problem, in fact, might well have been that he was too good, because the shah said "there can't be two Shahs in this country, and I am going to be the Shah." Reza disliked the Anglo-Persian Oil Company's monopoly on his country's largest potential source of revenues, but he had no way of eliminating it. For instance, he refused to look at the British refinery on Abadan Island when he passed by it on a boat in 1925 out of revulsion for what its presence represented.

In his opinion, the nation had to increase its production to become financially independent. He recognized the need for foreign capital investment and technological assistance, but he eschewed close relations with large countries and prevented any one foreign country or company from acquiring a major interest in any of his many development projects. Most development, therefore, occurred under government auspices or his own personal financing, since they were the main sources of investment capital in the land. As a millionaire several times over and the owner of more than three million acres of land, Reza was the wealthiest man in the nation by the end of his reign.

The National Bank, which he established in 1930, became a major instrument for financing the industrialization that was central to his quest for financial independence. It took over the function of printing government money from the British-owned Imperial Bank. In addition, it provided loans at a lower rate than the small bazaari bankers could afford to offer. The shah's close control over its policies and transactions also helped reward his supporters who obtained the right to establish enterprises he approved.

Taxes provided a reliable source of income for government sponsored projects, although most agree that a disproportionately large part of the tax burden fell on the lower classes. The levees on sugar, tea, and tobacco were especially onerous. Bazaari merchants also resented the taxes they paid on imports and exports, while the larger businesses, which were financed with government funds, enjoyed monopolies and paid little or no taxes. Peasants also paid high taxes, while large landowners, of which the shah was the greatest, made virtually no contribution to the state's coffers. The age-old practice of Persians evading taxes, however, ceased as the fairly efficient, and sometimes corrupt, servants of the new state could reach into every corner of the realm to collect the funds Reza's ambitions demanded.

TRANSPORTATION AND INDUSTRY

Virtual anarchy, the absence of capital, and foreign interference had prevented the development of a transportation infrastructure or industrialization in Persia prior to Reza's reign. Democrats and their Socialist successors had advocated the need to remedy this deficiency from the beginning of the century, but circumstances had made their development impossible. Under Reza, however, only development of the military had a higher priority, and, in fact, both industrialization and the development of improved transportation were vital ancillary complements to his quest for military strength.

The development of roads began in the earliest days after the *coup* propelled Reza into prominence. His original interests in better roads, which remained a major concern, were related to his need to move troops into rebellious tribal areas. Whenever possible he tried to settle the vanquished tribes near major roads as a reminder to them that national troops could quickly descend upon them if they caused trouble. The same roads became equally useful for transporting government authorities into the outlying areas to administer the nation and collect taxes. Without them, the vigorous improvement in the transportation of farm products, raw materials, and manufactured goods would have been impossible in Reza's relentless effort to create an integrated economy throughout his realm. About 17,000 miles of mostly unpaved highway existed by the time his reign ended in 1941.

Construction of a railway system in Iran became Reza's most abiding passion related to both military and economic development. The absence of railroads when he entered office made the movement of heavy goods almost impossible in the often treacherous terrain of the nation. The massive capital outlay that the development of the Trans-Iranian Railroad required seemed like an opening for major foreign interference in capital-poor Iran. Reza, of course, opposed such an approach and financed railroad development with Iranian funds, which he raised primarily through high taxes on the government-controlled monopolies on sugar and tea. He utilized foreigners in every aspect of railroad construction, just as he did in the construction of roads, but he confined their contracts to small, specific functions. Failure of any contractor to complete its share of the project, for whatever reason, could only impede completion of the system until the government found a replacement. While this approach was slow and required tremendous supervision, it resulted in the construction of a system unencumbered by foreign ownership or control. Its successful completion is all the more remarkable since much of it was constructed over some of the most treacherous terrain ever encountered in railroad construction and required more than two hundred tunnels.

Reza made construction of a rail line from the Caspian Sea in the north to the Gulf in the south his priority when he initiated railroad funding in 1925. The north, after all, was the economic heartland of the nation, which was primarily limited to trading with Russia. The north-south railroad had the appeal of connecting northern Iran to the world markets that were accessible through the Gulf ports. With completion of this vital new asset, trade with Europe, and especially Germany, surpassed trade with the Soviet Union in the later years of Reza's reign. Some criticize the failure to connect Iran's line with those in other nations, but it served the needs of Iran and could not serve as a conduit for transporting foreign armies into the country. East-west lines connecting most of the vital northern cities were well on their way to completion by the time Reza left office.

Efforts to industrialize Iran were surprisingly successful during Reza's reign, although no more than 4 percent of the labor force, including oil-field and railroad workers, was employed in industrial occupations. In this early stage of industrialization the emphasis was placed upon the development of products for domestic consumption, rather than for exportation. Textiles, sugar, tea, tobacco, silk, matches, electricity, cement, paper, chemicals, fish, and glass were the vital industries that developed to meet the most pressing consumer demands. All, except the electricity industry, had the additional appeal of requiring modest amounts of capital, which was within the means of Iranian investors to raise. Modest developments in mining promised the development in more heavy manufacturing in the future. Genuine efforts to consider larger projects only became possible in the late 1930s when Germany was willing to exchange capital and technology for long-range options on Iranian commodities.

The major rail lines and highways passed through Tehran as it became the financial and industrial center of Iran, while it was the undisputed center of political authority. The favoritism of the shah to developing the economy of the capital, plus the obvious advantage of conducting business at the seat of power, caused dissatisfaction in other urban regions. Tabriz, which had traditionally been commercially more important than Tehran, suffered from a decline in both its income and its status. Its predominantly Azeri population, its history for leftist radicalism, and its vulnerability to physical and ideological invasion from the Soviet Union, limited the attention the Persian-oriented shah was willing to provide Tabriz. Tehran's increased importance attracted a dramatic growth in population from about 200,000 in 1922 to 700,000 by 1941. Many of the new inhabitants could not find adequate employment, affordable housing, or a sense of individual meaning in the impersonal atmosphere of the big city, where they were divorced from their families and a way of life they understood. They could, however, observe and imagine even more how certain elements of Tehran's society benefited from the new Iran. Their numbers would grow in coming years to become a volatile force that could alter the society from which they felt increasingly alienated.

The new economic enterprises created opportunities to prosper that had formerly been confined to the landed aristocracy, the wealthier merchants, and people associated with the royal court. Industrialists, contractors, midlevel government workers, junior military officers, purveyors of various services, and dealers in nontraditional products began to constitute a new bourgeois class that owed its prosperity to the new shah's policies. While some responded to their good fortune with loyalty to their monarch, others resented the restrictions his policies placed on the fullest use of their ingenuity and their inability to participate in the policies that shaped the nation.

Reza's attention to transportation and industrialization took precedence over his attention to agriculture. This was understandable since both were so lacking and the nation of farmers and herdsmen had always been able to feed itself as well as export food. Conscription into the army and the migration of young men to the cities in search of a better way of life, however, reduced food production at the very time the larger urban populations required more commercial-level agriculture. Government campaigns against the tribes had killed large numbers of their livestock while the resettlement policies reduced milk product- and meat production even further. Experimental methods, which were used primarily on the shah's estates, were still in their early stages when he was forced from office. Irrigation projects and the construction of dams for agricultural purposes began to receive more attention by the late 1930s when, for the first time, Iran faced the prospect of having to import food.

OIL POLICIES AND DEVELOPMENT

Britain's continued presence because of the Anglo-Persian Oil Company's (APOC) concession was a constant reminder of Iran's weaker days. The company's unwillingness to reveal its accounts to government authorities created doubt that the nation received its fair share of the profits. Most Persians also believed that 16 percent of the profits, which the now discredited and dethroned Qajars had accepted, was a travesty, if not an insult. The government had only averaged about £1,000,000 a year income from the British concession. The fact that the nation had to import oil from the Soviet Union, although Persia was the fifth largest oil producer in the world, made matters worse. This oddity requires explanation. Most of Iran's use of oil occurred in the northern cities, but most of the oil was in the south and the country lacked the ability to transport it to the domestic markets until the railway system was completed. Much of the Soviet Union's best developed fields, however, were a short distance across the border, especially in the Baku region.

The Persian cabinet's unilateral cancellation of the oil concession on November 28, 1932 came as a surprise, although there had been Persian attempts to renegotiate the terms several times in the past. The British government, which owned controlling interest in the company, threatened to use force. Iran also made bellicose gestures, but did not impede the operation of production or exportation of the oil. The fact that the Depression had reduced the price and demand for oil, accompanied by the generally peaceful world situation, removed any sense of urgency in settling the dispute. There was good indication that the company's payment of just over £300,000 to Persia for its share of the 1931 profits was an important reason for the cancellation.

The crisis ended after five months when the two sides reached a new agreement on April 29, 1933. By the new agreement, Iran would receive a guarantee of nearly £1,000,000 ($4,850,000) annually, regardless of the level of profit the company experienced. APOC guaranteed to extract at least 5,000,000 tons annually. In addition, the Persian share of profits would be calculated at four shillings a ton based on publicly available figures of production. Use of the gold standard in all the calculations protected Persia from vacillations in British sterling, since Britain had abandoned the gold standard. The company also accepted an 80 percent reduction in the area of its concession, thereby removing its jurisdiction from 400,000 square miles of Persian territory. This was advantageous to Iran for nationalist purposes, but it also made room for competitors to enter the Persian market outside of the sensitive northern regions where the Soviet Union could cause trouble related to an earlier, but unratified, Russian concession. APOC agreed further to hire as many Persians as possible and to develop oil that was accessible to Persian markets in order to reduce or eliminate the necessity of importing Soviet oil. The Persians gained further when the company agreed to make a £2,000,000 payment in retribution for previous low payments and to pay all back taxes. This payment approximately equalled twenty percent of the nation's income from oil over the past decade. APOC's principal *quid pro quo* was a thirty-two year extension of its truncated concession, which had formerly been scheduled to end in 1961. This made it possible for the company to give the kind of attention to the development of oil in Iraq that both the Iraqis and the League of Nations had been demanding.

Many regard this arrangement as a major defeat for Reza Shah, since the British continued to control Persia's most important economic asset. The truth is that Persia had no capacity to do much with the concession if they had received full control of it, because Persians were unprepared to produce and market the oil. The Depression reduced the possibility that any other company would have taken the concession, especially since it would have had to deal with resistance from both APOC and the British government. In the meantime, the increased use of Persians in the company prepared them for the day when they would be able to play a larger role. The government had, in fact, negotiated a better agreement, and when the international recovery began shortly thereafter, its income increased steadily to about £4,000,000 by 1941.

EDUCATION

Reza Shah made more contributions to education than many of his critics care to recognize. He did not, however, attempt to implement compulsory education, although his desire to create a nation with a unified personality and value system made him a natural candidate to do so. More extensive education would have also conformed with his belief that the younger generation would be more constructive, since they were not embittered with the hostilities that permeated the older generation from the constitutional period. His limited funds and the resistance of both the clergy and the landed classes helps explain the limited attention he gave to education. Also, in theory all army recruits were supposed to receive a rudimentary education as part of their period of military service. This approach would have met the basic need for education and was an honest recognition that Iran could not afford to build schools for its widely scattered population. The nation also did not have enough educated people to serve as teachers for the entire population. Those with an education were inclined to enter more lucrative employment in private enterprise or with the government. A large percentage of the students his government sent abroad to study had to agree to enter the teaching profession upon their return to Iran.

The society he had in mind required the education of technocrats, since the alternative was to depend on foreign expertise. He saw no need for a literate public which could read newspapers, write poetry, construct models of utopian governments or economics, and vote in free elections. The educational institutions he constructed in Iran and the education he funded and endorsed for students abroad were designed to produce skills useful for his modern state. His emphasis was upon educating military officers, engineers, administrators, lawyers, and doctors, who could perform necessary functions and whose study generally did not involve close association with dangerous ideologies. Most higher education in Iran became centered in the University of Tehran, which he created in 1934 from existing colleges and the newly created School of Law. The law school was of primary importance as almost all jurisprudence passed from the ecclesiastical courts to his secular system. Just as the liberal constitutionalists had, he insisted on equal opportunity for women to receive an education and some women enrolled in the first classes of Tehran University.

He preferred a French education for the Persians he permitted to study abroad, whose numbers were up to two hundred a year by the end of his reign. This was in part because France had never played a significant role in threatening Persian independence. His preference of France, in fact, indicates as well as anything else his unfamiliarity with the outside world. He believed the French had the best army in the world. He thought that Persians would not only learn their specific skills but also become imbued with the love of nation that the French had exhibited in their defense of their country during World War I. He was apparently unaware that France also had the longest revolutionary tradition of any European nation and that only the Soviet Union nurtured a more leftist faculty.

Modest as the numbers of Persians who received higher education were, the government bureaucracy and other places of employment were unable to absorb their services by the end of Reza's reign. This calls into question critics who contend Reza did too little to educate his nation. The truth is that government financial support increased steadily throughout his reign and both the number of students and schools increased by more than 300 percent while he was in office. By contrast, enrollment in religious schools declined by nearly 90 percent during the same period. The newly educated, whom the economy could not utilize properly, often expressed their discontent in dissident activities. They realized that only a more open political system, a free press, and a commitment to universal education could utilize their talents and fulfill the aspirations their education inspired them to expect.

Reza was particularly interested in reeducating both the nation and the outside world about Persia's proud past prior to the Arab and Islamic conquest in the middle of the seventh century. He focused his attention on the Sassanian period (224–641 A.D.), which had rid the land of Greek influence and predated the domination of Arabs, Arabic, and Islam. The Sassanids had purged their language of foreign influence, which resulted in a pure Aryan language, Pahlavi, also known as Middle Persian. The nationalist dynasty had also reinstated the ancient traditional worship of Zoroastrianism. Reza's affinity for the period once his land was again free from foreign cultural domination prompted him to take the family name of Pahlavi for himself and his dynasty. A Society of Public Guidance used public facilities and the schools to create an awareness of the nation's ancient identity. Some complying officials changed their names, and streets and buildings received old Persian names, as did government and military departments and titles. In 1935 a special Persian Academy addressed the task of purging the language of words of Arabic and Turkish origin and replacing them with Persian words, many of which had to be fabricated because there was no appropriate Persian root. Non-Persian speakers found advancement in Reza's state very difficult and government authorities suppressed publications and presses of Persia's numerous non-Persian-speaking minorities. Place names, including the names of some provinces that formerly reflected the names of non-Persian tribes, received Persian designations.

From March 21, 1935, which was New Years Day on the newly installed old Persian solar calendar, Reza officially insisted that all references should designate that Iran was the official name of his nation. He blamed the Qajars for perpetuating the Greek-inflicted term of "Persia," which actually only applied to one tribe of Aryans. The Bible's use of the same term had made it difficult to overcome the use of the term, although the people of the empire had always referred to it as Iran, the land of the Aryans (Iranians). Foreign nations complied as instructed, but the change met with considerable international opprobrium, since the emphasis upon Aryan identity had become closely associated with Hitler's increased ignominy. The name change did signal the beginning of Iran's close relationship with the Third Reich that would force Reza's abdication six and a half years later.

THE CONSTITUTION AND POLITICAL PARTIES

The shah's ability to shape the composition of the Majlis, beginning with the Fifth Majlis in 1923, allowed him to rule dictatorially and maintain the constitution. The Majlis, for instance, theoretically retained the right to approve and dismiss cabinet ministers, but the shah enjoyed the service of the men of his choice without challenge. To his credit, he often placed very capable men in high office and allowed them great authority as long as they implemented his program and refrained from establishing an independent political base of their own. Many of his once trusted ministers ultimately fell into disfavor or under suspicion and met violent deaths or ended their lives either in prison or in exile. In some cases their demise appeared totally arbitrary as there was no obvious reason why their elimination was necessary. All realized, however, when they entered his service that he was a firm taskmaster, who brooked neither disloyalty nor sloth. He even tried to impose punctuality upon the entire government of a people who had no tradition of hurrying or performing their tasks at a specific time.

Iran had the distinction of developing something approximating genuine political parties earlier than any other Middle East country. The weakness of the central government in the near chaos of the constitutional period had allowed this to happen. Leaders had reasonably well-defined ideologies, which they promoted in their appeal to the fairly large electorate. The number of viable parties remained small enough that success at the polls easily translated into the ability to shape legislation and influence government policies. Reza, in fact, in his early years in office carefully cultivated legislative support and changed his affiliation with different coalitions in the Majlis to institute his program. His determination to transform the nation into a secular society alienated the Reformers, whose principal leader, Ayatollah Sayyed Hassan Mudarres, became one of his most outspoken critics. The Socialists, who provided the majority of the support for his earliest secularization of the nation, resented his rejection of a republic in favor of a monarchy. Reza transformed the Progress party, which had supported him more fully than any other group, into a court party. Once he abolished the Reformers and the Socialists when they fell into disfavor, there was no reason to maintain the fiction of a party system. He believed that any legislature he did not nominate and assure election was inclined to republicanism. In 1932, parties of all kinds ceased to exist and elections simply became a means of confirming the shah's candidates, who compliantly implemented his legislation. The demise of the parties did not destroy the affinity of their adherents to the ideas connected with each. In addition, important leaders of each party survived to maintain some level of coordination among the party supporters. Efforts persisted to revive party participation in a genuine parliamentary government, especially during the reign of Reza's successor. The defunct parties and the ideas they supported, therefore, periodically resurfaced in the future, particularly when the shah's policies caused significant discontent.

While the Persian Communist Party (PCP) received the harshest treatment of all the parties, a small but viable communist movement persisted. Following the suppression of the Soviet Republic of Gilan in 1921, the PCP rejected revolution and adopted a moderate approach of reform that Haydar Khan had advocated. In close cooperation with the Socialists, the PCP concentrated on the development of trade unions, which resulted in the establishment of the Central Council of Federated Trade Unions (CCFTU). CCFTU enjoyed modest success in organizing workers in Persia's limited crafts and industries, although it generally found the peasants unreceptive to attempts to organize them. Foreigners, especially Russian Azeris and Armenians, provided most of the leadership of the PCP. Native Armenians and Azeris, who had been exposed to communist influence in Azerbaijan and Gilan since the end of the nineteenth century, and who were heavily involved in Persian trades and crafts, also constituted a large percentage of the rank-and-file membership. The Socialists and the PCP agreed that Persia had to pass through a bourgeois-dominated stage in a strongly centralized democracy before a fuller socialist or communist society was feasible. The emergence of Tehran as the nation's economic center, accompanied by the economic decline of Azerbaijan, made the capital the focus of most communist activity after 1921, but it also spread to all the large urban centers. Communist success in organizing workers, strikes, and demonstrations resulted in the suppression of the PCP in the period from 1927 to 1931. Two of the more notable leaders, Seyyed Jafar Pishavari and Ardasher Ovanessian, went to prison, while others escaped to the Soviet Union to perish in Stalin's purges in the 1930s. When communism became illegal in 1931, most overt communist organization and activity shifted to Western Europe, first under the leadership of Avetis Sultanzadeh and later under Morteza Alavi.

Recently educated students of European and Iranian universities, who were considerably more leftist than their PCP predecessors, assumed control of the communist and other leftist movements in the 1930s. Taqi Arani, a German educated Azeri physicist, reestablished a Communist party in 1933 that engaged in disruptive activities centered on the University of Tehran. The new Communist party was composed of predominantly young, ethnically Persian middle-class membership, while the Azeris members also manifested a more national than provincial orientation. Increased communist activity after 1935 culminated in the arrest of most of the party's leadership in May 1937, when they attempted a large-scale penetration of the oil industry in Khuzistan. A famous group of "Fifty-Three" experienced a well-publicized trial in November 1938, which resulted in forty-five of them going to prison, where their differences with the imprisoned leaders of the PCP became more pronounced. Pishevari, who had fought real battles on behalf of his views, could not respect the new Soviet-connected communists, whom he regarded as armchair-intellectual revolutionaries. Ovanessian, who had always endorsed a strong central authority and possessed strong revolutionary zeal, gravitated toward the Fifty-Three to lay the foundation for the future Tudeh (Masses) party. These developments within the communist ranks had an important influence on later Iranian affairs.

REZA'S FOREIGN RELATIONS AND DEMISE

Somewhat ironically, Reza Shah made his enduring reputation as an iron-fisted nationalist who transformed his nation domestically. He lost his throne, though, because of a crucial miscalculation in foreign affairs. His absorption in domestic issues, Iran's weakness, his ignorance of foreign affairs, and the relative tranquility of world affairs during his reign prevented him from having to confront many major international questions prior to his fatal blunder. The Soviets' preoccupation with domestic affairs kept them from offering much of a threat, although almost every conflict among the contentious Soviet leadership had its counterpart among the Iranians and sometimes spilled across the border. Reza assumed that the Soviets were too weak to offer much real threat until well into the future.

The British continued to pose the only real threat to Iran's sovereignty and pride. While their oil concession was the most obvious cause for concern, British influence in Iraq and throughout the Gulf region thwarted any Iranian initiatives along its entire western border with Iraq. British policies toward the Arabs also helped arouse Islamic concerns throughout the region at a time Reza needed Iranian Muslims to forget the diminution of their status. Reza's desire to acquire a more favorable border with Iraq along the Shatt al-Arab seemed impossible because Iraq could always depend on British support. Britain alone stood between Iran's claim to the valuable island of Bahrain, whose population was approximately 90 percent Persian, but was under Arab control. On several occasions he had reason to believe that British interference had prevented him from establishing beneficial relations with the United States as a source of capital, technical assistance, and as an alternative developer of Iran's oil industry.

Iran took advantage of a respite in Britain's power in Iraq during the short period of Bakr Sidqi's tenure in office in Iraq to improve Iran's border with Iraq and obtain better navigation rights in the Shatt al-Arab. That agreement on July 4,

1937 signalled a much bigger agreement, called the Saadabad Pact, on July 8 among Iran, Iraq, Turkey, and Afghanistan. The pact, which was named after Reza's palace where it was signed, was essentially a nonaggression agreement and a promise to consult if either party were attacked. All four countries had in common a fierce desire to establish their independence from outside interference. The Soviets took umbrage at the pact as being directed toward them, when, in fact, it was much more an anti-British pact. Iraqi support for the pact ended with the overthrow of Sidqi on August 17 as Arab nationalists reasserted themselves and resented the concessions the aberrant Sidqi administration had made. A similar effort in the Baghdad Pact in 1955, this time with British approval, enraged Arab nationalists throughout the region. The Saadabad Pact never proved to be of any value to any of its signatories.

Iranian nationalists had searched for an affiliation with some third source that would break the strangle-hold Russia and Britain had held on Iran for so long. Hitler's reaction to Germany's degradation struck a note of admiration in the shah, whose increased relations of all kinds with Germany from 1936 received widespread Iranian support. Germany's rapid recovery under Nazi leadership and the timid response of the other nations to Hitler's aggressive behavior convinced Iranian officials and other Middle East nationalists that Nazi Germany was an unstoppable force. Nazi willingness to establish favorable trade relations and offer technical assistance was equally appealing. Germany also enjoyed a good reputation because it had never occupied any territory or made any extraterritorial claim in the entire Middle East. Iran, in turn, had special appeal to Germany, because every other area of the region, except Turkey, was either directly or indirectly under British or French control. Turkey's commitment to neutrality, therefore, made Iran the only country in the Middle East where Germany could establish a presence without encountering Anglo-French resistance.

Increased commercial relations between Germany and Iran after 1936 signalled a relationship that Great Britain and the Soviet Union perceived as threatening. Earlier German trade and participation in most phases of Iran's highway and railroad construction had been too modest to cause alarm. The roads and railways that connected the populous north with the Gulf, in fact, had been necessary before increased trade with Germany was possible. The approximately six hundred German technicians of all kinds became the dominant foreign presence in Iran outside of the oil fields. More than 40 percent of Iran's foreign trade was with Germany by the late 1930s and the two countries engaged in serious plans to develop heavy industry in Iran. The relationship seemed all the more promising as Germany's association with other nations declined. Iran's decimation of its Communist party at the same time it accelerated its relationship with Germany seemed less than coincidental to the Soviets.

By the mid-1930s, developments in Iraq also influenced British concern about both Germany and Iran. The Iraqi monarchy could prevent a strong German presence there, but it could not curtail a widespread affinity for Germany, especially among some government officials and even more of the military officers. Admiration for Germany had permeated the upper strata of Iraqi society from the late nineteenth century. The entire education system of Iraq had become preoccupied with cultivating Iraqi and Arab nationalism under very heavy German influence. German Minister Fritz Grobba capitalized on Iraqi sympathies to make

Baghdad the center of German propaganda to a receptive Arab world. Under British pressure, the Iraqi government broke diplomatic relations with Germany after World War II began. Grobba took his activities across the border into Iran. But Hajj Amin al-Husseini, the leader of the Palestinian resistance whom the British had expelled from Palestine, moved to Baghdad on October 16, 1939 to lead Arab nationalism, which favored an Axis victory. A pro-Axis military *coup,* with Hajj Amin's support, seized power in Iraq from April 12 to May 30, 1941. When British troops suppressed the so-called Rashid Ali *coup,* Hajj Amin and the *coup* leaders fled to Iran, which was the only place in the Middle East where they could find a safe haven. These developments tied British concerns with the greater Arab world to the already distressing pro-German developments in Iran.

Germany's easy victories in the war raised hopes in the Middle East for an Allied defeat and increased belief that Arabs and Iranians alike had finally supported the right side. It is, therefore, understandable that Reza Shah resisted British and Soviet efforts to gain permission to use Iran's new transportation infrastructure to transport supplies to the Soviet Union after the German invasion on June 22, 1941. The shah reminded his tormentors that Iran had declared its neutrality at the outset of the war. Anglo-Soviet needs were too dire, however, for them to honor Iran's neutrality. The Soviets were fighting for their lives and Great Britain could not allow the collapse of the Russian front to occur as it had in World War I. The Allies also had reason to believe that a combination of distaste for Reza and the pro-German sentiments of Iranian military officers could result in a pro-Axis *coup* against the shah that would ally with Germany. With Rommel's success in North Africa, and German tanks moving rapidly toward the Soviet oil fields in the Caucasus, Reza considered it foolish to comply with Anglo-Soviet demands on July 19 and August 16 that he essentially declare war on the Axis by allowing the Allies to use his nation to supply the Soviets.

An Anglo-Soviet invasion on August 25, 1941 resulted in their control of Iran, which would continue after the war ended. The army, which had used approximately 25 percent of Iran's budget during Reza's reign offered no resistance. The might of the attackers was no doubt a major factor in the army's failure to fight for its nation and its shah. Reza's loss of respect was probably just as strong a reason his army failed him. Few felt secure under his later regime as he had amassed all power under his authority and accumulated a personal fortune most suffered to help him acquire. It seemed that, since he had increasingly identified the nation with his person, defense of the nation was primarily a defense of the continuation of his rule.

Reza Shah, who had united and strengthened his nation, had no choice but deliver it back into the hands of its most persistent modern enemies. He did so with some dignity and attempted to lighten the humiliation by saying it was time for him to stand aside and leave the nation in the capable hands of his son, Muhammad Reza, who had been his designated heir since 1926. He hoped his own short reign had laid the foundation of a new dynasty that could withstand the trauma of its founder's demise. The marriage of his son to King Farouk of Egypt's sister in 1938 had provided the family with an infusion of royal blood that might help establish its legitimacy. British affinity for monarchy also offered him additional hope for his Pahlavi family. He abdicated on September 16 and moved very unceremoniously to the Gulf, where a British steamer took him to India. There the British immediately transferred him to another British ship that took him to the island of Mauritius, where he lived until March 27, 1942. His failing health and broken spirit did not respond well to the tropical climate, so the British allowed him to go to Johannesburg, South Africa where he died on July 26, 1944.

The overthrow of Reza Shah ushered in five years of Anglo-Russian-American control of the most important portions of Iran. Strong remnants of their control would remain after the foreign military forces and other officials withdrew soon after World War II finally ended. Most Iranians would believe more than thirty years passed before Iran's experience with imperialism ended. Adding to Iranian dismay and a feeling of exploitation was the fact that, despite the role foreign nations played in their internal affairs, Iran had never officially been part of any foreign empire.

12

Reoccupation

HISTORICAL TIMELINE

1940 ⇛ Paris fell to Nazis on June 14.
⇛ General Dentz, representing Vichy government, became Commissioner of Syria and Lebanon on June 17.
⇛ Zaki Arsuzi created *al-Baath al-Arabi.*

1941 ⇛ Uprising in Lebanon forced President Edde's resignation in April. Puaux appointed Alfred Naccache president.
⇛ Rashid Ali al-Galiani *coup* in Iraq on April 12.
⇛ Armed conflict between British and Iraqi troops on April 30.
⇛ British defeated Rashid Ali forces and took control of Baghdad on May 30. Rashid Ali fled.
⇛ Arab Legion helped subdue Rashid Ali in Iraq in May.
⇛ Arab Legion helped overcome Vichy government in Syria during June.
⇛ Leaders of Rashid Ali *coup* and Hajj Amin al-Husseini fled to Iran on May 30 after the British suppressed their movement in Iraq.
⇛ British and Free France troops invaded Vichy-controlled Syrian mandate June 8 and the Allied governments declared Syria and Lebanon free.
⇛ Anglo-Free French victory over Vichy government in Syria and Lebanon July 14.
⇛ British and Soviets demanded on July 19 and August 16 the right to use Iranian facilities for their war efforts.

⇛ Anglo-Soviet invasion of Iran on August 25 to establish transportation link from the Gulf to the Soviet Union.
⇛ British recognized Syrian and Lebanese independence September 21.
⇛ General Georges Catroux, Delegate General of Free France in Syria, declared Syrian independence, but did not restore the constitution on September 28.
⇛ Catroux appointed Shaykh Taj ed-Den al-Hasani president of Syria.
⇛ Reza Shah of Iran abdicated on September 16.
⇛ Muhammad Reza assumed throne of Iran on September 17.
⇛ Formation of Tudeh party in Iran on September 29.

1942 ⇛ Britain and Soviet Union agreed on January 29 to withdraw their troops from Iran six months after the cessation of hostilities of World War II.
⇛ British used show of force on February 4 to compel Farouk to appoint Nahas Pasha as prime minister.
⇛ Colonel H. Norman Schwarzkopf became commander of Iran Gendarmerie.
⇛ A regional Kurdish independence movement, centered in Mahabad, Persia, began under the leadership of Qazi Muhammad.
⇛ German forces pushed eastward toward Alexandria in the fall.
⇛ End of German threat to Middle East in October.
⇛ The Biltmore Program in 1942 called for a "Jewish Commonwealth" and signalled the switch from Great Britain to the United States as the primary supporter of Zionism.
⇛ Nasser became leader of the Free Officer Society.

1943–45 ⇛ Egypt played dominant role in the formulation of the League of Arab States. Other states followed Egyptian lead out of concern for the ambitions of the Hashemites.
⇛ Alexandria Protocol in March 1945 created the League of Arab States with its headquarters in Cairo.

1943 ⇛ United States forces entered Iran on January 1.
⇛ Dr. Arthur C. Millspaugh returned to Iran to become Treasurer-General.
⇛ Iraq declared war on Axis and Japan on January 16 and was the first Arab nation to do so.
⇛ Death of Shaykh Taj ed-Den al-Hasani on March 23 led to British pressure for France to restore the Syrian constitution.
⇛ General Catroux restored the constitutions of Lebanon and Syria on March 25.
⇛ Parliamentary elections in Syria and Lebanon were held during the summer.
⇛ Shukri al-Quwatly was elected president of Syria in July.
⇛ Leading politicians created a new distribution of Lebanon's Chamber of Deputies in July that guaranteed Christians a six-to-five majority in the Legislative Assembly.

- ⇛ Bishara al-Khoury was elected president of Lebanon September 21.
- ⇛ Al-Khoury and Riad al-Sulh formed the National Pact, which provided for a distribution of executive offices in Lebanon on a proportional confessional basis.
- ⇛ The Chamber of Deputies declared Lebanese independence on November 5.
- ⇛ The French arrested the Lebanese President al-Khoury and his cabinet on November 11 and Delegate-General Helleu suspended the constitution.
- ⇛ French put Edde back in presidential office of Lebanon on November 11.
- ⇛ Helleu was dismissed from office on November 17 after a large-scale Lebanese uprising.
- ⇛ Lebanese President al-Khoury and members of his cabinet were released from prison on November 22.
- ⇛ Michel Aflaq and Salah al-Din Bitar created the Baath Movement.
- ⇛ Saudi Arabia began to receive Lend-Lease funds, and the following year the United States government provided funds and allowed materials, which had formerly been needed for the war, to be used to develop Saudi oil production.

1944
- ⇛ Syria declared its independence January 22.
- ⇛ Reza Shah died on July 26 in Johannesburg.
- ⇛ Caltex changed its name to Arabian American Oil Company (ARAMCO).
- ⇛ Indications that American companies might obtain an oil concession in Iran prompted the Soviets to demand one for themselves.
- ⇛ *Irgun* began systematic destruction of British administrative centers. Stern Gang (*Lehi*) assassinated Lord Moyne on November 6.
- ⇛ Throughout the year, many countries, including the U.S. and the USSR, recognized Syrian independence.

1945
- ⇛ Roosevelt-Ibn Saud meeting was held on February 14.
- ⇛ Ahmad Maher of Egypt was assassinated on February 24 for declaring war against the Axis.
- ⇛ Syria declared war on Germany and Japan March 1.
- ⇛ Alexandria Protocol established League of Arab States on March 22.
- ⇛ Truman demanded in April termination of the provisions of the 1939 White Paper.
- ⇛ More French troops entered Syria and Lebanon on May 15.
- ⇛ Syrian uprising and French bombarded Damascus beginning May 28.
- ⇛ Churchill ultimatum to French stopped French slaughter May 31.

⇛ Attlee-Bevin labor government began in July.
⇛ French relinquished control of *troopes speciales* July 7.
⇛ Truman demanded the immediate acceptance of 100,000 Jews into Palestine on August 31.
⇛ Japan surrendered on September 2, which established March 2, 1946 as the latest date Allied forces should leave Iran.
⇛ Azerbaijan Democratic Movement was created under the leadership of Sayyed Jaffar Pishevaria on September 3.
⇛ Zionists increased efforts to smuggle more Jews into Palestine in September.
⇛ Zionists attacked Palestine railroad system in 153 places on October 31.
⇛ Approval of the Anglo-American Committee of Inquiry for Palestine on November 13.
⇛ Azerbaijan Democratic Movement seized control of provincial government on November 16.
⇛ Qazi Muhammad declared creation of Kurdish People's Republic in Iran on December 15.
⇛ Quota of Jewish migration to Palestine expired December 30.
⇛ Aflaq and Bitar referred to their organization as the Baath Party.
⇛ Britain had vital interests in the Middle East, especially in the Suez Canal, which prevented it from considering leaving the bases in Egypt.
⇛ Most Egyptians regarded continued British presence as an affront to their sovereignty.

1946 ⇛ United States forces left Iran on January 1.
⇛ Unprecedented Zionist attacks on the British during the first part of the year.
⇛ Ahmad Qavam became premier of Iran on January 26, after the Soviets refused to deal with his predecessor, Ibrahim Hakimi. His primary duty was to convince the Soviets to withdraw from Iran.
⇛ The British announced on January 30 that they would continue allowing the previous quota of Jewish migration until the Anglo-American Committee finished its study.
⇛ Return of Jamal al-Husseini to Palestine early in February.
⇛ Zionists and the United States refused to attend London Conference on Palestine scheduled for February.
⇛ On February 4, Syria and Lebanon appealed to the U.N. to remove France from their territory.
⇛ Stalin and Molotov demanded oil concession and major social changes in Iran when Qavam went to Moscow on February 18.
⇛ Abdullah crowned himself King of Transjordan on February 25.
⇛ British forces left Iran on March 2.
⇛ Iran raised an objection in the United Nations to Soviet refusal to leave Iran. Did the same on March 18.
⇛ Soviets agreed to begin removing their forces from Iran on March 24.

⇛ United Nations considered the problem of Soviet forces in Iran on April 3.
⇛ Qavam and the Soviets agreed on April 5 that the Iranian Majlis would consider a Soviet oil concession no later than November 24.
⇛ French withdrew from Syria on April 17.
⇛ Report of the Anglo-American Committee of Inquiry on Palestine on May 1.
⇛ Truman endorsed an Anglo-American Committee report on May 1.
⇛ Hajj Amin al-Husseini moved to Egypt in May.
⇛ Soviet troop withdrawal from Iran was completed on May 9.
⇛ Qavam reconciled most differences with the Azerbaijan Democrat Movement in Persia on June 13, but the movement's security forces remained in place.
⇛ "Night of the Bridges" Zionists destroyed ten bridges on June 17.
⇛ British arrested a large number of Zionist leaders on June 29.
⇛ Qavam created his Iranian Democrat Party on June 29.
⇛ Morrison-Grady committee conducted a study to determine a compromise between British and American positions throughout July.
⇛ *Irgun* bombed King David Hotel in Jerusalem on July 22.
⇛ Morrison-Grady committee report July 31.
⇛ United States rejected and Britain accepted Morrison-Grady report.
⇛ Tudeh organized massive strikes in Khuzistan oil fields in July, as well as huge demonstrations all over Iran throughout the summer.
⇛ The Zionists submitted their plan for immigration to Palestine August 6, which Truman accepted.
⇛ British sent Jewish refugees aboard *Haganah* ship to Cyprus on August 12.
⇛ Qavam appointed three Tudeh cabinet ministers and put other leftists into important Iranian government positions in August.
⇛ Qashqui tribal uprising in Iran during September, which spread to most of the south and southwest by October.
⇛ British officials met with Arab League officials on Palestinian problem policy on September 10.
⇛ Truman formally endorsed a Zionist plan for Palestine on October 4.
⇛ On October 6, Thomas Dewey, Republican candidate for president, called for an even higher rate of Jewish migration into Palestine.
⇛ Iran received military aid from the United States on October 18.
⇛ Iranian government and tribal forces destroyed much of Tudeh's political machinery and arrested or killed many of its leaders in October.

- ⇛ Qavam dismissed Tudeh cabinet members and other leftists from the Iranian government on October 19. He also released conservative political prisoners.
- ⇛ Zionists leaders arrested in Palestine on June 29 were released on November 5.
- ⇛ Hajj Amin and Jamal were elected to the two highest positions of the Arab Higher Committee in Palestine on November 22.
- ⇛ Majlis election in Iran had not occurred by November 24 deadline for considering Soviet oil concession.
- ⇛ Government troops under command of the Shah and General Ali Razmara destroyed the Kurdish and Azerbaijan independence movements from December 10–13.
- ⇛ World Zionist Organization refused to reelect Chaim Weizmann as president in December for his moderate position on Jewish immigration into Palestine.
- ⇛ French troops withdrew from Lebanon on December 31.
- ⇛ Zionists and United States refused to attend the London Conference on Palestine scheduled for February.
- ⇛ Assassination of Amin Osman, Finance Minister of Egypt.

1947

- ⇛ British submitted Palestine problem to the United Nations on February 18.
- ⇛ Standard Oil of New Jersey and Mobil bought 30 percent and 10 percent, respectively, of ARAMCO's stock in March.
- ⇛ Initial congress of the Baath Party on April 4.
- ⇛ Special session of General Assembly on Palestine question April 28–May 15. Appointed an eleven-member United Nations Special Committee on Palestine (UNSCOP) to recommend a solution.
- ⇛ UNSCOP arrived in Palestine June 14.
- ⇛ British returned the *Exodus*, a Zionist refugee ship, to its place of origin on July 19.
- ⇛ British executed three *Irgunists* July 29; *Irgun* followed with the execution of two British sergeants.
- ⇛ UNSCOP majority report on August 31 recommended partitioning of Palestine.
- ⇛ British announced on September 26 that they would terminate their mandate over Palestine.
- ⇛ General Assembly debate on Palestine from September through November.
- ⇛ The Lebanese Chamber of Deputies amended the constitution to allow al-Khoury to serve a second term as president.
- ⇛ Qavam and Majlis decided on October 22 to grant no further oil concessions and to begin to regain control over the British oil concession.
- ⇛ U.N. partition of Palestine into Jewish and Arab states, with Jerusalem as an international city, on November 29 by a 33–13 vote.
- ⇛ Two thousand people were killed or injured in Arab-Zionist

conflicts in Palestine during the six weeks following the U.N. vote.
- ⇛ British withdrew all forces in Egypt to the Suez Canal area.
- ⇛ *Irgun* carried out extensive attacks against Palestinian Arabs in December.
- ⇛ Qavam left Iranian premiership in fear of his life and liberty on December 10.
- ⇛ British announced on December 18 that they would withdraw from Palestine on May 15.

1948
- ⇛ Arab League organized and financed Arab Liberation Army under the command of Fawzi al-Qawaqji January 1.
- ⇛ Abd al-Qadir al-Husseini became commander of Palestinian guerrillas on January 1.
- ⇛ Opposition to the Anglo-Iraqi Portsmouth treaty erupted on January 5 because of rumors of its contents.
- ⇛ Haganah concluded a major arms deal with Czechoslovakia on January 14.
- ⇛ British and Iraqi officials agreed on January 15 to the Treaty of Portsmouth to replace the 1930 treaty.
- ⇛ *Wathbah* uprising in Iraq began on a large scale on January 16.
- ⇛ Fawzi al-Qawaqji entered Palestine as commander of the Arab Liberation Army March 5.
- ⇛ The United States was indecisive in March as to whether it still favored partitioning of Palestine. Truman categorically supported it.
- ⇛ Zionists completed Plan D by March 10.
- ⇛ Zionist offensive to implement Plan D began April 5 with the intention of conquering Jerusalem.
- ⇛ *Irgun* conducted a massacre of Deir Yassin April 9.
- ⇛ The United Nations appointed a commission to supervise implementation of partition, but violence in Palestine prevented the commission from conducting its duty.
- ⇛ Tiberius, Haifa, and Jaffa fell under Zionist control between April 20 and May 6. Most Arabs fled to become refugees.
- ⇛ Zionists gained control of scores of other Arab areas by the end of April and also moved up to the wall of the Old City.
- ⇛ Gush Etzion Bloc surrendered to Transjordanian troops on May 14.
- ⇛ Palestinian mandate ended on May 15.
- ⇛ British withdrew from Palestine on May 15.
- ⇛ Arab League armies invaded Palestine on May 15.
- ⇛ Zionists had control of much of eastern Galilee by the middle of May.
- ⇛ By May 15 Zionists were in control of the two northern sectors of the three the U.N. had assigned them.
- ⇛ Zionists pronounced the creation of the state of Israel on May 15.

⇛ The United States and the Soviet Union recognized Israel on May 15.
⇛ Israel declared creation of Israeli Defense Forces May 26.
⇛ U.N. appointed Count Folke Bernadotte as official mediator in Palestine on May 20.
⇛ U.N. called for a truce on May 29.
⇛ U.N. truce in Palestine began on June 11.
⇛ Count Bernadotte obtained an agreement for the U.N. truce on June 11.
⇛ War in Palestine resumed on July 9.
⇛ The second U.N. Truce in Palestine began on July 18.
⇛ *Lehi* assassinated Count Bernadotte on September 17.
⇛ Dr. Ralph Bunche became U.N. mediator after Bernadotte's death.
⇛ Hajj Amin al-Husseini declared the creation of the Government of All Palestine in Gaza on September 20.
⇛ The Palestinian delegation proclaimed Emir Abdullah king of All Palestine in September and a larger delegation proclaimed him king of Greater Syria in December.
⇛ War in Palestine resumed October 15.
⇛ General deadlock in the Iranian Majlis between opposing forces.

1949 ⇛ Egypt and Israel began armistice talks on the Island of Rhodes on January 12.
⇛ Hasan al-Banna, founder of the Muslim Brotherhood of Egypt, was assassinated on February 12.
⇛ Execution of Fahd, the communist leader of Iraq, took place in February.
⇛ All Palestinians under Transjordanian authority were given citizenship in February.
⇛ The Israeli-Egyptian armistice was signed on February 24.
⇛ The Lebanon-Israeli armistice was signed on March 23.
⇛ The Transjordanian-Israeli armistice was signed on April 3.
⇛ Colonel Husni Zaim seized control of Syria in a *coup* with broad initial support March 30.
⇛ Abdullah assumed the title of king of Jordan on April 25.
⇛ The U.N. recognized Israeli independence on May 11.
⇛ The Syrian Nationalist Party attempted a *coup* in Lebanon during July.
⇛ Execution of Antun Sa'ada on July 9.
⇛ Syrian-Israeli armistice signed on July 20.
⇛ Colonel Sami Hinnawi *coup* in Syria against Zaim on August 14.
⇛ Mossadegh created the National Front in Iran in October.
⇛ U.N. appointed Conciliation Commission on Palestine on December 11.
⇛ Colonel Abed Shishakli *coup* in Syria against Hinnawi on December 19.

- ⇛ Riots and demonstrations in Syria during December resulting from military failures in Palestine.
- ⇛ Kamal Jumblat formed Progressive Socialist Party in Lebanon.
- ⇛ Attempt on the Shah's life by a man associated with both the Tudeh and religious elements.
- ⇛ Shah summoned a constituent assembly that created a senate and gave the Shah greater control over the legislature.
- ⇛ ARAMCO increased production and Saudi Arabia's oil revenues increased from $10 million in 1946 to $50 million.
- ⇛ Saudis negotiated a much higher share of the profits from Aminoil and Great Western for the concession in the Saudi portion of the Neutral Zone.

Foreign domination of the Middle East continued to prevail a generation after the demise of the Ottoman and Qajar dynasties. After the armed clashes in the mid-1930s, the benign nature of this domination disguised the fact that Middle Eastern "nations" possessed only as much independence as the powerful Western nations deemed compatible with their own interests. The military and financial weakness of the Middle Eastern nations, coupled with their general political disarray, placed them at the mercy of the Western nations. Iran, which had undergone impressive changes under Reza Shah, proved no more capable of maintaining its sovereignty than tiny Lebanon. Westerners protected their strategic interests and resource requirements without consideration of Middle Eastern national aspirations and cultural concerns. Towards these ends, foreign powers overthrew five Middle Eastern governments during World War II. The establishment of Israel in Palestine following the war was, in addition to everything else, an attempt on the part of the West to solve a long-standing social and moral problem at the expense of Middle Eastern national sensibilities and territorial concerns.

EGYPT

Egypt during World War II

During World War II the independence of Egypt proved as ephemeral as it had been in other Arab areas under British and French control. As in Iraq and Transjordan, where the British also prevailed, Egypt broke relations with Germany when the war began. Unlike Iraq, Egypt also broke relations with Italy once it became a belligerent, since its neighbor, Libya, was an Italian colony. The prospect of Germany conquering Egypt was strong in 1942, as Rommel pushed eastward toward Alexandria before British forces stopped him at al-Alamayn in October. Many Egyptians applauded the German advances in the hope that a British defeat would remove them from Egypt. By 1941, former prime minister Ali Maher; General Aziz Ali al-Misri, the inspirational father of the Free Officer Corp and founder of al-Ahd; and Hasan al-Banna, the founder of the Muslim Brotherhood, were all in jail for pro-Axis sympathies. Anwar Sadat, a future president, was soon on his way to prison as well. The British suspected that King Farouk had pro-Axis inclinations and dealt with him accordingly. His stance was popular in Egypt but the British insistence that he dismiss his prime minister, Ali Maher, in June 1940 also piqued his personal and national pride. When Farouk balked at following British instructions to appoint Nahas Pasha as prime minister on February 4, 1942 the king felt the full fury of British domination. The British ambassador, accompanied by soldiers and tanks, confronted the king in his palace with the choice of making the appointment or losing his throne. Nahas Pasha, who had developed a warm relationship with the British since he negotiated the 1936 treaty, received the premiership. The king's humiliation endeared him to most Egyptians and marked the British and Nahas for later retribution.

Egypt was central to the regional war effort in no small part because of the Middle East Supply Center that was established there in 1941 to coordinate virtually all military and civilian goods of the region. This massive logistical enterprise reached out to every country and supplied them with necessities and fostered agricultural and manufacturing on a scale that brought prosperity to many. Egypt became the major center for rest and recuperation for Allied troops in Europe and North Africa. Much resentment in Egypt during and after the war resulted from the fortunes a small segment made during the war. The government of Egypt prospered, as well, but the wartime boom attracted many from the countryside to the cities where they watched their jobs disappear after the war as rapidly as they had appeared during the war. The needs of the troops often created food shortages in a land of plenty and wartime prices made the purchase of goods difficult for both the urban and rural poor.

Egypt in Arab Affairs

Egypt's monumental struggle to free itself from British control consumed most of its political attention and energy, but it was always active in Arab affairs. Egyptians, like other Arabs, displayed displeasure at the development of Zionist and British control in Palestine. Egyptians formed Palestine defense committees and attended international conferences like the one in Bludan on behalf of the Palestinians. In 1938 Cairo hosted the largest congress on behalf of Palestinian liberation, although British influence prevented the Egyptian government from issuing any statement on the partition plan of 1937. Cairo became the major center to coordinate Palestinian and Arab League opposition to Zionism after World War II. Most major delegations honed their presentations there before they presented them to either the British or the United Nations.

Egypt's opposition to Iraqi and Transjordanian Hashemite expansion helped it emerge as the leader of the Arab League, since none of the other Arab states who opposed the Hashemites were in a position to lead. Nahas Pasha's cordial relationship with the British enabled him to know the limits of cooperation among the Arabs that would be acceptable to the British. Nuri al-Said had equal experience, but Iraqi ambitions infringed upon the other Arab nations and threatened to make a union under Iraqi leadership more divisive than therapeutic. Egypt's sophistication, location, and apparent lack of inclination for territorial expansion suited it best as the leader of the Arab League, which was headquartered in Cairo after its formulation in 1944.

The Urge to Expel the British

In the opinion of most Egyptians, any justification the British had for reasserting their dominion over Egypt did not exist after the end of the war. Even the Wafd, which stood in disrepute in some circles for its close relationship with the British, endorsed the expulsion of the British. The Saadists, who regarded themselves as the true upholders of Saad Zaghlul's original Wafd principles, built their entire program upon freeing Egypt from foreign influence. Young Egypt, although small, expressed its most violent, fascistlike efforts against the British and their Egyptian allies. The Muslim Brotherhood regarded expulsion of the British as a necessary precondition for fulfilling its primary goal of creating an Islamic society. The Free Officers Society's agenda for abolishing corruption, favoritism, and ineptness required expelling the British support for King Farouk and his wealthy, privileged cohorts. The small communist movement took advantage of the strong anti-British feeling to escalate all kinds of demonstrations to higher levels of violence. Urban workers and students became willing pawns in the hands of all political groups, whose anti-British slogans could cause them to pour into the streets.

The British, however, remained committed to retaining bases in Egypt and the right to return in strength if Middle Eastern developments threatened their vital interests, especially those related to the Suez Canal. Much as in Iraq at the same time, nothing short of these provisions was acceptable to either Conservative or Labor British governments in the growing chill that became the Cold War. Anglo-Egyptian relations were even more complicated because any treaty arrangement also had to address control of Sudan, which both countries claimed. Adding to the awkwardness of their affairs, the still proud British Empire was financially in debt to Egypt at the end of the war with no prospect of repayment in sight. The Khedive Ismail might have enjoyed the irony of this development, which neither the British nor the Egyptians found comforting.

While Egyptian professional politicians could understand British concerns, they realized that any treaty relationship that allowed a continued British presence would bring personal disaster. All were well aware that anti-British feelings were responsible for Ahmad Maher's assassination after he symbolically declared war on Germany on February 24, 1945 after the war was essentially over. Prime Minister Mahmoud al-Nukrashi only lost his position amidst the violence that followed his apparent equivocation toward the British in 1946. He returned to the premiership in 1947, but died at the hands of a Muslim Brotherhood assassin in 1948 when he appeared more interested in suppressing that organization than expelling the British in the dark days following the defeat in Palestine. No Egyptian politician had the strength Nuri al-Said had in Iraq, where his Portsmouth Treaty in 1948 ignited the *wathbah* (uprising) in the less volatile situation before the Palestine disaster.

The Muslim Brotherhood

The Muslim Brotherhood became the most pivotal factor in Egypt in the absence of any other group to take the lead. The Turkish and Circassian senior officers, for instance, generally acquiesced to the policies of the king and his ministers and kept the military out of politics. The formerly dashing king seemed content to grow fat and indulge himself in every carnal way his immense wealth allowed. Memory of British tanks around his palace in 1942 engendered docility rather than confrontation. The conventional political parties habitually expressed their unwillingness to compromise on their demands for Britain's complete withdrawal from Egypt and recognition of Egyptian right to govern Sudan. They depended on the Muslim Brotherhood, Young Egypt, and small leftist groups like the communists to whip up the mobs that expressed Egyptian anger. The mainstream political parties, however, demonstrated no ability to change the status quo.

Neither the British, nor the king, nor the secular *Zeitgeist,* could deter the Muslim Brotherhood and its Supreme Guide, Shaykh Hasan al-Banna. This fiery advocate of traditional Islam ignored the trends of his region and elsewhere to turn to modern, secular, Western approaches for answers to social and political questions. For him and his growing following, *The Quran* and the *Shariah* (Islamic law) provided the answers and guide for religious, political, and social structures and behavior. In an Islamic society, the establishment of which was the reason God sent both *The Quran* and Muhammad, there could be no separation of religious and secular matters. Everything was under the jurisdiction of God's law since He created everything as an integral expression of His will.

Needless to say, the Muslim Brothers (*Ikhwan al-Muslimin*) found little in Egypt that met their standards. Foreign nonbelievers dominated almost everything worthwhile in collaboration with indulgent, misguided Egyptian transgressors of God's law. The same forces were imposing Zionist imperialism upon Palestine and Jerusalem, which contained the third most holy shrines for Muslims. Rectification of these abominations had to begin with expelling the British from both Egypt and Palestine.

The *Ikhwan* grew steadily, despite its often illegal status, after Shaykh Hasan began it in 1928. Its need to operate clandestinely and to guard the secrecy of its membership precludes an accurate estimate of its numerical strength, but most agree it numbered at least 500,000 members by the time of al-Banna's assassination in 1949. Since millions sympathized with its cause and its unwillingness to waver in the face of persecution, the *Ikhwan* commanded even more influence than its impressive numbers indicated. The use of small cells, whose members usually did not know the members of other cells or the overall structure of the organization, prevented the authorities from crushing the movement. Its real strength, however, probably resulted from its members' belief in their cause and the organization's capacity to provide spiritual, physical, health, and educational support, as well as a strong sense of direction for its members.

In keeping with the urbane nature of Egypt, al-Banna acknowledged that some things of non-Islamic origin were useful and even necessary in a modern Islamic society. He counselled, however, that Muslims should only assimilate from beyond their tradition after careful determination proved something was necessary, worthy, and compatible with Islam. Given the comprehensive nature of Islam, he was confident that anything that could stand such scrutiny represented no threat to Islam. He knew, however, that Islam prohibited ungodliness, wealth for a few and poverty for the many, and a majority of believers under the authority of a minority of unbelievers. It was unnecessary, therefore, to look beyond the simplest and most important tenets of Islam to find solutions for most of Egypt's problems.

Shaykh Hasan involved the *Ikhwan* in every issue in Egypt. He authorized demonstrations, strikes, riots, and assassinations. His followers generated many activities of their own and participated in activities of other groups that targeted British occupation and Egyptian misrule. Almost every major leader in Egypt, even

Farouk, flirted at some point with an affiliation with the *Ikhwan*. It spread beyond the confines of Egypt to all other Arab countries, where it endured the vagaries of acceptance and persecution. The brothers often silently waited for secular Arab nationalism to prove inept in meeting regional challenges before they resurfaced to offer their alternative based on Islam's oldest appeal. Their propensity to violence distracted many observers from the *Ikhwan's* quiet, deep, constructive growth, which met personal needs of the brotherhood that no amount of suppression could annihilate years after their leader's death.

IRAQ

Nuri al-Said and the Four Colonels

After a five-month interim government, Nuri al-Said was back in office as premier with the help of Colonel Salah al-Sabbagh, who, along with three colleagues of the same rank, determined the composition of the next six governments in Iraq until June 1941. Al-Said's ability to keep the premiership through the first three of these is a testimony of his political acumen, since he lacked the pan-Arabist credentials the colonels expected. The death of Ghazi on April 4, 1939 helped his cause, because the young king had never liked al-Said, whom he regarded as too pro-British. Al-Said had reciprocated his monarch's antipathy to the extent that he had entertained the possibility of working with the British to set Ghazi aside in favor of another Hashemite; and he had even investigated putting a member of the house of Saud on the Iraqi throne.

Ghazi's death was so convenient for both al-Said and the British that many Iraqis suspected they had conspired to cause his fatal automobile accident. Al-Said guaranteed his good favor in the Palace by promoting the elevation of Abd al-Ilah, the four-year-old Feisal II's uncle, to the role of regent. Abd al-Ilah was young, had no following of his own, and was inclined to follow the British lead as Europe drifted toward war and the White Paper indicated a more favorable British policy toward the Arabs in Palestine. Nuri was comfortable with this posture because he realized Iraq's legitimate treaty obligations to Britain, which he thought would prevail in a war with the Third Reich.

The colonels, most Iraqis, and other Arabs believed that the Germans would win and that an Axis victory would sever the Arab world from European imperialist and Zionist influence. Germany's early victories in 1939 and 1940 ended Nuri's efforts to keep Iraq neutral and in compliance with the British treaty. Hajj Amin al-Husseini, the exiled leader of Palestinian nationalism, had arrived in Baghdad in October 1939 to ignite an already receptive officer corp to embrace a pro-Axis posture. The Mufti was well connected with Iraqi officers because of his military training with some of them in the Ottoman Military College.

Hajj Amin's affinity for the Axis and his credentials as a fervent opponent of both the British and the Zionists made him a catalyst for Nuri's enemies and made semiindependent Iraq the center of Arab pro-Axis activities. Money and men flowed to the Mufti from Arab governments and the Axis members subsidized him liberally. Prominent politicians from the Arab countries, including the future president of Syria, Shukri al-Quwatly, flocked to serve on his "Arab Committee." Leading Iraqi politicians, both in and out of the government, rendered him service.

The claims some make for his influence over Iraqi affairs would have matched those of any Iraqi other than Feisal I. There was no doubt that for a year and a half in 1940 and 1941 Hajj Amin, a man without a country, was the arbiter of pan-Arab affairs and the principle liaison between Arab nationalists and the Axis.

The Mufti, however, was not anxious for Arabs to fight in the war, because he wanted to direct all Arab effort toward Arab goals when they were militarily strong enough and the time was right. The colonels and other pan-Arabists generally shared this view. Under the direction of Nuri, Iraq had already broken relations with Germany, but the colonels and other nationalists wished to prevent a break with Italy once it entered the war. The Italian legation, after all, provided an open conduit for communications with both partners of the Axis.

Confrontation with Great Britain

German victories in 1940 gave the nationalists reason to conclude that the time was near to expel Great Britain from Iraq and advance westward to liberate the Levant. They, of course, were badly in need of armaments of all kinds that both the Italians and the Germans never shipped, but always hinted they would ship. This quasi understanding led the nationalists to press their case against the British on the assumption that military assistance would arrive by the time a military confrontation would erupt. Taha al-Hashimi, the premier in early 1941, was less confident that this was the prudent course. As a seasoned military commander and planner, he understood Britain's military advantage.

The ardent, impatient colonels forced him out of office and placed the more pliant Rashid Ali al-Galiani in the premiership on April 12. Arab nationalists throughout the region welcomed the bold move and the Axis members and Japan recognized the new government. Rashid Ali, a lawyer, not a military man, understood Britain's rights under the treaty. Having been in several cabinets, he also had some appreciation of the fact that he held office by coup, since the regent had fled without giving his consent to Rashid Ali's cabinet. He was particularly concerned that the British would regard him as illegitimate and would treat him accordingly.

Both Taha al-Hashimi and Rashid Ali's fears proved correct. Axis arms did not arrive in time and Britain never acknowledged Rashid Ali's legitimacy. Instead, the British pressed the issue by sending troops in transit to Palestine from India to the Iraqi bases. Under pressure from the ardent nationalists, Rashid Ali militarily contested the British operation and entered into an armed conflict at the Habbaniyyah base on April 30. Iraq's failure to employ all their forces gave the British the advantage and they used the bases to bring in more men and supplies. Britain's early destruction of the Iraqi air force made the ground operation, with support coming in from Transjordan, a mopping-up operation. The Baghdad population, which had cheered when the war began, saw their city fall under British control one month later. The Colonels, the Mufti, and Rashid Ali fled, with, at best, a claim that they had won a "victory" through asserting the Arab right to obtain independence. Abd al-Ilah and Nuri al-Said returned and were able to bring all four colonels to trial and execution over the next five years. However, the colonels provided strong inspiration to later army officers who held Abd al-Ilah and Nuri responsible for helping thwart Iraq's opportunity to obtain sovereignty.

Iraq's Pro-Western Stance

Iraq remained tranquil following the suppression of Rashid Ali's government as the regent and Nuri al-Said returned and British troops arrived to discourage further nationalist adventures by the Iraqi military. American lend-lease aid to Iraq, along with Iraq's becoming a center for funnelling Allied aid to the Soviet Union, tied Iraq to the Allied cause. Iraq declared war on the Axis powers and Japan on January 16, 1943, a full two years before Egypt, Syria, and Lebanon did so. In doing so, it became the first Arab country to qualify to join the United Nations, just as it had been the first to qualify for membership in the League of Nations.

Iraq's good relationship with Great Britain and its support for the Allied war effort gave Nuri al-Said the upper hand in the early stages of negotiations to formulate a British-sponsored league for Arab cooperation and unity. Nuri, however, soon diminished Iraq's appeal to the other Arab states by proposing his Fertile Crescent Plan, which envisioned Syria and Lebanon either attached to Iraq or subservient enough to Baghdad to accomplish the same end. Nuri's plan, of course, alienated Abdullah of Transjordan since it conflicted with his own obsession to create a Greater Syria that would be under his control. Syria and Lebanon's fear of becoming part of either Hashemite regime moved both of them to accept Egyptian leadership as the only viable alternative. Ibn Saud's resentment of the Hashemites led Saudi Arabia into the Egyptian camp as well. Thus, a combination of the conflict between the two Hashemite regimes, and the other Arab states' apprehension of Hashemite ambitions assured that the Arab League would only be a loose league of sovereign states under Egyptian ascendancy.

Both Great Britain and the United States, however, courted the Iraqi regime and regarded it as the key to their policies in southwest Asia. Iraq's strategic location, its possession of large oil reserves, its financial solvency, and its tendency toward a pliant attitude toward the West explained its appeal. Nuri al-Said's appreciation of Iraq's limitations curbed the strong urges of some Iraqis, especially in the army, to liberate Palestine from the British and the Zionists and to provide leadership for the entire Arab world. Nuri also diminished Regent Abd al-Ilah's constant efforts to establish a kingdom for himself in Syria. The regent's ambition to obtain a Syrian throne remained one of the strongest destabilizing elements in Syrian and regional concerns from the end of World War II until his death in 1958.

Britain's desperation in Palestine by 1947, along with its general financial strain, increased the possibility of a different relationship with Iraq. Negotiations for a new treaty to replace the onerous one of 1930 began in May; in October Great Britain withdrew the large number of troops that had been in Iraq since 1941. Negotiators signed the Treaty of Portsmouth on January 15, 1948, whereby Britain relinquished control over the air bases at Habbaniya and Shubiah but retained the right to the continuous use of the bases, as well as the right to send troops to Iraq in the event of crisis. The treaty acknowledged Britain's exclusive right to equip and train the Iraqi military.

This reduction in British presence was, however, unacceptable to Iraqi and Arab nationalists since the United Nations had decided to partition Palestine on November 29, 1947. Advocates of democracy and communism also seized upon the resentment of the treaty to attempt to destroy the power of Nuri al-Said, if not the monarchy itself. Nuri's and the regent's ploy of placing a Shiah, Salih Jabr, in the premiership for the first time in the final stages of the negotiations could not diminish resistance to the treaty. Their failure to include leaders of the major parties in the negotiations denied them any sense of proprietorship in the treaty and guaranteed their opposition. The Istiqlal party, in fact, sent its members into the streets as early as January 5 to oppose the treaty; at that time they attracted other demonstrators and considerable police violence.

Rejection of Western Affiliation

The widespread opposition to the treaty was ideal for the communists under their almost mythical leader, Fahd (Yusuf Salman Yusuf). He managed to keep control of his movement from prison in Kut and was well prepared to present the monarchy with its greatest domestic challenge. Students and workers poured into the streets of Baghdad on January 16 to initiate the *Wathbah* (The Leap), which unusual police violence could not end. Abd al-Ilah, who was in Baghdad, denounced the treaty on January 21 in an effort to defuse the uprising, but Salih Jabr, Nuri al-Said, and Foreign Minister Fadil al-Jamali still advocated its ratification from the safety of London. Salih Jabr's public advocacy of the treaty when he returned to Baghdad on January 26 intensified the size and rhetoric of the demonstrations, as well as the police response. Close to four hundred people died and many more were wounded on the following day and Salih Jabr fled back to England in fear for his own life.

The *Wathbah* apparently ended with Salih Jabr's flight, but the government of Muhammad al-Sadr showed indecisiveness when it allowed an unprecedented outbreak of strikes and demonstrations throughout the spring of 1948. Communist leadership of the massive student and worker unrest, as well as its insistence upon the compatibility of social justice and Arab nationalism, raised the party's prestige. The intensification of developments in Palestine added to the confusion as the British mandate was scheduled to end on May 15. Iraq's and the Arab League's declaration of war against Israel on that date also brought the implementation of martial law and the framework for restoring domestic order. The Iraqi Communist party's endorsement of the partition of Palestine on June 6 made the task easier. Since few non-Communists could justify any cause greater than Palestinian liberation, the Communists lost credibility with elements that previously had followed their lead for general reform. Martial law gave the government extra-legal authority to deal decisively with the Communists. Fahd, (Yusuf Salman Yusuf), who had been in prison since January 1947, and two other prominent Communist leaders died on public gallows in the middle of February 1949. The zeal of their successors could not compensate for the sophistication their experienced leaders had used to turn various kinds of grievances in their favor.

SYRIA

Under Free France

After the fall of France in June 1940, Great Britain was concerned with the pro-German regime in Syria astride the oil pipeline from Iraq. Most of the Arab world, including the governments, assumed that an Axis victory would bring an end to the mandates. After British troops unseated the outwardly pro-Axis Iraqi government of Rashid Ali in May, 1941, British, Free French, Transjordanian, and Zionist forces invaded Syria and Lebanon on June 8 to expel the pro-Axis Vichy government. When the fighting ended on July 14, Bastille Day, Syrians had reason to believe that their liberation was complete. The assistance of Syrian volunteers to Rashid Ali and Vichy logistical support for the German effort to assist the Iraqi nationalists provided Britain an excuse to interfere in the French mandate. On the day of the invasion, the Free French government and Great Britain had promised Syria and Lebanon independence and freedom to form a single nation. Appealing as the promise was, it hardly mitigated their use of Zionist Palmach forces in the operation. Transjordan's participation on the side of the British in both Iraq and Syria diminished Abdullah's stature as a possible leader of Greater Syria.

Britain appeared sincere in its promise to allow Syrian and Lebanese independence and both countries benefited from being included in the Anglo-American Middle East Supply Center with its headquarters in Cairo. Syria's economy experienced a boom as capital, machinery, and technical assistance poured in to increase the production of food and materiel for the Allied Mediterranean war effort.

General Georges Catroux, who had the new title of delegate general of Free France, announced Syrian independence on September 28. He did not restore the constitution of Syria and appointed the elderly and compliant Shaykh Taj ed-Din al-Hasani as president. General DeGaulle and his Free France government, indeed, quickly reneged on the promise of independence and demanded that Syria accord Free France the same privileges the 1936 treaty, with the later debilitating concessions, had allowed prewar France. Free French officials, and the largest army France had ever had in the Syrian mandate, replaced their Vichy counterparts. Syria and Lebanon again fell under French mandatory control. DeGaulle's government maintained that it had no authority unilaterally to rescind the League of Nations mandate. Britain's official recognition of the independence of Syria and Lebanon made Anglo-French relations awkward and inspired regional politicians to take advantage of the impasse. By the end of October 1942, there was no longer a German threat in the Middle East and Great Britain and France were, again, the arbiters for the region.

Unfree Republic

Politicians in Lebanon and Syria maneuvered and consulted and the populations became increasingly restive despite overwhelming French strength. The British feared that violence would erupt and spread throughout the region. When Shaykh Taj ed-Din died on March 23, 1943, the British pressured Free France to restore the constitutions of Syria and Lebanon.

A regional frenzy followed in realization that a permanent configuration of borders and constitutions could occur. British encouragement of increased Arab unity seemed to invite at least an Arab alliance or, possibly, even a merger of two or more Arab states. The undefined nature of Syria made it the center of attention. Most Syrians and Lebanese and the governments of Egypt and Saudi Arabia feared a Hashemite assertion of reviving Feisal's kingdom. Syrians and Lebanese, with few exceptions, desired to reestablish their republics, while neither Egypt nor Saudi Arabia could abide the possibility of Iraq realizing Nuri al-Said's Fertile Crescent plan or Abdullah carrying out his Greater Syria plan, which he announced on April 8.

While the anti-Hashemite sentiment was too strong to make the success of either approach likely, both the Syrians and the Lebanese realized that they must act quickly. During the summer of 1943, elections followed in both countries that produced strong nationalist parliaments. Shukri al-Quwatly, who had recently revamped the National bloc into the National party, became the president of Syria. Bishara al-Khoury, whom the French had kept out of office for years, was elected president of Lebanon. Lebanon's unilateral declaration of its full independence on November 5 led to the new delegate general, Jean Helleu, suspending the Lebanese constitution and imprisoning the president and his cabinet. The scale of violent reaction and British pressure brought the reinstatement of the Lebanese government on November 22. France avoided the same problem in Syria by systematically transferring power to al-Quwatly's government, which declared its independence on January 22, 1944.

Syria was independent, but France kept much of its administration in place. It insisted upon a treaty to assure its diplomatic, political, economic, and military predominance. Of particular annoyance was continued French command of the *troupes speciales du Levant*, because they were Syrian, strongly Alawi, not French. Except for Transjordan, all the Arab states, Great Britain, the Soviet Union, and the United States had recognized Syrian independence by the fall of 1944. Syria had declared war on Germany and Japan on March 1, 1945 to qualify for admission to the United Nations in April and had become a charter member of the League of Arab States on March 22. Syria acknowledged the independence of Lebanon by joining it in membership in the Arab League. Its refusal to establish diplomatic relations with Lebanon, however, conveyed Syrian belief that they still constituted a single country. The arrival of additional French troops in the middle of May 1945 was a good indication of French intentions to stay, despite American and British objection. Protests, demonstrations, and riots throughout Syria and Lebanon in response to the new French intrusion met inexplicable force. French shelling and bombing of Damascus for three days caused about four hundred deaths, before Winston Churchill's virtual ultimatum to France ended the slaughter. Under continued pressure France slowly relented and relinquished control of the *troupes speciales* on July 7, 1945. When Syria and Lebanon finally took their case against France to the United Nations Security Council on February 4, 1946, France moved quickly to withdraw its troops from Syria on April 17 and from Lebanon on December 31, 1946.

Free and Dismembered Republic

A generation of French control left a mixture of results that are difficult to differentiate specifically between French influence and the mere passage of time. Most obviously, Syria and its estranged sister, Lebanon, were republics. Alexandretta and Cilicia were part of the Turkish republic to the great consternation of Aleppo, which depended on those areas for ports, water, grain, and trade in general. Likewise, Aleppo, which had always challenged Damascus for leadership of Syria, was cut off from its natural cultural and economic relations with Mosul and Baghdad, which were now in Iraq. Transjordan was a separate kingdom under Abdullah, who would go to his grave trying to establish his control over all of Greater Syria. As Transjordan's hope seemed to wane, an even greater threat arose of Iraq absorbing Syria, which was militarily weak, constitutionally shaky, Lilliputian through dismemberment, and beset with new ideologies to accompany its sectarian and ethnic diversity. Indications were strong that American assistance to Zionism would override Britain's reconsidered outlook and result in a Jewish state in Palestine. Out of tradition and pride Syria could not placidly accept a fate others had foisted upon it.

LEBANON

Lebanon during World War II

Lebanese efforts to negotiate and approve the 1936 treaty with France proved fruitless as the French government never ratified it. Lebanon was, therefore, still under the French mandate when World War II erupted in Europe in 1939. The French commissioner, Puaux, almost immediately suspended the constitution and retained Edde in office by appointment. General Dentz, a Vichy official, replaced Puaux after France collapsed in 1940. An uprising against Edde's weak administration led to his resignation in 1941, after which Dentz appointed Alfred Naccache to chair a special wartime government.

The Free France government's declaration of Lebanese and Syrian independence on June 8, 1941 signaled the British-Free France invasion to terminate Vichy control. General Catroux, who took the title of deputy-general, declared Lebanese independence on November 26, but he and the Free French officials continued to treat Lebanon as a mandate, to the dismay of both the Lebanese and the British. Catroux did not restore the Lebanese constitution until March 1943. Even then the French surrogate, Ayyub Thabit, who served as chief of state, attempted to rearrange representation in the Chamber of Deputies to favor pro-French elements. Violent reaction to these maneuvers forced Thabit from office and resulted in an agreement among the leading politicians to create a fifty-five man Chamber of Deputies with thirty Christian seats and twenty-five seats for the Muslims and Druze. This six-to-five ratio assured the Christians the ability to elect a Christian president. The arrangement was good politics that also accepted the validity of the 1932 census. (Fear in later years that a new census would reflect a Muslim-Druze majority and, therefore, dictate an alteration of the Chamber's composition, has prevented a census since 1932.)

Al-Khoury, who had been the popular choice for president since 1932, finally received the position and his administration marked a new beginning for the fledgling Lebanese nation. Al- Khoury and Riad al-Sulh, a Sunni, reached an agreement called the National Pact, which became an unwritten appendage to the constitution. According to this pact, a Maronite would always be president, a Sunni would be prime minister, a Shiah would be speaker of the chamber and other confessional groups would also have cabinet positions. They pointedly emphasized that Lebanon was an "Arab nation" that sought good relations with its Arab neighbors to reduce criticism from those who resented its close affiliation with France.

Six weeks after the presidential election, the Lebanese Chamber of Deupties unilaterally declared its independence from France on November 5. Additional French troops landed in Lebanon and French officials imprisoned al-Khoury and other high officials. Delegate-General Helleu suspended the constitution and placed France's ever-loyal Emile Edde back in power. Helleu's high-handed behavior created many Lebanese nationalists that had previously had no reason to feel loyalty to their country.

Lebanese resistance caused Helleu's dismissal and the restoration of al-Khoury and his administration back in office on November 22 in a much stronger position over a more united Lebanon. French intervention was far from ended, however, and French officials continued to perform most of their mandatory functions. Lebanon's official declaration of war on the Axis in the last two months of the war qualified it as a charter member of the United Nations. Similarly, Lebanon became a charter member of the Arab League after the predominantly Christian elements acknowledged its "Arab nature" and forsook their attachment to France, and the predominantly Muslim elements acknowledged the special status of Christians in Lebanon and promised not to attempt to merge Lebanon into any larger Arab state.

Although Lebanon had joined these two large international organizations, its true independence was far from secure as French mandatory officials were still in place. Additional French troops arrived immediately after the war ended. The French posture was apparently aimed at extracting a treaty from Lebanon that would tie it so closely to France that other countries could not enjoy normal relations with the former mandate. Only great pressure from Great Britain and the United States convinced France to withdraw its troops and officials late in 1946.

JORDAN

Opportunity for Independence and Expansion

Britain also modified its hold on Transjordan on the eve of World War II. Just before it announced the White Paper, it acknowledged that Transjordan would have its own diplomatic representatives, more control over its military, a more generous subsidy, more control over its internal affairs, and a larger role for Transjordanians at all levels of government.

World War II accelerated developments in the Middle East where most people hoped an Anglo-French defeat would lead to Arab liberation. In anticipation of such an attitude, the British made some adjustments of which the White Paper and the agreement with Transjordan were a part. All understood that the status quo would not prevail either during or after the war. Abdullah, in particular, saw some hope that he might gain the Syrian throne. For instance, Ghazi, Feisal's successor in Iraq, died suddenly in 1939 leaving a very young heir. This propelled Abdullah into the role as the undisputed head of the Hashemite family and, thus, as the natural choice of the Syrian monarchists. Abd al-Ilah, young Feisal II's regent, had other thoughts, of course, and continued to plot and disperse money and promises in Syria in his own behalf.

Abdullah's fetish for the Syrian throne was, however, not totally the product of his own dreams and ambitions. Various factions in Syria, including some of the leading nationalists, periodically kept his dream alive by suggesting they would like him to serve as their king. Granted, the invitations usually occurred when the political fortunes had turned against those who extended the offers. The Syrian government's refusal to grant him a visa even to travel through Syria indicated a genuine fear of the support he enjoyed. There was widespread sentiment among Arab nationalists to unite Greater Syria into a single Arab state, as most regarded Iraq, the Arabian peninsula, Egypt, and all of Arab-speaking Africa as clearly different entities. In this respect, too, Abdullah was not delusionary. He simply found it impossible to accept that he was not an acceptable leader for a goal Arab nationalists desired.

Transjordan during World War II

As in almost every other case, Transjordan pursued a course during World War II that was different from its Arab neighbors. A strong British presence, Abdullah's compliant attitude toward the British, and the absence of any effective political activism in the emirate account for this posture. While other Arab governments and populations yearned for an Axis victory, Abdullah openly supported the British war effort without causing internal unrest. The Arab Legion, under British officers, participated in the British suppression of the Arab nationalist movement of Rashid Ali al-Gaylani of Iraq in May 1941. Arab nationalists all over the Middle East resented Abdullah's assistance, even though it was on behalf of his Hashemite nephew. They regarded it more as an action to destroy a popular nationalist movement that the British believed was pro-Axis.

Most Arabs held the same opinion of the Arab Legion's small role in expelling the Vichy government from Syria early in June. The British and Free French justified their invasion of Syria on the grounds that the Vichy authorities had aided German efforts to support Rashid Ali in Iraq. Abdullah virtually intruded on the Anglo-French campaign because his participation afforded him the opportunity to assert himself openly for the first time in the country where he wanted to anchor the Greater Syrian state of his dreams. When Free France reneged on its pledge of independence for Syria and renewed Vichy France's mandate authority, Abdullah had no further opportunity to interfere in Syrian affairs until after the war. It is notable, however, that he alone among the Arab leaders did not recognize the republican government under Shukri al-Quwatli that Free France allowed to emerge in 1943. He still proclaimed his right to the Syrian throne as the legitimate heir of his brother, who had been elected king in 1920. Even though Syria was hardly any more independent than it had been any time since the French mandate began, Abdullah correctly understood that his chances of becoming its monarch diminished with every step it made toward sovereignty as a republic.

Abdullah's persistent pursuit of the Syrian throne harmed his relations with all the Arab states and Great Britain. An unusual flurry of Arab diplomatic activity following the end of a German threat to the Middle East in 1943 established the forum for his efforts. The Arab nations considered the future nature of their region, the relations of the Arab nations, and possibilities of reshaping national boundaries once the war ended with the likely end of the mandates. Several of the proposals supported a merger of Syria, Lebanon, Palestine, and Transjordan into a single state with the possibility of later including Iraq. Conflicting interests of Egypt and Iraq, both with pro-British prime ministers, complicated an already difficult subject. But Abdullah's single-mindedness for his right to Syria was perhaps the most bedeviling. Most Syrians did not want him as their king and Ibn Saud clearly opposed any enhancement of Hashemite status. Iraq was no more willing to support Abdullah than the other states for practical inter-Arab political reasons and because the Iraqi regent, Abd al-Ilah, had designs on a Syrian throne for himself once Feisal II reached his majority and assumed authority in Iraq. Great Britain, which tried to broker an amicable relationship among the Arab states, as well as one between itself and the Arab states, repeatedly had to restrain Abdullah's disconcerting efforts.

The Alexandria Protocol of March 22, 1945, which created the League of Arab States, was the most the Arab negotiations could produce. Even this level of affiliation disturbed Abdullah because in recognizing the sovereignty of each member state, it stamped a permanency on the existing borders. The Arabs, thus, seemed destined to remain divided and Abdullah's hope of encompassing the Levant in his royal arms diminished accordingly. Egypt, under the leadership of Prime Minister Nahas Pasha, had clearly emerged as the leader of the Arab nations at the expense of the two Hashemite states that had their own conflicting differences.

Kingdom of Transjordan

As likelihood of greater glory passed, Abdullah apparently received full independence for Transjordan in February, 1946. He assumed the title of king on May 25, which was the anniversary of the announcement of Transjordan's semi-independence in 1923. Interestingly, no other head of state attended his coronation. Despite his new status, all of the earlier limitations on his nation and himself continued. A population of about 400,000 with a capital city of about 25,000 indicated that Transjordan was no more capable of being a nation than before. Its heavy reliance on British administrators, British money, and British military officers had not changed. This dependency was the major reason both the United States and the Soviet Union justified their refusals to recognize Transjordanian independence and accept its request to join the United Nations.

Perhaps the fact that no one took him and his state seriously accounts for his even more constant assertions of his right to the Syrian throne and the unwillingness of the Arabs to realize their potential through the creation of his Greater Syria. His fomentations, including the call for an all-Syrian congress for the entire region, was more than annoying for the Arab states as they attempted to deal with their new independence, the emerging Cold War, and, most importantly, the dramatic terrorist and diplomatic attempts of the Zionists to create a state in Palestine. Even Abdullah had to recognize the situation in Palestine as the major regional concern once it became clear that the United Nations intended to create a Zionist state that the Arab states had pledged to oppose with force.

IRAN

Occupied Iran

In many respects Iran functioned throughout the remainder of World War II after the Allied invasion as if there were no foreign occupation. Arguably, government under the constitution proceeded in a predictable way with the absence of a strong executive authority. Perhaps the sudden removal of the formerly omnipotent

Reza Shah exacerbated Iran's tendency to follow the laws of centrifugal motion. The resentment and frustration of bending to Reza's will inspired all the special interests to attempt to establish positions that would prevent such subservience in the future. Iran's poor harvests and the inability to conduct normal international commercial activities in the early years of the war created an even more dire desperation. Near starvation in some regions of the nation inspired radical behavior, which the weak central government could neither address with repression nor relief.

Once again, however, the nation had an opportunity to determine if it could govern itself with its constitutional structure. Muhammad Reza, who was twenty-two years old, assumed the throne on September 17, the day after his father abdicated. His father, who had lost virtually all of his political support during the last few years of his reign, had not provided him with a political base in any element of the population and the young shah had not developed one of his own. Such central authority as there was devolved to the Majlis, which, constitutionally, had the authority to create and dissolve cabinets. Unfortunately, however, the small number of parties that had made government under a parliamentary majority theoretically possible in earlier times was unlikely during this period, when the large number of parties prevented any from being large enough to obtain a working majority. The close affiliation of many of the parties and their leaders with foreign interests cast suspicion upon them in a nation that, fractious as it was, could generally agree that Iran's greatest need was to eliminate foreign control and influence from their nation. Most of the parties, in fact, were committed to establishing a viable central government that could prevent national disintegration and foreign domination. While Azerbaijan and Gilan again developed provincial movements, even they expressed a willingness to rejoin the nation if they could receive guarantees of fair treatment. Only the Kurds seemed committed to leaving the nation to establish a separate state in union with their kinsmen in adjoining nations.

The British and Soviet occupiers, whom the United States later joined, remained surprisingly aloof from Iran's domestic deliberations. Their primary concern was a successful conclusion to the war against the Axis powers. The use of Iran to transport vital supplies for the Soviet war effort and the denial to the Axis of Iran as a base for operations made internal developments in Iran of decidedly secondary importance. Since there could be no clear separation of domestic and international matters, however, each of the Allied occupiers intervened in Iranian internal affairs when they perceived that failure to do so threatened their collective or individual interests. In time, therefore, each occupying power established an affiliation with important elements of Iranian society. This made the collaborating Iranians anathema to their countrymen and to the other Allies.

The British and the Soviets resumed control over the respective regions of Iran that they had established in 1907. They began a feverish effort to construct an efficient supply line between the Gulf and the Soviet Union. The Trans-Iranian Railroad and the highway system were the focus of their attention. Neither the rail nor the road system, however, were adequate for the constant flow of the millions of tons of heavy cargo required in modern war. Many Iranians profited from their participation in the massive reconstruction that followed. Individuals and companies that could provide any assistance to the war effort had the opportunity to improve their financial situation. Many made fortunes, especially those who had connections of any kind with the foreign governments that issued the contracts.

Iranian chauffeurs, chefs, clerks, or others of any rank in the foreign legations became contractors or paid expediters to fulfill the frantic attempt on the part of the Allies to use Iran's resources in the war. Iranian factories could not produce enough of their specialties to satisfy the appetite of the war machines. The Allies transformed some factories into manufacturers of the new products required for the war effort. Any Iranian who could provide labor, equipment, food, manufactured goods, services, or a connection to acquire something of value for the war effort could almost name his price.

Needless to say, while some prospered from this boom, others suffered as goods of all kinds became scarce and all prices soared. Iranians found themselves participating in a war in which they were neutral, but playing a vital role on behalf of the side most Iranians hoped would lose. The Germans, whose cause most Iranians supported, either left soon after the Allied occupation or were killed or arrested as quickly as the British and Soviets could locate them. As much as the Allies deplored the miserable condition of many Iranians at the beginning of the occupation, the war made it difficult to provide them much relief until several months later. The needs of Iran's population were simply another challenge that had to wait for the efficient but overworked and overextended Middle East Supply Center in Cairo to construct a means of getting supplies, especially bread, to the most desperately needy. To the distress of other regions, both the Iranian government and the Allies gave Tehran priority in receiving necessities from every source, in an effort to keep the population of the capital as tranquil as possible. With so many other forces tearing Iran apart, the Allies hoped that adequate necessities in Tehran could provide a modicum of stability for the capital. Even so, the cabinets, which exercised whatever executive authority there was for most of the war, assumed and lost office alarmingly often.

Majlis Government

Familiarity with the constitution, as well as an affection for it, were strong in the 1940s because it had provided the theoretical structure for Iran for more than thirty years. Reza Shah had retained it, although he had subverted it to his will and prevented anything approximating its actual provisions from operating for at least a decade. Its basic structure was intact and provided the framework for governing after Reza's autocracy ended. The absence of any major attempt to alter its structure indicated a general acceptance that the constitution was both fair and feasible.

The essentially nonfunctioning monarchy of Muhammad Reza deprived the government of executive leadership to direct or implement policies. It would be unjust, however, to blame the new shah for his failure to behave differently than he did. After all, in addition to the obvious problems of his youth, inexperience, and lack of political support, Muhammad Reza had to feel fortunate that any kind of monarchy remained, in view of the general lack of support for monarchy in his country or the world at large. His best hope, whether he consciously realized it or not, was to keep a low profile and allow circumstances and time to provide him the opportunity to reassert royal authority.

Well-intended and capable as many of Iran's parliamentarians were during this new time of troubles, their genuine ideological differences and their conflicting visions of the nation's needs and future prevented them from providing effective leadership. But, whatever else critics might say about Reza Shah, the nation he restructured was no longer a land where leadership could only come from the court and a combination of religious leaders, tribal chieftains, wealthy landlords, and a few prosperous merchants. Iran possessed a significant number of impressively educated people who dominated most parties and interest groups by the 1940s. Much as they differed in outlook, they loved their nation and most wanted it to prosper, regardless of how willing they were to increase their own wealth while in service to the national interests. Although few of the most active politicians and their supporters wished it, there was the strong possibility that another failure to make constitutional government work could lead to the equally unacceptable possibilities of national disintegration, annexation by foreigners, or dictatorship under a shah or whoever else could seize power.

Many parties filled Iran's political landscape in the 1940s in contrast to earlier times when a simpler dichotomy had existed between those who wanted gradual reform within a predominantly Islamic framework and those who had advocated more drastic changes to implement a secular society. The Iran party, with such notable leaders as Muhammad Mossadegh and Mehdi Barzagan, reflected the views of a large percentage of Iran's newly educated population. These unquestionable nationalists held views that could accommodate Iran's general heritage, including Shiah Islam, but emphasized the need to transform the nation into a democratic, socialist state that would be free from foreign exploitation and the ravages of a domestic privileged elite. This party eschewed affiliation with any foreign nation, as well as with other parties that had such affiliations. In sharp contrast, Seyyed Zia, who had been in Palestine most of the time since he had lost favor with Reza Shah, formed the National Will party. There was no question that this party was inclined to close cooperation with Great Britain. Unlike most other important Iranian parties, it supported a decentralized nation and opposed such sources of national strength as an army built on conscription. It courted more traditional Islamic sentiments, such as the suppression of non-Islamic publications and a return to the enforced use of traditional Islamic clothing.

Many parties appeared and dissolved soon afterwards. The new freedom for political expression provided the opportunity for almost anyone or any group to assume the august title of being a party to give credibility to their cause. This propensity was especially bedeviling to the more sincere nationalists who realized that the resulting chaos reduced the possibility for success of parliamentary government. The proliferation of parties produced the Comrades, Freedom, and Justice parties, to name a few, while the Persian Communist party also came back into existence. Parties and their members switched their allegiance for often undefinable reasons. This prevented premiers from being able to establish a parliamentary majority to implement a defined program or even maintain some continuity in administering ordinary government business. Ministers sometimes accepted cabinet posts under the leadership of prime ministers who advocated policies the opportunistic ministers could not possibly endorse. At times a prime minister with no party affiliation was the only acceptable course, while at other times cabinets governed without Majlis approval when no other choice seemed available.

The Tudeh (Masses) party thrived in this chaos and exerted influence that transcended both its numerical strength and public support. Its well-defined purpose and capable leadership elevated it into the most formidable party of the 1940s. Members of the "Fifty-Three," who had been imprisoned in 1937 for their Marxist views and activities, formed this new party on September 29, 1941. They and other political prisoners from Reza's reign had just been released from prison. Their imprisonment had given the founders time to evaluate their future and determine their best hope to implement their program, which was, in fact, to establish a Communist society in Iran. They realized, however, that Iranians were generally unreceptive to such a radical transformation of Iranian society. Also, they rejected a Leninist approach of seizing power and imposing a Communist regime upon the nation. They also had to face the simple truth that the 1931 law still existed that outlawed communism. They could not, therefore, participate in the constitutional process in support of an illegal doctrine.

Under Suleiman Mirza Iskandari's leadership, the Tudeh adopted the classic Marxist stance that communism could not evolve until a society passed through a bourgeois stage. Iran, which was still in many respects an agrarian society controlled by a small number of landowners, was far from ready to become a Communist society. The Tudeh, therefore, decided to help establish a more industrialized society in partnership with the middle class, while it accelerated an improvement in the lives of the workers and peasants. It refrained from emphasizing class differences, but hoped to cultivate genuine support in the lower classes by overt and clandestine means to guarantee these vital sources of strength in the parliamentary process. Accordingly, its platform offered a program of reform that all but the largest industrialists and landowners could find appealing. The Tudeh's commitment to the development of a strong national government was even appealing to nationalists. It had some difficulty in trying to reconcile its support for linguistic, religious, and ethnic minorities with its advocacy of a strong central government, but it had reasonable success in finding an acceptable posture even on these sensitive subjects. The party's restraint in its relationship with the Soviet Union improved its credibility as a nationalist movement, rather than an instrument of some ominous international cause. Soviet conflicts with the central government and with the other two occupying forces would in time make this approach impossible to follow and help diminish Tudeh's ascendancy in Iranian constitutional politics.

A strong trade union movement was central in Tudeh's immediate and long-range plans for extending its influence to the working and peasant classes. The leaders, therefore, revived the Central Council of Federated Trade Unions, which the Socialists and Communists had formed in 1921. Union organization gave them the opportunity and justification to move Tudeh cadres freely among the workers and peasants, where its largely educated, middle-class leadership had neither strong connections nor credibility. Many of the same elements that had embraced unionism in the past did so again, but Tudeh was never able to penetrate the rural area to any significant extent. Attempts to organize the workers in the British-controlled oil fields promised more success at this stage, although British concern for Tudeh's political intentions added to the ordinary problems Tudeh faced in organizing Iran's work force.

Visions of Postwar Iran

All parties realized that the unusual circumstances that resulted from the war and the occupying forces would end. Domestic factions and parties, as well as the occupiers, therefore, maneuvered to protect their interests when Iranians would become independent. Under American pressure, the British and Soviets agreed on January 29, 1942 to remove their troops within six months after the war ended. The United States, which entered Iran on January 1, 1943, pledged that it would also remove its troops from Iran on the same schedule that Britain and the Soviets had accepted. While the three wartime Allies cooperated in pursuit of their common interest of defeating the Axis, their conflicting views of postwar Iran caused frictions their common military goals could not overcome. Each found Iranian politicians who shared the conflicting visions.

Briefly stated, the three Allies viewed each other with a combination of jealousy and fear. The Soviets desired an Iran free from Western influence that could not endanger Soviet security. Preferably, Iran would reassume its natural role of economic subservience to the Soviet Union and would be receptive to Soviet influence in every respect. While the British wanted a stable Iran, they preferred that the provinces retain considerable autonomy because the British had a long history of working with the inhabitants in the southern provinces. Also, a stronger nationalist government would more likely take offense at Britain's continued monopoly on Iran's oil industry. The British could not, in fact, oppose Soviet pressure to obtain an oil concession because the principle that ruled against a Soviet concession would undermine Britain's concession. The British seemed to be more disturbed that the United States would enter this traditional Anglo-Soviet theater of conflict and cooperation to give the Iranians a means of getting free from foreign influence. An initial American concern for the plight of Iran and Iranians soon gave way to a realization that Iran was crucial to American interests in the entire region, especially in regard to American interests in the Saudi oil fields. Iran's potential as a vital link in commercial air traffic was also apparent. For these and other reasons the United States had determined by the end of the war that it could not abandon Iran to the domination of the Soviets or the British, or a combination of the two. America's aroused interest in Iran was welcomed among the elements of the nation, which had been seeking a policy of "positive equilibrium," meaning a third force to balance the traditional Anglo-Russian interference.

The United States offered the best choice for outside help among elements in Iran whose financial or ideological aspirations were not tied to either Britain or the Soviet Union. Ahmad Qavam, who was one of the most prominent Iranian policy makers during this period, helped bring the United States into Iran, primarily to counter British influence. An American, Colonel H. Norman Schwarzkopf, became the commander of Iran's gendarmerie in 1942 and he remained in that important function, which was always related to effective tax collection, until 1948. Arthur Millspaugh, whom Reza had fired in 1927, reappeared in Tehran as treasurer-general in 1943, along with a few dozen other American advisers. President Franklin D. Roosevelt believed that such an infusion of American expertise could move Iran toward greater self-sufficiency. The shah always seemed inclined to have a larger American presence as a means of asserting himself into the affairs of his nation. American policymakers reciprocated the shah's attention and decided by 1946 that increased royal authority offered the best possibility for ending the vagaries of Iranian policies, which alternatively responded to British and Soviet influence.

Knowledge that United States oil companies were exploring the possibility of obtaining an Iranian oil concession in September 1944 raised a sensitive subject that clouded Allied relations for the next several years. Some Iranians, including Shah Reza, had attempted to get the Americans involved in the oil industry for some years. The Soviets countered with a request for their own oil concession. At this point, Tudeh began to indicate its Soviet inclination by leading demonstrations on behalf of a Soviet oil concession. Concern spread in Iran that Tudeh was, for all its protests to the contrary, a front for imposing Soviet control over Iran. Tudeh's opposition, however, forced the cabinet of Muhammad Said from office and one under the leadership of Morteza Bayat replaced it. Bayat worked closely with the Tudeh and dismissed Millspaugh as part of his cooperation with them. In response to the entire oil question, the Majlis, with Mossadegh in the forefront, passed a law that delayed all consideration of any oil concessions until after the war. Further, it provided mandatory imprisonment for any cabinet minister who negotiated any oil concession without specific approval from the Majlis. Iran's oil reserves, which constituted its greatest economic asset, would become the center of attention in determining which internal and foreign forces would dominate Iran. Evidence of a merging of interests between the Americans and the shah indicated the possibility of an entirely new future.

The British and Soviets, however, had vital interests to protect in Iran that an American presence and a stronger shah threatened. The British remained as passive as possible to keep from drawing attention to themselves, their oil concession, and their alliance with the southern tribes. The Soviets cleverly ingratiated themselves to important dissident elements in Iran that offered the possibility for influence after they withdrew their troops. An ambivalent relationship between the Tudeh and the Soviets during the first years of the occupation raised questions on the part of both regarding exactly how they could affiliate. The picture was much clearer with the Kurds and the Azerbaijani separatist movements. Soviet occupation of Azerbaijan gave the Soviets ample opportunity to cultivate cordial relations with each movement, which, in turn, welcomed Soviet assistance. Both movements had special appeal that transcended their proximity to each other adjacent to the Soviet border. The Kurdish movement, for instance, offered the possibility of spreading Soviet influence among the Kurds in several states. The Azerbaijani movement was based upon a sound Soviet foundation that went back to the early part of the century, especially during the time of Muhammad Khiabani.

The Kurdish movement that began in Mahabad in 1942 under the leadership of a conservative clergyman, Qazi Muhammad, never had an ideological affinity for either the Soviets or the Tudeh. In fact, the Kurds did not allow Tudeh to organize in their region. The Kurds sought Soviet support, primarily because it was available. When Mulla Mustafa Barzani, the Iraqi Kurdish leader, joined the Mahabad movement, the Soviets found the movement too tempting to ignore. Soviet support continued for this genuinely nationalist Kurdish movement to weaken Iraq, Iran, and Turkey and improve its bargaining position in Iran. The Kurds consistently resisted Soviet attempts to merge the Mahabad movement with the considerably more leftist and Soviet-oriented Azerbaijan movement.

The separatist movement in Azerbaijan was an entirely different matter. Most of the province, with its large Azeri-speaking population and its significant Armenian and Assyrian Christian element, had a long history of leftist affinities. It harbored deep resentment for the unfavorable treatment it received from the central government dating back to the early constitutional period. Azeri discontent at attempts to suppress their language was as strong as the other differences they had with Tehran's insistence on Persian domination. Soviet military occupation provided protection for a strong antigovernment movement to develop under the two old rivals, Jafar Pishavari of the Iranian Communist party and Ardeshir Ovanessian, who was perhaps the most radical leftist leader of the Tudeh party. The appalling poverty in Azerbaijan provided fertile ground for a genuine leftist movement to grow. During the war, authorities had deprived the province of necessities to placate Tehran's volatile population. As the war ground to an end, widespread unemployment added to the other accumulated problems and grievances.

Beginning with the oil concession question, a series of cabinets passed in and out of office. Morteza Bayat's close cooperation with the Tudeh, which many had come to perceive as pro-Soviet, led to his dismissal in April 1945. The absence of either a strong leader or a viable coalition propelled Ibrahim Hakimi, who had no party affiliation, into the premiership. However, the Majlis would not confirm his position. The shah, who was disturbed by Tudeh's turn to the left and the increased activities in Azerbaijan and other provinces in the north appointed Mohsen Sadr, a strongly religious man with pro-British and anticommunist credentials, to the premiership. His immediate reprisals against the Tudeh, which included closing their newspapers, made it impossible for him to obtain Majlis approval because Tudeh; Mossadegh, in league with the Iran Party; and others boycotted the Majlis for three months. Sadr proceeded to administer the government under the authority he received from the shah. Sadr's affiliation with the shah, his conservative posture, and antileftist policies raised anxiety among the leftist parties, the Azerbaijani activists, and the Soviets. Clearly, there were indications that the Iranian situation had changed.

There was, however, no sense of urgency in Iran because the war in the Pacific theater portended to last for many more months and possibly for years. America's use of the atomic bomb against Japan on August 6 and 9 changed the situation rapidly. Japan's sudden surrender on September 2, 1945 provided an additional sense of the need to comprehend the new political situation in Iran because March 2, 1946 became the firm date on which the occupying forces were supposed to leave Iran. Domestic and foreign interests alike had a limited time in which to make their moves before Iran was scheduled to return to "normal." Northern Iran erupted into separatist movements in Azerbaijan, Kurdistan, Gilan, and Mazandaran during the fall of 1945, but the Soviets only supported those in Azerbaijan and Kurdistan, which they had cultivated in the earlier gestation periods. Pishavari formally declared the creation of the Azerbaijan Democratic party on September 3, 1945 and seized control of the provincial government on November 16. He adopted the name for the new movement Khiabani had used. He forcefully incorporated the Tudeh party and union organization into his movement, with Soviet approval and against the wishes of the Tudeh leadership. Tudeh was still trying to keep its distance from affiliation with the Soviet Union and had a strong commitment to the development of a strong central government. Since Pishavari's provincial concerns suited Soviet needs at the moment, it successfully opposed either government or Tudeh interference in the Azerbaijan effort for autonomy, if not independence. Pishavari, in fact, made it clear that Azerbaijan would seek total freedom unless Tehran assured the province its linguistic freedom, the right to govern its own affairs, and the right to utilize most of its revenue for provincial needs. Qazi Muhammad declared the creation of the Kurdish People's Republic on December 15, 1945 and made demands similar to those from the Tabriz rebels. Iran seemed on the verge of disintegrating as other provinces had strong grievances with the central government.

The approach of Sadr's government to such activities had become clear when it decisively suppressed the earliest of the uprisings in Khorasan in August. The avowed commitment of the Khorasan uprising's leader, Khosrow Ruzbeh, to class warfare did much to discredit all leftists, especially the Tudeh. Although Ruzbeh was a Tudeh member, and one of its principal military leaders, he strongly expressed his impatience with Tudeh's gradualist approach to gain control some time in the future by parliamentary means. Other elements of Tudeh, especially in the trade union movement, also expressed the possible need to resort to a violent takeover of the government. In the face of such threats, many could support Sadr's imposition of martial law in Tehran. Soviet military presence also suddenly seemed far less benign, since it obviously had the support of a formidable Fifth Column in the nation.

Suspicious as many Iranians were of Soviet intentions, there was a strong desire to accommodate their concerns adequately to obtain Soviet withdrawal as soon as possible. Sadr left office in October as a palliative to the Soviets, but his replacement, Ibrahim Hakimi, had a reputation of being pro-British. Hakimi, in fact, continued to deal harshly with the Tudeh and refused to make any accommodations with the separatist movements in the northern provinces. The Soviets were sure that Hakimi's cabinet would oppose a Soviet oil concession and treat Soviet-oriented Iranian groups brutally once the Soviet troops withdrew. The Soviets, therefore, refused all overtures from Hakimi to improve relations and insisted that they would only do business with Ahmad Qavam.

Qavam, indeed, assumed the premiership on January 26 and moved rapidly to improve relations with the Soviets. This suave, educated aristocrat, who spoke Russian, had personal and national interests in mind as he addressed one of the most delicate situations in modern Iran's history. His own vast estates in Gilan, after all, could be in danger if Soviet support led to a major change in the northern region. He enjoyed good relations with the Soviets and had worked closely with them as premier in the early months of Reza's reign and again in 1942, when he had negotiated the agreement for British and Soviet forces to leave six months after the war ended. Qavam had been consistently anti-British and most believed he was pro-American. His history of working closely with the Tudeh and his blood ties with Mossadegh gave him credentials the Soviets trusted. The Soviets had reason to believe Qavam had adequate parliamentary support to do whatever he said he would do. His nationalism and commitment to constitutionalism assured everyone he would do whatever served his country well. In this case, he had to convince the Soviets that they could withdraw their troops without suffering real or perceived reduction in their interests.

Exit Soviets: Deceit or Miscalculation?

Over the next few months Qavam accomplished his mission of obtaining the withdrawal of all Soviet forces by apparently giving them everything they wished. In doing so he alienated the more conservative elements of Iran, including the shah, as well as the United States and Great Britain. His failure to fulfill his promises to the Soviets and his destruction of the Tudeh and the separatist movements discredited him with the Soviets and the leftists. However much of this his devious mind could have planned from the beginning would not, in all likelihood, have included leaving him as politically isolated as it did in the end. His accomplishment in removing the Soviets was, nevertheless, masterful.

Within three weeks after returning to the premiership, Qavam went to Moscow on February 18, 1946, where he met repeatedly with Stalin and Molotov. Both shared with him their desire for a major transformation of Iran through extensive government guidance that would establish the basis for a genuine socialist society. Stalin again raised the sensitive topic of a Soviet oil concession and proposed the creation of an Irano-Soviet Oil Company with Iran having 49 percent ownership. Qavam found the offer tempting because it was much more favorable to Iran than the one with Britain that yielded approximately 20 percent of the profits to the Iranians. Like the original British concession, this one would last for fifty years. Qavam knew that many Iranians, including his cousin Mossadegh, opposed any further oil concessions. Also, there was a law that prevented so much as a discussion of a concession without specific instruction from the Majlis. It became clear, however, that the Soviets intended to insist on an oil concession and a genteel settlement between the government and the Azerbaijan and Kurdish movements as conditions for their withdrawal. The American troops had left on January 1 and the British troops had departed as scheduled on March 2.

The Fourteenth Majlis's term expired before Qavam could find a way to solve this conundrum. This situation offered him an opportunity for leverage that some believed elicited his most adroit maneuvering. Iranian law forbade the conduct of an election during the presence of foreign troops as a means of avoiding foreign influence on election results. Soviet troops, therefore, had to leave Iran before an election could occur. An election had to occur before a Majlis could convene to consider the oil concession. Unless the Soviets wanted to use brute force, they were going to have to trust Qavam to behave in good faith and obtain the oil concession they wanted, primarily to provide them entree into Iranian affairs and parity with the British. The Soviets, after all, had an abundance of proven petroleum reserves.

Qavam had to convince the Soviets to trust him and withdraw their troops to allow the Iranian constitutional process to operate. United Nations pressure also helped move the Soviets conceptually to action, but Qavam realized that his personal credibility was crucial to prevent the Soviets from returning after they withdrew. He even disclaimed any knowledge that the Iranian delegate planned to raise the question of Soviet troops in Iran at the United Nations on January 19 and again on March 18. Six days after the second time the U.N. heard the complaint, the Soviets pledged to begin their withdrawal that day. Two days after the U.N. considered the question on April 3, the Soviets said they would fully withdraw their troops within six weeks, if Iran proceeded in good faith toward the oil concession and fair treatment of the separatist movements. Qavam insisted that he would keep his promise and submit the proposal of an oil concession to the Majlis within seven months from March 24, when the Soviets had made their initial promise to withdraw. By this agreement the Fifteenth Majlis were expected to consider a Soviet oil concession no later than November 24. The notoriously long time it took to conduct elections in Iran and to validate the credentials of those elected made the seven-month period appear very reasonable.

Qavam had to keep the Soviets content with him during the period prior to the convening of the Majlis to prevent their return to Iran. He had assured them that with his positions as prime minister and minister of the interior, he could obtain the election of a new Majlis to approve an oil concession. He pointed out, however, that he could not hold an election with Azerbaijan in open resistance against the central government. Consequently, the Soviets reduced, and then terminated, their support for the Azerbaijan movement. Soviet troop evacuation proceeded and was complete by May 9. Iran was finally free from foreign military occupation.

Qavam gave every appearance of moving toward holding an election very quickly. The Azerbaijani movement agreed to tentative terms with the government on June 13, under which the movement's security forces remained in place and no government troops attempted to enter the area. The shah's and the military's resentment of this agreement, however, initiated a cooperation between them that soon influenced the elections and shaped much of Iran's future. Qavam formed his own Iranian Democratic Party on June 29, which appeared to have a more conceptually broad and inclusive platform than that of the Tudeh. This new instrument made it possible for almost anyone to stand for election under the umbrella of his new and amorphous creation. Tudeh enjoyed more freedom than it had ever had to pursue all of its political activities and organize workers into unions. This all seemed natural enough in view of the exceedingly cordial relations that existed between Qavam and the Soviets. Tudeh had experienced considerable hardship under the two previous cabinets and would need time to restore its political apparatus. Qavam's proposed legislative package and the policies he pursued in administering the nation caused concern in conservative circles, as it indicated that he intended to implement a major turn to the left.

Concern arose in Iran and abroad that Qavam had sold out to the Tudeh and the Soviets. In the view of some, Iran was quickly moving toward becoming the Soviet Union's first client state. The arrest of the conservative chief of staff, General Hassan Arfa; Sayyed Zia; and many pro-British politicians during his early days in office added to his reputation for radicalism to the distress of conservatives and to the delight of the Soviets. The new chief of staff, Ali Razmara, had a strong leftist reputation and enjoyed a cordial relationship with the increasingly active Tudeh party. Qavam began to distribute crown lands, moved toward establishing a minimum wage, and adopted policies to improve the general circumstances of peasants and workers vis-à-vis the landlords and capitalists. He arrested Ayatollah Abul Qassim Kashani, who emerged as the most vociferous spokesman on behalf of the traditional Islamic values Qavam's policies threatened. His incorporation of three Tudeh members into his cabinet in August, accompanied by the appointment of the leftist Muzaffar Firuz as deputy premier, enhanced his leftist reputation. Firuz's hatred of the Pahlavis, because of his father's death at the order of Shah Reza, indicated that his appointment threatened the institution of monarchy in Iran. No one could believe Qavam would refrain from electing a leftist, Soviet-oriented Majlis.

More ominously, there were indications that Tudeh, with which Qavam worked so closely, seemed as if it would be able to carry something approximating a free election. It was, no doubt, the strongest political force in Iran by the summer of 1946. Tudeh rallies, which sometimes reached 100,000, were the largest ever assembled in the entire Middle East. The massive general strike it organized in the oil fields of Khuzistan in July, 1946 had a similar distinction. Their success in organizing the oil workers was a recent accomplishment and particularly provocative. Tudeh had also finally penetrated the countryside, where peasants responded with political activity, including withholding grain that the cities needed for survival. In all, more than 300,000 Iranian workers belonged to Tudeh unions and the momentum indicated that the number would rise even further. Union organization had translated into political control of most of Iran's manufacturing cities. Tudeh control of public communication and transportation gave it the capacity to determine who could use these vital facilities and for what purpose. Tudeh success increased the leftist ardor of some of its members, who no longer confined their rhetoric and actions to the limited parliamentary goals its more responsible leaders had so cautiously stated since 1941. The "Red Menace" was clearly afoot in Iran and seemed both willing and capable of seizing control.

Months were passing, however, and Qavam failed to ask the shah to issue a decree to hold an election. The Soviets began to become disturbed with the delay, which they began to suspect was prevarication. As Soviet concern nearly reached the breaking point, a major uprising among the Qashgai tribes in September spread to other southern tribes. Much of the south-central portion of the nation fell under tribal control. No elections could occur in such an atmosphere. The tribesmen concentrated all their complaints against the unfettered actions of the Tudeh and its presence in the government at all levels. Muhammad Reza Shah endorsed the tribal demands. Fear arose that a civil war would occur between the army in alliance with the tribes against Tudeh and the union movement. Those who contend the tribal uprising was part of Qavam's effort to dupe the Soviets ignore more obvious facts. There was, for instance, no doubt that the conservative tribes feared Tudeh penetration into their regions, and even less doubt that the tribes abhorred the secular and antireligious ideology of Tudeh. The scope of the tribal uprising allowed the shah, whose power Qavam wished to diminish or destroy, to enter the political arena in his capacity as the Commander in Chief of the military. The shah, in fact, had played a major role in obtaining significant military assistance from the United States on October 18 as the American government was rapidly evolving toward the Truman Doctrine to deter the spread of communism. Qavam was in danger of facing a military obstacle in the hands of the shah that was as menacing as the one the Soviets might employ to accomplish their goals in Iran. Tudeh's rapid political growth also threatened Qavam and his party as much as the shah threatened him militarily. Qavam, therefore, needed to curb Tudeh activities for solely domestic concerns.

In response, Qavam not only dismissed the Tudeh cabinet ministers on October 19, he dismissed Tudeh governors of Tehran, Isfahan, and Kirmanshah. Muzaffar Firuz had to vacate his position as vice premier to accept his new duty as ambassador to the Soviet Union. Qavam tempered his conservative opposition additionally when he released Arfa, Sayyed Zia, Kashani, and other political prisoners. Government and tribal forces moved decisively against the Tudeh throughout the southwest of Iran and government forces used both the legal and military methods of martial law to suppress the Tudeh in other parts of the nation. Meteoric as Tudeh's rise had been, its apparent demise was much faster. Serious dissension within the party added to its collapse, as different factions blamed each other for adopting unsound doctrines and actions. The recently unbeatable party was in no condition to win an election once its natural enemies crushed its political machinery and, in turn, unleashed its internecine divisions.

The shah authorized the election on October 6 in the midst of the tribal uprising that led to Tudeh's destruction. The election gave the government a legitimate excuse to establish order in all provinces. Only the army, with the shah as Commander in Chief, could guarantee the proper tranquility to hold an election. This provided the shah and the army the opportunity to move against Azerbaijan and Kurdistan. Qavam was hesitant to issue the order to use the army against this region, which by the agreement of June 13 was still under the protection of the Democratic Movement's security forces. This was a sensitive situation, since it could cause a Soviet reprisal. Nevertheless, government troops under the command of General Ali Razmara, and with the shah in close supervision, moved against the troublesome provinces after Qavam reluctantly gave the order on December 10. There was no Soviet intervention, however, since they accepted that the troop movement was a precondition to the election and consideration of their oil concession. Government troops who were armed with new American weapons advanced into Azerbaijan. Tabriz came under government control on December 13, six months after the agreement it had made with the central government. Pishavari fled to the Soviet Union. Mahabad, which had become riddled with dissension, also succumbed to government forces and Qazi Muhammad and his fellow leaders, minus Mulla Mustafa Barzani, were hanged. Leftists of all stripes died, were imprisoned, or escaped as the government established its full authority over the traditional leftist stronghold. The Soviets had lost any vestige of a physical enclave in Iran in no small part because of an infusion of new American weapons and the more active role of the shah. The end of the separatist movements occurred more than a month after Qavam had agreed to submit an oil concession proposal to the Majlis, but the election for a new legislature had just begun on December 7.

Triumph and Deadlock in the Majlis

The tattered Tudeh party decided to boycott the elections for the Fifteenth Majlis, which they maintained Qavam and the shah had rigged. The accusation was, in fact, true, as each used its influence to elect its supporters. The shah and the army, for instance, did not allow Qavam to establish any organization for his party in the province of Azerbaijan. Consequently, the new legislature was unusually conservative because Qavam's Democrat party had also assumed a fairly conservative posture. Only Mossadegh's tiny contingent of four supported leftist social concepts, which significant elements of the population had come to embrace. The Majlis did not meet until July 1947 and conducted little business before October 22, when Qavam informed the legislature that the government no longer considered the possibility of granting an oil concession to the Soviet Union or any other foreign nation. He made it clear, in fact, that his government intended to take the necessary measures to obtain control of the Iranian oil industry, which was under British control. The Majlis approved his statement related to these and other provisions by a margin of 102 to 2, although the twenty-five members of the National Caucus coalition had strong pro-British sympathies. The Soviet threat of a year earlier had disappeared and the vote indicated that the British presence would soon come under attack. Qavam received permission from the Majlis to begin negotiations to revise the 1933 agreement that regulated the British concession.

Qavam's days were numbered, however, as he had lost the confidence of most of his former domestic and foreign supporters. The shah was additionally incensed when Qavam refused to support returning Reza's body from South Africa and the purchase of $10 million in military equipment from the United States. The prime minister's own party splintered into pieces as each of its disparate parts began to follow inclinations that had never fit into the party he had shaped around them. By December 10 his support had vanished and he left office after a vote of no confidence. He fled to France in fear that he might be arrested on several counts various people wanted to bring against him. The shah displayed his personal pique with the former prime minister when he stripped him of his title of "Noble Excellency."

National Unionists and National Caucus members, royalists and pro-British respectively, elected Ibrahim Hakimi to succeed Qavam by a one-vote margin over Mossadegh, whom the Democrats and independents supported. A virtual parliamentary deadlock ensued, which seemed to benefit the shah, who steadily increased the strength of the military. Royalists and Democrats, however, forced Hakimi from office in June and replaced him with Abdul Hussein Hezhir for the primary purpose of renegotiating the British oil concession. The new government's willingness to drop all charges against Qavam and support further military purchases from the United States inspired Kashani to organize large protests among the bazaari elements and religious traditionalists. Hakimi's cabinet fell in November after less than four months of ineffective leadership in the parliamentary stand-off. When the shah asserted himself and appointed Muhammad Said as prime minister, the Democrats raised the cry that the monarch intended to establish a military dictatorship. The shah's influence was evident as the new cabinet punished all criticism of the government and the monarchy. He obtained the return of his father's body and conducted an impressive state funeral for Reza, "The Great."

An attempt on the shah's life on February 4, 1949 increased his image and determination even further. His almost miraculous escape from death attracted support from many elements as he punished the Tudeh supporters and religious elements who seemed to have conspired to kill him. The shah declared martial law and deported Kashani to Beirut. A Constituent Assembly he convened revised the constitution to allow him to dissolve the Majlis and the Senate, which the Assembly created. He was, however, obligated to convene a new legislature within three months if he chose to dissolve the two legislative bodies.

For the shah to benefit from his new power and the deadlock in the legislature, he had to provide a program to satisfy both his domestic and foreign critics. Intense negotiations were occurring to revise the oil agreement with Great Britain. A relationship with the United States was the key to his hopes; the Americans, however, kept insisting on social improvements in Iran. Muhammad Reza, therefore, had to convince his potential American friends that efforts in those areas were as important to the shah as his desire to obtain increasingly large quantities of armaments. The shah announced the Seven-Year Plan, which had been developing for several years, and the creation of the Imperial Pahlavi Foundation. Both promised to improve the Iranian economy and improve the industrial and transportation infrastructure to the benefit of all classes. These seemed like reasonable answers to Iran's serious problems, which arose from a combination of high prices and high unemployment. The shah also announced plans to distribute crown lands to the peasants on easy payment terms and to purchase land from other large landowners for the same purpose. These plans, which received a favorable response in the United States, alarmed the landed elements in Iran, who welcomed a diversion from the land redistribution topic when the new Majlis met in February 1950.

13

Effective Defiance

HISTORICAL TIMELINE

1950

⇛ Nahas Pasha and Wafd had an impressive victory in the January election.

⇛ General Razmara became premier in June to curtail Mossadegh and the National Front, which wanted to make nationalization of oil the major issue of the Majlis. Many thought that only strong control under Razmara could avoid civil war.

⇛ Beginning in March Iraqi Jews left in large numbers for Israel. One hundred and sixty thousand left in fifteen months.

⇛ Establishment of Development Board to improve the Iraqi infrastructure with 70 percent of annual oil revenues.

⇛ United Nations-sponsored talks with Arab and Israeli delegations in Lausanne during the spring failed to resolve their differences.

⇛ Syria obtained a new constitution on September 5.

⇛ President al-Khoury of Lebanon dissolved the economic union with Syria.

⇛ Egypt was unable to arrive at an agreement with Britain to remove British troops from Egypt.

⇛ Britain, France, and the U.S. agreed to limit arms sales to all Middle Eastern countries.

⇛ Saudis obtained 50 percent of the profits from ARAMCO beginning on December 30.

1951 ⇛ General Razmara, premier of Iran, was assassinated on March 7.
⇛ Mossadegh introduced the oil nationalization bill in the Iranian Majlis on March 8.
⇛ Iranian Majlis approved the oil nationalization bill on March 15.
⇛ Iranian Senate approved the oil nationalization bill on March 20.
⇛ Final nationalization and implementation provisions passed in the Iranian Majlis and Senate on April 28.
⇛ Mossadegh became premier of Iran on April 29.
⇛ Huge May Day celebrations in Iran on May 1.
⇛ Shah approved Iranian oil nationalization on May 2.
⇛ King Abdullah of Jordan was assassinated on July 20. His son, Talal, became king.
⇛ Syrian Nationalist Party assassinated Riad al-Sulh of Lebanon.
⇛ British were forced to leave Iran on October 4.
⇛ Egypt under the leadership of Premier Nahas Pasha abrogated the 1936 treaty on October 16 and annexed the Sudan.
⇛ The issues of Egypt and Sudan were a major item on the agenda in the British election of October 25.
⇛ Shishakli overthrew the Syrian republic in November and ruled through a surrogate, Colonel Fawsi Salu. Syria became a military dictatorship.
⇛ Egyptians refused to work for the British; they also cut off food and water to the Suez Canal.
⇛ Egyptian army began to train and arm the *Ikhwan* (Muslim Brotherhood) and Young Egypt militias.
⇛ Saudi oil revenues nearly doubled from $57 million in 1950 to $110 million in 1951.

1952 ⇛ British attacked an Egyptian police station in Ismailiya, which caused more than one hundred casualties.
⇛ "Black Saturday" took place in Egypt on January 26 when large mobs destroyed or damaged most European-owned businesses in Cairo.
⇛ King Farouk of Egypt used five different premiers in six months in an attempt to maintain order.
⇛ Farouk decided to appoint General Amer as war minister to ferret out disloyalty in the military.
⇛ Mossadegh resigned on July 16 over the appointment of a war minister. Qavam became premier for six days before the demonstrations of July 21 forced the Shah to reappoint Mossadegh on July 22.
⇛ Free Officer Corps coup took place in Egypt on July 23.
⇛ Ali Maher became premier after the Free Officer's coup with King Farouk's approval.
⇛ King Farouk left for exile on July 26. His six-month-old son, Ahmed Fuad, became king under a regency.

- ⇛ Free Officer Society in Egypt changed its name to Revolutionary Command Council (RCC) on July 27.
- ⇛ King Talal of Jordan was deposed on August 11. His son, Hussein, became king but a Regency Council ruled until May 2, 1953 when Hussein assumed the full powers of his office.
- ⇛ General Neguib became president of RCC in Egypt during August.
- ⇛ Egyptian Agrarian Reform Program limited land ownership to two hundred acres.
- ⇛ Mossadegh received dictatorial powers in Iran in August.
- ⇛ RCC of Egypt dismissed Ali Maher on September 9. Neguib became premier but kept a civilian cabinet.
- ⇛ Socialist Front in Lebanon formed under leadership of Shamoun and Jumblat.
- ⇛ Socialist Front in Lebanon called a general strike on September 16 and forced President al-Khoury from office.
- ⇛ Chamber of Deputies of Lebanon elected Shamoun as president on September 23.
- ⇛ Britain and Iran broke diplomatic relations in October because of differences related to Iran's nationalizing the Anglo-Iranian Oil Company.
- ⇛ Saudi debts nearly equalled its oil revenues.
- ⇛ Iraq received 50 percent of profits from Iraq Petroleum Company, retroactive to 1951.
- ⇛ *Intifadah* (uprising) began in Iraq on November 22 to support giving the population a greater role in governing. The government responded with martial law.
- ⇛ Purge of army officers in Syria in December; arrest of opposition political leaders; Hourani, Aflaq, and Bitar fled to Lebanon.

1953

- ⇛ RCC in Egypt took all government authority under its control on January 16; disbanded all political parties and RCC members filled all cabinet posts.
- ⇛ Egypt and Britain agreed on February 12 to allow Sudan the choice of independence or union with either of them.
- ⇛ King Hussein assumed full duties as king of Jordan on May 2.
- ⇛ Feisal II was proclaimed of age and became king of Iraq on May 24.
- ⇛ Most prominent Lebanese leaders were in heated opposition to President Shamoun.
- ⇛ The Egyptian RCC abolished the monarchy in June and declared Egypt a republic with Neguib as president and premier. Nasser became deputy premier and interior minister. Abdel Hakim Amer became commander in chief of the military.
- ⇛ Shishali took personal control in Syria and was "elected" president July 10.
- ⇛ National Congress in Homs in July was made up of parties opposed to the Syrian dictator Shishakli.

- ⇛ Merger of Baath Party with Akram Hourani's Arab Socialist party.
- ⇛ Mossadegh received almost unanimous approval of his dictatorial rule in Iran in a July plebiscite.
- ⇛ Iranian Army officers, in an organization called the Committee to Save the Fatherland, under the leadership of General Fazallah Zahedi, attempted to arrest Mossadegh on August 17.
- ⇛ Large anti-shah demonstrations began on August 17.
- ⇛ Shah fled to Rome, by way of Baghdad, on August 17.
- ⇛ Mossadegh approved the use of the army to put down Iranian demonstrations on August 18.
- ⇛ American-financed pro-shah demonstrations took place on August 19. Army moved against Mossadegh on August 19. He went into hiding and surrendered on August 21.
- ⇛ The shah returned to Iran on August 23.
- ⇛ General Zahedi became premier of Iran in August, following Mossadegh's fall.
- ⇛ General suppression of Tudeh and other leftist elements followed the fall of Mossadegh in Iran, which resulted in the complete destruction of Tudeh by 1955.
- ⇛ Egyptian dissidents began to look to General Neguib to change the policies of the RCC.
- ⇛ Shishakli won nearly 90 percent of the seats in the Syrian parliamentary elections of October 9.
- ⇛ Uprising in Syria, especially in Aleppo; revolt in Jebal Druze in December.
- ⇛ Abdul Aziz of Saudi Arabia died November 8; his son, Saud, became king.

1954

- ⇛ Constitutional amendment in Jordan during January allowed simple majority to pass a no-confidence vote against the cabinet.
- ⇛ The United States extended $8,000,000 in aid to Jordan, which was the first Arab country to receive U.S. aid.
- ⇛ Saud dismissed the American Point Four team.
- ⇛ RCC forced General Neguib of Egypt to resign on February 25.
- ⇛ Restoration of diplomatic relations between Great Britain and Iran in February.
- ⇛ Army mutiny began in Aleppo and spread throughout Syria. The mutiny forced Shishakli to flee from Syria on February 25.
- ⇛ Early in March the Egyptian RCC promised to return to constitutional government beginning July 23.
- ⇛ By the end of March, Nasser announced that the constitutional government would not return until 1956, as originally planned. Nasser took the office of premier in April.
- ⇛ Major Muhi al-Din forced the Egyptian RCC to reinstate Neguib to all his former positions.
- ⇛ On October 19, Britain and Egypt agreed on the withdrawal of all British troops by 1956. Britain retained the right to return under certain circumstances.

- ⇛ Ikhwan actively opposed the new Egyptian treaty with Britain as a continuation of British influence.
- ⇛ Ikhwan member attempted to assassinate Nasser on October 26.
- ⇛ Creation of a new oil consortium composed of British, American, Dutch, and French oil companies to manage Iran's oil industry under the supervision of the National Iranian Oil Company. Iranian legislature approved the new arrangement on October 28.
- ⇛ Populist-dominated new Syrian government under presidency of Hashim al-Atasi begain in October. Had to deal with Nasser's growing popularity and decide whether to sign the Baghdad Pact.
- ⇛ Muslim leaders began to demand a larger role for Muslims in the Lebanese government and economy.
- ⇛ Muslim leaders demanded a new Lebanese census to justify more offices for Muslims.
- ⇛ Maronites demanded the right to include Maronites living abroad in their numbers to determine distribution of offices in Lebanon.
- ⇛ RCC in Egypt removed Neguib from his offices and placed him under house arrest on November 14.
- ⇛ Six members of the Egyptian *Ikhwan* were hanged and hundreds imprisoned; *Ikhwan* was declared illegal and went underground.
- ⇛ Jordan announced a Five-Year-Plan in November to spend $200 million on development projects.
- ⇛ Nuri al-Said received full authority to utilize all necessary measures to maintain order in Iraq. He essentially established authoritarian rule.
- ⇛ The Jordanian public became aware in December of the Iraqi-Turkish mutual defense agreement. Riots and demonstrations occurred against Jordan joining the pact.
- ⇛ The Jordanian cabinet resigned on December 19. Leftists called for abrogation of the treaty with Britain and acquisition of a replacement subsidy from Arab nations.
- ⇛ Some elements of Jordan advocated union with Syria; others advocated union with Saudi Arabia.

1955

- ⇛ Samir al-Rifai cabinet took office in Jordan on January 9 and declared martial law and restored order.
- ⇛ Egypt organized International Islamic Congress in January with Anwar Sadat as secretary general.
- ⇛ New government in Syria on February 13 was dominated by Khalid al-Azem. Pro-Soviet foreign policy was in place. Purchased arms from East Germany in December. Uncompromising anti-Western stance made Syria the darling of most Arab nationalists.

- ⇛ Turco-Iraqi treaty on February 24 became first part of the emerging Baghdad Pact.
- ⇛ Major Israeli raid on Gaza on February 28.
- ⇛ Anglo-Iraqi agreement on April 4 effectively replaced the 1930 treaty and made Britain part of the Baghdad Pact.
- ⇛ Zahedi was removed from premiership of Iran on April 6.
- ⇛ Brutal suppression of Syrian National Party during the spring on the accusation that it was pro-Western.
- ⇛ Nasser received warm reception at the Non-Aligned Nations Conference at Bangdung in April.
- ⇛ Shukri Al-Quwatly was elected president of Syria on September 5 and Populists dominated the new government. Did not endorse Baghdad Pact.
- ⇛ Iran joined the Baghdad Pact, a nonaggression agreement, on September 23 in alliance with Iraq, Turkey, and Pakistan.
- ⇛ Egypt announced in September that it had completed a major deal for sophisticated arms from the Eastern Bloc.
- ⇛ Egypt-Syrian mutual defense pact was signed on October 20.
- ⇛ Pakistan signed the Baghdad Pact on November 3.
- ⇛ Syria signed an economic pact with Saudi Arabia on November 9.
- ⇛ General Gerald Templer's mission to Amman took place from December 6–14.
- ⇛ Israelis raided Syrian outpost on Lake Tiberius on December 11.
- ⇛ New riots in Jordan on December 16 and 17 led to the cabinet's resignation.
- ⇛ U.S. agreed on December 16 to provide $56 million for the first stage of construction of Aswan High Dam; British and World Bank followed with offers to provide funds.

An intense volatility prevailed throughout the entire Middle East in the early 1950s. No small part of the discord and unrest resulted from Arab humiliation in their war with the new state of Israel. All Arab governments stood discredited, although mitigating circumstances had prevented a much better performance in the embarrassing war. Regional residents could agree that continued weakness was unacceptable. In the minds of most, new solutions under new leadership were obviously necessary. The appeal of Arab unity grew and became widely accepted as a precondition for Arab control over their own affairs. Arabs and Iranians alike resented the continued Western domination over the policies and resources of the region.

Globally, a new era was obviously afoot, which the United States and the Soviet Union dominated. However, British interests still dominated the Suez Canal and the petroleum resources throughout the Middle East. Great Britain also retained extensive direct and indirect political influence. Arabs regarded Israel as a new outpost of Western influence that the British had created, despite the recent conflicts between the British and the Zionists and the fact that the United States and the United Nations had played the most prominent role in transforming the Zionist entity from a "homeland" into a nation. The sheer longevity of foreign domination grated harshly upon people of the region who believed they should endure it no longer.

The population of the region had doubled since the West seized control at the end of World War I and a new generation of activists asserted themselves to demolish a status quo they did not create or respect. Oddly, however, an elderly Iranian, who appealed to the new generation of the entire region, struck the first significant blow against the continued Western domination. Mossadegh's later failure did not diminish his importance in the hearts and minds of his Middle Eastern contemporaries. In fact, his experience proved similar to those of others, especially Nasser, who met apparent defeat but scored "moral" victories. There was a general understanding in the region that the forces arranged against it were too strong to defeat. Acclaim went to individuals and groups that were willing to confront the oppressors. Those who dared to defy the West became heroes, while those who cooperated with the West suffered opprobrium.

Great Britain's prospects of retaining a presence in the region were strongest in Iraq, Jordan, and in the shaykhdoms on the shores of eastern and southern Arabia. Its most vital interests, however, were in the Suez Canal in Egypt and the petroleum industry of Iran. The British were confident that their holds on the Suez Canal and the petroleum industry of Iran were secure because they believed that neither Egypt nor Iran could operate those sophisticated facilities without British assistance.

Syria was the most unsettled part of the Middle East. A series of military coups failed to provide the republic with stable policies and a clear sense of direction. The absence of a strong central government transformed Syria into an incubator for radical ideas and experimentation. The Arab world marvelled at the near chaos in Syria, where no internal or external force could curb a full debate on the future of Syria and the entire Arab world. Supporters of the status quo could be thankful that Syria had no capacity to extend its adventurous ways beyond its own borders. Indeed, Syria also posed something of a problem because its weakness offered the possibility that it might disappear. Syria's disappearance would result in the enhancement of one or more of its neighbors and jeopardize the existing balance of power. There was even the possibility that Arab nationalism could prevail and result in Syria absorbing Jordan or Lebanon or part or all of Iraq. It became evident that developments in unstable Syria could well determine the shape and direction of the Middle East.

While Mossadegh's nationalization of Iran's oil gave hope of breaking the bond with Western domination, the Free Officers' coup in Egypt seemed to provide a political and military base for the Arab world to become a new and powerful factor in world affairs. The first couple of years following the Free Officers' coup was a period of cautious adjustment until Nasser could establish his authority in Egypt and define his relationship with nations outside of the region. By late 1955, Nasser was clearly the focus for Arab unity that most of the Arab population had yearned to find since freedom from the Ottoman Empire had delivered them into the control of Western powers. His appeal to the masses presented a large challenge to the Arab governments and the Western powers. They resented his popularity but hoped to find a way to work with him and protect their established interests.

Great Britain and the United States decided that Iraq was the best regional base to stem the tide of indigenous ferment and Soviet penetration. The small but strong Communist movement in Iraq persuaded Iraqi authorities that there was a genuine Communist threat to the region. There was also a much larger Communist movement in Iran and an openly active Communist element in Syria. There were even significant Communist sympathies in Jordan, although there, as in other regional states, it was difficult to differentiate between genuine affinity toward communism and nationalist support for enemies of the Western powers. For numerous reasons, however, a regional coalition called the Baghdad Pact evolved in 1955 to maintain the status quo for traditionalist regional governments and their British and American supporters. Nasser and Arab nationalists seized upon the non-Arab nature of the original signatories of the pact to discredit it as a new vehicle for maintaining imperialism in the region. After a generation of subservience to the West and its regional allies, "the street" found the accusation believable. If the Baghdad Pact was not stillborn, its early death was a clarion call that the Middle East was defiantly moving toward independence from Western control over its affairs.

EGYPT

Egyptian Disgrace in Palestine

Elements of the Egyptian army—both individual officers and soldiers—acquitted themselves with honor and heroism in the war against Israel in 1948 and 1949. Among those were General Muhammad Neguib and Colonel Gamal Abdel Nasser. The Egyptian defeat was both quick and decisive in combat with the more numerous and better armed Israeli forces. Previous discussion of the war eliminates the need to discuss it here. Egypt, however, engaged along by far the longest front of any Arab army in that war. Years of campaigning in the Sudan had in no way prepared it for the modern and determined enemy it faced in Gaza, the Negev, and near Hebron. Egyptian *Ikhwan* units left a strong impression of zeal, which failed to serve military purposes.

The Egyptian military and the citizenry in general refused to accept blame or feel shame for defeat against a fledgling nation. There was consensus that failure of leadership at the highest levels, a lack of preparedness, faulty equipment, and British complicity wasted the good effort of good men with a good cause. The British occupation and Egypt's corrupt leadership, the cause of all manner of domestic distress, also received responsibility for the international disgrace. Egyptian agony erupted in violence against its tormentors. Still, there was no hint of any capable and determined source of leadership that could offer redress and hope for Egypt's domestic injustice and international humiliation.

Firm Stand and Chaos

Nahas Pasha proved unexpectedly forceful in his attempts to gain a British withdrawal when he and the Wafd returned to power after the January 1950 elections. Anything less than a complete British withdrawal had become unacceptable to most Egyptians. The outbreak of the Korean War in June, however, eliminated any possibility of the British diminishing their capacity to secure the Suez Canal. The growing conflict with Iran over control and ownership of Iranian oil made unfettered British use of the canal additionally vital. Britain's questionable ability to engage in another major conflict improved Egypt's chances for success, except that the canal was central to much of Britain's other interests. They had, in fact, withdrawn all troops to the canal zone in 1947 in an effort to ease tension with Egypt and to prevent a United Nations resolution, on Egypt's request, for a complete British withdrawal. Nahas, who had worked so well with the British since 1936, made no progress toward a satisfactory treaty, because even in their intense struggle for power the British Conservative and Labor parties agreed on the necessity of keeping the canal.

Anglo-Egyptian conflict was inevitable when on October 16, 1951 Nahas broke with convention and obtained approval from the Chamber of Deputies for unilaterally abrogating the 1936 treaty and annexing Sudan. His announced intention to do so nine days earlier had already made Anglo-Egyptian relations a major issue in the British general election scheduled for October 25. Iran's nationalization of the Anglo-Iranian Petroleum Company in April and its eviction of the British on October 1 added to the magnitude of the Egyptian legislation.

Jubilant Egyptians prepared to make further British occupation untenable. Under government instructions Egyptians refused to work for the British and denied the isolated troops food and water supplies. When the Egyptian army began to train and arm *Ikhwan* and Young Egypt units, the British faced the prospect of encountering an entire nation in arms. The British occupation troops, therefore, came to regard all Egyptians as hostile enemies who not only endangered British control of the strategic canal but their lives as well.

Once British troops reacted as if they were at war, they escalated an already explosive situation. They destroyed an Egyptian village in an operation to secure its water supply in December 1951 and engaged in a battle with lightly armed police at Ismailiya on January 25, 1952. More than forty unfortunate policemen perished and twice that number were wounded in their conflict with British tanks.

The scale of violence the next day in Cairo, which the British called "Black Saturday," exceeded anything most could have expected from the obviously provocative slaughter at Ismailiya. Years of seething wrath ignited the destruction of property and loss of lives that was directed as much against Farouk's regime as it was against the British. The police, many of whom sympathized with the *Ikhwan,* made no effort to intervene and some outwardly went on strike. Perhaps no more than ten British nationals died, but few British and foreign-owned businesses and other establishments escaped destruction or severe damage. Most evidence indicated that the *Ikhwan* and Ahmad Husain's Young Egypt accounted for most of the damage thousands of others systematically helped inflict. The level of destruction was so great that most foreigners agreed it had to result from an existing plot that took advantage of enflamed attitudes following the Ismailiya incident. The Egyptian army restored order in Cairo by early evening.

Farouk, who regarded milder rioting against the British as acceptable, realized that the new level of violence endangered his ability to govern. He began to transfer his personal assets abroad in preparation for his possible exile. Farouk dismissed Nahas and reappointed Ali Maher, who was followed by a succession of three other premiers over six months in an attempt to avoid chaos. Egypt agreed to compensate foreigners for some of the damages to reduce the impact of the uprising on Egypt's relations with other nations and foreign investment in Egypt. His real problems, however, were internal.

The king was particularly concerned about the army, although it had never played a role in Egyptian politics, except for Arabi's brief period of prominence. Egyptian intelligence was aware that elements of the Egyptian army were disloyal to the government and that some belonged to a secret organization called the Free Officers Society. That group cleverly planted evidence implying that nothing of any significance existed.

Farouk, however, decided to install General Hussein Sirri Amer as War Minister to ferret out disloyalty among the officers. General Amer, in fact, knew enough about the Free Officers Society to cause its members concern. They feared that his appointment would bring their destruction, because, while they were well placed in strategic units, they were small in number and all were of only colonel rank or lower. They assumed that enough soldiers of all rank would follow their leadership if they could neutralize the predominantly Turkish and Circassian upper-echelon officers, whose fate depended on the king. They had the added concern that the Egyptian public did not know them. Their only hope was to accomplish a coup and present the king and the nation with a *fait accompli.* With Amer's impending appointment, the Free Officers realized, that their designs for deposing the king sometime in the future was no longer feasible. They had to act at once.

The Free Officer Coup

The Free Officer Society originated in 1939 among some newly commissioned officers in the Egyptian army under the leadership of Anwar Sadat. The association emerged out of their barracks discussions of the plight of Egypt under British control and Farouk's rule. The fact that almost all were of peasant origin gave them similar experiences and views toward remedying their country's ills. Their membership varied from fairly politically and socially conservative to a few Communists and other leftists. They received the blessing and advice of Shaykh Hasan al-Banna of the Muslim Brotherhood and Aziz Ali al-Misri, Inspector General of the Egyptian Army. Both endorsements encouraged the young men who believed themselves to be under the guidance of giants in Egypt's struggle for liberation.

Al-Misri had been a legendary figure in Egypt since 1913, when he had run afoul of his former colleagues in the Committee of Union and Progress, which had carried out the Young Turk Revolution in the Ottoman Empire. Uprisings on his behalf in Egypt had saved him from life in prison or a death sentence for suspicion of organizing Arab officers in the Ottoman army. This Egyptian of half Circassian lineage had, in fact, organized the tiny, secret group called al-Ahd among Arab officers, although he remained committed to the principles of Ottomanism as long as the Empire existed. He refused, for instance, to remain in the position of Chief of Staff of Shaykh Hussein at the beginning of the Arab Revolt once the Sharif decided to lead a liberation movement, rather than simply apply pressure to reform Ottoman policies toward Arabs. Under British pressure al-Misri lost his commission in the Egyptian army soon after the beginning of World War II because all knew he opposed British occupation to the point of being pro-German. The Free Officers were apt pupils of this revered nationalist who taught them his secrets for creating a clandestine organization within the army, obtaining assignments in strategic units and locations, and how to communicate with each other from scattered locations.

Gamal Abdel Nasser acquired control of the Free Officers after Sadat went to prison in 1942 for his pro-German espionage activities. This son of a postal clerk had lived much of his life in Alexandria and Cairo, although he had strong family ties and experience with village life. Nasser was among the activist students who demonstrated in the streets of Cairo and at one time or another considered joining one of the full spectrum of militant organizations. By all accounts, including his own, however, Nasser never seemed comfortable in groups until he gained control of his own. His serious, aloof demeanor also prevented others from being comfortable with him, but his sincerity and single-mindedness helped him become the leader of the Free Officers. There are indications that he would only have participated as the leader of the Constituent Council, the executive board of the Free Officers. His scars from British and Israeli-inflicted wounds provided him with additional credentials. Nasser took al-Misri's advice to heart and organized the Free Officers in a secretive fashion similar to those of al-Ahd and the Muslim Brotherhood.

The politically and administratively inexperienced young officers were unknown nationally. Sadat was an exception, as he obtained some fame because of his imprisonment in 1942 for pro-German espionage and in 1946 for planning the assassination of Amin Osman, an obsequiously pro-British Finance Minister. They persuaded General Muhammad Neguib to join their cause early in 1952 to give their movement some credibility when the time came for them to act publicly. His performance in the Palestine war, his agreement with the Free Officers on the needs of Egypt, and his acquiescence to their goal of taking control for a limited time to eradicate corruption gave him appeal to the officers and the public. Just as importantly, he had strong Muslim credentials at home and elsewhere in the Arab world. Nasser in no way relinquished his leadership position in the Free Officer Society when the senior officer joined. Two years would pass after the Free Officers entered the public before many realized that Nasser was the real power behind the movement.

Years of discussion, planning, and scheming paid dividends once the need to act became urgent. The conspirators staged a successful coup in the middle of the night of July 22–23, 1952 within a week from the time they decided it was necessary. Their well-placed members seized the important officers and installations of Egypt's military without allowing an alarm to go out to those who opposed such a move. Control of air and armor with adequate ammunition prepared them to meet resistance that never developed because of the ingenuity and execution of their plan. They gained control of the country virtually without shedding blood. The nation awoke on July 23 to hear Sadat announce on national radio the dramatic events that had occurred while Egypt slept. The normally noisy city of Cairo greeted the unexpected change with unusual silence that resulted from both relief and wonder about who their deliverers were and what kind of plans they had for the nation.

Free Officers in Power

Unknown to the public, except for Neguib and Sadat, the Free Officers had control of the government and the army, but they had no mandate to govern from the people or from any political parties. They had no affiliation with any of the foreign embassies and had no idea how foreign governments would react to their control of such an important country. They had no political, economic, or social ideology since they never intended to govern and, indeed, had believed it would take them another three years to prepare to seize the government. Unexpected developments had compelled them to act. They had seized Cairo, but the king was in Alexandria on vacation where he could possibly rally domestic and foreign support. They quickly turned to Ali Maher, whom the British had forced out of office ten years earlier with the use of tanks, to form a civilian government.

Farouk cooperated and approved Ali Maher as premier, but his compliance did not improve his status because the officers had decided to force the king out of office as their first priority. Free Officer troops besieged the royal palace in Alexandria on July 25 and skirmished with the king's guards. The Free Officers informed Farouk through Ali Maher that he must leave Egypt on July 26, which was the earliest they could have their forces in Alexandria and make proper arrangements for his departure. Farouk accepted the conditions and departed with his family at 6:00 P.M. as the Egyptian forces provided a proper, if hostile, salute. He sailed away aboard the royal yacht but with the understanding that the boat would return to Egypt. Farouk's six-month-old son became the king and a meaningless regency council managed royal affairs of the infant king, Ahmed Fuad, who was the last of Muhammad Ali's offspring to hold title in Egypt.

Nasser changed the name of the the Free Officers executive to the Revolutionary Command Council (RCC) the day after the king went into exile. He resigned at the same meeting, ostensibly because he favored democracy while the other members believed a period of their dictatorship was necessary. Most believe, however, that he assumed, correctly, that his colleagues would invite him back to wield even greater control with their renewed, overt authorization.

In an attempt to keep a constitutional face on their movement, the RCC instructed Ali Maher to reform the political parties and carry out land reform. Since the king was gone and British influence was neutralized, they regarded these two issues as central to establishing the "good government" they visualized and to eliminating the disparity of wealth and power in their country. Their Agrarian Reform Act proposed limiting individual landholding to a maximum of two hundred acres within five years. Landowners had a choice of selling their land in five-acre plots to individuals who owned no more than ten acres of land or allowing the government to acquire it for the nominal price of ten times its annual rental rate. The low compensation rate, which would be paid over thirty years, and the policy of taxing unsold excess at five times the normal rate, gave the large landowners an incentive to sell the land to their tenants. Land that the government seized would be sold to individuals in five-acre plots that the new owners would purchase over thirty years at the compensation rate plus administrative costs.

Ali Maher's government worked much too slowly to satisfy the impatient young officers who were accustomed to quick response to military orders and who were also impatient to change Egypt. The politicians' concern for the legal and legislative process, which included the sanctity of private property, made their continuation in office unacceptable to the RCC. Also, the RCC thought the changes in the political parties were too minor to constitute a genuine purge of corruption, attachment to the former regime, and affinity to British interests. Traditional politicians had also affiliated with elements in the military that had questionable loyalty to the RCC.

The RCC calmly dismissed Ali Maher on September 9, 1952 and General Neguib, who had become the titular head of the RCC in August, became premier of an otherwise civilian cabinet. The RCC arrested troublesome politicians and military officers before determining to take all government authority into their own hands for three years on January 16, 1953. With the end of parliamentary government the RCC disbanded the political parties and soon placed severe restrictions on the continuously troublesome Muslim Brotherhood. It abolished the monarchy in June and declared Egypt a republic with Neguib as president and premier. The RCC eliminated his potential independence by removing him from his previous posts of War Minister and Commander in Chief of the armed forces. Nasser became deputy premier and Interior Minister in the new government and took his first step out of the shadows of secrecy that veiled his role as the real power behind the revolution. Other RCC members took ministerial positions, with Nasser's trusted friend Abdel Hakim Amer, who was promoted to general, in the coveted role of Commander in Chief. Free officers entered most government operations to supervise the implementation of RCC policies and to use all means at their disposal to shape a new Egypt.

Dissatisfaction and Dissent

These structural changes in government were more than a response to inefficiency and the normal, cumbersome nature of parliamentary government. The revolution's slogan of "Discipline, Unity, and Work" still seemed to fall on deaf ears except in the Liberation Rally, which was the RCC's attempt to establish a political structure among the masses to support its approach to restructuring Egypt. Since the Liberation Rally was in a formative stage of development, it was ineffective and the RCC enjoyed no significant popular following. Ideological movements like the *Ikhwan,* the Communists and other leftists, who had risked their lives so many times against the king and the British, had no hope that the officers would shape Egypt in the way they visualized. All politicians and their followers had lost any reason for being. The Agrarian Reform Act starkly demonstrated to the wealthy landowners what their fate would be and other people of wealth feared a similar fate. Students and workers of all political persuasions hardly felt comfortable with a military regime that expressed no ideology. All these groups and others had allies in the military who might help them unseat the upstart RCC.

General Neguib seemed the best hope for relief for many dissidents. Many respected him for his distinguished career and sensed he was different from the other members of the RCC. Also, from all outward appearances he was in charge. Elements in the military and the *Ikhwan* were especially hopeful that Neguib would curb the zeal of his young colleagues. Neguib's apparent receptivity to their overtures led to his forced resignation on February 25, 1954, but two days later the leftist commander of the tank corps, Major Khalid Muhi al-Din, threatened to use force unless Neguib regained his positions. Muhi al-Din, indeed, had armored units in position that could have destroyed the RCC. Nasser relented and allowed Neguib to return to the presidency, but Nasser continued in the office of premier, which he had assumed when Neguib "resigned." These developments demonstrated that the RCC could not even rely on vital military units to keep its power. Ali Maher, who once again became their liaison with the nation, announced early in March that the RCC agreed to hold parliamentary elections and return to civilian government on

July 23, the second anniversary of the coup. Nasser seemed defeated because he also relinquished the premiership and the presidency of the RCC to Neguib. Many imprisoned opponents of the regime, including Nahas Pasha, gained their freedom as further indication of the RCC's weakened condition.

Nasser recovered quickly and learned how to get his supporters in the Liberation Rally into the streets to counter the demonstrations of the *Ikhwan* and the leftists. He brought dissidents within the RCC under control, exiled Major Muhi al-Din, and imprisoned suspected officers and some leaders of the *Ikhwan.* By the end of March Nasser felt strong enough to announce that military control would continue until 1956 as originally planned and he again assumed the position of premier in April.

Exit Great Britain and Neguib

Once the British realized that the RCC would not show weakness in negotiations for British withdrawal from the Canal and Sudan they began to seek a solution, although Foreign Minister Anthony Eden disliked the RCC. Both parties saved face by agreeing on February 12, 1953 to allow Sudan to choose affiliation with either of them or self-rule. Sudan chose the latter. Nasser had clearly subdued Neguib by October 19, 1954 when the British and Egypt reached an agreement on the canal question that had been the source of so much conflict since 1882. The British agreed to withdraw its 80,000 troops within twenty months but obtained consent to keep 1,200 technicians in the canal for seven years. While most Egyptians found this portion of the treaty honorable, some regarded Britain's right to return to the canal bases in case of an attack upon any Arab League member or upon Turkey as a continued British infringement on Egyptian sovereignty. Nasser, however, was proud of his accomplishment and had little difficulty convincing the RCC to approve it. He had, thus, rid Egypt of the British and was in position to accept the rewards commensurate with accomplishing what his royal predecessors and their lackeys had been unable to do.

While Nasser was willing to accept complete credit for removing the British, others, especially the *Ikhwan,* gave him full blame for accepting provisions that allowed the British to return. The *Ikhwan* also resented the diminished role of Neguib because Nasser, who apparently had no special regard for Islam, increasingly seemed to represent the RCC, if not the revolution itself. Their assessment was, in fact, accurate. Neguib had served his purpose of giving the obscure officers some respectability in Egypt and in the negotiations with the British. He had, with the aura of his rank and maturity, helped ease British apprehension about dealing with the revolutionary regime. The British did not realize that Neguib was merely the spokesman for Nasser in the direct negotiations.

Ikhwan resentment of the treaty with Britain, Nasser's treatment of Neguib, and his lack of interest in creating an Islamic society led to hostile speeches, demonstrations, and riots against the treaty. A Muslim Brother fired shots at Nasser on October 26 in Alexandria when he was giving a public speech. His calm reaction under fire and his bold public appearances the next day in Alexandria and Cairo, in defiance of the threat of assassination, galvanized his formerly lukewarm following, which spread to include others. That seemed to be the turning point in his life as Egypt's leader. The revolution, Egypt, and soon the Arab masses, were his.

The RCC removed Neguib from the presidency on November 14 and placed him under house arrest on charges of conspiring with the Muslim Brotherhood and other enemies of the government. The office of president remained vacant. Neguib's dismissal caused little stir in Egypt as the RCC had demonstrated for the first time in hanging six Muslim brothers that it was capable of using bloodshed as well as imprisonment and exile to deal with dissidents. Muslims in other parts of the Arab world expressed dismay and anger at the regime's treatment of the *Ikhwan* and Neguib. Nasser moved toward placating the Muslims when he formed the international Islamic Congress in January 1955 with Anwar al-Sadat as Secretary-General and by adopting the name of Islamic Arab Republic of Egypt in the new constitution of January 1956.

The wrath of the regime soon fell upon the Muslim Brotherhood after the spontaneous wrath of Nasser's supporters burned the brotherhood's headquarters and dealt harshly with all members they could lay their hands on. The attempted assassin, Mahmoud Abdel Latif, and five other *Ikhwan* went to the gallows; Shaykh Hasan al-Hudaibi, who had been Hasan al-Banna's successor as Supreme Guide since 1950, went to prison, as did hundreds of others. Al-Azhar university came under close supervision and served the needs of the regime from that time. The *Ikhwan* became illegal and went underground but it retained some organization and a full commitment to its principles. This vivacious and often violent movement, which had been in the forefront of Egyptian life for more than a quarter of a century, caused no further significant problems while Nasser was in office.

Domestic Needs and Financial Limitations

The driving force behind the Free Officer movement was to improve the lives of Egyptians, for which deposing Farouk and expelling the British were necessary preconditions. With them out of the way, Nasser and the RCC gave fuller attention to economic and financial concerns. Egypt's rapid population growth presented a microcosm of Malthus's predictions of the nightmarish inevitable disparity between the growth of population and the food supply. Even Egypt's good soil and climate could not feed the half million new mouths each year. Also, the RCC envisioned a life for their countrymen that provided more than subsistence. Egypt's concentration on exporting raw cotton added to the problem because it was the nation's primary source of foreign exchange to purchase goods Egypt was unable to manufacture due to a lack of raw materials and the absence of a modern industrial infrastructure. Landowners demanded that tenants grow cotton because the *fellahin* (peasants) could not eat it and deny the owners the full rent from their lands. The RCC's need for foreign exchange to improve Egypt's domestic and international status made any significant change in cotton production impossible. That led to the obvious conclusion that new land had to be developed for food production and Egypt's industrial production must increase.

Egypt lacked the capital and the technical knowledge it needed for agricultural and industrial expansion and for modernization in general. The United States and Great Britain proved responsive to early appeals for economic assistance for Egypt, but steadily refused to provide any significant increase in modern military assistance the RCC also sought. Great Britain, France, and the United States, the main suppliers of weapons outside the Eastern Bloc, had agreed in 1950 to limit all arms transfers to the Middle East as a means of encouraging the Arab countries and Israel to make peace. They were still technically at war since the Palestine war had ended in a truce, rather than a peace treaty. The adherence of the Western powers to their policy and the influence of Israeli pressure combined to deny Egypt any reason to believe it could obtain anything other than defensive weapons from the West. This disagreement smoldered in Egypt's relations with the West, but it did not prevent a basically cordial relationship from existing during the first three years of the RCC regime.

The RCC, after all, had enough monumental domestic challenges that required immediate attention to prevent dwelling on longer-term projects and possible foreign adventures. The purge of corrupt officials and disloyal military officers through special tribunals required time and effort that served more punitive than constructive needs. Land redistribution proved more complicated than expected as the large landowners used every legal means and prevarication they could devise in efforts of self-preservation and in hope that delays in divesting themselves of their land might outlast the RCC's control of power. The RCC restructured the legal and judicial system that all but eliminated any role for either the religious courts or Islamic law. The new regime built schools at a feverish pace, expanded health care and social services, imposed higher minimum wages, and frantically attempted to increase agricultural production with irrigation projects and attention to new agricultural techniques. The increasingly socialist nature of the RCC's approach was still, however, devoid of a specific ideological foundation. As Nasser's close relationship developed with Tito from early 1955, Egypt clearly took on characteristics of Yugoslavia's unique experiments in socialism, which were built upon no existing ideology or model.

Closer scrutiny of Egypt's problems and potential starkly informed the RCC of the impediments to an underdeveloped nation that aspired to achieve domestic improvement and military preparedness in the modern world. They began to consider every possible means of raising capital, including additional confiscations, higher taxes, and foreign borrowing. A group of legal and technical experts even began to study the possibility of nationalizing the Suez Canal Company, which showed a profit of about $100 million a year but paid less than $3 million to Egypt. Iran's experience in nationalizing the Anglo-Iranian Petroleum Company indicated that nationalization of the canal would be a risky venture, especially after it became clear that Egypt needed to borrow money from the Western countries that owned most of the shares.

Increasingly, the idea of building a high dam at Aswan became the focus for long-range planning, which would also provide the Egyptian public with hope that their poor living standard was temporary. The British had built the first dam at Aswan 450 miles south of Cairo in 1902. Heightening of the dam in 1912 and 1930 left the dam's utility far below the developing dreams for a high dam. The RCC, in fact, began further improvements in the dam in preparation for the needs of construction of one to fulfill the new goals. The high dam emerging on the drawing board would hold enough water to increase Egyptian agricultural production by more than 30 percent. It could generate sufficient hydroelectrical power to transform Egypt into a significant industrial nation. Not the least of its appeal was the prospect of providing electrical current to thousands of villages for schools, clinics, refrigeration, and the simple pleasure of radio and other small appliances.

Estimates pointed toward a cost for the dam of more than one billion dollars over a fifteen-year period of construction. This was a prohibitively high figure for Egypt, although estimates also indicated that it would more than pay for its cost through increased production. The United States and Great Britain were receptive to the project if for no other reason than that their participation would provide them high-profile cooperation in a strategic country that already demonstrated hesitation in joining their side of the Cold War. Egypt's independent, even provocative, policies throughout 1955 did not appear to deter U.S. and British assistance in beginning the dam. The U.S., in fact, promised on December 16, 1955 to provide $56 million and the British promised $14 million. This strong base of capital moved the International Bank for Reconstruction and Development (World Bank) to begin defining the conditions Egypt would have to satisfy to obtain a $200 million loan for the first stage of construction. Egyptians from Nasser down to village peasants believed they would soon enjoy the benefits of an engineering feat worthy of the land of the pyramids. The promises of capital also indicated that the West was generally comfortable with the RCC and hoped to maintain a working relationship with the new revolutionary regime.

IRAQ

A Return to Order in Iraq

Strong government control helps explain how the Iraqi government could withstand the Iraqi army's failure to distinguish itself in the Palestine war. A firm stand on behalf of the right of Palestinian refugees to return to their homes as a precondition for Iraq's participation in negotiations with Israel mitigated the military failure. In Iraq, as elsewhere, there was no initial appreciation of the fact that the international community would allow such wholesale displacement of people. Instead, Iraqi popular wrath focused on the numerous and important Jewish population, which was primarily centered in Baghdad. Iraq attempted to bargain better treatment of its own Jewish population for the right of Palestinians to return to their land. After that failed the Iraqis allowed the large-scale transfer of most of its Jewish population to Israel. From March 1950 to June 1951, 160,000 Iraqi Jews renounced their citizenship and migrated to Israel, leaving most of their assets behind.

Feisal II's approaching majority accelerated Abd al-Ilah's efforts to obtain a throne in Syria. Al-Ilah's relentless pursuit of this dream adversely affected Iraq's relations with its neighbors and Great Britain. His activities spawned three Syrian military coups in 1949 at considerable diplomatic and financial expense to his country. Nuri al-Said helped thwart the Regent's schemes because they presented unnecessary complications to his own domestic and international plans.

Challenges to the Old Order

Iraq's tradition as a difficult country to govern was never more apparent than in the 1950s. Failure of the war in Palestine and the Egyptian revolution in 1952 exacerbated an indigenous explosive situation. People who found life impossible in the countryside flocked to Baghdad to swell the slum population. Their plight provided inspiration for the various political parties that advocated democracy, Arab nationalism, social justice, and communism. In the popular mind, Iraq was an outdated monarchy under the domination of Great Britain, an insensitive regent, and a handful of elderly, reactionary politicians. While the government was, in fact, repressive, the very fact that a full spectrum of political activity was possible in Iraq attests to it being far from totalitarian. With all its imperfections, the complexities and vitality of Iraq were direct results of it being a constitutional state from its inception.

Nuri al-Said, more than any of his contemporaries, seemed to grasp the reality of Iraq's unique situation. Iraq, unlike Egypt, Syria, Saudi Arabia, Lebanon, Jordan, and Israel possessed fertile land, water, oil, and an adequate population to build a strong, modern constitutional state. Nuri believed that proper development of Iraq's resources would solve the social and economic problems that proved such fertile ground for the growth of leftist movements.

Toward this end he established the Development Board in 1950 to allocate 70 percent of Iraq's oil revenue into substantial government-sponsored projects to improve Iraq's agricultural, transportation, industrial, and flood-control infrastructure. Construction of the projects provided considerable employment, as well as large-scale use of technical skills. The true value of this approach, however, would take several years for manifestation. The agricultural regions received most of the earliest attention in an attempt to improve the plight of the small landowners and the landless, who could not afford the vital water pumps the wealthy, large landholders used to assure their prosperity. Prosperity in the countryside, after all, could eliminate the migration to the cities where neither adequate housing nor employment existed to meet the growing needs.

Prospects for this approach seemed to improve when Iraq obtained a better agreement with the Iraq Petroleum Company and other oil producers in 1952. Iraq demanded and received the same 50-50 split of profits before taxes, retroactive to 1951, that American companies granted Venezuela and Saudi Arabia in 1950. Iraq benefitted from Iran's failure to obtain the same kind of agreement, which led to nationalization and an international boycott of its oil, because the Iraq Petroleum Company increased production as Iraq had been urging for years.

Development, however, did not meet the increased expectations increased oil revenues seemed to offer, especially in urban areas. Baghdad exploded on November 22, 1952 in the *intifadah* (uprising) under the leadership of al-Chadirchi's Independent party and a coalition of other reform-minded parties and groups. This followed their unsuccessful attempt to persuade the regent to introduce one-stage voting, a reduced role of the monarchy, land reform, a truly neutral foreign policy, and the termination of the 1930 treaty with Great Britain. The fairly temperate initial demonstrations soon turned radical and violent as the Communists and the newly formed Baath seized control of "the street." Iraq's Communists were passing through a stage that probably gave them the distinction of being the most radical Communist party in the world at the time. Their activities made the *intifadah* violent, but the number of casualties was not as high as those of the *wathbah* in 1948. The regent appointed General Nur al-Din Mahmoud, the Kurdish chief of staff, as premier to invoke martial law and restore control. He did so and promulgated some changes that addressed the original grievances before returning government to civilian control.

The balance of opposing forces was so strong by 1953 that normal government became difficult. The reform-minded parties could obtain about as many seats in the legislature as the traditionalists. The ability of the dissidents to generate troublesome demonstrations gave them an advantage under these circumstances unless the traditionalists were willing to use police and military force against them. The hope that Feisal II's coming of age and becoming king on May 24, 1953 would improve matters proved illusory. He was popular in many circles and had the respect of many who were not particularly inclined toward monarchy. But the young, unassertive, and yet unmarried, king could not overcome the growing impasse between those who wanted immediate social, economic and political redress and the supporters of Nuri who wanted to keep matters much as they were or were only willing to implement gradual change through economic growth. Abd al-Ilah, who became crown prince until Feisal had a son, still held sway over his nephew and looked for the permanent security of a throne in Damascus.

Nuri's Authoritarianism

After three different governments were unable to implement a moderate course between the end of the *intifadah* and August 1954, the new king accepted Nuri's terms for establishing stability. Nuri proceeded to curtail Communist and union activities, throttle or abolish opposition newspapers, expand the powers of the police and ultimately abolish all political parties, including his own, the Union Constitutional party. The parliament that resulted from the Nuri-directed election was overwhelmingly supportive of both his domestic and foreign policy. He finally seemed to have the circumstances he needed to test his theory that Iraq could develop strong national institutions and prosperity that could reach to all classes if politicians were free from the influence of ideologues and the mob.

By most practical standards Nuri's approach succeeded. The economy enjoyed a significant improvement with the influx of income from the better oil prices that allowed increased investments and fuller employment. The cost of living for the poor, particularly in bread prices, declined enough to make them less inclined to take to the streets. The lower classes for the first time had reason to believe their lives would be something other than a penance of toil and despair.

The Communists presented a major disconcerting note to a pattern of improvement as they became increasingly combative. In a way, their unrealistic activities helped the regime as it did not have to hesitate in using its fullest capacity to deport, arrest, or kill the top Communist leaders and reduce the rank and file. Communist radicalism, as well as their domination of the 1952 riots and demonstrations, made other leftist groups avoid joining them against the government. While in the past the government had usually eased up after the main reason for crackdowns subsided, Nuri's stringent measures remained in place until the end of the monarchy. His approach gave the country stability and limited its opposition to clandestine activities.

The Baghdad Pact

Domestic calm created a favorable atmosphere in September 1954 for Nuri to begin negotiations for a treaty to replace the Anglo-Iraqi Treaty of 1930, which was to expire in 1957. The Communist excesses allowed him virtually to annihilate them and break diplomatic relations with the Soviet Union. Restrictions on the political and publishing activities of other leftist groups eliminated resistance to his policy which should have been at least as troublesome as the 1948 Portsmouth treaty.

Fear of the spread of communism in the region prompted Nuri's government to pursue a regional pact, rather than continue a bilateral pact with Great Britain. This approach was fraught with danger since it was not built upon an Arab base at the very time Nasser was arousing Arab nationalism to its highest level. But the ever realistic Nuri perceived the Arab states as still too weak to defend themselves either singly or collectively.

Against Nasser's advice in September 1954, Nuri pursued negotiations with Turkey, which was already aligned with Pakistan. Much to the discomfort of Syria, this led to a Turkish-Iraqi agreement to counter aggression on Feb. 24, 1955. On April 4, Great Britain agreed to the developing scheme and signed an agreement with Iraq to replace the Anglo-Iraqi Treaty of 1930. In this treaty, Iraq gained control over the two airbases at Habbaniya and Shuayba, but allowed Britain to retain landing and refueling rights there. Great Britain committed to come to Iraq's aid in case of aggression, and retained the right to equip and train the Iraqi military. These were essentially the same terms of the Portsmouth Treaty of 1948 that initiated the *wathbah.* Iran joined the antiaggression agreement on September 23 and Pakistan signed on November 3. The United States essentially acted as a member, although it never joined what came to be called the Baghdad Pact.

The participants in the pact hoped that all or most of the Arab states would join this thinly disguised anti-Communist pact. The pact fulfilled many of Iraq's defense needs, while it also soothed Kurdish and Turcoman desires for better relations with Turkey and Shiah desires for cordial relations with Iran.

It could hardly have been more provocative, however, in the Arab world as Nasser had enjoyed major successes with his iconoclastic arms purchase from the Eastern Bloc and his full acceptance in the nonaligned movement. Nasser immediately branded Iraq's overt alignment with non-Arabs as an alliance with "colonialism" and its "stooges." Clearly, the pact offered a test of whether Baghdad or Cairo would shape foreign relations in the Arab world. Nasser's appeal and prestige with the Arab masses and military was such that no other Arab government dared join the Baghdad Pact. Instead, Nuri's government lost untold credibility domestically and throughout the Arab world for its dependence upon Western support. Iraq's new prosperity and the suppression of leftist elements, however, prevented Iraqis from showing their distaste for the Baghdad Pact.

JORDAN

Transjordan and Palestine

Out of necessity Transjordan outwardly supported the Arab League opposition to the partition of Palestine, but privately Abdullah hoped partition would occur. The British, the United States, and the Jewish Agency all knew his real desires and others suspected them. He ostensibly thought partition was the best answer to a bad problem, but actually he saw partition as the opportunity to annex the Arab portion of Palestine to his impecunious new kingdom.

Many circumstances made Abdullah's new vision quite feasible. The

Palestinians had no significant political, diplomatic, or military capability of their own to expel the Zionists from their land. Great Britain steadfastly opposed partition when the United Nations established a Jewish state and an Arab state on November 29, 1947 and within a month declared it would withdraw completely from Palestine by May 15. The British preferred the annexation of the Arab portion of Palestine to Transjordan rather than have it become independent under the leadership of Hajj Amin al-Husseini. The British had many ways of helping Abdullah position himself to achieve this limited objective on the condition that he refrain from entering the Jewish state. The Arab armies were weak and unable to commit their full strength to a war in Palestine without risking foreign invasion and internal uprisings. However much the Arab League states might dislike Abdullah and distrust his intentions, they would need his military forces to have any chance for success. Transjordan's 7,500-strong Arab Legion was a formidable force for the kind of confrontation expected in Palestine. It was well-led under British officers and its members knew the terrain of the areas of Palestine in which it would operate. In addition, Abdullah had a long-standing relationship with the Jewish Agency, which would trust his word, his limitations, and British pressure to conduct the war on a limited basis for limited objectives.

Uncharacteristically, Abdullah played his strong hand so well that even his enemies could find little fault with his entry into and early conduct of the war. Indicative of his new stature in the Arab world as it faced its greatest challenge, the Arab League held its final planning session in Amman on May 13 and declared Abdullah the commander of their joint effort, although there never was, in fact, a combined army or centralized command. Arab Legion troops saw the first action of the Arab League states. They clashed with Zionist settlers of the Gush Etzion Bloc, south of Jerusalem, throughout May and forced its surrender on May 14, one day before the other Arab armies crossed into Palestine. This proved to be the only loss of colonies the Zionists experienced during the war.

Arab League armies did not invade until May 15 when the mandate officially ended and the British withdrew. Their entry simply escalated a war that was already several months old. By that time the Zionists had already achieved many of their military and political objectives and had sent approximately 300,000 Palestinian Arabs to flight along the same roads the Arab armies were trying to use. The Arab Legion immediately faced both a military and political problem because of the fighting in Jerusalem. According to the United Nations partition plan, Jerusalem and a considerable area around it was supposed to become an international city. Heavy fighting occurred there, however, because both the Israelis and the Palestinian Arabs wanted Jerusalem as their capital. Although Abdullah and Glubb Pasha, the British commander of the Arab Legion, were under strict British orders to confine their military activities to land of the proposed Arab state, they could not sit safely by and watch Jerusalem fall to the Israelis without suffering the opprobrium of the entire Arab and Muslim world. The Arab Legion joined the battle of Jerusalem and was able to retain control of the Old City. Its other major area of combat was related to the battle of Jerusalem because the Israelis attacked Latrun in the Arab state in an effort to secure a corridor from Jaffa to Jerusalem. In this confrontation, the Arab Legion was successful, but the level of combat nearly exhausted its limited ammunition. For the remainder of the war the Arab Legion was in little condition for combat because of political constraints and a lack of ammunition.

The Arab world had to regard Abdullah as a hero when a truce on June 11 ended the fighting. His legion had saved the Old City and its two major sacred mosques. No land his army defended fell into Israeli hands. By contrast, no other Arab army had acquitted itself with any distinction and none other, except the Egyptian, had demonstrated any zeal for the cause. Besides all of this, Abdullah's army, along with the small Iraqi contingent, held the area designated for an Arab state, except for eastern Galilee, which fit best with Transjordan.

The heads of state in Egypt, Saudi Arabia, and Iraq feted King Abdullah for his accomplishments when he visited them during the truce. Even as they did so, they began to maneuver to prevent him from realizing any territorial gains from his efforts. He alone seemed satisfied with the truce and desired it to continue until there could be a final peace settlement. Count Folke Bernadotte, the United Nations mediator, proposed a solution that pleased Abdullah because it would have attached the Arab portion of Palestine to Transjordan as he had suggested for some years.

That was not the least reason fighting resumed on July 9. Also, popular opinion in the Arab states could not accept the loss of any Palestinian land to Israel, which had also conquered considerable land beyond the areas the United Nations assigned it. Because of its ammunition shortage, the Arab Legion had no choice but to withdraw from both Lydda and Ramla, and put its limited resources into the defense of Latrun. Most of the Arab world regarded the abandonment of these two strategic and populous towns as treachery for which they held Abdullah and Glubb accountable. A United Nations truce after ten days of fighting prevented encounters, especially around Jerusalem, that might have led to additional losses.

Despite the Arab Legion's setback, the other Arab armies did not fare as well. Israel obtained virtual control of all of Galilee against Syrian, Lebanese, and Arab Liberation Army forces. It made considerable advances against Egypt's army near Gaza and south of Hebron. The Iraqis did not fight. Although embarrassed, the Arab Legion still had most of the land, including the Old City, it had before hostilities renewed on July 9. Abdullah, who was always an easy target for criticism, got verbal abuse from throughout the Arab world. There were even considerable demonstrations in Transjordanian towns that required force to subdue. Palestinians, in particular, expressed contempt for Abdullah and became convinced that the Arab Legion's failures were part of a Zionist-British plot that Abdullah carried out.

Since a state of war still existed, the situation in Palestine remained fluid. Arab hopes rested on international insistence on compliance with the United Nations resolution to prevent Israel from keeping its conquests. Arab League members and most Palestinians held the same attitudes toward Transjordanian acquisitions. The Palestinians tried to strengthen their case when Hajj Amin al-Husseini announced the formation of a Government of All-Palestine in the safety of Egyptian-held Gaza on September 20, 1948. This was a direct challenge to Abdullah, who responded with a hastily called conference of his Palestinian supporters in Amman that endorsed the union of Palestine and Transjordan under Abdullah's rule. In December he gathered nearly 3,000 Palestinians at Jericho that reiterated the earlier endorsement of the "King of All Palestine" with the added acknowledgement that he was the also the legitimate king of Greater Syria. The immediate threat of Hajj Amin's All-Palestinian government ended when Egypt lost a renewed stage of war with Israel for control of the Negev from October 15, 1948 through January 7, 1949. Egypt agreed to an armistice at that time and entered formal negotiations with Israel under U.N. auspices on the island of Rhodes.

The Armistice and After

The Egyptian-Israeli armistice essentially ended the war except for Israel's continued quest to establish control over a port facility on the northern tip of the Gulf of Aqaba. This put Israel on a collision course with both Great Britain and Transjordan even though the U.N. partition plan included it in an Israeli state. Many, including the larger international community, believed Israeli acquisitions in Galilee during the war obviated its claims to the entire Negev and Aqaba. Transjordan was the only Arab nation in a position to contest Israel's move to Aqaba, but it was totally incapable of deterring a significant Israeli force without overt British assistance. Enough British troops moved into Aqaba to establish a presence that would make an Israeli conquest awkward if not impossible. The Arab Legion forces in the region were too few to deter the two Israeli columns that moved toward Aqaba from early in March. The Legion withdrew and Israel pushed its border adjacent to Aqaba, which the British held to provide Transjordan with an outlet to the sea.

Transjordan had joined the official armistice negotiations at Rhodes on February 28, four days after the formal Egyptian-Israeli armistice. Israel had no interest in serious negotiation at that time because it enjoyed an overwhelming military advantage on every front and still had to establish a port at Aqaba. The real negotiations occurred on Transjordanian soil at Shuna, where, under duress and threat of Israeli attack, Abdullah agreed to cede vital Arab land around the West Bank towns of Jenin and Tulkarm.

Israel and Transjordan signed their armistice on April 3 and set off widespread violence on the West Bank, where the residents believed the armistice represented the latest chapter in the Zionist-British-Hashemite conspiracy. Indeed, the plight of most Palestinians was dire. Of the nearly 700,000 Palestinian refugees the war produced, more than 500,000 took refuge in land under Transjordanian control. About 100,000 actually moved to the East Bank to increase Transjordan's population to over 500,000. Thus, the population under Transjordanian care nearly tripled, because the nonrefugee population of the West Bank was close to 450,000.

Transjordan was different and drastically in disarray. Most Palestinians wanted their own state, while a few were content to be part of Transjordan. Others still wanted to be part of a Greater Syrian state. None accepted the creation of the state of Israel, which held the land and former livelihood of the refugees and more than 130,000 Palestinian Arabs. Only through the help of the United Nations Relief and Works Agency could Transjordan even provide the bare necessities to most of the refugees. All Palestinians received citizenship in Transjordan in February 1949, more than a year before Abdullah formally annexed the West Bank and officially took the title of King of Jordan on April 25, 1950.

The additional land and population increased the assets of the Hashemite realm, but it remained impecunious. The limited funds it could generate internally and from abroad favored the East Bank to add to the dissatisfaction of the West Bank. Since all permits for trade, business, and building emanated from Amman, only those in good standing with the regime could prosper. Needless to say, the same held true for all government positions. An attempt to establish parliamentary government that followed a heated election in April 1950 ended within a year because the Palestinian majority could not accept Hashemite policies.

Part of Abdullah's problem stemmed from knowledge that he and his highest ministers engaged in serious secret negotiations with the Israelis for two years after the armistice. The disdain for his treachery would have been no less if his dissatisfied subjects had known that much of his effort revolved around an attempt to gain access to a Mediterranean port as a means of improving Jordan's ability to trade with the west without having to use the cumbersome overland routes through Syria and Lebanon. None of his reasons could have satisfied the other Arab League members who resented his annexation of the West Bank. He remained a constant threat to break Arab solidarity against anything short of a comprehensive peace that would repatriate the refugees to their lands in Palestine.

Abdullah had saved considerable Arab land from Israeli occupation but neither the Palestinians nor the other Arab states and populations considered this accomplishment laudable. They could not regard him for what he was: an old Ottoman, who believed in the art of the possible; and an Arab nationalist, who had made a step toward uniting the Levant.

In both these roles he regarded all situations as transitory. This same man had grasped the opportunity to govern an impoverished Transjordan on a temporary basis and eventually gained the status of king. Abdullah had doggedly adhered close enough to British policies to gain their assistance in acquiring the West Bank, even though his military forces were inadequate to accomplish that task against a concerted Israeli resistance. He was always on the verge of being cast out of the Arab community of nations, but he had served as its titular leader in the war against Israel. Albeit begrudgedly, even most Palestinians came to accept him as their only viable ruler. Until his death, he always referred to all parts of the Levant as separate entities that, in time, must in an almost dialectical process evolve into its inevitable form as a single Arab state. He always made sure that his Arab brethren understood his willingness to lead that state.

Those who were willing to follow his leadership remained the few around him who benefited from his largess. His death at the age of sixty-nine was as much an enigma as his life had been. Plenty of witnesses saw the young tailor fatally shoot him at midday on July 20, 1951 as he approached al-Aqsa mosque in Jerusalem for the Friday prayers. So many individuals, groups, and nations resented him, however, that the number of suspects behind the plot include almost every person, group, and nation his life touched. Regardless of the reason he died, there was no noticeable alteration in the development of Jordan or the Middle East because of his death.

Abdullah's son, Talal, succeeded his father, although the two had been estranged for much of Talal's adult life. Abdullah's secret exclusion of his son from succession to the throne for many years was surprisingly unrelated to Talal's mental instability. The heir apparent's affinity for Arab nationalism, exclusive of Hashemite leadership, was a major cause of their differences. When, therefore, Abdullah's old advisers dethroned Talal within a year of his assuming the throne, rumors spread that Talal's Arab nationalism made him unacceptable. Medical evidence and testimony of his insanity could not satisfy those who saw Talal as the latest martyr for Arab nationalism. Talal's son, Hussein, soon demonstrated that he had many of the same survival skills of his grandfather, when he assumed the title and throne the former interloper from the Hijaz had created.

Hussein in Power

Hussein was still too young to reign when his father, Talal, was deposed on August 11, 1952 and he did not assume full powers until May 2, 1953. His tender age, alone, was adequate challenge for the new eighteen-year-old monarch, but the intense fervor of Arab nationalism under the leadership of Gamal Abded Nasser in Egypt could not wait for him to mature. Few, even among his military and administrative leaders, believed that either he or his tiny, penniless kingdom would survive. Few, in fact, could make a good case for Jordan's survival as an independent nation. It was, after all, dependent upon British financial and military assistance to meet its minimal needs. Large segments, arguably a majority of its citizens, sought citizenship in its own Palestinian state, or in Syria, or in an even larger Arab state that defied the European-imposed borders. The monarchy of Jordan appeared to be an empty title connected to a hopelessly impoverished land that remained unable to function as a modern state.

Ironically, the acquisition of the West Bank, which included the Old City of Jerusalem, weakened the Hashemite kingdom. The unification tripled Jordan's population, but nearly one-third of the new citizens were destitute and angry refugees who were within a cannon shot of their former homes. Much of the other third, composed of the 400,000 West Bank residents, felt betrayed as they became affiliated with the East Bank Hashemite regime. The challenge was even greater because no part of the newly created kingdom had access to the Mediterranean ports that had always connected Palestine and Transjordan to the rest of the world for travel and trade. The tiny outlet to the seas at Aqaba could never provide a substitute and it was totally undeveloped for international trade and tourism, as well as unconnected to the remainder of the kingdom with roads and other supporting infrastructure.

The constitution prevented any relief a dictatorial approach might offer. More than 300,000 of the nearly 1,400,000 citizens had the right to vote. The generally hostile West Bank actually had a majority of the eligible voters, but it, like the East Bank, which also contained a considerable number of Palestinians, could only elect twenty representatives to the Chamber of Deputies. In short, in a free election, the Palestinians could elect enough members to parliament to either shape policies contrary to Hashemite inclinations or cause a debilitating stalemate. Also, in conjunction with East Bank Arab nationalists, the Palestinians could vote Jordan out of existence and unite it with another Arab country. A constitutional amendment in January 1954 allowed a simply majority of the Chamber of Deputies, rather than the former two-thirds, to pass a no confidence vote against the cabinet.

The young king, who was sensitive to Palestinian concerns and Arab nationalist aspirations, also had a firm commitment to preserving the kingdom his beloved grandfather had created. If these were not challenge enough, he remained firmly under British tutelage and had to avoid military confrontation with his powerful Israeli neighbor. There is little wonder that hardly anyone believed he could preserve either his throne or his kingdom.

Following the alarming constitutional change in January 1954, the government dissolved all political parties and arrested or drove major political leaders into exile in order to achieve a favorable parliament in the October elections. The United States demonstrated its first interest in the fate of Jordan during this period when it extended $8,000,000 in aid in June. Jordan thus became the first Arab nation to receive American financial assistance. To placate the population the Jordanian government announced a Five-Year-Plan in November that projected the expenditure of $200 million in development projects.

Baghdad Pact Crisis

The revelation in December 1954 that Iraq was negotiating a mutual defense agreement with Turkey ignited riots and demonstrations in Amman and other major Jordanian towns. These outbreaks demonstrated widespread concern that Jordan might also join this British-sponsored diplomatic development that evolved into the Baghdad Pact. Britain, in fact, offered Jordan a significant increase in its subsidy as an inducement for it to join. In response to the public outcry, however, the cabinet resigned on December 19 and the king dissolved parliament. Arab nationalists and leftists openly called for an abrogation of the treaty with Britain and acceptance of aid from Egypt, Syria, and Saudi Arabia. Some called for union of Jordan with Syria, while a smaller element in the Maan region advocated union with Saudi Arabia. The atmosphere of national suicide was not conducive for others to speak out on behalf of Jordan remaining Jordan.

The respected statesman, Samir al-Rifai, formed a cabinet on January 9, 1955 that declared martial law and restored order. Many did not trust his pledge not to join the Baghdad Pact, because he did not pursue an alternative to the British subsidy. There was strong belief that Britain would demand adherence to the pact in return for the essential funds. These major questions remained the central concern in Jordan throughout the year as the pact developed to include Iran and Pakistan by the fall. Nasser took the initiative in opposing it with the outspoken support of Syria and Saudi Arabia. All resented any Hashemite initiative, especially since it occurred under British and American guidance. General Gerald Templer's mission to Amman from December 6 to December 14 indicated Britain's commitment to pressuring Jordan into compliance with the pact. New riots on December 16 and 17 led to the cabinet's resignation but did not clarify the intentions of the Jordanian government.

The anti-Baghdad Pact riots of January 6 and 7, 1956 proved to be a turning point in Jordanian history, as the army under General Glubb suppressed the riots with unusual severity. Prior to this, most could regard Glubb as a loyal instrument of the Hashemite throne. After this, however, he appeared to be a well-ensconced guarantee of continued British domination. Hussein's opponents portrayed him as little more than a British viceroy who relied on British officers in command of a native levy to implement British policies. Since this was the main theme of Cairo's "Voice of the Arabs," others felt comfortable in echoing these accusations. Glubb had become a liability to the king, whatever his contributions had been for the previous twenty-five years.

The strong possibility existed that both the king and his kingdom would cease to exist in the new atmosphere of the Arab world. Continued British financial support seemed increasingly untenable and Jordan was untenable without financial support, which simply did not exist within the Arab world.

SYRIA

Coups and Constitution in Syria

Recently independent and inexperienced in military matters, Syria was in no condition to fight a war in 1948. France had provided Syrian military protection and leadership for a generation under the mandate. The Syrian army, which was largely composed of minorities, had served as auxiliaries to the French and, even in that capacity, had seen no action. By contrast, the even newer state of Israel had a large army, a central command, and overseas sources of men, money, and materiel. The Syrian brigade of less that 2,000 men, therefore, had marginal military capacity when it entered the Palestinian war in the eastern Galilee theater in 1948. It acquitted itself as well as possible in the limited role it tried to play against the Israelis, but suffered defeat and dishonor. As in other Arab states, the Syrian army and the public blamed their government, Arab disunity, and western Great Power policies for the humiliation in Palestine.

Discontent over Syria's performance in Palestine, along with a sense of isolation and insecurity, set off a series of government changes through military coups. Colonel Husni Zaim, the army chief-of-staff, suppressed the antigovernment riots that erupted in December 1949 and then seized power for himself and the army on March 30. Initially, large portions of the population supported Zaim. His apparent inclination to affiliate with Iraq provided part of his appeal, especially to the Aleppo-centered People's Party (Populist), whose leaders had strong economic ties with Mosul and Baghdad. Baathists, Akram Hourani of the Arab Socialist party, and other secularist elements embraced Zaim's declarations for modern approaches, including the franchise for women.

Zaim quickly switched, however, to the anti-Hashemite camp of Egypt and Saudi Arabia, which was closely associated with the United States. His suppression of all political parties and unfavorable newspapers, along with his resort to martial law further alienated most of his original supporters. Zaim seemed particularly tainted for the terms he accepted in the armistice with Israel and for turning over Antun Sa'ada, founder and leader of the Syrian National Party, to Lebanon for execution.

Under the leadership of Colonel Sami Hinnawi, elements of the army overthrew and killed Zaim on August 14. Hashim al-Atasi became interim president and the Populists dominated the new constituent assembly, which actively pursued establishing a constitutional approach to union with Iraq. Most Syrians, civilian and military alike, opposed both Zaim's close tie to the west and Hinnawi's gravitation toward Baghdad. Foremost among them was Akram Hourani, who, as leader of the peasant-based Arab Socialist Party, was the most influential electoral politician in Syria. His friend, Colonel Adib Shishakli, overthrew Hinnawi on December 19 to place Syria on an independent course, unaffiliated with either America's influence over Egypt and Saudi Arabia or British influence over Iraq.

Shishakli's Rule

Although Shishakli's regime developed into a dictatorship, it began with an open debate among Syria's various factions to define a modern republic. No other Arab state had such an opportunity, as all were monarchies except Lebanon, which was a closely held oligarchy. By the time the new constitution emerged on September 5, 1950 it kept Syria's governmental structure essentially as it had been in the constitution of 1930. Other portions of the document, however, revealed the socially conscious influence of Hourani, who was an Arab nationalist of long standing, as well as a strong advocate of individual dignity and freedom.

These unique features, which were never implemented, nevertheless established Syria's claim as the leader of the modern Arab world and inspired reformers in other Arab nations. The constitution defined a nation devoid of large landowners through land redistribution. All citizens had the right to work under conditions that provided them security, dignity, education, health care, and appropriate housing. The nation obtained ownership over natural resources such as water, minerals, and forests. The parliament followed by nationalizing foreign-owned businesses and utilities. Foreigners could only conduct business in Syria in conjunction with Syrian partners. Syria withdrew from the restricting customs union with Lebanon and France. Large irrigation and marsh draining projects began under government sponsorship and financing. While most Syrians welcomed these policies, a strong coalition of large landowners, businessmen, and their foreign supporters found them threatening.

Likewise, Syria's foreign policy threatened regional and Western governments by example, rather than because of Syria's ability to marshall overt political, economic, or military forces. Syrians and other Arabs found the Shishakli government's militant opposition to the United States and Israel laudable. Khalid al-Azem, the prime minister, made favorable relations with other nations dependent upon support for restoration of Palestinians to the land they had lost to Israel. The popularity of Damascus's uncompromising stance made other Arab governments hesitant to accept western aid or join in anti-Communist pacts of the Cold War. Syria even overtly courted the Soviet Union as a better ally than the traditional colonial powers and their new leader, the United States. Frequent congruity between Syrian and Eastern Bloc foreign policies, however, did not diminish a general hostility of the government and public opinion toward communism. Al-Azem was an inveterate capitalist, but for political reasons he was the foremost proponent of close relations with the Soviets. The Muslim Brotherhood's leadership role in advocating a favorable relationship with the Soviet Union is perhaps the best indication that Syria's tilt to the Soviet bloc was the result of nationalist frustration, rather than ideological affinity.

Although Shishakli had made the coup, he did not hold office but allowed the republic, including President al-Atasi, to remain in office. Indeed, he was never comfortable with the increasingly socialist trend of domestic policies under Hourani's influence or the anti-Western foreign policy of Al-Azem. Under Hourani's influence, if not his leadership, an organized restlessness among Syria's rural population threatened the traditional structure of Syria's land ownership, as well as its political and social structure. Perhaps even more disturbing to him was the persistent inclination of some cabinet ministers, members of parliament, and sectors of the population to merge with Iraq. Shishakli and his followers preferred an independent course with a strong leaning toward Egypt and Saudi Arabia.

Indications that the cabinet intended to establish civilian control over the army and gendarmerie in late November 1951 prompted Shishakli to arrest the cabinet and other high officials. He allowed the untouchable President al-Atasi to resign. Still, Shishakli governed through a surrogate, Colonel Fawzi Salu, who held the principal portfolios. Syria became an unmitigated military dictatorship that abolished parliament and political parties, put the press and universities under government control, prohibited worker and student strikes, and drastically reduced normal cultural and economic relations with other nations. Shishakli relied on support from the big industrialists and landowners to make his repressive, fascist-style approach prove it could strengthen the Syrian economy and state.

Shishakli's End

Shishakli finally obtained his "election" as president on July 10, 1953, when the intimidated electorate also approved his new constitution. The fact that his party, the Arab Liberation Movement, was the only one fully free to campaign, assured his candidates nearly 90 percent of the seats in the October 9 elections for a new legislature. Six months before the presidential election he had purged his opposition from the army and arrested several leftist leaders. Akram Hourani and the two Baath party founders, Michel Aflaq and Salah al-Bitar, fled to Lebanon to avoid incarceration.

Despite Shishakli's repression, traditional political leaders retained boldness for independent action and some support in the Syrian army. Of this group, only the Syrian National Party had accepted the regime's restrictions and deigned to participate in the parliamentary elections. With strong support from Muslim religious leaders, the other parties held their own National Congress in Homs a week before the presidential election. Strangely, the regime the congress labeled as "tyrannical" allowed the congress to finish its business without impediment. Indeed, the regime not only permitted additional, fairly open political activities on the part of its opponents, it also released some political prisoners and allowed Hourani, Aflaq, and Bitar to return from exile.

Widespread protest in Aleppo in December 1953 signaled the end of Shishakli's regime. The government used heavy reprisals, numerous arrests, including that of former president al-Atasi, and martial law in certain regions in an attempt to restore order. A Druze uprising required major military effort that irretrievably turned that significant minority against Shishakli. A general mutiny in the army originated in Aleppo on February 25, 1954 under the leadership of Colonel Mustafa Hamdoun. Shishakli escaped to Lebanon and made his way to Brazil, where a Druze assassinated him in 1964 in retaliation for his brutality against his kinsmen.

The Struggle of Constitutionalism

The return to constitutional government indicated the appeal, if not the necessity, of dictatorship. Most successful candidates ran for office without any party affiliation. Much of the population that did not vote for independents, or for the National or Populist parties, had strong leftist or Arab nationalist inclinations. Although the National and the Populist parties represented much the same socioeconomic strata and could elect close to a majority, they could not work together, primarily because the National party leaned toward Egypt and the Arab League, while the Populist party, with its base in Aleppo and Homs, continued to favor union with Iraq. Socialists, Baathists, and Communists had growing appeal among the masses, but could not work together and found participation in the cabinets of the larger parties awkward. The Syrian National Party and the Muslim Brotherhood had unique agendas that precluded their easy relationship with other parties. The government that emerged, therefore, hardly had a mandate for a particular direction when it took office in October, 1954. It did, however, have the distinction of being the result of the most legitimate nationwide election in the Arab world. Hashim al-Atasi returned to finish his term as president, while the Populist party and independents filled most of the cabinet positions.

Regional concerns dominated both domestic and diplomatic developments under the new government. Nasser, for instance, had just consolidated his control in Egypt and had gained British consent to withdraw all of their forces from Egypt by 1956. His concern that Iraq was on the verge of becoming the regional leader impelled him to counter all Iraqi initiatives with his own. Most crucial in this regard was Nasser's opposition to the emerging Baghdad Pact, which he and other Arab nationalists regarded as a "betrayal of Arabism" and an alliance with imperialists. The Populist party found the Baghdad Pact appealing otherwise, because it satisfied their long-standing desire to affiliate with Iraq and establish better relations with Turkey. Endorsement of the pact, however, would have brought opprobrium from its domestic opposition and much of the Arab world, which was falling increasingly under Nasser's influence. There was, however, strong opposition to Nasser in Syria for his ousting General Neguib and suppressing the Muslim Brotherhood, which moved its headquarters to Syria. The Populist's inability to bring themselves to deny one of their main tenets led to their leaving the government to make way for a coalition of traditional opponents of union with Baghdad.

Turn to the Left

In the new government of Sabry al-Asali, a Nationalist, the policies of Khalid al-Azem were most notable. As Foreign and Defense Minister, he aggressively pursued a pro-Soviet policy in trade and military affairs. Syria, thus, was the leading Arab country in seeking aid from the Eastern Bloc, while Nasser was still pursuing the possibility of an Arab Collective Security Pact under American sponsorship. Al-Azem actually purchased military equipment from East Germany in December 1954, and soon thereafter obtained a pledge of Soviet assistance against Turkish or Iraqi attacks against Syria. Al-Azem's appreciation of the latent strength of the Populists and their pro-Iraqi posture caused him to be more cautious in considering a military pact with Egypt, which Nasser continued to suggest.

Syria, during this brief period of al-Asali's premiership, developed further credentials for independence of action. Unlike other Arab states, it refused to flirt with any of the western nations, despite being besieged by hostility from them, as well as from Iraq and Turkey. Arab nationalists admired Syria no less because it had neither the military nor economic ability even to defend itself without considerable help from some outside force. Syria's relentless, even brutal, reprisals against the Syrian National Party in the spring of 1955 demonstrated its commitment to annihilate anything that appeared even remotely pro-Western. The anti-SNP campaign created a furor in Syria and throughout the Arab world that more radical elements, especially the Baathists, thrived upon. Whenever large numbers took to the streets to demonstrate, they were usually knowingly or unknowingly under the influence of the Baath and their rivals, the Communists. The fever pitch of Syrian politics spilled over into other Arab countries and made politics under the traditional politicians, practiced in traditional ways, difficult.

Return of the Old Order

Syria was, however, a republic. It had demonstrated this fact at different times, despite its complexity and its bout with military dictatorship. The scheduled presidential election of September 5, 1955 presented the possibility of a new direction. Since the legislature chose the president, the traditional politicians had the opportunity to prevail, because "the street," where the Baathists and other radicals dominated, would have little influence. Populists and Nationalists disagreed on many policies, but they generally agreed that Syria under al-Asali and al-Azem's guidance was contrary to their fundamental desire to retain something of the status quo before it became too late.

The Populists, who remained the largest party, returned to power after seven months because of their support for Shukri al-Quwatly's successful bid for the presidency. Al-Quwatly was a National party member who had lived in Egypt since Zaim's coup. He shared more of the Populist views than his opponent, Khalid al-Azem, who was a vehement anti-Westerner.

Al-Quwatly had no strong agenda of his own and the Populists accompanied him in a pragmatic course that ignored the Baghdad Pact. Syria's conclusion of a mutual defense pact with Egypt on October 20, 1955 and an economic pact with Saudi Arabia on November 9, however, was a clear veto of Nuri al-Said's Baghdad Pact. Interestingly, the Populists had criticized the former government for considering the same alliances. Syria, thus, traded peace with Nasser for the enmity of Iraq and Turkey. The difficult choice satisfied more of the Arab nationalists than any other decision could have. This was especially true after the Israelis killed fifty-six Syrians in a raid on the southern border on December 11, 1955. The raid, and the earlier Israeli raid on Egyptian-held Gaza at the end of February, demonstrated general Arab vulnerability, which only collective action and additional weapons could eliminate.

Weak and fractious Syria was an inspiration to Arab nationalists. In many respects, it seemed to be dying. However, in a region where defiance of the West had become the new standard for measuring virtue, Syria had no equal.

LEBANON

Fractious Lebanon

Al-Khoury's administration proved to be less satisfactory than many had expected, given his long years of even-handed cooperation with different Lebanese factions. His favoritism to his family and closest supporters drove most political leaders to opposition against him. Their worst fears came true in 1947 when a favorable chamber, whose composition many believed he had illegally shaped, amended the constitution to allow al-Khoury a second term in office. The miserable showing of Lebanon, along with the other Arab armies, in the 1948 Palestinian war did nothing to improve al-Khoury's image. His acceptance of 150,000 Palestinian refugees softened the impact on some who would have otherwise demonstrated dissatisfaction. Failure in Palestine caused a coup in Syria in 1949 that the Syrian Nationalist Party attempted to duplicate in Lebanon. It failed and Riad al-Sulh specifically ordered the arrest and execution of Antun Sa'ada. Al-Sulh's assassination by a member of the Syrian Nationalist Party in 1951 deprived the president of his most helpful minister and the Muslims of their most respected leader.

The opposition coalesced around the leadership of a Maronite, Kamil Shamoun, and a Druze, Kamal Jumblat, both of whom were from the Shuf. It included Sunni and Shiah Muslims, Phalangists, the deceased Edde's former followers, and the Syrian Nationalist Party. Jumblat, whose family in Mukhtara had been in the forefront of Druze affairs for centuries, formed a separate Progressive Socialist Party in 1949. This unprecedented cross-section of confessions and ideologies called itself the Socialist Front, but its basic bond was opposition to al-Khoury's excluding them from the fruits of office. The Front's call for a general strike on September 16, 1952 forced al-Khoury from office, whereupon the Chamber elected Shamoun as president on September 23.

Ominously, Nasser's coup had occurred in Egypt two months before Shamoun became president of Lebanon. The ramifications of Nasser's rise to prominence in Arab affairs added uncontrollable external complications for Shamoun, who soon experienced enough internal problems to tax his abilities. Initially, however, Shamoun successfully improved relations with all his Arab neighbors and the great powers, while he made commendable administrative changes in Lebanon and increased the prosperity that had begun under al-Khoury. His policies won him widespread support from Lebanon's business community and among the masses. His exclusion from office of his former partners in the Socialist Front, however, created dissatisfaction among the political *zaims* who organized another opposition coalition.

Even though they had jointly founded the Socialist Front, Jumblat and Shamoun were political rivals, because Shamoun's political strength was centered in the Jumblat-dominated Shuf. Their cooperation to decrease al-Khoury's personal power ended once Shamoun obtained office and behaved like the former president and neither offered Jumblat a ministerial position nor sought his advice. Jumblat's largely personal pique impelled him to join Muslims and alienated Maronites against Shamoun.

Maronite leaders who opposed Shamoun had little in common ideologically with Jumblat and the Muslims, but they also resented exclusion from office and influence. Al-Khoury, Henri Faroun, Hamid Franjieh, Charles Hilou, and Nasim Majdalani were Shamoun's most important Maronite critics. The new Maronite patriarch, Paul Meouchy, who was an Al-Khoury supporter, enhanced the opposition's stature much to Shamoun's embarrassment. Illustrious as this group was, it would have been ineffective without Druze and Muslim support.

In 1954, Muslim leaders articulated substantial reasons for resenting Shamoun's administration and the entire structure of the Lebanese government and society. Lebanon's growing prosperity emphasized the economic and educational disparity between the Christians and the Muslims. The Muslims correlated the connection between Christian political power and financial success. Christian presidents, indeed, had rewarded their Christian supporters with lucrative government positions and contracts; Christian areas enjoyed better roads, schools, and other public services. Monetary and technological contributions from foreign Christian missionaries, and monetary remittances from the thousands of Maronite emigrants living abroad further widened the gap.

Muslims began to demand changes to reduce Christian advantages. Foremost in their demands was abolition of the distribution of offices by confessional allocation, and parity between the offices of president and prime minister. They also advocated reestablishment of the economic union with Syria, which al-Khoury had dissolved in 1950, and closer ties with the Arab world with a concomitant reduction of ties with the West. Muslims further demanded a new census that included the Palestinians to determine if the existing distribution of offices reflected Lebanon's actual population composition. The fact that coordinated Muslim discontent in Lebanon corresponded with Nasser's acquiring full authority in Egypt made it difficult to contain. The Muslims also enjoyed competent leadership from men such as Saib Salam, Rashid Karami, and Abdullah al-Yafi.

Shamoun's supporters, especially Pierre Gemayel, questioned both the motives and wisdom of the Muslim demands. They feared that Muslims really wanted to gain control and submerge Lebanon into a greater Arab state. They doubted that Muslims would give up their sectarian courts and submit to a secular judicial system. Provocatively, they agreed to accept a new census only on the condition that it include the thousands of mostly Maronite emigrants who lived abroad. This unusual proposal indicated the determination of strident Maronites to retain their unique role in Lebanon.

The problems of Lebanon were inextricably connected with the larger currents of the region, but the petty stage of Lebanon and the apparently petty and personal nature of the Lebanese disputes simply masked that reality. Lebanon's inconsequential military capacity allowed outside forces virtually to ignore Lebanese developments. Regardless of outside perceptions, the stakes were high for individual Lebanese and the many factions that heatedly contested to determine their role in Lebanon and Lebanon's role in the new pattern of the Middle East.

SAUDI ARABIA

Saudi Arabia's New Wealth and Prominence

The outbreak of World War II forestalled the development of Saudi financial capacity. Shipping lanes became unsafe for transporting either construction supplies or the end product, as well as the old standby of pilgrims to the Hijaz. Caltex continued to pay the annual rentals and extract a trickle of petroleum, but the resulting revenues failed to meet increased Saudi needs and expectations.

Great Britain's dire problems during the war enabled the United States to enhance its relationship with Saudi Arabia. In 1943 Saudi Arabia began to receive lend-lease funds, and the following year the United States government provided funds and allowed materials, which had formerly been needed for the war, to be used to develop Saudi oil production. Caltex changed its name to Arabian American Oil Company (Aramco) in 1944, but still found that it lacked the financial and marketing resources to develop fully its Saudi concession. With the encouragement of the U.S. government, Standard Oil of New Jersey and Mobil bought 30 percent and 10 percent, respectively, of Aramco's stock in March of 1947. The new funds and marketing capacity of Aramco dramatically increased production and the Kingdom's oil revenues grew from $10 million in 1946 to $50 million in 1949.

The increased Saudi income resulted from increased volume rather than from a larger share of Aramco profits. As Saudi officials became better informed about the international oil industry and pricing structure they also became dissatisfied with their Aramco arrangement. They negotiated a much higher share of the profits in 1949 from Aminoil and Great Western for the concession in the Saudi portion of the Neutral Zone. The Saudis were even more discontented when they learned that Venezuela was receiving 50 percent of the profits from her concessions. The U.S. State Department pressured Aramco to adopt the same profit split in a new agreement with Saudi Arabia on December 30, 1950. The combination of greater production and increased percentage of profits nearly doubled Saudi oil income from $57 million in 1950 to $110 million in 1951. By 1955 the Saudis further improved their share of the profits when they pressured Aramco to pay the 50 percent royalty of the higher price Aramco charged their customers, rather than the intermediate price they charged the companies of the cartel.

Ibn Saud's life was approaching its end by the time he gained the 50-50 split with Aramco. The new wealth presented problems that were understandably beyond his comprehension and weakened capacity to solve. The influx of great numbers of foreigners with their Western customs and technology, and Saudi involvement with international monetary systems, caused social and fiscal problems that even the most astute desert chieftain could be forgiven for finding difficult. By custom and nature Ibn Saud was generous with the members of his huge family and other members of the kingdom. As a result, his debts nearly equalled his oil revenues by 1952. U.S. fiscal advice through the Point Four program and better management of procurement for royal needs by a division of Aramco stabilized Saudi finances by the time Ibn Saud died on November 8, 1953.

Although Saud had been Crown Prince since 1933, he was not well acquainted with the affairs of the kingdom much beyond Nejd where he was viceroy. Unlike his brother, Feisal, he had travelled little outside of the kingdom except for a whirlwind tour of Arab capitals in 1953. He was equally unschooled on financial affairs and the oil industry upon which his country depended. His good intentions and the loyalty he had from the tribes because of his generosity were his only recommendations for the throne.

Once he became king, Saud became even more legendary for his luxurious life and extravagant beneficence. Palaces with all imaginable accouterments strained his income of over $230 million a year beyond his capacity to meet regular household expenses. Even the upkeep of his 107 children could not account for his squanderous excesses. The more responsible ministers who had served his father receded into the background to make way for men like Id bin Salem, a former mechanic, who advised Saud and controlled access to him. Under these circumstances, corruption became the rule rather than the exception in Saud's reign.

Saud's rise to power became even more difficult because it corresponded with Nasser's emergence as the quintessential Arab nationalist. Like other Arab leaders, Saud felt he had to appear to support Nasser's anti-Western policies. Saud, therefore, dismissed the American Point Four team, although he did not cancel the U.S. military base at Dhahran. While his actions against the U.S. might have been difficult, he had fewer qualms about supporting Nasser's anti-British activities. Saudi differences with Britain over Buraimi on the Abu Dhabi border had been brewing since 1949. The British also were closely allied to the Hashemite kingdoms of Iraq and Jordan, which Nasser and Saud mutually disliked. Consequently, Saud financially supported Nasser's anti-British campaign on all fronts and willingly lent his influence to prevent the extension of the Baghdad Pact to any Arab country other than Iraq.

IRAN

Mossadegh Triumphant in Iran

Shah Muhammad Reza appeared to be in a very strong position when the Sixth Majlis met in February 1950. His constitutional position was stronger, the Tudeh threat seemed past and his stated policies for reform and modernization seemed to preclude social unrest. There was a recognition that the landed elements' fear of the monarch's plans for land redistribution could cause conflict in the Majlis.

The fairly normal seven months of campaigning and certification produced the Sixteenth Majlis with a strong royalist majority. The new cabinet under Ali Mansur was the most royalist since Reza had left the throne. The royal influence in both the Majlis and the cabinet helped Muhammad Mossadegh attract a large following among the masses when he indefatigably pointed to the results of increased royal power. He said, as he had said many times in the past, that the monarch should reign, like the British monarch, but not rule. He and his tiny band of seven followers in the Majlis complained, as they had during the election, that the Majlis only reflected the will of the monarch and the privileged classes. He asserted that his loose confederation, called the National Front, represented the nation. Other National Front delegates voiced concern that the government and the Majlis favored large businesses over small business, landowners over peasants, irreligion over Islam, and fostered the growth of communism by their policies that increased class hatred. Ayatollah Kashani echoed similar sentiments from Beirut. Dire as these concerns were, the National Front made nationalization of Iran's oil the single issue they wished to emphasize in the Sixteenth Majlis. The overwhelming popular support in the nation for the small group's program led Mansur to resign without submitting the government's proposal for revising the British concession to the Majlis.

General Ali Razmara became the new premier with the shah's approval. The two of them had reconciled many of their differences as a result of the shah's efforts to improve the military. Razmara still had fairly substantial leftist credentials and made no secret of his continued affiliation with the Tudeh, although it was essentially an underground operation by the time he became premier. The Americans generally favored his appointment, since they believed he might carry out genuine reforms that the shah talked about but never implemented. Others agreed with the Americans and thought Razmara was the best hope for reform instead of revolution in Iran. His program went further than most moderates and the

United States preferred as he attacked corruption, raised the taxes on the upper classes, and began to redistribute crown lands. He improved relations with both the Soviet Union and the Tudeh to the point that some feared he would impose a socialist regime. His attempt to implement provincial assemblies raised the specter of a nation of soviets. His assassination by a member of the Fedaiyan-i Islam on March 7, 1951 met with widespread approval that ranged from the National Front, to the shah, to Washington. Of his many transgressions, Razmara's greatest deficiency was his insistence on revising, rather than revoking, Britain's oil concession. Nationalist fervor was not willing to accept Razmara's contention that Iran was not prepared to operate its own oil industry.

Mossadegh soon seized the initiative, during a short premiership of Hussein Ala, an anti-British landed aristocrat. Ala was in office long enough, however, to approve Kashani's return from Beirut. Mossadegh, who was a recognized authority on the oil question, chose March 8, the day following Razmara's assassination, to introduce a bill to nationalize Iran's oil. After the Majlis passed it unanimously on March 15 an observer remarked "Eight grams of powder did this" and Hussein Makki, the secretary of the National Front, said "This is one of the greatest days in the history of the Iranian nation." In the heated atmosphere of martial law, the Senate unanimously approved nationalization on March 20, which was New Year's Eve and the beginning of a three-week recess for the holiday. Impatience that Iran did not immediately take over operation of the oil industry following the legislative vote gave Tudeh an opportunity to reenter public affairs. Tudeh led strikes and demonstrations that aroused new concerns for class warfare. Ala attempted to maintain order by martial law. Contrary to Ala's desire, the Majlis and the Senate passed the final nationalization bill, with provisions for its implementation, on April 28. Ala resigned, and without a prior approval from the shah, the Majlis voted Mossadegh into the premiership on April 29 for the specific purpose of implementing the nationalization law. Huge May Day demonstrations by the Tudeh and celebrations of Mossadegh's triumph influenced the shah to approve nationalization and procedures for implementing nationalization on May 2.

The responsibility of the premiership was unusual for Mossadegh, who had been prominent in Iranian politics since the 1920s, but usually as an outspoken critic of both the monarchy and the government. He had, however, held cabinet positions for brief periods. His uniqueness was legendary in several different areas. No other premier, for instance, had led two *basts* onto the palace grounds on behalf of free elections as he had in 1947 and 1949. The committed constitutionalist had a doctorate in law from a Swiss university. A fervent nationalist, Mossadegh spurned all affiliation with foreign interests. His vast wealth came from his inherited estates rather than from taking advantage of his political prominence to steal or take bribes. This fourth largest landowner in Iran treated his own peasants well and consistently championed the cause of both the peasants and workers, while he lambasted the landlords and large capitalists. Even his critics could agree that Dr. Mossadegh was undoubtedly both incorruptible and a patriot. All could also agree that he had always been inflexible. This characteristic, which is becoming in a professional opposition member, could be a serious flaw if it persisted in a premier whose following was less than 5 percent of the legislature.

The National Front was a loose confederation that had emerged from the groups Mossadegh led in a *bast* on the palace grounds in October 1949. It remained loose in structure and ideology by design, as Mossadegh envisioned it as a nucleus that members of almost all other groups, except the most intransigent royalists and aristocrats, could join. It was first and foremost a nationalist movement, which was also anti-British, antimonarchist, antifeudal, and antimilitary. Most elements of the National Front embraced some form of socialism, but since all were avowedly Muslims, they rejected the secularism and atheism of many socialist ideologies. The aversion of the numerous religious elements to Marxism, and their commitment to the sanctity of private property, made their enduring affiliation with the National Front problematical. A strong coterie of middle-class intellectuals gave the Front direction, but its strength came from its ability to rally the masses into the streets, especially in Tehran. Religious traditionalists among the bazaari merchants and workers heeded the fiery rhetoric of Ayatollah Kashani and the strong-armed courage of athletes such as Shayban the Brainless. Tudeh joined in and gave the emotional and flamboyant Mossadegh a street following unmatched in previous Iranian experience.

The actual parties that comprised the heart of the National Front were not impressive for their numerical strength. Each possessed, however, a *raison d'etre* that most Iranians could respect and follow. Their nationalism alone was appealing to a nation that had been under some kind of foreign tutelage for most of the time for more than a century. Mossadegh's own Iran Party provided most of the direction for the movement. The Toilers shared the Iran Party's views, but was both more religious and more leftist than either Mossadegh or the Iran Party. The tiny Pan-Iranist Party was distinctive from the others with its vision of expanding Iran's boundaries to gather all Persian speakers under the national flag. Kashani's Society of Muslim Warriors advocated a full restoration of Islamic practice and strongly opposed the secular innovations that had become widespread in Iran through the Constitutional Movement and the reign of Reza Shah. The dramatic assassinations of Razmara, former prime minister Abdul Hussein Hezhir, and the historian Ahmad Kasravi, were all the work of the Fedaiyan-i Islam, who took orders from no one and scared everyone, including the *ulama*. Kashani was caught in the middle between the well-connected, educated *ulama* and the Islamic assassins. His motivations were always more strongly anti-British, however, than in support of a particular ideology. Kashani hated the British, who had killed his father and had expelled him from his native Iraq for his opposition to secular constitutionalism. Kashani arose to defend the interests of the bazaar and perished into obscurity after he had done all he could.

Ownership without Profits

The British slowly discovered that nationalization was a reality and not a negotiating ploy. The nationalist fervor in Iran militated against anything short of full Iranian control, although Mossadegh realized that British assistance and cooperation were necessary for nationalization to work and provide his nation with the funds it needed for other programs the National Front wished to implement. American efforts to bring the two sides to an agreement failed, as did efforts both Iran and Britain made before the United Nations. National pride on the part of both blinded each to the realities. Great Britain was also involved in the Korean war and a major conflict with Egypt regarding the Suez Canal at this time. In all of these conflicts, time was on the British side only in Iran, because the British realized that Iran could neither produce nor market its oil without British assistance. Mossadegh moved to take physical control of the oil operations in September, but the British withdrew all of their personnel by October 4. The complete cessation of oil production and sales had predictable results on Iran's economy and ability to withstand the British boycott of oil and other vital banking, commercial, and industrial transactions. Great Britain and Iran broke diplomatic relations in October 1952.

The mobs that put Mossadegh in power kept him in power and remained impervious to the hardships that Iran suffered. By the end of 1951 he had to use clever procedures to prevent a constitutional end to his authority in the Majlis. Prospects that his situation would improve in the upcoming Majlis were no better. Landlord control of the elections in the countryside would surely return legislators who realized that nationalization had failed, in no small part because of Mossadegh's attempt to achieve a total victory. The National Front won the elections in the cities, including all twelve seats in Tehran. Mossadegh cancelled all additional elections on June 24, 1952, once there was enough for a quorum of seventy-nine, of which he only had the support of thirty in the Seventeenth Majlis, which met in July. Faced with this problem and a clash with the shah over the appointment of a War Minister, Mossadegh resigned on July 16. Qavam became premier, but Mossadegh took his plight to the nation and angry mobs responded to Kashani and Tudeh's call to action. The mobs were so large and their anger so great that the shah decided to withdraw the army from the encounter on July 21 out of fear it would not remain loyal.

Mossadegh returned to the premiership on July 22 and rapidly took his revenge against the shah and the entire institution of monarchy. As self-proclaimed Defense Minister, Mossadegh took command of the military and expelled some officers and promoted others according to his perception of their loyalty to him. He confiscated royal lands, reduced the royal living expenses, forbade the monarch to contact foreign representatives without Majlis approval, and even exiled the shah's twin sister. These measures and others reduced Muhammad Reza to as much of a monarch as Mossadegh could tolerate. He could at most reign, but he had neither the funds nor the authority to rule. With both the army and the mobs for support, in August 1952 Mossadegh obtained a vote to rule dictatorially for six months, after which he got it extended for another twelve months. He pursued his goals of land reform, altered the tax burden from the lower to the upper classes, and changed the educational, judicial, and electorial procedures. The two legislative houses, however, remained a possible obstacle because of their capacity to raise both procedural and constitutional questions. He got the Majlis to vote the Senate out of existence and dissolved the Majlis by withdrawing the National Front, thereby denying it a quorum. The "Philosopher King" had seized power and neither the constitution nor any other force could deter him from shaping Iran into the society he had dreamed of during his many years in opposition. Mossadegh, who had always expressed confidence in the collective will of the nation, was confident that his seemingly arrogant seizure of power was just and justified. He had always maintained that the constitution was an instrument the wealthy classes had implemented to guarantee their privileges. In the tradition of many notable dictators, he held a carefully managed plebiscite in July, 1953, which indicated virtually unanimous approval to his personal rule.

Mossadegh's total victory was a brief prelude to his total defeat, because he lost the support of his original base of strength among the masses, while he threatened his enemies with annihilation. Throughout 1953 the Tudeh, which was an illegal organization, had played a larger role in the street demonstrations with his apparent approval. Tudeh's prominence, accompanied with Mossadegh's social reforms, raised questions among his religious supporters, especially Kashani, that a Marxist regime was imminent. The religious elements had been enthusiastic in support of the National Front's original goals of expelling the British and reducing the role of the monarch. Other features of the National Front program had little appeal to them from the beginning and increasingly seemed to endanger traditional religious values. Tudeh, which was the other principal source of mass demonstrations, never trusted Mossadegh, in no small part because of their previous experience with his cousin, Qavam. Tudeh supported him periodically because many of his actions were important for their own long-range goals, but they did not regard him as a partner in a permanent relationship. They seem to have determined that no group could maintain a permanent partnership with him. Tudeh later regretted their overt decision to abandon him, but only because his successors proved so onerous.

A Committee to Save the Fatherland, composed of ousted military officers, plotted to take overt action, while the religious and Tudeh elements grew passive in their support for Mossadegh. The officers, under the leadership of General Fazlollah Zahedi, weaned key commanders in the military to their cause and also obtained the support of important political and religious leaders. The Eisenhower Administration was receptive to their overtures and sent Kermit Roosevelt of the Central Intelligence Agency to assist in overthrowing Mossadegh. British intelligence officers also added the benefit of their better understanding of the Iranian situation.

The initial attempt to arrest Mossadegh on August 17, 1953 was a fiasco that briefly led to the resurgence of Tudeh-led mob support. The shah's departure for Rome on that day revealed his part in the plot. In the popular mind, the shah's flight was tantamount to abdication and mobs attacked his statues and other manifestations of royal authority. A shaken Mossadegh agreed, however, to use the army against the mobs under the impression that a restoration of order would finally bring the American aid he had been seeking. The army suppressed the demonstrators and cleared the streets on August 18. The following day, however, the army moved against Mossadegh and a hired mob demonstrated in behalf of the return of the shah. Mossadegh escaped temporarily but surrendered on August 21. The shah returned on August 23. Although the Iranian army was the obvious instrument that enabled the shah's restoration, most Iranians believed the United States' assistance was the actual reason for his return to power. From that point, he became "America's Shah." His future behavior, whether benevolent or despotic, would shape Iranian attitudes toward the new foreign power that seemed to hold their future in its grasp.

14

Apparent Freedom

HISTORICAL TIMELINE

1956

⇛ Anti-Baghdad-Pact riots in Jordan on January 6 and 7. The army under General Glubb suppressed the riot with unusual severity.

⇛ King Hussein of Jordan summarily dismissed General Glubb and his British chief of staff and director of intelligence on March 1.

⇛ General Ali Abu Nuwar became chief of staff in Jordan following Glubb's dismissal. General Ali al-Hiyyari became his deputy.

⇛ Last British troops left Egypt in June.

⇛ More leftist cabinet in Syria in June with Baath and al-Azem's Democratic Bloc dominant. Serious investigation of possibility of union with Egypt. Stronger ties with Soviet bloc.

⇛ The U.S. announced on July 19 that it would not help fund the Aswan High Dam. Britain and the World Bank soon withdrew their offers to finance a dam as well.

⇛ Nasser nationalized the Suez Canal on July 26. Iraq did not break relations with Great Britain.

⇛ Saudi Arabia broke off diplomatic relations with both Britain and France at the beginning of the Suez Canal Crisis.

⇛ Lebanon refused to break diplomatic relations with Great Britain and France during the Suez Canal crisis.

- ⇛ Syria broke off relations with Great Britain and France during the Suez Canal Crisis, disabled the IPC pipeline, and placed troops in Jordan to threaten Israel.
- ⇛ Hussein placed the Jordanian military under Arab Command during the Suez Canal Crisis.
- ⇛ The Canal Users Conference met in London in August.
- ⇛ The United Nations began to discuss the Suez Canal crisis on September 23.
- ⇛ A free election in Jordan on October 21 led to an Arab nationalist and leftist majority in the Chamber of Deputies.
- ⇛ Akram Hourani formed the National Front in Syria.
- ⇛ Baath joined the Syrian cabinet on the condition that Syria seek union with Egypt.
- ⇛ Syrians discovered an Iraqi plot to take control of Syria.
- ⇛ Israel attacked Egypt in Sinai on October 29.
- ⇛ Suleiman Nabulsi became prime minister of Jordan and formed a leftist cabinet on October 29.
- ⇛ Anglo-French ultimatum for end of Israeli-Egyptian hostilities was delivered on October 30.
- ⇛ Syrian, Saudi, and Iraqi troops were invited to enter Jordan on November 3 to thwart an Israeli attack.
- ⇛ U.S. and U.N. pressure brought an end to British and French hostilities on November 7.
- ⇛ U.N. Emergency Force went into place in Egypt.
- ⇛ All Anglo-French troops were withdrawn from Egypt by December 22.
- ⇛ Syrian leftists under Baath; Communists; al-Azem, and Colonel Sarraj had a free hand to implement leftist agenda.
- ⇛ Conservative President al-Quwatly of Syria agreed to new leftist orientation of his cabinet.

1957

- ⇛ Discredit of Britain and France after the Suez Canal crisis left the U.S. as the most powerful outside power in Middle Eastern affairs.
- ⇛ National Front government of Syria took office on January 2.
- ⇛ Eisenhower announced the Eisenhower Doctrine on January 5. (Senate approved it in March.)
- ⇛ In return for a $50 million aid program from the United States, Saud broke ranks with Nasser and agreed to the Eisenhower Doctrine of January 5, 1957. He also agreed to extend the right of the United States to retain the military base at Dhahran for an additional five years.
- ⇛ Jordan signed an Arab Solidarity Agreement on January 19 and received a promise from Egypt, Saudi Arabia, and Syria to replace the British subsidy.
- ⇛ Jordan suppressed Communist activities beginning in January.
- ⇛ Nabulsi cabinet negotiated termination of British treaty on March 13, which provided for the British to leave by June.
- ⇛ Nabulsi cabinet moved toward close relations with the Soviet Union and Communist China in March.

- ⇛ Israeli troops withdrew from Egyptian soil in March after strong pressure from U.S.
- ⇛ Lebanon accepted Eisenhower Doctrine on March 16.
- ⇛ National Front in Lebanon developed among most political leaders in opposition to Shamoun's apparent quest for a second term as president.
- ⇛ Armored troops moved into Amman and near royal palace on April 8.
- ⇛ Nabulsi cabinet dismissed Bahjat Tabara, director of security, without royal consent.
- ⇛ King demanded Nabulsi's resignation on April 10.
- ⇛ Apparent *coup* attempt in Jordan centered in the Zerqa military base on April 13. King sent General Abu Nuwar into exile.
- ⇛ General al-Hiyyari, Abu Nuwar's successor, fled on April 20.
- ⇛ Nabulsi supporters met in Nablus April 22 and made radical demands on King Hussein.
- ⇛ Jordanian government imposed martial law on April 25 and arrested Nabulsi.
- ⇛ United States extended $10,000,000 aid to Jordan in April and $40,000,000 more over the following four months.
- ⇛ United States dispatched the Sixth Fleet to the eastern Mediterranean.
- ⇛ The U.N. accepted Egypt's plan for operation of the Suez Canal on April 24.
- ⇛ The Saudis revealed in April of 1957 that they had uncovered an Egyptian plot to assassinate King Saud.
- ⇛ Lebanese security forces fired upon National Front demonstrators on May 30.
- ⇛ Shamoun candidates won an overwhelming victory in June elections and were in a position to reelect him as president.
- ⇛ Iraqi Free Officer Society and General Qasim's organization merged in June to plot overthrow of the monarchy.
- ⇛ Afif Bizri appointed Chief-of-Staff in Syria on August 17.
- ⇛ Syria obtained a large economic and technical aid agreement with the USSR in August.
- ⇛ There was growing concern by August that Communists might take control of Syria.
- ⇛ Throughout November Syrian and United States officials conferred and restored normal relations; Turkish troops were withdrawn from the Syrian border; the National Front disintegrated in the latter half of the month; fear of Communists led to cancellation of Syrian parliamentary elections.
- ⇛ Egyptian parliamentary delegation went to Syria in November to pursue possibility of total union of Syria and Egypt.
- ⇛ Egyptian delegation and Syrian parliament agreed on a confederation on November 18. Nasser rejected anything short of total union.
- ⇛ Al-Azem took the title of Deputy Premier of Syria in December to go along with defense and finance portfolios.

1958

⇛ Chief of Staff Bizri and other Syrian officers met with Nasser on January 12 to discuss a merger of Syria and Egypt. Bitar joined the talks later.
⇛ Formation of the United Arab Republic between Egypt and Syria on February 1. RCC abolished all political parties in Syria, just as it had in Egypt.
⇛ Formation of Arab Federation between Iraq and Jordan on February 14.
⇛ Plebiscite in Egypt and Syria on February 22 indicated that 99.9 percent of citizens approved of formation of United Arab Republic.
⇛ Huge crowds, including 300,000 Lebanese, greeted Nasser in Damascus on February 24.
⇛ Egyptians accused King Saud of Saudi Arabia in March of plotting to assassinate Nasser.
⇛ Saudi Arabia rescinded its agreement to sell Egypt oil below market price.
⇛ Members of the Saudi royal family transferred executive power to Feisal on March 24. Saud remained king and was free to perform ceremonial functions of his position. Saudis essentially admitted they had conspired to assassinate Nasser.
⇛ Assassination of Nasib al-Matni on May 8 set off full-scale civil war in Lebanon.
⇛ Phalangists and the Syrian National Party supported President Shamoun of Lebanon in the civil war against Arab nationalists.
⇛ Lebanese opposition declared a separate government on March 27.
⇛ Discovery of a conspiracy in Jordan to overthrow monarchy early in July.
⇛ Shamoun declared he would not seek another term as president of Lebanon early in July.
⇛ Overthrow of Iraqi monarchy on July 14.
⇛ U.S. Marines landed in Lebanon on July 15.
⇛ Jordanian Chamber of Deputies approved King's request to ask for British military assistance on July 16.
⇛ British paratroopers arrived in Amman on July 17.
⇛ Saudi government took no position on the overthrow of the Iraqi monarchy or the movement of U.S. and British troops into the region.
⇛ General Shihab was elected president of Lebanon on July 31. Rashid Karami formed a cabinet of the various factions that ended much of the cause for strife in the civil war.
⇛ King Hussein dissolved the Arab Federation between Jordan and Iraq on August 2.
⇛ United Nations resolution on August 21 called for all governments in the region to respect each other's borders and forms of government.
⇛ U.S. Marines left Lebanon on October 25.
⇛ British troops withdrew from Jordan on November 2.

Successful rejection of the Baghdad Pact indicated that the Middle East finally had the capacity to thwart attempts to impose alliances upon the region that primarily served Western purposes. During the late 1950s, the Middle East countries also seemed to establish their control over their internal affairs and resources in a manner to meet their needs irrespective of Western concerns. Dramatic developments shook the region as it began a new course that eliminated the direct involvement of both the Western nations and their closest local allies.

The Suez Canal crisis helped focus the issues. All of the Arab governments expressed some level of support for Nasser's dramatic action, which elated the region and the unaligned nations, while it stunned the rest of the world. The subsequent enhancement of Nasser's stature presented a problem to most Arab governments, although public support for Nasser gave Arab leaders little choice but to support him. Anglo-French military retaliation against Egypt in league with Israel discredited them and destroyed any vestige of respect they had in the region. The demise of the traditional Western forces opened the possibility for the United States to exercise greater influence, even though it was unprepared to play such a role.

Nasser's undisputed appeal to the Arab masses following the Suez Canal crisis seemed to signal some kind of affiliation of all the Arab states under his leadership. At least, it seemed inevitable that like-minded Arab nationalists would emerge in each Arab state to shape a major role for Arabs in world affairs. Unrest and turmoil in Jordan, Lebanon, and Syria reflected the concerns of the entire Arab region. Jordan experienced the fullest spectrum of pro-Nasser hysteria and seemed on the verge of overthrowing its monarchy and severing all ties with the British. Lebanon and Syria, which had no significant relationship with their former French mentor, were unstable and in danger of disintegration for different reasons. The Lebanese struggle was largely over the division of spoils among greedy leaders and their followers, although conflicts between advocates of a separate Lebanon and Arab nationalists played a role. Syria became a cauldron of debate and experimentation about its future and the Arab-speaking world it hoped to lead. The governments of Iraq and Saudi Arabia kept order and did not allow significant debate or demonstrations.

The dramatic conflicts among the Arabs caused considerable international concern, in part because the resolutions of their differences could affect alignments in the Cold War. From a Western perspective Nasser was already in the Soviet Bloc after he had accepted Soviet assistance on the High Dam project following the Suez Canal crisis. The activities of Middle Eastern Communists added to this concern, despite the fact that Nasser totally suppressed the small and insignificant Communist element in Egypt. The polarization of the United Nations prevented it from easing either the regional or international concerns. The Eisenhower Doctrine in 1957 assured the governments that the United States would help defend them against both the indigenous Communist movements and the Soviet Bloc.

Egypt and Syria merged early in 1958 as much in a desperate effort to prevent Syrian disintegration as to lay the foundation for a greater Arab political unity. The sudden creation of the United Arab Republic stimulated almost every interest in the Middle East to immediate action. Arab nationalists of all kinds were confident their dreams were about to come true. The traditional governments and their Western supporters believed their fate depended upon their ability to meet this greatest challenge. The bloody abolition of the Iraqi monarchy six months after the creation of the United Arab Republic seemed to foretell the end of the old ways and the beginning of Arab unification, which had hitherto been so illusive.

The new Iraqi regime's reluctance to join the United Arab Republic could not hide the fact that the Middle East was different by 1958. Iraq's pursuit of an independent course probably ensured the continuation of the independence of Jordan and Lebanon. British and American military forces, which landed in both of those countries, played no roles in shaping the future of either tiny nation. After those forces quickly withdrew, the Arab lands that had been either mandates or protectorates were free from foreign occupation and all were under the control of governments that had proved their capacity to exist within the context of strictly regional considerations.

Iran also seemed securely under the control of a beneficent regime that could provide order, prosperity, and security. Iran, like other nations in the region and elsewhere, contained elements that disliked the government and social order that prevailed. Dissidents in Iran and the other Middle Eastern nations took their new freedom in stride. They found it easy to overlook the fear that their problems were now among themselves after struggling for so long to expell foreign domination.

EGYPT

Nonalignment and Arabism in Egypt

Events in 1955 transformed Nasser, Egypt, and the Middle East without reducing either Egypt's existing needs or its goals. Before the year was over Egypt was on a collision course with the Western nations and Israel; a leader in the international nonaligned movement; the leader of the Arab masses in confrontation with other Arab governments, especially Iraq; and well on its way to becoming dependent upon the Soviet Union for military and technical assistance.

Iraq's pact with Turkey on February 24, against Nasser's advice, horrified the Syrians and angered other Arabs. Syria and Turkey were having serious disputes over numerous matters related to Turkey's holding land that the Syrians and other Arabs thought should be part of Syria. Turkey, the Arabs knew, was dependent upon NATO and particularly upon the United States. Iraq's participation in the pact was contrary to the Arab League agreement and appeared to be one of several Nuri al-Said's government had under consideration. Nasser regarded Iraq's initiatives, which were to become the Baghdad Pact, as the result of Anglo-American efforts to elevate Iraq to the role of leadership in the Arab world in the guise of developing a regional defense against Communist expansion. An uncontested acceptance of these developments was contrary to the interests of Nasser and Egypt's role as leader of the Arab League. Nuri al-Said's actions posed the real possibility of a major shift in Arab relations with the west. He, after all, had been working with the Western powers for more than a generation, while Nasser was a revolutionary who had been in power for only two-and-one half contentious years. After Nasser labeled the Baghdad Pact as a new form of imperialism and used the full force of Egypt's media and diplomatic pressure against it, no other Arab nation joined Nuri's new arrangement with Great Britain. The Arab public found Nasser's assessment easy to believe when Iran joined the pact in September and Pakistan signed in November. Both nations were closely allied to Great Britain and the United States.

Nasser also found himself in the forefront of international affairs in his role as protector of the Palestinians. In that role he had only recently been in Gaza, where he assured the Palestinians that they need not be concerned about fighting for their homeland. Egypt, he said, would soon acquire the necessary arms to accomplish their return. A major Israeli raid on Gaza on February 28 demonstrated that Nasser could not even protect the Palestinians who were under Egyptian custody. He almost immediately began to negotiate with the Soviets to acquire offensive military equipment and technical assistance in return for Egyptian cotton. The West had assumed that even as secular a regime as the RCC would never enter into such an agreement with the avowed atheistic Eastern Bloc. That attitude and Israeli pressure accounted for the West's persistent refusal to sell Nasser the arms he and his military believed were necessary. The Arab masses enthusiastically greeted the September announcement that Egypt had made a deal to acquire large quantities of offensive weapons, ostensibly from Czechoslovakia. Nasser's bold move had proved to them, as he had in scuttling Arab participation in the Baghdad Pact, that he would do anything necessary to restore Arab independence and dignity.

Nasser's regional and international stature received an additional boost when the leaders of the nonaligned nations and the international press treated him so respectfully at the Nonaligned Nations Conference in Bandung, Indonesia in April. Nasser seemed to be a welcomed and respected peer of Nehru, Chou En Lai, Tito, and Sukarno. No Arab had ever received so much respect during his own lifetime. Without premeditation, Nasser had led the Arab world into the sphere of the nonaligned nations because the Arab masses had concerns that neither the eastern nor western blocs of the Cold War shared. No Arab government was strong enough to join either side, especially the West, given the commitment to nonalignment of most Arabs and elements in every Arab military structure.

Nationalization of the Suez Canal

Nasser's nonalignment in the Cold War, his arms deal with the Soviets, and his trade with Red China led most in the West to conclude that his sympathies rested with the Communists. They did not bother to take note of his careful curtailment of Egypt's small and ineffective Communist movement, which indicated his real attitude toward communism. Western policymakers could understand that his opposition to the Baghdad Pact was a matter of inter-Arab concern, however harmful it was to Anglo-American efforts to contain communism. Likewise, they understood that Nasser's support of the Algerian liberation movement against France was part of his overt appeal to become both an African leader and an Arab leader. His high-profile popularity to the numerous constituencies he had developed in such a short time made it difficult for the West to ignore opportunities to work constructively with him. Thus, at the end of 1955, which had provided him with so many triumphs, the United States, Great Britain and the World Bank expressed their willingness to help him construct the Aswan Dam, which could make him as great a hero in Egypt as he was abroad. It was as yet uncertain how much of the acclaim he could generate in Egypt was the result of well-orchestrated rallies and the coercion of his opposition.

Nasser's behavior during the first half of 1956 tested the remaining Western patience just when the British were about to make their final withdrawal and Aswan Dam construction seemed about to begin. He flaunted the offer he had from the Soviet Union to finance and construct the High Dam more cheaply and with less control over the expenditure of the funds. The Soviets also did not express any reservations about Egypt's ability to pay for both the arms deal and the dam. He angered the British when King Hussein of Jordan suddenly and summarily dismissed Sir John Glubb, a British army officer, from his post of Commander in Chief of the Arab Legion on March 1. The British were certain Nasser had coerced Hussein into dismissing Glubb Pasha to embarrass Britain and eliminate all hope that Jordan would join the Baghdad Pact. France saw its prospects of subduing the Algerian rebels wane as they received inspiration and arms from Nasser. Israel, which could not use the Suez Canal, had genuine concern that Nasser would completely halt shipping from all countries in route to Israel through the Gulf of Aqaba. Egyptian restrictions on such shipping past Sharm al-Shaykh gave credence to Israel's concern.

Nasser's stock soared even higher in June. The last British troops left on June 18 and he was elected president for six years on June 22, with little restriction on his ability to conduct all Egyptian affairs. Nasser aggravated the West in general and Britain in particular when he spoke quite heatedly against the West at ceremonies that accompanied the British withdrawal from Suez. He invited the Soviet foreign minister, Dimitri Shepilov, to accompany him on that occasion and allowed him to add his antiimperialist comments to Nasser's.

John Foster Dulles, the American Secretary of State for Foreign Affairs, took the lead in trying to rein Nasser in. Egypt's ambassador to the United States had just received Nasser's approval on July 17 to accept the American offer to help with the dam. With no warning, Dulles chose the occasion of Nasser's crucial meeting with Tito and Nehru in Yugoslavia to release a statement to the press on July 19. He stated that the U.S. could not participate in financing the High Dam because of concern that the Egyptian government was financially overextended as a result of its arms deal with the Soviets. Failure to use official channels, rather than the press, embarrassed Nasser just as Dulles must have assumed it would. American withdrawal, which the British and the World Bank soon duplicated for the same reasons, did not endanger the High Dam project because Nasser already had substantial assurances that the Soviets would finance and supervise the construction. Nasser was particularly incensed that the stated reason for American reneging indicated that the Egyptian economy and, therefore, the revolution had collapsed. He was sure that Dulles, in collusion with Eden, wished to spread dissent and cause Nasser's overthrow from within.

On July 23, 1956, the fourth anniversary of the Free Officer coup, Nasser decided to nationalize the Suez Canal in retaliation for the Anglo-American rebuff and to obtain additional funds to construct the High Dam. Shepilov, who was back in Egypt for the celebrations connected with the revolution, also informed Nasser that the Soviets had decided to finance the dam. Egyptian officials took over the canal while Nasser was giving a speech in Alexandria on July 26, the anniversary of Farouk's departure. Egyptians took control at the very time he announced in his speech that Egypt had nationalized the canal. His mention of the name of Ferdinand de Lesseps, the builder of the canal, was the signal for his carefully positioned forces to move.

Thus, he accomplished another anti-Western coup to the elation of most Egyptians, other Arabs, and much of the nonaligned populations in Africa and Asia. He could hardly have done anything more provocative to both Great Britain and France, because of the pride and investment both had in the Suez Canal

Company, which reached beyond its utility. The United States had no such concern, but realized that Nasser's action jeopardized international peace because the British and French would probably retaliate with force against Nasser, who might well receive Soviet diplomatic and military assistance. The Suez Canal crisis portended to present the greatest possibility for armed confrontation between the alliances of the Cold War since the Berlin Crisis in 1948. Eisenhower's commitment to use the United Nations to solve the problem and the Soviet distraction due to the Hungarian uprising helped reduce such a risk. Also, Secretary of State Dulles' illness, which required an operation during the crisis, removed him and the views he shared with Eden from the deliberations.

Assumption that Nasser nationalized the canal solely in retaliation for his recent rebuff is simplistic. Serious problems of continued operation under the Suez Canal Company's mostly foreign directors were apparent. Of foremost concern was the need for repair and widening of the canal to accommodate the very large ships, especially oil tankers, that could constitute a large percentage of the canal tolls. Even normal dredging was in arrears and various buildings and machinery connected with the canal were in disrepair. These concerns and deficiencies resulted from the simple fact that there were only twelve years remaining on the company's ninety-nine year lease with Egypt. There was no way of knowing whether Egypt would grant a new lease. The directors were hesitant, therefore, to invest profits in long-range improvements they might lose if the canal devolved to Egypt in 1968. Egypt, in the meantime, was losing revenues and faced the possibility of acquiring a silted-up and outmoded facility when the company's lease expired.

Anthony Eden's claim, which other Westerners endorsed, that Nasser "stole" the canal, was incorrect. However, he made a strong impression in the heated atmosphere that followed the nationalization. Nasser agreed in his declaration of nationalization that shareholders would receive compensation at the closing price of the stock market that day. All the Western markets were closed when he made his remarks to an evening audience in Alexandria. The complete secrecy of his entire preparation for the takeover had prevented any hint that could have influenced the value of the shares from leaking out. Also, since the company was registered in Egypt it was subject to the laws of Egypt. Nasser had clearly stated at the time of nationalization that Egypt would abide by the 1888 convention that provided the basic international law connected with the canal. Further, Egypt continued to operate the canal and had every intention of continuing to do so because its revenues were of greater enduring concern than the shock value nationalization had in the short range.

Nasser expected a strong, perhaps even military, Anglo-French reaction. Toward that end Egypt prepared to meet a frontal invasion at Alexandria, where Europeans usually invaded. Egyptian forces were also on special alert along the northern end of the canal. He hoped, however, that his own commitment to operate the canal efficiently and normally would mobilize international diplomacy to avoid armed conflict.

President Eisenhower of the United States stated from the beginning of the crisis that the United States would not use force in settling the problem and would, in fact, use every peaceful means to avoid conflict between other interested parties. This sincere reflection of his attitude helped keep Soviet reaction to a minimum. Dulles initiated talks with Great Britain and France, neither of which indicated any desire to find a peaceful solution. Both seemed to welcome the opportunity to crush

Nasser, who repeatedly had proved to be their nemesis in all their dealings with the Arab world and North Africa. Britain, however, was too dependent upon the United States by 1956 to pursue an aggressive course until it demonstrated to the United States there was no other option.

Under American pressure, Great Britain and France agreed to call a conference on August 16 of the principal canal user nations in London. The Canal Users' Conference endorsed a suggestion of the three previous conferees that would have placed the canal under an international authority until negotiations with Egypt resolved the problem. Nasser categorically rejected such an approach on the premise that the canal was the property of Egypt and not subject to any international sanctions or supervision unless Egypt transgressed against the 1888 convention. He assured Prime Minister Sir Robert Menzies of Australia, the spokesman for the canal users, that Egypt would abide by all previous agreements, keep the canal open, operate it efficiently, and in addition, make the improvements that current and future traffic required. An attempt to solve the problem through another users' conference in September proved no more successful. By that time, Egypt's case was stronger because it had operated the canal to the satisfaction of shippers for two months.

The Anglo-French resort to the United Nations on September 23 was predicated on the assumption that Nasser would refuse a compromise and justify their use of force. Beginning in August they had developed plans for a joint military attack using Cyprus and Malta as bases for their amassment of troops and supplies. The strategy was heavily based upon the use of these British bases and the use of British bombers and naval assets. France, in other words, had no capacity to conduct an operation if Britain decided to withdraw.

France, however, added an incendiary element to retaliation against Nasser when it incorporated Israel into its plans. Guy Mollet, the French prime minister, was a strong supporter of Israel's socialist experiment. Alliance with Israel could bring French leftist support to complement rightist endorsement of French efforts to destroy Nasser's role in the Algerian revolution. Israel's new government under Ben-Gurion welcomed an opportunity to join the enterprise to terminate Egyptian-sponsored Palestinian attacks from Gaza. Israel wanted to counter Egypt's refusal to allow Israeli ships and ships from other nations carrying goods to Israel to use the canal. Israel was also concerned about Nasser's growing impediments to shipping to and from Israel through the Gulf of Aqaba.

The three partners developed a strategy by mid-October that involved Israel initiating the action with an attack on Egyptian forces in the Sinai that would drive toward the canal. Great Britain and France planned to issue an ultimatum that each party withdraw from within ten miles of the canal. Nasser would obviously refuse since the territory on both sides of the canal belonged to Egypt. The British and French would have their forces poised to strike, and launch their attack on Egypt on the pretense of keeping peace. They intended to inflict enough damage on Egypt to either destroy Nasser or cause his dismissal in disgrace.

United Nations debate on the Suez question throughout October revealed a strong similarity between Anglo-French demands and the Egyptian position. Egypt essentially continued to pledge its intention to provide good service to the users and abide by international law. It maintained that fees were negotiable and would be the same for all shipping. Egypt refused, however, to submit control of the canal even on a temporary basis to any international group and it rejected the right of any nation or group to employ "police activity" against Egypt for refusing to comply with Anglo-French demands for a return to the status quo prior to nationalization. The international community had reason to believe that Anglo-French and Egyptian talks with Dag Hammarskjold, Secretary-General of the United Nations, would work out remaining differences.

War

Egypt had no reason to expect an attack from any source since an apparently viable negotiating process was still unfolding. Israel's attack on Egyptian forces in the Sinai on October 29, therefore, surprised the Egyptians as much as it surprised the world. Egypt's preparations for a possible invasion elsewhere made the rapid advance of Israeli forces unusually easy. The Anglo-French ultimatum on October 30 was actually a little premature since Israel had not even reached to within ten miles of the canal. Great Britain and France vetoed a Security Council demand for a ceasefire and launched their own attack on Egyptian installations all along the Suez. Their destruction of the new Egyptian planes established almost instant air supremacy and determined a quick and total Egyptian defeat. Little of the new military equipment Egypt had recently acquired from the Soviets survived the onslaught that killed and maimed many and destroyed Egyptian properties of all kinds. Egypt impeded the use of naval vessels by sinking ships at strategic places in the canal, which made it inoperable for months after the war ended.

The Anglo-French attack ended as a result of United States pressure on Britain, as it and France had ignored a November 2, 1956, United Nations resolution to cease hostilities. Their cessation corresponded with another U.N. resolution on November 7, but Eisenhower's unequivocal demand that the attackers cease and desist was crucial. The United States had unusual leverage over Britain at this juncture. Britain desperately needed American financial assistance at the time. The week of hostilities had cut off Egypt's oil supplies just as winter was approaching. The canal was blocked and would remain so through the winter and Syrian sympathizers of Nasser had cut the pipeline from Iraq, which provided Britain's other source of Middle East oil. The United States, which was an oil exporter at the time, could provide Britain and other Europeans oil until Middle Eastern supplies were again available.

The United Nations agreed to send an Emergency Force (UNEF) into Egypt and the Sinai to supervise the truce and the evacuation of the occupying forces. Anglo-French forces all withdrew by December 22, but Israeli forces refused to leave Sharm al-Shaykh, which was their main strategic goal in the war. Israel refused all demands that it withdraw until Eisenhower threatened to prevent all American aid unless it withdrew. Israeli forces did not withdraw until March 8, at which time UNEF troops and observers took positions along the Egyptian-Israeli border. All U.N. forces, however, were on the Egyptian side of the border since Israel refused to trust any part of its security to any outside source. The UNEF were on Egyptian soil with the consent of the Egyptian government, which had the right to demand its departure at any time. Once they had been there for several months, however, their presence came to represent the status quo. An Egyptian demand that they depart anytime in the future, unless there was an improvement in Egyptian-Israeli relations, would become provocative as it did in May 1967.

Interestingly, the United Nations accepted Egypt's pledge on the operation of the canal on April 24, 1957, which was little different from the pledge Egypt made on October 12, 1956 before hostilities began.

Aftermath

The Suez Canal crisis marked several new departures in the Middle East. Nasser lost the war and emerged victorious with the canal and the veneration of the Arab world. Eden, far from destroying the man he repeatedly called a fascist, elevated him to increased popularity that could withstand an even greater military defeat. Britain and France won the war but lost all credibility to shape or even influence events in the Arab world to their favor. Their collusion with Israel, rather than the fact that they had used force, was their undoing, because while the Arabs were accustomed to highhanded imperialist actions, they could not forgive overt military operations with Israel. Israel, which was also militarily victorious, had to return the territory it conquered and intended to keep. It also learned that the United Nations, which had granted it legitimacy, held it accountable for acquiring territory of another sovereign member. The Soviet Union's representation of its role in stopping the aggression garnered it as much credit in the Arab world as Eisenhower received, although Nasser resented their basically passive role. Soviet ideology, especially its atheism, limited the appeal it could have among either Arab governments or the general population. Strangely, the Soviet Union, whose ideological premise opposed nationalist irredentism in a world of workers and peasants, became the champion of Arab nationalist hopes in each nation and as a macrocosm. The Soviets understood the limitations of their appeal, but were satisfied for even this level of entree into Middle Eastern affairs.

The Suez Canal crisis left the United States as the single outside state with the greatest influence in the Middle East. Its recent role in reestablishing the Shah in power in Iran and in resolving the oil question there had laid the foundation. But with Britain and France in total disrepute and the Soviet bloc only marginally influential, the Americans obtained the role of leadership, which they were unprepared to fulfill because of inexperience in the region and a general lack of understanding of the Middle East and its people in the highest levels of government and among the electorate. American ascendancy was assured, even though there was little receptivity to its attempts to maintain order and resolve differences that threatened peace. Eisenhower's failure to provide leadership through the doctrine that bears his name did not diminish the American role. He had formulated the thrust of his approach on November 8, the day after the ceasefire. He announced it on January 5, 1957 and Congress approved it on March 9, 1957. Other events, especially the overthrow of the Iraqi monarchy in July 1958, outstripped his good intentions. The Baghdad Pact and British influence ended with the death of Nuri al-Said and the Iraqi monarchy. It seemed, in fact, that the Arabs were finally in control of their own affairs.

Union with Syria

A triumphant Nasser, who claimed both military and diplomatic victory out of the defeat during the Suez Canal crisis, enjoyed even greater status among Arab nationalists. They were at greater liberty to express their hopes in Syria, Jordan, and Lebanon where governmental weakness reduced fear of repression. Elsewhere their aspirations seethed in the privacy of their minds and in small groups that appeared to offer no threat to the existing regimes.

Nasser's ego fed on the adoration across the Arab world, but he also realized the needs of Egypt were dire and still required help from beyond the region. Relations with the United States were proper and better than predictable in view of America's continued support for Israel and Great Britain. Egypt's need for American aid, particularly wheat, prevented Nasser from adopting the fullest strident anti-Western posture his supporters welcomed. The United States also remained a possible source of aid to repair the extensive war damage. Israeli destruction of much of the infrastructure in the Sinai made normal life there impossible and Anglo-French bombardment created extensive damage. Nasser's relations with the Soviet Union were strained because he resented their lack of assistance in the Suez crisis and because they resented his harsh treatment of Egyptian Communists. He maintained good relations with Saudi Arabia, which continued to regard Egypt's revolutionary regime as more acceptable than either of the Hashemite regimes of Iraq and Jordan. Egypt, Saudi Arabia, and Syria had remained closely associated from the earliest deliberations for forming the Arab League in the mid-1940s because of their mutual resentment of Hashemite ambitions. Contrary to western perception, they and most Arabs also shared a strong fear of Communist, rather than Soviet, growth in the Middle East. Their receptivity to Soviet diplomatic and financial support, and even the Soviet threat of military intervention in behalf of nationalist goals, was not an endorsement of Communist ideology.

Developments in Syria indicated the true Arab attitude toward communism. In many respects Syria had been on the brink of internal disintegration since 1949 and in danger of annexation to Iraq and of going to war with Turkey. Syria had turned to the Soviet bloc for military and technical assistance before Egypt had. Despite all of these problems, Syria posed as the leader of Arab nationalism while Nasser and the RCC gave most of their attention to expelling the British. The leftist regime of Khaled al-Azem from late 1954 allowed the Baathist and communist parties to thrive until Shukri al-Quwatly became president in September 1955. Al-Quwatly, who had lived in Egypt since 1949, had close relations with both Egypt and Saudi Arabia. He signed a mutual defense pact with Egypt on October 20 and an economic pact with Saudi Arabia three weeks later. He soon learned, however, that nationalist and leftist activities made Syria virtually ungovernable.

Al-Quwatly reduced some of the strain when he included two Baathists in his cabinet in June 1956. Their presence in the cabinet eased some of the Arab nationalist pressure, since they accepted posts on the condition that the president seek immediate union with Egypt. Syrian politics took another turn to the left early in 1957, however, when al-Azem again became Defense Minister and the government discovered a major plot among some of the more conservative politicians to merge Syria with Iraq. Baathists and Communists worked closely together throughout 1957 to subdue the conservative elements, although the two radical groups had totally conflicting long-range goals. Al-Azem also worked closely with the Communists, primarily because of their support among the masses and to curry favor with the Soviet Union to which he looked for additional military and financial aid. Syria's growing affinity with the Eastern Bloc was instrumental in the United States announcing the Eisenhower Doctrine on January 5, two months before it received congressional approval.

By August 1957, concern grew inside Syria and elsewhere that the Communists could take control of Syria under al-Azem's protection. During that month he concluded a major agreement with the Soviet Union and elevated a rabid leftist, Afif Bizri, to become Chief of Staff. Arab nationalists feared that the Communist threat might lead to annexation to Iraq with the support of Turkey because there was no public understanding of the exact provisions of the Baghdad Pact the two of them initiated in February 1955.

All regional governments, as well as the Western powers, were alarmed at the developments in Syria by the fall of 1957 but few were in a position to take preventive actions. The United States demonstrated its concern by restoring relations with Syria and pressuring Turkey to end its threatening posture. The Baathists terminated their cooperation with the Communists and began to work more closely with traditional political parties.

Nasser decided he had to consider the Baathists' overtures for union between Syria and Egypt, although he had been cool to the idea in the past. He had expressed concern that the intrinsic constitutional, economic, ethnic, and social differences between the two countries made union untenable. He had, however, insisted that any union had to be total rather than partial as the Baathists advocated. Events in Syria reduced his reluctance for further investigation of a possible union. Anwar Sadat, the deputy speaker of the Egyptian parliament, headed an Egyptian parliamentary delegation to explore possibilities of union in November. The delegation had no authority, however, to offer Syria anything short of total union and the abolition of all Syrian political parties. The Syrians resisted total submission and only agreed to a confederation on November 18 that was essentially an extension of their mutual defense treaty. Nasser declined the compromise and union no longer appeared to offer an escape from leftist supremacy in Syria. Al-Azem's power grew quickly thereafter when he also assumed the post of deputy premier.

The appeal and apparent need for union was stronger than Syrian leaders' concern for retaining either their party identities or Syria's independence. Arab unification, especially under Nasser's leadership, had reached such a fever pitch among the Arab masses that failure to do so seemed treasonous. Chief-of-Staff Bizri, who had caused so much apprehension only five months before for his Communist tendencies, took the initiative and flew to Cairo with four other officers at the end of January to make a direct appeal to Nasser for union. When Nasser refused to budge from his demand for total unity, the Syrian officers and Salah Bitar, who was one of the three founders of the Baath party, agreed to Nasser's terms.

Egypt and Syria merged into the United Arab Republic on February 1, 1958 and al-Quwatly demurely resigned. He was, after all, a good friend of Nasser and also recognized the overwhelming appeal of Pan-Arabism. Only the Syrian Communist party refused to disband and its leader, Khaled Bakdash, went into exile while the membership remained intact as an underground movement. The Baath complied earlier than the other parties under the conviction that they were destined to provide the U.A.R. and future Arab unity both its ideology and leadership. Salah Bitar stated their optimism later in the month when he said that the union could not succeed on "principles other than the Baath." The only indication this might be true beyond the Baathist concept that they were indispensable was in the adoption of Baathist nomenclature that designated Syria as the Northern Region and Egypt as the Southern Region of the U.A.R.. A plebiscite in both "regions" on February 22 revealed a 99.9 percent approval of the merger.

The elation of the Arab masses with these dramatic developments indicated that a plebiscite throughout the Arab world would have also won overwhelming approval. Almost every Christian, Muslim, and Druze leader in Lebanon, except President Shamoun and leaders of the Syrian National Party, went to Damascus to express their support. About 300,000 Lebanese swarmed to Damascus to get a glimpse of Nasser when he made his first trip to the Northern Region on February 24. Demonstrations in Jordan, which was in turmoil, expressed similar sympathies. The regimes in Iraq and Saudi Arabia did not permit such public expressions.

The merger of Syria and Egypt shocked the traditional regimes, which feared their own demise in the wake of Pan-Arab fervor. Nasser assured the other Arab states that the U.A.R. respected their independence, but his invitation for others to join the union was an invitation for the masses to force the other Arab states to join. Yemen, in fact, did, but little of substance ever developed in the strange relationship among these three disparate partners. While Shamoun sent a cursory note of congratulation to Quwatly, he expected the frenzy for unity to erupt in Lebanon where he was too weak to prevent its success. Iraq and Jordan responded with their own Arab Union on February 14, but their invitation for other Arab states to become members met a contemptuous silence from Arab governments and the Arab public. Saudi Arabia's cordial relationship with Nasser had ended about a year earlier when it turned strongly to the United States for financial, technological, and military aid. A desire to placate Nasser and its own Pan-Arabists, however, prevented it from joining the Hashemite alternative to Arab unity.

The six months following the formation of the U.A.R. proved that the concerns of the conservative regimes in Lebanon, Iraq, Jordan, and Saudi Arabia were valid. Egyptian and Syrian charges in early March that King Saud had plotted to assassinate Nasser led to Feisal's seizing control of executive authority on March 24 and virtually admitting that his brother Saud had paid for the assassination of Nasser. Saud kept his throne and Feisal, who had good credentials as an Arab nationalist, was able to mend relations with Nasser and the U.A.R. Civil war erupted in Lebanon in May for largely domestic reasons, but the question of union with the U.A.R. greatly enflamed the situation. Arab nationalists under the leadership of Suleiman Nabulsi and the Baathists nearly overthrew King Hussein in Jordan. Both Lebanon and Jordan appealed to the United Nations to end U.A.R. support of the dissidents, but American and Soviet disagreement on the cause of the eruptions prevented the U.N. from taking any action. The United States supported the charges of outside intervention, while the Soviets asserted that the problems were strictly internal matters.

Almost everyone assumed that the sudden and bloody end of the Iraqi monarchy on July 14 signaled Iraq's joining the U.A.R. Only massive non-Arab intervention could destroy an Arab nation composed of the three leading political and population centers of the Arab world. Since no one knew that General Abd-ul Karim Qasim, the leader of the coup, had no intention of presenting Iraq to Nasser's authority, the Arab masses welcomed it and most Western governments shuddered. American marines poured into Lebanon the day after the coup to save Lebanon from falling under "Communist" control and British paratroopers landed in Amman to save Jordan from the same suspected fate. The Saudi Arabian government remained discreetly silent in the hope that total neutrality would prevent the apparently relentless leftist Pan-Arab movement from sweeping it from power.

Concern that the entire Arab world would soon fall under Nasser's control was understandable, but the Middle East was intrinsically too complicated, regional jealousies and identities with Damascus and Baghdad were too strong, and outside forces were too concerned for an Egyptian government to prevail over the entire region. American interference provided stability in Lebanon, where the cause of civil war had run its natural course. British paratroopers and American economic assistance gave King Hussein the respite he needed to curb an uncontrollable political situation and govern through carefully chosen ministers with the unquestioned loyalty of his Bedouin army. The clear desire and ability of Qasim to concentrate on Iraqi affairs and turn his intentions for expansion toward Kuwait eliminated the possibility of Iraq contributing to Arab unity. Iraq under Qasim, in fact, soon became more of a challenge to Nasser and Arab unity than the monarchy had been.

Nasser's original fears of incompatibility between Egypt and Syria soon proved to be at least as real as he conjectured. Wealthy Syrians resented the imposition of the maturing Egyptian socialist experiments to Syrian business, landowning, and agriculture. Egypt's long standing bureaucratic practices, which ignored the preferential treatment Syria's multiethnic population customarily received, angered a broad spectrum of Syrians. Egyptian army officers, politicians, and administrators received high positions in Syria, while the few Syrians who found employment in Egypt seemed to receive such posts to remove them from their power bases in Syria. Syrian industry suffered as Egypt shipped raw materials to Egypt and flooded the Syrian market with Egyptian manufactured goods. In these and other respects Egypt became the senior partner in an obviously unequal relationship. Nasser's will prevailed in every aspect of the U.A.R. and he unabashedly reiterated the necessity of securing the revolution through a unitary political structure that allowed no legal opposition. Syrians could never expect any improvement of their situation through the election process since the Egyptian population supremacy was so great and showed no indication of ever ending.

Baathists soon learned that their participation in creating the U.A.R. as a foundation for developing a greater Arab unity under their guidance was illusory. Nasser resented public statements from Baathist leaders that credited their ideology for his pursuit of Arab unity and maintained that continuation of the process depended on Baath guidance for an otherwise philosophically unguided coterie of army officers. Baathist positions in the U.A.R. usually denied them any meaningful role in policy except for their early enthusiastic participation in implementing socialist regulations in Syria, which many Syrians despised. The continuation of a nascent Baathist organization in Syria after their apparent voluntary dissolution was also perturbing to Nasser. The easy access of the Baath to Syria through their active press in Beirut added to the problem. In addition, Hawrawni, Bitar, and Aflaq enjoyed control over an international Baathist organization while they were supposed to be servants of the new U.A.R. government. Baathists, as always committed to their mission, failed to realize any incongruity in their actions and only chafed at their unfair treatment. The fact that their former close ally, Interior Minister Abd al-Hamid Sarraj of the Northern Region, participated in diminishing their stature added to their dissatisfaction and frustration.

By the close of 1958 the Baath were well on their way out of any meaningful relationship in the union they had initiated. Nasser only had to allow the credit they assumed for forming the union to discredit them as the problems of the union became obvious to the more important elements among the former Syrian establishment and the military. Their elitist approach to membership and relations with the larger public brought their complete humiliation in popular elections. They were not allowed to infuriate crowds in behalf of Arab unity, which many believed was either well on its way to realization or a bad idea whose end was near. Nasser welcomed their discomfort and grew more confident that he could forge his own ideology of Arab socialist nationalism for a receptive Arab populace, which was firmly based on specific Arab needs rather than the fancies of Syrian wordspinners.

Nasser's unique hold on his country and the region embodied the special role Egypt had played through the centuries of being both peculiarly Arab and yet peculiarly Egyptian.

JORDAN

Dismissal of Glubb

To the surprise of everyone, King Hussein summarily dismissed General Glubb and his British chief of staff and director of intelligence on March 1,1956. Almost everyone, including the British, assumed this dramatic alteration in Jordan's relationship with Britain was the direct result of Nasser's pressure. This conclusion ignores Hussein's pride and Glubb's entrenched authority that was built upon his close association with Emir Abdullah. Glubb had every reason to believe that the young king needed more direct guidance than the Pasha had exercised over the king's two mature predecessors. The disparity in their ages and experience easily led to the perception that the king was little more than a cadet under Glubb's tutelage. Without realizing it, the instinctively loyal general might well have shared this belief.

Glubb overstepped his authority and piqued the king's dignity when he demanded the dismissal of some officers he believed were more strongly committed to Arab nationalism than to the Hashemite kingdom. Without consulting anyone, the young king decided to dismiss Glubb and to remove him immediately from Jordanian soil. It was a singular decision to demonstrate his determination to rule as well as reign. The decision appeared both brash and foolish, regardless of its popularity in Jordan and the Arab world, because it, no doubt, heralded the end of the life-giving British subsidy. Only the British seemed to have any vested interest in Jordan's existence and, even then they viewed it as a medium for British interests.

Glubb's dismissal appalled the British and elevated Hussein into a new status as an Arab hero. Arabs, in fact, generally interpreted the dismissal as the courageous act of Hussein on behalf of Arab independence, rather than the triumph of Nasser's pressure. Hussein for the first time appeared more the successor of his Arab nationalist father, Talal, than the reincarnation of his grandfather, Abdullah, whom most regarded as subservient to the British. Arab nationalists and leftists in Jordan assumed that Glubb's dismissal was a signal for their ascendancy. The National-Socialists, under Suleiman Nabulsi, and the Baathists and Communists became especially active.

Not the least of the questions that arose following Glubb's departure was who would fill the vacuum of leadership in the Arab Legion. When Britain withdrew its other officers, the Jordanians had to provide a new command structure from within their own ranks. The Bedouin officers were unquestionably loyal to the Hashemite throne, but the non-Bedouin officers were considerably better educated and prepared to formulate policy for a modern army. Many of the latter, however, were among the officers Glubb had wanted to dismiss because of their Arab nationalist and pro-Nasser proclivities. General Ali Abu Nuwar emerged as Chief of Staff because of his close friendship with the king, although there was reason to believe he was not the most qualified and also that he was tainted with Baathist inclinations. General Ali al-Hiyyari, Abu Nuwar's deputy, had a similar profile.

Suez Canal Crisis

Nasser's nationalization of the Suez Canal on July 23, 1956 elevated Arab nationalist expressions to an unprecedented height. Hussein remained a nationalist hero for his dismissal of Glubb and enjoyed his new stature as a nationalist supporter. He allowed unusually full political activities that the leftist elements dominated in preparation for parliamentary elections on October 21. Nabulsi became premier on October 29 since his party was the strongest, with twelve of the forty seats. His cabinet, which included a Baathist and a Communist, was the most radical to date in any Arab country. Its Arab nationalist and anti-Western composition portended to lead Jordan in a direction uncharacteristic of traditional Hashemite policies. It doubtlessly enjoyed popular support, but the question remained as to whether the king could continue his own Arab nationalist course.

Hussein indicated that he would not waver when he placed Jordan's army under the leadership of the Arab Command on October 25, with General Abdul Hakim Amer of Egypt in command. This was the king's initiative since Nabulsi's cabinet did not take office until four days later, when the Israelis launched their attack against the Egyptian Sinai. Jordan invited Syrian, Saudi, and Iraqi troops to enter Jordan on November 3 to defend Jordan and possibly open another front in the war. Britain assured all parties that it would abide by its obligation to defend Jordan against an Israeli attack but it would not participate in offensive actions against Israel, which, after all, was operating in collusion with the British and French against Egypt. Jordan broke relations with France after it joined the attack, but did not alter its relationship with Great Britain. Pressure from the United States and the United Nations ended the attack on Egypt within a week but the neighboring Arab troops remained in Jordan.

New Financial Assistance

Britain's participation with Israel in the attack upon Egypt made continuation of a close relationship between Jordan and Britain untenable. Jordan had to break the relationship, but it also had to find a source of financial assistance. Jordan simply could not function without outside aid. The announcement of the Eisenhower Doctrine on January 9 provided a possible source of funds, except that the Jordanian government could not endorse the doctrine in the anti-Western atmosphere of 1957. The United States, however, indicated that it might provide funds irrespective of Jordan's public announcements. Jordan signed the Arab Solidarity

Agreement on January 19, which provided for a 12.5 million Egyptian-pound subsidy from Egypt, Saudi Arabia, and Syria to replace the British subsidy. This was a popular alternative, although level-headed people had to question whether either of the Arab states could or would fulfill their promise. All, in fact, were also in need of foreign assistance.

The Nabulsi cabinet negotiated an agreement with Britain on March 13 that provided for an end of the British subsidy and the termination of all British personnel in Jordan by June. An American dispersal to Jordan of $10,000,000 in April indicated that Jordan had obtained a new source of funds without having to endorse the Eisenhower Doctrine. Better still, the Americans, unlike the British, placed no restrictions upon the expenditure of the funds. Another $40,000,000 from the United States over the next four months not only replaced the British subsidy, but gave Jordan financial independence from the Arab governments.

While the terms for American largess remain secret, the correlation between Jordan's restrictions upon its Communists and the announcement of the Eisenhower Doctrine indicated that Hussein privately endorsed the American policy. There is further evidence that this was the independent will of the king. The anti-Communist's actions, which included suppression of the Communist newspaper and the exclusion of Soviet propaganda, were under the personal direction of the king rather than the cabinet.

King versus Cabinet

The popular support for Nabulsi's cabinet and its origin in an unprecedentedly free election gave it a false sense of security. Its congruity with the Arab nationalist sentiments of the time added to its sense that it enjoyed the favor of destiny. Statements of cabinet ministers indicated that they were presiding over the demise of the Hashemite monarchy and preparing for an inevitable merger with Syria as the first step in uniting all the Arab states under a single government. Jordan's close relationship with both the Egyptian and Syrian governments virtually ignored the king as the monarch of a sovereign state. Both the British and the American governments seemed to expect that the uncontested constitutional process would lead inexorably to Jordan's disappearance. Nabulsi's open advocacy of full recognition of the Soviet Union and Communist China throughout March, without royal consent, indicated the extent of cabinet supremacy.

The king was the only possible impediment if he chose to use the army, which most believed was too much under Arab nationalist control to provide him with the necessary support. The sudden appearance of armored vehicles in Amman and adjacent to the royal palace on April 8 gave all indications of a military coup. The king firmly ordered them back to their bases and they obeyed. When the cabinet dismissed the king's director of security the next day, without royal consent, the king acted decisively. He demanded and received Nabulsi's resignation. Like Glubb, Nabulsi had exceeded his authority, but Nabulsi's acceptance of his ouster did not end the support he enjoyed for his subversion of royal authority.

Confusing and suspicious activities at the Zerqa military base twenty miles west of Amman on the evening of April 13 pointed toward a major coup attempt. Hussein rushed to Zerqa and boldly confronted the suspected leaders. Loyal Bedouin officers and soldiers restored order in the midst of protests from suspected officers that there was no threat to the regime. The strongest evidence indicated that

Ali Abu Nuwar, Hussein's trusted chief of staff and former aide-de-camp, was the leader of the aborted coup. The king allowed him to leave for Syria under military escort. He appointed General Ali al-Hiyyari as chief of staff only to have him flee to Syria on April 20, apparently in fear that an investigation would prove that he, too, had been a conspirator.

The king had won and preserved his throne, but the conspiracy indicated that few besides his trusted Bedouins were committed to the survival of his throne and his kingdom. His situation was so weak that he had agreed to Nabulsi becoming foreign minister in the cabinet of his successor, Fakhri Khalidi.

A group of Nabulsi supporters, who called themselves the Patriotic Congress, met at Nablus on April 22. This demonstrated that the crisis was not over. Appropriately, Nablus was the traditional center for Palestinian and Arab nationalism. The seventy-five dissidents included twenty-three members of the Chamber of Deputies, which, in fact, was a majority of three. Their resolutions demanded nothing short of the end of Jordan as a separate state. They demanded union of Jordan with Syria and Egypt a full seven months before those two nations discussed union. The congress insisted upon punishment of those who had mistreated loyal officials and officers, apparently the Nabulsi cabinet, Abu Nuwar, Hiyyari, and the other officers who were under arrest. The "loyalty" the resolution referred to was obviously to Arab nationalism, rather than to the Hashemite Kingdom of Jordan. The congress also called for solidarity between the people and the army, with a general strike as the first step toward implementing their agenda.

Normal constitutional government could not continue under these circumstances unless the king was willing to succumb and agree to his political death warrant. With a majority of the Chamber in rebellious opposition, Khalidi had no choice but resign. Samir al-Rifai, the deputy premier, was the real power in the succeeding cabinet that imposed martial law on April 25. The government dissolved all political parties and other troublesome organizations and arrested Nabulsi. The rapid arrival of the first American financial aid on April 29 signalled that the "plucky little king" had protection against further unacceptable manifestations of Arab nationalism and radical agendas. The United States moved part of the Sixth Fleet to the eastern Mediterranean, which gave further evidence that the king was not alone to face Nasser and the forces he commanded.

Jordan and the United Arab Republic

The continuous advocacy of merging Arab states into a single state created unrest and suspicion throughout the region following the end of the mandates. Union of Egypt and Syria, the two foremost leaders of Arab nationalism, into the United Arab Republic on February 1, 1958 seemed to signal the arrival of the millennium for Arab nationalists. Jordan and Lebanon seemed the most likely candidates to submit to nationalist ardor, since neither possessed strong credentials to remain independent. The unexpected forcefulness of Hussein had avoided Jordan's demise only ten months earlier.

Hussein was no more eager to allow Jordan to perish than he had been earlier. He seized the initiative and approached his cousin, Feisal II of Iraq, to advocate the establishment of a Hashemite alternative to the Syrian-Egyptian foundation for Arab unification. His approach was a recognition of the strong appeal for Arab political unification that prevailed throughout the region. Hussein's consent for his cousin to serve as president of the Arab Federation, which they announced on February 14, relegated Jordan to a secondary role in the new structure. This was a realistic acknowledgment of Iraq's intrinsically stronger military and financial capacity. It was also a desperate attempt to survive by endorsing Arab nationalism. Even though no other Arab state could strongly consider joining the Hashemite plan, it was awkward for Nasser to attack it since the Arab Federation, indeed, endorsed the principle of Arab political unity.

The Hashemites, in fact, made a good historical case for their claim to lead Arab unification. Hashemites, had, after all, initiated and led the Arab revolt against the Ottoman Empire in 1916. Feisal I had, by acclamation, been the first elected king of Greater Syria and Abdullah's role had earned the same congress's proclamation of him as king of Iraq. Further, Hashemite leadership had preserved part of Palestine, including Jerusalem, from Zionist domination. According to this scenario, no other family, group, or organization could match Hashemite credentials for the mantle of Arab leadership.

The July Crisis and the Great Power Rescue

Early in July, Hussein learned from foreign intelligence sources that another army element, in collusion with the Syrian region of the United Arab Republic, planned to carry out a coup. The conspiracy, under the leadership of Colonel Mahmud Rusan and his brother, proved to be remarkably similar to one that overthrew the Iraqi Hashemite regime later that month. The king's preemptive actions made the coup impossible, but he was unsure of the loyalty of his army after the successful coup in Iraq on July 14. Other conspirators could still be in place or the widespread elation that greeted the brutal Baghdad coup could inspire a spontaneous uprising on behalf of Arab nationalism. Most assumed, in fact, that the Iraqi developments as well as the civil war in Lebanon were a further unfolding of a bigger plot, which the formation of the United Arab Republic ignited.

With unanimous approval of a carefully elected Chamber of Deputies Hussein requested British military assistance on July 16. By July 17, British paratroopers flew into Jordan from Cyprus over Israeli airspace. No evidence of a coup emerged and Jordan remained calm. Hussein declared the termination of the Arab Federation on August 2. A United Nations resolution on August 21, on behalf of mutual recognition of all the governments in the region, implied that the United Nations might use sanctions against violators of its appeal. British troops withdrew on November 2 since there was no indication that the Hashemite regime was in any unusual danger.

Jordan and its king appeared secure as 1958 drew to a close. Britain had demonstrated its continued interest in maintaining Jordan's existence and there were strong indications that the United States would have provided the same kind of protection if it had not been preoccupied with ensuring Lebanon's independence at the same time that Jordan faced apparent danger. American financial assistance seemed assured unless Jordan became a center of anti-Israeli activities. Significant differences had already begun to surface within the United Arab Republic that made its immediate further expansion less likely. The Iraqi regime of General Qassim was preoccupied with solidifying its internal control and showed inclinations to move toward the Gulf rather than westward. Saudi Arabia could no longer afford to harbor its traditional anti-Hashemite posture as the new powerful forces in the region relegated that old feud to irrelevance.

Hussein had defied the British, the Arab nationalists, and his nation's financial and political inadequacies. He had survived in a fashion that impressed his Bedouin followers and his foreign supporters. Having passed through such an impassioned period of turmoil, he and his kingdom no longer seemed in imminent danger of extinction.

SYRIA

Syria's Gravitation toward Moscow and Cairo

The success of the conservatives in the Syrian presidential election of 1955 was ephemeral in the heated atmosphere of that year. Arab nationalist fervor reached new heights with Nasser's success at the Bangdung Conference and his Eastern Bloc arms deal; the furor over the Baghdad Pact; Turkish troops positioned on the Syrian border; and the Israeli raids on Gaza and Syria's Lake Tiberius community. The moment belonged to politicians who could address these problems, instead of showing primary concern for retaining their privileged positions. The Baathists had impeccable nationalist credentials. Despite their small number, they had the advantage of good international organization and the capacity to move the masses. Khalid al-Azem had a proven ability to combine a capitalistic outlook with a search for Soviet assistance to achieve nationalist ends. The communists, who were enemies of the Baath ideologically and because they appealed to much the same clientele, preyed upon both nationalist and class frustration to be an influential alternative.

Al-Quwatly shuffled his cabinet in mid-June 1956 to conform more closely with national and regional inclinations toward Nasser's Arab nationalism. The Baath consented to enter the cabinet on the condition that Syria seek union with Egypt as a step toward full Arab unification. Their receipt of the Foreign Affairs and Economics portfolios indicated their new strength, since they had never held cabinet positions before. The other major parties had cabinet positions, including al-Azem's Democratic Bloc. His assumption of the post of Defense Minister in early January 1957, after a period of illness, was the most notable.

The government change represented a major turn to the left for Syria in close alliance with Egypt and the Soviet Union. President al-Quwatly was a conservative, but he was not opposed to Arab nationalist goals and he had a good relationship with both Egypt and Saudi Arabia, which were still on cordial terms out of mutual fear of Iraq. Al-Quwatly's steadying hand and easy relationship with the Egyptian leadership helped to prevent precipitous developments when impatient forces within his country wanted to behave rashly. His equally good relationship with the Saudis helped limit the strain that occurred throughout the region as radical developments threatened the entire political and social structure of the Arab world. The president even reconciled himself to close association with the Soviet Union as it had become clear that Syria would not obtain modern weapons from France, its traditional supplier. He visited the Soviet Union soon after his election.

Soon after taking power, the new government witnessed the elation throughout the Arab world after Nasser's nationalization of the Suez Canal on July 26.

Syria broke relations with Great Britain and France, moved troops into Jordan to threaten Israel, and allowed Syrian "volunteers" to disable the IPC pipeline. Syria gave full support to the Nabulsi government, which emerged in Jordan as part of the strong nationalist movement in the fall of 1956. The discovery of an Iraqi-sponsored plot among Syria's conservative leaders bolstered the government's contentions that reactionary forces not only planned to crush Nasser but also to defeat all nationalist and liberation forces in the Arab world.

Left Again

Syrian policies became more radically leftist at the beginning of 1957 after disclosure that so many traditional politicians had conspired with Iraq. With mainstream leaders either discredited or on the defensive, the Baathists; al-Azem, in concert with the Communists; and Arab nationalist military officers under the leadership of Colonel Abdul Hamid Sarraj had unprecedented freedom to implement a radical agenda. Hourani constructed a National Front in parliament, which was primarily a merger of Baathists and Communists. This organization provided a legislative base to dominate domestic and foreign policies. This unique combination, in the unusual circumstances of 1957, was able to pursue a course that ultimately frightened almost everyone, even though the strange partnership was intrinsically incompatible. Hourani and Sarraj had the most in common, but even their efforts were predicated upon being able to dominate Nasser after they had engineered union with Egypt. They disliked the Communists and only found them convenient tools to help destroy the existing order they wished to replace. Al-Azem was a Syrian nationalist, who had no desire to subsume Syria in a larger Egyptian- or Baathist-dominated Arab state. He worked with the Communists because of their ability to help him with the masses and in his efforts to obtain Soviet assistance.

It is not coincidental that the National Front took office on January 2 and the United States issued the Eisenhower Doctrine on January 5. Syria, not Nasser's Egypt, appeared to present the Soviets with the opportunity to obtain a base in the Middle East. The Communists were outlawed in every other Arab country where they had to operate as persecuted, clandestine movements. Even in Syria, Communists operated at the sufferance of fellow travellers who intended to eliminate them once they had served their purpose. This was, however, too subtle a distinction even for those who understood the truth in the heat of the Cold War.

Al-Azem's conclusion of a broad economic and technical aid agreement with the Soviet Union early in August 1957 alarmed even the Baathists and Nasser, along with the Western Bloc. Syrian consent in April for Czechoslovakians to build a major oil refinery at Homs had already indicated Syria's dependence on the Soviet bloc for technical assistance. The scale of the new projected relationship, which was the first such Soviet agreement in the Arab world, dwarfed earlier Soviet military and technical efforts in Syria. By this agreement, Al-Azem and his Communist associates had exceeded acceptable bounds and became a liability, rather than an asset to Arab nationalists of all description. The appointment of Afif Bizri as Chief of Staff of the army on August 17 was decisively provocative. He enjoyed a high profile as an Arab nationalist going back to his participation in the Rashid Ali movement in Iraq and recently by presiding over the trial of those accused in the recent Iraqi conspiracy. His close association with the Communists led many, particularly outside of Syria, to conclude that his appointment gave the

Communists control of the army as well as the government. Regional opponents, especially Syrians, began to fear that the threat of a Communist takeover in Syria was as dire as the United States had been claiming. Since evoking the Eisenhower Doctrine was not an option, because all but Lebanon had renounced it, a union of Syria with Egypt seemed the only answer.

Union with Egypt

The shape of the future began to emerge in November 1957 in cooperation among anti-Communist elements, including the United States. The Americans had become sympathetic to the situation the Baathists faced in Syria. Secretary of State Dulles' statement at the end of September that there was no evidence any Middle East country was under Communist control signalled Syrians that the United States would work with Syria if it purged the Communists. The American Ambassador to the United Nations, Henry Cabot Lodge, met with Bitar early in November and the United States restored normal relations with Syria, which had broken down in August. Under U.S. pressure, the Turkish troops that had moved to the Syrian border in August withdrew. The National Front disintegrated on November 15 upon the initiative of the Baath, which joined most other parties in cancelling parliamentary elections that projected to return a stronger Communist contingent. An Egyptian parliamentary delegation visited Damascus to negotiate with the Syrian parliament on plans to unify their two countries. The Egyptians made it clear that they expected complete unity, while the Syrians insisted that a merger should be a confederation. They issued a joint resolution for confederation on November 18, but all knew that Nasser wanted either total unification into a single state or nothing. This resolution ignored Nasser's equally provocative demand that the abolition of all political parties was a precondition for union. Self-confident as the Baathists were of their ability to dominate Nasser once the union occurred, most resisted participation in their own destruction.

Al-Azem's assumption of the deputy premiership in December to supplement his posts of Minister of Defense and Finance moved army officers to take the initiative. His increased strength with the electorate through his alliance with the Communists, after all, had been crucial in accelerating the movement toward union. Chief of Staff Bizri proved that the fear of him as a Communist was misguided when he, accompanied by fellow officers, went to Cairo and conducted negotiations regarding the union with Nasser. Nasser's unwillingness to alter any conditions for merger gave the officers and Bitar, who later joined in the negotiations, no choice. The Syrians consented to total union on February 1, 1958. This meant the abolition of their independence and the abolition of all Syrian parties, as well as their independent military and legislature. President al-Quwatly, a close friend of Nasser, willingly endorsed the union as he resigned his office and proud Syria lost its separate identity to become the Northern Region of the United Arab Republic.

Syrian frustration with its dismemberment following World War I was compounded over the next forty years as it was not only unable to regain its lost provinces, but actually had difficulty maintaining its own limited borders. Western imperialists, Turkey, Israel, and neighboring Arab regimes subjected it to further territorial loss, constant danger, and fear of annexation. Unable to defend itself, Syria joined with the strongest Arab leader of modern times in the hope of obtaining, in partnership with him, a reunion with its lost provinces that it had been unable to obtain alone.

LEBANON

Lebanon's Dilemma

External developments exacerbated Muslim-Christian relations in Lebanon and provided President Shamoun's political opponents the opportunity to curb his otherwise strong support over a prospering nation. He had been vulnerable for some time because of his rumored connection with British and American intelligence agencies. His bad relations with Syria in 1955 and his good relations with Turkey and Iraq aroused suspicions that he intended to join the Baghdad Pact. While he did not, his failure to break relations with France and Great Britain during the Suez Canal crisis angered his detractors, who resented his rejection of Arab solidarity while he supported Western policies. His acceptance of the Eisenhower Doctrine, which many regarded as an American Baghdad Pact, on March 16, 1957 increased the resentment of Arab nationalists and various Lebanese who wished to avoid provocation of their Arab neighbors.

A combination of the outcry against acceptance of the Eisenhower Doctrine, and the upcoming parliamentary elections in June spurred the opposition to intense activity in April 1957. Shamoun's rejection of the Nasserist approach to Arab unity and nonalignment gave the opposition broad popular support, while each of the political leaders and groups pursued their different agendas. The opposition, which adopted the title of National Front, publicized their belief that Shamoun planned to pack the new chamber with his supporters in order to change the constitution and allow for his re-election. The situation worsened when security forces fired upon a National Front crowd demonstrating in Beirut on behalf of fair elections on May 30. The fact that two prominent leaders, Saib Salam and Nasim Majdalani, received wounds increased the Front's credibility. General Fuad Shihab, the Maronite Commander of the Army, helped negotiate procedures for the elections that avoided additional troubles before the elections began in June.

Shamoun's candidates won such an overwhelming victory that there was little doubt, as later research has proven, that bribery and overt intimidation accounted for the landslide that left even popular leaders like Jumblat, Salam, and Al-Yafi out of the chamber. Shamoun had won but he had to face momentous changes in neighboring countries with a divided nation, because he made no efforts to win any of the opposition to his side. Some overt acts of violence occurred against government installations from elements of the disaffected groups.

In such an atmosphere the union of Egypt and Syria into the United Arab Republic had a tremendous impact in Lebanon. Large, gleeful demonstrations occurred in all the major Lebanese cities in response to this concrete step toward Arab unification. Shamoun's government sent a perfunctory message of congratulation to Nasser, but almost every leader of the opposition, including Archbishop Meouchy, travelled to Damascus to congratulate Syrian President Quwatli. Others returned, along with perhaps three hundred thousand ordinary Lebanese, when Nasser visited Damascus on February 24. Shamoun, the more xenophobic elements of the Maronite community, and Muslims who had a vested interest in the smaller unit of Lebanon had reason to question whether Lebanon could resist the urge to join the U.A.R. They also shared the concern of the outlawed Syrian National Party that had worked from its inception in 1932 for the union of Greater Syria, but had no desire for union with Egypt. For the same reason the S.N.P. opposed the Ba'ath party's goal of unifying the entire Arab world.

Nasser, Quwatli, and the U.A.R.'s media promised to honor Lebanon's integrity, but made open invitations for Lebanon to join the union. Failure to accept such an opportunity was nothing short of treason in the view of fervent Arab nationalists. Nasser's pictures and U.A.R. flags appeared throughout Lebanon and more demonstrations on behalf of union erupted in the major cities. Shamoun supporters displayed his photograph in response in what is sometimes termed the "picture war." Banning of both photographs and demonstrations had little effect on avid believers on either side. Isolated, but often pointed, violence broke out periodically and numerous symbolic restraints prevented normal relations between the two main polarized groups. Differences seemed to have peaked on March 27 when the opposition actually formed an alternative government.

The assassination of Nasib Al-Matni on May 8 turned the previous posturing and sporadic violence into a full-scale civil war. This Maronite publisher of *The Telegraph,* a leading Beirut daily, had suffered imprisonment and an earlier attack on his life for his criticism of the Shamoun regime. Al-Matni's death soon ignited open warfare between the opposition and the government forces and their S.N.P. and Phalangist allies. Small numbers of Jordanian and Iraqi troops also supported the government. Since each side remained primarily in their respective sectors, fighting was limited in Beirut, where the opposition was under the command of Saib Salam. Heavy fighting occurred in Tripoli, as the army took an active part in subduing the opposition that was under the command of Rashid Karami. A prolonged series of battles occurred for over six weeks in the Shuf, where Jumblat's forces faced stiff resistance, particularly from the S.N.P. The opposition controlled most of the Biqa region, although in places they found the S.N.P. difficult to dislodge. Most of the fighting occurred between militias and government security forces as General Fuad Shihab, the commander of the army, generally reserved the army for limited use to prevent opposition forces from winning an overwhelming victory. He regarded the armed conflict as an abortive extension of the political process, which was not an army concern as the army should only defend Lebanon against foreign enemies. In addition, most of the opposition leaders were his close friends. He was also concerned that the army might disintegrate and join their brethren if ordered to fight against their families and friends.

When the fighting began, the Lebanese government appealed to both the Arab League and the United Nations to come to its rescue in face of its claim that the fighting resulted from U.A.R. interference in Lebanon. The Lebanese government refused to accept Arab League proposals for a solution, and the United Nations was severely divided on a course of action. The United States and its allies accepted Lebanon's accusation, while the U.S.S.R. and its allies claimed that the struggle was among Lebanese factions devoid of U.A.R. provocation.

The successful, bloody coup against the Hashemite monarchy of Iraq on July 14, 1958 moved Shamoun to invoke the Eisenhower Doctrine with the plea that his country would fall under Communist control unless he received American aid within forty-eight hours. Since the coup had taken everyone by surprise and most everyone assumed that it was an extension of the U.A.R. movement, U.S. marines began to land from nearby ships on July 15. Since the Lebanese army did not expect an American "invasion," confrontations nearly occurred before Shamoun and General Shihab could explain American presence to Lebanese commanders. The 15,000 U.S. troops occupied strategic areas such as the port and the airport and shared patrol duties with their Lebanese counterparts. The marines never had to use force as their strength seemed to have dissuaded serious attack from the opposition irregulars.

Developments in Iraq and Jordan that had precipitated the U.S. invasion as the real cause for the civil war had ceased when Shamoun finally stated early in July that he did not seek reelection. The Chamber of Deputies met on July 31 and elected General Shihab to succeed Shamoun, whose term ended on September 23.

Shihab's initial cabinet under Prime Minister Karami seemed to have awarded victory in the civil war to the opposition, because seven of the eight ministers had been opposition leaders. Pierre Gemayel and his Phalangists, who had regarded the civil war as a fight for Christian survival, erected new barricades and conducted violence against Muslims. After other supporters of the previous administration joined Gemayel, Karami's cabinet proved moribund because he had little support in the Chamber, which was the same one Shamoun had engineered in 1957. In the midst of an atmosphere of continued civil war Shihab met with all the leading *zaims* before deciding to adopt a policy of "no victor, no vanquished," which meant that Karami would form a new cabinet on October 14 with equal representation for Shamoun's supporters and the opposition. Gemayel, who joined this cabinet, had been the clear winner in this transaction and he emerged as a strong political force compared to his previous status as little more than a nuisance.

The broad-based cabinet signaled a return to normal in Lebanon. U.S. troops withdrew on October 25, 1958 and the Chamber authorized the cabinet to govern by decree for six months to restore order and prepare for a return to normal parliamentary democracy. Karami's cabinet resigned in May of 1960 to allow another broad-based cabinet composed of less controversial figures to conduct the June elections. The resulting, unusually fair elections returned a Chamber that represented most Lebanese factions. Saib Salam became the new Prime Minister of a huge, eighteen-member cabinet to include most interests. Lebanon's civil war had fully ended as most factions gained their expected share of power and no single person or group threatened the independence of any other.

President Shihab's administration centralized the power of Lebanon under a group of professional administrators with Ilyas Sarkis at the head of the presidential bureau. This approach reduced the influence of the traditional *zaims,* although Shihab had the steady support of Pierre Gemayel, Kamal Jumblat, and Rashid Karami, none of whom supported him for his administrative approach. Shihab won Gemayel's support by fostering the Phalangist's success over Raymond Edde, who had opposed Shihab's election. While Jumblat was the only major political leader who advocated a secular approach to government, he appreciated Shihab's good relations with Nasser and his apparent accommodation with Arab nationalism. Shihab's policies toward Nasser served Karami well with his largely Sunni constituents and made him comfortable to serve in the cabinet, usually as prime minister, from 1961 to 1970.

Shihab's approach to government was distinct enough that it became popularly known as the *Nahj al-Shihabi* (Method of Shihab) or Shihabism. In addition to close cooperation with Nasser, Shihab maintained good relations with the conservative Arab governments. But the "method" generally referred to internal administration that concentrated on continuing the economic liberalism of Al-Khoury and Shamoun, while providing better services to all sectors of Lebanese society, rather than favoring Christian areas. His *Deuxieme Bureau,* or military secret police, played a prominent role in the entire system, but especially in keeping dissident elements and the Palestinians under control.

Lebanon became a nation under President General Shihab. His extention of central authority throughout the tiny state forced even the most parochial and independent *zaims* to accept the superiority of national policy. His general respect for the traditional role of the local authorities helped him reach an accomodation with them that satisfied their pride. Shihab demonstrated a combination of wisdom and strength that prevented the other traditional Lebanese leaders from believing that a faction had control of the state for the enrichment of its members. The Middle East's least likely nation seemed to have a future as a functioning member of the region's economy and culture.

IRAQ

Stalwart Iraq

Nuri al-Said's control of Iraq enabled him and the monarchy to withstand the adverse regional reactions to the Baghdad Pact. The Iraqi government simply did not permit outward expressions of discontent with policies it regarded as necessary. The fast pace of events in the Middle East in the 1950s, however, did not allow the regime to recover from one major event before it faced a new challenge. Nasser's nationalization of the Suez Canal on July 26, 1956 aroused feelings of pride in Iraq and throughout the Arab world. The Israeli-Anglo-French attack on Egypt in late October was particularly troublesome for the Iraqi regime because of its close affiliation with Great Britain. It broke relations with France but maintained relations with its Baghdad Pact partner, although on a reduced level. While many Iraqis seethed at their government's posture, the firm clamp on opposition elements kept reactions to a minimum, except in the less secured city of al-Najaf and the small town of Hayy, where uprisings ended only after the authorities used strong force.

Nuri's masterful ability to control events within Iraq could not prevent regional problems, such as the factional ferment in Lebanon, the Communist threat in Syria, and the unrest in Jordan, from spilling across the Iraqi borders. Radio broadcasts from abroad kept Iraqis apprised of developments and interpreted them unfavorably against the regime. The establishment of the United Arab Republic between Egypt and Syria on February 1, 1958 proved more than the cauldron-like atmosphere of the Middle East could accommodate. It aroused Iraqi Pan-Arabists in behalf of unity and caused concern among such elements as the Kurds, Shiah, and Communists who opposed Pan-Arabism.

The regime could not speak for any of these groups as its main political and social philosophy was survival. Typically, it reacted by accepting the Jordanian offer to form a confederation called the Arab Union on February 14 and invited other conservative Arab states to join. None did. Also, the Hashemite union found little support in Iraq, where most regarded it as an effort to save an unpopular, outdated regime. The ferment in Lebanon developed into civil war in May and Nasserists appeared ready to topple King Hussein in Jordan.

The End of Monarchy

The Jordanian situation affected Iraq more, since Jordan was joined with Iraq as a result of the May 12 confirmation of the Arab Union. The movement of Iraqi troops to assist Jordan with its internal problems was the opportunity that approximately two hundred members of the Free Officer Society within the army had sought for several months.

The Free Officer group originated in 1952 under the leadership of two engineer majors, Rifat Sirri and Rajab Abd al-Majid, both of whom had strong Pan-Arab ideas and looked to Nasser as their model. They shared civilian discontent over the regime's non-Arab foreign policy, and its inability to eradicate social and economic injustice. Like the Baath, they adopted the Communist method of a secretive, selective approach to candidates for their society, whom they organized into cells of four.

Members were selected for their willingness to help overthrow the regime and their strategic placement in units, which could compose a proper combination for a successful coup. Like most of the officer corp, the Free Officers were predominantly Sunni Muslims. Most were better educated than their senior officers and had received their military training after 1932 when the British lost their hold on military affairs. By the end of 1956 the movement was under the control of a Supreme Committee, which alone knew all the members of the group.

General Abdul Karim Qasim and an officer who had served under him, Colonel Abd al-Salam Aref, formed their own clandestine group, which they merged with the Free Officers in June 1957. Qasim became the chairman of the Supreme Committee on the strength of his superior rank. But, contrary to his Free Officer oath, Qasim developed contact with the Communists and other leftist elements in pursuit of his own agenda.

The Free Officers concluded that a successful coup required seizing the king, the crown prince, and Nuri al-Said; preventing outside interference; obtaining live ammunition; and finding an opportunity when the movement of troops would not appear suspicious. They obtained prior commitments from both Nasser and the Soviet Union to prevent interference from Baghdad Pact nations. The conspirators accumulated ammunition in small amounts to avoid suspicion and made plans to seize more from specific arsenals when the three leaders of the regime were all in Baghdad and an excuse for moving troops coincided.

Their opportunity arose on July 3, 1958 when the Twentieth Infantry Brigade, in which Aref commanded one of the three battalions, received orders to move to Jordan to bolster King Hussein. Since it had to pass through Baghdad near the royal palace the time seemed ripe for a coup, especially since some of the younger Free Officers were impatient for action. The Free Officers and others who knew something was afoot realized the circumstances were ideal and waited for a signal from Qasim. He knew each of them understood their roles but did not want to include them in planning, which could increase their claims for special positions.

Aref's brigade moved to Baghdad as ordered on July 14 and he seized control to carry out the coup as agreed with Qasim. His battalion captured the palace, Nuri's house, and the radio station. Aref made a radio announcement at 6:30 A.M., called Proclamation Number 1, which informed the nation that the army had "liberated" Iraq. In the frenzy that accompanied the occupation of the palace, the entire royal family except the crown prince perished in a hail of gunfire after they had surrendered. Nuri al-Said escaped until the next day, when a soldier recognized him and promptly shot him. A mob discovered his secret grave and disinterred him to suffer untold mutilation before they burned his mangled remains. The mobs dragged the crown prince's body through the streets and hanged it at the Ministry of Defence, where he had hanged Colonel al-Sabbagh in 1945. All of this indicates the widespread glee that accompanied the fall of the royalist regime.

Approximately three thousand soldiers ignited a revolution, which others soldiers and the populace secured. By noon the coup was complete as General Qasim arrived in Baghdad from his base about sixty miles from the city. It was so swift and decisive that there was nothing to defend or rescue of the Hashemite regime.

World reaction assumed that the Iraqi revolution signalled a major triumph of Arab nationalism and that Iraq would soon affiliate in some way with Nasser's United Arab Republic. Colonel Aref seemed to have shared that belief. But Qasim had no such intentions. He sent Aref into exile as the ambassador to West Germany and imprisoned the reluctant diplomat, who returned to Baghdad without authorization to continue his advocacy of Arab unity. The Iraqi coup was the deciding factor in American troops landing in Lebanon in response to President Shamoun's plea on July 14 that, without American intervention, Lebanon would fall to the Communists (Nasser) within forty-eight hours.

Qasim, however, steadfastly pursued an anti-Nasser policy during his years as dictator of Iraq. The "Sole Leader," as he styled himself, ruthlessly implemented a personal regime that used the Iraqi leftists, especially the Communists, to subdue all opposition. His attempt to claim Kuwait when the British withdrew in 1961 raised the ire of all the Arab states, who cooperated with the British and the United States to prevent Qasim's annexation of Kuwait. Qasim's regime set Iraq on a radical course that put it outside of the mainstream of Arab affairs most of the time until 1980, when most of the Arab states found common cause with Saddam Hussein's war with Iran.

SAUDI ARABIA

Saudi Arabia's Quandary

King Saud dutifully broke diplomatic relations with both Britain and France at the beginning of the Suez Canal Crisis in 1956 in support of Nasser's bold stroke against lingering Western presence and unobliging policies. Nasser's pressuring of Jordan in the spring of 1956, which led to General Glubb's dismissal and the loss of the British subsidy, forced Saud's financial support of the Hashemite regime. He further agreed to sell Egypt oil one-third cheaper than the market price in 1957.

Nasser was a demanding and expensive partner, but he was not helpful as a source for the financial, technological, and military assistance Saudi Arabia needed unless Saud was willing to follow his lead and deal with the Soviet Union. His unwillingness to go that far forced him to respond favorably to the overtures of the United States, which were designed to retain American interests in the kingdom and create an alternative leadership to Nasser in the Arab world. In return for a $50 million aid program from the United States, Saud broke ranks with Nasser and agreed to the Eisenhower Doctrine of January 5, 1957. He also agreed to extend the right of the United States to retain the military base at Dhahran for an additional five years.

Predictably, Saud's moves toward the U.S. signalled the beginning of a disruption of his uneasy alliance with Nasser. A Saud-Nasser conflict emerged from personal, ideological, and financial reasons. The Saudis revealed in April of 1957 that they had uncovered an Egyptian plot to assassinate Saud. Eleven months later, the Egyptians presented evidence that Saudi Arabia had disbursed a large amount of money to assassinate Nasser. In the meantime, Saudi Arabia had rescinded its agreement to sell oil to Egypt at below market price. Both accusations were probably true, but they were particularly embarrassing to Saudi Arabia, which found itself facing the newly formed United Arab Republic of Egypt and Syria after February 1, 1958. Saud's bad relations with Nasser and some specific diplomatic efforts had improved his relations with both Jordan and Iraq. But Saud's policies had helped isolate Saudi Arabia, as the Arab Confederation of Jordan and Iraq soon followed the formation of the United Arab Republic. Making matters intolerable for Saudi Arabia was the fact that it was financially broke as it faced the new alignment of the major Arab nations. Saud's failure to involve his brothers, including Crown Prince Feisal, in the governing process attracted all blame to himself. It became clear that he could no longer be entrusted with uncontrolled management of the fiscal and diplomatic affairs of the Kingdom.

Turn to Feisal

Consultation of the oldest brothers and the intercession of Ibn Saud's brother, Abdullah bin Abdul Rahman, led to a transfer of executive power to Feisal on March 24, 1958. Feisal was well travelled and had served several important diplomatic and military functions during the reign of Ibn Saud. He had settled down from his youthful pleasures to a life of moderate tastes and devotion to his three wives and children. His children were, in fact, probably the best educated members of the entire royal family. His background and attitudes suited him well for the duties his unprepared brother had been unable to fulfill. Saud, however, remained king and was free to perform the ceremonial functions of the position. The question remained as to whether Saud would continue to accept his lowered status once the crisis passed and his own failing health improved.

Feisal was an enthusiastic Arab nationalist and apparently supported Nasser's leadership in the Arab world. Under Feisal's leadership the Saudi government essentially admitted it had interfered in Syrian affairs and paid for Nasser's assassination. Feisal made favorable gestures toward Nasser and other Arab leaders, while it backed away from the overtly pro-American posture of Saudi Arabia without adopting an anti-Western stance. His adroit beginning justified the hope that his leadership would provide a sounder future for Saudi Arabia and better relations with its international partners.

Events of the summer of 1958 tested Feisal's mettle and demonstrated his ability to accept developments in neighboring states. It appeared that all the Arab nations were going to fall under pro-Nasser regimes. But under his direction Saudi Arabia did nothing following the dramatic overthrow of the Hashemite regime in Iraq on July 14, 1958. The fact that it turned out to be anything but Nasserist could be no comfort to the foremost remaining Arab monarchy. Likewise, Saudi Arabia took no action and released no provocative statements after the U.S. Marines landed in Lebanon and the British paratroopers saved King Hussein in Jordan. All those events were beyond Feisal's capacity to alter. It was one of those rare times in the modern Middle East when doing and saying nothing was the best course of action.

Feisal's task of restoring order to Saudi finances and monetary stability was enough to have made him mute on foreign affairs. Here, too, he adopted a firm and resolute course, which displeased many who knew nothing of the government's problems, but were accustomed to receiving astronomical benefits and profits. Saud and all of his heavy pilferers were denied access to the treasury. The king received a liberal private fund for his habitual spending, which also allowed him a margin to continue his compulsive handouts and funding of projects. Feisal established a budget and required that all disbursements gain the approval of the Council of Ministers, which began to act as a responsible management branch of the government for the first time in Saudi history. He greatly restricted imports which had drained the Kingdom of vast quantities of its hard money. He devalued the Saudi riyal to a realistic level against the dollar and put the entire monetary system under consistent and responsible management. Feisal set aside a portion of the revenues to begin to retire the government's indebtedness. Feisal carefully avoided policies that were too onerous for the religious establishment, the military officers and the tribes to bear. Still, he gained the reputation for being hard and unfeeling. Such policies had never existed before in the open-handed regimes of his father and his brother. Such remedies were necessary and received desirable results, but he was also fortunate that the oil revenues rose substantially during his economic restructuring. By 1962 Saudi Arabia was truly solvent for the first time in its thirty-year history.

IRAN

New Direction in Iran

Serious discussion of reducing royal power was unacceptable in the immediate post-Mossadegh period, but the shah had to work closely with both the domestic and foreign elements that had restored him to power. He was, however, more than ever before in his reign the source from which direct and indirect power flowed. General Zahedi received the premiership as a reward for restoring the monarch. Other, undisputably loyal members of the political and military classes received appropriate rewards and joined with the shah to punish Mossadegh and his more ardent supporters. Mossadegh acquitted himself well in a public trial, which sentenced him to house arrest for three years, after which he lived out his life on his estates. Leftist elements, especially the Tudeh, received harsh treatment that included torture, imprisonment, and execution. By 1955 there was little remaining of the Tudeh structure that had survived its earlier suppression in the late 1940s. The new secret police of the revived regime, which evolved into the National Security and Information Organization (SAVAK) in 1957, did not hesitate to err on the side of caution, as they demonstrated a willingness to arrest anyone with a hint of leftist leanings. Fear of arrest became a very effective weapon to curtail antigovernment activities that had plagued the government since 1941. As even Zahedi learned when he was dismissed on April 6, 1955, Muhammad Reza was determined no individual or group could emerge with a power base that could threaten the shah's preeminence over Iranian affairs. Little approximating an opposition could get elected to the Majlis in the new structure, but the shah created an apparent two party system in 1957 when he instructed all Majlis members to join either the court's Nationalist Party or its supposed opposition, the People's party.

Settlement of the oil issue proceeded fairly rapidly after Iran restored diplomatic relations with Great Britain in December 1953. By the new agreement of October 1954 Iran's nationalization remained intact under the supervision of the National Iranian Oil Company. The former Anglo-Iranian Oil Company, which assumed the new name of British Petroleum, had to share exploration, production, and marketing with seven other companies. British Petroleum received 40 percent of the new consortium, as did the five largest American oil companies. Royal Dutch Petroleum (Shell) received a 14 percent share and the French Petroleum Company obtained the remaining 4 percent. The consortium and Iran shared all profits equally. This was a considerable improvement for Iran, which retained the right to grant future contracts to companies of its choice.

In foreign affairs Iran gravitated even closer to the United States, which provided both military assistance and large infusions of development capital. To the shah's great disappointment, the United States constantly refused his attempts to obtain more military equipment that the Americans believed he could neither afford nor needed. The United States contended that the shah should concentrate on improving the lives of his people, since social unrest was the main threat that could also lead to a Soviet invasion. The United States encouraged Iran to rely on a regional agreement and American assistance for defense against foreign attack. Under American influence Iran joined the Baghdad Pact in 1955, even though it strained the existing amicable relations between Iran and the Soviet Union. The collapse of the Iraqi monarchy in 1958 voided any merit of that pact, however, and Iran established a much closer defense relationship with the United States. The growing radicalism in the neighboring Arab states drew the United States and Iran closer together as Nasser led a concerted attack on all monarchies and conservative regimes in the region.

By 1958 Iran was solvent, stable, and, with the help of the United States, capable of defending itself against any of its neighbors. This security and the steady increase in oil revenues inspired Muhammad Reza to envision a glorious future for his nation that was worthy of its illustrious past. He realized that every social problem that had caused upheavals throughout the first half of the century still existed. Programs were already on the books to address many of the difficulties and he had ideas for addressing all of the others. Funds seemed to be literally "in the pipelines" to transform his dreams into a reality. It is understandable that his apparent good fortune and his increasing belief in his special relationship with God prevented him from remembering that Iran had a strong tradition of raising men to the pinnacle only to drop them.

15

The Challenge of Freedom after 1958

HISTORICAL TIMELINE

1960 ⇛ Creation of Organization of Petroleum Exporting Countries (O.P.E.C.) with Saudi Arabia and Iraq as the first members.

1961 ⇛ General Qasim of Iraq declared the annexation of Kuwait on July 25.
⇛ Syria withdrew from the United Arab Republic on September 28.
⇛ Shah Muhammad Reza of Iran began his White Revolution with an initial decree on land reform on November 11.

1962 ⇛ Nasser declared his intention to export the Egyptian revolution to other Arab countries.
⇛ The attempt of Yemeni army officers to overthrow Muhammad al-Badr led to a prolonged civil war that involved other Arab countries until 1967.

1963 ⇛ Baathist-dominated coup in Iraq overthrew General Abd al-Karim Qasim on February 8.
⇛ Baathist-dominated military coup in Syria on March 8.
⇛ Ayatollah Ruhollah Khomeini exiled to Turkey on June 15.
⇛ Baathists expelled from office in Iraq on November 11.

1964 ⇛ Israel completed its National Water Carrier that diverted water from the Sea of Galilee and the Jordan River.
⇛ First Arab Summit in Cairo in January; aggreed not to contest Israel's water diversion from the Sea of Galilee and the Jordan River; created the Palestine Liberation Organization.

1965 ⇛ Ayatollah Khomeini moved from Turkey to Iraq in October, where he lived until 1978.

1966 ⇛ Radical Baathist coup in Syria on February 23; Hafez al-Asad became Defense Minister; aggressive support for Palestinian commandoes; founders of Baathist party expelled to Iraq.
⇛ Syria and Egypt signed a mutual defense pact on November 13.

1967 ⇛ Israel shot down six Syrian jets on April 7.
⇛ Nasser ordered United Nations Emergency Force troops to withdraw from the Sinai on May 18.
⇛ Nasser closed the Straits of Tiran to Israeli ships on May 22.
⇛ King Hussein of Jordan signed a mutual defense pact with Egypt on May 30.
⇛ Six Day War between Israel and the Arab states began on June 5.
⇛ Israel occupied the Sinai peninsula, the Gaza Strip, the West Bank, and the Golan Heights at the end of the Six Day War.
⇛ Arab League Khartoum Conference in August agreed to remain at war with Israel; the oil producers made financial commitments to aid the military confrontational states; ended war in Yemen.

1968 ⇛ Creation of the Popular Front for the Liberation of Palestine (PFLP) under the leadership of Dr. George Habash.
⇛ Battle of Karameh on March 21 between Israeli and Palestinian commandoes.
⇛ Creation of Saiqa (Lightning) commando group of the P.L.O. under Syrian military control.
⇛ Creation of the Organization of Arab Petroleum Exporting Countries (O.A.P.E.C.).
⇛ Baathist coup regained power in Iraq on July 30.

1969 ⇛ Richard Nixon became president of the United States on January 20.
⇛ Yasser Arafat became chairman of P.L.O. in February.
⇛ Golda Meir became prime minister of Israel in March.
⇛ Cairo Agreement on November 3 between P.L.O. and Lebanon gave P.L.O. the right to administer their own affairs in the Lebanese camps and to use Lebanese bases for attacks on Israel.
⇛ Imam Musa Sadr created a separate Shiah Higher Council in Lebanon.
⇛ Druze leader, Walid Jumblatt, created a coalition of Lebanese leftists called the National Movement that challenged the status quo in Lebanon.
⇛ Creation of the Popular Democratic Front for the Liberation of Palestine (PDFLP) under the leadership of Naif Hawatmeh.
⇛ Colonel Muammar al-Khadafi led a successful coup against King Idris of Libya on September 1.

1970 ⇛ Rogers Plan for peace in the Middle East announced on June 20.

- ⇛ King Hussein of Jordan employed force during September to suppress Palestinian commandoes.
- ⇛ Nasser died September 28; Sadat became president of Egypt.
- ⇛ Armed Palestinian commandoes moved from Jordan to Lebanon during the fall following their military defeat in Jordan.
- ⇛ Hafez al-Asad seized power in Syria on November 13.

1973
- ⇛ Egypt and Syria attacked Israel to begin October War (also know as Ramadan War and Yom Kippur War).
- ⇛ Arab oil boycott connected with the October War quadrupled petroleum prices.

1974
- ⇛ Arab League recognized the P.L.O. as sole representative of the Palestinian people at the Rabat Summit.
- ⇛ Imam Musa Sadr of Lebanon created the Movement of the Disinherited on March 17, which indicated that the formerly passive Shiah were becoming activist.
- ⇛ Yasser Arafat addressed the United Nations General Assembly on November 13.

1975
- ⇛ Iran-Iraq rapprochement in Algeria on March 5, which altered their border along the Shatt al-Arab in favor of Iran and gave Iraq freedom to suppress Kurds without Iranian interference.

1976
- ⇛ President Suleiman Franjieh, a Maronite Christian, invited Syrian troops to interfere in the Lebanese civil war.

1977
- ⇛ Menachem Begin and his Likud coalition won the Israeli election and ended the Labor party's monopoly on Israeli politics.
- ⇛ Anwar Sadat went to Jerusalem and addressed Israeli Knesset on November 19.

1978
- ⇛ Large-scale Israeli invasion of Lebanon on March 14; large numbers of Shiah Muslims fled from southern Lebanon to cities in the north.
- ⇛ Under Israeli sponsorship, Major Saad Haddad established the Republic of Free Lebanon on the Israeli-Lebanese border.
- ⇛ Egypt and Israel signed the Camp David Accord on September 17.
- ⇛ Ayatollah Khomeini was exiled from Iraq to France where he provided focus for various opponents of Shah Muhammad Reza.

1979
- ⇛ Shah Muhammad Reza went into exile from Iran on January 16.
- ⇛ Ayatollah Khomeini returned to Iran on February 1.
- ⇛ Egyptian-Israeli Peace Treaty signed on March 16.
- ⇛ Saddam Hussein became president of Iraq on July 16.
- ⇛ Immam Musa Sadr of Lebanon disappeared in Libya on his way to Italy.

1980
- ⇛ Iraq abrogated the 1975 treaty with Iran and invaded Iran on September 22, which began the Iran-Iraqi war.

1981
- ⇛ Israel bombed Iraqi nuclear facility at Osirak on June 7.
- ⇛ The assassination of Anwar Sadat on October 6, the anniversary

of the beginning of the October War of 1973; Hosni Mubarak became president of Egypt.

1982 ⇛ The attempted assassination of the Israeli ambassador to Great Britain was used to justify a massive Israeli invasion of Lebanon that devastated Beirut on June 6.

⇛ P.L.O. military forces began withdrawing from Lebanon on August 21.

⇛ Bashir Gemayel was elected president of Lebanon on August 23.

⇛ U.S. Marines entered Lebanon on September 9 as part of an international peacekeeping effort.

⇛ Massacres of Palestinians in the Sabra and Shatila camps in Lebanon on September 18.

⇛ Bashir Gemayel assassinated on September 14; Amin Gamayel elected president of Lebanon on September 20.

1983 ⇛ Two hundred forty-one U.S. Marines killed in Lebanon on October 23 in a failed attempt by international peacekeepers to end the Lebanese civil war.

1987 ⇛ Large-scale Palestinian uprising (*Intifada*) began on December 9.

⇛ An Islamic movement called Hamas evolved in Gaza and spread among all Palestinians to become a new strong element in Palestinian and Palestinian-Israeli affairs.

1988 ⇛ Iran-Iraq War ended with a ceasefire on July 18.

1990 ⇛ Iraq invaded Kuwait on August 2 and annexed Kuwait.

1991 ⇛ United Nations coalition launched an air attack against Iraq on January 16.

⇛ United Nations coalition launched a land attack against Iraq on February 23 that led to the end of war and reestablished Kuwait's independence.

⇛ Middle East peace conference convened in Madrid, Spain on October 30.

1993 ⇛ Israel and the P.L.O. signed a treaty on September 13 after several months of secret negotiations with Norwegian mediators.

1994 ⇛ Israel and Jordan signed a peace treaty on October 26.

The future did not bear out the optimistic hopes Arabs and Iranians had once they had established their freedom from foreign domination. The importance of the Middle East region continued to attract extensive outside interference, especially related to the global conflict of the Cold War. Outside forces asserted themselves in various ways to determine control of the region's vital petroleum resources. Arab resentment of Israel, and Israel's own efforts to survive in a region hostile to its existence, kept the region in turmoil. The Arab nations competed intensely among themselves in a strange combination for leadership of the Arab world and in an effort to avoid extinction from neighboring Arab states. The personal interests of the Arab leaders were often as important as their philosophical differences regarding the ideal configuration of Arab society. The frustration of the dispossessed Palestinians erupted in increased activism, which attracted varying degrees of support from individual Arab nations and groups. Iran remained a monarchy, which became increasingly tied to United States interests. The nation prospered and became militarily powerful in return for adopting secular policies that created a sub rosa seething among traditionalists, which would erupt with startling results twenty years later. If the first half of the century represented the problems associated with infancy and early childhood for the new states of the region, the second half of the century was surely similar to the tumultuous problems that frequently accompany adolescence.

THE PARAMOUNT IMPORTANCE OF PETROLEUM

Without a doubt the region's possession of such a large percentage of the world's petroleum reserves exaggerated the importance of every other problem in the Middle East. It is virtually impossible to imagine modern life without the energy and products that are derived from petroleum. Ironically, the largest consuming nations of petroleum products either possessed no petroleum of their own or possessed far less than their way of life required. Many Middle Eastern nations, by contrast, had vast petroleum deposits, but had little capacity to utilize it in their preindustrial societies. They chose to sell their crude petroleum for cash, which they used to purchase luxurious consumer products and an extravagant lifestyle for a privileged few. (Iraq was the one notable exception to this practice.) Soon they began to direct an inordinate amount of their petroleum income to the purchase of military preparedness, which required the presence of foreign experts. Only later did they begin to invest their petroleum income in education, an industrial infrastructure, health care, and a better standard of living for their ordinary citizens.

Only Iraq and Iran of the major Middle Eastern petroleum producers had sufficient populations to produce and manage their petroleum industry; they were able to come close to providing most of the services the petroleum boom generated. Even those two nations were unable to restrain their frenzy for change within the technological capacity of their population, although, again, Iraq's dependence on foreigners was measurably less than that of Iran. The other Middle Eastern petroleum producers became inundated with foreigners to administer the most sophisticated tasks in all areas of the emerging new societies. An even larger group of foreigners poured into the petroleum-producing states to perform the more menial tasks of the petroleum industry, private business, public works, public security, and private household duties. Societies that had lived in virtual isolation for centuries suddenly became Towers of Babel with the influx of foreigners who spoke many different languages and dressed in every possible way from silk suits to rags.

The most politically active states of Egypt and Syria possessed no significant petroleum deposits. Neither did the stateless Palestinians. All of them, along with the Lebanese and Jordanians, vied to share in the wealth of the petroleum producers. There was, in fact, a widespread belief among Arabs that the riches from petroleum belonged to all Arabs and they demanded that the income should benefit all of them. More pointedly, there was a pervasive belief that the Arabs should use petroleum as a weapon against Arab enemies, i.e., all nations and groups that retarded Arab advancement and supporters of Israel. The petroleum producers had a delicate problem of balancing their obligations to the Arab world, while they attempted to maintain their political power and good relations with the industrial nations who purchased their petroleum. The interest of the petroleum-consuming nations in maintaining the status quo in the petroleum-producing nations usually met with the approval of the petroleum producers. Consequently, advocates of political and social change in the entire Middle East regarded the governments of the petroleum producers and the petroleum consumers as the enemies of Arab progress, strength, and national destiny.

The formation of the Organization of Petroleum Producing Countries (O.P.E.C.) in 1960, and its more limited Arab counterpart (O.A.P.E.C.) in 1968, fulfilled many of the aspirations to receive higher prices that came closer to reflecting the true market value of the precious but limited resource. Central to the success of the cartel was the willingness of the members to restrain production, which was based on quotas, to control petroleum prices. Saudi Arabia's vast capacity made it possible for it to influence both production levels and prices that could either reward or punish particular customers. Influence over Saudi Arabia became a primary goal of the petroleum consumer nations and the advocates of political and social change in the Middle East. Needless to say, the Saudis could never please both. With rare exceptions, the Saudis appeared to favor the needs of the petroleum-consuming nations, particularly the United States, since support from the consuming nations seemed to be the best means of continuing their prosperity and their regime. The Saudis and the other petroleum producers, however, also had to extend their largess to social and political advocates of change, even though those very elements threatened their regimes. The complicated manipulations related to this general theme produced tensions and conflicts that were not often obvious to the uninformed observer.

Iran's mixed blessings from petroleum wealth were accompanied by more direct pressure on the acceptable use of its dramatically increased income. Shah Muhammad Reza faced the major problem of the Soviet Union on his northern border, an aroused Arab world to his west, and considerable unrest among his own population. He was inclined to combat all his problems with increased military strength. Under the Kennedy Administration, the United States, which was his principal supplier of modern weaponry and military advice, insisted that he implement social changes in return for military and technological assistance. This American pressure and internal unrest prompted him to embark on a dramatic modernization program, which he called the White Revolution. The Western and secular nature of the radical changes he began in the early 1960s resulted in significant resistance from religious traditionalists under the leadership of Ayatollah Khomeini. The Shah suppressed the opposition with a minimum of force and forced Khomeini into exile in Turkey, but he soon moved to neighboring Iraq. Khomeini would remain in Iraq as little more than a nuisance factor for the next fourteen years while the Shah implemented his secularist policies on an ever increasing scale. The United States generally approved of the Shah's approach and extended increased military assistance to him while it also allowed him a large role in maintaining stability in the entire Gulf region.

INTERNECINE CONFLICTS

Meanwhile, the Arab governments became embroiled in internecine conflicts that ranged in importance from the grand to the petty. Nasser was such an overwhelming force by 1958 that other Arab leaders, states, and even the Arab League, paled into insignificance.

Nasser's hasty union with the Baathists and Syria, which seemed to augur quick Arab unity, soon proved untenable. The Baathists resigned from the government in 1959 when they determined that Nasser would not follow their leadership. He neither forgave nor trusted the Baathists for the remainder of his life. Other Syrians quickly discovered that they were destined to a subservient role in the United Arab Republic. Syria withdrew from the Union in 1961 to the embarrassment of Nasser and to the disappointment of most Arab nationalists.

The revolutionary regime of General Qasim in Iraq, which had overthrown the Iraqi monarchy in 1958, pursued an agenda that Nasser and other Arab nationalists correctly concluded was contradictory to Arab unity. The Qasim regime, in close association with Iraqi Communists, rapidly mortified all the neighboring Arab states. Its attempt to annex Kuwait when the British withdrew in 1961 met the collective resistance of the other Arab states, which sent troops to prevent the annexation.

A revolutionary coup in Yemen in 1962 failed to eliminate the monarchy, which was able to establish a resistance movement. Nasser became embroiled in a prolonged civil war in support of the revolutionary regime, while the monarchists received assistance from Saudi Arabia and Jordan. Large-scale armed conflict persisted in Yemen until 1967.

Successful Baathist coups in Iraq and Syria in 1963 revived the possibility of a union among these revolutionary states with Egypt. Nasser's anger with the Baathists for their undermining of the Egyptian-Syrian union and the awkward incompetence of the Baathists in their efforts to reconcile with Nasser spelled disaster. The recriminations among them at least equalled those of the Arab nations that were at war with each other. Nasser subjected the Baathist leaders to unprecedented public humiliations. By 1963 he had developed his own brand of Arab Socialism which he began to advocate throughout the Arab world. His open call for revolution among the Arab masses against all existing governments made normal relations among any of them impossible.

Israel seemed to benefit from the multifaceted Arab conflicts. Its diversion of water into Israel from the Jordan River in 1964 was provocation for war, except that the Arabs were both too weak and too divided to do more than protest. At a Cairo summit to address this problem, the Arab states managed to create the Palestine Liberation Organization. This, too, was a manifestation of their collective weakness, as the principal reason for creating the P.L.O. was to provide some order and control for Palestinian frustrations. The Arab states feared that the uncoordinated actions of various Palestinian groups could provoke a war with Israel, which the Arabs were unable to fight.

A coup in Syria in February 1966 by young, radical Baathists spelled an end to the intense but comparatively minor conflicts in the Middle East. Their accession to power also began a decisive split between the Baathists of Syria and Iraq, as Iraq became the home of the Baathist founders, who were all native Syrians. The new Syrian regime unabashedly criticized Nasser's leadership of the Arab world and asserted their own intention to lead. Support for the Palestinians and an aggressive posture toward Israel were foremost on their agenda. Their assistance to Palestinian commando attacks upon Israel and their own confrontation with Israel in aerial combat destroyed the status quo.

Nasser answered the challenge to his leadership with reconciliation. He agreed to a mutual defense pact with the new Syrian regime. Under this agreement the provocative policies of Syria could easily lead to war between Israel and Egypt.

Governments that had suffered Nasser's attacks in recent years chided him for his soft policies against Israel, while he constantly expressed his support for the Palestinians. Even though his best troops and air units were fully engaged in the Yemeni war, Nasser took the bait and moved inexorably toward war with Israel. He demanded the removal of the United Nations Emergency Force from the Sinai, which was unquestionably legal if unwise. His blockade of the Gulf of Aqaba shortly thereafter was a violation of international law and a deprivation of access to the seas that Israel could not tolerate, since it had never had the use of the Suez Canal. Inability to use the Gulf of Aqaba denied Israel access to East Africa and the entire orient.

THE ARAB-ISRAELI WAR: AN ISRAELI TRIUMPH

The ensuing Arab-Israeli war was a debacle for the Arabs and an indescribable triumph for Israel. Israel won the war in the first moments when it destroyed most of Egypt's air force on the ground. Israeli command of the air made the remainder of the Six-Day War a mopping up operation. The Arab rush to war caused immeasurable Arab embarrassment and humiliation as the world watched their televisions and were able to witness the dancing and singing Israeli troops rounding up hordes of dirty, shoeless Egyptian soldiers. Retreating Syrian and Jordanian armed forces, accompanied by thousands of new Palestinian refugees, was an equally pathetic sight. There was no graceful way to accept such a devastating defeat and the magnitude and ease of the Israeli victory generated an outbreak of celebration in Israel and among its supporters abroad that no Arab could forget or forgive. The non-Arab world basically agreed that the Arabs were simply incapable of fighting a modern technological war. Desire to dispel this belief became a passion among most Arab leaders and the Arab masses.

Israel continued to hold vast Arab lands after the war ended. It refused to return the Sinai peninsula, the West Bank and the Old City of Jerusalem, the Gaza Strip, and the Golan Heights unless the Arab nations recognized its right to exist. As in 1949, however, the Arab states refused to negotiate or recognize Israel's legitimacy. United Nations efforts to reconcile the two enemy camps were unsuccessful.

THE PALESTINIAN PLIGHT: A QUEST FOR LIBERATION

Oddly, the Palestinians were the only Arab beneficiaries of this war, even though it created thousands of new Palestinian refugees. Many of them, in fact, were refugees from the 1948 war who had to move again. Their plight became more visible to the world as they settled into the makeshift camps in Jordan. An aroused younger element among the Palestinians seized control of the Palestinian community and vowed to carry on the fight for their liberation, which they had formerly entrusted to the Arab governments. Few, including the Arab governments, could disagree with this assessment. With the Arab military hardware destroyed and its leadership discredited, the Arab governments found themselves unable to counter Palestinian assertiveness. All recognized that it would take years to rebuild a conventional Arab military capability. The petroleum-producing states of Saudi Arabia, Kuwait, and Libya agreed to pay significant sums of money to Egypt, Syria, and Jordan to speed up the process of rebuilding their armed forces.

Thousands of Palestinians flocked to the various elements of the P.L.O., which promised to wage a guerilla war to liberate Palestine. Jordan, which had formerly used all means to suppress Palestinian activities against Israel, became the unwilling but primary host for the burgeoning Palestinian effort. Arab governments and private individuals contributed money in large sums to arm the guerrillas. After all, they were the only possible force that could strike militarily against Israel. Yasser Arafat, who lead the Fatah group, emerged as the new secretary general of the entire P.L.O. His unideological approach to liberating Palestine attracted more financial and diplomatic support than the very leftist elements such as George Habash's Popular Front for the Liberation of Palestine or Nayif Hawatmeh's Popular Democratic Front for the Liberation of Palestine. These latter two Marxist groups intended to revolutionize the entire Arab world in preparation for Palestinian liberation, while Arafat was willing to work with all existing governments. These and many other smaller groups vied for support and funds from the Arab governments. Syria, in fact, created its own group, Saiqa, to give it additional influence within the P.L.O.

Sporadic Palestinian guerilla attacks from bases in Jordan and Lebanon made little impression, except for the fairly large engagement between the commando forces and Israel at Karameh early in 1968. In the view of Jordan, however, the number of armed Palestinians grew to a dangerous level from 1968 to 1970. P.L.O. forces exercised considerable authority in Jordan and became an almost parallel government to that of King Hussein. The P.L.O. extracted an agreement from the Lebanese government in 1969 that permitted them to use Lebanon as a base for operations against Israel. In addition, the so-called Cairo Agreement recognized the P.L.O.'s right to administer the affairs of Palestinians in the refugee camps. Impatient elements of the P.L.O. turned to dramatic actions in their effort to make a larger impression on international public opinion. They called attention to the Palestinian plight by hijacking several international air carriers in 1970.

King Hussein struck against the Palestinians in September 1970 in an effort to reestablish his control over his nation and to prevent Israeli and international reprisals. The small arms of the Palestinians were no match for the conventional forces of Jordan. The Arab world expressed horror at the Jordanian use of force against the Palestinians. Nasser brokered a truce between Hussein and Arafat on September 27 and died the following day. Over the next few months the Jordanians expelled the armed Palestinians from their country.

Lebanon was the only Arab country too weak to deny the Palestinian commandoes a haven after their expulsion from Jordan. The Palestinian's sheer numbers, financial support, and sense of commitment soon propelled them into the midst of Lebanese politics. The simultaneous development of a leftist and Arab nationalist coalition under the leadership of the Druze, Kamal Jumbalat, threatened the delicate balance of Lebanese factions. Neither the Palestinians nor Jumbalat's National Movement were willing to accept the status quo that had prevailed among Lebanon's traditional political leaders for the previous forty years. Few could imagine, however, that any kind of development in Lebanon could develop into anything more than a minor blip on the Middle East, where so many powerful political and military forces operated.

POST NASSER DRIFT

Drift seemed to dominate the post-Nasser Middle East as the Arabs lacked any single leader and Arab military power remained weak because of Soviet hesitance to provide the kind and quantity of modern weapons the Arab countries attempted to purchase. The Baathist regimes of Syria and Iraq faced considerable internal problems and expended much of their energies on mutual recriminations. Iran, by contrast, enjoyed a dramatic growth in military strength and was moving rapidly to develop a credible industrial infrastructure in close association with the Western nations. The Shah even had a favorable image in the West in part because most people did not realize he was a driving force behind the increased petroleum prices O.P.E.C. demanded.

Israel seemed unusually secure because of the weakness of the leaderless and recently defeated Arabs. The Israeli government of Golda Meir exploited its overwhelming military superiority to extract the most favorable concessions form the Arabs. Aroused Jewish pride throughout the world urged Meir's receptive government either to keep the Arab lands or return all or part under conditions that enhanced Israel's national security. Unprecedented as it was for a female to lead any Middle Eastern government, there was no doubt that this Ukrainian-born woman from Milwaukee, Wisconsin was as formidable as any contemporary leader of the region. She became prime minister within months of the time that Yasser Arafat, Muammar al-Qadhafi, Richard Nixon, Henry Kissenger, Anwar al-Sadat, and Hafez al-Asad assumed their auspicious leadership roles.

The general absence of women from public affairs was customary enough that there was virtually no mention of the fact. Although women obtained the right to participate in Zionist affairs from the earliest immigrations into Palestine, few Jewish women held prominent leadership positions in their parties or in public office. Only the Middle Eastern nations of Iran and Turkey provided opportunities similar to those in Israel for women to participate in public affairs in the post-World War I period.

Golda Meir's emergence in a male dominated world, therefore, was notable. The ease with which she conducted herself made her prominence appear normal. Meir prepared carefully for her migration to Palestine in 1921. She worked her way up from membership in a small kibbutz to important leadership positions in the Histadrut, which was the economic organization of the Labor Party that dominated most labor, manufacturing, financial, political, and social affairs of the Zionist community in Palestine. She was in the forefront of laying the foundation for the state of Israel and held diplomatic and cabinet positions from its birth to prepare her for the prime ministership, which she obtained in March 1969.

There was hope for peace despite Israel's inflexible position under Meir's leadership. Even Nasser had demonstrated some interest in American efforts to negotiate a peace agreement between the Arabs and Israel. Not the least reason for many of the P.L.O. actions was their fear that the Arab states intended to make peace with Israel without restoring the Palestinian homeland.

EGYPT IN TRANSITION: THE CHALLENGE TO SADAT

To the surprise of almost everyone, Anwar al-Sadat managed to survive considerable resistance from his Egyptian colleagues and moved from the vice presidency to the presidency of Egypt upon Nasser's death. He made no effort to replace Nasser as the leader of the Arab world. Sadat had, in fact, strong inclinations to concentrate on the welfare of Egypt in contrast to the pan-Arab ambitions that had driven Nasser. He desired the benefits of peace that could help his nation face the challenge that the long confrontation and three wars with Israel had brought about.

Egyptian pride and the stark reality of power politics demanded, however, that Egypt improve its military position before Sadat could achieve an honorable peace settlement that would also regain land Israel had occupied during the 1967 war.

In short, Sadat planned to wage another war against Israel to lay a foundation for a peace settlement and future Egyptian prosperity. He said as much, but few believed him. Most regarded him as a weak man who was fortunate to keep his office in the giant lingering shadow of Nasser. To his benefit, however, there was a genuine desire among both the Egyptians and the most other Arabs to rectify the humiliation of 1967. Egyptian officers had taken much more seriously their study of modern warfare, which was based upon a much better educational foundation than a few years earlier. Also, the Syrians under the wiser leadership of Hafez al-Asad demonstrated an inclination to cooperate in a joint effort. King Feisal of Saudi Arabia, whom many regarded as cautious and non-aggressive, had expressed his willingness to use petroleum as a weapon if it could serve the genuine cause of restoring Arab dignity. Few others knew that Sadat and his staff were carefully laying specific plans to attack Israel.

THE 1973 WAR: A WATERSHED FOR THE REGION

After careful planning and elaborate deception to lull the Israelis into lethargy, Egyptian forces attacked the Israeli forces on October 6, 1973 when the Arabs were keeping Ramadan and the Israelis were celebrating Yom Kippur. Syria launched a simultaneous attack upon the Israelis in the Golan Heights. The Egyptians had the limited goal of establishing a presence on the east bank of the Suez Canal, which they believed they could hold under the protection of their significant supply of Soviet surface-to-air (S.A.M.) missiles. The plan also required the use of daring and technologically complicated hardware and strategy. Success in the campaign would prove the Arab's ability to fight a modern war and restore Arab pride. Egypt and the other Arab states could then pursue the possibilities of a fuller peace settlement with Israel.

"The Crossing" went even better than Egyptian planners had hoped. A stunned Israel and the world watched the Egyptian forces conduct a clinic in modern warfare, while the Syrians made a good showing in their own theater of the Golan Heights. The Arab petroleum-producing countries declared their intention of depriving supporters of Israel of access to their oil. Petroleum prices sky rocketed throughout the world to a level that would never again subside to where they had been before the Arab oil boycott began. The United States was hardest hit because it had established a supply line to provide Israel with massive quantities of goods for its war effort. Lines began to form at gasoline stations in the United States before the short war ended. The Israelis recovered from the shock of the early Arab advances and began to push both the Egyptians and Syrians back from their earlier advances. The Soviets, who had also poured massive war materiel into the Arab effort, joined the United States and the United Nations to arrange a ceasefire.

Most analysts agree that the ceasefire saved Egypt and Syria from another major military defeat. The mere fact that there was doubt was a victory in the eyes of most Arabs. The Egyptians and the Syrians had fought masterfully with modern weapons to restore Arab self-respect. The military effort, in conjunction with a successful Arab attack upon the industrial world through its control of much of the petroleum reserves, presented a convincing case for the prominent Arab role in modern society. Arabs from all nations expressed as much pride in the role "their" oil had played in the war as they did in the intelligence and performance of the Egyptian and Syrian military.

The 1973 war was clearly a watershed in the history of the world, as well as in the Middle East. Oil prices remained high after the war. The resultant enhancement of Arab wealth spread fear that Arabs would soon own unacceptably high portions of the world's land and businesses. Academic study of the Arab world increased to an unrecognizable extent in no small part because businesses wanted people who could sell goods and services to the wealthy Arabs. The high price of petroleum drove up the cost of business, and home ownership. Higher oil prices were reflected in anything that required heating, cooling, or transportation. It also increased prices on a plethora of petroleum bi-products. Obviously, very little escaped the influence of the war that lasted far beyond when most people remembered anything about the war. Several years would pass, however, before the war seemed to produce any significant alteration in Arab-Israeli relations.

SIGNIFICANT NEW DIRECTIONS

An agreement between Iraq and Iran in 1975, which Algeria brokered, proved far more significant than was obvious at the time. Iraq agreed to allow Iran's border to extend westward a few hundred feet in the Shatt al-Arab. This provided Iran with an equal share of the shipping channel of this vital waterway, much to the dismay of many Iraqis. The Iraqi government of Ahmad Hasan al-Bakr and Saddam Hussein did not like their concession, but it was a necessary step for their immediate needs. They hoped the future would provide an opportunity to rectify their agreement to share Iraq's only outlet to the seas with Iran. Iraq's problems with its Kurdish population was the dominant problem of the time. By the terms of the Iraqi-Iranian agreement Iran agreed to cease its support of Iraq's Kurdish rebels. Iran also promised to terminate the passage of arms from Iran to the Kurds and agreed that Kurds could no longer find safe haven in Iran to avoid Iraqi retaliation. Iranian adherence to the agreement enabled the Baathist regime to suppress the Kurds and reestablish government control over the Kurdish region.

Lebanon was coming unraveled in the early 1970s because of the conflict between the National Movement-Palestinian coalition and the conservative establishment forces over Lebanese and Arab nationalist issues. The government's inability to stop Israeli air raids and assassinations of P.L.O. leaders discredited the government even further. The widespread ferment among students and workers indicated the desire of the younger generation to reject the formula for cooperation among the old traditional leaders that had governed Lebanon since French mandatory days. Militia units sprang up in most identifiable groups.

Virtually unnoticed at the time was a growing dissatisfaction among the Lebanese Shiah population. Few noticed or cared that the Shiah had become the largest single group in Lebanon. The popular conception was that the Shiah were a politically insignificant element "that only knows how to have babies." Most Lebanese believed the Shiah were insignificant, had always been insignificant, and always would be insignificant. The Shiah's traditionally minor role in Lebanese affairs substantiated this belief. They had, however, become much more unified and had a greater sense of their worth due to the activities of Imam Musa Sadr, the leader of the Shiah Higher Council. The massive migration of Shiah from the rural south to the northern cities to avoid Israeli raids provided him a large following few bothered to notice. He created the Movement of the Disinherited in 1974 and soon thereafter stated that unless the Shiah received greater economic equality and social justice they would take it by force if necessary. An opportunity for the Shiah to make good on their promise soon occurred when Lebanon erupted into a civil war.

CIVIL WAR IN LEBANON

Lebanon's civil war, which began in 1975, almost defies understanding because of the complex relationships among the various participants, which continued to shift repeatedly throughout its duration. The fact that many foreign nations from all over the Middle East and elsewhere supported different factions at different times added to the confusion and made it virtually impossible to end the war. Among the Lebanese and the Palestinians who lived there, it was a struggle for power between conservatives and advocates of change. Conservative Arab regimes supported the conservative factions, which were basically Maronite Christian, and revolutionary Arab regimes generally supported the revolutionary factions and the Palestinians. The conservative factions received substantial support from Israel, which benefited from the chaos the Lebanese cauldron spread throughout the Arab world. At a crucial juncture in 1976 the Lebanese revolutionary forces and the Palestinians faced the combined efforts of almost all the foreign elements, which used Lebanon as a surrogate theater to accomplish their goals. The only thing it is safe to say about the Lebanese civil war is that it was not a religious war. In time, however, it created much more animosity among Lebanon's many religious groups than had ever existed before.

The very fact that a Maronite Christian president, Suleiman Franjieh, could invite the secular, Alawi, Baathist regime of Ḥafez al-Asad in Syria to intervene in 1976 indicates the nonreligious nature of the struggle. The revolutionary Syrian regime, which posed as the primary supporter of the Palestinians, accepted the invitation to intervene to prevent a victory of the leftist-Palestinian coalition. This is further indication of the complexity of the Lebanese situation. Syria also entered Lebanon as an official peacekeeping force of the Arab League, whose members had dramatically conflicting interests in the Lebanese crisis. The unwillingness of the Arab League, Israel, and the United States to allow Syria a free hand in Lebanon assured that even their strong military presence would not end the fighting. Many ceasefire agreements collapsed before the ink dried on the paper. Killing and war became the principal business in tiny Lebanon, the former "Switzerland of the Middle East." The numerous but formerly insignificant Shiah could find an opportunity to assert themselves in this kind of chaos only if they could acquire a strong sense of direction and a source of military equipment.

CAMP DAVID ACCORD

A peace treaty between Israel and Egypt on March 26, 1979 added to the chaos of the Arab world and the Middle East. This resulted from the unexpected electoral victory of Menachem Begin in 1977 over the Labor Party, which had held power in Israel since mandatory days. Begin, who was the most notable advocate of an expanded Israel, stated soon after coming to office that he was willing to make peace with Egypt. To the surprise of almost everyone, Anwar Sadat flew to Israel and began a flurry of negotiations that resulted in the Camp David Accord in 1978. President Jimmy Carter of the United States had facilitated this treaty by offering generous financial incentives to Egypt and Israel. Israel returned Egypt's Sinai peninsula and obtained peace with its only significant Arab military foe, as well as a substantial amount of aid from the United States. Egypt regained possession of the Sinai and received American assistance at a level second only to that of Israel. Most Egyptians warmly welcomed the agreement that gave them peace and the promise of prosperity, which they assumed would occur almost immediately. Anwar Sadat quickly became one of the most popular men in the United States. He also received international acclaim when he shared the Nobel Peace Prize with Begin. The world was relieved because an Arab-Israeli war seemed impossible once Egypt was removed from the Arab military equation.

Sadat initially received support among most Egyptians for his unilateral peace treaty with Israel, but Egypt and its leader suffered the opprobrium and hatred of the entire Arab world for destroying Arab solidarity against Israel. Iraq led the "Rejectionist Front," which first attempted to change Egyptian policy and later expelled Egypt from the Arab family of nations. The Arab League and the Islamic Congress moved their headquarters from Cairo to Tunisia and all the Arab states broke relations with Egypt. Egypt, the traditional leader of the modern Arab states, thus became a pariah in the Arab world. Egypt's peace with Israel embodied one of the greatest fears of the Palestinians, who realized the absence of Egypt from confrontation with Israel destroyed the leverage necessary to regain control over Palestine. While Palestinians participated in the ostracism of Egypt, they went further in committing terrorist attacks that kept the region in turmoil. The heated atmosphere in the Middle East prevented foreign investors and tourists from participating in Egypt's anticipated prosperity. The large numbers of Arabs who usually visited Egypt and conducted business there also ended. Peace, thus, failed to bring prosperity to Egypt and left most Egyptians feeling betrayed by both their president and their new American friends. Religious traditionalists felt particularly betrayed as Israel continued to hold Jerusalem while facing no real threat to deprive them of it.

IRAN'S ISLAMIC FERVOR

The provocative impact of the Camp David peace settlement soon paled in comparison to the dramatic developments in Iran. Confrontations between government forces and demonstrators escalated throughout 1978. Each encounter grew in size and violence, in part because each commemorated the deaths and injuries that had occurred in the previous one. The many different elements of Iranian society both at home and abroad became emboldened as the phenomenon unfolded. There had been little belief that anything of this nature could occur, because the Shah's many opponents had so little in common and lacked a common leader. The United States, which had assisted the military and industrial growth of the Shah's regime, cautioned him to be patient and refrain from using the force at his disposal. The sick and vacillating Shah docilely accepted the American approach.

An important turning point occurred when Iraq submitted to Iranian pressure and expelled Ayatollah Khomeini in the fall of 1978. This firebrand religious opponent of the Shah's White Revolution had been in Iraq since 1963, where he had been something of a nuisance to the Iranian regime as he joined in Iraq's frequent diatribes against the Shah. His increased activities from Iraq during the 1978 troubles in Iran ignited his numerous followers in Iran to become more active in the anti-Shah demonstrations. In a major miscalculation, the Iranian government requested that the Iraqi government expel the troublesome cleric from Najaf, the most important center of Shiah Islamic studies. Iraq complied and the Ayatollah journeyed to a residence near Paris, where the international press and many Iranian political exiles flocked to him. During his little more than three months' stay in France, he became an international media star and the rallying point for all the Shah's many enemies. The anti-Shah demonstrations in Iran took on a decidedly pro-Islamic flavor, even though many of the most significant opponents of the Shah had little affiliation with traditional Islamic beliefs or practice. The Islamic emphasis had a broad appeal, however, since it emphasized the genuine Iranian cultural roots that the Shah's rapid Westernization had obscured.

Opportunists with different agendas attached themselves to the Islamic fervor and the beturbaned Ayatollah because he had attracted a massive following. These opportunists assumed that he could help topple the Shah. They had little reason to doubt that they, in turn, could set him aside once he had served their purposes. These Western-educated intellectuals were confident that religious traditionalism, which had been systematically dismantled over the better part of a century, was a thing of the past. They also knew that Khomeini's activism was contrary to the modern tradition of the important Shiah leaders of Iran, at least a good dozen of whom outranked Khomeini and regarded him as their theological and intellectual inferior.

Tehran, which had belonged to the wealthy for so many decades, fell under the control of the millions of recent migrants from the countryside who had been unable to find fulfillment in the glitzy opulence of modern Iran. They had little trouble convincing the Shah's ordinary troops, who came from the same background, to join their cause. Soldiers accepted the flowers that demonstrators placed in the muzzles of their guns and expressed their support of Khomeini. The Shah followed the Americans and his highest military officers followed him as he had trained them to do over the previous decades. There was not, therefore, any military resistance as pro-Khomeini supporters made life untenable for the Shah. As a result, the Shah appointed a new government under the leadership of an old opponent, Shahpour Baktiar, and went into exile on January 16, 1979. The Ayatollah landed in Iran on February 1 to find himself the leader of an unexpected and successful revolution. Baktiar resigned on February 11 and Khomeini's supporters established an Islamic Republic a few weeks later.

A struggle for power in Iran raged throughout much of 1979 and into 1980, but at every turn the supporters of Khomeini prevailed. Their commitment to restoring complete Iranian revolutionary control over their society and way of life was uncompromising. Khomeini's characterization of the United States as the "Great Satan" and the United States embassy as a "den of spies" drowned out other possible orientations for post-Shah Iran. Iranian recollections of American assistance in restoring the Shah to power in 1953 inspired them to take every precaution against it happening again. Khomeini supporters seized control of the American embassy and held American diplomats hostage, to the mortification of the entire United States population. Large-scale executions of former supporters of the Shah and the gradual demise of revolutionaries with different agendas secured the forces of Khomeini's Islamic Revolution.

A wave of Islamic fervor spread throughout the Middle East, which had generally moved toward a secular approach to life throughout the twentieth century. Khomeini's Shiaism and Iranian heritage proved no obstacle to his appeal to the predominantly Sunni and Arab population of the region. People under twenty-five years of age, who constituted about half of the population of the region, flocked to the banner of revived traditional Islam. The older generation fell under the pressure of their juniors to adopt Islamic dress. They began to crowd the mosques to hear militant sermons that demanded militant action. Governments responded with laws that reflected a new conformity with traditional Islamic teachings.

Iraq's secular Baathist regime received special attention from Iran's Islamic Republic in part because more than half of Iraq's population was Shiah, but also because the Iraqi regime had dealt harshly with Khomeini after the Iran-Iraqi agreement in 1975. Iran's call for an Islamic revolution in Iraq embittered relations between the two states and led to some serious confrontations along their borders. Saddam's regime was too strong and the Iraqi Shiah were both too weak and too Arab to heed the Ayatollah's call for revolution.

While the entire region quaked from Iran's activities, Iran was in chaos as factions continued to battle for control. Most Iranian military officers had either been executed or fled the country. The absence of foreign technicians rendered much of the sophisticated military equipment useless. Iran, therefore, was in no position to carry its revolution beyond its borders with military aggression. There was no reason to believe it could even defend itself from attack by forces far less dangerous than those of the Soviet Union, which is situated to its immediate north.

THE IRAN-IRAQ WAR

Saddam Hussein, who had become president of Iraq in July 1979, thought that the situation in Iran was propitious for him to abrogate the 1975 treaty and perhaps also obtain control of much of Iran's petroleum industry, which was located in the predominantly Arab province of Khuzistan. The agitation of Islamic Iran caused real concern for the safety of his regime in Iraq. Of perhaps equal importance was the possibility that a successful war with Iran could establish Iraq superiority in the Gulf, which Iran had exercised before its revolution. Saddam was also aware that the Arab world had been leaderless since the death of Nasser in 1970. Egypt's expulsion from the Arab League left Iraq as the largest military force among the Arab states. Iraq had the added advantage of a large income from petroleum and a reserve that was second only to that of Saudi Arabia. In addition, revolutionary Iraq had been on the periphery of Arab affairs since the overthrow of the monarchy in 1958. There were strong indications from the militarily weak Gulf states that they would welcome a fatal military blow to Khomeini's Islamic Republic, because all of the Gulf states had considerable ethnic Iranian Shiah populations.

Saddam abrogated the 1975 treaty on September 17 and invaded Iran on September 22 in anticipation of a quick and fruitful victory. Instead, the Iranians ceased fighting among themselves and mounted a resistance that would nearly bleed both nations to death over the next eight years. The war also ruined each nation financially and placed great strain on the economies of all the Arab states that provided much of the financing of Saddam's unremitting effort. The war transformed Iraq from the outcast nation that all the other Arab nations feared and detested into the hope of the Arab world. The petroleum-rich Gulf states opened their treasuries to purchase the war materiel Iraq needed for a prolonged war of attrition. Iraq used much of its own financial capacity not only to fight the war but also to provide new benefits and services for its often neglected Shiah population in a successful effort to kept them loyal during a war against their fellow believers in Iran. The quick recovery of Iraq after the war and its abundance of sophisticated weapons indicate that Iraq utilized considerable assets during the war in order to develop its military capacity for future needs.

When Iraq's minimal port facilities on the Gulf became impassable during the war, Iraq had to depend on a long and expensive supply line from Aqaba in neighboring Jordan. This established a mutual relationship between the two states that had varied from terrible to strained since the Iraqis had overthrown their own Hashemite monarchy in 1958. The war enhanced Iraq's awareness that its fragile outlet to the seas, which the British had established at the end of World War I, inhibited Iraq's potential. Kuwait was hesitant throughout the war to allow Iraq to use its ports in fear that Iran would retaliate against their country. Kuwait shipping, in fact, was possible only because the United States agreed to place Kuwaiti ships under the American flag to justify American naval protection of them in the treacherous Gulf war zone.

DISILLUSION IN EGYPT

The Egyptians, who had accepted the peace treaty with Israel as a relief from their years of carrying the principal military responsibility for the Arab world, were soon disappointed. Sadat had promised them that prosperity would accompany peace. Visions of vast Western capital investment and extensive tourism were appealing to the overpopulated nation that possessed inadequate natural resources to meet its needs. Regional resistance to Egypt that kept the Middle East in turmoil had failed to attract any significant new economic activity. The Arab boycott had actually cost Egypt income. American aid obviously had not affected the lives of ordinary Egyptians. Resentment from other Arabs toward Egypt's independent course gained greater significance once peace seemed to offer no rewards. To add to their discontent, Khomeini's Islamic militancy swept across the region at the same time Egyptians were expecting their peace dividends. The deep-rooted Islamic traditionalism that the Muslim Brotherhood had fostered for half a century enjoyed greater appeal among many disillusioned Egyptians. The Brotherhood provided a much better standard of living, as well as spiritual support, to the people who embraced it than the government could provide for those who looked for assistance from its secular institutions.

Egypt's mosques became centers of resistance to Sadat's dependence upon Western assistance. His emphasis upon his commitment to Islam was insufficient, since his concept of Islam obviously included considerable compromise with ideas and practices that the traditionalists regarded as non-Islamic. Sadat openly criticized Khomeini more than any other Arab leader, as he heatedly stated that Khomeini's teaching was "not Islam." His wife's public support of birth control and other controversial causes also tainted his image in the eyes of traditionalists. Overt criticism of Sadat increased in the mosques throughout 1981 to the point that he dismissed hundreds of the leaders of the Friday prayers in September and replaced them with men with more moderate views.

Religious traditionalists in the army assassinated Sadat while he sat on the reviewing stand on October 6, 1981 to celebrate "The Crossing" of the Suez Canal, which had occurred in 1973. World leaders from the West converged on Egypt to honor their friend, who had bravely attempted to establish peace in the Middle East. Middle Eastern leaders did not attend his funeral and Egypt was strangely silent, in strong contrast to the anguish tens of millions had displayed upon the death of Nasser eleven years earlier.

Sadat's vice president, Hosni Mubarak, quietly assumed the presidency as Sadat's assassination had not been connected with an attempt to take control of the government. His assassins had simply concluded that Sadat's non-Islamic policies required punishment. Millions of Egyptians agreed with them. Most who did not remained silent. Mubarak vowed to maintain Sadat's basic policies, including the peace treaty with Israel. He did not, however, initiate dramatic new pro-Western policies. Instead, he patiently watched for opportunities to ease Egypt back into the mainstream of the Arab community. Egypt's exile ended when the Arab League admitted Egypt back to membership in the later 1980s and the Arab states reestablished normal diplomatic relations with the errant Egyptians.

LEBANESE TROUBLES PERSIST

Lebanon's troubles increased and became more complex as the civil war continued in defiance of apparent efforts to end it. A particularly bloody Palestinian raid on Israel in March 1978 resulted in escalation of the conflict. Israel retaliated with heavy air attacks and deployed 30,000 troops into southern Lebanon. Approximately 200,000 Lebanese, who were mostly Shiah, fled their homes and lived as homeless refugees in the slums of Sidon and Beirut. Unusually strong American pressure convinced the Israelis to withdraw after three months. They had used the time well, however, to establish even closer ties to elements of the Maronite community in Lebanon. The Israelis established a small enclave on the Lebanese border called the Republic of Free Lebanon under the control of Major Saad Haddad, a former Lebanese army officer. His small forces helped suppress anti-Israeli activity in southern Lebanon and the area he controlled provided Israel a safe passageway for future incursions into Lebanon. While Haddad's affiliation with Israel might appear to be an aberration, it soon became obvious that Israel and some of the mainstream leaders of Lebanon's Maronite community enjoyed a close and lethal relationship.

The migration of increased numbers of Shiahs from the south to the northern cities as a result of the Israeli incursion helped change the course of the Lebanese civil war. Less than a year after the Israeli raid, Khomeini's revolution in Iran inspired the Shiah to action. Iran's revolutionary government poured leadership, money, and arms into the Lebanese Shiah community. The formerly docile Shiah, who were the single largest group in Lebanon, began to play a prominent role in Lebanese affairs. Even the mysterious disappearance of Imam Musa Sadr in Libya in 1979 did not impede their activities. In fact, astute Shiah leaders facilely claimed that the absent Imam had made statements, which, even if spurious, continued to guide Lebanon's Shiah community.

The aroused Shiah community had never played a major role in earlier periods of Lebanon's affairs. They did not have a vested interest, therefore, in restoring the old order, which provided rewards to the traditional power brokers at the expense of the Shiah. There is little wonder that few Lebanese could understand that something close to normal could not occur in Lebanon until the Shiah obtained what they felt was their "fair share." The number of homeless Shiah and the pervasive Islamic militancy among them demanded concessions that other Lebanese factions found unacceptable.

Violent as Lebanon was during the civil war, no part of it was more brutal and ruthless than the internecine struggle that occurred among the Maronite Christian leaders. Their right to provide Lebanon's president exacerbated the conflicts among the strong, egocentric Maronite leaders. These conflicts arose because the strongest among them had the power to become president or to determine who would hold that office. The civil war created an atmosphere in which incivility was an asset in a country where, despite its outward appearance, violence and coercion had usually determined political leadership.

Lebanon's chaos was a perfect milieu for Bashir Gemayel to catapult past other possible contenders into the Lebanese presidency. This second son of the founder of the Phalangist party defied his father and all of the other powerful Maronite leaders to assert leadership over the Maronite community. His single-mindedness, ruthlessness, and propensity to brutality made him infamous in the non-Maronite community. Through a combination of murder, intimidation, and bribery he gained control of the Lebanese Forces, which was a well-armed, predominantly Maronite fighting force. By 1980 he had either destroyed or merged all other Maronite militias, including that of his older brother, under his control. In close association with Israel he had developed the strongest military force in Lebanon, except, of course, for the Syrians whom the Israelis and the international community restricted. Bashir's success won him widespread respect throughout Lebanon, where the ability to wreak the most havoc had become the principal measure of a man.

A flurry of activity in the spring and summer of 1981 ended in an unusual lull thereafter. The Syrians moved surface-to-air missiles into Lebanon, the Palestinians launched intense rocket attacks upon northern Israel, and Israel retaliated with extensive air raids from the south all the way to Beirut. In an almost nonchalant aside Israel destroyed Iraq's nuclear power plant at Osirak on June 7 with a bold and unexpected aerial assault. By the end of June something approximating a truce occurred between Israel and the P.L.O. Arafat had, in fact, moved the P.L.O. to a posture that defied its popular international reputation as primarily a terrorist organization. It had become increasingly a Palestine government in exile with observer status in the United Nations since 1974. The organization depended much more on diplomacy, as well as financial and moral leverage to accomplish its goals, while it struggled to keep dissident elements from tarnishing its image with unauthorized terrorist acts.

Ariel Sharon's acquisition of the portfolio of Defense Minister in Begin's new cabinet in August 1981 was a good indication that Israel would become more aggressive. Israel's annexation of the Golan Heights in December, just four months before it was supposed to withdraw from Sinai, was a good indication of the new government's lack of commitment to either a greater peace settlement or regional tranquility. Sharon moved large numbers of troops and support materiel to the Lebanese border in the spring of 1982 with the apparent intention of conducting a major campaign into Lebanon. He would need an adequate provocation to justify whatever purpose he had in mind. Presumably, his goal was to eliminate the

P.L.O.'s military capacity. The wary Syrians and P.L.O. leadership were determined not to provide Sharon and Begin with an excuse to unleash their lethal forces.

An abortive attempt in London on June 3, 1982 upon the life of Israel's ambassador to Great Britain furnished the Israeli leadership the provocation it needed to launch an unprecedentedly massive attack upon the Palestinians in Lebanon. In their view, the fact that the assassins were members of the mercenary, renegade faction of Abu Nidal, whom the P.L.O. had expelled from their organization and sentenced to death, did not exonerate the Palestinians from responsibility. The Israelis had reason to believe that Alexander Haig, the American Secretary of State, approved a larger than usual Israeli retaliation. Despite announcements that they intended to penetrate only twenty-five miles as they had in 1978, the heavily armored Israeli forces drove quickly to the outskirts of Beirut. Syria greeted the Israeli invasion with a timid resistance that cost it the loss of eighty-three airplanes and the destruction of the missiles it had placed in Lebanon in 1981. But the P.L.O. and other "terrorists" were the real targets of Israel's wrath.

The Israelis proved that they were willing to destroy most of war-torn Beirut to achieve their goal. Nearly constant bombardment of Beirut from the air, land, and sea continued for more than two months as the world witnessed events on their televisions. Even the Arab governments expressed only the mildest of objections and made no effort to retaliate against Israel or its allies with either military or economic sanctions. A nearly continuous stream of Israeli trucks hauled captured weapons and stolen property south while the inferno of Beirut raged. A significant amount of human cargo was also in the seemingly endless convoy as the Israelis captured thousands of Lebanese and Palestinians, whom they transported to Israel for internment in huge prison camps. Many Shiah, whom had welcomed the Israeli invasion, soon turned against their supposed benefactors and began a retaliation that would cost the Israelis dearly when they began their withdrawal later.

The invasion proved how deeply Israel had penetrated Lebanese society. Well-placed beggars and others who had blended into the Lebanese society abandoned their disguises and joined the triumphant Israeli forces. Christian Lebanese openly entertained Israeli officers as old friends and acquaintances. Life in Christian East Beirut, which was under the protection of the Lebanese Forces and Israel, proceeded fairly normally while the western sector was perishing. The Maronite forces provided some vital logistical support but refrained from engaging in the fighting. They were satisfied to allow their Israeli allies to cleanse Lebanon of the Palestinian curse, while they laid their plans for electing Bashir Gemayel to the presidency. Gemayel's forces took advantage of the Israeli presence to move into areas they had never occupied before. Such actions were indiscreet, because even in lawless Lebanon there was a recognized agreement on territoriality, based in part on the assumption that sanity would someday return and the groups would again work together in harmony. Since the Israelis could not stay in Lebanon forever, the day would come when the other factions would extract their vengeance from the opportunistic Maronites.

This particular "war" was different from all others involving the Arabs and Israelis, because most of the media was trapped in Beirut when it began. For the first time, reporters were on the receiving end of Israeli firepower. The hardship to Arabs and the wanton destruction of Beirut tarnished Israel's former image as an underdog that heroically won its wars against great odds. Accounts from Beirut indicated that Israeli forces were killing a defenseless city and its inhabitants.

In Israel's defense, the Palestinians refused to surrender to their overwhelming foe. Although they had no opportunity either to win or even retaliate very effectively against the long-range Israeli bombardment, the Palestinians demonstrated bravery and tenacity in their confrontations with the Israelis on the periphery. Palestinian success in the close man-to-man fighting, as well as the success of the Shiah during Israel's withdrawal, helped dispel the belief in Israel's military invincibility.

As the carnage dragged out, increased international efforts under American leadership sought a means of allowing the Israelis to withdraw. Long before this final stage Arafat, the leader of the Palestinians, had decided to seek an end because it was obvious that the Palestinians would receive no assistance. In mid-August, the P.L.O. agreed to withdraw its armed fighters from Lebanon after it received assurance that Israel would withdraw and that international forces would enter Lebanon to protect the civilian Palestinian population from both the Israelis and the Lebanese. The Palestinian armed forces left Lebanon by ship. Their exit lasted from August 21 until the end of the month in a hail of celebrative gunfire usually associated with victory. The nature of their defeat *was* a type of moral victory, as they had not perished, and, in fact, they had forced their Israeli tormentors to behave in a fashion that disgusted observers in Israel and throughout the world.

Dramatic developments prevented a fair assessment of the affect of the expulsion of the Palestinian commandoes from Lebanon. In the early stages of the Palestinian withdrawal, the Lebanese Forces and the Israelis supervised the election of a new president for Lebanon. They carefully arranged the gathering of a bare minimum for a quorum of the Lebanese legislators at an army barracks on August 23. Bashir Gemayel was the only candidate for the position, but a full meeting of the legislature might well have denied him the election. Few who did not support Bashir were allowed to attend. With no votes to spare, Gemayel became Lebanon's president-elect. As is the case with many who accede to high office, he seemed more mellow once he achieved his goals. It became quite clear that he would not, as had been expected, bend to Israel's will and sign a peace treaty.

Bashir was assassinated before he took office when his political headquarters exploded on September 14. There was a great deal of speculation about who was responsible, although a member of the Syrian Nationalist Party was arrested and charged with the crime. Emotions were running too high for the actual cause to really matter. Israeli forces moved into West Beirut on September 15, contrary to their earlier promises, for the ostensible purpose of keeping peace. During the next two days Phalangist and Lebanese Forces military units entered two Palestinian refugee camps and killed many unarmed refugees in retaliation for Bashir's assassination. Most agree that the killers were Maronite Christians who operated under Israeli protection. Estimates of the number of dead vary from several hundred to several thousand, depending on the view of the appraiser. All except the perpetrators and their supporters could agree that a major new atrocity had occurred in Lebanon's tragedy. It was also clear that Lebanon would not be tranquil as new blood required additional revenge.

In a remarkable unity of grief, almost all political and religious leaders expressed their sorrow at Bashir's assassination. Going even further, the legislature elected Bashir's brother, Amin, to the presidency on September 21 by a 77-to-3 vote. Amin had never been very much involved in politics, and had suffered very harsh treatment from the brother he replaced. He proved much more pliable for the Israelis and troublesome for the United States from which he received assistance that other powerful factions in Lebanon could not tolerate.

Lebanon's various factions perceived the small multinational force of the United States, France, Great Britain, and Italy as allies of Amin and his Lebanese Forces. To the foreign nations, Amin was the president of Lebanon, but to the other factions he was a weak reflection of themselves. They felt that he took undue advantage of foreign troops to extend his control over their regions of Lebanon. Lebanon had long since ceased to function as a nation.

The Western nations, Israel, Syria, and the many Lebanese factions became embroiled in a new and different stage of the civil war. Israel gradually pulled back toward southern Lebanon, but was unable to extricate itself until 1985, during which time it suffered many casualties, while, of course, it caused many more among its adversaries. The Shiah finally emerged at this stage to become the strongest force in West Beirut. Failure of the United States to understand Syria's legitimate concerns in Lebanese affairs ignited fierce relations between the two countries and Syria's Lebanese allies. The baffled Americans lost many lives and seemed certain to lose more if they remained in the conflict. Their withdrawal in February 1984 was a recognition that it was difficult to play in a game with too many players, definite but obscure rules, and apparent widespread disregard for the score.

Lebanon in general, and Beirut in particular, would claim many more victims over the following years as it continued to be the modern showcase of anarchy. Real groups and mythical groups kidnapped and killed people all over the world on behalf of both large and very personal causes. Few could recall when Amin Gemayel left office or who his successors were, because the government became irrelevant. In a twist of fate, geographical Lebanon, which many had contended had no validity from its inception, remained very much intact. The Lebanese nation disappeared.

REALITIES OF THE 1980s

Most dramatic activities that occurred during the 1980s in the Middle East were centered in the quagmire of Lebanon and in the continued bloodbath between Iraq and Iran. The Cold War theme that had been so strong for forty years almost imperceptibly disappeared as Gorbachev adopted a warm relationship with his American counterparts in his search for Western help to save the Soviet Union from economic collapse. Internal problems of the Eastern Bloc nations diverted them from their former assistance to international terrorism and other adventurous international activities. After withdrawing from Lebanon, Israel became preoccupied with the dual challenge of a grassroots Palestinian uprising called the *Intifada* and absorbing the unusually large number of Jews the Soviet Union allowed to migrate to Israel. Mubarak's unassertive policies enabled Egypt to return gradually into the mainstream of Arab affairs in no small part because he supported the general Arab war effort against Iran. Syrian and Libyan support for Iran reduced their credibility and influence in Arab affairs. The debilitating cost of the Iran-Iraq war essentially ended the previous spree of economic expansion in the Gulf petroleum-producing states. The petroleum producers could do little more than maintain the status quo, even with Iranian and Iraqi petroleum removed from the international market. They also began to use more of their assets in the purchase of sophisticated military preparedness. The two Yemens even enjoyed better relations as they moved toward a full merger on a sound basis. Ironically, the absence of any strong source to promote the political unity of the Arab states created an unusual level of cooperation among them.

PALESTINIAN REORIENTATION

The P.L.O. had a lower profile in the 1980s than it had displayed in the previous decade. The P.L.O. had moved its headquarters to Tunisia after its expulsion from Lebanon; this removed it from the heartland of the Arab world. Arafat spent about as much time in the air as on the ground, both to preserve his life and to be able to move at a moment's notice to maintain his influence. Arafat's terrible relations with Syria greatly reduced the P.L.O.'s effectiveness when the other Arab nations were absorbed in the Iran-Iraq war. His improved relations with Jordan indicated to many that he no longer endorsed strong revolutionary goals. The youths in the Occupied Territories of the West Bank and Gaza who threw rocks at the Israeli soldiers and settlers seized the leadership of the Palestinian cause and captured the fascination of the Arab world. *Hamas*, a religious fundamentalist movement that began in Gaza, grew in influence among Palestinians under Israeli occupation. Its effectiveness and zeal transformed life among the occupied Palestinians and challenged the leadership of the predominantly secular P.L.O. Arafat deftly handled these crises, as well as the loss of his closest associates in Fatah to Israeli and Palestinian assassins. With no military option, there was a growing consensus among the Palestinians that they had to make some accommodation with Israel. While the Israelis and the United States refused to negotiate directly with the P.L.O., there was a broad agreement among the Palestinians that the P.L.O. was, indeed, its spokesman. By surviving, Arafat and the P.L.O. were the real coordinators of the Palestinian efforts to obtain an acceptable compromise with Israel that would improve their lives and regain their national dignity.

IRAQI EMERGENCE

The Iran-Iraq war dwarfed all previous confrontations in the region as hundreds of thousands perished on both sides. Their economies collapsed from a combination of military actions, the absence of petroleum income, and the diversion of their human and materiel resources into the war effort. Iraq, however, enjoyed a much more favorable situation because of the financial and logistical support it received from its Arab neighbors. Iraq's superior financial capacity enabled it to acquire weapons from all over the world as it steadily moved away from its dependence on the Soviet Union for military hardware, advice, and technological assistance. Iran's acquisition of a modest number of missiles from the United States in return for using its influence to obtain the release of American hostages in Lebanon only delayed its eventual collapse. Even Iran's religious zeal could not endure in a war of such senseless devastation.

POSTWAR IRAN AND IRAQ

Contrary to the popular American perception that "there is no such thing as a moderate Iranian," cooler heads prevailed in Iran to accept peace. Khomeini, who had vowed he would not cease the war effort until he had destroyed the "Godless regime of Saddam Hussein," agreed to peace in 1988. The war ended. Iran's unique orientation and its continued isolation from most of the rest of the world retarded its recovery in the postwar period. The Ayatollah's death in 1989 neither ended Iran's isolation nor freed its frozen financial assets in the West. Iran's condition dictated that it would experience a period of reduced importance in regional and world affairs.

In contrast, the Iraq of Saddam Hussein emerged from the war as the indisputably strongest military power of the region. Its immense oil reserves assured it of rapid economic recovery. Iraq's years of improving its technological base and its aggressive acquisition of technological expertise from abroad propelled it into the forefront of international affairs. The fact that most of Iraq's attention had concentrated upon military technology began to cause considerable alarm, especially in Israel. Other nations were less concerned because they welcomed a strong Iraq to counterbalance the aberrant Iranian regime.

Iraq's strength, which had been the hope of the Arab world during the war with Iran, became troublesome to many elements in the Arab world after the peace. Syria could not match Iraq in the quest to provide leadership for the Arab world. It had suffered increasing isolation from the Arab nations, in large part because of its support for Iran during the war. The collapse of the Soviet Union and the Eastern Bloc, upon which Syria depended, weakened the Asad regime, which also lacked economic resources. Iraqi support of the Maronite Christian, General Michel Aoun, destabilized Lebanon at the expense of Syria. This self-proclaimed president of Lebanon used Iraqi military and financial support to embark on a level of destruction that only the Israelis could match. Aoun's violence was all the more distressing because it often appeared random and toward no particular purpose. The Gulf governments understandably felt uneasy with the prospect of an Iraqi revolutionary colossus dominating the region. Some of their citizens, however, and particularly the hundreds of thousands of Palestinians in the Gulf countries, began to regard Saddam as the first hope since Nasser who could deal forcefully with Israel. Most of the often highly placed Palestinians in the Gulf were true refugees from the 1948 war. They had neither home nor country, because most were subject to instant deportation from the host Gulf states, regardless of their positions or periods of residence in the Gulf. The advanced ages of the original Palestinian refugees made them particularly anxious, since they would die before returning to Palestine unless its liberation could occur soon. The Palestinians were also becoming expendable in the Gulf societies, which the Palestinians had helped build, as the indigenous population became sufficiently well educated, with extensive Palestinian assistance, to manage their own affairs. The Palestinians and Jordan, with which Iraq retained a sound symbiotic trade and logistical relationship, were the only reliable allies Iraq had by 1990. Egypt, which was far enough removed from Iraq to fear no immediate threat, had a level of correct relations, as Mubarak carefully guided his country to a position to obtain assistance from every possible source.

The Economic and Military Buildup in Iraq

An international economic decline that accompanied the end of the Cold War and the disruption following the collapse of the Eastern Bloc countries benefitted Iraq. Businesses and governments were willing to sell Saddam virtually anything his planners could imagine. Government regulatory agencies either ignored or rescinded restrictions upon the flow of goods, technology, and services to Iraq that would not have received approval in more prosperous times. The Iraqis used an immensely complicated web of dummy companies and financial institutions such as B.C.C.I. throughout the world to assist in their prevarications. Of the few who understood Iraq's machinations, most had a vested interest in keeping them secret. An even tinier few who suspected the truth found that others took virtually no interest in their accusations. Iraq took full advantage of the situation to purchase everything possible with its actual assets and extensive credit.

Throughout the beginning of 1990, a steady stream of information and speculation indicated that Iraq represented a real danger to world peace. Its armed forces of half a million men equipped with air power, armor, and missiles of all descriptions ranked it as the fourth largest military power in the world. Solid information existed that it possessed chemical weapons, which it had used against both the Iranians and its own Kurdish population. Speculation abounded that it also had biological weapons and was on the brink of possessing a nuclear capability. Israel, of course, led the growing chorus of pronouncements concerning the Iraqi menace.

Most Arabs were surprised to learn that an Arab nation had arrived at such a high state of readiness to engage in modern warfare. They also recalled that, less than two years before, Iraq had accepted a peace with Iran that was far short of total victory. Those observations aside, a perceptible stir began to surge through the Arab world. This was a combination of pride that an Arab country, and thereby the Arab world, could be taken seriously as a military power and the belief that Arab armed strength could lead to a satisfactory solution with Israel. The Palestinians, who had already favored Saddam, gravitated toward him as their possible savior.

The Iraqi acquisitions had placed a strain upon Iraq's finances that its only partially restored petroleum capacity could not solve. Indications that the Gulf states intended to collect the loans they had extended to Iraq during the war added to Saddam's concerns. The low price of petroleum on the international market was another factor in Iraq's financial strain. Saddam openly criticized the Kuwaitis and the United Arab Emirates for keeping the price of oil low by selfishly exceeding their O.P.E.C. quotas. He accused the Kuwaitis of stealing Iraqi oil through the use of slant drilling into Iraqi oil fields on the borders between the two countries. Kuwait displayed little regard for any of Saddam's concerns, despite major efforts on the part of some Arab governments, especially Jordan and Egypt, to prevent a crisis. Saddam was offended that the Kuwaitis, whom he believed he had saved from Iranian aggression, denied the validity of Iraq's claims. They also turned a deaf ear to his request for some kind of arrangement to provide Iraq access to Bubyian Island, which Kuwait did not use, to relieve Iraq's landlocked condition. Kuwaiti recalcitrance prompted Saddam to increase his demands to include a Kuwaiti forgiveness of his debt; he also expected Kuwait to make a major contribution to the thirty billion dollar sum he was trying to obtain from the Gulf countries. Saddam moved military units to the Kuwaiti border in what most assumed was a combination of bluff and military exercise. Other participants in the discussions were sure the two principals would reach an accommodation. Saddam maintained that the Gulf countries should meet his demand for financial support in compensation for the deprivation Iraq had suffered in defense of them during the Iranian war. Personal pique between him and the Kuwaiti Emir helped create an impasse that concerned mediators could not overcome in the last days of July.

Iraq's Invasion of Kuwait

Iraq invaded Kuwait on August 2 on the pretense of supporting a "coup," which had sent the Kuwaiti government of Prince Emir Jaber al-Ahmad el-Sabah and most of its military leadership to exile in Saudi Arabia. The magnitude of Iraqi's forces caused concern that he would also invade Saudi Arabia. Saddam responded to United Nations resolutions by annexing Kuwait. The United States and Great Britain deployed a small number of troops to Saudi Arabia and Saddam increased his forces in the region to more than three hundred thousand. A huge military operation would be required to dislodge Iraq's occupation. Saddam was confident that the world community would be unable to mount such an effort and would be unwilling to pay such a price. He had, however, overlooked that the end of the Cold War removed the Soviet Union as a major player in military affairs.

Most Arab states joined the United States and Britain in the coalition against Saddam. Crucially, Syria and Egypt took very firm stands against Saddam's annexation of Kuwait. Only Jordan wavered in response to the support Saddam's actions received among Jordan's Palestinian majority. In short, Saddam faced the real, unexpected, and unprecedented prospect of confronting the wrath of the entire world with only a few weak Arab states, the P.L.O., and perhaps Arab public opinion for support. His concessions to Iran at this time of all the gains he had made in the war was a sign of his desperation and reduced the likelihood that he could afford to leave Kuwait. It would have been impossible for him to justify, even to his closest associates, the sacrifices of the eight-year-war and the international opprobrium from his Kuwait adventure with nothing in return.

The Security Council decided, however, to use economic sanctions rather than force against Iraq. Iraq's neighbors stopped the flow of Iraqi oil to the world's markets and a blockade soon cut off Iraqi imports. The blockaders even regarded commodities such as tea, sugar, and coffee as contraband. They expressed confidence that economic sanctions would expel Saddam from Kuwait.

In response Saddam detained thousands of foreign "guests" in Kuwait and Iraq. Stories abounded of Iraq's harsh treatment of Kuwaitis and the wholesale transport of everything of value to Iraq. These developments brought additional U.N. resolutions and broader international support for sanctions. Saddam's behavior also deterred many Arabs, who would have liked to support his claim that he was rectifying wrongs of the "haves" against the "have-nots." They also feared the power of their governments, which supported the U.N. resolutions. Saddam tried even more diligently to gain support among the Arab and Islamic masses. He maintained that he would leave Kuwait only if Israel would withdraw from occupied Arab lands in the West Bank and the Golan Heights and Syria would withdraw from Lebanon. Saddam, who had never manifested significant religious convictions, called for a "holy war" on the part of all Muslims against the forces arraigned against him. Only the Palestinians in Jordan and the West Bank openly applauded his actions, because they felt that their fate was tied to his. They feared that, if he failed, it would be another generation before a new Arab leader could emerge to liberate them.

Assad of Syria benefitted from his support of the U.N. resolutions. After years of a mere holding action, he forcefully ousted Saddam's Maronite client, General Aoun, from the presidential palace in Lebanon without any objections from either the United States or Israel. President Elias Hrawi assumed uncontested authority for the first time since he had assumed office several months earlier. The militias ceased their activities and Beirut reunited and remained calm for the first time in fifteen years.

This quick, apparent end of Lebanon's long civil strife seemed to vindicate those who claimed that the conflict existed to serve the purposes of Western powers. The fact that the United States could signal Syria and Israel to end the Lebanese conflict because of the urgency of the Gulf War clearly indicated the war could have ended any time in the past. Nothing had eliminated irreconcilable conflicts that had caused war among the Lebanese. Lebanese leaders had not met to work out reasons and procedures to end their war. How could a genuine war end without the combatants participating in the process? Cynics observed that the United States had essentially allowed Syria to annex Lebanon as a reward for supporting American policies against Iraq and ordered its client, Israel, not to interfere. People who embraced this theory blamed the United States for most of the consequences of fifteen years of civil war in Lebanon.

The Response to Saddam's Aggression

Saddam gave no indication that economic sanctions would drive him from Kuwait. With the United States in the lead, the coalition partners obtained a resolution from the Security Council on November 29 that approved the use of force if he failed to remove his forces from Kuwait by January 15, 1991. The diplomatic efforts of the U.N. Secretary General, the Soviets, Algeria, Jordan, and France proved fruitless. Neither the United States, on behalf of the coalition, nor Saddam Hussein budged one iota from their August positions. On January 12 both houses of Congress approved American use of force if Saddam did not leave Kuwait by January 15.

Optimists hoped that Saddam would go up to, or a couple of days past, the deadline and then agree to withdraw. They reasoned that a show of courage against overwhelming foes would provide him with a moral victory that would make him a hero among the Arab masses but would preserve his entire military capacity. There was, however, strong sentiment in other circles that he was too dangerous to leave for later, regardless of what he did in Kuwait. For them it was unacceptable to withdraw the large forces without reducing Saddam's military capacity.

There was little time for speculation because, just past midnight of the January 15 deadline, coalition forces struck military and strategic targets all over Iraq and Kuwait. Allied air supremacy systematically destroyed strategic targets with an accuracy that astounded the world. Military briefings treated the world to T.V. footage of "smart" laser and radar-guided bombs that entered rooftop vents and exploded entire buildings. B52 bombers and other planes also began a systematic reduction of the fighting effectiveness of Saddam's half-million troops in Kuwait and southern Iraq. Iraq's much-touted SCUD missiles caused great alarm, and preoccupation with them diverted the normal pursuit of the war in an inordinate time and effort spent "chasing SCUDs." A few of the missiles hit Saudi Arabia and Israel, but they were militarily inconsequential.

Iraq had no capacity to resist the Allied ground offensive on February 23. Weeks without adequate food, water, and sleep, as well as the inability to communicate with their superiors had rendered the Iraqi troops hapless. Allied troops rolled through the desert to encounter more surrendering Iraqis than they could handle. As the end of the conflict unfolded on television the allied commanders ended the supporting air attack upon the retreating Iraqi troops to spare the world the sight of a monumental slaughter. The Iraqi forces were, in fact, helpless.

LIFE AFTER THE GULF WAR

Critics, many of whom had originally opposed the war, began to complain that the Allies, especially President George Bush, had stopped short of expelling Saddam from power. That, of course, had never been a stated objective of the United Nations resolutions. The war had driven Iraq out of Kuwait, whose leaders returned to a devastated country where hundreds of oil wells were ablaze from fires the Iraqis had deliberately set. The United Nations placed Iraq under greater restrictions that it had ever placed upon any country. The economic blockade remained in place to punish Iraq even further.

The severity of the world community's punishment of Iraq arose from its brutal occupation of Kuwait and the environmental havoc it inflicted upon the region. Saddam's treatment of the Shiah and Kurds, who rose in rebellion in the last stages of the war, added to the international dissatisfaction. The Shia and Kurds had believed that Saddam would perish after leading Iraq into such a disaster. Their premature uprising, in fact, rallied the military to his support in order to put down domestic foes that threatened the Iraqi social and political structure. In addition, they knew they enjoyed military superiority over these minority groups.

By the end of the war, the Arabs once again had a marginal military capacity. Syria had rejoined the mainstream of the Arab community and had fuller custody of Lebanon than it had ever exercised before. A single, powerful force in Lebanon promised stability for that troubled land, albeit from a source beyond its borders. Jordan shared much of the opprobrium the other Arab countries and the world heaped upon Iraq. Jordan faced the overwhelming problem of assimilating tens of thousands of Palestinians, which the Gulf states had expelled from their countries. Interestingly, during the war, both Iraqi and Jordanian officials referred to King Hussein as "Sharif Hussein" to resurrect Hashemite claims to parts of Saudi Arabia. Parallel references to the Saudi regime as the "government of Nejd" called into question the Saudi's legitimacy over any part of their kingdom other than the central province of the nation, which had no petroleum. King Hussein's unprecedented popularity following his illness in 1992 and the bad relations between Saddam and Jordan aroused the appeal of a Hashemite government in Iraq to replace Saddam's totalitarianism. The Palestinians took Saddam's defeat as their own and faced a future without the financial and political support they had received for the previous twenty years. Egypt was still the cultural leader of the Arab world, but its excessive population and the presence of a strong Islamic traditionalist element portended an explosion that could destroy the delicate balance in the region. Saudi Arabia had proven to be the best possible military ally in the Middle East with its combination of wealth, oil, location, and logistical flexibility. Iran had sat out the war with an equal antipathy toward all its participants. Its gradual recovery indicated that it would still be a major force in the future under an Islamic system that was maturing and free from the chaos of earlier experimentation. Israel was safe for the moment and in a somewhat improved position, because the large influx of immigrants forestalled the day that Arabs would outnumber Jews in Israel and the Occupied Territories.

The Gulf War ended any semblance of traditional Arab unity. Each Arab leader had ignored the principles of the Arab League and pursued his own agenda during the war. While the war only devastated Iraq and Kuwait many perceptive Arabs regarded the war as a disaster for all Arabs. The resignations of Clovis Maksoud, the Arab League's venerable ambassador to the United Nations, and Marwan al-Qassem, Jordan's august foreign minister, out of revulsion of Arab disarray are more than symbolically important. In the New World Order of reduced resources and a single Super Power the premium seemed reserved for those who acted first.

A MODICUM OF PEACE

When and how, rather than if, peace would occur between the Arabs and the Israelis seemed the important questions after the Gulf War. High level government proponents genuinely in search of peace began to outnumber opponents of peace for the first time since the beginning of the Arab-Israeli conflict. Those who subscribed to a peace only their side could dictate lost credibility. The Arabs had no military option and had no prospect of acquiring one for many years. Soviet assistance was no longer available and the war had added the latest chapter in discrediting Soviet military equipment. The P.L.O., which had supported Saddam, shared his disgrace and virtually eliminated the "plight of the Palestinians" as the foremost issue of Arab diplomacy for the first time since the end of World War I.

A Middle East peace conference convened in Madrid, Spain on October 30, just seven months after the Gulf War ended. Belief abounded that President Bush and Secretary of State James Baker would use the unprecedented prestige of the United States to force the Arabs and Israelis to face the new reality and make peace. Participation of Arab and Israeli diplomats in the same conference was a major breakthrough and led to additional talks among the delegations in other locations over the next few months. Quite soon, however, President Bush's status deteriorated as strong elements of opinion criticized Saddam Hussein's continuation in office and his alleged mistreatment of Iraqi minorities. The peace process experienced a rapid dispersement and dissipation. Even so, months of meetings occurred among the Palestinian, Jordanian, and Israeli representatives at all levels. Perhaps the discussions among their technocrats were the most meaningful, if for no other reason than that the participants learned how human, sophisticated, and knowledgeable their counterparts were. Respect, which had never existed before, replaced hatred, rage, and feelings of superiority. Negotiations went far past catch phrases and long standing general goals in a meaningful search to determine how to share such things as water resources, law enforcement information and duties, and the freer flow of people across borders.

The sudden announcement during the first week of September 1993 that the

P.L.O. and Israel would sign a peace treaty the following week was a surprise to everyone except a few Israelis, Palestinians, and Norwegians. The assertive and imaginative initiative of Terje Rod Larsen, a Norwegian, succeeded where all others had failed during previous decades. Numerous secret meetings in Norway between Israeli and Palestinian officials produced an agreement. Yitzhak Rabin and Yasser Arafat signed their historic agreement at the White House in Washington on September 13. The dramatic event was less than cordial and it seemed that the world stood still for a moment as all watched to see if Rabin would accept Arafat's offer of a handshake. He did.

Similar to the Camp David Accord, this agreement provided for a gradual, stage by stage establishment of P.L.O. control over the West Bank and the Gaza Strip. While only time would determine the sagacity of this approach, both sides finally agreed to recognize the existence of their enemy. It was beyond doubt that elements in each camp would expend every possible effort to destroy this modest move toward peace between Israel and the Palestinians. It was crucial for Israel to make this peace agreement since so much of the rancor throughout the Arab world and elsewhere related to the official state of war that had existed between Israel and the Palestinians. Peace between Irael and the Palestinians was an essential step for establishing peace with the Arab states. One could make a case for the observation that once Israel satisfied the Palestinians, there was little justification for the Arab states to continue a state of war.

In the process of using its good office to establish the Israeli-Palestinian rapprochement, Jordan had improved its often properly functional relationship with Israel. Jordan finally determined that advantages outweighed disadvantages and signed a treaty of peace with Israel on October 26, 1994. As with the P.L.O., this treaty was a declaration of the end of a state of war. It was not a treaty of friendship nor an alliance to pursue joint ventures. Anything more amicable would require time to develop mutual trust after half a century of conflict.

MATURITY AND HOPE

The gradual growth of regional relationships among the populations of the Arab countries over their years since independence provided a unity that had never existed before. Professionals of all kinds crossed borders and communicated by mail and electronic methods to share ideas and dreams. Most such intercourse had nothing to do with politics. Common citizens of all countries increasingly read the same books, viewed the same movies, listened to the same music, and engaged in other activities that became increasingly similar throughout the Arab-speaking world. Time and maturity were providing a genuine Arab unity that political leaders, philosophers, military people, wars, and scathing verbal conflicts had failed to achieve. Despite evidence to the contrary, an inexorable sense of community that recognized regional peculiarities, and differing forms of political and social organization was much stronger than in the earlier years when the people of the region had struggled to deal with their new freedom. This new situation enabled Arabs to express allegiance to the countries in which they resided without feeling a sense of guilt for betraying the cause of Arab unity. Knowledge of the dramatic events in Eastern Europe in the early 1990s inspired many to believe that Arabs, too, could find relief from their troubled past sometime in the future. Israel and Iran obviously were different from the general character of the region, but somewhere along the way, they would have to adjust to the region and forego the improbability of imposing their set of beliefs on the Middle East.

In some respects the ancient Middle East, which had so recently obtained its freedom in a panorama of new, individual states, was showing signs of maturity by the mid 1990s. The region was free to chart its course through relationships with nations of its own choice from beyond the region. A greater sense of self-worth reduced the need to rush into actions to prove that it was a legitimate force in the larger world.

Selected Bibliography

Any bibliography of this length will be incomplete because new books appear constantly, many more books exist than we can list, and compilers have unique interests. The following list contains books on a broad spectrum of topics, that should lead the reader to additional works. Some older books have the distinction of either being the best or at least essential. Frequently new theories or observations first appear in the professional journals. There are numerous small journals, but the largest ones in the field are *The International Journal of Middle East Studies* of the Middle East Studies Association (MESA) and *The Middle East Journal* of the Middle East Institute, the *Journal of Near East Studies,* and the *Journal of Palestine Studies.* The book review sections of these journals are also the best source of information on new books.

The inclusion of a work in this bibliography is an indication that it either is among the best, or is the only one on a subject, or has peculiar merit. We have chosen to forego commentary on the books in order to include more titles. We ask the forgiveness of authors who have produced meritorious works which we inadvertently omitted.

For many years a tiny number of scholars worked on the Modern Middle East and produced the classic works in the field. Literature in this field proliferated after 1973 when the Arab military showing and their use of oil as a weapon sparked wider interest in the Middle East. Large areas still have not received proper scholarly attention and that will remain the case due to the demanding requirements in linguistic skills and the inaccessibility of resources. Surprisingly, satisfactory biographies do not exist for numerous modern Middle Eastern figures. Increased scholarship on social issues is attempting to fill the shortages in that area. Likewise, attention to the role of women is receiving the emphasis it merits. Many scholars are giving economic and agricultural topics increased attention. Future bibliographies will reflect these important trends. These developments are the result of increased awareness of the importance of these areas in understanding the region. It is notable how little attention Islam received prior to 1979. The number of works on Islam after 1979 indicates the increased role of Islam in Middle Eastern affairs.

GENERAL WORKS ON THE MIDDLE EAST

Abu-Lughod, Ibrahim, *The Arab Rediscovery of Europe*. Princeton, NJ: Princeton University Press, 1963.

Adams, Michael, ed., *The Middle East: A Handbook.* New York: Facts on File, 1988.

Amin, Samir, *The Arab Nation*, (2nd ed.) trans. Michael Pallis. London: Zed Press, 1978.

Ayalon, Ami, and Haim Shaked, eds., *Middle East Contemporary Survey*. Boulder, CO: Westview Press, annual.

Bill, James A., and Robert Springborg, *Politics in the Middle East* (3rd ed.). Glenview, IL and London: Scott, Foresman/Little, Brown Higher Education, 1990.

Cleveland, William L., *A History of the Modern Middle East.* Boulder, CO: Westview Press, 1994.

Denoeux, Guilain, *Urban Unrest in the Middle East*. Albany, NY: SUNY Press, 1993.

Fisher, Sidney Nettleton, and William Ochsenwald, *The Middle East, A History* (4th ed.). New York: McGraw-Hill Publishing Company, 1990.

Hasou, Tawfig Y., *The Struggle for the Arab World.* London: Routledge and Kegan Paul, 1985.

Hourani, Albert, *A History of the Arab People.* Cambridge, MA: The Belknap Press of Harvard University Press, 1991.

———, Philip S. Khoury, and Mary C. Wilson, eds., *The Modern Middle East.* Berkeley: University of California Press, 1993.

Hudson, Michael, *Arab Politics: The Search for Legitimacy*. New Haven, CT: Yale University Press, 1977.

Kedourie, Elie, *The Chatham House Version and Other Middle-Eastern Studies*. Hanover, NH and London: Published for Brandeis University Press by University Press of New England, 1970.

Khoury, Philip S., and Joseph Kostiner, eds., *Tribes and State Formation in the Middle East*. Berkeley: University of California Press, 1990.

Luciani, Giacomo, *Nation, State and Integration in the Arab World*, 4 vols. London and New York: Croom Helm, 1987–1988.

Malone, Joseph, *The Arab Lands of Western Asia*. Englewood Cliffs, NJ: Prentice Hall, 1973.

Mansfield, Peter, *A History of The Midle East*. New York: Penguin Books, 1991.

The Middle East and North Africa (37th ed.). London: Europa Publications, 1990.

Olson, Robert, Asaf Hussain, and Jamil Qureshi, *Orientalism, Islam, and Islamists*. Brattleboro, VT: Aman Books, 1984.

Ovendale, Ritchie, *The Middle East Since 1914*. London and New York: Longman, 1992.

Peretz, Don, *The Middle East Today* (5th ed.). New York: Praeger, 1988.

Safran, Nadav, *From War to War: The Arab-Israeli Confrontation, 1948–1967*. New York: Pegasus, 1969.

Yapp, M.E., *The Making of the Modern Middle East, 1792–1923*. London and New York: Longman, 1991.

———, *The Near East Since the First World War*. London and New York: Longman, 1991.

Zeine, Zeine, *The Struggle for Arab Independence* (2nd ed.). Delmar, NY: Caravan Books, 1977.

The Middle East in World Affairs

Al Marayati, Abid A., ed., *International Relations of the Middle East and North Africa*. Cambridge, MA: Schenkman Publishing Company, 1984.

Brown, L. Carl, *International Politics and the Middle East: Old Rules, Dangerous Game*. Princeton, NJ: Princeton University Press, 1984.

Hurewitz, J. C., ed., *The Middle East and North Africa in World Politics*, (2nd ed.), 2 vols. New Haven, CT: Yale University Press, 1975, 1977.

Ismael, Tareq, *International Relations of the Contemporary Middle East*. Syracuse, NY: Syracuse University Press, 1986.

Kirk, George, *The Middle East in the War*, London: Oxford University Press, 1952.

Korany, Bahgat, and Ali E. Hillaal Dessouki, eds., *The Foreign Policies of Arab States*. Boulder, CO: Westview Press,1984.

Lenczowski, George, *The Middle East in World Affairs* (4th ed.). Ithaca, NY: Cornell University Press, 1980.

Reich, Bernard, ed., *The Powers in the Middle East: The Ultimate Strategic Arena*. New York: Praeger, 1987.

Economic Developments

Hershlag, Zvi Yehuda, *Introduction to the Modern Economic History of the Middle East*. Leiden, Netherlands: E.J. Brill, 1980.

Issawi, Charles, *The Fertile Crescent, 1800–1914: A Documentary Economic History*. New York: Oxford University Press, 1988.

Owen, Roger, *The Middle East in the World Economy, 1800–1914*. London: Methuen, 1987.

Richards, Alan, and John Waterbury, *A Political Economy of the Middle East*. Boulder, CO: Westview Press, 1990.

Social Developments

Ahmad, Leila, *Women and Gender in Islam: Historical Roots of a Modern Debate*. New Haven, CT: Yale University Press, 1992.

Bates, Daniel, and Amal Rassam, *Peoples and Cultures of the Middle East*. Englewood Cliffs, NJ: Prentice Hall, 1983.

Beck, Lois, and Nikki Keddie, eds., *Women in the Muslim World*. Cambridge, MA: Harvard University Press,1978.

Botman, Selma, et al., *Women in the Middle East*. London: Zed Books, 1987.

Eickelman, Dale F., *The Middle East: An Anthropological Approach*, (2nd ed.). Englewood Cliffs, NJ: Prentice Hall, 1989.

El-Saadawi, Nawal, *The Hidden Face of Eve: Women in the Arab World*. London: Zed Books, 1980.

Esman, Milton J., and Itamar Rabinovich, eds., *Ethnicity, Pluralism, and the State in the Middle East*. Ithaca, NY: Cornell University Press, 1988.

Farsoun, Samih K., *Arab Society: Continuity and Change*. London: Croom Helm,1985.

Fernea, Elizabeth Warnock, ed., *Women and the Family in the Middle East: New Voices of Change*. Austin: University of Texas Press, 1985.

———, and Basima Qattan Bezirgan, *Middle Eastern Muslim Women Speak*. Austin: University of Texas Press, 1976.

Gerber, Haim, *The Social Origins of the Modern Middle East*. Boulder, CO: Lynne Rienner Publishers, 1987.

Weekes, Richard, ed., *Muslim Peoples: A World Ethnographic Survey*, (2nd ed.), 2 vols. Westport, CT: Greenwood Press, 1984.

Philosophical and Conceptual Development

Abdel-Malek, Anouar, ed., *Contemporary Arab Political Thought*. London: Zed Books, 1989.

Burke, Edmond, III, and Ira M. Lapidus, eds., *Islam, Politics, and Social Movements*. Berkeley: University of California Press, 1988.

Halliday, Fred, and Hamza Alawi, *State and Ideology in the Middle East and Pakistan*. New York: Monthly Review Press, 1988.

Hodgson, Marshall, *The Venture of Islam*. 3 vols. Chicago: University of Chicago Press 1974.

Karpat, Kemal, ed., *Political and Social Thought in the Contemporary Middle East* (2nd ed.). New York: Praeger, 1982.

Khadduri, Majid, *Arab Contemporaries: The Role of Personalities in Politics*. Baltimore and London: The Johns Hopkins University Press, 1973.

Sharabi, Hisham, *Neopatriarchy: A Theory of Distorted Change in Arab Society*. London and New York: Oxford University Press, 1988.

Middle East Relations with the West

Busch, Brinton Cooper, *Britain and the Persian Gulf, 1894–1914*. Berkeley: University of California Press, 1967.

Dann, Uriel, ed., *The Great Powers in the Middle East 1919–1939*. New York: Holmes and Maier,1988.

Hirshowitz, Lukaz, *The Third Reich in the Arab East*. Toronto: University of Toronto Press,1966.

Lewis, Bernard, *The Middle East and the West*. Bloomington: Indiana University Press, 1963.

Louis, William Roger, *The British Empire in the Middle East, 1945–1951: Arab Nationalism, the United States, and Postwar Imperialism*. Oxford: Oxford University Press,1984.

Monroe, Elizabeth, *Britain's Moment in the Middle East, 1914–1956*, (2nd ed.). Baltimore: Johns Hopkins University Press, 1981.

Robinson, Ronald, and John Gallagher, *Africa and the Victorians: The Official Mind of Imperialism*. New York: St. Martin's Press, 1961.

Sachar, Howard, *Europe Leaves the Middle East, 1936–1954*. New York: Knopf, 1972.

OTTOMAN EMPIRE

General Works

Creasy, Sir Edward S., *History of the Ottoman Turks*. London: R. Bentley, 1854–1856; reprint, Beirut: Khayats, 1961.

Davison, Roderic H., *Essays in Ottoman and Turkish History, 1774–1923: The Impact of the West*. Austin: University of Texas Press, 1990.

Gibb, H. A. R., and Harold Bowen, *Islamic Society and the West: A Study of the Impact of Western Civilization, Volume l: Islamic Society in the Eighteenth Century*, 2 parts. London: Oxford University Press, 1950.

Inalcik, Halil, *The Ottoman Empire in the Middle East and the Balkans*. Bloomington, IN: Indiana University Turkish Studies Series, Vol.9, 1993.

———, *The Ottoman Empire: The Classical Age, 1300–1600*. London: Weidenfeld and Nicolson, 1973.

Kinross, Lord, *The Ottoman Centuries: The Rise and Fall of the Turkish Empire*. New York: Morrow Quill, 1977.

Kuneralp, Sinan, ed., *Studies on Ottoman Diplomatic History, Volume I*. Istanbul: Isis Press, 1987.

Lampe, John R., and Marvin R. Jackson, *Balkan Economic History, 1550–1950: From Imperial Borderlands to Developing Nations*. Bloomington, IN: Indiana University Press, 1982.

Lewis, Bernard, *The Emergence of Modern Turkey* (2nd ed.). London: Oxford University Press, 1968.

Olson, Robert W., *The Siege of Mosul and Ottoman-Persian Relations, 1718–1743*. Bloomington, IN: Indiana University Press, 1975.

Pears, Edwin, *Life of Abdul Hamid*. London: Constable, 1917.

Pierce, Leslie P., *The Imperial Harem: Women and Sovereignty in the Ottoman Empire*. New York: Oxford University Press, 1993.

Polk, William R., and Richard L. Chambers, eds., *Beginnings of Modernization in the Middle East: The Nineteenth Century*. Chicago: University of Chicago Press, 1968.

Quataert, Donald, *Ottoman Manufacturing in the Age of the Industrial Revolution*. New York: Cambridge University Press, 1994.

Shaw, Stanford J., *Between Old and New: The Ottoman Empire Under Selim III, 1789–1807*. Cambridge, MA, Harvard University Press, 1971.

———, and Ezel Kural Shaw, *History of the Ottoman Empire and Modern Turkey*. 2 vols. Cambridge: Cambridge University Press, 1976.

Wittek, Paul, *The Rise of the Ottoman Empire*. London: Royal Asiatic Society, 1938; reprint, New York: B. Franklin, 1971.

Ottoman Social Developments

Celik, Zeynep, *The Remaking of Istanbul: Portrait of an Ottoman City in the Nineteenth Century*. Seattle: University of Washington Press, 1986.

Davis, Fanny, *The Ottoman Lady: A Social History from 1718 to 1918*. New York: Greenwood, 1986.

Findley, Carter V., *Ottoman Civil Officialdom: A Social History*. Princeton, NJ: Princeton University Press, 1989.

Karpat, Kemal H., *Ottoman Population, 1830–1914: Demographic and Social Characteristics*. Madison, WI: University of Wisconsin Press, 1985.

Pears, Edwin, *Forty Years In Constantinople, 1873–1915*. New York: Appleton, 1916.

Rosenthal, Steven T., *The Politics of Dependency: Urban Reform in Istanbul*. Westport, CT: Greenwood Press, 1980.

Ottoman Economics

Blaisdell, Donald C., *European Financial Control in the Ottoman Empire: A Study of the Establishment, Activities and Significance of the Ottoman Public Debt*. New York: Columbia University Press, 1929.

Earle, Edward Mead, *Turkey, the Great Powers and the Baghdad Railway: A Study in Imperialism*. New York: Macmillan, 1923.

Islamoglu-Inan, Huri, ed., *The Ottoman Empire and the World-Economy*. New York: Cambridge University Press, 1987.

Issawi, Charles, ed., *The Economic History of Turkey, 1800–1914*. Chicago: University of Chicago Press, 1980.

Kasaba, Resat, *The Ottoman Empire and the World Economy: The Nineteenth Century*. Albany: State University of New York Press, 1988.

Pamuk, Sevket, *The Ottoman Empire and European Capitalism, 1820–1913: Trade, Investment, and Production*. New York: Cambridge University Press, 1987.

Quataert, Donald, *Social Disintegration and Popular Resistance in the Ottoman Empire, 1881–1908: Reactions to European Economic Penetration*. New York: New York University Press, 1983.

Administrative Reform

Davison, Roderic, *Reform in the Ottoman Empire, 1856–1876*. Princeton, NJ: Princeton University Press, 1963.

Devereux, Robert, *The First Ottoman Constitutional Period: A Study of the Midhat Constitution and Parliament*. Baltimore, MD: Johns Hopkins Press, 1963.

Findley, Carter V., *Bureaucratic Reform in the Ottoman Empire: The Sublime Porte, 1789–1922*. Princeton: Princeton University Press, 1980.

Midhat, Ali Haydar, *The Life of Midhat Pasha*. London: J. Murray, 1903.

Minorities

Andrews, Peter Alford, *Ethnic Groups in the Republic of Turkey*. Wiesbaden, Germany: Dr. Ludwig Reichert Verlag, 1989.

Betts, Robert Bretton, *Christians in the Middle East: A Political Study*. Athens: Lycabettus Press, 1975.

———, *The Druze*. New Haven, CT: Yale University Press, 1988.

Braude, Benjamin, and Bernard Lewis, eds., *Christians and Jews in the Ottoman Empire: The Functioning of a Plural Society*. 2 vols. New York: Holmes & Meier, 1982.

Entessar, Nader E., *Kurdish Ethnonationalism*. Boulder: Lynne Rienner Publishers, 1991.

Guest, John S., *The Yezidis: A Study in Survival*. London: Routledge, 1987.

Hourani, Albert, *Minorities in the Arab World*. London: Oxford University Press, 1947.

McCarthy, Justin, *Muslims and Minorities: The Populations of Ottoman Anatolia and the End of the Empire*. New York: New York University Press, 1983.

McDowell, David, *The Kurds*. London: UK Minority Group, 1991.

Olson, Robert, *The Emergence of Kurdish Nationalism and the Sheikh Said Rebellion, 1880–1925*. Austin: University of Texas Press, 1989.

van Bruinessen, Martin, *Agha, Shaikh and State: The Social and Political Structure of Kurdistan*. London: Zed Press, 1992.

Turkish Nationalism

Berkes, Niyazi, ed. and trans., *Turkish Nationalism and Western Civilization: Selected Essays of Ziya Gokalp*. Westport, CT: Greenwood Press, 1981.

Haddad, William, and William Ochsenwald, eds., *Nationalism in a Non-National State: The Dissolution of the Ottoman Empire*. Columbus: Ohio State University Press, 1977.

Heyd, Uriel, *Foundations of Turkish Nationalism: The Life and Teachings of Ziya Gokalp*. London: Luzac, 1950.

Kushner, David, *The Rise of Turkish Nationalism, 1876–1908*. London: Frank Cass, 1977.
Parla, Taha, *The Social and Political Thought of Ziya Gokalp, 1876–1924*. Leiden: Brill, 1985.

Young Ottomans and Young Turks

Ahmad, Feroz, *The Young Turks: The Committee of Union and Progress in Turkish Politics, 1908–1914*. Oxford: Clarendon Press, 1969.
Mardin, Serif, *The Genesis of Young Ottoman Thought: A Study in the Modernization of Turkish Political Ideas*. Princeton, NJ: Princeton University Press, 1962.
Ramsaur, Ernest, *The Young Turks*. Princeton, NJ: Princeton University Press, 1957.
Zurcher, Erik Jan, *The Unionist Factor: The Role of the Committee of Union and Progress in the Turkish National Movement, 1905–1926*. Leiden, Netherlands: E.J. Brill, 1984.

The Balkans

Anderson, M.S., *The Eastern Question, 1774-1923*. New York: St. Martin's Press, 1966.
Crampton, R. J., *A Short History of Modern Bulgaria*. Cambridge: Cambridge University Press, 1987.
Crampton, R. J., *Bulgaria, 1878-1918: A History*. Boulder, CO: East European Monographs; New York: Distributed by Columbia University Press, 1983.
Helmreich, E.C. *The Diplomacy of the Balkan Wars, 1912-1913*. Cambridge, Mass.: Harvard University Press, 1938.
Hitchens, Keith, *Rumania: 1866-1947*. Oxford: Clarendon Press, 1994.
Jankovic, Branimir, *The Establishment of Balkan National States, 1804-1920*. Seattle: University of Washington Press, 1977.
Jelavich, Barbara, *History of the Balkans*. Cambridge: Cambridge University Press, 1983.
Jelavich, Charles and Barbara Jelavich, *The Establishment of the Balkan National States, 1804-1920*. Seattle: University of Washington Press, 1977.
Petrovich, Michael Boro, *A History of Modern Serbia, 1804-1918*. New York: Harcourrt Brace Jovanovich. 1976.
Pollo, Stefanaq, *The History of Albania: Fromn its Origins to thr Present Day*. London: Routledge & Kegan Paul, 1981.
Rossos, Andrew, *Russia and the Balkans: Inter-Balkan Rivalries and Russian Foreign Policy, 1908-1914*. Toronto: University of Toronto Press, 1981.
Stavrianos, Leften Stavros, *The Balkans Since 1453*. New York: Rinehart, 1958.
Treadway, John D., *The Falcon and the Eagle, Montenegro and Austria-Hungary, 1908-1914*. West Lafayette, Indiana: Purdue University Press, 1983.
Wolff, Robert Lee, *The Balkans in Our Time*. Cambridge: Harvard University Press, 1956.

EGYPT

Politics

Ansari, Hamied, *Egypt: The Stalled Society*. Albany: State University of New York Press, 1986.
Berque, Jacques, *Egypt: Imperialism and Revolution*. New York: Praeger, 1967.
Binder, Leonard, *In a Moment of Enthusiasm: Political Power and the Second Stratum in Egypt*. Chicago: University of Chicago Press, 1978.
Cromer, Lord, *Modern Egypt*. 2 vols. London: Macmillan, 1908.
Deeb, Marius, *Party Politics in Egypt: The Wafd and Its Rivals, 1919–1939*. London: Ithaca Press, 1979.
Efendi, Huseyn, *Ottoman Egypt in the Age of the French Revolution*, trans. by Stanford J. Shaw. Cambridge: Harvard University Press, 1964.
Goldschmidt, Arthur, Jr., *Modern Egypt: The Formation of a Nation-State*. Boulder, CO: Westview Press, 1988.
Herold, Christopher, *Bonaparte in Egypt*. New York: Harper & Row, 1962.
Holt, P. M., *Egypt and the Fertile Crescent, 1516–1922: A Political History*. London: Longmans, 1966.
———, ed., *Political and Social Change in Modern Egypt*. London: Oxford University Press, 1968.
Hopwood, Derek, *Egypt: Politics and Society, 1945–1981*. Winchester, MA: Allen & Unwin, 1982.
Hunter, F. Robert, *Egypt Under the Khedives, 1805–1879: From Household Government to Modern Bureaucracy*. Pittsburgh: University of Pittsburgh Press, 1984.
Marsot, Afaf Lutfi al-Sayyid, *A Short History of Modern Egypt*. New York: Cambridge University Press, 1985.
———, *Egypt in the Reign of Muhammad Ali*. New York: Cambridge University Press, 1984.
———, *Egypt's Liberal Experiment, 1922–1936*. Berkeley: University of California Press, 1977.

Safran, Nadav, *Egypt in Search of Political Community: An Analysis of the Intellectual and Political Evolution of Egypt, 1804–1952*. Cambridge, MA: Harvard University Press, 1961.

Terry, Janice J., *The Wafd, 1919–1952: Cornerstone of Egyptian Political Power*. London: Third World Center for Research and Publishing, 1982.

Tignor, Robert, *Modernization and British Colonial Rule in Egypt, 1882–1914*. Princeton, NJ: Princeton University Press, 1966.

Vatikiotis, P. J., *The History of Egypt from Muhammad Ali to Mubarak* (4th ed.). Baltimore: Johns Hopkins University Press, 1991.

Economy

Davis, Eric, *Challenging Colonialism: Bank Misr and Egyptian Industrialization, 1920–1941*. Princeton, NJ: Princeton University Press, 1982.

Gran, Peter, *Islamic Roots of Capitalism: Egypt, 1760–1840*. Austin: University of Texas Press, 1979.

Issawi, Charles, *Egypt in Revolution: An Economic Analysis*. New York: Oxford University Press, 1961.

Landes, David, *Bankers and Pashas: International Finance and Economic Imperialism in Egypt*. Cambridge, MA: Harvard University Press, 1958.

Mabro, Robert, *The Egyptian Economy, 1952–1972*. London: Oxford University Press, 1974.

Owen, Roger, *Cotton and the Egyptian Economy, 1820–1914*. Oxford: Clarendon Press, 1969.

Richards, Alan, *Egypt's Agricultural Development, 1800–1980: Technical and Social Change*. Boulder, CO: Westview Press, 1981.

Rivlin, Helen, *The Agricultural Policy of Muhammad 'Ali in Egypt*. Cambridge, MA: Harvard University Press, 1961.

Saab, Gabriel S., *The Egyptian Agrarian Reform, 1952–1962*. London: Oxford University Press, 1967.

Tignor, Robert L,. *State, Private Enterprise, and Economic Change in Egypt, 1918–1952*. Princeton, NJ: Princeton University Press, 1984.

Social

Abdel-Malek, Anouar, *Egypt: Military Society*. New York: Random House, 1968.

Baer, Gabriel, *History of Land Ownership in Modern Egypt, 1800–1950*. London: Oxford University Press under auspices of Royal Institute of International Affairs, 1962.

———, *Studies in the Social History of Modern Egypt*. Chicago: University of Chicago Press, 1969.

Beinin, Joel, and Zachary Lockman, *Workers on the Nile: Nationalism, Communism, Islam, and the Egyptian Working Class, 1882–1954*. Princeton, NJ: Princeton University Press, 1987.

Brown, Nathan J., *Peasant Politics in Modern Egypt*. New Haven, CT: Yale University Press, 1990.

Golbert, Ellis, *Tinker, Tailor, and Textile Worker: Class and Politics in Egypt, 1930–1952*. Berkeley: University of California, 1986.

Hussein, Mahmud, *Class Conflict in Egypt: 1945–1970*. New York: Monthly Review Press, 1973.

Kramer, Gudrun, *The Jews in Modern Egypt, 1914–1952*. Seattle: University of Washington Press, 1989.

Lane, E.W., *Manners and Customs of the Modern Egyptians*. New York: Dutton, 1923.

Reid, Donald M., *Cairo University and the Making of Modern Egypt*. Cambridge and New York: Cambridge University Press, 1990.

———, *Lawyers and Politics in the Arab World, 1880–1960*. Minneapolis: Bibliotheca Islamica, 1981.

Springborg, Robert, *Family, Power, and Politics in Egypt: Sayed Bey Marei—His Clan, Clients, and Cohorts*. Philadelphia: University of Pennsylvania Press, 1982.

Toledano, Ehud R., *State and Society in Mid-Nineteenth-Century Egypt*. New York: Cambridge University Press, 1990.

Tucker, Judith, *Women in Nineteenth Century Egypt*. Cambridge: Cambridge University Press, 1985.

Ziadeh, Farhat J., *Lawyers, the Rule of Law, and Liberalism in Modern Egypt*. Stanford, CA: Hoover Institution on War, Revolution, and Peace, Stanford University, 1968.

Egypt under Nasser

Baker, Raymond William, *Egypt's Uncertain Revolution Under Nasser and Sadat*. Cambridge, MA: Harvard University Press, 1978.

Dekmejian, R. Hrair, *Egypt Under Nasir: A Study in Political Development*. Albany: State University of New York Press, 1971.

Lacouture, Jean, *Nasser, A Biography*. New York: Knopf, 1973.

Nutting, Anthony, *Nasser*. New York: Dutton, 1972.

Stephens, Robert, *Nasser: A Political Biography*. New York: Simon & Schuster, 1971.

Vatikiotis, P.J. ,*Nasser and His Generation*. New York: Croom Helm, 1978.

Waterbury, John, *The Egypt of Nasser and Sadat: The Political Economy of Two Regimes*. Princeton, NJ: Princeton University Press, 1983.

Foreign Affairs

Bowie, Robert R., *Suez 1956: International Crisis and the Role of Law*. New York and London: Oxford University Press, 1974.
Daly, N.W., *Empire on the Nile: The Anglo-Egyptian Sudan, 1898–1934*. Cambridge: Cambridge University Press, 1986.
———, *Imperial Sudan: The Anglo-Egyptian Condominium, 1934–1956*. Cambridge: Cambridge University Press, 1991.
Darwin, John, *Britain, Egypt, and the Middle East: Imperial Policy in the Aftermath of War, 1918–1922*. New York: St. Martin's Press, 1981.
Dawisha, A. I., *Egypt in the Arab World, 1952–1970: The Elements of a Dynamic Foreign Policy*. New York: Halsted Press, 1976.
Dawisha, Karen, *Soviet Foreign Policy Towards Egypt*. New York: St. Martin's Press, 1979.
El-Hussini, Mohez M., *Soviet-Egyptian Relations, 1945–85*. New York: St. Martin's Press, 1987.
El-Shazly, Saad, *The Crossing of the Suez*. San Francisco: American Mideast Research, 1980.
Farnie, D.A., *East and West of Suez: The Suez Canal in History, 1854–1956*. Oxford: Clarendon Press, 1969.
Heikal, Mohammed Hassanein, *Cutting the Lion's Tail: Suez Through Egyptian Eyes*. London: Andre Deutsch, 1986.
———, *The Cairo Documents*. New York: Doubleday, 1973.
———, *The Road to Ramadan*. New York: Ballantine Books, 1975.
———, *The Sphinx and the Commissar: The Rise and Fall of Soviet Influence in the Middle East*. New York: Harper & Row, 1979.
Kerr, Malcolm, *The Arab Cold War: Gamal 'Abd al-Nasir and His Rivals, 1958–1970*. (3rd ed.) London: Oxford University Press, 1971.
Kyle, Keith, *Suez*. New York: St. Martin's Press, 1991.
Lorenz, Joseph P., *Egypt and the Arabs: Foreign Policy in Search of Identity*. Boulder, CO: Westview Press, 1990.
Louis, William Roger, and Roger Owen, eds., *Suez 1956: The Crisis and Its Consequences*. Oxford: Clarendon Press, 1989.
Love, Kennett, *Suez- The Twice-Fought War: A History*. New York: McGraw-Hill, 1969.
Marsot, Afaf Lutfi al-Sayyid, *Egypt and Cromer: A Study in Anglo-Egyptian Relations*. London: John Murray, 1968.
Mitchell, Timothy, *Colonizing Egypt*. New York: Cambridge University Press, 1988.
Neff, Donald, *Warriors at Suez: Eisenhower Takes America into the Middle East*. New York: Linden Press, 1981.
Thomas, Hugh, *Suez*. New York: Harper & Rowe, 1967.

Egyptian Nationalism

Ahmad, Jamal, *The Intellectual Origins of Egyptian Nationalism*. London: Oxford University Press, 1960.
Ahmed, Mohammad, *The Intellectual Origins of Egyptian Nationalism*. London: Oxford University Press, 1960.
Gershoni, Israel, and James P. Jankowski, *Egypt, Islam, and the Arabs: The Search for Egyptian Nationhood, 1900–1930*. New York: Oxford University Press, 1986.
Scholch, Alexander, *Egypt for the Egyptians! The Socio-Political Crisis in Egypt, 1878–1882*. London: Ithaca Press, 1981.
Zayid, Mahmud, *Egypt's Struggle for Independence*. Beirut: Khayats, 1965.

Islam

Adams, Charles, *Islam and Modernism in Egypt*. London: Oxford University Press, 1933; reprint, New York: Russel, 1968.
Ayubi, Nazih, *Political Islam: Religion and Politics in the Arab World*. London: Routledge, 1991.
Jansen, J.G., *The Neglected Duty: The Creed of Sadat's Assassins and Islamic Resurgence in the Middle East*. New York: Macmillan, 1986.
Kepel, Giles, *Muslim Extremism in Egypt: The Prophet and the Pharaoh*, trans. by Jan Rothschild. Berkeley: University of California Press, 1986.
Kerr, Malcolm, *Islamic Reform: The Political and Legal Theories of Muhammad 'Abduh and Rashid Rida*. Berkeley: University of California Press, 1961.
Mitchell, Richard, *The Society of the Muslim Brothers*. London: Oxford University Press, 1969.
Qutb, Sayed, *Milestones*. Lahore, Pakistan: Kazi Publications.

PALESTINE AND ISRAEL

Abboushi, W. F., *The Unmaking of Palestine*. Boulder, CO: Lynne Rienner Publishers, 1985.
Abu-Lugod, Ibrahim, ed., *The Transformation of Palestine*. (2nd ed.) Evanston, IL: Northwestern University Press, 1987.

———, ed., *The Transformation of Palestine: Essays on the Origin and Development of the Arab-Israeli Conflict.* Evanston, IL: Northwestern University Press, 1971.

Bowle, John, *Viscount Samuel: A Biography.* London: Gollancz, 1957.

Cohen, Michael J., *The Origins and Evolution of the Arab-Israeli Conflict.* Berkeley: University of California Press, 1987.

ESCO Foundation for Palestine, *Palestine: A Study of Jewish, Arab, and British Policies* (2 vols. New Haven, CT: Yale University Press, 1947.

Flapan, Simha, *Zionism and the Palestinians.* London: Croom Helm, 1979.

Hurewitz, J.C., *The Struggle for Palestine.* New York: Norton, 1950; reprint, New York: Schocken Books, 1976.

Kayyali, A.W. ,*Palestine: A Modern History.* London: Croom Helm, 1978.

Khalidi, Walid, ed., *From Haven to Conquest: Readings in Zionism and the Palestine Problem Until 1948.* Beirut:Institute for Palestine Studies, 1971.

Khouri, Fred J., *The Arab-Israeli Dilemma.* (3rd ed.) Syracuse, NY: Syracuse University Press, 1985.

Laqueur, Walter, and Barry Rubin, eds., *The Israel-Arab Reader: A Documentary History of the Middle East Conflict.* (4th revised ed.) New York: Penguin, 1984.

Lesch, Ann Mosely, *Arab Politics in Palestine, 1917–1939: The Frustration of a Nationalist Movement.* New York: Cornell University Press, 1979.

———, and Mark Tessler, *Israel, Egypt, and the Palestinians: From Camp David to the Intifada.* Bloomington: Indiana University Press, 1989.

Lukacs, Yehuda, and Abdalla Battah, eds., *The Arab-Israeli Conflict: Two Decades of Change.* Boulder, CO: Westview Press, 1988.

Masalha, Nur, *Expulsion of the Palestinians: The Concept of "Transfer" in Zionist Political Thought, 1882–1948.* Washington, DC: Institute for Palestinian Studies, 1992.

Moore, John Norton, *The Arab-Israeli Conflict.* Princeton, NJ: Princeton University Press, 1974.

Morris, *The Birth of Israel and the Palestinian Refugee Problem, 1947–1949.* New York: Cambridge University Press, 1987.

———, Benny, *1948 and After: Israel and the Palestinians.* Oxford University Press, 1991.

Neff, Donald, *Warriors Against Israel.* Brattleboro, VT: Amana Books, 1988.

———, *Warriors for Jerusalem: Six Days That Changed the Middle East.* New York: Linden Press, 1984.

Ovendale, Ritchie, *The Origins of the Arab-Israeli Wars.* New York: Longman, 1984.

Porath, Yehoshua, *The Emergence of the Palestinian-Arab National Movement, 1918–1929.* London: F. Cass, 1974.

———, *The Palestinian National Movement: From Riot to Rebellion: 1929–1939.* London: F. Cass, 1977.

Quigley, John, *Palestine and Israel: A Challenge to Justice.* Durham, NC: Duke University Press, 1990.

Rodinson, Maxime, *Israel and the Arabs.* New York: Pantheon, 1968.

Safran, Nadav, *From War to War: The Arab-Israeli Confrontation, 1948–1967.* Indianapolis, IN: Pegasus, 1969.

Smith, Charles D., *Palestine and the Arab-Israeli Conflict.* New York: St. Martin's Press, 1988.

Smith, Pamela Ann, *Palestine and the Palestinians, 1876–1983.* New York: St. Martin's Press, 1984.

Smooha, Sammy, *Arabs and Jews in Israel.* Boulder, CO: Westview Press, 1989.

Stein, Kenneth W., *The Land Question in Palestine, 1917–1939.* Chapel Hill: University of North Carolina Press, 1984.

Taylor, Alan, and Richard Tetlie, eds., *Palestine: A Search for Truth.* Washington, DC: Public Affairs Press, 1970.

Waines, David A., *A Sentence of Exile: The Palestine/Israel Conflict, 1897–1977.* Wilmette, IL: Medina Press, 1977.

Zionism

Avineri, Shlomo, *The Making of Modern Zionism: The Intellectual Origin of the Jewish State.* New York: Basic Books, 1986.

Avishai, Bernard, *The Tragedy of Zionism: Revolution and Democracy in the Land of Israel.* New York: Farrar, Straus and Giroux, 1985.

Brenner, Lenni, *The Iron Wall: Zionist Revolutionism from Jabotinsky to Shamir.* London: Zed Books, 1984.

———, *Zionism in the Age of the Dictators.* London: Croom Helm, 1983.

Cohen, Israel, *Theodor Herzl, Founder of Political Zionism.* New York: Thomas Yoseloff, 1959.

Cohen, Mitchell, *Zion and State: Nation, Class and the Shaping of Modern Israel.* New York: Basil Blackwell, 1987.

EAFORT and AJAZ, *Judaism or Zionism: What Difference for the Middle East?* London: Zed Books, 1985.

Feuerlicht, Roberta Strauss, *The Fate of the Jews: A People Torn Between Israeli Power and Jewish Ethics.* New York: Times Books, 1983.

Halevi, Ilan, *A History of the Jews: Ancient and Modern,* trans. by A.M. Barrett. London: Zed Books, 1987.

Halpern, Ben, *The Idea of the Jewish State.* (2nd ed.) Cambridge, MA: Harvard University Press, 1969.

Hertzberg, Arthur, ed., *The Zionist Idea: A Historical Analysis and Reader.* Garden City, NY: Doubleday, 1957.

Katz, Samuel, *Days of Fire.* Garden City, NY: Doubleday, 1968.

Kayyali, Abdul Wahhab, ed., *Zionism, Imperialism and Racism.* London: Croom Helm, 1978.

Kimmerling, Baruch, *Zionism and Territory: The Socio-Territorial Dimensions of Zionist Politics.* Berkeley, CA: Institute of International Studies, 1983.

Laqueur, Walter, *A History of Zionism*. New York: Schocken Books, 1976.
Lehn, Walter, and Uri Davis, *The Jewish National Fund*. London: Kegan Paul International, 1988.
Rubinstein, Amnon, *The Zionist Dream Revisited: From Herzl to Gush Emunim and Back*. New York: Schocken Books, 1984.
Ruether, Herman J., and Rosemary Radford Ruether, *The Wrath of Jonah: The Crisis of Religious Nationalism in the Israeli Palestinian Conflict*. San Francisco: Harper & Row, 1989.
Schoenman, Ralph, *The Hidden History of Zionism*. Santa Barbara, CA: Veritas Press, 1988.
Segre, Dan V., *A Crisis of Identity: Israel and Zionism*. New York: Oxford University Press, 1980.
Smith, Gary V., ed., *Zionism: The Dream and the Reality, A Jewish Critique*. New York: Barnes & Noble, 1974.
Taylor, Alan, *Prelude to Israel*. New York: Philosophical Library, 1959.
———, *The Zionist Mind: The Origins and Development of Zionist Thought*. Beirut: Institute for Palestine Studies, 1974.
Tekiner, Roselle, et al., eds., *Anti-Zionism: Analytical Reflections*. Brattleboro, VT: Amana Books, 1988.
Vital, David, *The Origins of Zionism*. Oxford: Clarendon Press, 1975.
———, *Zionism: The Crucial Phase*. Oxford: Clarendon Press, 1987.
———, *Zionism: The Formative Years*. Oxford: Clarendon Press, 1982.

Israel

Arian, Asher, *Politics in Israel: The Second Generation*. (2nd ed.) Chatham, NJ: Chatham House,1989.
Beit-Hallahmi, Benjamin, *The Israeli Connection: Who Israel Arms and Why*. New York: Pantheon,1987.
Eisenstadt, S.N., *The Transformation of Israeli Society: An Essay in Interpretation*. Boulder, CO: Westview Press, 1985.
Elon, Amos, *The Israelis: Founders and Sons*. New York: Holt, Rinehart and Winston, 1971.
Flapan, Simha, *The Birth of Israel*. New York: Pantheon, 1988.
Harkabi, Yehoshafat, *Israel's Fateful Hour*, trans. by Nenn Schramm. New York: Harper & Row, 1988.
Jiryis, Sabri, *The Arabs in Israel, 1948–1966*. New York: Monthly Review Press, 1976.
Lucas, Noah, *The Modern History of Israel*. New York: Praeger, 1975.
Lustick, Ian, *Arabs in the Jewish State: Israel's Control of a National Minority*. Austin: University of Texas Press, 1980.
———, *For the Land and the Lord: Jewish Fundamentalism in Israel*. New York: Council on Foreign Relations, 1988.
O'Brien, Conor Cruise, *The Siege: The Saga of Israel and Zionism*. New York: Simon & Schuster, 1986.
Oz, Amos, *In the Land of Israel*. New York: Harcourt Brace Jovanovich, 1983.
Peretz, Don, *The Government and Politics of Israel*. (2nd ed.) Boulder, CO: Westview Press, 1983.
Reich, Bernard, *Israel: Land of Tradition and Conflict*. Boulder, CO: Westview Press, 1985.
Rodinson, Maxime, *Israel: A Colonial Settler State?* New York: Monad Press, 1973.
Sachar, Howard Morley, *A History of Israel from the Rise of Zionism to Our Time*. New York: Knopf, 1976.
———, *A History of Israel, Vol.II: From the Aftermath of the Yom Kippur War*. New York: Oxford University Press, 1987.
Segev, Tom, *1949: The First Israelis*. New York: Free Press,1986.
Sykes, Christopher, *Crossroads to Israel*. New York: World Publishing Company, 1965; reprint, Bloomington: Indiana University Press, 1973.
Weizmann, Chaim, *Trial and Error: The Autobiography of Chaim Weizmann*. New York: Harper, 1949.
Wolffsohn, Michael, *Israel, Polity, Society, and Economy 1882–1986: An Introductory Handbook*, trans. by Douglas Bokovoy. Atlantic Highlands, NJ: Humanities Press International, 1987.

Palestine and Palestinians

Abu-Ghazaleh, Adnan Mohammed, *Arab Cultural Nationalism in Palestine During the British Mandate*. Beirut: Institute for Palestine Studies, 1973.
Curtis, Michael, et. al., *The Palestinians: People, History, Politics*, New Brunswick, NJ: Transaction Books, 1975.
John, Robert, and Sami Hadawi, *The Palestine Diary*, 2 vols. (New York: New World Press, 1971.
Khalidi, Walid, *Before Their Diaspora: A Photographic History of the Palestinians*. Washington, DC: Institute for Palestinian Studies, 1984.
Lesch, Ann Mosley, *Arab Politics in Palestine, 1917–1939*. Ithaca, NY: Cornell University Press, 1979.
Miller, Ylana N., *Government and Society in Rural Palestine, 1920–1948*. Austin: University of Texas Press, 1984.
Morris, *The Birth of the Palestinian Refugee Problem, 1947–1949*. New York: Cambridge University Press, 1987.
———, Benny, *1948 and After: Israel and the Palestinians*. New York: Oxford University Press, 1991.
Muslih, Muhammad Y., *The Origins of Palestinian Nationalism*. New York: Columbia University Press, 1989.
Nakhleh, Khalil, and Elia Zureik, eds., *The Sociology of the Palestinians*. New York: St. Martin's Press, 1980.
Palumbo, Michael, *The Palestinian Catastrophe: The 1948 Expulsion of a People from Their Homeland*. London and Boston: Faber and Faber, 1987.

Porath, Yehoshua, *The Emergence of the Palestinian National Movement, 1918–1929*. London: Frank Cass, 1973.
———, *The Palestinian Arab National Movement, from Riots to Rebellion: 1929–1939, Volume II*. London: Frank Cass, 1978.
Quandt, William B., et al., *The Politics of Palestinian Nationalism*. Berkeley: University of California Press, 1973.
Said, Edward W., *The Question of Palestine*. New York: Times Books, 1979.
———, and Christopher Hitchens, et al., *Blaming the Victims: Spurious Scholarship and the Palestine Question*. New York: Verso, 1987.
Smith, Pamela, *Palestine and the Palestinians, 1876–1983*. New York: St. Martin's Press, 1984.
Zureik, Elia, *The Palestinians in Israel: A Study in Internal Colonialism*. London: Routledge & Kegan Paul, 1979.

JORDAN

Abidi, Agil Hyder Hasan, *Jordan: A Political Study, 1948–1957*. New York: Asia Publishing House, 1965.
Aruri, Naseer H., *Jordan: A Study in Political Development (1921–1965*. The Hague: Martinus Nijhoff, 1972.
Baily, Clinton, *Jordan's Palestinian Challenge, 1948–1973: A Political History*. Boulder, CO: Westview Press, 1984.
Bar-Joseph, Uri, *The Best of Enemies: Israel and Transjordan in the War of 1948*. London: Frank Cass, 1987.
Dann, Uriel, *King Hussein and the Challenge of Arab Radicalism: Jordan, 1955-1967*. New York: Oxford University Press, 1989.
———, *Studies in the History of Transjordan, 1920–1949: The Making of a State*. Boulder, CO: Westview Press, 1984.
Day, Arthur R., *East Bank-West Bank: Jordan and the Prospects for Peace*. New York: Council on Foreign Relations, 1986.
Glubb, John Bagot, *The Story of the Arab Legion*. London: Hodder & Stoughton, 1948.
Gubser, Peter, *Jordan: Crossroads of Middle Eastern Events*. Boulder, CO: Westview Press, 1983.
Lewis, Norman N., *Nomads and Settlers in Syria and Jordan, 1800–1980*. Cambridge: Cambridge University Press, 1987.
Lunt, James, *Hussein of Jordan: Searching for a Just and Lasting Peace*. New York: Morrow, 1989.
Salibi, Kamal, *The Modern History of Jordan*. New York: St. Martin's Press, 1993.
Satloff, Robert B., *Troubles on the East Bank: Challenges to the Domestic Stability of Jordan*. New York: Praeger, 1986.
Shlaim, Avi, *Collusion Across the Jordan: King Abdullah, the Zionist Movement, and the Partition of Palestine*. New York: Columbia University Press, 1988.
Wilson, Mary C., *King Abdullah, Britain and the Making of Jordan*. New York: Cambridge University Press, 1988.
Wilson, Rodney, ed., *Politics and the Economy in Jordan*. New York: Routledge, 1991.

LEBANON

Ajami, Fouad, *The Vanished Imam: Musa al-Sadrand the Shi'a of Lebanon*. Ithaca, NY: Cornell University Press, 1986.
Bulloch, John, *Final Conflict: The War in Lebanon*. London: Century, 1983.
Cobban, Helena, *The Making of Modern Lebanon*. Boulder, CO: Westview Press, 1985.
Deeb, Marius, *The Lebanese Civil War*. New York: Praeger, 1980.
Evron, Yair, *War and Intervention in Lebanon: The Israeli-Syrian Deterrence Dialogue*. Baltimore: Johns Hopkins University Press, 1987.
Fawaz, Leila Tarazi, *Merchants and Migrants in Nineteenth Century Beirut*. Cambridge, MA: Harvard University Press, 1983.
Fisk, Robert, *Pity and the Nation: Lebanon at War*. London: Deutsch, 1990.
Friedman, Thomas, *From Beirut to Jerusalem*. New York: Farrar, Straus and Giroux, 1989.
Gilmour, David, *Lebanon: The Fractured Country*. New York: St. Martin's Press, 1983.
Gordon, David C., *The Republic of Lebanon: Nation in Jeopardy*. Boulder, CO: Westview Press, 1983.
Goria, Wade R., *Sovereignty and Leadership in Lebanon, 1943–1976*. London: Ithaca Press, 1986.
Harik, Iliya, *Politics and Change in a Traditional Society: Lebanon, 1711–1845*. Princeton, NJ: Princeton University Press, 1968.
Hiro, Dilip, *Lebanon: Fire and Embers, a History of the Lebanese Civil War*. St. Martin's Press, 1992.
Hudson, Michael, *The Precarious Republic*. New York: Random House, 1968; reprint, Boulder, CO: Westview Press, 1985.
Khalaf, Samir, *Lebanon's Predicament*. New York: Columbia University Press, 1987.
———, *Persistence and Change in 19th Century Lebanon: A Sociological Study*. Beirut: American University of Beirut Press, 1979.
Khalidi, Walid, *Conflict and Violence in Lebanon: Confrontation in the Middle East*. Cambridge, MA: Harvard University Center for International Affairs, 1980.
Petran, Tabitha, *The Struggle over Lebanon*. New York: Monthly Review Press, 1987.

Polk, William R., *The Opening of South Lebanon, 1788–1840*. Cambridge, MA: Harvard University Press, 1963.
Qubain, Fahim I., *Crisis in Lebanon*. Washington, DC: The Middle East Institute, 1961.
Randal, Jonathan C., *Going All the Way: Christian Warlords, Israeli Adventurers, and the War in Lebanon*. New York: Viking Press, 1983.
Salibi, Kamal, *A House of Many Mansions: The History of Lebanon Reconsidered*. Berkeley: University of California Press, 1989.
———, *Crossroads to Civil War: Lebanon, 1958–1975*. Delmar, NY: Caravan Books, 1976.
———, *The Modern History of Lebanon*. New York: Praeger, 1965.
Sayigh, Rosemary, *The Palestinians in Lebanon*. Atlantic Highlands, NJ: Humanities Press International, 1979.
Spagnola, John, *France and Ottoman Lebanon, 1861–1914*. London: Ithaca Press for the Middle East Centre, St. Anthony's College Oxford, 1977.
Zamir, Meir, *The Formation of Modern Lebanon*. Ithaca, NY: Cornell University Press, 1985.

SYRIA

Bodman, Herbert, *Political Factions in Aleppo, 1760–1826*. Chapel Hill: University of North Carolina Press, 1963.
Commins, David Dean, *Islamic Reform: Politics and Social Change in Late Ottoman Syria*. New York: Oxford University Press, 1990.
Devlin, John F., *The Ba'th Party: A History from Its Origins to 1966*. (Stanford, CA: Hoover Institution Press, 1976.
———, *Syria: Modern State in an Ancient Land*. Boulder, CO: Westview Press, 1983.
Gaunson, A. B., *The Anglo-French Clash in Lebanon and Syria, 1940–45*. New York: St. Martin's Press, 1987.
Hinnebusch, Raymond A., *Authoritarian Power and State Formation in Ba'thist Syria: Army, Party, and Peasant*. Boulder, CO: Westview Press, 1990.
———, *Authoritarian Power and State Formation in Ba'thist Syria: The Political Economy of Rural Development*. Boulder, CO: Westview Press, 1989.
———, *Peasant and Bureaucracy in Ba'thist Syria*. Boulder, CO: Westview Press, 1989.
Khoury, Philip S., *Syria and the French Mandate: The Politics of Arab Nationalism, 1920–1945*. Princeton, NJ: Princeton University Press, 1987.
———, *Urban Notables and Arab Nationalism: The Politics of Damascus 1860–1920*. New York: Cambridge University Press, 1983.
Lesch, David W., *Syria and the United States: Eisenhower's Cold War in the Middle East*. Boulder, CO: Westview Press, 1992.
Longrigg, Stephen, *Syria and Lebanon Under the French Mandate*. London: Oxford University Press, 1948.
Ma'oz, Moshe, *Asad, the Sphinx of Damascus: A Political Biography*. London: Weidenfeld and Nicolson, 1988.
———, *Ottoman Reform in Syria and Palestine, 1840–1861*. Oxford: Clarendon Press, 1968.
———, and Avner Yaniv, eds., *Syria Under Asad: Domestic Constraints and Regional Risks*. New York: St. Martin's Press, 1986.
Marcus, Abraham, *The Middle East on the Eve of Modernity: Aleppo in the Eighteenth Century*. New York: Columbia University Press, 1989.
Olson, Robert, *The Ba'th and Syria: From the French Mandate to the Era of Hafiz al-Assad*. Princeton, NJ: The Kingston Press, 1982.
Petran, Tabitha, *Syria*. New York: Praeger, 1972.
Pipes, Daniel, *Greater Syria: The History of an Ambition*. New York and London: Oxford University Press, 1990.
Rabinovitch, Itamar, *Syria Under the Ba'th, 1963–1966*. New York: Halsted Press, 1966.
Roberts, David, *The Ba'th and the Creation of Modern Syria*. New York: St. Martin's Press, 1990.
Schilcher, Linda Schatkowski, *Families in Politics: Damascene Factions and Estates of the 18th and 19th Centuries*. Stuttgart: Franz Steiner Verlag, 1985.
Seale, Patrick, *Asad: The Struggle for the Middle East*. Berkeley: University of California Press, 1988.
———, *The Struggle for Syria: A Study of Post-War Politics, 1945–1958*. New Haven: Yale University Press, 1987.
Tibawi, A. L., *A Modern History of Syria, Including Lebanon and Palestine*. New York: St. Martin's Press, 1969.
van Dam, Nikolaos, *The Struggle for Power in Syria: Sectarianism, Regionalism, and Tribalism in Politics, 1961–1980*, 2nd ed. New York: St. Martin's Press, 1980.
Zuwiyya-Yamak, Labib, *The Syrian Social Nationalist Party: An Ideological Analysis*. Cambridge, MA: University of Harvard Press, 1966.

IRAQ

al-Khalil, Samir, *Republic of Fear: The Politics of Modern Iraq*. Berkeley: University of California Press, 1989.
Axelgard, Frederick W. ,*A New Iraq? The Gulf War and Implications for U.S. Policy*. New York: Praeger, 1988.
———, ed., *Iraq in Transition: A Political, Economic and Strategic Perspective*. Boulder, CO: Westview Press, 1986.
Batatu, Hanna, *The Old Social Classes and the Revolutionary Movements of Iraq: A Study of Iraq's Old Landed and*

Commercial Classes and of Its Communists, Ba'thists, and Free Officers. Princeton, NJ: Princeton University Press, 1978.
CARDRI [Committee Against Repression and for Democratic Rights], *Saddam's Iraq: Revolution or Reaction*. London: Zed Books, 1989.
Farouk-Sluglett, Marion, and Peter Sluglett, *Iraq Since 1958: From Revolution to Dictatorship*. London: I.B. Tauris & Co. Ltd., 1990.
Fernea, Robert A., and William Roger Louis, eds. *The Iraqi Revolution of 1958*. London: I.B. Tauris, 1991.
Gunter, Michael M., *The Kurds of Iraq: Hope and Tragedy*. New York: St. Martin's Press, 1992.
Helms, Christine Moss, *Iraq: Eastern Flank of the Arab World*. Washington, DC: Brookings Institution, 1984.
Kelidar, Abbas, ed., *The Integration of Modern Iraq*. New York: St. Martin's Press, 1979.
Khadduri, Majid, *Independent Iraq, 1932–1958: A Study in Iraqi Politics*. (2nd ed.) London: Oxford University Press, 1960.
———, *Republican Iraq: A Study in Iraqi Politics Since the Revolution of 1958*. London: Oxford University Press, 1969.
Kienle, Eberhard, *Ba'th v. Ba'th: The Conflict between Syria and Iraq, 1968–1989*. London: I.B. Tauris, 1990.
Marr, Phebe, *The Modern History of Iraq*. Boulder, CO: Westview Press, 1985.
Miller, Judith, and Laurie Mylroie, *Saddam Hussein and the Crisis in the Gulf*. New York: Times Books, 1990)
Niblock, Tim, ed., *Iraq: The Contemporary State*. New York: St. Martin's Press, 1982.
Silberfarb, Daniel, *Britain's Informal Empire in the Middle East: A Case Study of Iraq, 1929–1941*. New York: Oxford University Press, 1986.
Simon, Reeva S., *Iraq Between the Two World Wars: The Creation and Implementation of a Nationalist Ideology*. New York: Columbia University Press, 1986.
Sluglett, Peter, *Britain in Iraq, 1914–1932*. London: Ithaca Press for the Middle East Centre, St. Anthony's College, Oxford, 1976.

ARABIAN PENINSULA

Abdullah, Mohammed, *The United Arab Emirates: A Modern History*. New York: Barnes & Noble, 1978.
Abir, Mordechai, *Saudi Arabia in the Oil Era: Regimes and Elites, Conflict and Cooperation*. Boulder, CO: Westview Press, 1988.
Al Farsy, Fouad, *Saudi Arabia: A Case Study in Development*. (4th ed.) New York: Routledge and Kegan Paul, 1986.
Allen, Calvin H., *Oman: The Modernization of the Sultanate*. Boulder, CO: Westview Press, 1987.
Anthony, John Duke, *Arab States of the Lower Gulf*. Washington, DC: Middle East Institute, 1975.
Beling, Willard, ed., *King Faisal and the Modernization of Saudi Arabia*. Boulder, CO: Westview Press, 1980.
Bidwell, Robin, *The Two Yemens*. Boulder, CO: Westview Press, 1983.
Burrowes, Robert D., *The Yemen Arab Republic: The Politics of Development, 1962–1986*. Boulder, CO: Westview Press, 1987.
Busch, Brinton Cooper, *Britain and the Persian Gulf, 1894–1914*. Berkeley: University of California Press, 1967.
Goldberg, Jacob, *The Foreign Policy of Saudi Arabia: The Formative Years, 1902–1918*. Cambridge, MA: Harvard University Press, 1986.
Halliday, Fred, *Arabia without Sultans*. New York: Vintage Books, 1974.
Hawley, Sir Donald, *Oman and Its Renaissance*. (4th ed.) London: Stacey International, 1987.
Helms, Christine Moss, *The Cohesion of Saudi Arabia*. Baltimore: Johns Hopkins University Press, 1980.
Holden, David, and Richard Johns, *The House of Saud: The Rise and Rule of the Most Powerful Dynasty in the Arab World*. New York: Holt and Reinhart, 1981.
Howarth, David, *The Desert King: The Life of Ibn Saud*. New York: McGraw-Hill, 1964; New York: Quartet, 1988.
Ismael, Jacqueline S., *Kuwait: Social Change in Historical Perspective*. Syracuse, NY: Syracuse University Press, 1982.
Ismael, Tareq Y., and Jacqueline S. Ismael, *The People's Democratic Republic of Yemen: Politics, Economics and Society*. Boulder, CO: Westview Press, 1986.
Kostiner, Joseph, *The Making of Saudi Arabia, 1916–1936: From Chieftancy to Monarchy*. New York: Oxford University Press, 1993.
———, *The Struggle for South Yemen*. New York: St. Martin's Press, 1984.
Lackner, Helen, *A House Built on Sand*. London: Ithaca Press, 1978.
———, *P.D.R. Yemen: Outpost of Socialist Development in Arabia*. London: Ithaca Press, 1985.
Landon, Robert, *Oman in the Late Nineteenth Century and After*. Princeton, NJ: Princeton University Press, 1967.
Lawson, Fred H., *Bahrain: The Modernization of Autocracy*. Boulder, CO: Westview Press, 1989.
Long, David E., *The United States and Saudi Arabia: Ambivalent Allies*. Boulder, CO: Westview Press, 1985.
Mackey, Sandra, *Inside the Desert Kingdom*. Boston: Houghton Mifflin, 1987.
McLoughlin, Leslie, *Ibn Saud: Founder of a Kingdom*. New York: St Martin's Press, 1993.
Ochenswald, William, *Religion, Society, and the State in Arabia: The Hijaz Under Ottoman Control, 1804–1908*. Columbus: Ohio State University Press, 1984.

Peck, Malcolm C., *The United Arab Emirates: A Venture in Unity*. Boulder, CO: Westview Press, 1986.
Peterson, J.E., *The Arab Gulf States: Steps Toward Political Participation*. New York: Praeger, 1988.
Peterson, John E., *Yemen: The Search for a Modern State*. Baltimore: Johns Hopkins University Press, 1982.
Philby, St. John, *Arabian Jubilee*. New York: The John Day Company, 1953.
———, *Sa'udi Arabia*. London: Benn, 1955.
Phillips, Wendell, *Oman: A History*. Mystic, CT: Verry, 1972.
Pridham, B.R., ed., *Contemporary Yemen: Politics and Historical Background*. New York: St. Martin's Press, 1985.
———, ed., *Economy, Society and Culture in Contemporary Yemen*. London: Croom Helm, 1985.
Reza, A., S. Islami, and Rostam Mehraban Kavoussi, *The Political Economy of Saudi Arabia*. Seattle: University of Washington Press, 1984.
Risso, Patricia, *Oman and Muscat: An Early Modern History*. New York: St. Martin's Press, 1986.
Rumaihi, Muhammad, *Beyond Oil: Unity and Development in the Gulf*, trans. by James Dickins. London: Al Saqi Books, 1986.
Safran, Nadav, *Saudi Arabia: The Ceaseless Quest for Security*. Cambridge, MA: Harvard University Press, 1985.
Salibi, Kamal, *A History of Arabia*. Beirut: Caravan Books, 1980.
Shaw, John, and David Long, *Saudi Arabian Modernization*. New York: Praeger, 1982.
Sindelar, H. Richard, III, and J. E. Petersen, eds., *Crosscurrents in the Gulf: Arab, Regional and Global Interests*. London: Routledge, 1988.
Stookey, Robert W., ed., *The Arabian Peninsula: Zone of Ferment*. Stanford, CA: Hoover Institution, 1984.
———, *Yemen: The Politics of the Yemen Arab Republic*. Boulder, CO: Westview Press, 1978.
Thesiger, Wilfred, *Arabian Sands*. Harmondworth: Penguin Books, 1964.
Troeller, Gary, *The Birth of Saudi Arabia*. London: Frank Cass, 1976.
Wilkinson, John C., *Arabia's Frontiers: The Story of Britain's Boundary Drawing in the Desert*. London and New York: I.B. Taurus, 1991.
Winder, R. Bailey, *Saudi Arabia in the Nineteenth Century*. London: Macmillan, 1965.
Zahlan, Rosemarie Said, *The Creation of Qatar*. London: Croom Helm, 1979.
———, *The Making of the Modern Gulf States: Kuwait, Bahrain, Qatar, and the United Arab Emirates and Oman*. London and Boston: Unwin Hyman, 1989.

MODERN TURKEY

Ahmad, Feroz, *The Making of Modern Turkey*. London: Routledge, 1993.
———, *The Turkish Experience in Democracy, 1950–1975*. Boulder, CO: Westview Press, 1977.
Berkes, Niyazi, *The Development of Secularism in Turkey*. Montreal: McGill University Press, 1964.
Gunter, Michael M., *The Kurds in Turkey: A Political Dilemma*. Boulder, CO: Westview Press, 1991.
Hale, William, *The Political and Economic Development of Modern Turkey*. New York: St. Martin's Press, 1981.
Heper, Metin, Ayşe Öncü, and Heinz Kramer, *Turkey and the West: Changing Political and Cultural Identities*. London: I.B. Tauris, 1993.
Karpat, Kemal, *Social Change and Politics in Turkey*. Leiden, Netherlands: E. J. Brill, 1973.
———, *Turkey's Politics: The Transition to a Multiparty System*. Princeton, NJ: Princeton University Press, 1959.
Kazancigil, Ali, and Ergun Ozbundun, eds., *Ataturk: Founder of a Modern State*. Hamden, CT: Archon Books, 1981.
Keyder, Caglar, *State and Class in Turkey: A Study in Capitalist Development*. New York: Verso Press, 1987.
Kinross, Lord, *Ataturk: A Biography of Mustafa Kemal, Father of Modern Turkey*. London: Weidenfeld and Nicolson, 1964.
Lewis, Bernard, *The Emergence of Modern Turkey*. (2nd ed.) London: Oxford University Press, 1968.
Ozbudun, Ergun, *Social Change and Political Parties in Turkey*. Princeton, NJ: Princeton University Press, 1976.
Renda, Gunsel, and C. Kortepeter, eds., *The Transformation of Turkish Culture: The Ataturk Legacy*. Princeton, NJ: Kingston Press, 1986.
Robinson, Richard, *The First Turkish Republic*. Cambridge: Harvard University Press, 1963.
Weiker, Walter F., *The Modernization of Turkey: From Ataturk to the Present Day*. New York: Holmes and Meier, 1981.
Zürcher, Erik Jan, *Political Opposition in the Early Turkish Republic: The Progressive Republic Party, 1924–1925*. Leiden, Netherlands: E.J. Brill, 1991.
———, *Turkey: A Modern History*. London: I.B. Tauris, 1993.

WORLD WAR I AND PEACE

Andrew, Christopher M., and A.S. Kenya-Forstner, *The Climax of French Imperial Expansion, 1914–1924*. Stanford, CA: Stanford University Press, 1981.
Busch, Brinton Cooper, *Britain, India, and the Arabs, 1914–1921*. Berkeley: University of California Press, 1971.
Fromkin, David, *A Peace to End All Peace: Creating the Modern Middle East, 1914–1922*. New York: Henry Holt, 1989.

Hovannisian, Richard G., *Armenia on the Road to Independence, 1918*. Berkeley: University of California Press, 1967.
———, *The Republic of Armenia*. Berkeley: University of California Press, 1971.
Howard, Harry, *The King-Crane Commission*. Beirut: Khayats, 1963.
———, *The Partition of Turkey*. Norman: University of Oklahoma Press, 1931; reprint, New York: F. Fertig, 1969.
Kedourie, Elie, *England and the Middle East: The Destruction of the Ottoman Empire, 1914–1921*. (3rd ed.) London: Mansell; Boulder, CO: Westview Press, 1987.
Kent, Marian, ed., *The Great Powers and the End of the Ottoman Empire*. London: George Allen & Unwin, 1984.
Nevakivi, Jukka, *Britain, France, and the Arab Middle East, 1914–1920*. London: Athlone Press, 1969.
Sachar, Howard, *The Emergence of the Middle East, 1914–1924*. New York: Knopf, 1969.

ARAB NATIONALISM

Allen, Roger, compiler and ed., *Modern Arabic Literature*. New York: Ungar, 1987.
Antonius, George, *The Arab Awakening: The Story of the Arab National Movement*. London: H. Hamilton, 1938; reprint, New York: Capricorn Books, 1965.
Badawi, M.M., *Modern Arabic Literature and the West*. London: Ithaca Press, 1985.
Boullata, Issa J., *Trends and Issues in Contemporary Arab Thought*. Albany: State University of New York Press, 1989.
Dawn, C. Ernest, *From Ottomanism to Arabism: Essays on the Origins of Arab Nationalism*. Urbana: University of Illinois Press, 1973.
Duri, A.A., *The Historical Foundation of the Arab Nation: A Study in Identity and Consciousness*, trans. by Lawrence I. Conrad. London and New York: Croom Helm, 1988.
Farah, Tawfic E., ed., *Pan-Arabism and Arab Nationalism: The Continuing Debate*. Boulder, CO: Westview Press, 1987.
Haim, Sylvia, ed., *Arab Nationalism, an Anthology*. Berkeley: University of California Press, 1962.
Hourani, Albert, *Arabic Thought in the Liberal Age, 1798–1939*. (2nd ed.) London: Oxford University Press, 1983.
Khadduri, Majid, *Political Trends in the Arab World: The Role of Ideas and Ideals in Practice*. Baltimore: Johns Hopkins University Press, 1970; reprint, Westport, CT: Greenwood Press, 1983.
Khalidi, Rashid, et. al., *The Origins of Arab Nationalism*. New York: Columbia University Press, 1991.
Khuri, Ra'if, *Modern Arab Thought: Channels of the French Revolution to the Middle East*, trans. by Ihsan 'Abbas, ed. by Charles Issawi. Princeton, NJ: Kingston Press, 1983.
Kritzeck, James, *Modern Arabic Literature: From 1800 to the Present*. New York: New American Library, 1970.
Porath, Yehoshua, *In Search of Arab Unity, 1930–1945*. London: Frank Cass, 1986.
Sharabi, Hisham, *Arab Intellectuals and the West: The Formative Years, 1875–1914*. Baltimore: Johns Hopkins University Press, 1970.
Zeine, Zeine, *The Emergence of Arab Nationalism*. (3rd ed.) Delmar, NY: Caravan Books, 1973.

IRAN

Politics

Abrahamian, Ervand, *Iran Between Two Revolutions*. Princeton, NJ: Princeton University Press, 1980.
Algar, Hamid, *Religion and State in Iran, 1785–1906*. Berkeley: University of California Press, 1969.
Amirahmadi, Hooshang, and Monoucher Parvin, *Post-Revolutionary Iran*. Boulder, CO: Westview Press, 1989.
Amjad, Mohammed, *Iran: From Royal Dictatorship to Theocracy*. Westport, CT: Greenwood Press, 1989.
Arjomand, Said Amir, *The Turban for the Crown: The Islamic Revolution in Iran*. New York: Oxford University Press, 1988.
Avery, Peter, *Modern Iran*. New York: Praeger, 1970.
Azimi, Fakhreddin, *Iran: The Crisis of Democracy, 1941–1953*. New York: St. Martin's Press, 1989.
Bakhash, Shaul, *Iran: Monarchy, Bureaucracy and Reform Under the Qajars, 1858–1896*. London: Ithaca, 1978.
———, *The Reign of the Ayatollahs: Iran and the Islamic Revolution*. New York: Basic Books, 1984.
Banani, Amin, *The Modernization of Iran, 1921–1941*. Stanford, CA: Stanford University Press, 1961.
Bill, James, *The Politics of Iran*. Columbus, Ohio: Merrill, 1972.
Bill, James A., and Wm. Roger Louis, eds., *Musaddiq, Iranian Nationalism, and Oil*. Austin: University of Texas Press, 1988.
Binder, Leonard, *Iran: Political Development in a Changing Society*. Berkeley: University of California Press, 1962.
Bosworth, Edmund, and Carole Hillenbrand, eds., *Qajar Iran: Political, Social, and Cultural Change, 1800–1925*. Edinburgh: Edinburgh University Press, 1983.
Browne, Edward G., *The Persian Revolution of 1905–1909*. New York: Barnes and Noble, 1966.
Cottam, Richard, *Nationalism in Iran*. (2nd ed.) Pittsburgh: University of Pittsburgh Press, 1979.
Diba, Farhad, *Mohammed Mossadegh: A Political Biography*. London: Croom Helm, 1986.
Fischer, Michael, *Iran: From Religious Dispute to Revolution*. Cambridge: Harvard University Press, 1980.

Ghods, M. Reza, *Iran in the Twentieth Century*. Boulder, CO: Lynne Rienner Publishers, 1989.
Goodell, Grace E., *The Elementary Structure of Political Life: Development in Pahlavi Iran*. New York: Oxford University Press, 1986.
Halliday, Fred, *Iran: Dictatorship and Development*. (2nd ed.) Baltimore: Penguin, 1979.
Katouzian, Homa, ed., *Musaddiq's Memoirs: The End of the British Empire in Iran*. London: JEBHE, National Movement of Iran, 1988.
Keddie, Nikki, *Modern Iran: Religion, Politics and Society*. London: Frank Cass, 1979.
———, *Roots of Revolution: An Interpretative History of Modern Iran*. New Haven, CT: Yale University Press, 1981.
———, and Eric Hooglund, eds., *The Iranian Revolution and the Islamic Republic*. (2nd ed.) Syracuse, NY: Syracuse University Press, 1986.
Lambton, Ann K.S., *Qajar Persia: Eleven Studies*. Austin: University of Texas Press, 1987.
Lenczowski, George, ed., *Iran Under the Pahlavis*. Stanford, CA: Hoover Institution, 1978.
McDaniel, Robert A., *The Shuster Mission and the Persian Constitutional Revolution*. Minneapolis, MN: Bibliotheca Islamica, 1974.
Milani, Mohsen M., *The Making of Iran's Islamic Revolution: From Monarchy to Islamic Republic*. Boulder, CO: Westview Press, 1988.
Nashat, Guity, *The Origins of Modern Reform in Iran, 1870–80*. Urbana: University of Illinois Press, 1982.
Ramazani, R.K., ed., *Iran's Revolution: The Search for Consensus*. Bloomington: Indiana University Press, 1989.
———, *Revolutionary Iran: Challenge and Response in the Middle East*. Baltimore: Johns Hopkins University Press, 1986.
Roosevelt, Kermit, *Countercoup: The Struggle for the Control of Iran*. New York:McGraw-Hill, 1979.
Saikal, Amin, *The Rise and Fall of the Shah*. Princeton, NJ: Princeton University Press, 1980.
Salehi, M.M., *Insurgency Through Culture and Religion: The Islamic Revolution of Iran*. New York: Praeger, 1988.
Schultz, Ann Tibbits, *Buying Security: Iran Under the Monarchy*. Boulder, CO: Westview Press, 1989.
Wilber, Donald N., *Riza Shah Pahlavi: The Resurrection and Reconstruction of Iran, 1878–1944*. New York: Exposition Press, 1975.
Wright, Martin, ed., *Iran: The Khomeini Revolution*. Essex, UK: Longman, 1989.
Zabih, Sepehr, *The Iranian Military in Revolution and War*. New York and London: Routledge, Chapman and Hall, 1988.
———, *The Mossadegh Era: The Roots of the Iranian Revolution*. Chicago: Lake View Press, 1982.

Foreign Affairs

Bill, James A., *The Eagle and the Lion: The Tragedy of American-Iranian Relations*. New Haven, CT: Yale University Press, 1988.
Cottam, Richard W., *Iran and the United States: A Cold War Case Study*. Pittsburgh: University of Pittsburgh Press, 1988.
Graham, Robert, *Iran: The Illusion of Power*. (2nd ed.) London: Croom Helm, 1980.
Heikal, Mohammed, *Iran: The Untold Story*. New York: Pantheon Books, 1981.
Kazemzadeh, Firuz, *Russia and Britain in Persia, 1864–1914: A Study in Imperialism*. New Haven, CT: Yale University Press, 1968.
Keddie, Nikki R., and Mark Gasiorowski, eds., *Iran, the Soviet Union and The United States*. New Haven, CT: Yale University Press, 1990.
Lenczowski, George, ed., *Russia and the West in Iran, 1918–1948, A Study in Big Power Rivalry*. Ithaca, NY: Cornell University Press, 1949.
Millspaugh, Arthur C., *Americans in Persia*. Washington, DC: The Brookings Institution, 1946.
———, *The American Task in Persia*. New York: Century, 1925.
Olson, William J., *Anglo-Iranian Relations During World War I*. London: Frank Cass, 1984.
Ramazani, Rouhollah, *The Foreign Policy of Iran: A Developing Nation in World Affairs, 1500–1941*. Charlottesville: University Press of Virginia, 1966.
———, *Iran's Foreign Policy, 1941–1973*. Charlottesville: University Press of Virginia, 1975.
Wright, Denis, *The English Among the Persians During the Qajar Period, 1787–1921*. London: Heinemann, 1977.

Economics

Amuzegar, Jahangir, and M. Ali Fekrat, *Iran: Economic Development Under Dualistic Conditions*. Chicago: University of Chicago Press, 1971.
Bharier, Julian, *Economic Development in Iran, 1900–1970*. London: Oxford University Press,1971.
Hooglund, Eric J., *Land and Revolution in Iran, 1960–1980*. Austin: University of Texas Press, 1982.
Issawi, Charles, ed., *The Economic History of Iran, 1800–1914*. Chicago: University of Chicago Press, 1971.
Katouzian, Homa, *The Political Economy of Modern Iran: Despotism and Pseudo-Modernism*. New York: New York University Press, 1981.

Social Affairs

Bonine, Michael E., and Nikki Keddie, eds., *Modern Iran: The Dialectics of Continuity and Change*. Albany: State University of New York Press, 1981.

Lambton, A.K.S., *Landlord and Peasant in Persia*. London: Oxford University Press, 1953.

Sansarian, Elizabeth, *The Women's Rights Movement in Iran: Mutiny, Appeasement, and Repression from 1900 to Khomeini*. New York: Praeger, 1982.

Zonis, Marvin, *The Iranian Political Elite*. Chicago: University of Chicago Press, 1971.

Religion

Akhavi, Shahrough, *Religion and Politics in Contemporary Iran*. Albany: State University of New York Press, 1980.

Arjomand, Said Amir, *The Shadow of God and the Hidden Imam: Religion, Political Order and Societal Change in Shi'ite Iran from the Beginning to 1890*. Chicago: University of Chicago Press, 1984.

Bayat, Mangol, *Mysticism and Dissent: Socioreligious Thoughts in Qajar Iran*. Syracuse, NY: Syracuse University Press, 1982.

Hussain, Asaf, *Islamic Iran: Revolution and Counter-Revolution*. New York: St. Martin's Press, 1985.

Keddie, Nikki R., *Religion and Politics in Iran: Shi'ism from Quietism to Revolution*. New Haven, CT: Yale University Press, 1983.

———, *Religion and Rebellion in Iran*. London: Frank Cass, 1966.

Khomeini, Ayatollah, *Islam and Revolution: Writings and Declarations of Imam Khomeini*. Hamid Algar, trans.. Berkeley, Calif: Mizan Press, 1981.

Martin, Vanessa, *Islam and Modernism: The Iranian Revolution of 1906*. Syracuse, NY: Syracuse University Press, 1989.

Mottahedeh, Roy, *The Mantle of the Prophet: Religion and Politics in Iran*. New York: Pantheon,1985.

ISLAM

Ahmad, Jalal Al-I, *Occidentosis: A Plague from the West*, trans. by R. Campbell, Hamid Algar, ed. Berkeley: Mizan Press, 1984.

Arjomand, Said Amir, ed., *From Nationalism to Revolutionary Islam: Essays on Social Movements in the Contemporary Near and Middle East*. Albany: State University of New York, 1984.

Banisadr, Abolhassan, *The Fundamental Principles and Precepts of Islamic Government*, trans. by Mohammad R. Ghanoonparvar. Lexington, KY: Mazda Publishers, 1981.

Binder, Leonard, *Islamic Liberalism: A Critique of Development Ideologies*. Chicago: University of Chicago Press, 1988.

Burgat, Franşois, and William Dowell, *The Islamist Movement in North Africa*. Austin: University of Texas Press, 1993.

Cole, Juan R.I., and Nikki R. Keddie, eds., *Shi'ism and Social Protest*. New Haven, CT: Yale University Press, 1986.

Dekmejian, R. Hrair, *Islam in Revolution: Fundamentalism in the Arab World*. Syracuse, NY: Syracuse University Press, 1985.

Donahue, John J., and John L. Espositio, eds., *Islam in Transition: Muslim Perspectives*. New York: Oxford University Press, 1982.

Enayat, Hamid, *Modern Islamic Political Thought*. Austin: University of Texas Press, 1982.

Esposito, John L., *The Islamic Threat: Myth or Reality?* New York: Oxford University Press, 1992.

———, *Islam and Politics*, 2nd ed. Syracuse, NY: Syracuse University Press, 1987.

———, *Islam the Straight Path*. New York and Oxford: Oxford University Press, 1991.

———, ed., *Voices of Islam Resurgent*. New York: Oxford University Press, 1983.

Gibb, H. A. R., *Modern Trends in Islam*. Chicago: University of Chicago Press, 1945; reprint, New York: Octagon Books, 1972.

Haddad, Yvonne Yazbeck, *Contemporary Islam and the Challenge of History*. Albany: State University of New York Press, 1981.

———, ed., *The Islamic Impact*. Syracuse, NY: Syracuse University Press, 1984.

Heper, Martin, and Raphael Israeli, eds., *Islam and Politics in the Modern Middle East*. New York: St. Martin's Press, 1984.

Keddie, Nikki R., *An Islamic Response to Imperialism: Political and Religious Writings of Sayyid Jamal al-Din al-Afghani*. (2nd ed.) Berkeley: University of California Press, 1983.

———, *Sayyid Jamal al-Din al-Afghani: A Political Biography*. Berkeley: University of California Press.1972.

———, ed., *Scholars, Saints, and Sufis: Muslim Religious Institutions in the Middle East Since 1500*. Berkeley: University of California Press, 1972.

Kedourie, E., *Afghani and Abduh*. London: Frank Cass, 1966.

Khomeini, Ayatollah, *Islam and Revolution*, trans. and annotated by Hamid Algar. Berkeley, CA: Mizan Press, 1981.

Kramer, Martin, *Shi'ism, Resistance and Revolution*. Boulder, CO: Westview Press, 1981.
Mortimer, Edward, *Faith and Power: The Politics of Islam*. New York: Random House, I982.
Munson, Henry, Jr., *Islam and Revolution in the Middle East*. New Haven, CT: Yale University Press, 1988.
Nasr, Sayyed Hossein, *Traditional Islam in the Modern World*. London: Kegan Paul International, 1987.
Pipes, Daniel, *In the Path of God: Islam and Political Power*. New York: Basic Books, 1983.
Piscatori, James P., *Islam in a World of Nation-States*. New York: Cambridge University Press, 1986.
———, ed., *Islam in the Political Process*. New York and Cambridge: Cambridge University Press, 1983.
Qutub, Seyd, *Milestones*. Lahore, Pakistan: Kazi Publications.
Rahman, Fazlur, *Islam and Modernity: Transformation of an Intellectual Tradition*. Chicago: University of Chicago Press, I981.
Sivan, Emmanuel, *Radical Islam: Medieval Theology and Modern Politics*. New Haven, CT: Yale University Press, 1985.
Smith, Wilfred Cantwell, *Islam in Modern History*. New York: New American Library, 1963.
Stowasser, Barbara Freyer, ed., *The Islamic Impulse*. London: Croom Helm, 1987.
Voll, John Obert, *Islam: Continuity and Change in the Modern World*. Boulder, CO: Westview Press, 1982.
von Grunebaum, Gustave, *Modern Islam: The Search for Cultural Identity*. Berkeley: University of California Press, 1962.
Williams, John, *The Word of Islam*. Austin: University of Texas Press, 1994.
Wright, Robin, *Sacred Rage: The Wrath of Militant Islam*, 2nd ed. New York: Simon & Schuster, 1986.

Index